Using DOS

Developed by Que® Corporation
Text written by David W. Solomon

Que®
CORPORATION
LEADING COMPUTER KNOWLEDGE

Using DOS

David W. Solomon is a Que product development specialist and staff writer who specializes in operating systems, database management, and programming. Since 1978, he has worked with a variety of operating systems on both minicomputers and microcomputers, and he has developed and written custom software for scientific and business applications on a worldwide basis. In addition to being the author of this book, he is also the author of *MS-DOS QuickStart*, the principal author of *MS-DOS User's Guide,* Special Edition, the coauthor of *dBASE IV Applications Library*, 2nd Edition, and a contributing author of *Using Turbo Prolog*, all published by Que Corporation.

Publishing Director

David Paul Ewing

Product Development Director

David W. Solomon

Acquisitions Editor

Terrie Lynn Solomon

Production Editor

Mary Bednarek

Editor

Jeannine McDonel

Technical Editors

Caroline M. Halliday
Jeff Sabotin
Timothy S. Stanley

Editorial Assistant

Stacey Beheler

Indexer

Sharon Hilgenberg

Proofreaders

Jodi Jensen
David Kline
Lori Lyons
Bruce Steed

Book Design and Production

William Hartman, Hartman Publishing
Ellen J. Sickle

Pasteup

Dennis Sheehan
Mary Beth Wakefield

Composed in Garamond by

Hartman Publishing

Contents at a Glance ▼

▼ TABLE OF CONTENTS

▼ Part One: The Role of DOS in Personal Computers

Part Two: Putting DOS to Work for You

6   Understanding Disk Preparation and Management

Part Three: Getting the Most from DOS

▼

Part Four: Command Reference

Part Five: Appendixes

▼ ACKNOWLEDGMENTS

Using DOS is the result of the dedicated contributions of a team of true microcomputer publishing professionals. All of the people who worked many long, hard hours deserve special thanks.

Tim Stanley, a Que Corporation "staffer," compiled the Command Reference for this project. Tim also acted as a technical editor for several chapters.

Publishing Director David P. Ewing provided guidance and support to help make this book possible.

Production Editor Mary Bednarek directed the book's editing, established the style and conventions for the book, and worked with the production department to complete the project in an effective, time-efficient manner.

Editor Jeannine McDonel worked with Tim Stanley to refine and condense the Command Reference into its final form.

Caroline M. Halliday acted as a technical editor for the Command Reference, providing critical technical expertise and guidance. Caroline also contributed to this project through her involvement as a contributing author for the *MS-DOS User's Guide,* Special Edition. Her material from that book provided a basis and direction for some command-specific sections of *Using DOS* that appear in Parts One and Two.

Jeff Sabotin also acted as a technical editor on sections of *Using DOS*. His contribution helped to ensure the quality and technical accuracy of this project.

David Busch contributed to this project through his involvement as a contributing author for the *MS-DOS User's Guide,* Special Edition. His material from that book provided a basis and direction for some sections that appear in Part Three of *Using DOS*.

Stacey Beheler provided editorial support throughout the project. Her many hours spent at the photocopier are greatly appreciated.

Bill Hartman spent many hours designing, revising, correcting, refining, and desktop-publishing *Using DOS*. Bill's dedication to quality and his talented desktop-publishing skills made this book a creative, attractive final product.

Graphics artist Ellen Sickle provided the design elements and enhanced the book's appearance. Her skills and efforts are greatly appreciated.

Sharon Hilgenberg was both precise and exact, not to mention speedy, in her creation of the book's index.

Proofreaders David Kline, Jodi Jensen, Bruce Steed, and Lori Lyons spent many diligent hours examining this project's contents to ensure its accuracy. Their efforts are greatly appreciated.

And finally, Que owes thanks the vendors who supplied software for this project:

Microsoft Corporation, and especially Tanya Van Dam, Public Relations. Microsoft's assistance with MS-DOS and OS/2, as well as Windows, has been a great help.

International Business Machines Corporation (IBM) for its supply of all versions of PC DOS and OS/2.

*T*RADEMARK *A*CKNOWLEDGMENTS ▼

Que Corporation has made every attempt to supply trademark information about company names, products, and services mentioned in this book. Trademarks indicated below were derived from various sources. Que Corporation cannot attest to the accuracy of this information.

1-2-3, Freelance, Lotus, and Magellan are registered trademarks of Lotus Development Corporation.

Andrew Tobias' Managing Your Money is a registered trademark of MECA (Micro Education Corporation of America).

Apple, Macintosh, and Mac are registered trademarks of Apple Computer, Inc.

AutoCAD is a registered trademark of Autodesk, Inc.

COMPAQ Personal Computer DOS Version 4.00 is a trademark, and COMPAQ and COMPAQ DeskPro 386 are registered trademarks of COMPAQ Computer Corporation.

CompuServe Information Service is a registered trademark of CompuServe Incorporated and H&R Block, Inc.

CP/M and GEM are registered trademarks of Digital Research Inc.

dBASE IV is a trademark, and dBASE III Plus is a registered trademark of Ashton-Tate Corporation.

DeskMate is a trademark of Tandy Corporation.

DESQview and Quarterdeck QEMM/386 are trademarks of Quarterdeck Office Systems.

DisplayWrite 4, IBM Personal Editor, IBM ProPrinter, IBM Token Ring, Micro Channel, OS/2, Presentation Manager, Systems Application Architecture (SAA), and TopView are trademarks, and IBM, PC XT, PS/2 Models 25, 30, 50, 50Z, 60, 70, and 80, and Quietwriter are registered trademarks of International Business Machines Corporation.

Dow Jones News/Retrieval is a registered service mark of Dow Jones & Company, Inc.

DUMP.EXE is a trademark of Phoenix Technologies Ltd.

EPSON is a registered trademark of Epson Corporation.

Epson Equity is a trademark of Epson America, Inc.

First Publisher and Harvard Graphics are trademarks of Software Publishing Corporation.

FLASH is a trademark of Software Masters, Inc.

Hercules Graphics Card is a trademark of Hercules Computer Technology.

Keyworks is a trademark of ALPHA Software Corporation.

GW—BASIC, Microsoft Excel, Microsoft QuickBASIC, Microsoft Windows/386, Microsoft Windows Development Kit, Microsoft Windows Write, Microsoft Word, MS-DOS, and XENIX are registered trademarks of Microsoft Corporation.

Introduction

Since its introduction in 1981, MS-DOS has grown to be the most widely used operating system in the world. Thousands of applications programs have been written for the MS-DOS operating system. With over 40 million users worldwide, MS-DOS affects more people than any software product ever written.

As MS-DOS has evolved, Que Corporation has helped hundreds of thousands of personal computer users get the most from MS-DOS. *Using DOS* represents Que's continuing commitment to provide the best microcomputer books in the industry.

MS-DOS is the operating system of choice for most personal computer users and will remain so for the foreseeable future. *Using DOS* offers DOS users a source of information to organize their work with the PC more effectively, make their hardware respond more efficiently, and provide a resource of answers to questions about the capabilities of DOS.

Who Should Read This Book?

Using DOS is written for PC users who need a tutorial reference to DOS. The book explains the key concepts of DOS without being technical and intimidating. Developed to address the majority of your DOS needs,

1

Using DOS also recognizes that your learning time is limited. Whether you are just beginning to use DOS or you have been using DOS and need a better understanding of it, *Using DOS* is for you.

What Hardware Is Needed?

This book applies to the family of IBM personal computers and their close compatibles. This list includes the IBM Personal Computer, the IBM Personal Computer XT, the IBM Personal Computer AT, and the IBM PS/2 series. Dozens of other computers which use MS-DOS, and are manufactured or sold by COMPAQ, Zenith Data Systems, EPSON, Leading Edge, Tandy, Dell, Northgate, CompuAdd, and others are also covered by this book. If your computer runs the MS-DOS operating system, you have the necessary hardware.

What Versions of DOS Are Covered?

This book specifically covers MS-DOS and PC DOS versions 3 and later. Special attention is given to versions 3.3 and 4.0. Users of DOS V2 will also find their version covered to their satisfaction. If you use DOS V2, you can generalize much of the book to that version, but many useful DOS features and commands included in the newer DOS versions are not available to you.

What Is Not Covered?

Some of the more esoteric DOS commands and less frequently used switches and parameters are not covered in the text, but are included in the Command Reference. *Using DOS* does not include coverage of the DEBUG or LINK commands, nor does it include a technical reference to the applications programming interface that DOS provides programmers. If you are interested in programming at the operating system level, you will find that Que offers a complete line of books that cover DOS programming.

Also not included in this book are computer-specific setup or configuration commands, such as IBM's SETUP for the PS/2 and Toshiba's CHAD for laptop displays. Although these commands are often distributed with the same disks as MS-DOS, they are too variable to be covered adequately here. Your computer-supplied manuals and your PC dealer are the best sources of information about these machine-specific features.

The Details of This Book

You can flip quickly through this book to get a feeling for its organization. *Using DOS* begins with fundamentals and builds your DOS capabilities to a practical level. The Command Reference provides you with a rapid resource to commands as well as an information base to complete your DOS expertise. The book also includes a set of useful appendixes.

Part One—The Role of DOS in Personal Computers

Part One is an introductory tutorial on the PC and DOS. If you are a DOS beginner, Part One lays a foundation of understanding that you will draw upon while reading this book.

Chapter 1, "Understanding the Personal Computer," takes a look at today's PCs. The chapter explores the major components of the PC and addresses the use of system and peripheral hardware. In this chapter, you not only get a feel for your system, but also for systems with different keyboards, displays, and peripherals.

Chapter 2, "Understanding the Role of DOS," introduces DOS as the PC's operating system. This chapter examines DOS from a product-oriented point of view as well as from a software-oriented point of view. This chapter's explanation of the parts of DOS and how they interact clears up the confusion of what DOS does on your PC.

Chapter 3, "Starting DOS," steps through the process of booting DOS while explaining important concepts along the way. The DOS Shell, the graphical user interface provided with DOS V4, is introduced through a quick tour of its main screens.

Chapter 4, "Using DOS Commands," introduces DOS commands and how to use them. You will learn the concepts behind issuing commands at DOS's command prompt. The chapter explains syntax, parameters, and switches in an easy-to-learn fashion. Important keys and various examples of the DIR command are also covered.

Chapter 5, "Understanding Disks and Files," recognizes the important job DOS performs in managing disks and files. This chapter defines files and explains how they are named. File-naming conventions are clearly explained. Also explored are the uses of hard disks and floppy disks and the common disk capacities available with DOS.

Part Two—Putting DOS to Work for You

This part of the book covers the DOS commands and concepts that make up the core of DOS's utility. With your knowledge of Part Two, you will be able to use DOS effectively to manage your PC work.

Chapter 6, "Understanding Disk Preparation and Management," examines the process of formatting disks. You will learn what formatting does and how DOS uses formatted disks to store your files. Also presented are the disk-level DOS commands that copy and compare floppy disks and analyze disks for damage. You will also learn how to partition a hard disk into sections that DOS can use as logical disks.

Chapter 7, "Understanding Hierarchical Directories," explains the important concept of DOS tree-structured directories. This major feature of DOS is explained from the ground up. This inside look at DOS's file-management strategy will prepare you to manage the DOS file system.

Chapter 8, "Managing Directories," picks up where Chapter 7 leaves off. In this chapter, you use DOS directory-level commands to customize a multilevel file system on your PC. You will learn how to create, change, and remove DOS subdirectories. Included are commands that enable you to view your directory structure.

Chapter 9, "Keeping Files in Order," illuminates the file-level DOS commands. Because you are likely to spend most of your time with DOS working with files, this chapter offers an in-depth view of these commands. Each command includes examples that will help you appreciate the full power of the important file-level commands.

Chapter 10, "Understanding Backups and the Care of Data," offers some important considerations for protecting your data. DOS provides several important commands that enable users to maintain diskette backup sets of a hard disk's contents. These commands and the concept of developing a backup policy are discussed in this chapter.

Part Three—Getting the Most from DOS

Part Three provides the information you need to tap the expanded power available with DOS. This part of the book will help you utilize the many features provided with DOS as well as help you customize your computer system.

Chapter 11, "Using EDLIN," provides a tutorial approach to DOS's built-in text-file editor. The examples developed in this chapter show you how to use EDLIN as a day-to-day utility. With the careful attention given to EDLIN's practical use, you will learn the skills needed to quickly compose a text file. Practical examples of using EDLIN to create memos and batch files are also presented.

Chapter 12, "Using Batch Files," guides you through the process of creating batch files. The commands related to batch files are explained in a tutorial style. Useful examples help make mastering the basics of batch files easier. The important concept of the AUTOEXEC.BAT file is also explored.

Chapter 13, "Configuring Your System and Managing Devices," is a comprehensive collection of DOS commands and directives that are explained to help you get the best performance from your PC. By using these commands, you can control the way DOS sees your system's drives and directories and controls your peripheral devices. You will also learn several useful techniques—from creating a CONFIG.SYS file to using disk-caching software with extended memory.

Chapter 14, "Using the DOS Shell," directs the configuration and use of the graphical user interface included with DOS V4. You will see the features and benefits of the DOS Shell.

Part Four—Command Reference

Part Four contains the comprehensive Command Reference. The commands, which are arranged in alphabetical order, are shown with syntax, applicable rules, and examples. When a command is also covered elsewhere in the book, a chapter reference is provided. You can use the section both as a reference when you have problems and as a source of practical advice and tips during "browsing sessions." In all, the Command Reference is a complete, easy to use, quickly accessed resource on the proper use of DOS commands.

Part Five—Appendixes

Using DOS includes nine appendixes containing useful summary information. Appendix A lists the main commands and keystroke sequences you need to know to navigate successfully in DOS. Appendix B is a list of the most common error messages displayed by DOS as well as possible explanations for each message. Appendix C is a guide to installing DOS on your computer. Appendix D outlines the preparation of a hard disk. Appendix E lists the changes and additions of commands between version changes. Appendix F explains the DOS control and editing keys. Appendix G provides ASCII and extended ASCII code charts. Appendix H lists the ANSI control sequences supported by DOS through ANSI.SYS. Appendix I lists character tables of the standard code pages.

Learning More About DOS

If *Using DOS* whets your appetite for more information about DOS, you are in good company. Thousands of Que's readers have gone on to purchase one or more additional Que books about DOS.

No one book can fill all of your DOS and personal computer needs. Que Corporation publishes a full line of microcomputer books that complement this book.

If you are a corporate trainer, need to teach beginners about DOS, or feel that you need a more visual approach to DOS, you may be interested in purchasing Que's *MS-DOS QuickStart*. This book features a graphics approach to learning DOS and is geared to the beginner. Que also offers the *DOS Workbook and Disk*—an interactive learning tool for the classroom environment or motivated self-starters.

MS-DOS User's Guide, Special Edition, is a comprehensive learning tool and reference volume for users of MS-DOS and PC DOS. This book is especially well-suited for readers who are proficient with applications programs, but who have grown beyond elementary tutorials and could benefit from a more in-depth understanding of DOS.

You are probably using DOS on a PC equipped with a hard disk drive. The key to efficient computer use is effective hard disk management. *Managing Your Hard Disk*, 2nd Edition, provides you with the in-depth information you need to get the most from your hard disk.

Newer versions of DOS support powerful equipment to help your programs run quickly and efficiently. If your current hardware is not up to the task of running the extensive new software packages, examine Que's *Upgrading and Repairing PCs*. This informative text shows you how to get the most from your hardware and how to upgrade your system to handle the new breed of high-powered software, such as Lotus 1-2-3 Release 3, dBASE IV, Microsoft Windows, and WordPerfect. According to Mark Brownstein of *InfoWorld*, *Upgrading and Repairing PCs* is "one of the best books about the workings of personal computers I've ever seen; it will be a useful, easy-to-read, and interesting addition to most anyone's library."

Other reference tools for the DOS user include *DOS Programmer's Reference*, 2nd Edition, *DOS Tips, Tricks, and Traps*, 2nd Edition, and *DOS QueCards*. *DOS Programmer's Reference* offers comprehensive coverage of the programming aspects of MS-DOS. Que's *DOS QueCards* is a desktop reference tool that DOS users of any experience level will find invaluable. *DOS Tips, Tricks, and Traps*, 2nd Edition, provides a topical collection of in-depth DOS tidbits.

All of these books can be found in better bookstores worldwide. In the United States, you can call Que at 1-800-428-5331 to order books or obtain further information.

Using DOS follows the Que tradition of providing quality text that is targeted appropriately for the DOS user. Because of the dedication to this goal, Que ultimately has only one way of getting better—by hearing from you. Let Que know how you feel about this book or any other Que title. Que wants to keep improving its books, and you are the best source of information.

Conventions Used in This Book

Certain conventions are followed in this edition to help you more easily understand the discussions. The conventions are explained again at appropriate places in the book.

Special Typefaces and Representations

Uppercase letters are used to distinguish file names and DOS commands. In most cases, the keys on the keyboard are represented as they appear on your keyboard, with the exception of the arrow keys. Both arrow symbols and their corresponding terms, such as "up arrow" or "up-arrow key," have been used.

Ctrl-Break indicates that you press the Ctrl key and hold it down while you press also the Break key. Other hyphenated key combinations, such as Ctrl-Z or Alt-F1, are performed in the same manner.

Words or phrases that are defined for the first time appear in *italic* characters. Words or phrases you are to type appear in **boldface** characters.

Uppercase letters are usually used in the examples for what you type, but you can type commands in either upper- or lowercase letters. For a few commands, the case of the letters makes a difference. When the case is significant, the difference is specifically mentioned in the discussion of the command.

All screen displays and on-screen messages appear in the following special typeface:

```
This is a screen message
```

The system prompt (A>, C>, and so on), which appears on-screen, also appears in the special typeface.

Command Syntax

The notation for issuing commands and running programs appears, in fullest form, in lines like the following:

*dc:pathc***CHKDSK** *filename.ext /switches*

In any syntax line, not all elements of the syntax can be represented in a literal manner. For example, *filename.ext* can represent any file name with any extension. It also can represent any file name with no extension at all. However, command names and switches can be represented in a literal way. To activate the command **CHKDSK.COM**, you must type the word **CHKDSK**. To use the CHKDSK command with the /V (verbose) switch, you can type the following:

CHKDSK /V

Any literal text that you can type in a syntax line will be shown in uppercase letters. Any text that you can replace with other text (variable text) will be shown in lowercase letters.

7

As another example, note the following syntax line:

FORMAT d:

This representation means that you must type **FORMAT** to format a disk. You must also type the drive represented by **d:**. However, **d:** can be replaced by any disk drive. If **d:** is to be drive A:, you would type the following:

FORMAT A:

Mandatory vs. Optional Parts of a Command

Not all parts of a syntax line are essential when typing the command. You must be able to distinguish mandatory parts of the syntax line from those that are optional. Any portion of a syntax line that you see in **boldface** letters is mandatory; you must always give this part of a command. In a previous example, to issue the CHKDSK command, you must type the word **CHKDSK** as it appears. In the example of the FORMAT command, you must type **FORMAT** as well as substitute the drive letter you want for **d:**.

It is not, however, always mandatory to type certain items in a command line. Portions of a syntax line that you see in *italic characters* are optional; you supply these items only when needed. In the CHKDSK example, you substitute for *dc:pathc* the appropriate disk drive and path name. You substitute for *filename.ext* a file name or other item. You use the appropriate character or characters for */switches*. If you do not type an optional item, DOS will use its default value or setting for the item.

In most cases, the text will also help you distinguish between optional and mandatory items, as well as those mandatory items that are variable.

Part One

The Role of DOS in Personal Computers

Understanding the Personal Computer

Understanding the Role of DOS

Starting DOS

Using DOS Commands

Understanding Disks and Files

Understanding the Personal Computer

Until a few years ago, computers were large, expensive machines that were not available to individual users. Early computers were room-sized cabinets filled with thousands of tubes and transistors. The few users who knew anything about computers had to share the resources of these early machines with other users.

As recently as the early 1970s, computers were filled with thousands of discrete electronic parts and integrated circuits called *chips*. During that decade, however, advances in computer technology resulted in the production of chips that incorporated the jobs of hundreds of these discrete components. Most of the essential electronic building blocks a computer needed could be contained on one of these miniature chips, or *microprocessors*. Computers that use these chips are called *microcomputers*. By the end of the 1970s, several companies had begun to sell microcomputers. Microcomputers were small enough and inexpensive enough so that individuals could purchase them for use in their businesses or homes. It was through the notion of having a microcomputer dedicated to a single user that the term *personal computer* developed.

Reading about those old personal computers now is like reading about the first automobiles. By today's standards, both were slow and temperamental. To maintain these early machines, the owner needed to be somewhat of a scientist. Without those pioneering automobiles, however, your driving experience might be far less routine today.

Likewise, without the early microcomputers, you might still be doing all of your automated work by hand. While automobiles took nearly 40 years to become practical personal transportation, it has taken microcomputers less than 10 years to revolutionize the way people approach their work.

In the early 1980s, International Business Machines (IBM) introduced the IBM Personal Computer, which was an immediate success. Before long, the IBM PC captured the infant microcomputer industry and shaped its formative years. The IBM microcomputer was so popular that it became a de facto standard for personal computers.

Today, many manufacturers sell computers that are nearly functionally equivalent to the IBM Personal Computer. Today's personal computers—PCs—often employ advanced technology over the original IBM design. Yet nearly all programs developed for the IBM microcomputers will run on the personal computers offered by various manufacturers. PCs that follow the de facto IBM standard have been dubbed *compatibles*. The primary software that IBM's personal computers and the compatibles have in common is the MS-DOS disk operating system introduced by Microsoft for the original IBM PC. In this chapter, you will learn about system elements that can be generalized to any IBM PC or compatible.

Key Terms Used in This Chapter

Display	The screen or monitor.
DOS	An acronym for Disk Operating System. In IBM PC, XT, AT, PS/2, and functional compatibles, both PC DOS and MS-DOS refer to DOS.
Peripheral	Any device (aside from the main components) that is connected to the computer to help it perform tasks.
Disk	A plastic or metal platter coated with magnetic material that is used to store files. A disk drive records and plays back information on disks.
Modem	A device for exchanging data between computers through telephone lines.
Input	Any data a computer reads.
Output	Any data the computer puts out.
Bit	A binary digit. The smallest discrete representation of a value that a computer can manipulate.
Byte	A collection of eight bits that a computer usually stores and manipulates as a unit.
K (kilobyte)	1,024 bytes, used to show size or capacity in computer systems.

M (megabyte)   1,024 kilobytes. Used to measure values or capacities of millions of bytes.

Data   A catch-all term that refers to words, numbers, symbols, graphics, photos, sounds—any information stored in bytes in computer form.

File   A named group of data in electronic form.

Exploring the Components of Computer Systems

To read this chapter, you won't need to switch on your PC. You might find it handy, however, to have your PC visible. The topics covered here discuss what your computer is all about.

Personal computer systems based on the IBM PC are functionally the same, despite the wide variety of configurations available. As long as you have the main components, the shape and size of your computer matter very little. For example, you can find equally powerful machines in the traditional desktop configuration, in portable laptop models, or in compact lunchbox-sized computers. The wide variety of PC software operates equally well in any of these cosmetic configurations.

Hardware and software are the two main segments of a computer system. Both must be present for a computer to do useful work for its operator. Both hardware and software work together in a manner similar to a VCR and a videocassette. The VCR unit itself is like the hardware because it is electro-mechanical. The videocassette is like the software because it contains the information and control signals necessary for the VCR to display pictures on the TV screen.

Understanding Computer Software

You may at one time, use your VCR to view a videocassette that contains cartoons. At another time, you may watch a taped, public television special on the crisis in education. Even though you use the same hardware (VCR) at both viewing sessions, the software (the videocassettes) stores different pictures and sounds. Likewise, your PC can be a word processor during one work session and be a database manager during the next. The software program that you use is designed to work in a specific way.

Your computer has the potential to do useful work. By using various software packages or applications programs, you determine what kind of utility you get from your computer. Software enables a PC to be a flexible tool. You can program (instruct) a computer to perform a wide variety of operations. Almost anything you can reduce to calculations can be made into a program and then entered into the computer.

You probably use many small "computers" that have been programmed. Calculators, telephones with number memories, VCRs that can automatically record television programs, and arcade games are all examples of small computer-assisted devices that use a form of software. These devices have built-in software, so their usefulness is limited to their built-in functionality. Because personal computers are designed to accept outside software, they are quite versatile.

You can teach your computer to perform chores much as these everyday machines do. With the proper software, your computer will serve as a word processor, a spreadsheet, a project manager, a mailing list generator, or even a wily chess opponent! Table 1.1 illustrates some of the variety of software you can purchase for your computer.

Table 1.1
Computer Software

Type of Software	Example
Operating systems	MS-DOS; UNIX
Databases	dBASE IV; Reflex; Q&A
Spreadsheets	Lotus 1-2-3; SuperCalc; Quattro
Word processors	WordPerfect; WordStar; Microsoft Word
Sales management	Act!
Utilities	SideKick; DESKMATE (calendar, note pad, calculator)
Graphics	AutoCad; Map Master; Freelance; Harvard Graphics
Integrated programs	Smart; Symphony; Microsoft Works
Games	Flight Simulator; Jeopardy
Home finance	Managing Your Money; Quicken 3
Desktop publishing	First Publisher; Ventura Publisher; Aldus PageMaker

The operating system, DOS, is the most important type of software for the PC. Operating systems provide a foundation of services for other programs. These services, for their part, provide a uniform means for programs to gain access to the full resources of the hardware. Operating systems that help programs access disk resources are called disk operating systems. Chapter 2 gives you an introduction to disk operating systems.

This book shows you how to use the most common operating system for the IBM PC and compatibles. The IBM versions of DOS and the various versions of Microsoft Corporation's DOS are highly compatible. For this reason, DOS will be used as the generic term to refer to both.

Understanding Computer Hardware

A PC's *configuration* is based on its components and the PC's overall outward appearance. The PC sitting on your desk is a configuration of component parts or hardware.

Hardware is the collection of electro-mechanical components that make up your PC. In general, the term *hardware* refers to the system unit, the keyboard, the screen display, the disk drives, and printers. The components exist in a wide variety of configurations, but the computers all operate in essentially the same manner. Figure 1.1 presents three common PC configurations. Notice that in all three cases, the PCs have system units, keyboards, displays, and disk drives. Internally, the PCs have many common components that make up the microprocessor support circuits.

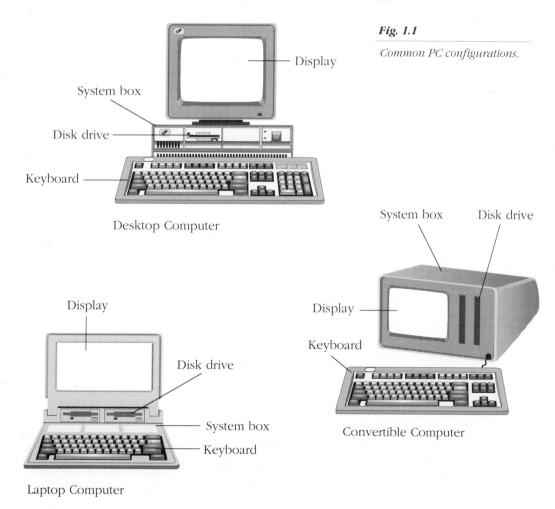

Display

System box

Disk drive

Keyboard

Desktop Computer

Fig. 1.1

Common PC configurations.

System box   Disk drive

Display

Keyboard

Convertible Computer

Display

Disk drive

System box

Keyboard

Laptop Computer

Hardware falls into two main categories: system hardware and peripheral hardware. *System hardware* is directly associated with processing or computing activity. The microprocessor is the system-hardware component that is central to the computer's ability to function. Because of its central role, the microprocessor is also called the *central processing unit* or *CPU.*

Technically, any device used by a computer for input or output of data is a *peripheral.* Displays, printers, modems, keyboards, and disk drives are all items of peripheral hardware. Peripheral hardware supports the system hardware's computing activity.

System Hardware

A PC's system hardware consists of the microprocessor and its support components and circuits. The microprocessor is a chip which does the computing in the computer. System hardware is often soldered or socketed to circuit boards within the computer.

The computer's random access memory, or RAM, performs a system-hardware function by storing programs and data while the PC is turned on. System read-only memory, or ROM, is also considered system-level hardware. ROM contains program pieces that are permanently stored. The PC's microprocessor can retrieve information from the ROM but cannot store any new information in ROM. Because the contents of ROM are not very flexible, ROM is often called *firmware.*

The microprocessor steps through a program in order to execute it. To coordinate the complex interactions between the microprocessor and the rest of the electronic parts, such as RAM and ROM, the microprocessor relies on a constantly timed set of pulses. These pulses are produced by a clock-timing generating circuit. Don't confuse this clock-timing generating circuit with the clock-calendar that keeps the time of day and date. The timing generator is more like a metronome that ticks at a determined speed to provide a beat for musicians to follow.

 If you don't understand how a computer "computes," don't worry. The details of system-level computing are fairly complicated. In a short time, you will better understand how your computer computes.

Peripheral Hardware

System hardware must have outside input in order to compute. The input comes from various devices called *input devices.* The keyboard is an example of an input device.

When the system hardware has completed some aspect of its work, it must output the result for you to see or store in order for the work to be useful. The system hardware's output goes to *output devices.* Your PC's display monitor is an example of an output device.

A great deal of your interaction with the PC will take place between you, the keyboard, and the display. Fortunately, the basic concepts of using a keyboard or viewing a display are simple. Some differences do exist, however, between different keyboards or different displays. In the next two sections, you will see some of the principles that control keyboards and displays. Understanding these principles will help you avoid confusion or mix-up when working with this book, DOS, and your applications programs.

Exploring the Computer Display

The *display*, also called the *monitor* or the *screen*, is the part of the computer's peripheral hardware that produces visual output. The display is the normal or *default* location for output for the PC. Your display is your PC's primary output device.

Most displays offered with PCs work on the same principle as your television set. Like televisions, most PC displays employ a *cathode ray tube* or *CRT* as the means to display output. Some PC users refer to the PC's display as the CRT. Manufacturers also incorporate other types of technology into computer displays. For example, to produce flatter (and thinner) displays, manufacturers use a technology known as a *gas plasma* display. Gas plasma displays produce an orange color against a dark background.

Another technology adapted to computer displays is liquid crystal. *Liquid crystal displays* (LCDs) work on the same principle as digital watch displays. Most LCDs produce dark characters against a lighter background. The LCD works well in brightly lit rooms because the light striking the display increases the contrast of the display output. Some LCDs also employ a backlight that increases display contrast.

Regardless of the display type, all displays have one function in common. They take electrical signals and translate them into patterns of tiny picture element dots or *pixels* that you can recognize as characters or figures. Not all displays produce the same total number of pixels. Some displays are noticeably sharper than others. The more pixels available with a display, the sharper the visual image. The sharpness of the visual image, the *resolution*, is a function of both the display and the display adapter.

The *display adapter* is a collection of circuits which interface with the system hardware. The display adapter controls the computer display. In some PCs, the display circuitry can be part of the motherboard. It can also be on a separate board that fits into a slot in the computer. The display adapter can be a monochrome display adapter (MDA), color graphics adapter (CGA), enhanced graphics adapter (EGA), video graphics array adapter (VGA), or some less common type of special display adapter. All of these display adapters fall into one of two main categories. The adapter displays *text* only, or the adapter displays *text* and *graphics*.

Text Displays

When you see letters, numbers, or punctuation on your display, you recognize these images as text. This text comes from your computer's memory where it has been stored as a code in accordance with the standard that most computers recognize, the *American Standard Code for Information Interchange (ASCII)*.

Most programs set an operating mode for the display called *text mode*. In text mode, predetermined ASCII coded characters compose the visual display. Each ASCII code represents a letter or a symbol. Letters or symbols are sent to the display adapter so that you can see the characters on the screen. Because ASCII is the standard, the display adapter can use an electronic table to pull the correct pixel pattern for any letter, number, or punctuation symbol. The display adapter uses the electronic table like a set of stencils.

The principle is actually very close to the method used to display scores on a lighted sports scoreboard. Instead of lighting a pattern of bulbs, the display adapter illuminates a pattern of pixels. Each number on the scoreboard is simply a different arrangement of illuminated bulbs.

Although ASCII codes may seem like a recent development, the basis for the code for each letter, number, and punctuation symbol can be traced to the origins of the teletype machine that delivered news and information before the age of computers. When the classic movie shows the radio announcer telling the audience that the news bulletin is "hot off the wire," the "wire" is the teletype interconnect that sends the encoded characters as patterns of "blips."

You may occasionally see references to *extended* ASCII codes. The ASCII-to-pixel table can have 256 different combinations, which is more than are needed to represent all the letters, numbers, and punctuation commonly used in English. With 128 remaining possible ASCII codes, equipment manufacturers are free to use the remaining codes as they see fit. The makers of compatible PCs put these remaining codes—the extended ASCII codes—to good use. Display adapters use the leftover ASCII values for pixel patterns of lines, corners, and special images like musical notes.

Programs can use combinations of these extended ASCII characters to produce boxes and other graphics-like characters. Because text adapters and displays can only produce predetermined characters and special shapes, these extended ASCII codes are quite useful for giving a screen a graphics-like look. The extended codes enable a text display to incorporate a wide variety of borders, boxes, and icons. If, however, a program requires a pixel or a pattern of pixels on the screen that is not included in the ASCII-to-pixel table, you are out of luck if you use a text display. Of the various display adapters available, the monochrome display adapter (MDA) is the only adapter that is a text-only display adapter. All adapters, however, produce the standard text and extended special characters. If you are interested in seeing all of the possible characters that your PC can display in its text mode, look at the code page tables in Appendix I to get a good idea.

Graphics Displays

Graphics displays can produce any pixel or pattern of pixels. The PC enters a special graphics-display mode through program control. In graphics mode, the display adapter can select any pixel on the screen for illumination. Thus, complex figures with curves and fine details can be displayed. Graphics-based screens are perhaps the most pleasing to view. Charts, drawings, digitized pictures, animated game characters, and What-You-See-Is-What-You-Get (WYSIWYG) word processing text are all graphics-based outputs.

The computer must work harder to create a graphics image than a text image, however. There is no electronic stencil for a graphics screen. In order to light the correct point on the display, the display adapter must find the screen coordinate points for each pixel. No table of predetermined pixels exists as in text mode. And, unlike text mode, graphics modes are variable. For graphics displays, no one standard exists.

Graphics displays differ in the number of pixels available. The greater the number of pixels, the finer the detail of the display (and the greater the cost for the display). Each computed pixel has characteristics that tell the graphics adapter what the color or intensity of the pixel should be. The greater the number of colors and intensities, the more storage space in memory is required. Graphics adapters offer varying combinations of pixel densities, colors, and intensities. Table 1.2 lists the various display types, including the colors available and the pixel resolution.

Table 1.2
Resolution and Colors for Display Adapters

Adapter Type	Graphics Mode	Pixel Resolution	Colors Available
CGA	Medium resolution	320 × 200	4
CGA	High resolution	640 × 200	2
EGA	All CGA modes		
EGA	CGA high resolution	640 × 200	16
EGA	EGA high resolution	640 × 350	16
MGA	Monochrome graphics	720 × 348	2
MDA	Text ONLY	N/A	N/A
VGA	All CGA and EGA modes		
VGA	Monochrome	640 × 480	2
VGA	VGA high resolution	640 × 480	16
VGA	VGA medium resolution	320 × 200	256

Figure 1.2 demonstrates the principle of resolution that affects the quality of a graphics display. The higher-resolution image (left) uses four times as many pixels as the low-resolution image (right).

Fig. 1.2

Resolution in a graphics display.

The most important thing to remember about displays is the difference between the various displays. DOS works in the text mode, so you will always be able to use DOS. Your applications programs may use text mode or one of the various graphics modes. Before you decide to buy software that uses a graphics mode, let your dealer help you determine if the package is suitable for your display.

Exploring the Computer Keyboard

Like displays, keyboards can vary from PC to PC. The impact of a keyboard's variance from others is not as critical as the variance among displays and display adapters. Programs don't normally require one type of keyboard over the other types. Like displays, keyboards have some core common characteristics. This section will help you get familiar with your keyboard. Because DOS and other programs use special keys, your understanding of these keys will make learning about DOS and other programs easier.

The computer keyboard has the familiar QWERTY layout. (The name QWERTY comes from the letters found on the left side of the top row of letters on a standard typewriter.) But a computer keyboard is different from a typewriter keyboard in several important ways.

The most notable difference is the presence of the "extra" keys—the keys that do not appear on a typewriter. These keys are described in table 1.3. Depending on the type of computer you use, you will also find ten or twelve special function keys.

Many of the function keys are designed for use in combination with other keys. For example, pressing the Shift key and the PrtSc key in combination causes DOS to print the contents of the current screen. Pressing the Ctrl and PrtSc keys simultaneously causes DOS to continuously print what you type. Pressing Ctrl and PrtSc a second time turns off the printing. Table 1.4 describes the more common key combinations used in DOS.

The function keys are shortcuts. Not all programs use these keys, and some use only a few of them. When used, however, they automatically carry out repetitious operations for you. For example, the F1 key is often used for on-line help.

On-line help displays instructions from the computer's memory to help you understand a particular operation. The DOS V4.0 Shell uses the F3 key to automatically back out of one operation and move into another. The F10 key in a DOS Shell session moves the cursor to various parts of the screen. These and other keys will be explained in later parts of this book.

The keyboard is the way you put information into the computer. Each character you type is converted into code the computer can process. The keyboard is therefore considered an input device.

Table 1.3
Special Keys on the Computer Keyboard

Key	Function
Enter	Signals the computer to respond to the commands you type. Also functions as a carriage return in programs that simulate the operation of a typewriter.
Cursor Keys	Change your location on the screen. Included are the left arrow, right arrow, up arrow, and down arrow.
PgUp/PgDn	Scroll the screen display up one page or down one page.
Home/End	Home moves the cursor to the upper left corner of the screen; End moves the cursor to the lower right hand corner.
Backspace	Moves the cursor backwards one space at a time, deleting any character in that space.
Del	Deletes, or erases, any character at the location of the cursor.
Insert (Ins)	Inserts any character at the location of the cursor.
Shift	Creates uppercase letters and other special characters. When pressed in combination with another key, can change the standard function of that key.
Caps Lock	When pressed to the lock position, all characters typed are uppercase. Caps Lock does not shift the keys, however. To release, press the key again.
Ctrl	The Control key. When pressed in combination with another key, changes the standard function of that key.
Alt	The Alternate key. When pressed in combination with another key, changes the standard function of that key.
Esc	In some situations, pressing Esc allows you to "escape" from a current operation to a previous one. Sometimes Esc has no effect on the current operation.

Special Keys on the Computer Keyboard (cont.)

Key	Function
Num Lock	Changes the numeric keypad from cursor-movement to numeric-function mode.
PrtSc	Used with Shift to send the characters on the display to the printer.
Print Screen	Found on Enhanced keyboards. Same as Shift-PrtSc.
Scroll Lock	Locks the scrolling function to the cursor-control keys. Instead of the cursor moving, the screen scrolls.
Pause	Suspends display output until another key is pressed. (Not provided with standard keyboards.)
Break	Stops a program in progress from running.
Numeric Keypad	A cluster of keys to the right of the standard keyboard. The keypad includes numbered keys from 0 to 9 as well as cursor-control keys and other special keys.

Table 1.4
DOS Key Combinations

Keys	Function
Ctrl-Num Lock	Freezes the display; pressing Ctrl-S or any other key restarts the display.
Shift-PrtSc Print Screen	Prints the contents of the video display (print-screen feature).
Ctrl-PrtSc	Sends lines to both the screen and to the printer; giving this sequence a second time turns this function off.
Ctrl-C Ctrl-Break	Stops execution of a program.
Ctrl-Alt-Del	Restarts MS-DOS (System reset)

AT Keyboards and Enhanced Keyboards

Many early PC-compatible computers use a standard keyboard like that of the IBM PC. Other machines use Personal Computer AT keyboards. IBM's new PS/2 computers use the 101-key Enhanced Keyboard. Some users prefer the keyboard arrangement of the standard keyboard, and others prefer the enhanced keyboard.

You can determine whether your computer has a standard keyboard, a Personal Computer AT-style keyboard, or an Enhanced Keyboard. Certain keys are found only on specific keyboards. For example, you find the Print Screen and Pause keys only on the Enhanced keyboard. You can, however, simulate these keys by using a combination of keys on the standard keyboard.

The 102-key Keyboard

Some keyboards enable you to change key caps and switch key definitions for the Caps Lock, Ctrl, Esc, and ~ (tilde) keys. Northgate Computer Systems, for example, offers these options as well as an enhanced-style keyboard.

Northgate's enhanced-style keyboard locates the first ten functions keys to the left instead of across the top of the alphabet and number keys. Because this arrangement requires one more key than the 101-enhanced keyboards, this type of keyboard is called the 102-key keyboard.

Nonstandard Keyboards

Small computers, such as "lunchboxes" and laptops, use nonstandard keyboards, usually to conserve space. On some, space is so restricted that you need an external numeric keypad for use with software that performs advanced calculations.

Your computer manuals will explain how to use the special functions of your nonstandard keyboard. Usually, the "missing" keys are functionally available to you through multiple-key sequences. Normally, though, a nonstandard keyboard will not affect your work with DOS.

Exploring the System Unit

If you look at a standard desktop PC, you will find a box-shaped cabinet to which all other parts of the PC are connected. This box is called the *system unit*. The devices connected to it are the *peripherals*. The system unit and the peripherals make the complete computer system. Peripherals such as the display and the keyboard make their electrical connections to the system unit.

The system unit houses all but a few parts of a PC. Included are various circuit boards, a power supply, and even a small speaker. System units vary in appearance, but a horizontal box shape is the most common. A vertical "tower" shape is becoming popular because it frees desk or table space.

The system unit houses the main circuit board of the computer. This circuit board, called the *motherboard*, holds the main electronic components of the computer. The microprocessor and the various circuits and chips that support it are the primary components on the motherboard.

Normally the motherboard secures electrical sockets where users can plug various adapter circuit boards for additional peripherals. The electrical socket areas are often referred to as *expansion slots* because of their slot-like mounting of adapter boards.

Chips that provide the computer with its memory are located on the motherboard and, in some cases, an additional memory adapter can be plugged into an available expansion slot to increase the system's memory. The number of available expansion slots varies with the PC's manufacturer. Most motherboards have a socket for a math coprocessor. Math coprocessors help number-intensive programs perform calculations more quickly and accurately.

Most system units house hardware devices or their associated adapter boards. The hardware devices are peripherals that are internal to the system unit's cabinetry. Much variety is possible in a PC's included devices, but a few types are the most common. Figure 1.3 shows the parts of a typical system unit, and the following sections take a look at these parts in more detail.

Fig. 1.3.

A hypothetical system unit and related peripherals.

Hard disk platters are sealed inside the hard disk drive.

Floppy disks are encased in either a flexible 5 1/4-inch jacket or a rigid 3 1/2-inch jacket.

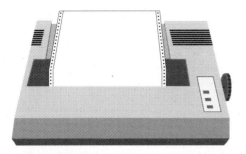

A printer is like a typewriter without a keyboard. It accepts input from the computer and renders it as characters on paper.

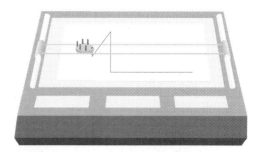

A plotter lets you draw with the computer. Unlike the printer, it moves up and down as well as back and forth.

A mouse is a computer input device whose shape is vaguely reminiscent of a real mouse.

A modem allows you to transfer signals between computers by using telephone lines.

A digitizer tablet provides a work surface that many users find more natural than using a mouse. The "puck" is moved across the tablet and the display shows the position of the puck on the tablet.

Understanding Disk Drives and Disks

Disk drives are complex mechanisms, but they carry out a basically simple function. They read and write information from and to disks. *Disks* are circular platters or pieces of plastic that have magnetized surfaces. As the disk rotates, the drive converts electrical signals that represent data into magnetic fields on the disk. This process is called *writing data to the disk*. Disk drives also recover or read the magnetically stored data and present it to the computer as electrical signals that the PC can use.

When a computer writes to a disk, DOS ensures that the data is stored as a named collection of information called a *file*. A disk's primary job, therefore, is to act as a storage medium for files. Unlike data stored in silicon memory chips, magnetically stored disk data is not lost when the computer's power is turned off.

You know that a drive is reading or writing the disk when the small light on the front of the disk drive comes on. Generally, you should not open a disk drive door or eject a disk until the light goes out. The light is the drive's signal that the drive is in use.

Two types of disks (and their drives) are available in a variety of sizes. Disks are either *floppy* or *hard*. Floppy disks, also called *diskettes*, are removable, flexible, and have a lower capacity than hard disks. DOS, as well as other software, is supplied on floppy disks (diskettes). Hard disks, also called *fixed disks*, are nonremovable, high-capacity rigid platters. Several platters can be stacked within a single hard disk drive resulting in increased storage capacity.

The components of a disk drive are similar to those of a phonograph. The disk, like a record, rotates. A positioner arm, like a tone arm, moves across the radius of the disk. A head, like a pickup cartridge, translates the encoded information to electrical signals. Unlike phonographs, however, disk drives do not have spiral tracks on the disk's surface.

The disk's surface is recorded in concentric rings or tracks. The tighter these tracks are packed on the disk, the greater the storage capacity of the disk. Chapter 5 explains in more detail how DOS uses the drives and disks on a PC.

Both sides of the disk are used for encoding information. Most DOS-based disk drives operate in this two-sided manner and are thus called double-sided disk drives.

Floppy Disks

Floppy disks store from 360K to 1.44M bytes of data and come in two common sizes. *Minifloppies* are 5 1/4-inch disks, and *microfloppies* are 3 1/2-inch disks. The measurement refers to the size of the disk's jacket. Unless size is important, floppy disks are generally referred to as *floppies* or *diskettes*.

Make sure that you know your drive's specification before you buy or interchange floppies. Floppies of the same size but with different capacities can be incompatible with a particular disk drive.

Fixed Disks

In 1973, IBM developed a hard disk technology and code-named it "Winchester." Over the years, the term Winchester has become practically synonymous with hard disks.

Hard disks often consist of multiple, rigid-disk platters. The platters spin at approximately 3,600 RPM, which is much faster than a floppy disk drive spins. As the platters spin within the drive, the head positioners make small, precise movements above the tracks of the disk. Because of this precision, hard disks can store enormous quantities of data—from 10M to more than 100M.

Despite their precision, hard disks are reasonably rugged devices. Factory sealing prevents contamination of the housing. With proper care, hard disks should give years of service.

Hard disks range from 3 1/2 to 8 inches in diameter. The most common size, 5 1/4 inches, holds between 2 1/2 and 10 megabytes of information per side.

Understanding Peripheral Devices

Besides the display and the keyboard, a variety of peripherals can be useful to a user. Many state-of-the-art computer programs require that you use a mouse to take the most advantage of the program's features. Other peripherals, such as printers and modems, enable you to use the output of your computer as you want.

The Mouse

The mouse is a device that moves on the surface of your work space and causes the computer to correlate the movement to the display. The mouse is contoured so that your hand comfortably fits over it. The contoured shape and the cable tailing from the unit gives the vague appearance of a mouse sitting on the table. The mouse has one, two, or three switch buttons that are positioned beneath the fingers of the operator's hand.

Not all software supports mouse input, but many popular programs do. Generally, mouse-based programs expect the user to point to options on the display and click one of the buttons on the mouse to carry out a task.

Printers

Printers accept signals (input) from the CPU and convert those signals to characters (output), which are usually imprinted on paper. You can classify printers in two ways: the manner in which they receive input from the computer, and the manner in which they produce output.

The manner that your printer gets its input from your PC is important in determining the type of printer assignments you will make with DOS and other software. The type of output your printer produces is a matter of print quality, graphics capability, and speed.

The terms *parallel* and *serial* describe the two methods of output from personal computers to printers. The terms *dot-matrix*, *daisywheel*, and *laser* are the generic names of printers that produce their output in three different ways.

Serial printers operate at longer cable lengths than parallel printers. A serial printer can be 50 feet or more from your PC, while a parallel printer may have trouble getting its input from a cable over 15 feet long. Having your printer close is convenient, but it can be noisy. When buying a printer, ask your dealer to demonstrate both serial and parallel printers before you decide.

Printers are usually rated by their printing speed and the quality of the finished print. Some printers print by using all the addressable points on the screen, much as a graphics display adapter does. Some printers offer color prints.

Parallel and Serial Printers

You connect printers to the system unit through a port. A *port* is an electrical doorway through which data can flow between the system unit and an outside peripheral. A port can have its own expansion adapter or can share an expansion adapter with other ports or circuits, such as a CGA.

The terms parallel and serial relate to the way the electrical data is delivered from the port to the printer. A serial port delivers the bits of the data byte one after another in a single-file manner. It takes longer to send one complete byte (character) using serial communications, but communications require fewer wires in the cable. Serial printers can communicate with the port over longer distances than parallel printers.

With a parallel port, all of the bits of data are synchronously sent through separate wires in the parallel cable one complete byte (character) at a time. Parallel printer connections are more common than serial connections.

Dot-Matrix, Daisywheel, and Laser Printers

All printers have the job of putting their output onto paper. Most of the time this output is text, but it may also be a graphics image. Three classifications of printers exist, distinguished by the mechanical method of getting output on the page.

The most common printer is the dot-matrix. Dot-matrix printers use a print head that contains a row of pins or wires that produce the characters. A motor moves the print head horizontally across the paper. As the print head moves, a vertical slice of each character forms as the printer's controlling circuits fire the proper pins or wires. The wires press corresponding small dots of the ribbon against the paper, leaving an inked dot impression. After several tiny horizontal steps, the print head leaves the dot image of a complete character. The process continues for each character on the line.

The daisywheel printer also steps the print head across the page, but strikes the page with a complete character for each step. All the characters of the alphabet are arranged at the ends of holders that resemble spokes on a wheel. The visual effect of this wheel is similar to a daisy's petals arranged around the flower head. Because the characters are fully formed, rather than made of dots, the quality of daisywheel printing is high.

Laser printers use a technology that closely resembles that of photocopying. Instead of a light-sensitive drum picking up the image of an original, the drum is painted with the light of a laser diode. The image from the drum transfers to the paper in a high-dot density output. With high-dot density, the output characters look fully formed. Laser printers can also produce graphics image output. The high quality text and graphics combination can be very useful for desktop publishing.

Modems

Modems are peripherals that enable your PC to communicate over standard telephone services. Modems are serial-communications peripherals. They send or receive characters or data one bit at a time. Modems can communicate with other modems at speeds from 30 to 960 bytes per second. Modems require communications software to coordinate their communications with other modems.

Modems can be installed within the system unit in an expansion slot. If the modem is built into the system unit, it is called an *internal* modem. Most modems attach to the system unit through a serial communications connector. The modem itself is contained in its own stand-alone case. This stand-alone type of modem is called an *external* modem.

Modems differ in their speed of communicating information. Some modems can communicate at about 30 characters per second. Most popular modems communicate between 120 and 240 characters per second. Some special modems are capable of 1,920 characters per second. As a rule of thumb, faster modems cost more than slower ones.

Understanding How Computers Work with Data

Now that you have been introduced to the essential parts of a computer system, you are ready for a general overview of how these parts carry out the job of computing. The world inside a computer is a strange and different place. Fortunately, you do not have to know the details of a computer's operation to use a computer effectively in your work. Most of the highly technical aspects of computing are better left to computer professionals. But if you do undertake some exploration, you will adjust more quickly to using your computer. The fundamentals of computing are easier to understand than many people think.

Computers perform many useful tasks by accepting data as input, processing it, and releasing it as output. Data is any information. It can be a set of numbers, a memo, an arrow key to move a game symbol, or just about anything else you can conceive. Input comes from you and is translated into electrical signals that move through a set of electronic controls. Output can be thought of in three ways:

- Characters the computer displays on-screen
- Signals the computer holds in its memory
- Signals stored magnetically on disk

Computers receive and send output in the form of electrical signals. These signals are stable in two states: on and off. Think of these states as you would the power in the wire from a light switch you can turn on and off. Computers contain millions of electronic switches that can be either on or off. All forms of input and output follow this two-state principle.

The computer name for the two-state principle is *binary*, which refers to something made of two things or two parts. Computers represent data with two binary digits, or *bits*—0 and 1. For convenience, computers group eight bits together. This eight-bit grouping is called a *byte*. Bytes are sometimes packaged in two-, four-, or eight-byte packages when the computer moves information internally.

Computers move bits and bytes across electrical highways called *buses*. Normally, the computer contains three buses. The *control* bus manages the devices attached to the PC. The *data* bus is the highway for information transfer. The *address* bus routes signals so that data goes to the correct location within the computer. The microprocessor is connected to all three buses and supervises their activity.

Because the microprocessor can call upon the memory at any address and in any order, the memory is called *random access memory* or *RAM*. Some RAM information is permanent. This permanent memory is called *read-only memory* or *ROM*. ROM is useful for holding unalterable instructions in the computer system.

The microprocessor depends on you to give it instructions in the form of a program. A *program* is a set of binary-coded instructions that produce a desired result. The microprocessor decodes the binary information and carries out the instruction from the program.

You can begin from scratch and type programs or data into the computer each time you turn on the power. But, of course, you wouldn't want to do that if you didn't have to. Luckily, the computer can store both instructions and start-up data, usually on a disk. Disks store data in binary form in files.

As far as the computer is concerned, a file is just a collection of bytes identified by a unique name. These bytes can be a memo, a word processing program, or some other program. The job of the file is to hold binary data or programs safely until the microprocessor calls for that data or program. When the call comes, the drive reads the file and writes the contents into RAM.

Displaying a word on a computer screen seems to be a simple matter of pressing keys on the keyboard. But each time you press a key to enter a character, the computer carries out a series of complex steps.

A personal computer is very busy on the inside. Program instructions held in random-access memory (RAM) are fetched and executed by the CPU. Resulting computations are stored in RAM. The CPU controls internal operations by using electrical highways called buses. The CPU uses the data bus to determine WHAT the data should be, the control bus to determine HOW the electrical operations should proceed, and the address bus to determine WHERE the data or instructions are located in RAM.

Summary

This chapter provided a quick overview of personal computers. DOS is much easier to learn when you are familiar with your PC and its component parts. In this chapter, you learned the following important points:

- ❏ IBM and compatible computers operate basically in the same way.

- ❏ A computer's hardware works with software to do useful work.

- ❏ System hardware does the "computing" in the PC.

- ❏ Peripheral hardware provides the PC with input and output capability so that the PC can work with you.

- ❏ PCs have text displays or graphics displays. Text displays cannot display the output of many graphics based software programs. Graphics displays can display both text and graphics.

- ❏ The PC's keyboard offers standard typewriter keys as well as special keys such as the function keys. Programs like DOS and the DOS Shell determine how the special keys will work.

- ❏ The PC's main box is the system unit. The system unit houses the disk drive(s) and the motherboard where the system hardware resides.

- ❏ Disk drives are either fixed hard disk drives, or removable floppy disk drives.

- ❏ Many PC systems include a printer, modem, or mouse. PCs accommodate these outside peripherals as well as other attachments.

❑ Computers "compute" by operating on binary representations of information. The source of the information is called input. The destination of the resulting computational result is called output. Computers store information in 8-bit bytes.

You will pick up more insight into computers as you progress through this book. The next chapter introduces the role of DOS in the personal computer. DOS was designed around the system hardware and peripherals discussed in this chapter, so you will want to move directly to Chapter 2 while this chapter is fresh in your mind.

Understanding the
Role of DOS

2

Chapter 1 introduced personal computer systems and their component parts. The chapter described software and showed how data moves in the computer. This chapter introduces an important link between the hardware, the software, and you. This link is the disk operating system—DOS.

As with Chapter 1, you can read this chapter without being at your computer.

An *operating system* is a collection of computer programs that provide recurring services to other programs or to the user of a computer. These services consist of disk and file management, memory management, and device management. Computers need software to provide these services. If the computer's operating system software did not provide these services, the user or the user's applications program would have to deal directly with the details of the PC's hardware, file system, and memory utilization.

Without a disk operating system, for example, every computer program would have to contain instructions telling the hardware each step the hardware should take to do its job, such as storing a file on a disk. Because an operating system already contains these instructions, however, any program can call on the operating system when a service is needed. The operating systems are called *disk operating systems* because most of the commands are kept on the *disk* (either floppy or hard) rather than in memory. As a result, the operating system requires less memory to run.

IBM-compatible personal computers use as an operating system either MS-DOS or its close relative, PC DOS. MS-DOS is the disk operating system developed by Microsoft Corporation to provide a foundation of services for operating an IBM PC or compatible computer. Manufacturers of personal computers, such as Zenith, IBM, and COMPAQ, tailor MS-DOS for use on their computers. In fact, hundreds of PCs use some form of MS-DOS. The manufacturers may put their own names on the disks and include different manuals with the DOS packages they provide. But all of these types of DOS are very similar when they operate on a PC. When you read about DOS in this book, you can safely assume that what you read will apply to the version of DOS used by most manufacturers. In special cases, differences will be noted.

Key Terms Used in This Chapter

Program   Instructions that tell a computer how to carry out tasks.

BIOS   Basic Input/Output System. The software that provides in a PC the basic functional link between DOS and the peripheral hardware.

Redirection   A change in the source or destination of a command's normal input or output.

Application   A program. A set of instructions that tell the computer to perform a program-specific task, such as word processing.

Interface   A connection between parts of the computer, especially between hardware devices. Also refers to the interaction between a user and an applications program.

Batch file   A series of DOS commands placed in a disk file. DOS executes batch-file commands one at a time.

What is DOS?

DOS is an acronym for *Disk Operating System*. Nearly every computer has some sort of disk operating system. Those that do not are severely limited in reliable data storage. Disk operating systems manage many of the technical details of computers as well as disk-file storage. Disk management, however, is perhaps the most important service these operating systems provide.

Many computers, including personal computers and large, multiuser computers, use these three letters—DOS—as part of their operating system's name. Microsoft's MS-DOS and IBM's version of MS-DOS, PC DOS, are examples. So are Apple's DOS 3.3 and ProDOS.

These various operating systems are all called DOS. But if numbers count, more people associate the term DOS with MS-DOS than with any other disk operating system in the world. There are millions of MS-DOS users. When you read the term DOS in this book, you will be reading about MS-DOS. MS-DOS is a single-user, single-tasking disk operating system that provides the framework of operation for millions of today's personal computers.

Examining the Variations of MS-DOS

MS-DOS is an operating system that accommodates variation in its exact makeup while retaining its core characteristics. Just as a car model can have differences in style, color, and standard equipment, DOS can have variations. The basic framework for the car (and DOS) allows for differences to be introduced as the final tailoring of the finished product. This capability for variation enables various computer manufacturers to adapt MS-DOS to their computers. Both IBM PC DOS and COMPAQ DOS, for example, are variations of MS-DOS. As DOS has matured as a product, it has been enhanced. Enhancements have been released as new versions of DOS. Each new version has built upon its predecessor while retaining the original version's primary design features.

Product-Specific Variations of DOS

Today, all commonly available variations of MS-DOS are very close in design and operation. There is a good reason for this closeness. MS-DOS works with computers designed around Intel's 8086 microprocessor family. This family includes the 8088, 8086, 80286, 80386, and 80486 microprocessors. When conceiving the original IBM Personal Computer, IBM designers selected the Intel 8088 microprocessor to be the "brains" of their computer.

IBM's Personal Computer was a grand success. The enormity of the original IBM PC's influence on the PC market convinced other PC manufacturers using the 8086 family to follow closely IBM's personal computer design. Because IBM used an open approach to designing the IBM PC, other companies were able to configure their computers to use programs and hardware designed for the IBM PC. From DOS's point of view, these various computers are virtually alike, even though the PCs may be more advanced than the original IBM PC.

The closeness of its design to the IBM PC determines to what degree a PC is said to be *IBM-compatible*. No industry standard concerning compatibility has been written down. The standard is instead a de facto standard—one which grew out of the principle of supply and demand. The buying public has demanded a high degree of IBM compatibility in PCs. Most PCs (and their respective variations of MS-DOS) that were not designed to be highly compatible with the IBM PC have either been discontinued, sell in specialty markets, or are available in countries other than the United States. Because of this "shaking out" of the market, most compatible PCs successfully operate using a version of IBM's PC DOS even though most compatible manufacturers usually offer their own variation of MS-DOS.

The variations in MS-DOS implementations among PC manufacturers are seen by users as subtle differences, usually limited to the names of a few commands or the way parameters are given. Some manufacturers include in their MS-DOS packages additional utilities that work with a feature of that manufacturer's model of PC. Yet, as a general rule, if you are proficient at using one variation of MS-DOS, you are proficient with all variations of MS-DOS. In a practical sense, the terms MS-DOS, PC DOS, and DOS are interchangeable. You will be able to use just about any compatible computer that runs DOS as its operating system by using what you know about DOS from working with another PC.

Changes between Versions of DOS

Another type of variation involves the evolution of the product itself. As MS-DOS has evolved, the core product has been enhanced several times. Each release of enhancements is a distinct version of the program. Since its appearance in the summer of 1981, DOS has evolved through four major versions. Table 2.1 lists the important differences between versions of DOS, beginning in 1981. (More detailed coverage of these changes can be found in Appendix E.)

Table 2.1
Quick Reference to Versions of DOS

MS-DOS Version	Significant Change
1.0	Original version of DOS.
1.25	Accommodates double-sided disks.
2.0	Includes multiple directories needed to organize hard disks.
3.0	Uses high-capacity floppy disks, the RAM disk, volume names, and the ATTRIB command.
3.1	Includes provisions for networking.
3.2	Accommodates 3 1/2-inch drives.
3.3	Accommodates high-capacity 3 1/2-inch drives; includes new commands.
4.0	Introduces the DOS shell and the MEM command; accommodates larger files and disk capacities.

Even with the introduction of Microsoft's OS/2 and the presence of several versions of the UNIX operating system, DOS remains strong. You can expect your investment in learning DOS to continue paying dividends in any future computing. Most industry experts predict that DOS will have a presence in the PC picture for years to come.

TIP

Operating systems such as OS/2 and UNIX are getting a great deal of media attention. Perhaps one of these operating systems will eventually emerge as the replacement for DOS in everyday personal computing. Even if you move to OS/2 or UNIX at some point, however, you will find that much of your DOS expertise can be used with these operating systems.

Examining the DOS Package

Chances are very good that your purchase of a computer included a DOS package. You may have purchased DOS as a separate item if your computer did not include DOS, but most dealers and manufacturers supply or sell DOS as a stand-alone package or as an accessory package to a PC. Most often the DOS package includes one or more manuals and two or more disks. The DOS software itself is on the disk(s).

PC DOS V4.0, for example, comes packaged with 2 or 5 disks depending on the model of computer intended for the software. PC DOS V3.3 comes in a package with 1 or 2 disks. COMPAQ supplies DOS V4.0 with 2 DOS disks and 1 supplemental disk. DOS packages supplied by other computer manufacturers may have more or fewer disks. The disks may contain supplemental programs for the PC such as GW—BASIC and MS-LINK. These supplemental programs are often considered part of DOS because the manufacturer included them in the physical DOS package. Depending on the context, supplemental programs may be associated with the term *DOS package*, but for the purpose of this book, you should consider such supplemental programs to be outside of DOS.

Normally, the DOS package contains a DOS reference manual. The manual is an important supplement because it contains specific information about your version of DOS. Many PC users, however, prefer to use another book, such as this book or other books about DOS published by Que Corporation, for their daily DOS reference. It's not surprising that DOS users may prefer another, perhaps more specialized, book to the package's DOS manual. DOS users can select a book that fits their needs closely, whether they are beginning, intermediate, or advanced DOS users. On the other hand, the DOS reference manual included in the DOS package must attempt to supply an accurate description of that version of DOS to new and advanced users alike.

Many manufacturers include in the package other manuals that look similar to the DOS reference manual and contain information specific to the computer model or its auxiliary software. COMPAQ, for example, supplies a manual describing the operation of the tape unit included in some COMPAQ models. Although the discussion of the tape unit includes references to DOS, this manual is not considered to be a standard part of DOS for all PCs. The topics in these specialty manuals are not covered in this book, so keep those additional manuals at hand for reference.

Understanding the Purpose of the DOS Disks

DOS disks that come in the DOS package are special disks. What makes the disks special is that they contain DOS files—the files that are needed to start your PC and subsequently support your commands and applications. These DOS files contain the computer-level instructions that provide the functional aspects of DOS. The PC doesn't have these computer-level functions built in. In a way, the DOS disks serve as the key that unlocks the potential of the computer. When the operating system information stored on these disks is loaded into your PC, your programs can exploit the PC's computing potential.

> ***On using the disks that came in your DOS package . . .*** If you are fairly new to DOS, here's a word of wisdom: Don't use the master DOS disks that came in your DOS package for everyday work. The manufacturers intended for you to make copies of these master DOS disks; the copies can then be used when you need to use the DOS disks. Be sure to store your masters in a safe place. You should have at least one known good (tested) set of working DOS floppies even if your computer has a hard disk that contains the DOS files.
>
> Even if DOS is installed on your hard disk, do not be without floppy-based copies of your DOS package disks. You may need them if your hardware experiences problems or some software holds your hard disk hostage.

You can hold the DOS disks in your hand because the disks are physical. The instructions that the disks hold, however, are logical—not physical. In the world of computers, you view something in a logical way by understanding the concept of its operation.

This conceptual view includes the steps that make the computer "compute." Each time it is turned on, the PC must refresh itself by reading in the DOS instructions from the DOS system files on the PC's start-up disk to the PC's working memory. The PC is then ready to run your favorite software. DOS, your PC, and your favorite software work together to produce the computing result. If you remove any of the ingredients, you won't be computing.

When you mow your lawn, you count on the operation of the mower and the application of your mowing technique on the lawn to get the job done. Mowing the lawn is conceptually the interplay between you, the mower, and the lawn. If you simply push a dead mower over the grass, you are going through the motions, but the grass is not mowed. If you start your mower, but let it sit in one spot, the potential of the spinning blades is available, but the grass is still not mown. Only when you start the mower and push it correctly across your lawn is the lawn mown as you intend.

Likewise, you can start DOS on your computer and let it sit, but you won't be doing any useful computing. You can attempt to use your computer without starting DOS, but nothing will happen. Conceptually, DOS is the go-between that links you with the computer's capability to do useful work. You have to know how to start DOS from the files on the DOS disks or their equals on a hard disk. Once DOS is started, you can mow through a memo or a spreadsheet.

All disks must be prepared by DOS before they can be used by DOS. Only disks prepared with the DOS system files can start your PC. Disks which include the DOS system files are the DOS boot disks. In fact, many people refer to a bootable disk as *being* DOS.

Examining the Files on the DOS Disks

Like the files on other disks, the files on the DOS disks have specific purposes. Every file available to DOS has a file name. The file name can have two parts with a period separating the parts. The first part, called the *root file name*, can include up to 8 characters. The second part of the file name, called the *file name extension*, can be up to 3 characters long. The extension is optional. On the DOS disks, a file's extension helps to describe the general mission of the file in a working PC. Each version or variation of DOS has an individual assortment of file names on the DOS disks. Even with this variation, you can benefit by looking at the file names of one particular DOS disk. The following list shows the names of the DOS files on the PC DOS V4.0 disks.

```
ASSIGN   COM
BACKUP   COM
BASIC    COM
BASICA   COM
CHKDSK   COM
COMMAND  COM
COMP     COM
DEBUG    COM
DISKCOMP COM
DISKCOPY COM
EDLIN    COM
FDISK    COM
FORMAT   COM
GRAFTABL COM
GRAPHICS COM
KEYB     COM
LABEL    COM
MODE     COM
MORE     COM
PRINT    COM
RECOVER  COM
RESTORE  COM
SELECT   COM
SHELLB   COM
SYS      COM
TREE     COM
```

The COM file extension identifies a *command* file. Command files are derived from one of the earliest operating system for personal computers, CP/M-80. As you learn DOS, you will recognize that most of the file names with COM extensions are the names of external DOS commands.

```
5202      CPI
4208      CPI
4201      CPI      ── Files with CPI extensions operate the display screen.
EGA       CPI
LCD       CPI
SELECT    DAT      ── A file with the extension DAT is a data file.
012345    678      ── Files used by a program that teaches aspects of DOS V4.0.
012345    678
MORTGAGE  BAS      ── A program file written in the BASIC language has a BAS
                      extension.
AUTOEXEC  BAT      ── A BAT or batch file. In this case, AUTOEXEC.BAT is a
                      special batch file that runs automatically when you start
SHELL     CLR         the computer.

ATTRIB    EXE         A color configuration file that instructs DOS V4.0 how
FASTOPEN  EXE         to display the DOS Shell program.
FILESYS   EXE
APPEND    EXE
FIND      EXE
IFSFUNC   EXE         EXE files are executable program files. Except for the
JOIN      EXE         technical details of their internal structure, they are
MEM       EXE         much like COM files. By entering the root name of an
NLSFUNC   EXE         EXE file, you cause a program to run.
REPLACE   EXE
SELECT    EXE
SHARE     EXE
SHELLC    EXE
SORT      EXE
SUBST     EXE
XCOPY     EXE

SELECT    HLP      ── HLP files are used to display on-screen help.
SHELL     HLP

DOSUTIL   MEU      ── MEU extensions indicate that the files handle on-screen
SHELL     MEU         menus from which you make selections.

PCIBMDRV  MOS      ── MOS file extensions identify files that operate the
PCMSDRV   MOS         mouse.
PCMSPDRV  MOS

GRAPHICS  PRO      ── The GRAPHICS.PRO file contains profiles of graphics-
                      mode printers supported by DOS V4.0.
ANSI      SYS
CONFIG    SYS
COUNTRY   SYS
DISPLAY   SYS         SYS files are system files. They are also called device
DRIVER    SYS         drivers. SYS files are used to add or modify hardware
KEYBOARD  SYS         support to the basic PC operation.
PRINTER   SYS
VDISK     SYS
XMA2EMS   SYS
XMAEM     SYS
```

Understanding the Parts of DOS

Remember that the DOS disks contain the files necessary for DOS to do its job. When DOS is loaded in the PC, it acts as a go-between so that you and the PC can do useful computing. You can also look at DOS as an entity that is divided into modular parts. This modularity allows DOS to "divide and conquer" the various operating system requirements placed upon DOS by users and programs.

DOS can be viewed as having three main functional components:

- The command interpreter (COMMAND.COM)
- The basic input/output system (BIOS)
- The DOS utilities

All three of these components are contained in files that come with the disks in your DOS package. In the following sections, you will be introduced to the components and to their duties.

A note from the author . . . Don't worry if you haven't completely grasped the significance of a computer's operating system at this point. This chapter will go a long way towards setting the stage for you. An operating system is a multifaceted software creation. Some facets are easier to master than others. You may benefit from reading this chapter again after you've completely read through the rest of the chapters in Part One. Many of the ideas presented in this chapter are touched on again in later chapters. Rest assured that once you start using DOS, you will quickly develop your own personal definition for this versatile operating system.

The Command Interpreter

The command interpreter is DOS's "friendly host." It interacts with you through the keyboard and screen when you operate your computer. The command interpreter is also known as the *command processor* and often is referred to simply as COMMAND.COM (pronounced *command dot com*). COMMAND.COM accepts your DOS commands and sees that they are carried out.

COMMAND.COM prints on your display the DOS *prompt* (C>, A>, and so on). The DOS prompt is a request for input. When you enter a command, you are communicating with COMMAND.COM, which then interprets what you type and processes your input so that DOS can take the appropriate action. COMMAND.COM, through DOS commands, handles the technical details of such common tasks as displaying a list of the contents of a disk, copying files, and, of course, starting your programs.

When you go to a restaurant, you may be attended by a waiter whose job it is to see to your needs. COMMAND.COM is like the waiter. You communicate your dining requests to the waiter as you communicate your command requests to COMMAND.COM. In the process of ordering, for example, the waiter may inform you that an entree is not available or that a combination of additional side dishes isn't included with a certain dinner. COMMAND.COM communicates to you when a command is not available or when an additional part of a command is not allowed.

Your waiter doesn't prepare your meal in the kitchen. The waiter communicates your instructions to the personnel in the kitchen in a way that the cooks understand. Likewise, COMMAND.COM doesn't carry out most of the DOS commands itself, but instead communicates to other modules of DOS which specialize in the requested service. Your waiter may provide you with some simple services, such as pouring more water or offering condiments. These simple services are built into the waiter's job. COMMAND.COM has some simpler DOS commands built-in also. These built-in commands are available whenever you are using DOS. With these built-in or *internal* commands, COMMAND.COM does not have to rely on the presence of other DOS modules to carry out the work of the internal commands.

COMMAND.COM is a very important part of DOS. Perhaps PC users think of COMMAND.COM's operation as being the essence of DOS because it is so visible. DOS does many things behind the scenes, but COMMAND.COM is very up-front (see fig. 2.1). PC users equate issuing commands with performing DOS-level PC-management work because issuing DOS commands is the primary area of their DOS activities.

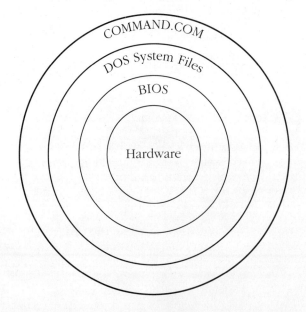

COMMAND.COM

DOS System Files

BIOS

Hardware

Fig. 2.1

All of your communications with DOS are actually instructions to COMMAND.COM. COMMAND.COM is a special type of software that lets you address the file and input/output systems of the computer through the keyboard. Because you instruct COMMAND.COM rather than the hardware directly, you need never know the details of how the hardware operates.

Chapter 4 discusses DOS commands more fully, and Part Two of this book is devoted to the DOS commands users most often issue. But issuing commands is only a part of using DOS to manage a PC. Many of the commands you issue at the DOS prompt work with the file system. Chapter 5 provides an inside view of the file system that makes using disk- and file-related DOS commands more meaningful.

The Basic Input/Output System

The so-called "hidden" or *system* files are another part of the operating system. These two or three special files (the number depends on your computer) define the hardware to the software. When you start a computer, these DOS system files are loaded into RAM. Combined, the files provide a unified set of routines for controlling and directing the computer's operations. These files are known as the input/output system.

The hidden files interact with special read-only memory (ROM) on the motherboard. The special ROM is called the *ROM Basic Input Output System* or simply *BIOS*. Responding to a program's request for service, the system files translate the request and pass it to the ROM BIOS. The BIOS provides a further translation of the request that links the request to the hardware (see fig. 2.2).

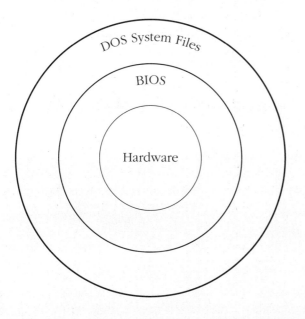

Fig. 2.2

DOS provides a uniform service to the hardware by getting assistance from the permanent ROM BIOS in the computer. ROM BIOS can vary among computer makers, but the computers will be highly compatible if the design of the ROM BIOS is integrated with DOS.

In large part, it is the DOS input/output system, through the special BIOS, that determines the degree to which a PC is "IBM-compatible."

The Hidden Core of DOS

Inside a working PC, DOS is the collection of services that DOS offers in the form of built-in groups of related instructions or software routines. These routines provide the core of the services DOS provides to your applications programs. The extensive file-system management provided by DOS, for example, is made up of these routines. Programmers can access these software routines to perform a variety of internal operations with the PC. These functions are common and repetitive actions that operating system designers have included in DOS to make life easier (and programs more uniform) for those people who write programs for PCs. DOS commands themselves rely on these service routines to do standard low-level computer work. By accessing the built-in DOS service routines, a program doesn't need the details of how DOS works with the PC. With the interface to DOS service built-in, computer languages and the programs they produce can use DOS uniformly.

The internal file system and input/output aspects of DOS are often as invisible to DOS users as interaction with COMMAND.COM is obvious. When you order from a waiter, you don't need to know the details of how your meal is prepared. You just want timely service and satisfaction with your food. In a similar way, you (or your program) want timely and appropriate services to be conducted by the internal parts of DOS. You don't care how DOS goes about doing its internal job, detailed though it may be.

Fortunately, you do not have to know much about these internal DOS programming concerns to operate your PC. Having some idea of what goes on at the internal level, however, may give you more insight into how a DOS command or your word processor works. Programming at the DOS level is fascinating and rewarding to many, but this book will not attempt to teach you the programming aspects of DOS. If you want to know more about programming at the DOS level for additional insight or to write actual programs, you can refer to one of the books published by Que Corporation on this topic. *DOS Programmer's Reference*, 2nd Edition, by Terry Dettmann, and *Using Assembly Language*, by Allen Wyatt, are suggested.

If the programming aspects of DOS do not interest you, do not feel alone. Most DOS users are generally uninformed about "what goes on in there," and they do just fine. As your DOS skills increase, however, you may find that having a general layman's notion of "what goes on in there" will enable you to become a more self-reliant PC user. Throughout this book, you'll get simple explanations of internal operations. There is a whole world in this invisible but essential part of DOS.

The DOS Utilities

The DOS utilities carry out useful housekeeping tasks, such as preparing disks, comparing files, finding the free space on a disk, and printing in the background. Some of the utilities provide statistics on disk size and available memory; others compare disks and files. The utility programs are files that reside on disk and are loaded into memory by COMMAND.COM when you type their command names. They are called *external* commands because they are not built into DOS. An example of one of these external commands is the DOSSHELL command, which provides access to the DOS Shell program included with DOS V4.0 (see fig. 2.3).

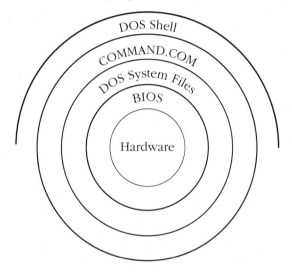

Fig. 2.3

The DOS 4.0 Shell is a user-friendly program interface between your need for DOS services and the details of DOS commands. The Shell is a final layer that insulates you from having to know how to electronically control the details of the computer's hardware.

Disk operating systems insulate you and your programs from the need to know exactly how to make the hardware work. For example, to list the contents of a disk in a disk drive, you don't need to know the capacity or recording format of the disk or how to get the computer to direct the output to the screen. An applications program that needs to store data on the disk does not have to reserve space on the disk, keep track of where on the disk the data is stored, or know how the data was encoded. DOS takes care of all these tasks.

Understanding the Functions of DOS

By now, you no doubt suspect that DOS does many "technical" things that do not seem to be easy to comprehend. It is certainly true that much of DOS's activity falls into a category that could be called technical. But most DOS activities that you need to understand to make DOS work effectively for you are not at all difficult to comprehend. This section briefly describes the common DOS functions you will use again and again as your computing expertise grows. Later sections treat each of these topics in detail.

Managing Files

One of DOS's primary functions is to help you organize the files that you store on your disks. Organized files are a sign of good computer housekeeping. Good housekeeping becomes crucial once you begin to take advantage of the storage capacity available on today's disks.

Think, for example, about the fact that the smallest-capacity floppy disk can hold the equivalent of 100 letter-sized pages of information. Now, imagine that each sheet of information makes up one file: you have 100 files to keep track of. If you use disks that can hold more information than a standard floppy (such as a hard disk), file organization becomes even more crucial.

Fortunately, DOS gives you the tools to be a good computer housekeeper. DOS lists files for you, tells you their names and sizes, and gives you the dates when they were created. And you can use this information for many organizational purposes. In addition to organizing files, DOS can duplicate files, discard files that are no longer useful, and replace files with matching file names.

Managing Disks

Certain DOS functions are essential to all computer users. For example, all disks must be prepared before they can be used in your computer. This preparation is called *formatting* and includes checking disks for available space. Other functions in DOS's disk-management category include the following:

- Labeling disks electronically
- Making restorable backup copies of files for security purposes
- Restoring damaged files on disk
- Copying disks
- Viewing the contents of files on a disk

Redirecting Input and Output

DOS expects its input to come from a standard place, such as the keyboard. DOS sends its output to a standard place, such as the display screen. Designers of DOS recognized that it would sometimes be convenient to send output to another device, such as a printer. DOS designers provided DOS with the ability to redirect, or send in another direction, the output that normally goes to the standard output. Through redirection, a list of files that usually appears on the screen can be sent to the printer. You will see useful examples of the redirection of common commands when the commands are discussed.

DOS also contains commands that enable you to tailor your PC's hardware environment to your specific needs. In fact, DOS provides much versatility in its configuration capabilities. Fortunately for users just starting with DOS, the standard configuration of the PC will work fine. In this book, you will, however, learn how to make simple alterations of the PC's DOS configuration.

Adding configuration control to your DOS activities isn't an every day occurrence. Usually, a user will establish a tailored configuration using the CONFIG.SYS file. Once established, the CONFIG.SYS file remains relatively unchanged. Chapter 13 covers the topic of configuration. Don't worry about configuration for now. You will be ready to understand it later.

Running Applications Programs

Computers require complex and exact instructions—programs—to provide you with useful output. Computing would be impractical if you had to write a program each time you had a job to do. Happily, that is not the case. Programmers spend months doing the specialized work that allows a computer to function as many different things: a word processor, database manipulator, spreadsheet, or generator of graphics. Through a program, the computer's capabilities are *applied* to a task—thus the term *applications programs.*

Applications programs, like DOS, are distributed on disks. DOS is the go-between that gives you access to these programs through the computer. By simply inserting a disk into a computer's disk drive and pressing a few keys, you can instantly have an astonishingly wide variety of easy-to-use applications at your disposal.

Applications constantly need to read data *from* or write data *to* disk files. You need to see what you have typed by viewing text information sent to the screen or printer. The program you are using needs you to enter information from the keyboard or move the mouse in a certain way. These input and output tasks are common, repetitive computer tasks. Electronically, these tasks are not trivial. Thanks to DOS, you can take the repetitive tasks for granted. DOS takes responsibility for the technical detail of input and output. DOS provides applications with an easy-to-use connection or program interface that sees to the details of these repetitive activities. As the user of the computer, you want easy-to-understand information about disk files, memory size, and computer configuration. DOS provides these services.

When you walk up to a soft-drink machine, you concern yourself with having the right coins and making a selection that will satisfy your desire. You probably don't think of the wires, motors, refrigeration equipment, and the mechanism that calculates change. You know to put the coins into the slot, press the correct button, and pick up your drink from the dispenser. The maker of that soft-drink machine has provided you with an easy-to-use interface that has relatively simple input and provides straightforward output. You have a need, and through your actions, the machine carries out many detailed steps internally to provide you with a service that fills that need. DOS's service provisions are not unlike that of the soft-drink machine. DOS is perhaps a bit more complicated, but the concept of internal details that you don't see is the same for DOS as it is for the soft-drink machine.

Running Batch Files

Most of your interaction with DOS will take place through the keyboard. You type commands for COMMAND.COM to carry out. Commands, however, can also be placed in a disk file called a *batch file* and "played back" to COMMAND.COM. Chapter 12 covers batch files and how you can create them.

COMMAND.COM responds to these batches of commands from the file just as it would respond to commands typed from the keyboard. Batch files can automate often-used command sequences, making keyboard operation simpler.

Difficult-to-remember command sequences are ideal candidates for batch-file treatment.

Handling Miscellaneous Tasks

Some of the functions of DOS fall into a "miscellaneous" category. One example is the setting of the computer's clock and calendar so that files and applications programs can have access to dates and times. Or, you might need to use DOS's text editor to create text files such as memos, notes, or batch files. You can even see the amount of RAM available for applications programs through DOS.

Developing a Working Knowledge of DOS

Anyone who intends to use a personal computer can benefit from a working knowledge of DOS. Consider the fact that you can't use your computer to run most popular programs at all unless you start it with DOS. While it may true that someone you know is always more or less willing to do the DOS-related work for you, you will become much more proficient at computing if you learn a little DOS. Besides, the results will greatly exceed the effort you spend learning DOS.

Summary

In this chapter, you learned some facts about the role of DOS in personal computing. Following are some important points to remember:

- ❏ The term DOS is an acronym for *Disk Operating System*. Many computer operating systems have the term DOS in their names.
- ❏ MS-DOS is the name of an operating system for IBM PCs and close compatibles. To most PC users, DOS means MS-DOS.
- ❏ When PC users use the term DOS, they may be referring to only one contextual part of the whole of DOS.
- ❏ DOS works with the Intel 8086 family of microprocessors.
- ❏ The DOS package includes a number of disks that contain the files necessary for DOS to do its job.

❏ The files on the DOS disks include extensions that indicate the purpose of the file.

❏ The BIOS layer of a PC is contained in permanent ROM which works with the hardware and provides a foundation of services for DOS.

❏ COMMAND.COM is the DOS command processor. COMMAND.COM executes DOS commands.

❏ The DOS Shell program available with DOS V4.0 provides a windowed interface that enables the user to execute DOS commands by selecting an item from a menu.

❏ DOS has many functions, including managing files and disks, redirecting input and output, running applications programs and batch files, and handling miscellaneous tasks such as setting the computer's date and time.

As you read the following chapters, you will find that DOS can be useful in a variety of ways. There are more than seventy DOS commands and functions possible. This book emphasizes those that are essential to using a personal computer for running off-the-shelf programs. You will quickly become familiar with the essentials of DOS through this approach.

Starting
DOS

Now that you have an overview of both the PC and DOS, it's time to start your PC and learn more about the practical operation of DOS. This chapter is an overview of the start-up process. The first time you start your computer, you may not know what to expect. Once you learn a few computer terms and perform the basic start-up procedure, however, you will begin to feel at ease. Before you flip the PC's switch, take time to understand some preliminary information about the start-up process.

The operators of early computers started their computers by entering a short, binary program and then instructing the computer to run the program. This binary program was called the "bootstrap loader" because the computer, through the bootstrap program, figuratively pulled itself up by the bootstraps to perform tasks. The early computer operators shortened the name of the start-up process to *booting*. The term stuck. Today, *booting the computer* still refers to the start-up procedure. Fortunately, the process of booting is now relatively automatic.

This chapter assumes that you do not know how to boot or know the process behind booting. A few commands are necessary to show you the start-up process, but don't worry if you do not know them. Just type in the examples; you will read about the commands in detail in later chapters.

Key Terms Used in This Chapter

Cold boot	The process of starting a PC from a power-off condition.
Warm boot	The process of restarting a PC while the power is on.
Cursor	The blinking line or solid block that marks where the next keyboard entry will appear.
Default	A condition or value that the computer, the program, or DOS assumes if you choose not to supply your own.
Prompt	A symbol, character, or group of characters which indicate that you must enter information.
DOS prompt	The characters that COMMAND.COM displays to inform you that you can enter a DOS command. An example of a DOS prompt is C>.
Command	A text directive to COMMAND.COM, issued at the DOS prompt, that instructs DOS to provide an operating system service.
Parameter	Additional instructions given with a command to let DOS know how to carry out the command.
Syntax	The formation of commands and parameters at the prompt. COMMAND.COM interprets the syntax as your instructions to DOS.
Logged drive	The current default disk drive that DOS uses to carry out commands that involve disk services. Unless you change the prompt with a command, the letter of the default drive will be the DOS prompt.

Performing a Cold Boot

The term *cold boot* is derived from the fact that the computer's power is off and that the unit is not yet warm. (In reality, computers don't heat up very much.) The word "boot" may seem odd, but it is the preferred expression. Just remember that the key idea behind a cold-boot startup is that the computer's power switch is off. If the booting process is new to you, you will want to make a few preliminary checks part of your booting routine. The next section reviews these preliminary checks before the cold-boot process.

Making Preliminary Checks

If you take airplane trips, you may have noticed that before taking off, a pilot checks to make sure that all equipment is in working order. Just as this preliminary check of the airplane is important, so is your check of your computer's equipment. Your PC isn't as complicated as an aircraft, but a few preliminary checks help you avoid the potential of "crashes."

Computers like clean, steady power sources. Choose a good electrical outlet that does not serve devices like copy machines, hair dryers, or other electrical gadgets. Ask your computer dealer about a line conditioner if you must share an outlet.

Make sure that the switch is off before you plug in your computer. Some computers have switches marked with 0 and 1. The switch side marked 0 is the off switch position. Many PCs will keep themselves turned off after a electrical "drop out" even when the PC's switch is in the on position. This feature ensures that unsettled power conditions have passed before you switch the unit off, then on again.

Ventilation is important to computers. Make sure that your PC has room to breathe. Computers must dissipate the heat generated by their internal electronic components. PCs do not need a blanket of paper to keep warm. Keep paper, books, beverages, and other clutter away from the system unit's case.

If you stand your computer's system unit on end on the floor, make sure that the cooling fan is not obstructed by the back of a desk or some other furniture. Use one of the commercially available vertical floor stands to make the system unit more stable. Watch out for dust accumulation in the fan area from the extra dust on the floor.

Place this book, your DOS manual, DOS disks, and your PC system manual nearby for reference. The disk you use to boot your computer can be labeled "Startup," "System," "Main," or "DOS." Check your DOS manual if you are not sure which disk is bootable, or ask your computer specialist to provide a bootable DOS system disk. From this point on, the bootable disk(s) supplied in your DOS package will be referred to in this book as the *DOS Master disk(s)*.

Inserting the Disk

For the initial cold boot, you will use your DOS Master disk. To ensure that the DOS disk (or any other disk for that matter) does not get accidentally erased, you should write-protect the disk. To write-protect a 3-1/2-inch microfloppy disk, locate the write-protect shutter (see fig. 3.1) and slide the plastic shutter so that the window is open. To write-protect a 5-1/4-inch minifloppy disk, locate the write-protect notch (see fig. 3.2) and cover the notch with a write-protect tab so that the notch is covered. When write-protected, the drive is unable to write new information on the disk even if you inadvertently issue to DOS a command that attempts to write data to the disk.

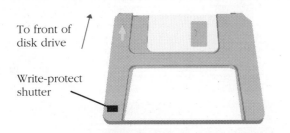

To front of
disk drive

Write-protect
shutter

Figure 3.1

*Microfloppy (3 1/2-inch) disk
showing built-in write-protect
shutter.*

To front of
disk drive

Write-protect
notch

Figure 3.2

*Covering the notch on a
minifloppy disk protects the
information from accidental
erasure or alteration.*

Insert the write-protected DOS Master disk in drive A. Check your PC's system manual
for the location of drive A and for disk-insertion instructions. When you have properly
inserted a disk, the label usually faces the top on horizontal drives and the left on
vertical drives (see fig. 3.3). If the disk does not go in, make sure that the drive
doesn't contain another disk. Never jam or buckle a disk during insertion; you could
cause permanent damage to the disk (see fig. 3.4).

For this exercise, you will be booting from a floppy disk. Even if you have a
hard disk with DOS installed, learn how to boot from a floppy in case your hard
disk becomes unbootable. Booting from a prepared hard disk is the same as
booting from a floppy. The difference is that you do not need to insert a disk in
the floppy drive.

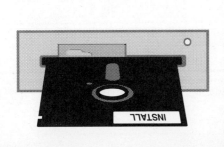

Fig. 3.3

*Insert disks into horizontal
and vertical drives in the same
way. To complete the insertion
of a 5 1/4-inch disk, close the
drive door or turn the latch
clockwise.*

54

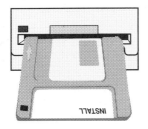

Fig. 3.4

Insert 3 1/2-inch disks gently, pushing until you hear a click. The drive closes by itself.

After you load the disk, close the drive door. (Microfloppy drives close themselves.) If you have a key lock on the front of the system unit, unlock the unit.

Finally, turn on the display switch, if necessary, and give your screen a few seconds to warm up. Some displays are powered from the system unit and do not have a switch. Locate the computer's power switch. It is usually on the right side toward the rear of the system unit. Snap on the switch. At this point, the cold boot has begun.

Always let the spring action of the PC's power switch snap the switch on or off. If you hold the switch arm between your fingers and ease the switch on, the switch will not make immediate and decisive electrical contact. Easing the switch on may cause fluttering power, and the PC may fail to turn on.

If your computer supplier installed DOS on your hard disk, you can automatically boot from the hard disk simply by turning on the computer. To understand the elements of booting, however, you should learn to boot from a floppy disk.

Tech note . . . The term *booting* is derived from the old concept that someone with no external help can "pull himself up by his bootstraps." In other words, someone can start with nothing and turn it into something useful. Needless to say, the act of creating something from nothing requires some wide interpretation of what "nothing" is. When you boot your PC, the PC is nothing on a scale of computing output. The potential is there, but you can't compute with it.

Much of this computing potential resides on the DOS boot disk in three disk files. The file that contains the core of DOS, the file that contains the basic input and output additions for ROM BIOS, and COMMAND.COM are all waiting on the disk to be loaded into the PC. Before the PC can load these files and make DOS available to you, the PC must test itself, initialize external hardware, and load the three DOS files from disk into random access memory (RAM).

Special instructions built into the PC enable the PC to access a predetermined part of the boot disk and read the boot sector into RAM. The boot sector contains a short machine language program that finds and loads two DOS hidden system files. The boot program then looks for the CONFIG.SYS file in the root directory of the boot disk. (CONFIG.SYS is discussed in Chapter 13.) If CONFIG.SYS is found, the boot

Tech note . . . (cont.)

program opens the file and installs into memory any device drivers that CONFIG.SYS refers to.

By loading device drivers at the time of booting, the PC is given the provision to operate in a configuration tailored to the specific needs of the PC's individual hardware and running requirements. Most device drivers are built into DOS's BIOS extensions, but CONFIG.SYS device drivers are selectable and included under your control.

The boot program locates the COMMAND.COM file and loads it. When COMMAND.COM is found, it is loaded into memory. The boot program turns control of the PC's resources over to COMMAND.COM. COMMAND.COM searches the root directory of the boot disk for a file named AUTOEXEC.BAT. If the AUTOEXEC.BAT file is found, its contents are executed as a series of DOS commands. (Chapter 12 discusses AUTOEXEC.BAT.) By providing for this special batch file to be executed at boot time, DOS can tailor the start-up of every PC to meet the specific needs of the user.

When AUTOEXEC.BAT has been executed by COMMAND.COM, you will see the DOS prompt, or *system prompt* (assuming that one of the commands does not start a program like the DOS Shell). COMMAND.COM is then ready to receive your command.

Watching the Progress of the Boot

The instant you snap on the switch, the computer's electronics do a *power on reset* (POR). The RAM, the microprocessor, and other electronics are zeroed out, which is something like cleaning the slate. The system then begins a *power-on self test* (POST). The POST ensures that your PC can deal responsibly with your valuable data. The POST can take from a few seconds to a couple of minutes. During the POST, you may see a description of the test or a blinking cursor on the display, similar to the following:

```
ABC Computer Co.
Turbo
RAM check
640K
OK
```

When the POST concludes, you will hear one beep and drive A will start activity. The bootstrap loader then loads DOS from the Master DOS disk into RAM.

Viewing DOS

When the cold boot completes its preliminary loading of DOS, you will see DOS appear on your screen. With DOS V4.0, you have two view options:

- The prompt view (DOS's only view prior to V4.0)
- The DOS Shell view

The prompt view is the traditional look of DOS. The prompt view appears on a plain screen with one letter of the alphabet representing the current, or active drive (see fig. 3.5). DOS V3.3 and earlier versions have always used this view. The drive letter is followed by a greater-than symbol (>). The most common DOS prompts are A> for floppy disk systems and C> for hard disk systems. If you are using V3.3 or earlier versions, or if you or your dealer has enabled the prompt view, the plain DOS prompt view will be your view.

Fig. 3.5

The traditional DOS prompt view.

If you are using V4.0 and you booted from a master DOS disk, you may see the V4.0 installation program. You can stop the installation program by pressing Esc; you will then see the DOS prompt. Appendix C provides complete installation instructions. You may want to install DOS V4.0 at this time.

The DOS V4.0 Shell view is a new look for DOS. The Shell view provides a full-screen "window" with various menus, pop-up help screens, and graphic representations of directories and files (see fig. 3.6). You can issue some standard DOS commands by pointing and selecting with a mouse.

The Shell view is the friendliest way to use DOS, but you should learn the basic commands from the prompt view. The reason becomes clear as you gain experience. With the DOS Shell, you must learn not only the Shell's command actions, but the DOS commands for which they stand. There is another complicating factor. Working with the DOS prompt is the traditional way to use DOS.

Just remember that even though using the Shell is easy, you still need to know something about DOS commands and terminology. They remain substantially unchanged from previous versions of DOS. The Shell can be viewed as simply a shortcut for someone who already understands the basics of DOS. Don't worry if you have V4.0 and want to learn about the Shell. Chapter 14 is devoted to the use of the DOS Shell. For now, press the F3 key to exit the DOS Shell. You will see the DOS prompt appear. When the prompt appears, you are in the standard prompt view.

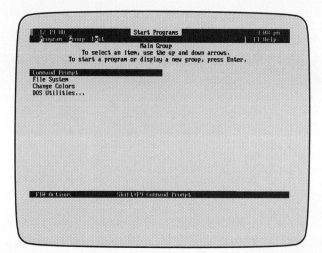

Fig. 3.6

The DOS Shell view.

*A **word about Shells** . . .* The DOS Shell that comes with V4.0 isn't the only graphical user interface to DOS. Many independent companies sell add-on software that does essentially the same job as the DOS Shell. In fact, the term *shell* is often used to describe any program that adds a layer of user friendliness to an existing program.

Programs such as XTreePro and Lotus Magellan give you a graphical user interface to DOS similar to the DOS Shell. Many users find that shell programs enable them to use the features of DOS more competently. Others discover that without some knowledge of the DOS prompt view, they are at a disadvantage when they must operate a PC other than their own. This book encourages you to learn the prompt view because of its universal availability on PCs. However, if reading about the DOS Shell causes you to become interested in the concept of shells, you should talk to your dealer about the features and benefits of the various shells available for your version of DOS.

Entering the Time and Date

DOS uses the time and date to indicate or stamp the time and date of a file's creation or last change. If your system has no automatic AUTOEXEC.BAT start-up file, DOS will ask you for the time and date so that file stamping will be accurate. If your PC has an AUTOEXEC.BAT file, you should still check the time and date using the DOS commands explained shortly. But first, there are a few considerations about keeping time that you should review.

Most contemporary computers come with a built-in, battery-powered calendar and clock. The clock keeps correct time even when the unit's power is off, so that the correct time and date are always the default values. Many older PCs, or PCs based on the original IBM PC, do not have built-in clocks. These PCs keep time when the power is on, but you must establish the correct time as a follow-up of the boot process to ensure proper time and date stamping.

At the keyboard, a *default* value is a suggested response or recommended choice or action. If you make no specific choice when the computer prompts you, DOS accepts the built-in suggestion by default. You usually press Enter to accept the default. You will find out more about defaults when you read about commands in later chapters.

When a computer boots, it automatically enters the time and date from the system, offers default values, or requires you to enter each manually. You can determine which of these three cases fits your situation. Remember that the other situations may exist on a different PC so that you will know what to do if you boot a different PC. You can always set the time with the TIME command and the date with the DATE command. In fact, the prompts you see in the boot operation for time and date are the same as those DOS uses when you enter the DATE and TIME commands at the DOS prompt.

If your computer is set up to record automatically the time and date, DOS will not prompt you for the time and date during the boot process. Otherwise, DOS prompts you to enter the correct time and date.

The DOS prompt for the current time is as follows:

```
Current time is 11:17:00.75a
Enter new time:
```

When prompted, enter the current time. The template for time is hh:mm:ss. The hours are in 24-hour (military) clock format for DOS V3.3 and earlier versions. With V3.3 or earlier versions, you won't see the a or the p in DOS's time prompt. V4.0 will accept 12-hour time with a trailing a or p for A.M. or P.M. You can include the seconds, but it isn't required. Again, if you enter something that DOS doesn't like, (isn't programmed to accept) DOS will prompt you again.

DOS is programmed to issue error messages to the screen when something is incorrect in your response. Different mistakes will produce different error messages. Appendix B is a useful guide to error messages that DOS is programmed to provide. You will want to review that appendix as you read this book. Reviewing the various error messages helps you understand DOS's handling of the mistakes that it detects.

The DOS prompt for the correct date is as follows:

```
Current date is Tues 10-31-1989
Enter new date (mm-dd-yy):
```

Unless you have an automatic system clock, you will need to enter the current date at the prompt. Look at the date template that DOS shows in parentheses. You enter the calendar month as 1 through 12 in place of the mm. Likewise, you enter the day between 1 and 31 in the place of dd. When you enter yy, you do not have to include the century. DOS will accept the year as the decade and the year as in **90** for 1990.

If you enter a value that DOS is programmed to reject, DOS will let you know with an error message. Don't worry about making a mistake; DOS prompts you again for the date, and you can reenter the date correctly.

The role of the Enter key . . . Enter is an important key to DOS. Enter is often called *Return* or *New Line* by some computer people. You press Enter to activate the command line you type. You can type at the DOS prompt a command line or a response to a command's prompt, but the response you type won't be acted on by DOS until you press Enter. Enter is like a "Go" key that instructs DOS to execute a command or accept a response. You can always correct a line that you are typing by using the Backspace key. Once you press Enter, however, you won't be able to correct the line. If you press Enter without a command at the prompt, DOS simply scrolls up a new line.

If your PC prompts you for the time and date and you respond, the boot operation is complete. If your clock is maintained automatically or your AUTOEXEC.BAT file bypasses the time and date steps, the boot operation is completed without a time and date step.

Using the Booted PC

Once the boot is complete, the system prompt indicates the logged drive. The logged drive is the active drive—the drive that responds to commands. For example, an A> and a blinking cursor tells you that DOS is logged onto drive A, which is usually a floppy disk drive. A C> and a blinking cursor means that DOS is logged onto drive C, which is usually a hard disk drive.

You can change the logged drive. Just enter the drive letter followed by a colon, and then press Enter. DOS reads the drive letter and colon as the disk drive's name. For example, you can change from drive A to C by typing **C:** at the prompt and pressing Enter. The sequence on-screen would be as follows:

```
A> C:
C>
```

Your DOS prompt may contain other characters and look like A:\> or C:\DOS>. Don't worry if this is your case. The prompt, which can be changed in DOS, is capable of providing more information than just the drive. You will learn in later chapters more about the information that can be included in a prompt.

Understanding the Logged Drive

DOS remembers the logged drive as its *current* drive. Many commands use the current drive and other current information without your having to actually specify them in the command. You will learn more about this focusing of DOS's attention later as part of the *rule of currents*.

Remember that you need not specify the drive if you are requesting information from the logged drive. (If you are using two floppy drives, substitute B: for C: in the examples and exercises.) Just because DOS provides special attention to the logged drive doesn't mean that the other drive(s) in your system are out of DOS's reach. You can use any drive on your system at any time by using a drive specifier in a command. You will learn later how to include the drive name when you request information from a drive that is not current.

Stopping the Computer's Action

You may occasionally want to stop the computer from carrying out the action you requested through a DOS command. You may, for example, want to stop a command that produces long output or takes a long time to complete. You may also want to stop a command that you issued in error. Besides switching the power off (the last resort), there are three key sequences you can use to stop a command in DOS:

Sequence	Action
Ctrl-C	Stops commands in which DOS pauses for you to type in further information. Be aware that DOS carries out many commands too quickly for you to intervene with Ctrl-C.
Ctrl-Break	The Break key is located next to the Reset key on some keyboards. (Make sure that you do not press the Reset key when you perform a Ctrl-Break.) On some keyboards, Break shares the same key with Scroll Lock or Pause. For this reason, you may want to use Ctrl-C if you frequently type the wrong keys. In certain instances, however, Ctrl-Break will work when Ctrl-C will not.
Ctrl-Alt-Del	The warm-boot key sequence. Ctrl-Alt-Del should not be your first choice to stop a command, but sometimes Ctrl-C or Ctrl-Break will not work. If this approach fails, turning off the power is the last resort.

As in all Ctrl-key sequences, you hold down the Ctrl key and then press the other key(s) in the sequence.

You can think of these key sequences as the "panic" buttons to stop DOS. Don't worry that you will constantly have to use them to stop disasters. If you need to use them, they will be handy.

Performing a Warm Boot

The warm boot differs very little from the cold boot. You perform a warm boot when the PC's power is on. A warm boot restarts DOS without your needing to touch the power switch. You may need to warm boot your PC for several reasons. If you change your system's start-up configuration (described in Chapter 13), you will have to restart the PC. If your system becomes "hung" or unresponsive to keyboard input, you can perform a warm boot. You can even start a different version of DOS from another disk by performing a warm boot.

For the cold boot, you inserted the DOS system disk and then switched on the computer. For the warm boot, your PC is already switched on. Make sure that you have the DOS system disk in drive A. You then press three keys.

Look at the keyboard and locate the Ctrl, Alt, and Del keys. The warm boot takes no more effort than holding down both Ctrl and Alt and then pressing Del. The PC skips the preliminary POST operation and immediately loads DOS.

Whether you have cold booted through a power-up or warm booted through a Ctrl-Alt-Del combination, your PC is reset, refreshed, and ready for a computing session.

Taking a Look at the DOS Shell

If you have DOS 4.0, take some time to read this section. If you do not have DOS 4.0 installed, see Appendix C for installation instructions. More information about the DOS Shell is also provided in Chapter 14.

The Shell provides a visual presentation of DOS with "action options" from which you make selections. You can manage your computer from the action options, which are selectable versions of the DOS prompt-view commands.

This book presents the basics of DOS from the command-prompt view. The Shell, however, may be where your system starts after a boot. The following sections highlight the basic structure of the Shell.

Issuing the DOSSHELL Command

You type **DOSSHELL** at the DOS prompt to load the DOS Shell into memory if the Shell is not already loaded. DOS then establishes the system configuration selected when DOS 4.0 was installed. (A batch file holds the configuration commands for the DOS Shell.) For now, assume that the options selected are satisfactory for your computer.

The DOS Shell takes a few seconds to load after you enter the DOSSHELL command at the DOS prompt. If your system goes directly to the Shell, it is not necessary to type **DOSSHELL**.

Start Programs is the first screen you see in the Shell (see fig. 3.7). Start Programs lists the main items in the Shell; you can add your own applications programs to this list to make accessing them easier.

Group contents   Action bar   Display title   Group title

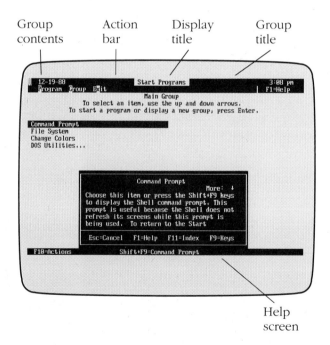

Help screen

Fig. 3.7

The Start Programs menu from the DOS Shell.

On either side of the screen title are the time and date. Under the title is the action bar, a line which displays the kinds of actions you can select. Positioned under the action bar are the group title line and the group contents. The Start Programs menu serves as your base to explore the important keystrokes you use in the DOS Shell.

DOS V4.0 also includes an on-line help feature. On this screen, the item Command Prompt is highlighted. Pressing F1 brings up information about the command prompt.

63

Accessing On-line Help

Fortunately, you can always get information or explanations about DOS when you use the Shell. If you press F1, a help window appears. On-line help assists you with the current selection or action so that you can make an informed selection.

F11 displays a directory of different help topics (see fig. 3.7). If your computer does not have the F11 key, use the Alt-F1 key combination.

You can press F9 to get a display of the keys and their Shell meanings. Within a window, you can move up or down a window's worth of text with PgUp or PgDn. The Shell sounds a beep when you press keys that it doesn't have an action for. Press Esc to cancel the help window and resume your session.

Moving from Shell to Prompt

You can move temporarily from the Shell to the DOS prompt, keeping the Shell in memory. To do so, use the cursor-arrow keys to place the highlighted bar on `Command Prompt` and press Enter. (The bar is called the *selection cursor*—a highlighted, reversed video, or different-colored section of text that will be the object of an action if you press Enter or push the mouse button.)

When you press Enter, the DOS prompt appears. You now can enter DOS commands. To return to the Shell, type **Exit** and press Enter. For convenience, you can also press Shift-F9 to get to the command prompt. By selecting `Command Prompt` from the group items, however, you will see how the selection process works.

If you cannot move your selection cursor, check to make sure that Num Lock is off and that the actions on the action bar are highlighted or reversed in intensity. Use the right- and left-arrow keys to move the highlight accordingly. F10 moves the activity area of the selection cursor between actions and items. Press F10 until no action item stands out from the rest.

The other way to get to the DOS command prompt is to leave the Shell. This method causes the Shell to leave memory. To stop the Shell, press F10 and place the selection cursor on `Exit`. Now press ENTER. Move the selection cursor to `Exit Shell` and press Enter. The Shell returns you to the DOS prompt. Remember, you have exited the Shell, so you must restart the Shell by typing **DOSSHELL** when you want to use it again.

The Main Group Menu

Now that you know how to get to the DOS command prompt from within the Shell, you can look at the Main Group items. The Main Group of the opening Start Programs menu shows the main areas where you will do work in the Shell. By selecting one of these items, you are asking the Shell to usher you to a screen so that you can work in that item's subject area.

When you select an action item and press Enter, additional selections pull down from under the selected item automatically. As with other selected items in the Shell, selected pull-down items are not carried out unless you press Enter. You move to other items in pull-down menus using the up- and down-arrow keys. You exit pull-downs by pressing Esc. The action bar gives you options for how the Shell presents the activity in the window below the action bar. In other words, you do DOS work in the lower part of the screen and give the Shell instructions with the action bar. The Shell knows the items in a selection list that are not usable at that point and places an asterisk in the item's name. If you have an EGA or VGA display, the Shell makes the item's name "fuzzy," rather than using the asterisk.

The F10 key toggles the selection cursor between the action bar and the lower work area of any Shell screen. Press F10 a few times and watch the selection cursor jump between the lower part of the screen and the action bar. If you have a mouse, you can move the pointer freely across area boundaries on the screen. One click selects an item. Two quick clicks select an item and tell the Shell to execute that item.

The Start Programs menu offers a Main Group of Shell items. These items come with DOS 4.0, but advanced users can add their own. Some software makers offer installation procedures for their programs that add their programs to the item list.

Use F10 to move the selection cursor to the Main Group's item list. Then try the arrow keys and watch the selection cursor highlight each item in succession.

The File System Screen

The second item listed on the Start Programs menu is File System. Use the arrow keys to select File System and press Enter (see fig. 3.8).

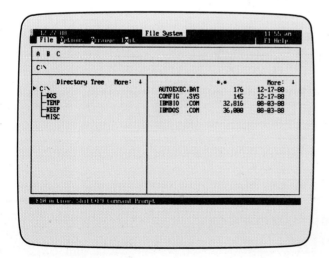

Fig. 3.8

The File System screen from the Start Programs menu.

Because DOS is a disk operating system and because disks store information in files, the Shell pays ample attention to the file system in this screen. The general layout of this screen is similar to that of the Start Programs screen. Notice, however, that the action items in the action bar at the top of the screen are not the same as those on the Start Programs menu. Just below the action bar, the remainder of the screen is divided into sections that are bounded by bars or included in colored blocks. Look at the screen until you clearly see the individual sections. If you are familiar with DOS's hierarchical file structure, you will see the logic of this screen. Chapter 6 should clear up any confusion you may have about directories.

For now, you can concentrate on learning to move around this screen. Press the F10 key a few times. Notice that the selection cursor toggles between the action bar and one of the lower items. F10 works the same here as in Start Programs. Press F10 until a lower item is selected and then press the Tab key. The selection cursor moves to an item in the next area of the lower part of the screen. Press the Tab key a few more times. The selection cursor moves from section to section. Use the Tab key to move to the next screen section. If you press Tab enough times, the Shell selects the action bar. You can tab so quickly that you may find using the Tab key more convenient for reaching the action bar than using F10.

Tab to the list of file names on the right side of the screen. Press the down-arrow key and see that the selection cursor moves to the next name. Use the up- and down-arrow keys to move to items that are listed vertically and use the right- and left-arrow keys on items that are listed horizontally. A beep tells you when you have reached the end of the list.

Press F10 again to move to the action bar. Press Enter to pull down additional information items about the selection (see fig. 3.9). Use the left- and right-arrow keys to move to other main action bar items. You'll notice that the pulled-down list from the first selection allows the other item's pull-down menus to appear automatically.

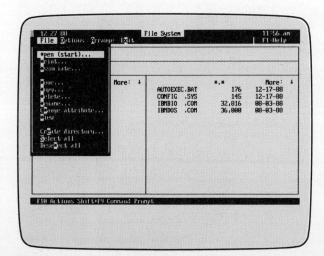

Fig. 3.9

To display the file-system pull-down menus, select an item from the action bar by pressing F10 and then Enter. Pressing the left- and right-arrow keys displays menus for other file-system options.

You have all the selection possibilities available for viewing when you use the right- and left-arrow keys. The File pull-down menu gives you actions for the Shell to perform on files and directories you have selected from the lower part of the screen. The Options and Arrange pull-down menus control the way the Shell displays files and also prompt you for confirmation when you erase or rename files.

The Change Colors Utility

If you have a graphics display adapter, select Change Colors from the Start Programs menu and press Enter. You are now in the Change Colors utility. You can choose from available color schemes to give the Shell the look you prefer. If you have a text-only display, the Shell knows that you can't change colors, so you won't be able to try this item. If you have a black-and-white, green, or amber screen, you will see the colors as shades. Press the right- or left-arrow keys; your screen will take on a different look each time. Don't forget to use F1 for help if you need it. Look at all the combinations and stop on your favorite. Press Enter to keep that combination and then press Esc to return to the Start Programs menu.

The DOS Utilities Screen

The DOS Utilities screen is the last item on the Start Programs menu. All the selections in this group are disk utilities that enable you to set the time and date, copy and compare files, and format, back up, and restore disks. You will learn how to do these activities at the DOS prompt in later chapters. For now, try setting the time and date.

Select DOS Utilities by using the arrow keys; then press Enter. You are now in the DOS Utilities menu, but you are just passing through. Use the arrow keys to select Set Date and Time; then press Enter. A new block of the screen, a *window*, pops up. This is a Shell pop-up window and in this case, it is the Set Date and Time utility.

You will see a prompt for a new date and a "picture" of what format the Shell expects. Press F1 (Help) for an explanation of the format. Then enter the date; press Enter at the cursor. Now you are prompted for the correct time. Enter the time at the cursor in 24-hour format and then press Enter. The Shell tells you to press any key, so press the space bar. The Shell then brings you back to the DOS Utilities screen. From that screen, you can press Esc to get back to Start Programs, F10 to move to the action bar, or Shift-F9 to get to the command prompt.

When you have finished entering the time and date, press Esc to return to the Start Programs menu. You have successfully navigated the DOS Shell! You will find more information about the DOS Shell in Chapter 14.

Summary

This chapter has presented the boot process that starts your PC. You were introduced to the following key points:

❑ The boot process resets your computer for a fresh DOS session.

❑ The DOS disk must be inserted in drive A to boot unless you have a hard disk with DOS installed.

❑ When you perform a cold boot, the PC performs a POST test before prompting for time and date.

❑ You can set the time and date at the DOS prompt with the DATE and TIME commands.

❑ Systems without an AUTOEXEC.BAT file will prompt for time and date as part of the boot operation.

❑ In the prompt view, DOS shows a prompt that indicates the logged drive.

❑ In the V4.0 Shell view, DOS presents a graphical user interface which enables you to select actions you want to carry out.

The next chapter introduces the concept of DOS commands. Now that you know how to boot your PC, you will be ready to try some commands to get the feel of managing your computer through DOS.

Using DOS Commands

To communicate your need for service to DOS, you enter DOS *commands* at the DOS prompt. Commands are made up of groups of characters which are separated or *delimited* by certain other characters. A command you give to DOS is similar to a written instruction you might give to a work associate. Both the DOS command and the written instruction must communicate your intentions using proper form or *syntax*. Both must communicate what action you want carried out and what the objects of that action are.

For example, if you need to duplicate a sign on a bulletin board so that you can post it on another bulletin board, you might tell a work associate: "Copy sign A to sign B. Be sure to verify that you have made no mistakes." Similarly, if you want DOS to copy the contents of disk A to disk B, you would give DOS the following instruction:

DISKCOPY A: B:

To verify that the copy is the same as the original, you would instruct DOS to compare the two disks:

DISKCOMP A: B:

DISKCOPY and DISKCOMP are the DOS commands that determine what action is to be carried out. The drive letters A: and B: indicate where the action is to be carried out. Although the instructions to duplicate a sign look more natural than the DOS DISKCOPY command, the two are quite similar.

DOS recognizes and responds to well over 75 commands. The most useful of these are built into the command processor and are immediately available at the system prompt. Because of the built-in availability of these commands, they are called *internal commands*.

Other commands are stored as utility programs on your DOS disk(s) or in a hard disk directory. Because these commands must first be loaded and executed when you enter their names at the system prompt, they are called *external commands*. External commands can be executed from the system prompt in functionally the same way as internal commands.

Learning the "ins and outs" of issuing DOS commands takes some practice. Fortunately, DOS commands have a familiar structure, and you will soon branch out from the examples in this book to your own forms of the DOS commands.

Key Terms Used in This Chapter

Command	A group of characters that tell the computer what action to take.
Syntax	A specific set of rules that you follow when issuing commands.
Parameter	An additional instruction that defines specifically what you want the DOS command to do.
Switch	A part of the command syntax that turns on an optional function of a command.
Delimiter	A character that separates the "words" in a command. Common delimiters are the space and the slash.
Wild card	A character in a command that represents one or more characters. In DOS the **?** wild card represents any single character. The * wild card represents the remaining characters in a "word" in the command.

Understanding the Elements of a DOS Command

You issue commands to tell DOS that you need its operating-system services. Although each DOS command provides you with an individual service, all DOS commands conform to standard rules. Using DOS is easier when you understand the concepts behind the commands. You can then generalize many of these rules to different commands.

To begin to understand DOS commands, you need to know two fundamental facts:

- DOS requires that you use a specific set of rules or syntax when you issue commands.

- Parameters, which are a part of a command's syntax, can change the way a command is executed.

Syntax is the order in which you type the elements of the DOS command. Using proper syntax when you enter a DOS command is like using proper English when you speak. DOS must clearly understand what you are typing in order to carry out the command.

You can think of the command name as the action part of a DOS command. In addition to the name, many commands require or allow further directions. Any such additions are called *parameters*. Parameters tell DOS what action to take or how to apply the action. Using DOS commands is really quite easy as long as you follow the rules of order and use the correct parameters.

Most software incorporates the issuance of commands as part of the software's operation. The commands discussed in this book are DOS commands. Be sure that you know the difference between the DOS commands and the commands you learn to use with your applications software.

The Command Syntax

Command syntax can be compared to the phrasing of a spoken or written sentence. The order of the words, the punctuation, and the vocabulary are important ingredients for good communication. When you communicate with DOS, you need to use the proper ingredients so that DOS can interpret your intentions correctly. Like most PC programs, DOS cannot decide to ignore what you "say" and then do what you mean. Unfortunately, PCs don't have the capacity for intelligence that people do. If you use improper syntax in a DOS command, DOS will object with an error message—even if the mistake is minor.

This chapter uses a symbolic form to describe a command's syntax. With this symbolic form, the parts of the command are given names that you can relate to. When you actually enter the command, however, you substitute real values for the symbolic names. In other cases, the examples are commands that you can enter exactly as shown. Don't worry that you will not be able to tell the symbolic form of a command from a literal example. They are clearly marked in both cases. If you make a mistake and enter a symbolic word in the command line, DOS will simply object with an error message. You won't damage anything.

Because many DOS commands have various parameters, switches, and defaults, various forms of these commands may be correct. Even though the simple versions of

DOS syntax work effectively, most DOS manuals show the complete syntax for a command, making the command look complex. For example, the symbolic syntax for the DIR command can look like the following:

DIR *d:\path\filename.ext /W/P*

You use the DIR command to display a directory of a file or files stored on a disk. This command may look very formidable, but don't worry. Command syntax is much easier to understand if you look at the elements on the command line one at a time.

Some parts of a DOS command are **mandatory**. These parts represent information that must be included for the command to work correctly. Mandatory parts of a command are the minimum that DOS can understand. When you read that an element of syntax is required or mandatory, be sure to include a proper value for that element when you enter the command. In this book, mandatory elements are signaled by **boldface type**.

When you enter only the mandatory command elements, DOS in many cases uses default parameters for other elements. Thanks to defaults, many commands are simple to issue. DOS recognizes the default values either because the values are programmed into DOS or because you established the value in a previous command or directive. Recall the discussion of the logged drive in Chapter 3. When you log to another drive, that drive becomes the *current*, or *default* drive. If you omit from a command the drive's command-line specifier, DOS will use the default drive.

Syntax elements for which DOS maintains default values are considered *optional*. You do not have to enter optional elements. If you do not intend for DOS to use a different value in place of the default, you can save keystrokes by omitting the optional syntax element. DOS will accept commands with all syntax elements present, even though some elements are optional. By including all syntax elements, however, you assert full control over what DOS will do. In this book, optional elements are signaled by *italic type*.

When you enter all syntax elements, DOS uses the exact instructions in place of default values. For the DIR command example, the **DIR** is mandatory. The rest of the command, *d:path\filename.ext /W/P*, is optional. The elements represented by *d:path\filename.ext* can also be considered as *variable*. In other words, you can substitute the drive and file name of your choice for this element. Remember that *d:path\filename.ext* is a symbolic example of parameters. A real command would have actual parameters instead of symbols.

Certain commands require that you enter a file name or other element; that element, the file name, would then be both mandatory and variable. In such cases, the item (such as **filename.ext**) would be represented in lowercase letters and boldface type. Don't worry about being confused; ample discussion of each command's requirements is included in a neighboring discussion.

You can type upper- or lowercase letters when entering DOS commands. DOS converts lowercase to uppercase letters. You must type the syntax samples shown in this book letter for letter, but you can ignore case. Items shown in lowercase letters are variables. You type in the appropriate information for the items shown in lowercase.

The Command-Line Parameters

In addition to the command's name, a DOS command line contains the syntax elements known as *parameters*. You have been reading about parameters (sometimes called *arguments*) in previous sections and chapters. Parameters are the additional parts or elements of a command line that provide DOS with the objects of the command's action. The objects might be files, system settings, or hardware devices.

In the DIR example, the lowercase *d:* identifies the disk drive the command will use for its action. *d:* represents the drive parameter in the command line. You substitute for *d:* the drive letter of your choice (A:, B:, or C:) when you give the command.

path, a parameter that will be introduced in Chapter 7, refers to the directory path which leads to the command. For now, don't worry about *path*.

filename.ext stands for the name of a file, including its extension. When you see *filename.ext* in a syntax presentation, the symbolic term represents a file name and extension parameter. In DOS, file names can include up to eight letters. The name can also contain an extension, which consists of a period and up to three more letters. In this case, you might type in the file name **MYFILE.123**.

If you pay close attention to the example syntax and commands, you will note that spaces separate or *delimit* the command name and some parameters. Other commands use the slash (/) character to separate parameters. Delimiters are important to DOS because they help DOS break (or *parse*) the command apart. For example, the command **DIR A:** is correct; **DIRA:** is not. Make sure that your disk is in drive A and try both examples, but use the letter of your disk drive. If you type **DIRA:**, DOS will display an error message, such as Bad command or file name.

The Optional Switches

A *switch* is a parameter that turns on an optional function of a command. Switches are special parameters because they are usually not the objects of a command's action; rather, switches modify the command's action. Switches can give a basic command more versatility. In the DIR example, /W and /P are switches. Note that each switch is a character preceded by a slash. Not all DOS commands have switches. In addition, switches consisting of the same letter may have different meanings for different commands.

You can use the /W switch with the DIR command to display a *wide* directory of files. Normally, the DIR command displays a directory with one file listing per line. The date and time you created the file is displayed next to the file name. As the screen fills, the first files scroll off the top of the display. The /W switch produces a directory that contains only file names and extensions.

Sometimes a disk may contain too many files to display on one screen. When you use the /P switch with the DIR command, 23 lines of files, or approximately one screen, are displayed. The display *pauses* when the screen fills. At the bottom of a paused directory, DOS prompts you to Press any key to continue to move to the next screenful of files. By using the /P switch, you can view all the files in the directory, one screen at a time.

When you see the message Press any key to continue, DOS really means that you should press *almost* any key. If you press the Shift, Alt, Caps Lock, Num Lock, or Scroll Lock keys, DOS ignores you. The easiest keys to press are the space bar and the Enter key. When DOS asks for a key press, you do not have to finish the action by pressing Enter.

Issuing DOS Commands

Take a moment to become familiar with the instructions used for entering commands in this book. The notation helps you distinguish between what you type and what the computer displays. If you feel that issuing commands is going to be difficult, relax. You will not be required to instantly memorize commands; instead, you will learn by doing. If you get lost, just back up a few sections and reread the text. Millions of people use DOS commands; most of them had to go through a learning process to start with.

Figure 4.1 breaks down the different elements that make up a typical DOS command—the DIR command.

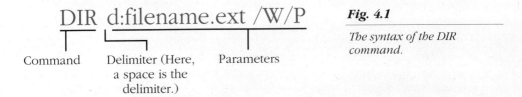

Fig. 4.1

The syntax of the DIR command.

Figure 4.2 is a diagram of the DIR command explained in the preceding section. The diagram illustrates the steps of issuing a DOS command that are covered in the next sections.

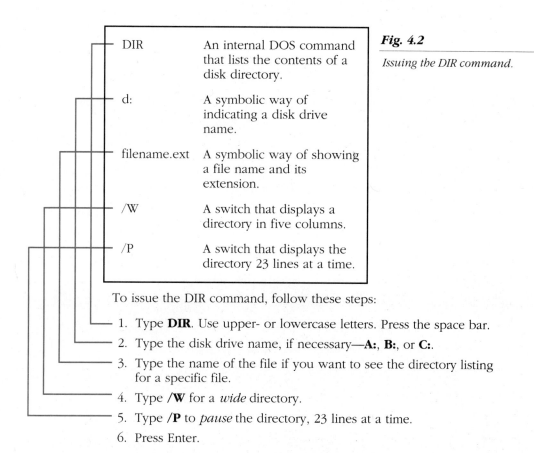

Fig. 4.2

Issuing the DIR command.

DIR	An internal DOS command that lists the contents of a disk directory.
d:	A symbolic way of indicating a disk drive name.
filename.ext	A symbolic way of showing a file name and its extension.
/W	A switch that displays a directory in five columns.
/P	A switch that displays the directory 23 lines at a time.

To issue the DIR command, follow these steps:

1. Type **DIR**. Use upper- or lowercase letters. Press the space bar.
2. Type the disk drive name, if necessary—**A:**, **B:**, or **C:**.
3. Type the name of the file if you want to see the directory listing for a specific file.
4. Type **/W** for a *wide* directory.
5. Type **/P** to *pause* the directory, 23 lines at a time.
6. Press Enter.

Typing the Command Name

You enter a command when the screen displays the DOS prompt. This prompt usually consists of the drive letter followed by the greater-than character >. Notice that immediately following the > is the blinking cursor. You will recall that the cursor marks the point where your keystrokes will be displayed.

The command name is like a key to the DOS operating system. A command's name identifies the action that the command is programmed to perform. COMMAND.COM is the DOS command processor that reads the command you type. COMMAND.COM can carry out several "built-in" (internal) commands. It also knows how to load and run the external utility command programs whose names you enter at the DOS prompt. Because you enter both internal and external commands at the DOS prompt, both are referred to as command names.

When you type a command, do not leave a space after the > of the DOS prompt. Enter all DOS command names directly following the prompt. If the command has no parameters or switches, press the Enter key after you type the last letter of the command name.

75

Remember that you can take advantage of default parameters when you enter a command line. For example, you can type the directory command at the prompt as follows:

   C>**DIR**

Then press Enter. DOS knows to supply the drive parameter even though you omitted the drive parameter from the command line. DOS will use the logged (default) drive, in this case, drive C.

Adding Parameters

When you are instructed to enter parameters that are not switches, this book will show them in one of two ways—lowercase and uppercase. You are to supply the value for the lowercase text. The lowercase letters are shorthand for the full names of the parts of a command. As in the command name, uppercase means that you enter letter-for-letter what you see—the literal meaning of the command.

To add a file-name parameter to the DIR command, you can type the following:

   C>**DIR C:MYFILE.TXT**

In symbolic notation, MYFILE.TXT would be shown as *filename.ext*.

Remember that you delimit parameters from the rest of the command. Most of the time the delimiter is a space, but other delimiters, such as the period (.), the backslash (\), the slash (/), and the colon (:) are available. Look at the examples in this book to see the correct delimiter.

You will recognize any switches in the example text by the leading slash character (/). Always enter the switch letter as shown. Do not forget to type the slash.

If you were to enter the DIR command with a switch character, the command would be as follows:

   C>**DIR/W**

The / serves as the delimiter and tells DOS that a switch is about to follow.

Ignoring a Command Line (Esc)

You may occasionally make a mistake when you are entering a command. Remember that until you press the Enter key, DOS does not act on the command. You can correct a mistake by using the arrow keys or the Backspace key to reposition the cursor. Press the Esc key, however, if you want to type in an entirely new command. The Esc key cancels the entry and gives you a new line. Just remember that these line-editing and canceling tips only work *before* you press the Enter key. Some commands can be successfully stopped with the Ctrl-C or Ctrl-Break sequence, however. To restore the system prompt, press Esc.

Executing a Command

The Enter key is the action key for DOS commands. '
what you just typed before you press the Enter key
computer gets busy and carries out your command.
command, DOS does not display your keystrokes. DOS ⌐
keystrokes, however, so be aware that the characters you typ⌐
next command. DOS stores unactioned keystrokes in a *typeaheaσ*
typeahead buffer, a temporary storage area in RAM, can fill with keysι
when your PC is hung. When the typeahead buffer fills, your PC will beep
you press an additional key. DOS's use of buffer storage areas gives DOS some
special editing capability also.

Using the DOS Editing Keys

When you type a command and press the Enter key, DOS copies the line into an
input *buffer*—a storage area for command-line keystrokes. You can pull the last
command line from the buffer and use it again. You will find this feature helpful
when you want to issue a command that is similar to the preceding command you
used. Table 4.1 lists the keys you use to edit the input buffer.

Table 4.1
DOS Command-Line Editing Keys

Key	Action
|← →|	Moves the cursor to the next tab stop.
Esc	Cancels the current line and does not change the buffer.
Ins	Enables you to insert characters in the line.
Del	Deletes a character from the line.
F1 or →	Copies one character from the preceding command line.
F2	Copies all characters from the preceding command line up to, but not including, the next character you type.
F3	Copies all remaining characters from the preceding command line.
F4	Deletes all characters from the preceding command line up to, but not including, the next character typed (opposite of F2).
F5	Moves the current line into the buffer, but does not allow DOS to execute the line.
F6	Produces an end-of-file marker (^Z) when you copy from the console to a disk file.

...g DIR To Look at Files

...DIR command is one of the first commands most DOS users learn. The command ...ckly gives a list of files, along with the date and time of creation, and the file sizes.

It can be quite important to know what files are on your disks and when you created them. You can manually keep a list of files, but this can be quite a task. You can use the DOS DIR command to get a list of files contained on each of your floppy disks or your hard disk.

Issuing the DIR Command

DIR stands for *DIR*ectory. A directory is a list of files. The DIR command displays a volume label, five columns of information about the files, and the amount of unused space on the disk.

Try the DIR command now. Type the following:

DIR

Then press Enter so that DOS can execute the command. You have just told DOS to display a list of files from the logged drive. You can also type **DIR A:** to specify drive A or **DIR C:** to list the files on drive C. The A or C is the optional drive parameter. If you specify no drive, DOS uses the logged drive by default.

You can change the logged drive by first typing the drive letter, then typing a colon, and finally pressing Enter. For example, typing **A:** at the DOS prompt changes the logged drive to drive A. A disk must be in a drive before DOS can make it the logged drive. Remember that you can only log to a drive that your system contains. By changing the logged drive, you can switch between a hard disk and a floppy disk.

Using Scroll Control

Scrolling describes how a screen fills with information. As the screen fills, information scrolls off the top of the display. To stop a scrolling screen, you press the key combination Ctrl-S (hold down the Ctrl key and then press S). Press any key to restart the scrolling. On enhanced keyboards, press the Pause key to stop scrolling.

With the DIR command, you can have scroll control by using the /P switch or the /W switch.

If you want to see more of the files at once, you can use the /W switch. The command **DIR /W** displays only the file names in a wide format, which fits many more files on a single screen (see fig. 4.3). The directory listing is displayed in a wide arrangement, but you do not receive the additional information about the individual files that is usually included in a directory listing.

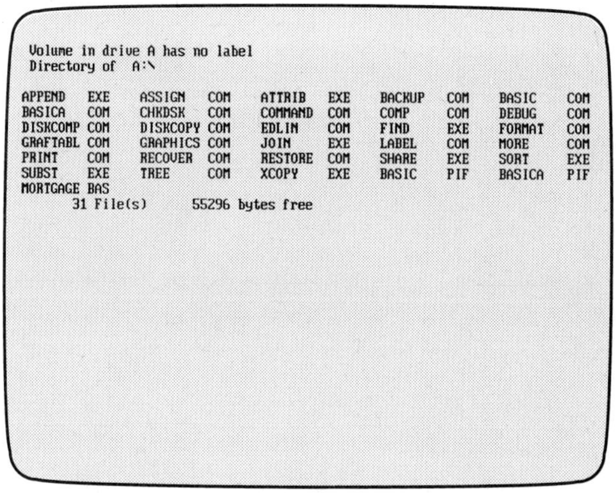

```
Volume in drive A has no label
Directory of  A:\

APPEND   EXE    ASSIGN   COM    ATTRIB   EXE    BACKUP   COM    BASIC    COM
BASICA   COM    CHKDSK   COM    COMMAND  COM    COMP     COM    DEBUG    COM
DISKCOMP COM    DISKCOPY COM    EDLIN    COM    FIND     EXE    FORMAT   COM
GRAFTABL COM    GRAPHICS COM    JOIN     EXE    LABEL    COM    MORE     COM
PRINT    COM    RECOVER  COM    RESTORE  COM    SHARE    EXE    SORT     EXE
SUBST    EXE    TREE     COM    XCOPY    EXE    BASIC    PIF    BASICA   PIF
MORTGAGE BAS
       31 File(s)      55296 bytes free
```

Fig. 4.3

The display produced by the command DIR /W.

For a complete and convenient listing of the directory, use the /P switch. The command **DIR /P** pauses the display so that the listing is presented page-by-page. Pressing any key will display the next page of information.

For example, if your DOS V3.3 Operating disk is in drive A, typing **DIR /P** will produce the following listing of the directory:

```
Volume in drive A has no label
Directory of  A:\
APPEND    EXE      5825 03-17-87  12:00p
ASSIGN    COM      1561 03-17-87  12:00p
ATTRIB    EXE      9529 03-17-87  12:00p
BACKUP    COM     31913 03-18-87  12:00p
BASIC     COM      1063 03-17-87  12:00p
BASICA    COM     36403 03-17-87  12:00p
CHKDSK    COM      9850 03-18-87  12:00p
COMMAND   COM     25307 03-17-87  12:00p
COMP      COM      4214 03-17-87  12:00p
DEBUG     COM     15897 03-17-87  12:00p
DISKCOMP  COM      5879 03-17-87  12:00p
DISKCOPY  COM      6295 03-17-87  12:00p
EDLIN     COM      7526 03-17-87  12:00p
FIND      EXE      6434 03-17-87  12:00p
FORMAT    COM     11616 03-18-87  12:00p
GRAFTABL  COM      6128 03-17-87  12:00p
GRAPHICS  COM      3300 03-17-87  12:00p
JOIN      EXE      8969 03-17-87  12:00p
LABEL     COM      2377 03-17-87  12:00p
```

```
MORE      COM        313 03-17-87   12:00p
PRINT     COM       9026 03-17-87   12:00p
RECOVER   COM       4299 03-18-87   12:00p
RESTORE   COM      34643 03-17-87   12:00p
Press any key to continue . . .
SHARE     EXE       8608 03-17-87   12:00p
SORT      EXE       1977 03-17-87   12:00p
SUBST     EXE       9909 03-17-87   12:00p
TREE      COM       3571 03-17-87   12:00p
XCOPY     EXE      11247 03-17-87   12:00p
BASIC     PIF        369 03-17-87   12:00p
BASICA    PIF        369 03-17-87   12:00p
MORTGAGE BAS       6251 03-17-87   12:00p
     31 File(s)      55296 bytes free
```

Examining the Directory Listing

Notice the directory listing in the preceding section. The first line you see in the directory listing is the *volume label*. A volume label is an identification that you specify when you prepare the disk. The volume label is optional, but including it can ease your organization of disks.

The next lines in the directory listing contain file information. Each line in the directory describes one file. You see the file name, extension, and size of file in bytes. You also see the date and time you created or last changed the file (assuming that you entered the time and date when you booted your computer). The next sections look at this information more closely.

File Names and Extensions

The file name contains two parts—the name and the extension. A period delimits the file name and its extension. In the directory listing, however, a space separates the file name from the extension.

In any single directory, each file must have a unique full name. DOS treats the file name and the extension as two separate parts. The file names MYFILE.123 and MYFILE.ABC are unique because each file has a different extension. The file names MYFILE.123 and YOURFILE.123 are also unique. Many DOS commands make use of the two parts of the file name separately. For this reason, it is a good idea to give each file a file name and extension.

File names should help you identify the contents of a file. Because a file name can contain only eight alphanumeric characters and the extension can contain only three, meeting the demand of uniqueness and meaningfulness can require some ingenuity.

DOS is particular about which characters you use in a file name or an extension. To be on the safe side, use only letters of the alphabet and numbers—not spaces or a period. DOS truncates excess characters in a file name.

File Size and the Date/Time Stamp

In the directory listing, the third column shows the size of the file in bytes. This measurement is only an approximation of the size of your file. Your file can actually use somewhat more bytes than shown. Because computers reserve blocks of data storage for files, files with slightly different data amounts may have identical file-size listings. This explains why your word processing memo with only five words can occupy 2K of file space.

The last two columns in the directory listing display a date and a time. These entries represent when you created the file or, in the case of an established file, when you altered the file. Your computer's internal date and time are the basis for the date and time "stamp" in the directory. As you create more files, the date and time stamp become invaluable tools in determining which version of a file is the most recent.

The last line of the directory tells you the total number of files that a disk contains and the amount of free space available. Free space is measured in bytes. This is useful when you want to determine how many more files a disk can hold.

Using Wild-Card Characters with DIR

Perhaps you have seen a Western movie in which a poker-playing cowboy says, "Deuces are wild!" Of course, this means that the number two cards can take on a meaning other than their own. Computer linguists borrowed this wild-card concept and applied it to file-name operations on computers. You can use wild-card characters in file names to copy, rename, delete, list, or otherwise manipulate file names.

DOS recognizes two wild-card characters. You can place the **?** character in any full file name. The **?** matches any one character in that position. The * in a file name or in an extension matches all characters in that part of the full file name.

Remember that if you type **DIR** followed by the file name, the selected list of files is displayed. The long form of the DIR command looks like the following:

> **DIR** *d:filename.ext*

Remember to substitute your actual drive letter for the **d:**. In place of *filename.ext*, you can type something like **MYFILE.123**. The DIR command you just typed tells DOS to list a directory of all files that match MYFILE.123. The directory listing would list only one file, MYFILE.123. When you use DIR alone, DOS lists all files in the directory. When you use DIR with a file name and extension parameter, DOS lists only files that match that parameter.

The DIR command, however, becomes more powerful when used with wild cards. If you want to see a listing of all files that have an extension of 123, you can use the * wild-card character. The * replaces every character from the asterisk to the end of the part of the command where the asterisk is located.

For example, you can type the following:

DIR *.123

DOS will list any file that bears the 123 extension, including files such as MYFILE.123 and YOURFILE.123. If you issue the command **DIR MYFILE.***, you may get a listing of MYFILE.123 and MYFILE.XYZ.

You can name your letter files with a LET extension and your memo files with an extension of MEM. This technique enables you to use the DIR command with a wild card to get a separate listing of the two types of files.

The **?** wild card differs from the * wild card. Only the character that is in the same position as the **?** is a match. If you issue the command **DIR MYFILE?.123**, files like MYFILE1.123, MYFILE2.123 are displayed, but MYFILE10.123 is not. The same rules apply to other commands that allow wild cards.

The wild-card designation **.** replaces every character in the root file name and every character in the extension. **.** selects *all* the files in a directory.

The **.** specification is a powerful tool; be sure to use it with caution. When used with commands such as DEL, the specification can be dangerous. For example, the command **DEL *.*** will delete *all* files in the directory.

Other examples of wild-card uses with the DIR command are shown in the following list:

Command	Result
DIR MYFILE.123	Presents directory information for the file MYFILE.123.
DIR *.123	Lists each file in the directory that has the extension 123.
DIR M*.*	Lists each file whose name begins with the letter M.
DIR *.*	Lists all files in the directory; the same as typing just **DIR**.
DIR *.	Lists all files that have no extension.
DIR ???.BAT	Lists all three-letter files that have a BAT extension.
DIR MYFILE.???	Lists all the files named MYFILE that have three-letter extensions.

Reviewing the DIR Command

The DIR command displays more than a list of file names. As your computing expertise grows, you will find many uses for the information provided by the full directory listing (see fig. 4.4).

```
Volume in drive A has no label
Volume Serial Number is 0FD9-2E4E
Directory of  A:\

COMMAND   COM     37637 06-17-88   12:00p
CHKDSK    COM     17771 06-17-88   12:00p
DISKCOPY  COM     10428 06-17-88   12:00p
PCIBMDRV  MOS       295 06-17-88   12:00p
PCMSDRV   MOS       961 06-17-88   12:00p
PCMSPDRV  MOS       801 06-17-88   12:00p
PRINT     COM     14163 06-17-88   12:00p
SHELL     CLR      4438 06-17-88   12:00p
SHELL     HLP     66977 06-17-88   12:00p
SHELL     MEU      4588 06-17-88   12:00p
SHELLB    COM      3937 06-17-88   12:00p
SHELLC    EXE    153975 06-17-88   12:00p
DOSUTIL   MEU      6660 06-17-88   12:00p
012345    678       109 06-17-88   12:00p
DOSSHELL  BAT       184 10-14-88    8:22a
SHELL     ASC         0 10-21-88    4:45p
        16 File(s)     35328 bytes free
```

Fig. 4.4

The elements of a directory listing.

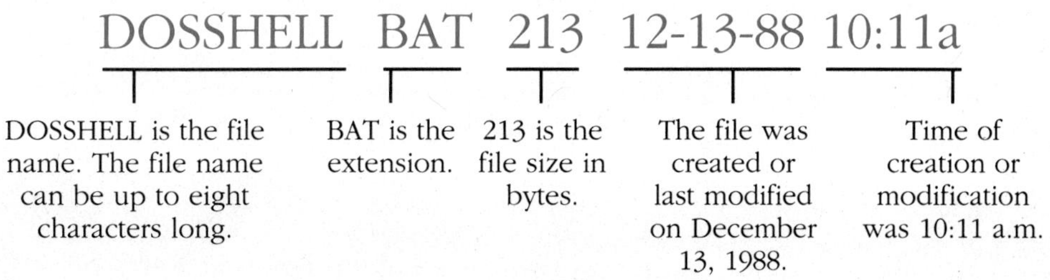

DOSSHELL BAT 213 12-13-88 10:11a

DOSSHELL is the file name. The file name can be up to eight characters long.

BAT is the extension.

213 is the file size in bytes.

The file was created or last modified on December 13, 1988.

Time of creation or modification was 10:11 a.m.

Summary

As you can tell, there is an underlying logic to issuing DOS commands. Even though each DOS command has its own personality, each command has a defined syntax which can include parameters and switches. The basic knowledge of how to issue DOS commands is an important ingredient in your mastery of DOS. Following are the key points covered in this chapter:

❏ You issue commands to DOS for operating system services.

❏ The proper phrasing of each DOS command is called the command's syntax.

❏ In addition to the name of the command, a syntax line can contain parameters and switches.

❏ The DIR command, like many other DOS commands, uses optional parameters. When the optional parameters are omitted, they are supplied as DOS defaults.

❏ You can edit a DOS command line using special DOS editing keys.

❏ Some commands allow wild-card characters (? and *) as substitutes for position-matching in file-name parameters.

The next chapter completes your introduction to DOS by covering the important subject of disks and files. Although you are moving on from this chapter, you will want to review the ideas presented here when you begin to use DOS commands.

Understanding Disks and Files

5

One of the primary roles of a disk operating system is to provide the service of storing and retrieving data to and from disks. Providing this service involves many factors. The operating system must oversee the many technical details of the disk hardware as well as provide a bookkeeping method for file storage and retrieval on disks. DOS's file-bookkeeping method includes the way the operating system shows you what it has stored and where it has stored it.

DOS's internal file-bookkeeping system is responsible for accounting for unused disk space as well as the contents of used disk space. The details of how DOS implements its bookkeeping system are, for the most part, hidden from you. DOS manages its file system behind the scenes. To enable you to control the files that you create while computing, DOS offers a full complement of commands. DOS's file-related commands enable you to manage all aspects of data storage—ranging from preparing disks to performing safety backups. Finally, the disk operating system should provide these services without your needing to know the internal details of the operations.

You shouldn't have to be burdened with technical details in order to save a memo from a session with your word processor. Nor should your word processor have to supervise elemental disk-output tasks to save that memo. A disk operating system assumes responsibility for getting data, in the form of files, to and from a disk through a predefined organization using predefined commands or methods. The predefined organization is called the *file system*. Disk hardware and file commands are closely linked to this file system. These fundamental disk operations are discussed in this chapter because of this close link. The disk and file commands are discussed in Part Two of this book.

Key Terms Used in This Chapter

File system	The predefined organization used by a disk operating system to get data, in the form of files, to and from a disk.
File	A variable-length collection of related information that is referenced by a name.
Root	A file-name prefix which can include up to eight characters. Usually describes the contents of a file.
Extension	A file-name suffix which can include a period and up to three characters. Usually describes the type of file.
Parse	The process of breaking out the components of the command line.
Disk	The predominant means of file storage for DOS.
Disk drive	The electro-mechanical components that record and play back data using the magnetic surfaces of a disk.
Hard disk	A built-in, fixed disk drive.
Floppy disk	Any lower-capacity disk in a jacket that you remove from your PC's drive.
Minifloppy	5 1/4-inch disk.
Microfloppy	3 1/2-inch disk.
Diskettes	Another term for 5 1/4- and 3 1/2-inch disks.
Platter	A disk contained in a hard disk drive.
Track	A circular section of a disk's surface that holds data.
Cylinder	The conceptual alignment of heads on the same track position on different sides (and platters) of the same disk.
Sector	Manageable, fixed-size component parts of a track.
Format	The specification for a disk's use of its physical space.

Introducing the DOS File System

A file system is an organized collection of files. As a user, you see the DOS file system at work in the files you organize into directories and subdirectories on your disks. Each file is a named group of data that DOS appears to manipulate as one continuous unit. Behind the scenes, however, DOS employs a structured management strategy whose complexity is hidden from you. The DOS file system reflects this strategy. A file system includes not only the files, but also the internal tables that record the file organization as well as the built-in rules that ensure the consistency of file organization.

Understanding Files

A *file* is a variable-length collection of related information that is referenced by a name. You can picture a file cabinet full of file folders, each with a name on the tab. Neither the cabinet nor the individual pieces of paper in the folders are files. Only the named collection in one folder is considered a file. Think about the file cabinet, the folders, and the papers for a moment to understand the relationship (see fig. 5.1).

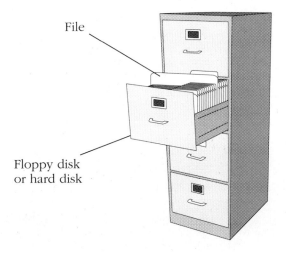

File

Floppy disk
or hard disk

Fig. 5.1

Electronic files can be compared to a traditional file cabinet. The drawers are like floppy disks or hard disks. The file folders are like files.

A file cabinet is an information storage medium; likewise, DOS disks serve as an information storage medium. The file cabinet alone, however, is not informational; rather, the file folders in the cabinet are informational because they are named. Yet the named folders alone do not serve as the information.

DOS files are informational because you name them. You find file names helpful in locating the information in the correct file. Yet, the file name itself is not the memo, spreadsheet, or other information that you use. The information stored on the individual papers in the folders is the source of record for the subject named on the file folder. Without the properly named folders to group the related papers, access to the information is greatly hindered. Likewise, DOS automatically provides the grouping of related information in the form of files. DOS and DOS-based applications software provide for opening named files whenever information is to be stored on a disk.

In a computer setting, a file can contain data (information), programs (instructions that guide computer tasks), or both. A file can exist on a disk, on magnetic tape, on punch cards, and even in a computer's memory. Files are made of elements of data or programs. The individual elements can be stored as patterns of holes in a paper tape, or patterns of magnetic fields on the surface of a disk, or in many other ways. Physical storage techniques for files vary greatly. In all likelihood, however, when you reach for some stored files, you reach for a disk. Disks are the predominant means of file storage for DOS. When you see the term *file* in this book, you can count on it to mean *disk file*.

DOS uses file names to identify files. Full file names consist of up to eight characters of a name prefix followed by an optional period character (.) and up to three optional characters of suffix or extension. The full file name is often referred to as the *file name plus extension*.

The prefix or root of a file name is usually named to describe the *contents* of the file. Extensions, on the other hand, are traditionally used to describe the *type* of file. Someone using a word processor, for example, might use as a root file name the name (or a close approximation) of a person who will receive a memo. The memo's extension might then safely be named .MEM. The memo to be sent to Mr. Duncan could be called DUNCAN.MEM. Likewise, the extension .DOC is commonly used for office policy document files. A monthly policy statement might be named JAN.DOC. DOS enables you to use a wide variety of full file names. You are free to develop your own file-naming conventions as long as you stay within the character limits imposed by DOS.

Using first and last names makes it much easier to differentiate among people. DOS conventions borrow from this naming concept by providing for a root name (first name) and an extension (last name). When you name your files, you should use both parts of the file name to help you better identify the file at a later time. Some applications programs add their own file extensions, however, and you simply supply the root file names.

Selecting File Names

DOS ensures that every one of your files has a name. In fact, DOS provides no method of putting file data on a disk without a file name. When a file is created, either by your applications software or a DOS file-service routine, DOS places the name of a file in one of its directories. A directory is DOS's equivalent to a library card file. You will learn more about directories later. For now, just consider a directory as a table for holding file names and locations.

DOS provides room in a directory entry for eight characters of a file-name prefix and three characters of a file-name suffix. The file-name prefix is what you think of as the *root* file name; the suffix is the file-name *extension*. When you include a file name in a command, you place a period (.) between the file name and extension.

DOS does not store the period character in the directory. DOS internally separates the file name from the extension by knowing the position of the extension in the directory field. You include the period to indicate to DOS the point where the extension begins.

DOS could have been designed so that a file name consisted of seven characters of file name and four characters of extension—or nine characters of file name and two characters of extension. The UNIX operating system, for example, has no provision for file-name extensions. The OS/2 operating system provides for file names·that can include dozens of characters. DOS, however, allows up to eight characters of file name and up to three characters of extension because a DOS directory can accommodate those numbers.

The origin of DOS file names . . . DOS utilizes the file-naming convention of the once dominant CP/M operating system. DOS designers felt that using the CP/M file-naming convention would provide an easier transition for users from CP/M-based computers to DOS-based computers. The DIR command that shows a listing of the file names in a directory is also used in the CP/M operating system. Many file-related concepts were adapted for DOS from the CP/M operating system. As DOS has matured, the DOS file system has been enhanced well beyond the capabilities of the original CP/M file system.

Characters that you see on your computer screen are the ASCII-code representations of bytes of data. One character is stored in one byte. The name field of a directory entry is 11 bytes long (8 for file name plus 3 for extension). DOS accepts for file names most characters you would use for "everyday" names. You can use in file names the upper- and lowercase letters a through z; DOS automatically stores them in uppercase format in a directory entry. The numeric characters 0-9 can be used as well as the alternate graphics characters of a PC's keyboard. (The alternate characters, ASCII values 128-255, are produced by holding down the Alt key while pressing the number keys on the numeric keypad for the desired ASCII value.) Many punctuation characters are also allowed in file names.

Following are the rules for file names.

Rules for File Names

1. A file name consists of the following:
    a. A root name of one to eight characters.
    b. An optional extension of one to three characters.
    c. A period between the root name and the extension name if an extension is used,

2. The following characters are *allowed* in a file name:
    a. The letters A to Z. (Lowercase letters are transformed automatically into uppercase.)
    b. The numbers 0 to 9.
    c. The following special characters and punctuation symbols:
       $ # & @ ! & ( ) - { } ' _ ~ ^ `

3. The following characters are *not allowed* in a file name:
    a. Any control character, including Escape (27d or 1Bh) and Delete (127d or 7Fh).
    b. The space character.
    c. The following special characters and punctuation symbols:
       + = / [ ] " : ; , ? * \ < > |

4. If DOS finds an illegal character in a file name, it usually stops at the character preceding the illegal one and uses the legal part of the name. (There are a few exceptions to this rule.)

5. A device name can be part of a root name but cannot be the entire root name. For example, CONT.DAT or AUXI.TXT are acceptable; CON.DAT or AUX.TXT are not.

6. Each file name in a directory must be unique.

7. A drive name and a path name usually precede a file name. (Path names are discussed in Chapter 7.)

To understand why DOS objects to some characters in file names, you must look below the surface of DOS. Certain characters are not allowed because DOS will not pass those characters from the keyboard to the command or external command program that controls a file's name. You cannot, for example, use the Ctrl-G (^G) character in a file name. Ctrl-G tells an input device to sound the computer's bell or beep signal. The Escape character produced by the Esc key is another character that DOS will not accept as part of a file name. DOS interprets the Esc key as your request to cancel the command line and start again.

Another example of a disallowed character is Ctrl-S (^S). DOS and other operating systems use Ctrl-S to stop the flow of characters from the input device to the output device. Ctrl-S stops a scrolling screen, for example. If you press Ctrl-S while entering a file name, DOS assumes that you are entering an input-stopping character—not part of a file name. When you type **DIR** immediately followed by Ctrl-S, and then press Enter, DOS does nothing. DOS sees the ^S and Enter sequence as a stop, and then start, flow. DOS interprets the press of the Enter key as the signal to start sending keystrokes again. The temporarily stopped command processor then executes the DIR command.

You cannot use in a file name any characters that COMMAND.COM and external command programs use to divide the parameters and switches from the command in a command line. Because DOS must break out, or *parse*, the components of the command line, certain predefined characters are seen by DOS as delimiters of parameters or parts of a parameter. The backslash character (\), for example, separates directory names in a path specifier. DOS always reads the backslash on the command line to indicate part of a path.

Tech note . . . Surprisingly, DOS does not allow spaces embedded in file names that are created by applications programs. Most programs ensure that file names are legal before asking DOS to create a file using the name. Others do not. Microsoft QuickBASIC, a program used for writing BASIC programs, is an example. A program written in QuickBASIC allows files to be created with spaces embedded in a file name. The following directory listing of files (from a DIR command) shows two entries that include spaces and one without spaces.

```
Volume in drive C is LAP TOP
Directory of  C:\QUICK
1234567   123        13    8-25-89    7:58a
1 2 3 4   123        14    8-25-89    7:58a
S P A CE  123        14    8-25-89    7:59a
     3 File(s)    1996800 bytes free
```

DOS accepts the file names that contain embedded spaces and displays them in a directory listing with no objections.

If, however, you try to use one of the files with embedded spaces in a command line, DOS objects with the following message:

```
Invalid number of parameters
```

The space you try to enter in a file name at the command line confuses COMMAND.COM when it breaks apart the elements of the syntax. The space looks like a delimiter to COMMAND.COM, not like part of a file name. You cannot use COMMAND.COM to get to one of the files with embedded spaces in its name, so it is impractical to use a space, even when a program allows it.

Avoiding Reserved Names

DOS reserves names for its built-in character devices. You recall that DOS can treat some devices in a PC in a high-level way by accepting their names as input or output parameters in a command line. Before DOS looks for a file using the file name parameters from a command line, DOS checks whether the name is a device name. Table 5.1 lists the DOS character device names and their purposes.

Table 5.1
DOS Device Names

Device Name	Purpose
COM*x* or AUX	Identifies the serial communication port(s)
LPT*x* or PRN	Identifies the parallel printer port(s)
CON	Identifies the screen and keyboard
NUL	Identifies the "throw away" or "do nothing" device

If you intend for DOS to use one of these device names as a file name, you may be disappointed with the outcome of your command. DOS will intercept the device name, even if you add an extension, and try to use the device—not the file that you intend—to complete the command. The rule on the reserved device names of DOS is simple: Use a device name only as a device parameter in a command. Never expect to write a disk file with a root file name that is a device name.

Observing File-Naming Conventions

A convention is an informal rule that is not explicitly enforced. DOS file names follow a certain convention. Although you can use any file name that passes DOS's character rules and device-name rules, you will want to observe file-naming conventions whenever possible. You can, for example, name a memo file using a BAT extension, DOS would not know that you were not saving a conventional batch file. As long as you do not try to execute the memo as a batch file, DOS is happy. If you try to execute the memo file, however, DOS sees the BAT extension and tries to execute it. Of course, the memo cannot be executed.

You can also name an EXE file with a COM extension. Although both files are executable, they have internal differences. DOS does not take the extension's name to mean that the file is indeed an EXE or COM file. DOS inspects a key part of the file before deciding how to load and execute the program file. If you name a spreadsheet file as an EXE or COM file, for example, DOS is not fooled into executing the nonprogram file. In all likelihood, your system will simply "lock-up" and you will have to warm boot to begin again.

Many software manufacturers use certain extensions for special files in the applications programs. To avoid confusion as to the contents of a file, av certain extensions. Table 5.2 lists conventional file-name extensions and meanings.

Table 5.2
Common File-Name Extensions

Extension	Common Use	Extension	Common Use
.ARC	Archive (compressed file)	.LET	Letter
.ASC	ASCII text file	.LST	Listing of a program (in a file)
.ASM	Assembler source file		
.BAK	Backup file	.LIB	Program library file
.BAS	BASIC program file	.MAC	Keyboard macro file (Superkey)
.BAT	Batch file		
.BIN	Binary program file	.MAP	Linker map file
.C	C source file	.MEU	Menu file (DOS visual shell and SELECT)
.CBL	COBOL source file		
.CFG	Program configuration information	.MOS	Mouse driver file (DOS visual shell)
.CNF	Program configuration information	.MSG	Program message file
		.NDX	An index file (dBASE III)
.CHP	Chapter file (Ventura Publisher)	.OBJ	Intermediate object code (program) file
.COM	Command (program) file	.OLD	Alternative extension for a backup file
.CP1	Code page information file (DOS)	.OVL	Program overlay file
		.OVR	Program overlay file
.DAT	Data file	.PAK	Packed (archive) file
.DBF	Database file (dBASE III)	.PAS	Pascal source file
.DCT	Dictionary file	.PCX	A picture file for PC Paintbrush
.DEV	Program device driver file		
.DIF	Data Interchange Format file	.PIF	Program Information File (TopView/Windows)
.DOC	Document (text) file	.PRO	Profile (configuration file (DOS GRAPHICS)
.DRV	Program device driver file		
.DTA	Data file		
.EXE	Executable program file	.PRN	Program listing for printing
.FNT	Font file	.PS	PostScript program file
.IDX	Index file (Q&A)	.RFT	Revisable Form Text (Document Content Architecture)
.IMG	GEM image (graphics) file		
.HLP	Help file		
.KEY	Keyboard macro file (ProKey)	.SAV	Alternative extension for a backup file

93

Table 5.2—(cont.)

Extension	Common Use	Extension	Common Use
.SYS	System or device driver file	.$xx	Temporary or incorrectly stored file
.STY	Style sheet (Ventura Publisher)	.WK1	Worksheet file (1-2-3, Release 2)
.TIF	A picture file in tag image format	.WK3	Worksheet file (1-2-3, Release 3)
.TMP	Temporary file		
.TST	Test file	.WKQ	Quattro spreadsheet file
.TXT	Text file	.WKS	Alternative extension for a worksheet file

Don't worry—you don't have to memorize all of these file-naming conventions. You can always keep this table handy for reference. Even when you do use with your software a file name that causes file-name conflicts, you can easily rename the file by using the RENAME command covered in a later chapter. Normally, the worst that happens when you use an inappropriate convention when naming a file is that the file will trip you up later in a case of mistaken identity.

Avoiding Bad File Names

When you enter file names in the command, DOS may not simply reject the bad file name. In some cases, DOS takes some unusual actions. As an example, you will look at the COPY command. Don't worry about learning all about COPY from this example; the command is covered in detail in Chapter 9. The general form of COPY takes a source-file parameter and copies the file to the destination-file parameter. If the destination file doesn't yet exist, DOS creates it. The example assumes that the source file, TEST.TXT, already exists on the default drive. To create a new file from the file TEST.TXT, you can, for example, enter the COPY command as follows:

COPY TEST.TXT 123456789.1234

Notice that both the root file name and the extension given for the destination file name have an extra character. The root file name has the extra character **9** and the extension has the extra character **4**. You might predict that DOS will issue some message to warn that the file name and extension were both too long. DOS does not issue a warning but silently chops-off, or *truncates*, the file name to eight characters and the extension to three characters. DOS then completes the COPY operation by creating a new file. The resulting file, named by DOS, is **12345678.123**. DOS always discards excess characters in the file name and extension and uses the remaining characters as the file parameter.

Illegal characters in a file name can also stop DOS from carrying out a command. The following interaction with DOS is an example. Again, the example assumes that the source file exists.

COPY 12345678.123 1[3.123

```
File creation error
     0 File(s) copied
```

As you might expect, the illegal character [in the target file's extension stopped DOS from completing the copy operation. If you assume that the [character will always produce a file-creation error when the character is used in a file name, however, you may be surprised. The following interaction with DOS shows a surprising result.

COPY 12345678.123 87654321.12[

```
File cannot be copied onto itself
     0 file(s) copied
```

DOS sees the destination (target) file name as being the same as the source file name. The only peculiar aspect of either file name is the [character in the last character position of the target file's extension. Although the error message this command invokes is not what you would predict, DOS does stop the command.

If you use the same [character in a reporting command such as DIR, you might predict that DOS would issue an error message because of the illegal character in the file parameter. The following sequence shows that no error message is issued.

DIR [

```
Volume in drive C is LAP TOP
Directory of  C:\DATA
File not found
```

DOS performs a directory search for something and finds nothing. No error message is issued even though the only file parameter is an illegal character.

Not every character that is illegal in a file name stops DOS from carrying out a command. In the following example, the semicolon character is at the end of the destination file's extension.

COPY 12345678.123 12345678.12;

```
1 File(s) copied
```

DOS carries out the COPY command and creates a new file from the destination parameter. To see the new file's name, issue the DIR command and view the listing:

```
Volume in drive C is LAP TOP
Directory of  C:\DATA
TEST     TXT       5    8-25-89     9:25a
12345678 123       5    8-25-89     9:32a
12345678 12        5    8-25-89     9:35a
      3 File(s)  1978368 bytes free
```

DOS adds the `12345678.12` file. DOS reads the `;` in the command as a closing delimiter. The remaining part of the target-file parameter becomes the new file's name.

Not many DOS users with some experience would use illegal characters in a file name on purpose. Typos, however, can easily creep into your command lines and introduce illegal characters into file-name parameters. Just remember that the reaction of DOS to an illegal file name isn't always predictable.

Examining Disks and Drives

The use of files for storing named collections of data is not useful to you without some convenient medium for storing the files themselves. PC designers chose disks as the file-storage medium of choice. Disks, both removable and fixed, have a virtual monopoly on file storage in PCs. Tape and CD ROM (Compact Disk Read Only Memory) finish a distant second and third. Disk drives, DOS's warehouse for file storage, offer convenience, reliability, reusability, and rapid access to files. Disks play the primary role as the file's storage medium, so it helps if you have some understanding of how disks perform this storage job.

Understanding the Disk's Magnetic Storage Technique

Disk drives are electro-mechanical components that record and play back data using the magnetic surfaces of a disk. Normally, the data is in the form of a file. During the recording or *writing* of a file, an electronic circuit translates the PC's electrical data into a series of magnetic fields. These magnetic fields are mirrored (very weakly) by the oxide coating of the disk in the drive. In effect, the original data is magnetically imprinted on a disk. The information has changed its state. Electrical information is changed to magnetic information.

During the playback or *reading* of data from the disk's surface, an electronic circuit translates the magnetic fields back into electrical signals, and the data is once again in the electrical form. The disk's original magnetic imprint, the file, is not destroyed by the reading operation. The file is still on the disk after it is read. Under normal use, only recording over the old imprint, called *overwriting* the disk, will change the imprint. Many file-related commands will overwrite the previous contents of files. Commands that overwrite must be used with respect.

Unless you overwrite a file, the file is permanent. The recorded magnetic imprint on the disk is resistant to weakening and will last for years. Other magnetic fields, however, such as those produced by motors, magnetic paper clip holders, ringing telephones, and televisions, can weaken the magnetic imprint on a disk, and the disk's files can become unreadable in a short time. If the data being magnetically translated from a disk has some loss of integrity, your computer will not be able to fill in what is missing or wrong. The result is a *read error*. Read errors can end a work session unpleasantly because DOS will stop your computing when it detects a critical error. Disk drive designers must strive for perfect data reproduction from computer disks. One bad spot on a disk can result in a message similar to the following:

```
General Failure error reading drive A:
```

This message signals the unrecoverable loss of all data on a disk.

Looking into Disk Drives

The mechanical parts and electrical circuits of disk drives are complex. Although disk drives are parts of PC systems, the drives are machines in their own right. DOS relies on the driver programs of the BIOS to signal a drive's electronic circuitry to control the actions of the drive's mechanical components. You don't have to be concerned with the drive's complexity.

All disk drives have in common certain components: read/write heads, head-positioner mechanisms, and disk-spinning motors. All disk drives record on disks. Some disks are removable; some are built into the drive. Both fixed disks and removable disks are spun on a center spindle within the disk drive.

Many of today's PCs have both fixed disks and removable disks installed in their system units. DOS includes provisions in its BIOS extensions for both types of drives. Even with their common features, fixed and removable disk drives have some important distinctions. Knowing these distinctions will help you understand each drive type's operation in your system.

Hard Disk Drives

Non-removable media disk drives have their disks built in. Drives with built-in disks are called *fixed disk drives*. This term is often shortened to *fixed disk* or *hard disk*. Both terms are suitable substitutes. Fixed disk drives are often called hard disk drives because their disks are made of a hard, rigid metal. In this book, the term *hard disk* is used to describe the built-in, fixed disk drive. A hard disk drive can contain more than one hard disk or *platter*. Multiple platters are arranged in a stack with space between the individual platters. Hard disk drives have large storage capacities in the order of millions of bytes.

Figure 5.2 shows a cut-away view of a typical hard disk. The circular platters in the figure are the drive's magnetic disks. A head-positioner arm holds the read/write heads above and below each surface of each platter. When the drive leaves the factory, the inside components are not open; the drive is sealed closed. The seal keeps dust, hair, dirt, smoke, and other contaminants out of the delicate mechanical parts within the drive.

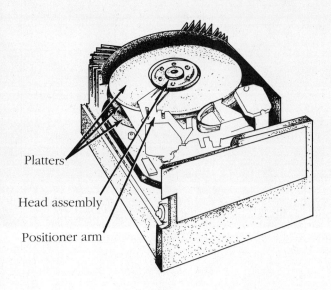

Fig. 5.2

*An inside view of the main
components of a hard disk.*

Platters

Head assembly

Positioner arm

Many users refer to hard disks as *Winchester* disks. Winchester is a name derived from
an IBM code name for the sealed disk-drive technology developed by IBM. Hard
disks have the advantages of quick operation, high reliability, and large storage
capacities. Hard disks have the disadvantage of tying the data stored on the disk to
the PC in which the drive has been installed. Because the hard disk's platters cannot
be removed, the data is tied to the drive. Hard disks are installed in a PC with
mounting hardware and interconnecting power and data cables. To move an entire
hard disk to another computer just to use the hard disk's data is impractical. When
you need to move data between the hard disks of two computers, you can use the
XCOPY command, or the BACKUP and RESTORE commands. These commands are
covered in Part Two of this book.

Floppy Disk Drives

In a PC system, the disadvantages of tying data to the hard disk is compensated by
the PC's floppy disk drive. By far the most common class of removable disk is the
floppy disk. Floppy disks are protected by a permanent jacket which covers the
flexible mylar disk and is coated with a magnetic-sensitive film. The first floppy disks
were 8 inches in diameter. By today's standards, the early 8-inch floppy disks didn't
store much data considering their size. Some 8-inch floppies could only store 320K of

data. Today's 5 1/4-inch and 3 1/2-inch floppy disks store from hundreds of thousands of bytes to nearly 1 and 1/2 million bytes.

Some early microcomputers used these 8-inch floppies as their standard. For three or four years, the pioneering microcomputer makers offered 8-inch floppy drives as the alternative to primitive off-line file storage such as paper tape and cassette recording.

A smaller version of the 8-inch floppy, the 5 1/4-inch *minifloppy*, quickly became the floppy of choice for PC designers because of its size. The 3 1/2-inch *microfloppy* is yet another departure from its larger, older cousins because it incorporates a rigid plastic case (its jacket) as a protective cover. The 3 1/2-inch mylar circular medium inside a microfloppy disk is flexible like the media in 8-inch and 5 1/4-inch floppies.

Figure 5.3 shows a microfloppy disk being inserted into a drive. It is not possible to interchange disks between size (diameter) classes of floppy drives.

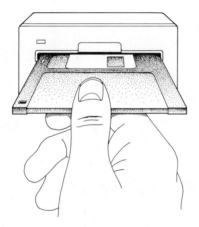

Fig. 5.3

Inserting a microfloppy (3 1/2-inch) disk into a drive.

The smaller two sizes of floppy disks are officially called *diskettes*; the 8-inch version is called a *disk*. The term *floppy disk* (or just *floppy*) refers to any lower-capacity disk in a jacket that you remove from your PC's drive. If identifying the type of floppy is important, many users use the size qualifier as in "3 1/2-inch floppy" to make a distinction. *Minifloppy* always refers to 5 1/4-inch floppy disks; *microfloppy* always refers to 3 1/2-inch floppy disks. You'll likely read or hear the term *disk* used to mean any floppy or hard disk when the disk type is clear in context. In other contexts, the term *diskette* is used to refer to both 3 1/2-inch and 5 1/4-inch disks.

Understanding the Dynamics of the Disk Drive

The dynamics of the disk drive are a function of the drive's electronics. The drive contains many components that interact with each other to provide performance. These components are covered in the next sections.

Disk Drive Heads

Disk drives utilize one or more record/pickup or read/write *heads*. The heads of a disk drive are analogous to the pickup cartridge of a phonograph. The cartridge "picks-up" vibrations from the stylus riding in the track and converts them to electrical energy. Disk heads convert magnetic energy to electrical data. Although several heads can be employed in a disk drive, the electronics of the disk drive accept data from one head at a time.

Disk drive heads come in various shapes. Figure 5.4 illustrates two common head configurations. The heads themselves are held in position by flexible metal head-holder assemblies. A set of wires carrying electrical signals connects to the head and passes through the head-holder assembly where the set connects to a flexible ribbon cable. The ribbon cable absorbs wire movements when the head assembly moves. The hard-disk head assembly is lower in mass to allow for greater start-stop control during high speed head positioning.

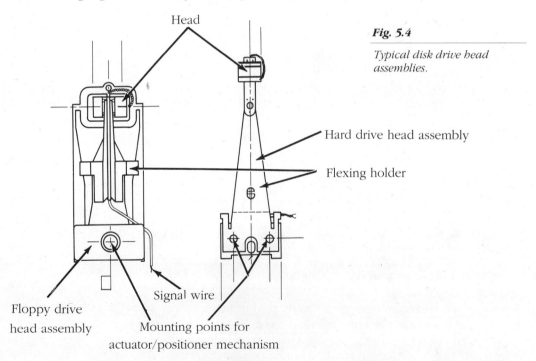

Head

Fig. 5.4

Typical disk drive head assemblies.

Hard drive head assembly

Flexing holder

Floppy drive head assembly

Signal wire

Mounting points for actuator/positioner mechanism

Most floppy disks have data recorded by a head on each of their two sides or surfaces. Floppy drives that use a head on each side of the floppy disk are called *double-sided* drives. Hard disk drives can accommodate more than one double-sided platter because the drives incorporate heads on both sides of each platter. Using both sides of a disk or platter doubles its capacity. Incorporating multiple platters in a hard disk further multiplies its capacity by the number of heads employed.

Disk Tracks

Regardless of the type of disk drive, all disks spin on a center axis like a record spinning on a phonograph. A floppy disk spins at 360 revolutions per minute. The rotational speed of a hard disk is 10 times higher (approximately 3,600 RPM). The heads, which are positioned above the spinning surface of the disk, are held and moved in distinct steps by an actuator arm and head positioner. The heads of a floppy disk drive touch the medium's surface; the heads of a hard disk ride above the surface of the media on a cushion of air. At each step position, the alignment of the head and the spinning disk produces a circular track.

The track is not a physical track like the groove in a record, but rather a ring of magnetically recorded data. Unlike the phonograph, which plays a record's contents by following a single, spiraling track, the disk drive steps from track to track to retrieve data. Figure 5.5 gives some idea of the position of the tracks. Notice that the tracks are not depicted as a spiral. All the tracks on a disk's surface are perfect concentric circles. The number of concentric tracks available on one disk's surface is determined by the head positioner's mechanical movements. The smaller the stepping distance, the tighter the track pattern, and consequently, the greater the number of tracks.

Tracks · Sectors

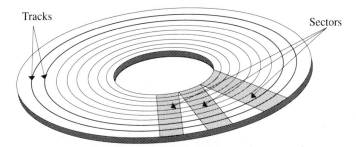

Fig. 5.5

Concentric tracks on a disk's surface.

Disk Cylinders

A disk drive's multiple heads are affixed to a single positioner mechanism. When one head moves one track on its side of a platter (or floppy), the other heads all move one track on their respective sides of their respective platters. Picture a top head riding over track 10 of side one of a platter, while the bottom head is riding under track 10 of side two. If the disk has more than one platter, all the heads of that disk are positioned on track 10 of their associated side and platter. This conceptual alignment of heads on the same track position on different sides (and platters) of the same disk is called a *cylinder* (see fig. 5.6). The term cylinder is derived from the imaginary shape of the stacked circular tracks at any one stopping point of the positioner mechanism.

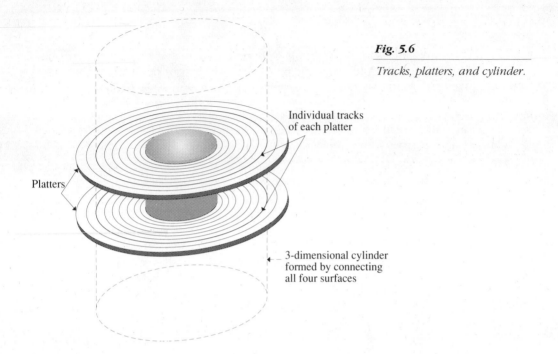

Fig. 5.6

Tracks, platters, and cylinder.

Individual tracks
of each platter

Platters

3-dimensional cylinder
formed by connecting
all four surfaces

Because only one head can be active at one time, the drive must activate all of its heads in sequence to write (or read) all tracks at the cylinder position. Head activation starts at the top head. To fill a cylinder, a 4-head drive writes a track with head 1, then head 2, then head 3, and finally head 4. The head positioner moves one cylinder, and the sequence repeats. Processing all tracks of a cylinder before moving to the next cylinder is efficient because all heads are already at new track positions. You will see how DOS uses this efficiency in a moment.

Disk Sectors

When a disk is blank, as it is when it comes from the factory, it contains no tracks and therefore no information. DOS has to prepare the disk to accept data. This preparation exercise is known as *formatting*. Formatting, as the name implies, places a uniform pattern of format information in all tracks as it steps through each cylinder of the disk. This format information within each track allows DOS to slice each track into smaller, more manageable, fixed-size component parts. These component parts are called *sectors*. Figure 5.7 shows the sectors of a floppy disk represented as slices of the disk's surface. The figure shows the boundaries for every other sector. The concentric arcs between the indicated sectors are the disk's tracks. Notice that each track has the same number of sector boundaries (and therefore sectors).

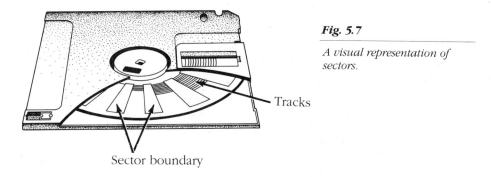

Tracks

Sector boundary

Fig. 5.7

A visual representation of sectors.

DOS reads and writes disk data one sector at a time. Some of its internal file-system bookkeeping is done by sectors. To DOS, a sector is the disk's most manageable block of data. DOS uses 512-byte sectors with disks, but DOS has provisions to use a different sector size. DOS has been using 512-byte sectors since its beginning, so a change in sector size is unlikely (but not impossible) in the future.

The number of sectors formatted into each track is tied to the data density that the drive uses when reading or writing data. The more dense the recording in a track, the greater the number of sectors that can be formatted. The more tracks, the greater the number of sectors per disk.

Designers select the number of tracks and the number of sectors per track with reliability in mind. Floppy disk drives are designed with more margin for error than hard disks. It's easy to see why some margin for error is desirable for a drive that must ensure the mechanical alignment of each disk a user shoves in the door. Floppy disk drives must read disks that may have been stored in a place where the disk's magnetic information has been weakened. Even with the protective jacket, the magnetic-coated surfaces of many floppy disks become contaminated with smoke, dust, or finger prints. The drive must be able to tolerate some contamination on a disk and still perform its function without numerous errors. Of course, no disk drive can avoid errors if the disks it uses are abused. Drive heads can't read through liquid spills or ballpoint pen dents.

Hard disk drives have higher capacities than their floppy cousins. The higher capacity is due in large part to the precision of the drive's critical components in conjunction with the special oxides used to magnetically coat the platters. In addition, the working parts of the drive are sealed at the factory in a way that protects the platters, positioners, and heads from particles and contamination. With outside influence over these critical components sealed out, the hard disk drive can offer more tracks and sectors in the same physical space. When you consider that most hard disks have more than one platter, each capable of two-sided operation with more tracks, you can begin to see how hard disks get their large storage capacities.

Understanding Disk Formats

Disk drives have a universal way to divide a disk's available physical space in a logical manner. The number of platters, the number of sides, the number of tracks, the number of bytes per sector, and the number of sectors per track are the specific details that allow this logical division of a disk's physical space. The specification for a disk's use of its physical space is called its *format*. PCs employ a variety of disk-drive sizes and formats. PCs equipped with both 5 1/4-inch and 3 1/2-inch floppies are available. Most PC users and software manuals differentiate a format from other formats by using the byte-capacity figure for the desired format. Each new version of DOS has maintained support for disk formats supported by its predecessors. This support ensures that disks made with older drive formats will be usable with current versions of DOS.

Floppy Disk Drive Formats

The first DOS-supported disk drives allowed for double the number of tracks on a 5 1/4-inch floppy disk than the standard 5 1/4-inch disk formats of the time. These DOS formats were called *double-density* formats. The original PC disk size and format was 5 1/4-inch, single-sided, 40 tracks, with 8 sectors per track and 512 bytes per sector. These disks are called *single-sided, double-density* disks or *SSDD*. The capacity of this 8-sector single-sided format is 160K.

The early format was extended by making the disk format double-sided in DOS V1.1. All floppies are double-sided in the sense that they have two sides. The term *double-sided* in the formatting sense means that data is recorded onto both sides of the disk. Only drives equipped with a second head can accommodate double-sided recording. By using the other side of the disk, disk capacity is doubled. To differentiate these two-sided disks from disks that used only one side for storage, disk makers called them *double-sided, double-density* disks or *DSDD*. By using both sides for storing data, the format capacity was 320K. Today it is rare to find a PC with a single-sided disk drive. The majority of 5 1/4-inch floppy drives are equipped with two heads.

As disk drives became more sophisticated in design and magnetic materials made great improvements, the number of sectors per track was increased from 8 to 9 in DOS V2.0 with no reliability problems. Both DSDD and SSDD formats were given the extra sector per track. The extra sector per track allowed this format to store more data than the previous DSDD and SSDD formats, and the new format quickly became popular with users. To differentiate between the DSDD and SSDD, 8-sector formats, and these DSDD and SSDD, 9-sector formats, you can think of these formats as *DSDD-9* and *SSDD-9*. Of course, referring to the DSDD and SSDD, 8-sector formats as DSDD-8 and SSDD-8 provides additional clarification. The single-sided, 9-sector version has a capacity of 180K; the double-sided version has a capacity of 360K.

The evolution of DOS to V3.0 provided for drives with quadruple the number of tracks of those early standard disks. These new 80-track *quad-density* formats were applied to 5 1/4-inch drives as well as the newer 3 1/2-inch drives. DOS provided one quad-density format of 9 sectors per track, used primarily on 3 1/2-inch drives. This quad-density, 9-sector format is called *QD-9*, and sometimes just *quad*. The QD-9 disk capacity is 720K. A second quad-density, high-capacity quad format of 15 sectors per track was incorporated by DOS designers at the same time. This high-capacity format is used primarily on 5 1/4-inch drives. The quad-density, 15-sector format is called *HC* for High Capacity even though it is just as proper to refer to it as *QD-15*. The QD-15 format, with a capacity of 1.2M, was popularized by the IBM PC/AT.

DOS V3.3 added a high-capacity format for 3 1/2-inch drives that supports the 80-track quad density but provides 18 sectors per track. The high capacity format offers 1.44M of storage space from a microfloppy. This *QD-18* format is sometimes called 3 1/2-inch HC.

Table 5.3 summarizes the common floppy disk formats. Some versions of DOS enable you to use the FORMAT command to place a format on a disk other than the normal format. Chapter 6 explains the details of the FORMAT command.

Table 5.3
DOS Floppy Disk Formats

Format	Tracks	Sectors/Track	Total Sectors	Usable Capacity
SSDD	40	8	320	160K
DSDD	40	8	640	320K
SSDD-9	40	9	360	180K
DSDD-9	40	9	720	360K
QD-9	80	9	1420	720K
QD-15	80	15	2400	1.2M
QD-18	80	18	2880	1.44M

Raw Capacity and Usable Capacity

The process of formatting a blank disk places some data on the disk that is not part of the total capacity of the disk. A 1.44M disk, for example, holds more than 1.44M bytes of information. This extra space is not available to you, though. It is the space used by the sector-identification and error-checking information. If you buy disks for a 1.44M drive, the disk's identification label may say that the disk has a 2M capacity. Disks for a 720K drive may indicate a 1M capacity.

This apparent discrepancy is explained by looking at the difference between total or raw capacity and usable or formatted capacity. The larger of the two numbers for the same disk is considered the *raw* capacity of the disk. Raw capacity includes the capacity that the formatting information will use at format time. The lesser of the two numbers for the same disk is the *usable* capacity of the disk. This number of bytes is available for storing files after the formatting information has been put on the disk.

Fortunately, most hard disk manufacturers state the capacity of their drives as the formatted capacity. Hard disks also lose some overhead space. If you have any doubt as to the meaning of a hard disk's stated capacity, ask the dealer if the capacity is determined before or after formatting. In this book, *disk capacity* refers to usable capacity after formatting-overhead information has been applied to the disk.

Hard Disk Drive Formats

Formats for hard disks nearly always employ 17,512-byte sectors per track. You can understand the concept of hard disk capacity by remembering the concept of cylinders. Hard disks, as you recall, have two or more heads. Remember that a cylinder is the alignment of all of the heads on the same track on both sides of each platter. If a disk has 306 tracks on one side of one platter, the disk has 306 cylinders. The total number of tracks on the disk is the number of cylinders times the number of heads. The disk's capacity in bytes is the number of tracks times the number of sectors per track, times the number of bytes per sector. To obtain the capacity in kilobytes, divide the result by 1,024. To obtain the capacity in megabytes, divide the kilobyte total by 1,024. For approximations of capacity, you can divide by a rounded 1,000.

DOS does not actually provide the low-level format data for a hard disk as it does a floppy disk. Hard disks are normally prepared at the factory with a low-level format. End users seldom (if ever) need to initiate a low-level format on a hard disk. DOS uses the low-level format to perform its high-level format. When discussing hard disk formatting, the term *format* refers to the high-level format initiated by the DOS FORMAT command. During the formatting of a hard disk, DOS initializes its bookkeeping tables and then writes "dummy" data into the disk's tracks. From your point of view, formatting a hard disk is the same basic operation as formatting a floppy. DOS keeps the details of the low-level format hidden and out of your way.

Table 5.4 shows some typical hard disk formats. An increasing number of hard disk sizes are being used in PCs, and each size or type uses the same basic principle of format.

Table 5.4
Hard Disk Formats

Typical Disk	Sectors/Track	Heads	Cylinders	Capacity
IBM PC/XT	17	4	306	10M
IBM AT	17	4	615	20M
IBM AT (Late Model)	17	5	733	30M

> **Tech note ...** Computers generally store data in groups of eight bits. This eight-bit group of data is called a *byte*. By design, digital computers are most efficient when working with numbers as some power of 2. Numbers that are powers of two can be represented directly in a binary annotation.
>
> Computer programmers and designers apply this power-of-2 convention to the expression of a quantity of bytes. A kilobyte, for example, is 2^{10} or 1,024 bytes. Two kilobytes = 2,048 bytes or 2K. One megabyte, or 1M, equals 1,024K. It's not important for you to know about numbers in the power of 2 except to note that capacity in kilobytes or megabytes has this 1,024 rather than 1,000 multiplier. You can, for scaling purposes, think of 1K as approximately 1,000 bytes.
>
> The capacity of disk drives is stated in bytes as either kilobytes or megabytes. The storage capacity of a hard disk is in the order of millions of bytes; megabyte is the usual capacity descriptor. The capacity of floppies is in the order of hundreds of thousands to just over a million bytes. Both kilobyte (K) and megabyte (M) can be used as a multiplier to describe the capacity of a floppy.

Trying Some Disk Commands

The DOS file system and its provisions to handle disks and files are made useful to you through commands. To get some hands-on practice with disks, try the commands in the following sections. You will learn a few disk commands as well as some other common DOS commands. The exercises will build on your knowledge of commands from the last chapter and help reinforce the information about disks and files in this chapter.

Determining Your DOS Version with VER

Not all PCs run the same version of DOS. DOS has evolved through four major versions with minor version changes along the way. Not all commands are available in all versions, nor do all commands work exactly the same in all versions. You will find it useful to determine your exact version. DOS includes the VER command to help you to do just that.

VER is one of the DOS commands that has no parameters or switches, so it's an easy command to learn and use. VER is an internal command built into COMMAND.COM. Because VER is internal, COMMAND.COM does not have to find the VER program on the DOS disk (or as you will learn later, the DOS subdirectory).

Of course, you need to boot DOS on your PC before you can issue any commands. If you haven't started your PC, do so now. If you are cloudy on how to boot, check back to Chapter 3. If you want to perform a warm boot (reboot), remember to put the working DOS disk in drive A and press Ctrl-Alt-Del.

Issuing VER is easy. When you see the DOS prompt, simply enter the command as follows:

VER

Don't forget to press Enter to send the command line to DOS. DOS will report the version of DOS that you used to boot the PC. What you see on your screen will look similar to the following:

```
IBM DOS Version 4.00
```

Manufacturers who adapt DOS to their PCs may include other information. You might see something like the following:

```
Toshiba MS-DOS Version 3.30 / R3C00US
```

In both of these VER reports, you see a manufacturer's name and the version number of DOS. As with the output of many DOS commands, your particular VER report may vary slightly.

When you boot with one version of DOS and, later in the session, use the external commands from another version, DOS may object with an error message. Implementations and versions of DOS don't often mix due to slight differences. If you get an Incorrect DOS Version message, chances are good that you've mixed external commands from one version with the booting of another.

Clearing the Screen with CLS

When you issue a series of DOS commands, your screen can soon become cluttered with output text. In most cases, the text scrolling off the top of the screen won't bother you. While you are learning to use DOS commands, however, you may want to clear your screen before issuing your next command. Just use the internal CLS command, and the job is done.

Clearing your screen is easy. Like VER, CLS has no additional parameters or switches on the command line. Simply enter the following command:

CLS

When you press Enter, DOS clears the screen and places the cursor in the top left corner of the screen. Because DOS commands fill the screen from a top down fashion, you will have an entire 25-line screen (possibly more lines in some modes) to fill with command input and output.

If your applications software exits to DOS with an image of the last screen or other clutter, a CLS command will clear the screen as you clear your thoughts before you issue a DOS command.

Copying an Entire Disk with DISKCOPY

Copying one disk (a source disk) to another disk (the target or destination disk) is a practical and useful exercise. DOS's DISKCOPY command is the external DOS command that carries out the exercise. DISKCOPY makes a near mirror-image copy of a source disk. DISKCOPY is an ideal command to use when you need to make a copy of a disk, such as a master applications program disk. DOS provides other commands to copy the contents of one disk to another, (you'll learn more about these commands in Part Two), but DISKCOPY is the only disk-level copy command offered by DOS.

When you use DISKCOPY, you copy the format and content of the source disk. DISKCOPY uses the formatted capacity of a source disk to determine if the destination disk is the same format. If you have a 360K source disk, you will end up with a 360K destination disk. A 1.2M floppy will DISKCOPY to a 1.2M floppy.

One type of disk that DISKCOPY won't copy is a hard disk. DISKCOPY is a floppy-disk-only command. Don't be concerned that you will harm your hard disk with DISKCOPY in an errant command line. DISKCOPY will issue an error message if the disks involved in the operation aren't compatible, but the command won't hurt a hard disk.

DISKCOPY is an external command that you load from disk. You must have the disk that contains DISKCOPY in your default drive or set the correct path with the PATH command (see Chapter 6 for information on the PATH command). Use the DISKCOPY command to copy floppies only.

The correct syntax for DISKCOPY is as follows:

    DISKCOPY *sd: dd:*

sd: represents the optional name for the drive that holds the disk that you want to copy; this drive is called the *source* drive. *dd:* is the optional name of the drive that holds the disk to receive the copy. This *destination* drive is sometimes called the *target* drive (see fig. 5.8).

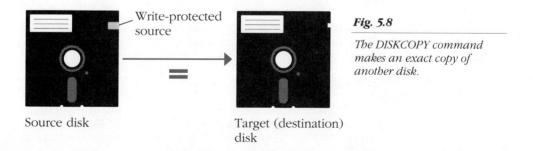

Write-protected source

Source disk

Target (destination) disk

Fig. 5.8

The DISKCOPY command makes an exact copy of another disk.

As always, type a colon (:) after the drive name. COMMAND.COM needs the colon as an indicator that you are naming a drive as a specifier. Insert a space between the source and destination drive names. The space delimits the source and destination drive parameters. If you use a blank disk as the destination disk, DOS first formats it. An example of the DISKCOPY command is as follows:

DISKCOPY A: B:

After you issue the DISKCOPY command, DOS prompts you to put the disk(s) into the proper drive (see fig. 5.9). Make sure that you put them in the correct drives and then write-protect the source disk. If you write-protect the source disk, you safeguard its contents in case of a disk mix-up.

```
A>DISKCOPY A: B:

Insert SOURCE diskette in drive A:

Insert TARGET diskette in drive B:

Press any key to continue . . .

Copying 40 tracks
9 Sectors/Track, 2 Side(s)

Copy another diskette (Y/N)? N

A>
```

Fig. 5.9

A typical DISKCOPY command sequence and messages from DOS.

When the disks are in place, you are ready to continue. Press a key, and the disk copy process will begin. When the copy process finishes, DOS asks if you want to make another copy. Answer Y to make another copy or N to exit the command. If you answer Y, you do not have to access DISKCOPY again because DOS has the external DISKCOPY program in memory.

If you leave out the drive names in the DISKCOPY command line, DOS uses the default drive as the specifier. To avoid confusion, you can always give both the source and destination drive names.

If the drives or disks are not compatible, you will get an error message, and no copy will take place (see fig. 5.10).

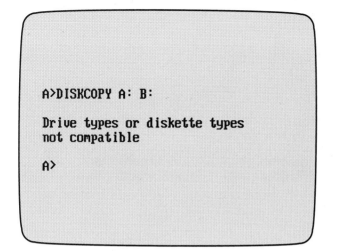

Fig. 5.10

An error message produced by the DISKCOPY command.

If the DISKCOPY command is issued with no drive parameters, DOS will copy using just one drive. DOS will prompt you to alternately switch between inserting the source and destination disks. Depending on your system's memory, you will swap disks once or several times (see fig. 5.11). By entering DISKCOPY alone, remember that you are telling DOS to use one drive. Make sure that you don't get the disks confused during swapping.

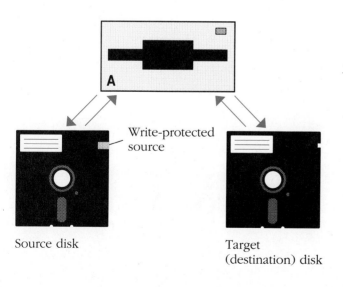

Write-protected source

Source disk

Target (destination) disk

Fig. 5.11

Using the DISKCOPY command alone with no parameters may require you to swap disks several times.

111

How One Floppy Drive Can Be Two . . . The designers of DOS provided for PCs with a single floppy drive to work with source and destination disks. Many DOS commands, such as DISKCOPY, COPY, and DISKCOMP, treat the one drive as two by dividing their operation into two phases. If you have one floppy drive (even if you have a hard disk) and you issue the command **DISKCOPY A: B:**, DOS reads the source disk from the floppy drive as A: and then asks you to insert the destination disk for B:. On a single floppy drive system, drive B is really drive A. Even though you have one physical drive, DOS treats it logically as two. DOS is able to use the drive name B: for some commands by viewing the single drive logically. For your part in the one-drive-as-two operation, you should ensure that you have inserted the correct disk in the drive when DOS prompts you. DOS keeps the identity of the drive straight internally.

Comparing Disks with DISKCOMP

You can confirm that two disks are identical by using the external command DISKCOMP. DISKCOMP compares each track of one disk to another sector by sector. Like DISKCOPY, DISKCOMP is a floppy-only command. You cannot use DISKCOMP to compare two hard disks. Remember that the disks and capacities must be the same for both disks in the comparison. Any difference in disks made with DISKCOPY is a sign of a problem disk. One practical use of DISKCOMP is to compare a master disk included with an applications software package to a working copy; DISKCOMP will confirm whether or not the working copy is good.

The DISKCOMP command compares two disks of equal size and capacity to confirm that both are the same (see fig. 5.12). Normally, you use DISKCOMP to test disks that were made from originals using the DISKCOPY command. Because DISKCOMP doesn't write any information to either disk, both disks can be write-protected. If the disks compare, DOS gives the message Compare OK.

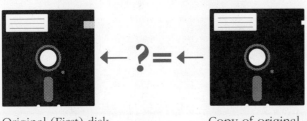

Original (First) disk

Copy of original
disk (Second)

Fig. 5.12

The DISKCOMP command compares two disks of equal size and capacity to confirm that both are the same.

The syntax for DISKCOMP is very similar to that of DISKCOPY. Again, remember that on a single drive system, one drive can act logically as two. Issue the command in the following form:

DISKCOMP *d1: d2:*

Notice that the syntax for DISKCOMP is much like the syntax for DISKCOPY. Because the disks are being compared, not copied, they are referred to as *d1:* and *d2:* rather than source and destination. The drive specifiers *d1:* and *d2:* are optional. Load the two disks at the DOS prompt, and DOS will confirm the comparison or point out the differences. As with DISKCOPY, you can repeat the DISKCOMP command. An example of the DISKCOMP command is as follows:

DISKCOMP A: B:

Again, if you omit a drive designator, DOS uses the default drive.

In the sequence shown in figure 5.13, a working copy of a master disk is compared to the original master. Notice the compare errors. The working copy is no longer reliable, or other files have been added to the disk since DISKCOPY was first used to make a working copy from the master. To solve the problem, the best bet would be to make a new working copy.

```
A>DISKCOMP A: B:

Insert FIRST diskette in drive A:

Insert SECOND diskette in drive B:

Press any key to continue . . .

Comparing 40 tracks
9 sectors per track, 2 side(s)

Compare error on
side 0, track 0

Compare error on
side 0, track 3

Compare another diskette (Y/N) ?N

A>
```

Fig. 5.13

A working copy of a master disk compared to the original disk.

If the DISKCOMP command is issued with no drive parameters, DOS will carry out the comparison using just one drive. DOS will alternately prompt you to switch between inserting the first and second disks. Depending on your system's memory, you will swap disks once or several times (see fig. 5.14). By entering DISKCOMP alone, you are telling DOS to use one floppy drive even if your system contains two. Make sure you don't get the disks confused during swapping. By confusing which disk DOS wants in the drive, you may end up comparing part of a disk to itself.

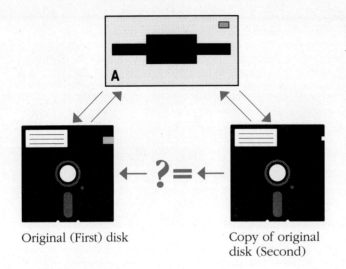

Fig. 5.14

The DISKCOMP command issued without parameters may require that you swap disks several times.

Original (First) disk

Copy of original disk (Second)

Summary

In this chapter, you have taken a look at drives, disks, and files. You also learned about the internal DOS commands VER and CLS, and the external disk-level commands DISKCOPY and DISKCOMP. Following are the key points covered in this chapter:

❑ DOS organizes files into a file system which DOS manages.

❑ Disks are the main storage media of a DOS-based PC.

❑ Files are the storage units of disks.

❑ All files have names of up to 8 characters of root file name and up to 3 characters of extension. File-name characters must be "legal" to DOS.

❑ DOS tracks file names in a disk directory. Each file name in a directory must be unique.

❑ By convention, certain file names refer to specific types of files. You can override file-naming conventions, but observing file-naming conventions helps keep file contents more meaningful.

❑ DOS uses one of its standard devices when you use a file name that contains the device name as root-file name. You should avoid using the names PRN, CON, NUL, LPT, and COM in file names.

❑ During formatting, disks are divided by DOS into tracks, cylinders, and sectors. The storage capacity of a disk is governed by the total number of sectors on the disk.

❑ Typical floppy-disk storage capacities are 360K, 720K, 1.2M, and 1.44M. Each floppy drive is designed to work optimally at one of these capacities.

❑ The VER command reports your current DOS version.

❑ The CLS command clears the screen.

❑ The DISKCOPY command is an external command that makes a mirror-image copy of a source disk.

❑ The DISKCOMP command is an external command that compares two disks for equality and reports any comparison errors that are encountered.

The next chapter of the book begins Part Two. Part Two introduces many DOS commands as well as some additional file-system concepts. Part One has given you a foundation, and you may want to review some of the concepts and rules presented in Part One as you work through the chapters of Part Two.

Part Two

Putting DOS to Work for You

Understanding Disk Preparation and Management

Understanding Hierarchical Directories

Managing Directories

Keeping Files in Order

Understanding Backups and the Care of Data

Understanding Disk Preparation and Management

In Chapter 5, you learned the basics of using disks and files in DOS. This chapter builds on that knowledge and introduces useful disk-related DOS commands. You will learn about preparing blank floppy disks and hard disks, assigning volume labels, transferring the system files, and analyzing disks for problems.

Key Terms Used in This Chapter

Format	Initial preparation of a disk for data storage
Volume label	A disk-level name that identifies a particular disk
Track	A circular section of a disk's surface that holds data
Sector	A section of a track that acts as the disk's smallest storage unit
Disk partition	A division of a hard disk that DOS sees as an individual area of access.
Logical drive	A partitioned section of a hard disk that DOS views as an additional hard disk.

Boot sector	A special area in track 0 of each DOS disk. DOS uses the boot sector to record important information about a disk's format. DOS later uses this information when working with the disk.
Internal command	A DOS command that is built into COMMAND.COM.
External command	A DOS command that must be located from a file loaded by COMMAND.COM before it can be executed.

Understanding Disk Preparation

A blank disk is not like a blank audio tape. You can't just drop it in and use it. You must electronically prepare disks before you can store information on them. This electronic preparation process is called *formatting*.

DOS's FORMAT command performs this preparation process for disks. You do nothing more than enter the command. FORMAT analyzes a disk for defects, generates a root directory, sets up a storage table, and makes other technical modifications.

Think of unformatted and formatted disks as being comparable to unlined and lined sheets of paper (see fig. 6.1). The lines on the sheet of paper provide you with an orderly way to record written information. The lines also act as a guide for the reader of your information. New disks (unformatted disks) are like unlined sheets of paper to DOS.

Fig. 6.1

Formatted disks are comparable to lined paper. Just as the lines on the paper are guides for the reader, so are the tracks and sectors on the disk guides for the computer.

When you format a disk, DOS *encodes*, or programs, data-storage divisions on the surface of the disk. As you learned in Chapter 5, these divisions are concentric circles called *tracks* (see fig. 6.2). DOS decides what type of drive you have and then positions the tracks accordingly. DOS also writes data on the disk's first track—track 0—that records the vital information about the disk's format. Later, DOS can quickly read this information to determine how to work with the disk.

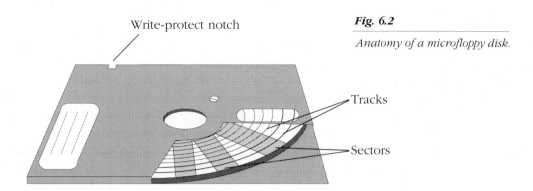

Write-protect notch

Fig. 6.2

Anatomy of a microfloppy disk.

Tracks

Sectors

Each track is further divided into segments called *sectors* (see fig. 6.2). DOS stores data in the sectors and uses the track number and sector number to retrieve the data. Disk-level commands use tracks and sectors as road maps to carry out their operations. DOS tracks the utilization of the sectors in a special disk table called the *File Allocation Table* or *FAT*. The FAT logs every sector on a disk. One of FORMAT's primary responsibilities is to set up the disk's FAT in track 0. Based on the capacity of the disk (and the version of DOS), The FAT may track a disk's sectors in units of multiple sectors called *clusters*. A cluster is DOS's minimum file allocation unit.

A standard floppy disk (one that holds 360K of data) has 40 tracks per side. A standard microfloppy disk (720K) has 80 tracks per side. Disks with larger capacities have more tracks and more sectors. DOS provides for FATs and directories to accommodate the relative capacities of disks.

Formatting disks will become a routine job for you, but remember to always use care during the process. Formatting erases all information that a disk contains. If you format a disk you previously used, everything stored on that disk will disappear. Be careful not to format a disk that contains files you want to keep.

Labeling your disks can help you avoid such a mishap. Another precaution is to write-protect the 5 1/4-inch disk with a tab or set the write-protect switch on 3 1/2-inch disks. In any case, you should use the DIR command to see the files the disk holds before you attempt to format a previously used disk.

Understanding the FORMAT Command

NOTE

With some external commands like FORMAT, DOS prompts you to place the proper disk into the drive before the command is carried out. If you have a floppy disk system, you can remove the DOS working copy that contains the FORMAT program, insert the disk to be formatted, and press any key. Hard disk systems are normally set up to search for and load an external command from a directory on the hard disk. Chapter 7 explains this process.

The FORMAT command prepares disks for use as external data storage media. Both floppy disks and hard disks must be formatted to be used. You can also format disks that have already been formatted. Reformatting a disk effectively erases the previous contents of the disk.

FORMAT is one of the DOS commands that can quickly wipe out the entire contents of a disk. Before you use the FORMAT command, make sure that you are familiar with its syntax. FORMAT issues warning messages on-screen and prompts you for verification before formatting a hard disk. Get in the habit of exercising extreme care when using FORMAT. Read the screen prompts, verify that the disk you are formatting is correct, and keep backups of your data. FORMAT is an easy-to-use command, but the formatting operation relies on you to be sure that you are formatting the correct disk.

Issuing the FORMAT Command

Before you use the FORMAT command, study its syntax carefully. You will see that FORMAT has several switches. Don't worry about the complexity of the command's parameters and switches. Examples will make them clearer.

The syntax assumes that the FORMAT command resides on the logged drive. Remember that when you boot your computer, DOS displays the name of the drive that holds the DOS disk from which you booted. This drive is the *default* (or *current*, or *logged*) drive. To issue an external command to be executed from another disk drive, enter the drive letter for that disk drive before you type the command's name.

The syntax for FORMAT is as follows:

FORMAT d: */switches*

d: is the drive which holds the disk you want to format; */switches* are one or more optional switches. FORMAT's switches are explained in the section "Using FORMAT's Switches." For now, you only need to know one switch—the */V* switch which places a *volume* label on the disk you format.

The next sections describe the process of formatting floppy disks in floppy disk drives and in a hard disk drive. Formatting the hard disk itself is covered in a later section of this chapter, "Formatting a Hard Disk."

Formatting Floppy Disks

The process of formatting floppy disks varies depending on the number of drives in your system. Because FORMAT is an external command, COMMAND.COM must load it from the DOS disk (or the hard disk).

Before you begin, you should have a floppy disk that you can format. It is very easy to mix formatted disks with unformatted disks when you are working with a fresh box of disks. To avoid a mixup, place an indicator on the label of each disk you format. The indicator may be as simple as a dot, a check mark, or the letter "F" for "Formatted." For these exercises, the indicator is the more literal identifier: the word "Formatted."

To format a floppy disk, write "Formatted" on the label and follow the directions for your system. Insert the working DOS disk into drive A, boot your computer, and follow the subsequent directions for your system.

These exercises assume that you are using your working DOS disk. The DOS V4.0 installation process creates a working disk. If you have an earlier version of DOS, you will need a working copy of the system disk. See Appendix C for instructions.

Formatting on a Single Floppy Disk Drive System

Step 1. Close the drive door if necessary.

Step 2. Type **FORMAT B:/V** and press Enter.

No matter what disk arrangement you have on your computer, after you type the command to format the disk, you will receive a message similar to the following:

```
Insert new diskette for drive A:
and strike ENTER when ready . . .
```

Step 3. Replace the working DOS disk in drive A with the disk labeled "Formatted."

Step 4. Press Enter.

The indicator on the drive will glow, and the formatting process will begin.

Versions of DOS prior to V3.0 do not require that you specify the drive that holds the disk you want to format. If you simply issue the FORMAT command with no drive parameter and the logged disk holds the DOS working copy, DOS will attempt to format the working copy. If you have write-protected the DOS working copy, FORMAT cannot format the DOS disk.

Formatting on a Two Floppy Disk Drive System

Follow the DOS messages throughout as in the preceding section.

Step 1. Close the drive door if necessary.

Step 2. Insert the disk labeled "Formatted" in drive B.

Step 3. Type **FORMAT B:/V** and press Enter.

Formatting on a Hard Disk Drive System

The following steps discuss formatting a floppy disk in a hard disk drive system. To format a hard disk, see the section "Formatting a Hard Disk."

Step 1. Check to see that drive C is your logged disk drive and that the C> prompt is displayed.

Step 2. Insert the disk labeled "Formatted" in drive A.

Step 3. Type **FORMAT A:/V** and press Enter.

Looking at FORMAT's Reports

Versions of DOS earlier than V4.0 show the track and sector numbers as formatting proceeds. With DOS V4.0, the FORMAT command gives you a continual update of what percentage of the disk has been formatted.

You next will see a report as to the capacity of your diskette. The report will show the total disk space and total bytes available on the disk. If FORMAT finds *bad sectors*, that is, bad spots on the disk, it will mark them as unusable, and display how many bytes are unavailable due to the bad sectors. DOS V4.0 will display how many bytes each *allocation unit* (sector) can contain, and how many allocation units are available on the disk for storage. The DOS V4.0 report for a 1.44M formatted disk may look like the following:

```
1457664 bytes total disk space
1457664 bytes available on disk
    512 bytes in each allocation unit
   2847 allocation units available on disk
   Volume Serial Number is 3952-OBE4
```

For DOS V3.3, the numbers for various sizes of disks are as follows:

```
360K            362496 bytes total disk space
                 78848 bytes used by system
                283648 bytes available on disk

1.2M           1213952 bytes total disk space
                 78336 bytes used by system
               1135616 bytes available on disk

720K            730112 bytes total disk space
                 78848 bytes used by system
                651264 bytes available on disk
```

```
1.44M                1457664 bytes total disk space
                       78336 bytes used by system
                     1379328 bytes available on disk
```

Remember that the numbers for different versions of DOS V3 will be slightly different.

You will then see the following report if you have issued FORMAT with the /V switch (V4.0 users see this report automatically):

```
Format complete
Volume label (11 characters, ENTER for none)?
```

You can give the disk a volume name of up to 11 characters, or you can press Enter to omit the volume name. Remember that with DOS V4.0, the volume label is automatic.

The next part of the report prompts for additional formatting activity:

```
FORMAT another (Y/N)?
```

By answering Yes to the prompt and pressing Enter, you can format another disk while the FORMAT program is loaded in system RAM.

Using FORMAT's Switches

As with many DOS commands, you can add switches to modify and add versatility to the FORMAT command. You separate, or delimit, the switch from the command with the slash (/) character. You can add more than one switch to a command. For example, **FORMAT B:/V/S** is a valid command. This command tells DOS to load the FORMAT command from the logged drive, format the disk in drive B, prompt for a volume label, and transfer the system files to the new disk to make it bootable. By changing the drive specifier from B: to A:, you tell DOS to format drive A.

The Command Reference section provides more detail on allowable switch combinations and which switches are available with different versions of DOS. You will be relieved to know that most FORMAT commands that you issue will be simple. As with many of the switches available with DOS commands, only a few switches are needed by the average DOS user. Remaining switches provide advanced features or allow compatibility with older versions of DOS. Table 6.1 lists the switches available with the FORMAT command.

Table 6.1
FORMAT Switches

Switch	Action
/1	Formats a diskette as a single-sided disk. /1 is often used with the /8 switch to format 8-sector-per-track diskettes to be compatible with V1.0 and V1.1 systems.
/4	Formats a 5 1/4-inch diskette with 40 tracks per side (360K) in a HC (1.2M) drive. The resulting disk may be unreadable by a standard 360K (double-sided, double-density) drive.
/8	Formats a diskette with 8 sectors per track instead of 9 or 15.
/B	Leaves space on a formatted diskette so that the DOS system files can later be placed on the diskette.
/F:size	Formats a diskette to the capacity specified by size. Some possible values for size include 160, 180, 320, 360, 720, 1200, and 1400. Each size refers to kilobytes (K) of capacity. This switch is new with V4.0.
/N:nn	Formats a diskette with the number of sectors specified by nn. nn can range from 1 to 99. The disk drive, controller electronics, and the driver must support the specified number of sectors.
/S	Produces a bootable DOS system disk that contains the hidden DOS system files and COMMAND.COM.
/T:nn	Formats a diskette to the number of tracks (per side) that you specify in nn. nn can range from 1 to 999.
/V	Causes FORMAT to prompt for a volume label of up to 11 characters. When you have entered the volume label, press Enter.
/V:volume_label	Causes FORMAT to label the disk being formatted with the volume label in volume_label. This version of the /V switch is new with V4.

The next sections look at some of the features of FORMAT switches.

The /4 (Reduce Capacity) Switch

The /4 switch enables you to format a disk in a high-capacity disk drive for double-sided, double-density disk drive use. Use this switch to prepare a disk in your 1.2M drive for use in a 360K drive. You will need to use the /4 switch if you are formatting a disk on a 1.2M drive system such as an AT, but are using the disk in a 360K system such as an IBM PC-XT. If you use the /4 switch, be sure that the disk you are formatting is designed for the 360K capacity.

Despite the provision of the /4 switch for downward compatibility, disks prepared in this way are often not readable on the 360K drive. Drive electronics are optimized for the drive's highest capacity. Reducing the capacity of a disk with /4 may amplify any alignment or electronic problems that a subsequent 360K drive has while working with the disk. Most often, however, you won't have a problem when you use the /4 switch.

The /1, /8, /B, /N, /F:size, and /T Switches

These FORMAT switches allow current versions of DOS to format disks for very early computers, or to format a lesser-capacity disk in a higher-capacity drive. Although you may never need to use these switches, brief descriptions may be helpful.

/1 tells DOS to prepare a single-sided disk for use in a single-sided disk drive.

/8 prepares a disk with 8 sectors per track.

/B allows room for the system files on an 8 sectors-per-track disk.

You use these switches when formatting disks that need to work with DOS V1. Using V1 is extremely rare today, but a few users do utilize V1.

The /N and /T switches enable you to vary the *number* of *tracks* and sectors on high-capacity floppy disk drives. These switches are useful when you are preparing 720K microfloppies on a 1.44M drive.

A switch that is even more useful for formatting different capacity disks is the /F:size switch available with V4.0. With this switch, you do not need to remember the number of sectors and tracks of each capacity of disk; you can use the /F:size switch to enter the actual size. For example, to format a 720K disk in a 1.44M drive, you can use the switch /F:720.

The Command Reference section includes syntax for the use of these switches with the FORMAT command. If you need to use the less common switches, consult the Command Reference for more information.

The /V and /V:volume_label (Volume Label) Switches

DOS reserves a few bytes of data space on disks so that you can place an electronic identification—a *volume label*—on each disk. A volume label is simply a name to help you identify the disk. Think of a volume label for a disk in the same context as the title of a book. DOS V4.0 automatically builds this switch into the FORMAT command. The */V:volume_label* switch transfers the volume label to a formatted disk. You substitute an 11-character name for the new disk for *volume_label*. As you will see later in the chapter, the DOS LABEL command can do the same disk-naming job.

Newer versions of DOS also reference a disk's volume label when an operation involves disk swaps or when disks may have been changed. To assign a volume label during formatting if you have a version of DOS prior to V4.0, you must use the */V* switch. DOS V4.0 automatically includes the */V* switch in the FORMAT command.

After formatting a disk using **FORMAT /V** (or automatically in V4.0), DOS prompts you for an 11-character volume name:

```
Volume label (11 characters, ENTER for none)?
```

The rules for volume labels are included in the following list:

Rules for Volume Labels

You can use as a volume label any of the following characters in any order:

- The letters A to Z and a to z
- The numerals 0 to 9
- The following special characters and punctuation symbols:
    ~ ! @ # $ ^ & ( ) - _ { } '
- A space character (V3.3 and later)

The following characters are *not* allowed in a volume label:

- * ? / \ | . , ; : + = < > [ ] Esc Tab
- Any control characters (ASCII 31 and lower) and the DEL character (ASCII 127).

When you enter too many characters or an illegal character in the volume label, DOS V3.3 and later versions will use the characters you typed, up to the mistake. Earlier DOS versions ask you to enter the volume label again. If you do not want to name the disk, just press Enter.

The /S (Transfer System Files) Switch

The */S* switch places the DOS *system* files on the formatted disk. Use this switch if you want to be able to boot your PC with the disk you are formatting. As part of the formatting operation, DOS transfers the hidden DOS system files from the DOS disk to the formatted disk. COMMAND.COM is also transferred. You cannot see these hidden files in the directory of the disk, but the files are there, along with COMMAND.COM, which you can see. The /S switch reduces the available storage capacity of the disk by as much as 110K.

Don't use the /S switch with FORMAT unless you actually plan to boot from the disk. Hard disk users rarely use the /S switch.

You normally use FORMAT with the /S switch to format a floppy disk. If you are using one floppy drive, your computer will act as though it has two drives. It will treat your single floppy drive as both drive A and drive B, just as in formatting without system files.

If you have two floppy drives, DOS will format the disk in drive B with system files. If you are using a hard disk, DOS will format the floppy disk in drive A.

When formatting is complete, a report similar to the following report for a 360K disk is displayed on-screen:

```
System transferred
362496 bytes total disk space
108544 bytes used by system
253952 bytes available on disk
  1024 bytes in each allocation unit
   248 allocation units available on disk
```

Reviewing the Concept of Defaults

In Part One of this book, you learned that a single alphabetical letter, followed by a colon, designates a disk drive. When used in a command, DOS understands that letter and colon as the drive specifier. You also used the DIR command, which leaves the drive specifier out of the command line. In this case, DOS assumed that you wanted the directory for the previously logged drive to serve as the *default* directory.

The concept of defaults is important if you want to be effective with DOS commands. DOS uses certain prepackaged, or default, values to carry out its services. You can override many of these values through commands or switches. Some values, such as the /S switch for FORMAT, remain in effect only for one instance.

Changing other defaults, like the logged drive, causes the default to change to the new value. When you boot your computer, DOS automatically logs to the drive that holds the bootable disk. This drive is the default drive. DOS normally displays the default drive name in the DOS prompt and uses this drive to execute commands.

If the drive specifier is the same as the default drive, you do not have to enter the drive letter. If you want to issue a command to another disk drive, you must enter the drive specifier for that disk in the command line. The command is shorter and cleaner if you leave out the defaults. Many command examples you use in this book assume some default values. The logged drive is a frequently used default.

Using FORMAT on Another Drive

In Chapter 4, you learned that COMMAND.COM contains certain built-in DOS commands, called *internal* commands. Commands that reside on disk are called *external* commands. COMMAND.COM must find and load external commands before executing them. If the external commands are not on the logged disk, you must enter a drive specifier before the command name.

The drive specifier is the name of the drive that contains the command's program file. You will learn in Chapter 7 how to give DOS the correct path to the external commands.

Suppose that your computer has a hard disk and two floppy drives. You want to format a disk in drive B. You have FORMAT.COM on a disk in drive A and a blank disk in drive B.

Type **A:** and press Enter to make the drive holding the DOS working disk your default drive. Then type **FORMAT B:** to format the unformatted disk in drive B.

If you had changed to drive B, the command **FORMAT B:** would produce an error message. Because drive B is not the default drive, DOS would not find FORMAT.COM.

One solution to this dilemma is to issue the command **A:FORMAT B:**. DOS finds the FORMAT command on the DOS disk in drive A as specified in the command. The formatting is done on the unformatted disk in drive B as specified in the command.

Understanding FORMAT's Error Messages

Errors that can occur during formatting activity are usually not serious. For example, if you insert an unformatted disk in the drive where DOS expects to find the FORMAT command and then issue the FORMAT command, DOS displays the following message:

```
General failure reading drive A
Abort, Retry, Fail?
```

Because DOS could not find the internal file tables on the blank disk when it attempted to load FORMAT, DOS assumed that the disk, the drive, or the drive electronics had failed. The solution is to place the DOS disk in the drive and press R to Retry the command.

When you insert and remove disks during formatting sessions, you can sometimes give DOS the "go ahead" too soon when you are prompted to `Strike ENTER when ready . . .`. When you make this error, DOS displays the following message:

```
Not ready error reading drive A
Abort, Retry, Fail?
```

This message usually means that the drive door is still open or that you forgot to insert a disk into the drive. An open drive door isn't uncommon when you are swapping disks in and out of floppy disk drives. To recover, make sure the disk is properly inserted in the drive, close the drive door, and answer R to Retry.

If the FORMAT command detects errors on the disk, you will see a line describing the problem in the report. For example, the line might state something like the following:

```
2048 bytes in bad sectors
```

The `bytes in bad sectors` message means that DOS found bad sectors on the disk. These sectors cannot be used to hold information. The total amount of free space on the disk is reduced by the number of bytes in bad sectors.

You can have your dealer replace a floppy disk, or you can use the disk as is. Before you do either, though, try formatting the disk again. Some disks do not format properly the first time. If, after the second format attempt, the bad sector message is still present, you may want to use a different disk. Bad sectors can cause trouble with the disk.

You can usually run FORMAT a second time by answering Y to the question `Format another (Y/N)?`, and pressing Enter.

The worst disk error message is the following:

```
Invalid media or track 0 bad - disk unusable
```

This message may mean that the areas on the disk that hold key DOS system data are bad. If you get this error message, take the disk back to your dealer if you just bought it. If the disk is an old floppy disk, throw it away.

You may see this message if you are using a disk whose capacity is wrong for your computer system. The magnetic oxides on disk surfaces differ among particular capacities. Using a higher capacity disk than necessary will cause disk errors.

If your system is set up with a RAM disk and you try to format the disk, you may also see this message. A RAM disk is a portion of system memory that software treats collectively as a disk drive. RAM disks are also called *virtual* disks or *memory* disks. You cannot format a RAM disk.

The following list presents some FORMAT command sequences, error messages, and possible explanations and solutions.

Command and Message Sequence

```
C>FORMAT A:
Insert new diskette for drive A:
and press ENTER when ready . . .

Not ready
Format terminated
Format another (Y/N)?
```

Possible Explanation

DOS was unable to read from the disk drive. For floppy disk drives, the drive door may be open or the disk may not be inserted.

Remove the disk and reinsert it, close the drive door if necessary, and issue the FORMAT command again. Abort the operation by pressing A.

Command and Message Sequence

```
A>FORMAT A:/V
General failure reading drive A
Abort, Retry, Fail?
```

Possible Explanation

The disk is not correctly formatted, the disk's formatting is wrong for the computer you are using, or the disk is damaged.

Format the disk again, making sure that the disk is formatted for your system. If the disk is damaged, replace it.

Command and Message Sequence

```
A>FORMAT A:/V
```
```
A>FORMAT A:/V
Insert new diskette for drive A:
and press ENTER when ready . . .

Write-protect error
Format terminated
Format another (Y/N)?
```

Possible Explanation

This error occurred because DOS attempted to format a write-protected disk. Write protection saved the disk from accidental erasure.

Command and Message Sequence

A>**FORMAT A:**
```
Insert new diskette for drive A:
and press ENTER when ready . . .

Invalid media or Track 0 bad - disk unusable
Format terminated
Format another (Y/N)?
```

Possible Explanation

This disk had a scratched surface, and DOS was unable to read disk-level information on the first track. Discard the disk.

Command and Message Sequence

A>**FORMAT A:**
```
Insert new diskette for drive A:
and press ENTER when ready . . .

Format complete

Volume label (11 characters, ENTER for none)?

1213952 bytes total disk space
 107520 bytes in bad sectors
1106432 bytes available on disk

    512 bytes in each allocation unit
   2161 allocation units available on disk

Volume Serial Number is 0B75-13FB

Format another (Y/N)?
```

Possible Explanation

Because bad sectors cannot hold information on the disk, the total amount of free space is reduced by the number of bytes in bad sectors.

Try reformatting the disk. If it still has bad sectors, you can have your dealer replace the disk, or you can use the disk as is. Before you do either, though, try formatting the disk again.

Command and Message Sequence

A>**FORMAT A:/V**
```
General failure reading drive A
Abort, Retry, Fail?
```

Some disks do not format properly the first time. If, after the second format attempt, the error message is still present, you may want to use a different disk. Bad sectors can cause trouble with the disk.

Preparing the Hard Disk

The next sections deal with dividing and formatting the hard disk. More information on this subject is found in Appendix D. Be sure to heed all warnings and read all explanations carefully.

Many computer dealers install the operating system on a computer's hard disk before you receive it. If your dealer has installed an applications program such as a word processor, **DO NOT FORMAT THE HARD DISK!** If you reformat your hard disk, all programs and data will be erased.

Dividing a Hard Disk with FDISK

The hard disks used by today's PCs can be logically divided into partitions. Before you can format a hard disk, you must partition it. A partition is simply a section of the storage area of a hard disk. Many operating systems, including DOS, can utilize disk partitions, and most have some utility program that creates and manages partitions. DOS's utility program for partition creation and management is the external command FDISK. The DOS installation considerations of FDISK are presented in Appendix D. Use the presentation in Appendix D when you need to use FDISK; the Appendix contains step-by-step instructions for using the command with different versions of DOS. This chapter's view of FDISK provides a more general view of the command.

Many dealers have already used FDISK on a system's hard disk before the system is delivered to the end user. If your hard disk contains files, it has already been partitioned with FDISK and formatted. If you have any questions about the state of your hard disk's preparation, consult your dealer.

Most hard disk users choose a DOS partition size that includes all of the hard disk. In other words, their one physical hard disk appears to DOS as one logical hard disk. FDISK enters information in a hard disk partition table that indicates that the entire disk is available to DOS and that the disk is bootable.

Some PC users want another operating system to reside on a hard disk along with DOS. Different operating systems employ file systems that are not compatible with each other. FDISK provides a means to divide the hard disk into separate sections which are isolated from each other. DOS can use one partition section while another operating system, such as UNIX, uses another. Through separation, the operating systems are "tricked" into seeing their partitions as their own hard disks. The operating system that is booted is called the *active* partition. FDISK controls which partition is active in a multipartition situation.

Hard disk capacities have increased over the last few years. FDISK enables DOS users to divide these larger hard disks into a *primary* DOS partition and also additional *extended* partitions. To DOS, the primary and extended partitions look like distinct disk drives. The extended DOS partition consists of fixed-size logical disks. A *logical* disk doesn't exist physically; it just appears to exist to DOS. Through logical disks, one hard disk drive can have, for instance, logical drives C:, D:, and E:. DOS treats each of these logical drives as though they were individual hard disks.

Until DOS V4.0, the largest drive that DOS could manage as one partition was 32M. Drives with capacities of more than 32M have been available for some time. FDISK and the extended-partition capability of DOS give users of large capacity drives a means to put to work these capacities greater than 32M.

WARNING

The FDISK command has provisions to delete an existing partition from the disk partition table. If you delete an existing partition, all of the data in the files contained in that partition will be lost. Be sure that you have backed up or copied any data from a partition that you are about to delete. FDISK is not a command to experiment with unless your hard disk contains no data. Be cautious when you use FDISK.

Issuing the FDISK Command

The syntax for FDISK is as follows:

FDISK

Notice that there are no parameters for FDISK. Because FDISK handles the partitions of any hard disks on your system in a sequential fashion, there is no need for a drive parameter. In fact, until FDISK logs a partition in the partition table, DOS has not assigned the partition a drive letter.

Tech note . . . DOS started out supporting floppy disks only, so prior to V2.0, DOS did not need to address hard disk partitioning. As hard disk drive innovation and competition drove hard drive prices lower, however, the IBM PC/XT with its 10M hard disk and DOS V2.0 brought DOS out of the floppy disk category and into the high capacity storage category. With over 25 times the storage of the 360K floppy, the PC/XT's 10M disk was an ideal candidate for using an additional operating system such as Microsoft's UNIX-derived XENIX. From a capacity standpoint, the XT has no problem accommodating DOS and XENIX on the same hard disk. The real problem is that the two file systems are incompatible. The obvious solution is to partition the disk into two parts.

Microsoft and other operating system suppliers uniformly left a reserved area of the hard disk available for the partition table's data. Operating system vendors understood that a user might want to install an additional operating system on the hard disk. Most operating systems are not compatible with other operating systems. An operating system, such as DOS, wants to establish the disk as its own. Fortunately, most operating systems consult the hard disk's partition table when booting from the hard disk. The partition table establishes the boundaries of the physical disk that each operating system can call its own.

Tech note . . . (cont)

DOS uses the disk-level boot record and bookkeeping tables that DOS places in track 0. If another operating system "owns" track 0 as part of the other operating system's partition, DOS cannot use track 0 without damaging the internal tables of the other operating system or seeing the other operating system's data as gibberish. DOS avoids the problem by consulting the partition table at the time of start-up. If DOS does not "own" track 0, DOS simply uses the first track that it does own as its track 0. DOS therefore translates the first physical cylinder of its partition into a logical first cylinder of a disk. DOS also considers the last physical cylinder of the DOS partition as being the logical end of the hard disk. Other operating systems use the partition table information to "peacefully coexist" on the same physical disk with another operating system.

Understanding the Operation of FDISK

The primary function of the FDISK program is to provide the DOS user with high-level access to the disk's partition table. FDISK allows DOS to participate in a multioperating system disk-sharing arrangement. Other operating systems, such as XENIX, have their own versions of FDISK to manage the partition table. You can use FDISK to create a DOS partition of the size you specify, to make the DOS (or another operating system's) partition active, and to delete an existing DOS partition. You can also use FDISK to define partitions for up to four different operating systems.

If you have another operating system to install on your hard disk, use the instructions supplied with the FDISK or similar command of the other operating system.

With DOS V3.3, FDISK can be used to create more than one DOS partition. After you define a *primary* DOS partition with FDISK, you can define an *extended* DOS partition which you divide into one or more logical drives. All primary DOS partitions and logical drives must be properly formatted using the FORMAT command before they can be used. When DOS is the active operating system as reflected in the partition table, DOS will boot from the active DOS partition. You can then log to one of the logical drives. The primary DOS partition is normally assigned the drive name C:. The extended DOS partition can be further divided by FDISK into additional logical drives.

Before you format a new hard disk, you must ensure that the disk has been prepared with FDISK. DOS cannot work with a hard disk that has no DOS values in its partition table. In fact, if you have in your computer system another physical hard disk that has been partitioned, DOS will move the drive letter that would apply to the unpartitioned drive to the next physical drive's primary DOS partition. Remember that DOS uses drive letters as names for drives in a multidisk system.

Once you partition your hard disk(s), DOS will respect the logical drives and create a file system for each drive when it is formatted. If you use FDISK to delete a partition and subsequently create another partition, all the data in the original partition will be destroyed. Don't worry about FDISK doing something rash when you run it. You will see warnings when you are electing to do something with FDISK that destroys data. In order to proceed beyond the warnings, you must answer a confirmation prompt.

Before FDISK deletes a partition, for example, you will see the following warning message:

```
Warning: Data in the DOS partition
will be lost. Do you wish to
continue (Y/N). . . . . . . . . . . . . ? [N]
```

Respond with N if you do not want to continue with the partition deletion operation. Respond with Y if you are sure that deleting the partition is your intention.

Because of its potentially dangerous effects, FDISK is one DOS command you should not practice with often. There are, however, some opportunities to work with FDISK. If you decide to reformat your disk, for example, and you have one DOS partition on the whole disk, you can run FDISK first and experiment. If you are upgrading to a hard disk from a floppy-only system, you can experiment with FDISK before you make your "official" partition decisions. Just remember that you will need a bootable floppy disk that contains the FDISK and FORMAT programs. As always, you should have a working copy of your DOS master system disks. Deleting partitions can cause you to rely on the system's floppy disk until the hard disk is again partitioned and formatted.

Formatting a Hard Disk

Like floppy disks, hard disks must be formatted before use. The SELECT command in V3.3 and earlier versions carries out a format of the hard disk as part of the DOS installation process. The installation program of V4.0 also automatically formats an unformatted hard disk. Appendix D covers the topic of preparing your hard disk. If you haven't read that appendix, you should do so now. This chapter's discussion of hard disk formatting assumes that you are familiar with the FDISK command discussed in the previous section.

Assume that the hard disk (or logical disk) that you are going to format is drive C. If you are formatting another drive, use its drive name (letter) in place of C. Note that if your drive is not the primary DOS partition, you do not need the /S switch because DOS will boot from the primary DOS partition only. Put your working copy of the DOS master system disk in drive A, log to that drive by typing **A:**, and then type the following:

FORMAT C:/S/V

If the drive has already been formatted, it has a volume label; if you are using V3.2 or later versions, FORMAT will display the following prompt:

```
Enter current Volume label for drive C:
```

Enter the current volume label for the drive. If the volume label does not match what FORMAT found on the disk, you will see the following message:

```
Invalid Volume ID
Format failure
```

If this message is displayed, make sure that you are formatting the correct drive. Check the volume label again. If the label appears to be correct, it may include a hidden character. You can change the volume label of the disk to one of your choosing with the LABEL command (discussed later in this chapter) and use the new volume label to successfully answer the volume label confirmation prompt.

FORMAT will issue the following warning message and confirmation prompt:

```
WARNING, ALL DATA ON NON-REMOVABLE DISK DRIVE C:
WILL BE LOST!
Proceed with Format (Y/N)?
```

This is an extremely important prompt. Examine this prompt to confirm the disk drive name (letter) before you answer Y. If you get in the habit of answering Y to the confirmation prompts of less dangerous commands, you may make a serious mistake with this final FORMAT confirmation prompt. If the drive is the one you intend to format, answer Y. If not, answer N to terminate FORMAT.

If you answer Y, FORMAT will update the display with progress reports on its operation. V4.0, as in the preceding example on formatting floppy disks, reports percentage completion. Other versions report the head and cylinder count. The process can take from a few minutes to more than a half-hour; the length of time depends on the capacity of the disk being formatted. Larger disks take more time. When the disk has been formatted, FORMAT issues the following message:

```
Format complete
```

FORMAT may not be finished, however. If you used the /S switch, you will see the following message:

```
System Transferred
```

If you used the /V switch, or if you are using V4, FORMAT prompts for the volume label with the following:

```
Volume label (11 characters, ENTER for none)?
```

Enter the label text you want. The discussion of the /V switch in the preceding discussion of FORMAT's switches includes a list of allowable volume label characters. If you need to change this label, you can use the LABEL command in V3.1 (PC DOS V3.0) and later versions.

Finally, FORMAT will display a report showing the disk space formatted, the bytes used by the system files, defective sectors marked (if any), and the number of bytes available on the disk. Don't be surprised if your hard disk shows some bad sectors in the report. It is not uncommon for hard disks to have a few bad sectors, especially if the formatted capacity exceeds 21M. These bad sectors are marked in the FAT and will not be allocated to a file.

Tech note ... Until the introduction of V4.0, DOS used 16 bits (binary digits) to represent sector numbers internally. In binary notation, 16^2 is 65,536. In order to use the 16-bit sector numbers, DOS must hold the number of sectors on a disk to 65,536 or fewer. Because all versions of DOS have used 512-byte sectors, the largest drive capacity (or partition) DOS could manage was 512 bytes for each of 65,536 (64K) sectors or 32M. By introducing the extended partition in V3.3, DOS allowed an extended partition of more than 32M, even though no logical drives of the V3.3 extended partition can be larger than 32M.

DOS V4.0 allows a disk or partition to be larger than 32M. V4.0 adds a second field in a disk-description table called the *boot record* for disks or partitions with more than 64K sectors. If a disk is formatted with more than 64K sectors, the new sector-number field is used and the previous sector-number field is set to 0. When DOS V4.0 builds the disk's FAT, it adjusts the cluster's sector multiple upward as disk capacity increases. By adjusting the cluster, the FAT's size can remain constant while covering the additional sectors of a disk larger than 32M.

Because DOS versions prior to V4.0 are not designed for extensions that accommodate disks larger than 32M, you cannot expect to find everything you stored on a large capacity disk (larger than 32M) if you boot your PC with an earlier version of DOS. Some third party disk utility applications programs do not allow for DOS V4.0's extensions to the boot sector, either. If you have DOS V4.0, before you use a disk optimizer such as the Norton Utilities or a rapid backup program such as FASTBACK, be sure that the application's version expressly handles DOS V4 disks.

Naming Disks with LABEL

The external command LABEL adds, modifies, or changes the volume label of a disk. In DOS, a volume label is a character name given to a physical or logical disk (the volume). The LABEL command is available with PC DOS V3.0 and later versions and MS-DOS V3.1 and later versions. If a disk's volume label is blank (if the user pressed Enter when FORMAT or LABEL prompted for the label), you can use the LABEL command to add a volume label.

DOS displays the volume label when you issue commands such as VOL, CHKDSK, DIR, and TREE. DOS V3.2 FORMAT asks for a hard disk's volume label before reformatting the disk. It is a good idea to give each disk (physical and logical) a volume label. You can more easily identify the disk when it has a unique volume label.

The syntax for the LABEL command is as follows:

LABEL *d:volume_label*

d: is the drive name that holds the disk to be labeled. *volume_label*, the optional label text that you supply as the new volume label, can include from 1 to 11 characters. If you do not supply the *volume_label* parameter, LABEL will automatically prompt for a new label.

The allowable characters for a volume label are discussed in the section on the */V* and *V:volume_label* switches of the FORMAT command.

The command sequence for the LABEL command looks like the following:

LABEL

DOS responds:

```
Volume label in C is BOOT DISK
Volume label (11 characters, ENTER for none)?
```

You enter the text for the volume label; DOS assigns the new label. If you simply press Enter in response to the prompt, you are telling DOS to delete the current label and leave it blank. DOS confirms your decision by prompting as follows:

```
Delete current volume label (Y/N)?
```

When you press Y and then Enter, DOS deletes the current label. If you press only Enter or with any character other than Y or N, DOS repeats the prompt.

When you issue a LABEL command with the optional *volume_label* parameter which can include from 1 to 11 characters, DOS immediately updates the specified or default drive's label with no warning prompt. If you enter an incorrect volume label, simply enter the LABEL command for the drive again and correct the label. Some special restrictions affect your use of LABEL:

- You cannot use the LABEL command on a networked drive.
- With V3.2 and later versions, you cannot use LABEL on a disk in a drive that is affected by the SUBST or ASSIGN commands.

Some third party programs can edit the volume label of a pre-V3.1 (PC DOS V3.0) formatted disk in a manner similar to LABEL. Check with your dealer for a recommendation of one of these third party programs.

Examining Volume Labels with VOL

The internal command VOL is a convenient command for viewing a disk's volume label or verifying that a label exists. VOL is a display-only command. It will not modify the current volume label. VOL will show the volume label created during the disk's formatting or modified by a subsequent LABEL command. .

VOL accesses the disk's volume label from the root directory and then displays the label. VOL does not change any files or the label name, so you can use it freely. The command accommodates an optional drive specifier and uses the default drive if no drive specifier is given.

The syntax of the VOL command is simple:

VOL *d:*

d: is the optional drive name of the drive whose volume label you want to see. If you omit a value for *d:*, DOS displays the label for the default drive.

To see the volume label of the disk in drive A:, enter the following command:

VOL A:

DOS will respond with the following or similar message for your disk:

```
Volume in drive A: is WORK_DISK1
```

CHKDSK, TREE, and DIR include the volume-label display as part of their outputs.

Transferring the DOS System Using SYS

All DOS disks have a DOS file system, but only disks with the DOS system files and COMMAND.COM can be used to boot DOS. The external command SYS transfers (copies) the hidden system files from a bootable system disk. You then must use COPY to transfer COMMAND.COM to the target disk, if desired, because SYS does not transfer COMMAND.COM.

You learned in a previous section that you can make a disk bootable by using the /S switch with the FORMAT command. Normally, users know in advance that they want a bootable disk and use this command sequence. The SYS command is provided for use when a formatted disk must be made bootable.

SYS makes bootable a disk that was not formatted with the /S switch. In addition, SYS can transfer a new version of the operating system to existing bootable disks. There is, however, no guarantee that SYS will be able to transfer the system files to a disk. The disk must have room for the system files SYS intends to transfer, and those system files must be compatible with the version of operating system the PC is currently running.

141

DOS loads the two system files from the boot disk into memory where the files act as the default system drivers and the operating system kernel. You do not see these hidden files when using a DIR command. The two system files are also marked with a system attribute and read-only attribute in their directory entries.

To use SYS successfully, you need to observe the following rules:

- SYS requires the destination disk to be formatted.

- The destination disk must be empty (containing no files or directories), or the disk must already contain the two system files or have been formatted with the /B switch. Otherwise, the system files will not transfer.

- With versions of DOS prior to V4, if the destination disk contains the two system files, the system files that SYS tries to transfer to the destination disk must not be too large to replace the existing system files. SYS V4 can transfer the system files as long as there are two root directory entries available on the disk you are putting the system on.

- With V3.3 or earlier versions, if a disk already contains user files and does not contain the two system files, DOS will issue the following error message:

    ```
    No room for system on destination disk
    ```

    If the existing system files are too small to allow a new version's system files to take their space, DOS will issue the following error message:

    ```
    Incompatible system size
    ```

- A disk formatted with the /B option can be the destination disk for SYS even if the disk is not empty because the /B switch reserves room on the disk for the system files.

    The /B switch with FORMAT forces the disk to an eight-sector-per-track format which is compatible with V1 disk formats. Because an eight-sector-per-track format is normally not desirable, you should not use the /B switch with FORMAT simply to reserve space on a disk for the system files should you decide to store files on the disk and subsequently use SYS on the disk.

- You cannot use SYS on a networked drive. If you want to use SYS on a networked drive, you must either log off the network or pause your drive to perform the SYS command. For exact restrictions, consult your system's network documentation.

- You must give the destination drive parameter for the SYS command. SYS is a command that does not use the default drive for the destination parameter. The source drive for the system files is always the default drive unless you specify a source-drive parameter when using SYS V4.

- Although it is possible to use SYS to transfer the system files between some different versions and implementations of DOS, some versions or implementations are not compatible with certain others. If DOS detects incompatibility, the system files will not transfer, and the error message `Incorrect DOS version` will appear.

 If you are in doubt about the version of DOS on the boot disk, you can issue the VER command; DOS will then display the version. Remember that one of the hidden files is the input-output (IO) system which contains device drivers for the implementation of DOS on a particular computer. Although many implementations of the IO system file are compatible with one another, some may not be. For this reason, you should not mix DOS versions or implementations when using the SYS command.

The syntax for the SYS command is as follows:

SYS d:

If you are using DOS V4, you can also provide the source drive for the system files as in the following:

SYS ds: dd:

The drive specified by **dd:** is the target or **destination** drive for the system files. You must include a drive name (letter) for drive **dd:**. The drive specified by **ds:** (V4 only) is the drive that is used for the **source** of the system files.

Assume that you are using DOS V4 with a hard disk and have an empty diskette that you want to make bootable to use with another computer. Put the formatted diskette in drive A and be sure that your current PATH setting includes the directory that contains SYS (see Chapter 7 for information on the DOS path). Then, enter the following command:

SYS C: A:

The C: is optional; if you are logged to drive C, C: is already the default source for the system files. SYS will reply with the following message:

```
System transferred
```

The system files are now on the disk in drive A. To complete the process of making the disk in drive A a bootable disk, copy COMMAND.COM from the root directory (on some systems, from the DOS subdirectory) of C to the disk in A with the following command:

COPY C:\COMMAND.COM A:

The disk in drive A is now a bootable disk. SYS transferred the system files, and COPY transferred COMMAND.COM.

Analyzing a Disk with CHKDSK

The external command CHKDSK analyzes a floppy or hard disk. CHKDSK checks the FAT, the directories, and, if you want, the fragmentation (the spreading out of parts of a file) of the files of a disk. Optionally, CHKDSK will repair problems in the FAT due to lost clusters and write the contents of the lost clusters to files. CHKDSK also provides an option to display all of a disk's files and their paths (paths are covered in Chapter 7). Upon completion, CHKDSK displays a screen report of its findings.

It is good practice to run CHKDSK periodically on your hard disk and important floppies. Because the FAT and the hierarchical directory system work together to track file names and locations, a problem in either the FAT or one of the directories is always a serious problem. In all likelihood, CHKDSK will find and fix most problems it finds in a disk's internal bookkeeping tables.

Issuing the CHKDSK Command

You issue the CHKDSK command with the following syntax:

CHKDSK *d:path\filename.ext /F/V*

d: is the optional drive name to be checked. If the drive name is omitted, the current (default) drive is assumed.

path is the optional path to the directory containing the files to be analyzed for fragmentation. If a path is omitted and a file specifier is given in the command line, the default directory is assumed.

filename.ext is the optional file name and extension for the file(s) to be analyzed for fragmentation. If a file-name specifier is not present on the command line, CHKDSK does not check for fragmentation.

/F is the optional *fix* switch which instructs CHKDSK to repair any problems encountered.

/V is the *verbose* switch which instructs CHKDSK to provide file names to the screen as the files are being analyzed.

Understanding the Operation of CHKDSK

CHKDSK is DOS's self-test command. CHKDSK makes sure that the internal tables that keep files in control are in order. The technical details of how CHKDSK does its analysis are beyond the scope of most casual DOS users. Yet, the more you understand CHKDSK, the more comfortable you will be when the command uncovers problems. Just because you don't understand exactly how CHKDSK works doesn't mean that you should avoid using it. CHKDSK checks for the following problems in the FAT:

1. Unlinked cluster chains (lost clusters)

2. Multiple linked clusters (cross-linked files)

3. Invalid next cluster-in-chain values (invalid cluster numbers)

4. Defective sectors where the FAT is stored

CHKDSK checks for the following problems in the directory system:

1. Invalid cluster numbers (out of range)

2. Invalid file attributes in entries (attribute values DOS does not recognize)

3. Damage to subdirectory entries (CHKDSK cannot process them)

4. Damage to a directory's integrity (its files cannot be accessed)

CHKDSK then produces a screen report which summarizes disk and system RAM memory usage. Figures 6.3 and 6.4 show typical CHKDSK reports.

You should issue the CHKDSK command without the */F* (*fix*) switch before you subsequently use the /F switch. CHKDSK has the capability to make a "dry run" of its checking routines. CHKDSK without /F will prompt you if it finds a problem as though you used the /F switch. Take advantage of CHKDSK's "dry run" capability to assess reported problems. After you have assessed the findings of CHKDSK and have taken remedial actions (such as those that follow), you can issue CHKDSK with the /F switch so that the command can fix problems that it finds.

```
D:\>chkdsk

Volume LOGICAL D    created 09-07-1989 11:20p

  33454080 bytes total disk space
     51200 bytes in 18 directories
  13004800 bytes in 766 user files
  20398080 bytes available on disk

      2048 bytes in each allocation unit
     16335 total allocation units on disk
      9960 available allocation units on disk

    655360 total bytes memory
    409856 bytes free

D:\>
```

Fig. 6.3

A typical report produced by CHKDSK issued with no parameters.

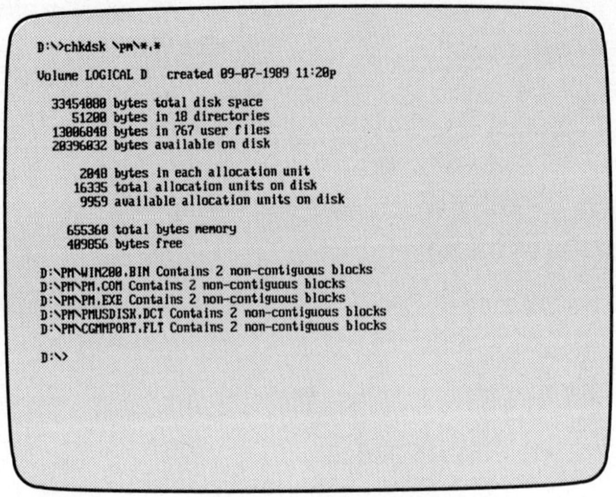

```
D:\>chkdsk \pm\*.*

Volume LOGICAL D   created 09-07-1989 11:20p

   33454080 bytes total disk space
      51200 bytes in 18 directories
   13006040 bytes in 767 user files
   28396032 bytes available on disk

       2040 bytes in each allocation unit
      16335 total allocation units on disk
       9959 available allocation units on disk

     655360 total bytes memory
     489056 bytes free

D:\PM\WIN200.BIN Contains 2 non-contiguous blocks
D:\PM\PM.COM Contains 2 non-contiguous blocks
D:\PM\PM.EXE Contains 2 non-contiguous blocks
D:\PM\PMUSDISK.DCT Contains 2 non-contiguous blocks
D:\PM\CGMPORT.FLT Contains 2 non-contiguous blocks

D:\>
```

Fig. 6.4

Report produced when CHKDSK is issued with an optional path to the directory to check for fragmentation.

CHKDSK has the ability to read the FAT and directories. DOS's file allocation method gives CHKDSK its method. CHKDSK knows that every file on the disk has its sectors allocated as clusters from the FAT. In addition, CHKDSK knows that each file's directory entry should contain a starting cluster which points to the appropriate entry in the FAT to the file's chain of clusters.

CHKDSK processes each directory starting at the root and following each subdirectory. The indicated cluster chain is checked using the directory entry's FAT pointer. The size of the file in bytes is also compared to the size of the FAT's allocation in clusters.

CHKDSK expects to find enough chained clusters in the FAT to accommodate the file, but not more than necessary. If CHKDSK finds too many clusters, it issues the following message:

```
Allocation error,
size adjusted
```

The file is truncated (excess clusters deallocated) if the /F switch is in effect. You should copy the reported file to another disk before running CHKDSK with the /F switch in case the number of bytes indicated in the directory entry for the reported file is incorrect. If the directory entry has an errant (too low) number of bytes indicated, CHKDSK will effectively "chop off" some of the file. With a copy of the file on another disk, you can recover in the unlikely case the directory entry was wrong.

CHKDSK makes sure that each of the FAT's clusters are allocated only once. In rare circumstances such as power problems or hardware failures, DOS can give two different files the same cluster. By checking each cluster chain for cross-linked files, CHKDSK can report "mixed-up" files. Each time you see the message `filename is` `cross-linked on cluster` X, copy the file reported in `filename` to another disk. You will find that CHKDSK reports another file with the same message. Copy the second file to another disk also. There's a good chance that the contents of the two files will be mixed up, but you will have a better chance of recovering the files if you save them to another disk before CHKDSK "fixes" the problem.

Unfortunately, if CHKDSK encounters a file allocation chain that loops back to itself, CHKDSK will run in a circle reporting errors. If the /F switch is active, you can easily find your root directory swamped with CHKDSK-produced recovery files. In all likelihood, the action that will terminate CHKDSK when it is chasing a circular allocation chain is the filling of all root directory entries. You can press Ctrl-C to stop the process. If you detect that a circular reference episode is taking place with CHKDSK, don't reissue the command with the /F switch. Try erasing the file and restoring it from your backup.

CHKDSK expects that every cluster in the FAT will either be available for allocation, part of a legitimate directory-based cluster chain, or a marked bad cluster. If CHKDSK encounters any clusters or cluster chains that are not pointed to by a directory entry, CHKDSK issues the following message:

`    x lost clusters in Y chains`

CHKDSK then prompts as follows:

`    Convert lost chains to files (Y/N)?`

If the /F switch is active, CHKDSK will turn each cluster chain into a file in the root directory. Each created file will have the name `FILEnnnn.CHK`. `nnnn` is a number, starting with `0000`, which increments for each file created by the CHKDSK command's current execution.

You can use the DOS TYPE command to examine the contents of a text file, and you may be able to put the text back into its original file using a word processor. If the file is a binary (program or data) file, the TYPE command won't do you any good. If the problem was with a program file, you may need to use COMP or FC to compare your disk's binary files with their counterparts from your master disks.

The disk does not actually lose any sectors physically. A lost cluster report does not indicate that the clusters are bad. Lost clusters only indicate that DOS made a bookkeeping error in the FAT that makes some cluster or clusters appear to be lost to DOS. The clusters aren't tied to a directory entry, yet the clusters are marked as being in-use. The lost cluster problem is most likely to occur when you are running disk-intensive programs such as dBASE IV or WordPerfect. The programs are not to blame for lost clusters, but the programs increase DOS's exposure to bookkeeping errors. Programs that use disk files to swap sections of program and data too large for memory may ask DOS to read and write work files hundreds of times in an afternoon of computing. Power "glitches" or interruptions, heated hardware components, and electrical interference can turn a cluster chain number into a different number at the critical moment that DOS is writing the number into the FAT. Still, when you consider the millions of bytes that DOS is responsible for in a typical PC, DOS's reliability record is superb. CHKDSK recovers most clusters that bookkeeping errors in DOS lose.

When you use CHKDSK, the following rules apply:

- CHKDSK begins execution immediately after you enter the command. If you use a one-disk system, you use the drive B: specifier to allow for changing from the disk containing CHKDSK to the disk to be analyzed if necessary.

- CHKDSK will not repair problems found during operation unless you issue the /F switch in the command line.

- You should run CHKDSK at least weekly. Run CHKDSK daily during periods of extreme file activity.

- You must press Enter after answering (Y/N) ? prompts before CHKDSK will continue.

- CHKDSK may report three hidden files on a DOS system disk. Two hidden files are the DOS system files; the third file is a volume label file.

- CHKDSK will convert lost clusters to files if you answer Y to the Convert lost chains to files (Y/N) ? prompt. CHKDSK places the files in the disk's root directory with the name FILEnnnn.CHK.

  If CHKDSK terminates because the root directory has no more entries available for converted chain files, clear the current FILEnnnn.CHK files by erasing them or copying them to another disk. When the files are cleared from the root, reissue CHKDSK.

Using CHKDSK To Repair an Allocation Size Error

For this example exercise of CHKDSK, suppose that you are copying a group of files from your hard disk to a floppy. During the copy, the lights flicker and then go out completely. In a few seconds, power is restored to normal. Your computer reboots DOS V4.0 and awaits your input.

Power problems during file operations such as COPY can cause DOS's bookkeeping job to be interrupted. The directory and the FAT can contain errors. To ensure that no errors go undetected, you issue the CHKDSK command on the floppy disk:

CHKDSK A:

CHKDSK begins to analyze the floppy disk in A: and then reports as follows:

```
Volume SCRATCH DISK created 09-12-1989  11:23a
Errors found, F parameter not specified
Corrections will not be written to disk

A:\DBASE1.OVL
Allocation error, size adjusted

  730112 bytes in total disk space
  415744 bytes in 4 user files
  314368 bytes available on disk

    1024 bytes in each allocation unit
     713 total allocation units on disk
     307 available allocation units on disk

  655360 total bytes memory
  409856 bytes free
```

Because you did not specify the /F switch, CHKDSK did not repair the problem. You have the opportunity to examine the problem further before reissuing CHKDSK with the /F switch. You look at a directory listing of the files on drive A to see whether you can determine the nature of the allocation problem. The directory listing shows the following:

```
Volume in drive A is SCRATCH DISK
Volume Serial Number is 0000-0000
Directory of  A:\

DBSETUP   OVL    147968 10-21-88   12:22a
DBASE3    OVL     85024 12-28-88    9:04p
DBASE6    OVL    114832 10-20-88   11:22p
DBASE1    OVL         0 09-12-89    1:46a
        4 File(s)      314368 bytes free
```

The last directory entry, DBASE1.OVL, shows a file size of 0 bytes. A 0-byte file size should never result from a COPY operation. The file's directory size entry is suspicious. To further clarify the nature of the allocation error, you use the CHKDSK report to compare with the directory listing for the same files.

The CHKDSK report shows 415,744 bytes in the 4 files. When you total the bytes in the directory listing, you can only account for 347,824 bytes in the 4 files. Both CHKDSK and the directory listing show 314,368 bytes available on the disk. CHKDSK and DIR both report available disk bytes as the number of bytes in unallocated disk clusters—not the difference between the capacity of the disk and the number of bytes in the disk's files. Both commands get the disk's remaining capacity indirectly from the FAT.

Because both commands agree on the FAT's calculation, you must assume that the directory entry for DBASE1.OVL is incorrect in its reflection of the file's size. CHKDSK can repair the directory entry. Issue the CHKDSK command again using the /F switch:

CHKDSK A: /F

CHKDSK then reports the following:

```
Volume SCRATCH DISK created 09-12-1989   11:23a
A:\DBASE1.OVL
Allocation error, size adjusted
 730112 bytes in total disk space
 415744 bytes in 4 user files
 314368 bytes available on disk

   1024 bytes in each allocation unit
    713 total allocation units on disk
    307 available allocation units on disk

 655360 total bytes memory
 409856 bytes free
```

To confirm that the problem you suspect in the directory is repaired, list the directory of the disk again. You see the following:

```
Volume in drive A is SCRATCH DISK
Volume Serial Number is 0000-0000
Directory of  A:\
DBSETUP   OVL    147968 10-21-88  12:22a
DBASE3    OVL     85024 12-28-88   9:04p
DBASE6    OVL    114832 10-20-88  11:22p
DBASE1    OVL     65536 09-12-89   1:46a
        4 File(s)      314368 bytes free
```

Notice that DBASE1.OVL shows 65,536 bytes instead of 0. The available capacity of the disk remains unchanged. Now the total bytes shown in the directory listing is within a few thousand of the difference between the disk's capacity and the bytes free total. You can account for this small difference by considering that some of the files do not completely fill their last allocated cluster. The error in the directory is corrected, and the disk is ready for use again.

Summary

This chapter has presented the important FORMAT command as well as other disk-level DOS commands. The following key points were presented in this chapter:

❏ Hard disks and floppies must be formatted before they can be used to store files.

❏ Formatting sets up a directory for file-name and status information and a File Allocation Table (FAT) for tracking the disk's cluster availability.

❏ FORMAT accepts several switches that add versatility. The /S switch makes the disk bootable. The /V switch enables giving the disk a volume label.

❏ Hard disks must be partitioned using FDISK before they can be formatted.

❏ Disk partitions can be DOS partitions or partitions of another operating system.

❏ DOS partitions are either a Primary (bootable) partition or an Extended partition divided into one or more logical drives.

❏ DOS views logical drives as being the same as physical disks and assigns each logical drive its own drive name letter.

❏ The LABEL command adds or changes a disk's volume label.

❏ The VOL command displays a disk's volume label.

❏ The SYS command transfers the hidden DOS system files from a bootable disk to another disk. SYS can be used to upgrade a disk's DOS version.

❏ CHKDSK is a disk-level command that finds and fixes problems. CHKDSK analyzes a disk's FAT and directory system.

❏ When you include the /F switch, CHKDSK can repair most problems it encounters.

In the next chapter, you will be introduced to DOS's hierarchical directory system. With knowledge of the hierarchical directory system, you will be able to use DOS commands in a multilevel directory system.

Understanding Hierarchical Directories

7

Chapter 6 introduced you to several disk-level DOS commands. Disks are the major building blocks of the DOS file system. The FORMAT command (and FDISK for hard disks) prepares disks for storing files. One of DOS's major duties is moving information to and from disks in the form of files. To you and your programs, the process of managing files is based on referencing files by name. DOS must bridge the technology gap between your requesting a file by name and the data reading and writing methods of the disk's electronic and electro-mechanical operation. DOS employs a strategy or method for taking file names from your command line and ensuring that the data held in those files is acted upon by the command. When you consider the millions of bytes available on a typical hard disk, you can appreciate that a file-management strategy must be effective. Without such a strategy, accessing files would be like finding a needle in a haystack.

An operating system's job is to provide routine services to you and your programs while keeping the burden of understanding the details of the services away from you. When it comes to dealing with files, DOS provides many commands that copy, delete, rename, compare, and change the attributes of files that you ask for by name. As part of its strategy, DOS keeps the names of files in a directory system along with other information about each file. Understanding the DOS directory system is important because every file-management command you use goes through DOS's directory entries.

DOS enables you to add to the basic directory system of each disk. You can create new, named directories to hold file names; you can work with

153

those files as though they were the only files on the disk. The system DOS employs is far more versatile than simply dividing a disk into areas by giving each area its own directory. DOS enables you to maintain an interdependent hierarchy of directories that you control.

This chapter introduces you to the DOS hierarchical directory system. You will get to see a little below DOS's surface as you learn how DOS employs its file-management strategy.

Key Terms Used in This Chapter

Directory   A disk-based table of file names and other file-related information that DOS uses in conjunction with the File Allocation Table (FAT) to access a file's data content.

Root directory A master directory created on each disk by FORMAT and referenced by the \ character.

Subdirectory   An additional named directory created by a user.

Attribute   A directory-based indicator of a files status. Attributes include read/write, hidden, system, archive, and volume label.

Reviewing Disks

To set the stage for looking at directories, you should review some of the concepts of DOS disks. As you recall, DOS references each disk drive on your system by using a drive name or specifier. The names DOS uses for drives are letters such as A, B, and C. Before DOS can use a disk in a drive, the disk must be formatted. The FORMAT operation establishes key tables on each disk along with some vital information about the disk's format. DOS uses the tables and disk information as a template for managing the disk's storage capabilities. A root directory and File Allocation Table are included in this FORMAT-provided disk preparation.

Because each disk has the tables necessary to stand on its own as a storage medium, DOS can treat your hardware as a multidisk environment. DOS keeps track of the logged drive and uses the drive as the current or default drive. Internally, DOS stores the logged drive's name. When you issue a command without an optional drive specifier, DOS uses the stored logged drive letter by default. For example, if you type the command **DIR**, DOS will produce a directory listing from the default drive. In this case, DOS seems to approach its file system as a single set of files.

If you use a drive specifier with a command, DOS accesses the file-system tables from the specified disk. If you type the command **DIR B:**, DOS will produce a listing of the disk in drive B even if drive A is the logged drive. By adding the drive specifier to the command, you are actually invoking DOS's multidisk capabilities. Because DOS uses the same set of guidelines for establishing the method to use various types of disks,

DOS commands can access files on all types of disks. If DOS can format a disk on your system, DOS can use the disk. With a drive specifier, you have immediate access to any disk on your system, and you access the files on any disk using commands that work with any other disk.

Understanding the Role of Directories

One of the important tables established on each disk by FORMAT is the *directory*. Each DOS-prepared disk has one directory. This directory is called the *root directory* because it is the root of each disk's file system. DOS uses a directory as a kind of index system for finding desired files. Individual members of this index system are called *directory entries*. DOS provides for a fixed number of directory entries in the root directory. The fixed number is the same for the same types of disk formats, but varies with differing formats. Disks with larger capacities are given more root directory entries.

By using DOS commands, you can see a good deal of the makeup of a directory. The DIR command, you will remember, accesses and displays selected parts of directory entries:

```
Volume in drive A is SCRATCH DISK
Volume Serial Number is 0000-0000
Directory of  A:\
DBSETUP   OVL    147968 10-21-88  12:22a
DBASE3    OVL     85024 12-28-88   9:04p
DBASE6    OVL    114832 10-20-88  11:22p
DBASE1    OVL     65536 09-12-89   1:46a
        4 File(s)      314368 bytes free
```

The DIR command does not display all of the elements of a directory entry, however. Table 7.1 lists the component parts of a directory entry.

Table 7.1
The Main Features of DOS Directories

Feature	What is Stored	Example
File name	Eight-character file prefix	THANKYOU
File-name extension	Three-character file suffix	DOC
File Attributes	Special status information about this file used by DOS.	R (Read-only)
Time	The time of creation or last modification	10:22
Date	The date of creation or last modification	11-14-89
Starting cluster	The number of the first cluster allocated to this file by DOS in the FAT	576
File Size	The number of bytes in this file.	1024 bytes

You recognize the file name, extension, time, and date components of a directory entry as being displayed by the DIR command. The file size is also displayed by DIR. These components or *fields* of a directory entry contain information useful to you as well as DOS (see fig. 7.1). DIR displays this information because it is useful for your file-management DOS activities.

Fig. 7.1

File Name	Extension	Attributes	Reserved	Time	Date	Starting Cluster	Size

The fields of a directory entry.

DOS also stores volume labels (see Chapter 6) in directory entries. DOS uses the combined file-name and extension fields to form an 11-byte (character) field when the directory entry is for a disk's volume label. The commands FORMAT/V and LABEL write your choice of a volume name into the root directory entry for a disk. DOS knows that the directory entry is a volume label because the volume label attribute for the entry is set.

The starting-cluster and file-attribute fields shown in table 7.1 and in figure 7.1 are not included in the displayed output of DIR. The starting-cluster field contains the cluster number of the first cluster DOS allocated for a particular file's storage. The file-attribute field contains special status information about the file that DOS uses to determine how the file is to be managed internally. Because these two fields are not as visible or as self explanatory as the fields displayed in the DIR listing, the next two sections will look at them in a bit more detail.

Chaining Through a File

The starting cluster field of a file's directory entry is the key to the file's storage allocation as tracked in the FAT. You will recall that DOS creates a FAT for each disk during formatting. Every sector on the disk is represented by an entry in the FAT as part of (or all of) a cluster.

If you have ever walked into a restaurant and had the hostess look at a table chart for a place to seat you, you've got the concept of the FAT. DOS looks for available clusters when a file is created or enlarged. When you arrive early at the dining hour, the restaurant is nearly empty, and the hostess seats you in the general vicinity of other guests while other sections of the restaurant remain unused. When DOS allocates files on a freshly formatted disk, DOS uses the first cluster and sequences through a connected series of clusters, leaving many never-used clusters at the end of the FAT. When you leave the restaurant, the hostess marks your table as being available again. Likewise, when you erase or shorten a file, DOS marks the released clusters in the FAT as being available again. DOS can use them when storing another file.

Files, like diners at a busy restaurant, don't have a choice of where they go. They are serviced on a "next available" basis. DOS checks the FAT and finds the next available cluster, and a portion of the file is stored there. If the file is larger in size than a cluster can accommodate, DOS finds the next available cluster and stores part of the file there. If the disk has a great deal of file activity, the two clusters might not be connected to each other. The two clusters might be in completely different areas of the disk's surface or even on different surfaces. This disconnected cluster condition is known as *file fragmentation.*

You might have had a similar dining experience when a hostess did not have enough adjacent tables to seat your entire party. In all likelihood, your group was fragmented across two or more tables with other parties seated at tables between the parts of your group. You can remain connected as a group by telling the waitress, "We're with those people over there," as you point to the other table.

DOS connects all clusters of a file by entering where the next cluster is located in the current cluster's entry in the FAT. When a file is allocated more than one cluster, each cluster "points" to the next cluster that contains more of the file. The "pointer" is the next cluster number. The result is a chain of clusters that comprise the map of a file's disk storage. Even though fragmentation slows DOS's access to the whole of the file, the FAT as a storage map tells DOS exactly where to go on the disk to get all parts of a file.

When you ask for a file by name by using a DOS command, DOS looks in the directory for the "who" identity of the file. The directory stores file names. To access the file from the disk, DOS needs to know the "where" identity of the file. Because the directory contains the starting-cluster number for each file, DOS can get a file's starting-cluster number when accessing the directory, and then consult the FAT with the starting number to unlock the chain of clusters that holds the "where" values for the file.

Assuring the integrity of the FAT . . . DOS uses the directory and the FAT in a file allocation and accessing strategy. If the values in these DOS tables become corrupted due to power surges, errant programs, or media failure, DOS becomes unable to access the disk's files and storage areas effectively. If you have important files on a damaged disk, you may be able to reduce the damage by using certain DOS commands.

The CHKDSK command (see Chapter 6) uses the directory and the FAT to account for the proper tracking of each cluster and directory entry on a disk. CHKDSK detects improper relationships in the cluster chains of files and the sizes of directory entries. CHKDSK fixes a disk by adjusting improper file allocation sizes, eliminating circular references in cluster pointers, and making other technical adjustments in the FAT and directories.

Assuring the integrity of the FAT... (cont.)

The RECOVER command (see the Command Reference) can reestablish a file under a new allocation chain and directory entry if the existing FAT or directory entries are damaged. Some of the recovered file's content will probably be lost, however. RECOVER includes a provision to recover an entire damaged disk. This full version of the command is meant for informed users only, and even then, should be used only as a last resort.

Many third party software companies offer programs that can repair FATs and directories that have become corrupted. Ask your dealer about these programs. These programs are generally easier to use than RECOVER and can save your disks or files from being unusable. Some programs can bring back files from a disk that you have formatted. Third party disk maintenance programs fill a gap that DOS leaves open.

Understanding File Attributes

The file attribute is special status given to files by DOS. You can manage some file attributes through DOS commands; others are managed directly by DOS. The values of a file's attributes do not appear in the displayed directory listing of the file. DOS provides storage room in each directory entry for all available attributes, regardless of whether any attributes are used or not. The attribute field in the directory entry is therefore made up of individual attributes, each capable of indicating a unique status. These individual attributes are often referred to as *attribute bits*; one bit represents one attribute. Table 7.2 lists the attributes and their purposes in DOS.

Table 7.2
File Attributes and Their Meanings

Attribute Bit	Meaning
Read-only	This file can be accessed for information, but cannot be erased or overwritten.
Hidden	This file will be bypassed by most DOS file-management commands and will not appear in a directory listing.
System	This file is a DOS system file.
Volume label	This entry is the volume label for this disk, not an actual file.
Subdirectory	This entry is for an additional directory stored in this file, not data or a program.
Archive	This file has been created or modified since the last DOS command that resets this attribute processed this file.

The *volume label attribute* indicates that the directory entry involved is not for a file at all. This attribute tells DOS that the file name and extension fields should be combined to provide an 11-character volume label ID for the disk. Only a volume label entry will have this attribute indicated (turned on).

The *subdirectory attribute* indicates to DOS that the entry is not intended for a user file but for an additional directory called a subdirectory. Subdirectories are explained in later sections of this chapter. DOS knows to bypass a file with the subdirectory attribute turned on when conducting file-management commands.

A file entry with the *hidden attribute* turned on is "invisible" to most DOS file-management commands. Hidden files have file names and extensions like normal user files, but a DIR listing or a COPY command will not process a hidden file. The two DOS system files on the boot disk are examples, as are many copy-protection files. Volume labels are also hidden file entries. You can detect the presence of hidden files with the CHKDSK command. CHKDSK does not indicate the identity of the hidden files, but it does tell you how many hidden files are present on a disk.

The *system attribute* indicates that a file is an operating system file. The two DOS system files have this attribute in addition to the hidden attribute. You won't need to worry about the system attribute because its presence is of no consequence to your DOS work.

The *archive* and *read-only attributes* are the only attributes that you can manage. DOS controls the other attributes. Because you control the archive and read-only attributes, you can concentrate your understanding of attributes on these two.

The archive attribute works in harmony with certain DOS file-management commands to add conditional selectivity to which files the commands will process. XCOPY, for example, includes an optional switch that causes XCOPY to examine a file's archive attribute before copying the file to its destination. If the archive attribute is not turned on (set), XCOPY bypasses the file. The underlying reason for archive attributes is similar to the reason for having a small metal flag on a rural mailbox.

The rural mail carrier passes by each mailbox each delivery day as part of the mail delivery and pickup operation. If there is no mail to deliver to a box on a particular day, and no letters are being mailed from the box, stopping at the box to process the possible mail is a waste of the mail carrier's time. The owner of the mailbox can raise the red metal flag as an indicator that the box contains letters to mail, and the carrier, seeing the flag, stops to pick up the letters. Emptying the box, the carrier drops the flag back down. The flag acts as a synchronizer of activity so that only necessary stops are made.

Likewise, the archive attribute of a file is a flag for the command that processes the file. When DOS adds or modifies the contents of a file, DOS sets the archive attribute just like a flag. Commands that have the capability to use the archive attribute can optionally look to see if the flag (archive attribute) is raised. Only if the archive attribute is raised will the command process the file. When commands like XCOPY and BACKUP see that the archive attribute is turned on in a file's directory listing, the

159

commands assume that the file has changed since the last XCOPY or BACKUP command processed the file. You can use these capabilities of the archive attribute to make backups of files that have changed since your last backup or copy using XCOPY. If only a few files have been added to a disk or changed on a disk, only a few files will be included in the operation. DOS will bypass the files whose "flags" are not raised, thus saving time and destination disk space.

DOS commands change the archive attributes for files when the files are added or modified, or when commands like XCOPY reset the attributes. DOS also supplies you with a command to directly change a file's archive attribute. The command is the ATTRIB command. ATTRIB in V3.2 or later versions can turn an archive attribute on (set it) and turn it off (reset it). With ATTRIB, you can control which files that commands such as XCOPY will process while operating with the archive switch. You may want to override the default setting of the attribute for a file. ATTRIB is the command to use.

Establishing Read-Only Files

The ATTRIB command also gives you control over a file's read-only or read/write attribute. The read/write attribute controls the capability of DOS to overwrite or erase a file. Commands such as COPY, ERASE, and XCOPY have the capability to remove or overwrite an existing file. When DOS (or an application through DOS) adds a file to a directory, the read/write attributes are established so that the file can be overwritten or erased. The default value of the read/write attribute enables DOS commands to perform destructive operations on the file. If you change the read/write attribute of a file to make the file "read-only," the DOS commands that normally overwrite or erase files will not affect the read-only file. Marking a file as read-only protects the file in a way similar to that in which write-protecting a disk protects the contents of a disk. You can use the ATTRIB command to effectively write-protect important files and have insurance that an errant COPY or ERASE command will not destroy the marked files.

 The FDISK and FORMAT commands do not observe the read-only status of a file. FDISK and FORMAT are disk-level commands that do not look at the disk's directories when doing their jobs. Don't rely on the read-only attribute of a file to protect the file from a disk-level command.

After you use the ATTRIB command to mark a file as read-only, you can use the ATTRIB command again to mark the file as read/write. In other words, you can reverse your decision at any time. The file will then be subject to DOS commands that can overwrite or erase the file.

Issuing the ATTRIB Command

Remember that each directory entry provides some fields to record a file's attributes. The external command ATTRIB enables you to manipulate the file's read/write and archive attributes. Both of these attributes are given default values by DOS when the file is added to the directory.

You can issue the ATTRIB command in three basic ways.

1. Use the following syntax form to receive a screen report of a file's current attribute values:

   ATTRIB *d:path***filename.ext**/*S*

2. Use the following syntax form to set (turn on a file's attribute(s):

   ATTRIB *+R +A d:path***filename.ext**/*S*

3. Use the following syntax form to reset (turn off) a file's attribute(s):

   ATTRIB *−R −A d:path***filename.ext**/*S*

d: is the optional drive that holds the disk containing the selected files, and *path* is the optional directory path that contains the selected files. You will learn about paths later in this chapter.

filename.ext, the selected file specifier, can contain wild cards. Remember that by using wild cards, several files that match the wild-card pattern are included in the command's operation. A file name must be specified.

The optional */S* switch (DOS V3.3 and later versions only) instructs ATTRIB to additionally process files that match the file specifier in all *subdirectories* of the path directory. You will learn about subdirectories in this chapter.

The *+R* and *+A* attribute indicators instruct ATTRIB to set (add) the read-only and archive attributes respectively.

The *−R* and *−A* attribute indicators instruct ATTRIB to reset (clear) the read-only and archive attributes respectively.

The R and A attributes can be specified individually or together in the command line. Specifying both enables you to use one command to manipulate both attributes.

The R and A attributes can have the same action (+R and +A or −R and −A) or opposite actions (−R and +A or +R and −A).

If neither an R nor an A attribute specifier is included in the command line, the ATTRIB command produces a screen report showing the attribute status of desired files. You view this screen report to see the current attributes of the files specified in the command line.

Making COMMAND.COM Read-Only with ATTRIB

COMMAND.COM is an important program file. To protect the file against accidental erasure or overwriting, you can make COMMAND.COM read-only. Making COMMAND.COM read-only is a good example of using ATTRIB. Because ATTRIB can write a new attribute value to a disk, be sure that the disk you specify is not write-protected. Assume that COMMAND.COM is in the root directory of your logged disk, and then issue the following command:

ATTRIB +R \COMMAND.COM

COMMAND.COM is now a read-only file. To verify that the file has its read-only attribute set, issue the following command:

ATTRIB \COMMAND.COM

DOS replies as follows:

```
R   C:\COMMAND.COM
```

If you didn't make COMMAND.COM read only, don't use the ERASE command sequence that follows. Erasing COMMAND.COM causes the disk to be unbootable, and you will have to boot the PC from a working DOS disk or the DOS master disk.

If you then issue the command **ERASE COMMAND.COM**, DOS reports as follows:

```
Access Denied
```

DOS will not erase the file. The same type of command can make another file read-only. By using wild cards in the file specifier, you can make groups of files read-only. To return a file's read-only status back to read/write, you reverse the process. In the case of COMMAND.COM, you issue the following command:

ATTRIB –R \COMMAND.COM

The file can now be erased or overwritten.

Expanding the File System through Subdirectories

DOS designers designed one master directory with a predetermined number of file entries to keep the space occupied by the directory small. You will recall that FORMAT establishes one fixed-length directory for each disk. Keeping this directory small is important, because the larger the directory, the smaller the space left on the disk for your files. The designers first established a cap on the number of entries in the directory to fix its size. The cap number was proportional to the capacity of the disk the designers were dealing with. Floppies had fewer file entries in the master directory (less bytes) than hard disks. Each DOS user is different, as are the file-storage needs of each DOS user. For most DOS users, one directory is not sufficient to encourage effective file management by users.

The FORMAT-provided directory is not intended to accommodate every possible file that a disk can hold (unless the disk is a floppy used to store a few files). The FORMAT-provided directory, as the *root* of the system, is called the *root directory*. DOS does not limit directory entries to those of the root directory. Many of the disk's files can be entered into subcategory expansion directories or *subdirectories*. DOS provides a disk with a root directory, but you add subdirectories to the file system. You add as many as your personal computing needs require.

In the root directory or in a subdirectory, DOS can still enter the name and the first cluster number of a file's FAT entry. The DOS subdirectory is a special file that DOS uses like the root directory. When you work with DOS commands, you can't tell that the root directory is a reserved section of the disk, and that the subdirectory is a special file. DOS appears to work with them in the same way. DOS manages the root directory and subdirectory difference internally and provides uniformity on the surface. For this reason, it is quite common for DOS users to call subdirectories "directories." Unless the context of the term dictates otherwise, subdirectories can be called directories.

DOS can implement an entire system of subdirectories and still retain the general advantages of a single directory. From a space-economy point of view, a subdirectory system overcomes many of the drawbacks of a single directory system such as an excessively large number of dedicated file entries. Of course, DOS has to provide a few commands to manage the subdirectory system. Commands to create, remove, and change the current directory are examples. You will learn about these commands in detail in the next chapter.

On a freshly formatted disk, you have access to the disk's only directory, the root directory. With the MKDIR (Make Directory) command, you can create a subdirectory called LETTERS. The actual name you use can be any file name that DOS accepts. You might use the name LETTERS as the subdirectory name to categorize the letter files that you will keep in this new subdirectory. Subdirectories have the advantage of holding files of some common type or purpose.

To focus DOS's attention on the LETTERS subdirectory as though it were the only directory on the disk, you can use the CHDIR (Change Directory) command to change the current directory to LETTERS. DOS keeps track of the current directory just like it tracks the current drive. Once you change to a directory, that directory is the default for that disk. The default directory of the logged disk is your working directory. When you boot DOS, the working directory is the root directory of the boot disk.

If you later want to remove the LETTERS subdirectory because you no longer need it, you can use the RMDIR (Remove Directory) command to do so. If you want to remove the directory, the directory must contain no files. DOS will not enable you to delete a directory while making orphans of the files the directory contains.

Subdirectories in DOS V2 and later versions, as well as the commands that support them, are a great advancement over the single fixed directories of V1. The feature that gives the most efficiency to the DOS file system is the relating of the subdirectories hierarchically.

Understanding the Hierarchical Directory System

A hierarchy is an organization or arrangement of entities (things). Entities can refer to people, objects, ideas, files, or many other things. Coins, for example, can be arranged by denomination, and soldiers can be organized by rank. There are, of course, many ways to organize entities besides hierarchically. Stones in a driveway are arranged randomly; bricks in a wall are arranged in parallel rows; and telephone book listings are arranged in alphabetical order. The arrangement of the stones, bricks, and listings is not hierarchical. What makes hierarchical organization useful is that you can name each entity by its relationship to other entities. If this organization confuses you, don't despair. You will soon be able to understand it.

To a genealogist, entities may be people in a family tree. To DOS, entities are directories in a directory system. In either case, the hierarchy begins with the essential core or root entity. In a family tree, the core entity might be great-great-grandfather Isaac Watson. In DOS, this core entity is the root directory. In genealogy, people can trace their roots through their parents and their parents' generations. People know who their forefathers are based on the relationships of the family tree. In DOS, subdirectories can trace their paths back to the root directory. DOS subdirectories and their files are identifiable by their relationships to other subdirectories. It is easy to see why the DOS hierarchical file system is called a tree-structured file system. At the base of this tree structure is the root directory.

In a family tree, David might be son of Wayne, who is son of Alex, who is son of John. John is the head or root of the family tree for David. Another way to represent David's identity in this family tree is as follows:

John\Alex\Wayne\David

In this example, each level of the family tree is separated by a backslash character. This David is different from the following David:

Issac\Virgil\Robert\David

Both share the name David, but their relationships to their parents are unique. DOS directories share the same kind of identity relationships as families. In fact, since V2.0, every DOS disk is capable of having a family of subdirectories that stems from the root directory.

DOS enables you to add subdirectories in levels like generations. The subdirectory LETTERS is a first-level subdirectory. LETTERS is created as an offspring of the root directory. LETTERS is a subdirectory name that you supply. The root has no name as such, and is simply referenced on the command line as the \ (backslash) character.

To refer to the file MEMO.DOC located in the LETTERS subdirectory, you can use the name \LETTERS\MEMO.DOC. If the MEMO.DOC file is located on a drive other than the logged drive, you can give a full file-name parameter of C:\LETTERS\MEMO.DOC.

The drive specifier is C:. \LETTERS is the directory specifier, and MEMO.DOC is the file specifier. The root directory of C: is the parent directory of LETTERS.

You can create many directories from the root. The root will be the parent of each of these directories. You can also create subdirectories that stem from other subdirectories. These new subdirectories have a subdirectory as their parent directory. Figure 7.2 illustrates how subdirectories are arranged hierarchically from the root. The arrangement looks like that of a family tree. The DOS directory system is often called a tree-structured directory system.

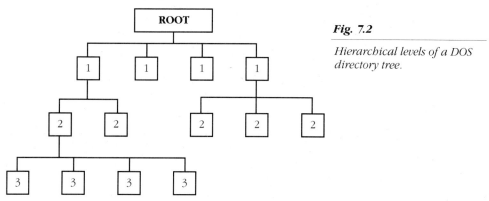

Fig. 7.2

Hierarchical levels of a DOS directory tree.

Three levels of subdirectories are represented in figure 7.2. Because you determine the subdirectories on your disks, your directory may have more or fewer levels. Regardless of the number of levels, the relationship of the subdirectories is important. Each subdirectory, as well as the root directory, can contain user files. Two files can have the same file name and extension as long as the files reside in different directories. Because DOS needs to know which of two same-named files your command specifies, DOS needs the name of the directories, starting from the root, that lead to the desired file. This sequence of directory names leading to a file is called a *path*.

Understanding Path Names

A path name is a chain of directory names that tell DOS how to find a file that you want. Each directory is separated from the others by a \ character. The \ is DOS's directory delimiter. A file's full path name (including the drive specifier) is the absolute indicator of where the file is located. Using symbolic notation, the path name for a file looks like this:

  d:\dir1\dir2\dir3...\filename.ext

d: is the drive letter. The first \ is the DOS name for the root. *dir1\dir2\dir3...* indicates a chain of directories in which the directory to the left of another directory is the parent. The (...) indicates that more (or fewer) directory names are allowed. All

165

characters between the first \ and the final \ comprise the directory path. *filename.ext* is the name of the file that is in the final directory of the directory path.

 Some software packages create hidden subdirectories when you install them on a hard disk. Some of the directories on your hard disk may have been created in this way. Don't worry that you won't be able to find the files that these packages produce. The files will be in one of the created subdirectories.

To see how the path specifier works with DOS, look again at the DIR command. Recall that issuing DIR alone on the command line displays the directory of the logged drive. DOS supplies the drive specifier for the command by using a default. DOS accepts a path specifier with DIR also. Up to now, you haven't issued a path specifier with DIR, and DOS hasn't complained. That is because, like the drive, the path is a default value. DOS has been supplying the path specifier for you. If you don't give a path specifier with most DOS commands, the command will use the current directory.

When DOS is booted, the current directory is the root directory of the boot disk. The boot disk is always the first default (logged) disk. If you want to see the files in the \DOS subdirectory, for example, you must include the path specifier in the directory command. Remember that the current directory is the root (\). DOS does not display the files in other directories with the DIR command. When you include a path specifier in the command, DOS looks only at the specified directory for the files. To see the COM extension files in \DOS from the root of the logged drive, you issue the following command:

DIR \DOS*.COM

If your logged drive is A and you want to see the COM files on drive C in the \DOS directory, you issue the following command:

DIR C:\DOS*.COM

If you log to the \DOS directory with the command **CHDIR \DOS**, \DOS is your default directory on the logged disk. DOS knows that if you omit the path specifier, \DOS is the default to use. Now when you want to see the COM files in the \DOS directory, you can issue the following command:

DIR *.COM

This command produces the same list of files as the command **DIR \DOS*.COM** issued from the root directory. DOS supplied the \DOS path by default. Many DOS commands work with optional path specifiers. When you don't supply a path, DOS uses the current directory. Check the syntax for each command to see whether you can take advantage of the default path.

Using PROMPT To Display a Full Path

While you are reading about the hierarchical directory system, you might want to confirm that your DOS prompt is displaying the current full path (drive and path) of your current directory. To give you visual confirmation of your current logged drive and any logged directory, DOS provides the internal command PROMPT to display the full path as part of the DOS prompt. DOS V4 supplies this command automatically in the AUTOEXEC.BAT file that runs after you boot. You can establish a more meaningful prompt by issuing the following command:

PROMPT pg

If you are logged to the \DOS directory on drive C, the prompt will be displayed as follows:

```
C:\DOS>
```

The **$p** specifier in the PROMPT command tells DOS to display the full path as part of the prompt. The **$g** tells DOS to display the > character as the end of the prompt. With your prompt established in this way, you will have a visual reminder of where you are working in the hierarchical directory system.

As soon as you reboot, the prompt returns to its former look. If you want to include the path as a permanent part of your DOS prompt, read the section on PROMPT in Chapter 13.

You can include the PROMPT command in your AUTOEXEC.BAT file (see Chapter 12) to make the new prompt appear at boot time. If you don't include the PROMPT command in your AUTOEXEC.BAT, you will have to issue a PROMPT command each time you boot to change the prompt from the default.

Helping DOS Find External Commands

When you issue an external command, DOS must know where to find the file containing the command's program code before the external command can be loaded and executed. There are three basic ways to tell DOS where the command is located.

1. Log to the disk and directory that contains the command.
2. Supply the command's path in the command line.
3. Establish a DOS search path to the command's directory.

So far, you have logged to the drive and directory that contains the external command file. DOS finds the command in this circumstance by using the default drive and path.

If you want to use an external command that is located on a drive and (or) directory that is not the default, you can supply the drive and path information that DOS needs directly before the command's name in the command line. For example, if you want to analyze the logged disk in drive B, and the DOS external commands are on the working DOS disk in drive A, you can issue the following command:

B:\>**A:CHKDSK**

DOS looks for the CHKDSK program on drive A and analyzes the logged disk in drive B. The same principle applies to the path of the command. For example, if the CHKDSK command is in a directory called \DOS on drive C, and you are logged to drive B, you can analyze the disk in B with the following command:

B:\>**C:\DOS\CHKDSK**

Notice that the command was issued with B: as the logged drive as indicated in the prompt. C: is the drive specifier for the location of the \DOS directory where CHKDSK resides. A final \ separates the path from the command-file specifier. With the path to the command given in the command line, DOS will find and execute the CHKDSK command analyzing the disk in drive B. Actually, the paths to the external command are the same as the first method, but the drive and the path are not the default.

The most convenient method to help DOS find external commands is to establish a search path for DOS to use. A search path is established through the PATH command. DOS designers anticipated that you would not want to log to the drive containing an external command or give the command's path in order to use the command. The PATH command enables you to inform DOS of the most likely directories to contain external commands, batch files, and program files.

Tech note ... The PATH command enables DOS to locate program files with COM and EXE extensions for execution. Batch files with BAT extensions are also located and executed through the search path. If you supply a path to a program on the command line, DOS will not search the path alternatives if the program is not in the directory you specified.

You can include up to 64 characters in the parameters for the PATH command. DOS saves 64 characters of space in memory to store the search alternatives. If you are unsure of your current PATH setting, you can issue the SET command at the DOS prompt. DOS will show the PATH setting as well as any other settings such as PROMPT in a screen report. The SET command reports variable values from an area of special memory called the *environment*. All programs, as well as DOS commands, can consult the environment to find the current values of environment variables.

The PATH command does not help DOS find data files. A similar command, APPEND, has the ability to search for data files that are not in the current directory. The APPEND command is outlined in the Command Reference section.

168

The syntax of the PATH command is as follows:

PATH=*d1:path1\;d2:path2\;...*

The equal sign (=) (assignment character) is optional; you can simply use a space. *d1:* is the first drive containing *path1*. The semicolon (;) character following *path* tells DOS that the end of the first path has been reached in the command. *2:path2* is a second alternative drive and path combination for DOS to search if the desired program is not in the first path. *;...* indicate that you can add other alternative paths to the command. DOS will search for a program from left-to-right ordering of the path alternatives. You do not have to give the drive specifiers with the path specifiers, but you always should. You don't want DOS to be searching for a directory on the default drive that is really on another drive.

Nearly all hard disk users take advantage of the PATH command. Many program packages add an alternative that stores their files to the PATH command in the AUTOEXEC.BAT file. Program package instructions usually recommend what path alternative you should add. For DOS use on a hard disk, you will almost certainly want to include the directory that holds the DOS external commands. You can then issue external commands without logging to their drives or including their paths in the command line. Thanks to the PATH command, internal and external commands are equally as convenient.

For an example of setting a search path with PATH, suppose that you have a hard disk named C:. The DOS external program files are located in a directory named \DOS as they would be if you install DOS V4 on your hard disk. To include the external commands in your search path, issue the following command:

PATH=C:\DOS

DOS will look in C:\DOS for a program that is not located in the current directory. If you have other program packages, you might add their directories to the path. Some packages, such as dBASE IV, add their search alternatives for you. If you added dBASE's directory yourself, the command would look like the following:

PATH=C:\DOS;C:\DBASE

Notice that the semicolon separates the two alternatives. DOS will search C:\DOS first for the dBASE program, and failing to find it there, will search C:\DBASE where the file is located.

You can add search paths to your AUTOEXEC.BAT file so that the desired paths will be automatically established when you boot. See Chapter 12 for more information.

169

Summary

In this chapter, you were introduced to hierarchical directories and related concepts. You saw how the FAT and directories contain the what-and-where values for a file that DOS uses to locate a file's data. Understanding how DOS directories relate to one another is an important step towards mastering the DOS directory-level commands and effectively using file-level commands. The following key points were discussed in this chapter:

❏ Directories store the entries for each file. Each file has a name, time and date of creation or modification, file attributes, and file size.

❏ The starting cluster stored in a file's directory entry points to a chain of clusters in the FAT which log the file's actual location on the disk.

❏ File attributes indicate special statutes for a file. Attributes are read-only (read/write), hidden, system, volume label, subdirectory, and archive.

❏ The ATTRIB command enables you to control the read-only and archive attributes.

❏ DOS provides the root directory (\) through the action of FORMAT, and you provide subdirectories through the MKDIR command. You name subdirectories using any legal DOS file name and optional extension.

❏ The root directory and subdirectories form a hierarchically related tree structure. Any subdirectory can be found by tracing the path to it from the root through its parent directories.

❏ You can log to a directory with the CHDIR command. That directory then becomes the current directory on that disk.

❏ The command **PROMPT=pg** causes the DOS prompt to include the current drive and directory. By viewing the prompt, you can determine your current location in the directory system.

❏ The path specifier is part of a file parameter which tells DOS the directory location for the file.

❏ The PATH command sets search path alternatives which DOS uses to find and execute a program file, such as an external command, when the program file is not in the current directory.

❏ When the search path contains the drive and directory holding the external DOS commands, you can issue external commands as conveniently as internal commands.

In the next chapter, you will use the directory-management commands to learn how to manage your subdirectories. With the background of this chapter, the next chapter will have you well on your way to being in control of DOS's hierarchical directory system.

Managing
Directories

One of the primary features of DOS is its hierarchical directory system. Chapter 7 explains how DOS uses directories in conjunction with the file allocation table (FAT) to log the physical location of files on a disk. DOS uses internally related directories and the FAT to provide a framework for the management of the hierarchical file system.

This chapter's focus is your view of the file system. This is the view you have of directories when you work with applications programs and DOS commands. From this external point of view, a freshly formatted disk is ready for you to give it a tree-structured file system any way you see fit. DOS directory commands enable you to design, manage, and modify your directory tree.

Many DOS commands deal with directories in some way or another. For example, you can copy a file from one directory to a different directory with COPY. Yet COPY is a file-level command because it deals primarily with files. The directory commands, on the other hand, have a definite connection with directories. This chapter explains how you can design, manage, and modify your directory system based on the directory-level commands provided with DOS. The chapter also offers some suggestions for efficient management of the hierarchical directory system on your hard disk.

Key Terms Used in This Chapter

Relative path   The path from the current directory where the root and intervening directories are taken from DOS defaults.

Absolute path   The path named from the root directory with all intervening subdirectories.

Redirection   The sending of the input or output of a command to other than the device to which the output or input normally goes.

Reviewing Subdirectories

A subdirectory is a file that DOS uses in the same general way that it uses the root directory. Recall from Chapter 7 that the root directory is a fixed-length directory table that resides in the control area of each disk. Subdirectories share with the root directory the common 32-byte entry size used to record information about a file. You can think of the root directory and subdirectories as being just "plain" directories because most of your DOS commands use the root directory and subdirectories in a similar way. For a discussion of DOS commands, it is nearly always as meaningful to say "directory" when referring to the root or a subdirectory as it is to use "root" or "subdirectory."

When working with files, you can easily get the impression that DOS keeps the files themselves rather than entries about the files in directories. This is an erroneous impression. There is no physical division of a disk into subdirectories of files. A directory's files may be spread randomly across the disk.

Yet it is logical to think of a file's data as being in a particular directory because a file's data is tied to an entry in that directory. You give directory parameters in commands by including paths. When most commands with path parameters carry out their actions, the objects of the actions are files. DOS does a good job of hiding from users the random locations on disk of most files by keeping a hierarchical order in the directories.

For the purpose of discussing the contents of a directory, when the contents are files—not file entries, thinking of a directory as a "place" on the disk does no harm.

Specifying a path in the syntax line ... Good syntax representation is always accompanied by an explanation of each element of the syntax. If you have any doubts about how to form a command line with a path included, read the explanation of each element of the syntax. To make path specification more meaningful, you can follow three guidelines for specifying a path:

- If the path specifier begins with the backslash character (\), DOS interprets the path as being from the root.

> ### *Specifying a path in the syntax line . . .* (cont)
>
> - If the path specifier does not begin with the \, DOS interprets the path as being relative from the current directory.
>
> - If the path specifier is omitted, DOS assumes that the path is the path of the current directory and that you are supplying the object of the command's action in a command line parameter. The object may be a file name and extension, or in the case of the directory commands, a directory name.

Making Directories with MKDIR (MD)

Because the only automatically available directory on a DOS disk is the root, any additional directories must be added by you. DOS provides the internal MKDIR, or MD, command which you use to tell DOS to make a new directory.

The MKDIR and MD names for this command are identical in operation. You can use either name for the command.

When you issue the MKDIR command, you are instructing DOS to add a new subdirectory to some part of the file-system tree. Remember that any time you can use MKDIR, you can use MD in its place. The following syntax and examples use the MKDIR version of the command. The syntax for the MKDIR command is as follows:

MKDIR *d:path***directoryname**

d: is the optional target-drive specifier containing the disk where the new directory is to be added. If *d:* is omitted, the default drive is used.

path\ is the optional path specifier to which the new directory will be added.

directoryname is the name for the new directory; a directory name must be given.

The length of the full path (drive, path, and new directory name) must not exceed 63 characters, including delimiters. The full path name is the measure for length. If you are creating a directory relative to your current directory, you must count your current directory's full path length from the implied root \ character as being part of the 63-character limit.

About relative paths . . .   When you begin a path specifier with the \ character, you are telling DOS how to locate the directory or file from the root directory. DOS provides another way to specify a path that takes advantage of your current directory. The second way to specify a path is the *relative* way. Because DOS tracks your current directory for each disk on your system, you do not have to give the path that leads to the current directory for DOS to know where you are.

If you specify a path that does not begin with the \ character, DOS assumes that you are specifying a path relative to your current directory. For instance, if your current directory is \DOS and you want to add the directory \DOS\DRIVERS, you can get the job done by issuing the command **MKDIR DRIVERS**. Notice that there is no leading \ in front of the new directory name DRIVERS. Remember that DOS expects directory references in commands to be a chain of directory names starting at the root and separated by the \. When you omit the leading \, DOS adds the current directory's path to your path specifier to form the complete path specifier.

Relative path specifiers work with other DOS commands besides MKDIR. You will see examples of relative paths as path specifiers in other examples.

Understanding the Operation of MKDIR

When you issue the MKDIR command, DOS does some work behind the scenes. First, DOS verifies that the given (or implied by default) parent directory exists. DOS will not allow you to create two directory levels with one command. Then, DOS confirms that the new directory has a unique name. To confirm uniqueness, DOS looks in the proposed new directory's parent directory to ensure that the name is unique. The parent directory cannot contain an entry for a file with the same name as the proposed directory's name. Because subdirectories are files, DOS has no convenient means of separating a directory from a normal file with the same name. When creating a directory, a file name can be a possible naming conflict.

After confirming that the new directory name is unique in the parent directory, DOS allocates a file for the new directory and marks the new file's entry in the parent directory as a subdirectory. When the new directory file is allocated, the directory is technically created. MKDIR is not yet finished making the new directory, however. The new directory must be linked to its parent in another way.

DOS completes two entries in the new directory. The first directory entry's name is always . (pronounced "dot") regardless of the true name of the new directory. Except for the name difference, the dot entry in a subdirectory is the same as the subdirectory's entry in its parent directory. DOS uses a directory's . entry internally.

The second entry is always named .. (pronounced dot-dot). DOS can use this dot-dot entry to find the current directory's parent directory regardless of what that parent directory is named.

About the . and .. entries . . . Every subdirectory you create automatically contains the **.** and **..** entries. If you use the DIR command to view a subdirectory's file entries, you will always see the **.** and **..** entries. You won't be able to delete these two entries, but you never have to. DOS manages them.

The usefulness of the **.** and **..** entries may not be immediately obvious. On the command line, COMMAND.COM accepts the **.** and **..** entries as legitimate parts of path specifiers. By using the dot-dot alias as a path specifier, you can access the parent directory of your working directory—no matter at what point in the directory tree your working directory is located. (This same shorthand mechanism is available to DOS for internal use as well.) You will see some examples of **..** aliases in commands in this chapter's examples.

Understanding the General Rules of MKDIR

- MKDIR and MD are different names for the same command. Both commands produce identical results.

- All characters allowed in a normal file name can be used in a directory name.

- A directory name cannot be the name of a standard DOS device such as AUX, PRN, and CON.

- A directory name cannot duplicate a file name in the intended parent directory.

- The specified or implied parent directory of the intended directory must exist. MKDIR cannot make more than one directory at a time. On a disk with only a root directory, for example, the command **MKDIR \PROG\DATA** will not work.

- MKDIR (MD) does not change the current directory to the new directory. To change to the new directory, use CHDIR (CD).

Creating a Directory with MKDIR

For this example, assume that you are currently logged to the root directory of a newly formatted floppy disk in drive A. If you are using DOS on a hard disk, the examples that follow assume that you have established a path to the directory that contains the external DOS commands with PATH (see Chapter 7). To create the directory \DATA on the disk in drive A, enter the following command:

MKDIR \DATA

DOS will make the new directory—DATA—on the disk in drive A. You can issue a DIR command to see the new directory. Another way to confirm the new directory's existence on drive A is to enter the CHKDSK command from the DOS directory of your hard disk. The following command produces a report of the disk in drive A:

C:\DOS\CHKDSK

DOS displays the following:

```
730112 bytes total disk space
  1024 bytes in 1 directories
729088 bytes available on disk
655360 bytes total memory
603152 bytes free
```

Notice that the available space of this disk has been reduced by 1K because DOS allocated a two-sector cluster to the newly created \DATA directory. DOS allocated disk space to the directory because a subdirectory is actually a file with special attributes.

You can achieve the same result by issuing the MKDIR command while logged to the root directory of drive A. You use the relative path form of a path specifier as in the following:

MKDIR DATA

The directory is created directly from the root even though no disk name or beginning backslash is given in the command line. DOS uses the current (default) drive, drive A, and makes the directory relative to the current directory, the root. If you do not specify a path, DOS makes the current directory the parent directory of your new directory.

Changing the Current Directory with CHDIR (CD)

DOS remembers the current directory path as well as the current drive name. You issue the CHDIR or CD command to change the current directory to a new current directory. The directory you make current with CHDIR is the directory that DOS will search first to find files if you omit a path specifier in most commands.

 Both CHDIR and CD initiate the same command; their usage is identical.

The CHDIR command is the hierarchical directory system's navigation command. It is the command you use to position yourself in different working directories.

If you use the CHDIR command with no path specifier, DOS will report the current directory's path name for the specified or default drive on the display. CHDIR alone (with no parameters) is the "Where am I?" command. Issuing only CHDIR tells DOS to report where commands using no drive and path specifiers will do their work. Using only CHDIR (no parameters) in the command line does not change your current directory.

The syntax for CD or CHDIR is as follows:

CHDIR *d:path*

d: is the optional drive-name specifier. Use of the CHDIR command with a drive specifier and no path specifier will not log the default drive to the drive in the drive specifier. If you omit the drive specifier, DOS uses the logged disk.

path is the name of the directory you want to make the default directory on the disk in drive *d:*. The path specifier can begin with the **..** alias.

Understanding the Operation of CHDIR

DOS stores the name of the current directory in an internal location. When you boot your PC, DOS makes the root directory the default, and CHDIR stores the new directory name internally. If you omit the path, and DOS must provide a path for a command line, DOS receives the current value of the path.

Each drive that DOS recognizes on your system has its own current directory value stored by DOS. When you issue CHDIR with a path specifier, but no drive specifier, DOS first consults the logged drive storage area to determine which drive is the current drive. When DOS knows the current drive, DOS verifies that the path from the CHDIR command exists. If the path is not found, DOS issues the `Invalid directory` message and does not change the current directory, which is stored internally. If the path does exist, DOS stores the path's name in the internal storage area as the current directory.

If the CHDIR command is issued with no parameters, DOS determines the logged disk internally, finds the name of the logged disk's current directory, and then displays the current directory. CHDIR issued with only a drive parameter will report the specified drive's current directory.

Understanding the General Rules of CHDIR

- CHDIR and CD are different names for the same command. Both names produce identical results.
- The drive and path specifiers in the command line must be valid.
- If the path specifier begins with a \, CHDIR assumes that the directory specified in path is absolute from the root.

- If the path specifier does not begin with a \, CHDIR assumes that the directory given in path is relative from the current directory.

- When the path specifier is omitted from the command line, CHDIR reports the current working directory for the disk in the drive specifier.

- When the path specifier and the drive specifier are omitted from the command line, CHDIR reports the current working directory of the logged drive.

You can always change to the root directory of the logged disk by typing **CHDIR ** or **CD **.

Using the Two Forms of CHDIR To Change Directories

CHDIR has two operational forms. One form returns a report of a disk's logged directory's path name. The second form of CHDIR replaces a disk's logged directory with the directory given in the command line. The action of the command in the two cases is identical.

Suppose that the current directory on drive A is \DIR1. To receive a report of the logged (default) directory of a disk, you issue the CHDIR command in the following form:

CHDIR A:

CHDIR reports drive A's logged directory as the following:

    A:\DIR1

Suppose that the logged disk is drive C, and that the current directory of C: is \KEEP. To see the default directory or working directory (the one where DOS will carry out commands if no drive and path specifiers are used in a command that accepts them), issue the command in the following form:

CHDIR

CHDIR reports as follows:

    C:\KEEP

To change the default directory of the disk in drive A to \FILES when the logged drive is C:, issue the command in the following form:

CHDIR A:\FILES

DOS changes the default directory in A: to \FILES. To confirm the change, issue the command in the following form:

CHDIR A:

CHDIR replies as follows:

    A:\FILES

The subdirectories \WORDS\MEMOS and \WORDS\DOCS both have \WORDS as their parent directory (as their names imply). To change the directory in the current drive C from \WORDS\MEMOS to \WORDS\DOCS, issue the command in the following form:

CHDIR ..\DOCS

Notice that the alias for the parent directory (.. with no leading \) of the current directory acts as a shorthand substitute for the same full command you issue in the following form:

CHDIR \WORDS\DOCS

To change from the \WORDS\DOCS directory on the current drive to \WORDS (the parent directory of \WORDS\DOCS), you issue the command in the following form:

CHDIR ..

DOS will log \WORDS as the current directory of the logged disk. The use of the .. alias as the only parameter of the command always logs to the parent of the current directory, unless the current directory is the root. The root has no parent.

Listing Directories with TREE

The files in your hierarchical directories probably are (or will be) organized in a manner similar to the way you would physically organize floppy disks. Perhaps you keep subdirectories for letters, for applications programs, for memos, or many other categories just as you would keep disks with categories of files. As the number of directories and files grows, however, your ability to remember which directory holds which file decreases. Instead of asking yourself which disk holds your file, your question becomes "Which directory holds my file?"

DOS provides an external command—TREE—that lists all the directories of a disk. TREE will also list the files in the directories. If you have a hard disk computer, you will find the TREE command especially useful.

TREE's command syntax is as follows:

TREE *d:path\ /F/A*

d: is the optional name of the disk drive that holds the directories you want to list. If you omit *d:*, TREE lists the directories on the current disk drive.

TREE V3.3 and earlier versions accept only the single switch */F*, which directs TREE to list the *files* in the directories. Use this switch if you are trying to locate a file. If you do not give the switch, TREE displays only a list of the disk's directories—not the disk's files.

TREE with MS-DOS V3.3 and PC DOS V4.0 accepts the optional *path* specifier. The path specifier names the directory where TREE starts processing the listing. If the path specifier is omitted, TREE begins processing from the root directory.

In V4, TREE's output displays the directory tree with line graphics characters. The */A* switch available with V4 enables you to use an alternate graphics character set of "typewriter" characters.

Understanding the Operation of TREE

TREE is not the same as the DIR command; you do not give a path or file name with the drive name. The TREE command—available with PC DOS through V3.3 and MS-DOS through V3.2—automatically starts its listing with the root directory of the specified or current disk drive; you do not give TREE the choice of where it starts. Also, you cannot specify a file for which you want to search. With TREE, you get an all-or-nothing listing of the disk's hierarchical directory specification.

MS-DOS V3.3 and DOS V4 accept an optional path specifier which causes TREE to list the directory structure for the specified directory and lower directories. With certain implementations of MS-DOS V3.3 and DOS V4, the /F switch displays the file names of each directory in a wide format next to each directory (see fig. 8.1). This feature compresses TREE's lengthy /F report format.

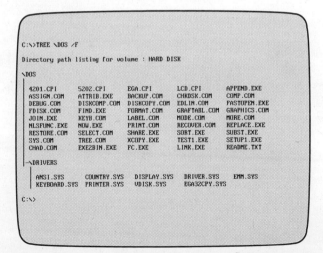

Fig. 8.1

The output of **TREE /F** *showing listed files.*

The MS-DOS V3.3 and DOS V4 TREE listing uses line drawing characters to draw the tree structure (see fig. 8.2). With V4, if you specify the /A switch with V4, TREE displays line drawing characters which consist of normal keyboard characters (see fig. 8.3). Although the characters produced by the /A switch are not as well suited to drawing lines as TREE's default characters, the characters produced by /A can be printed on any printer. If your printer does not follow the IBM printer character set for extended (ASCII 128 or greater) characters, use the command **TREE /A >PRN** to direct the output to your printer.

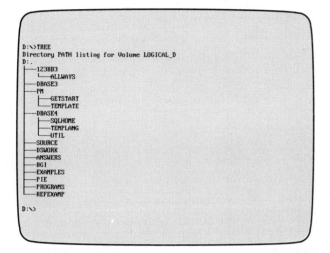

```
D:\>TREE
Directory PATH listing for Volume LOGICAL_D
D:.
├───123BB3
│   └───ALLWAYS
├───DBASE3
├───PM
│   ├───GETSTART
│   └───TEMPLATE
├───DBASE4
│   ├───SQLHOME
│   ├───TEMPLANG
│   └───UTIL
├───SOURCE
├───DSWORK
├───ANSWERS
├───BGI
├───EXAMPLES
├───PIE
├───PROGRAMS
└───REFEXAMP

D:\>
```

Fig. 8.2

The TREE command showing line graphics characters.

```
D:\>TREE /A
Directory PATH listing for Volume LOGICAL_D
D:.
+---123BB3
|   \---ALLWAYS
+---DBASE3
+---PM
|   +---GETSTART
|   \---TEMPLATE
+---DBASE4
|   +---SQLHOME
|   +---TEMPLANG
|   \---UTIL
+---SOURCE
+---DSWORK
+---ANSWERS
+---BGI
+---EXAMPLES
+---PIE
+---PROGRAMS
\---REFEXAMP

D:\>
```

Fig. 8.3

*The output of **TREE /A** showing alternate graphics characters.*

181

Using TREE To View a Disk's Hierarchical Structure

The following examples show the TREE command used on a practice disk. The example provides a display similar to that found with PC DOS V3.3. For DOS V4, TREE's output uses block graphics and indenting to show the hierarchical nature of the directory structure a bit more clearly.

The first example shows the output of the command **TREE A:**

```
C>TREE A:
DIRECTORY PATH LISTING FOR VOLUME PRACTICE
Path: \COMS
Sub-directories:  SAMPLES
Path: \COMS\SAMPLES
Sub-directories:  TEST
Path: \COMS\SAMPLES\TEST
Sub-directories:  None
```

The next example shows the output of the TREE command when the /F switch is included:

```
C>TREE A: /F

DIRECTORY PATH LISTING FOR VOLUME PRACTICE
Files:           None
Path: \COMS
Sub-directories:  SAMPLES
Files:           COMMAND .COM
    ASSIGN   .COM
    BACKUP   .COM
    BASIC    .COM
    BASICA   .COM
    CHKDSK   .COM
    COMP     .COM
    DEBUG    .COM
    DISKCOMP.COM
    DISKCOPY.COM
    EDLIN    .COM
    FDISK    .COM
    FORMAT   .COM
    GRAFTABL.COM
    GRAPHICS.COM
    KEYB     .COM
    LABEL    .COM
    MODE     .COM
    MORE     .COM
    PRINT    .COM
```

```
     RECOVER  .COM
     RESTORE  .COM
     SELECT   .COM
     SYS      .COM
     TREE     .COM
Path: \COMS\SAMPLES
Sub-directories:   TEST
Files:             MORTGAGE.BAS
Path: \COMS\SAMPLES\TEST
Sub-directories:   None
Files:             BASICA   .COM
```

CHKDSK /V is the "verbose" mode of CHKDSK. CHKDSK /V produces a list of directories and their files similar to that produced by TREE.

Controlling the Output of TREE with Filters and Redirection

With TREE (and CHKDSK /V), the resulting output can be lengthy. This type of output is ideally suited for redirection. Redirection is the sending of input or output of a command to other than the device that the output or input normally goes. Filters are special DOS commands that intercept output and perform an additional operation on it. You can, for example, use the MORE filter to display one screen's worth of information at a time. The normal output of TREE might scroll off of the screen too fast to be useful. MORE intercepts the output and sends it to the screen a few lines at a time. The command syntax for using MORE for output redirection with TREE is the following:

TREE | MORE

You can redirect the output of TREE to the parallel printer device with this command:

TREE > PRN

You can place TREE's output into a disk file with this command:

TREE > treelist.txt

If you store the output in a disk file, you can print the output at any time. It's a good idea to occasionally run TREE on your hard disk to get a printed copy of your disk's entire contents, which you can keep near your computer. This type of output is a good road map of your hard disk's structure and can help coworkers or friends when they must use your computer.

183

Removing an Unneeded Directory with RMDIR (RD)

When you need to remove a directory from your directory tree structure, use the RMDIR or RD command.

The two command names RMDIR and RD are different names for the same command; the action of both names is identical.

RMDIR removes directories that are at the end of a path branch of the directory tree. In other words, you can remove a directory at the lowest level of a directory path. Just as you can create a directory structure with MKDIR, you can remove a directory structure with RMDIR. RMDIR lets you rearrange your directory system if you change your mind about your current choices for directories or their names.

DOS does not provide a command to rename directories. To rename a directory, you must remove it and then create a new directory with the desired name.

The syntax for RMDIR is as follows:

RMDIR *d:path***directoryname**

d: is the optional drive name that holds the disk where the command will search for directory to be removed. If *d:* is omitted from the command line, DOS assumes that the current (logged) disk holds the directory to be removed.

path\\ is the valid, existing path to **directoryname**. If the path specifier is omitted, DOS assumes that **directoryname** is a subdirectory of the current directory of *d:*. If *path* begins with a backslash (\\) character, DOS assumes that the path to the directory name is absolute from the root. If the path specifier does not begin with a backslash, DOS assumes that the path to the directory name is relative from the current directory of *d:*.

directoryname is the name of the directory to be removed. The directory name is required in the command line.

Understanding the Operation of RMDIR

Deleting a subdirectory is similar to deleting a user file. Subdirectory entries are special files to DOS. Unlike user files, however, subdirectories may contain user files *and* subdirectory entries. DOS will not "orphan" a subdirectory's files and lower subdirectories by simply deleting the subdirectory as it does a user file.

When you issue the RMDIR (RD) command to delete a subdirectory, DOS checks to ensure that the subdirectory is empty.

An empty subdirectory will contain the **.** and **..** file entries, but DOS knows that these two entries are part of the subdirectory bookkeeping function. The presence of only the **.** and **..** files in the directory tell DOS that the directory is empty.

DOS also checks to ensure that the current directory is not the directory you are deleting. You can't delete a current directory.

Hidden files which do not appear in a DIR command listing of the directory are considered user files; the directory cannot be removed if it contains hidden files. Use the CHKDSK command to discover the presence of hidden files on a disk.

After determining that the subdirectory to be deleted is empty, and not the current directory, DOS removes the directory from the file system.

Understanding the General Rules of RMDIR

- The directory you remove must be empty.
- The root directory is not a subdirectory. You cannot remove a root directory.
- The number of characters in the full path name (drive, path, and directory) to be removed cannot exceed 63.
- A directory affected by a SUBST command cannot be removed.
- Do not remove directories from a drive which is affected by a JOIN or ASSIGN command.

The SUBST, JOIN, and ASSIGN commands are covered in Chapter 13.

Deleting an Empty Directory with RMDIR

When you are maintaining files, you may create a directory to contain files for a special purpose of limited duration. Perhaps you keep in a special directory a few files that need to be checked. After you check the files, you no longer need to keep the files separate, or you may not need the files at all. The directory itself may have no further use to you, and you now want to remove the directory from your disk.

As an example, assume that drive E of your system includes the directory \PROLOG\DSWORK\DONE, which contains program files which have been checked by their author. The files and the directory are no longer needed, so they can be removed. You can log to drive E and change to the \PROLOG\DSWORK directory by using the following command:

CHDIR \PROLOG\DSWORK

You will then be logged to the parent directory of \PROLOG\DSWORK\DONE. Because the directories in this example do not use the dot (.) character as an extension delimiter in their names, you can see the directory to be deleted in its parent directory's listing by using the following command:

DIR *.

DOS reports the directory on-screen as follows:

```
Volume in drive E is LOGICAL E
Directory of  E:\PROLOG\DSWORK
.            <DIR>        7-05-89    11:54a
..           <DIR>        7-05-89    11:54a
DONE         <DIR>        7-11-89     9:42a
       3 File(s)     200704 bytes free
```

The directory to be deleted, DONE, is displayed in this DIR listing because the *. wild card parameter for DIR displays files and directories with no extensions. You know you are in a subdirectory's parent directory when the subdirectory's name appears in a DIR command with no path specifier.

From the parent directory of the directory to be deleted, you can issue the RMDIR command with no drive and path specifiers as in the following:

RMDIR DONE

DOS may respond with the following message:

```
Invalid path, not directory,
or directory not empty
```

This DOS message tells you that one of the following situations is the case:

1. The full path name you gave (or that was implied by default) is not on the disk.
2. The full path name you specified names a file, not a directory.
3. The directory you are asking DOS to delete still contains files other than the . and .. entries.

You must determine which message applies to your situation by using the process of elimination. Don't worry. The process is easy. Simply keep these checks in mind.

First, check the current directory with the CHDIR (no path specifier) command. Or, you can look at the prompt (if you have incorporated a current directory indicating the PROMPT command) to verify that the path is valid. If your current directory isn't what you think it is, you may be logged to the directory you want to delete. Use CHDIR to get to the parent directory of the directory you want to delete and try again.

If you still get the error message, the directory you are trying to delete may not exist. By looking at the parent directory with DIR and seeing that the directory (\DONE in this case) is listed as a directory, you can be assured that the directory name you are using really is a directory, not a file name. If the directory isn't in the full path you think it is, use TREE to find it.

The remaining error possibility of the message indicates that the directory is not empty. To determine whether the DONE directory contains user files or subdirectories, you can change to that directory by using the following command:

CHDIR DONE

Notice that you did not have to give a absolute path to change to DONE. DOS changed to DONE relative to the current directory. You can accomplish the same directory change by issuing the following:

CHDIR \PROLOG\DSWORK\DONE

This second form you will recognize as the absolute path form of CHDIR. Either form will work in this example. When you are logged to DONE, issue the DIR command for all files. For this example, you will see the following directory listing:

```
Volume in drive E is LOGICAL E
Directory of  E:\PROLOG\DSWORK\DONE
.            <DIR>        8-11-89    10:23a
..           <DIR>        8-11-89    10:23a
DWIMDOS PRO     3439      6-03-89     5:23p
DWIM1   PRO     5414      6-04-89    11:07a
DWIM2   PRO    11625      6-06-89     5:39p
        5 File(s)     200704 bytes free
```

The directory listing of the DONE directory shows that the directory is not empty. You can erase all files that contain the .PRO extension to empty the directory (erasing files is covered in the next chapter); then verify that it is empty by issuing another DIR command. The DIR command will report the following:

```
Volume in drive E is LOGICAL E
Directory of  E:\PROLOG\DSWORK\DONE
.            <DIR>        8-11-89    10:23a
..           <DIR>        8-11-89    10:23a
        2 File(s)     255280 bytes free
```

Now only the . and .. alias directory entries remain. You can change to the parent directory by using the following shorthand command:

CHDIR..

From DONE's parent directory, you can remove the now empty DONE with the following command:

RMDIR DONE

The E:\PROLOG\DSWORK\DONE directory is removed.

Trying Hands-On Examples

The hypothetical examples given with the explanation of the directory-management commands are good for illustrating how the commands work, but hands-on examples that you can try are helpful as well. The exercise in this section is one that you can try because it uses a practice disk in drive A. You will be able to try the MKDIR, CHDIR, TREE, and RMDIR commands on a disk that won't be hurt by command mistakes. The exercise assumes that DOS is in drive C and that a PATH command tells DOS where the external FORMAT, LABEL, and TREE commands are located on drive C.

If you don't have a hard disk, but you have two floppy disks, use DOS in drive A and perform the exercise on a disk in drive B. B: should be your logged drive. You will need to give the location of the drive that contains your external commands when using the FORMAT, LABEL, and TREE command, as in **A:TREE**. Be sure that your working DOS disk is write-protected.

If you have only a floppy drive, you can use drive parameters that make DOS use the one drive as two. DOS will be on the disk designated as A. Start by formatting a disk with the command **FORMAT B:**. Log to drive B. DOS will ask you to insert the disk for B:. You leave the newly formatted disk in the drive. When you issue the TREE and LABEL commands, issue them as **A:TREE** and **A:LABEL**. DOS will ask you to insert the disk for drive A:. At that time, remove the practice disk and insert the DOS disk. Be sure that your working DOS disk is write-protected.

Your version of DOS may produce slightly different messages and displays as those shown. As usual, these differences are minor and won't affect the exercise.

Preparing the Exercise Disk

For this exercise, to avoid disturbing a useful disk, you should prepare a blank or surplus floppy disk. If you have a formatted blank diskette, you can skip this part of the exercise. If you are using a diskette that is already formatted, use the DIR command on the diskette to ensure that it is empty.

Insert the blank disk in drive A and issue the following command:

FORMAT A:

DOS responds with the following message:

```
Insert new diskette for drive A:
and press ENTER when ready . . .
```

Press Enter; the formatting process will begin. When FORMAT is finished, you will see the following message:

```
Volume label  (11 characters, ENTER for none)?
```

Respond to this prompt by pressing Enter. You will add a volume label for the disk in a later step. DOS will report the results of the formatting of the floppy and prompt you with the following:

```
Format another (Y/N)?
```

Press N; FORMAT will terminate. You will see the DOS prompt again. Now, for the practice, issue the LABEL command as follows:

LABEL

DOS responds with the following:

```
Volume in drive A has no label
Volume Serial Number is 394A-17EE
Volume label (11 characters, ENTER for none)?
```

Enter the volume label as **PRACTICE**. You can use this disk later for other command practicing if you want, but for now, you will use it to work with the directory commands.

Issue the DIR command on the newly formatted disk and you will see the following:

```
Volume in drive A is PRACTICE
Volume Serial Number is 394A-17EE
Directory of  A:\
File not found
```

Notice that the directory report is for A:\. You might be used to reading this report as a report for the entire disk, but it is actually a report for the contents of drive A's root directory. The line `File not found` is a good indicator that the disk has no files or subdirectories, but remember that a hidden file will not be listed by DIR. Because this disk is freshly formatted, it contains no files or subdirectories, just the root directory provided by FORMAT.

Issue the following command:

MKDIR \LEVEL1

DOS will create a directory named \LEVEL1 that stems from the root directory. You should see your disk light come on momentarily as DOS writes the directory entry for

\LEVEL1 into the root. Now issue the DIR command again. The DIR report will look like the following:

```
Volume in drive A is PRACTICE
Volume Serial Number is 394A-17EE
Directory of  A:\
LEVEL1        <DIR>        10-31-89    4:54p
        1 File(s)     1457152 bytes free
```

Notice that the directory listing is still of the root of drive A. Making the new directory did not change the current directory from the root. The new directory is listed in its parent (the root) directory now. To make \LEVEL1 the current directory, issue the following command:

CHDIR LEVEL1

If you have set up your prompt with the command **PROMPT=pg**, your prompt should be A:\LEVEL1>. Notice that the path parameter for the CHDIR command did not begin with a \. DOS made the directory change by moving from the current directory's path, \, and adding the path parameter from the CHDIR command, LEVEL1. To DOS, the effective path of the command was \LEVEL1. In the command's case, using a relative path parameter saved the \ keystroke.

Now issue the DIR command again. You see the following directory listing:

```
Volume in drive A is PRACTICE
Volume Serial Number is 394A-17EE
Directory of  A:\LEVEL1
.               <DIR>        10-31-89    4:54p
..              <DIR>        10-31-89    4:54p
        File(s)     1457152 bytes free
```

The listing verifies that the directory being shown is of A:\LEVEL1. The two "dot" files are the only files in the directory. Notice that the two "dot" files are listed as directories also. Remember that the . directory is representative "shorthand" for \LEVEL1 itself. To test this representation, issue the DIR command as follows:

DIR .

You will see the \LEVEL1 directory again. The . entry isn't of much use to you, but DOS makes use of it internally. The .. entry is representative of a directory's parent directory. Try the following command:

DIR ..

You will see the A:\ (root) directory listing again. DIR used the .. parameter as meaning "list this directory's parent directory's contents." Using .. as a path specifier is a quick way to reference a path from a parent directory while a subdirectory is the current directory.

Now you will add a subdirectory to \LEVEL1. Issue the following command:

MKDIR LEVEL2

Again, the path specified in the command is a relative path because no leading \ is used. DOS will create a new directory named \LEVEL1\LEVEL2 by adding the current directory, \LEVEL1, and the parameter of the MKDIR command, LEVEL2. Issue the DIR command now. You will see the following:

```
Volume in drive A is PRACTICE
Volume Serial Number is 394A-17EE
Directory of  A:\LEVEL1
.              <DIR>       10-31-89    4:54p
..             <DIR>       10-31-89    4:54p
LEVEL2         <DIR>       10-31-89    4:56p
      3 File(s)    1456640 bytes free
```

The new directory is listed in the \LEVEL1 parent directory. Now change to the new directory with the following command:

CHDIR LEVEL2

Again, the CHDIR parameter is a relative path to the new directory from its parent. Your DOS prompt should look like A:\LEVEL1\LEVEL2>. The disk now has two subdirectories as a single branch off of the root directory. It's important to note that LEVEL2 can only be reached by passing through LEVEL1. LEVEL1 is part of LEVEL2's path.

Now issue the **CHDIR** command to make the root the current directory. The prompt should be A:\> again. To see the directory structure that you have created on drive A, issue the TREE command. You should see something like the following:

```
A:\>TREE
Directory PATH listing
Volume Serial Number is 394A-17EE
A:.
└───LEVEL1
    └───LEVEL2

A:\>
```

You can see that the structure is a main branch from the root to \LEVEL1 and an additional branch from \LEVEL1 to \LEVEL1\LEVEL2. DOS enables you to create directories in a branch—one level at a time. The next command tries to create two levels of a new branch. Issue the following command:

MKDIR \SUB1\SUB2

Because \SUB1 has not been created, DOS refuses to create \SUB1\SUB2. You get the following error message:

```
Unable to create directory
```

If you create SUB1 and then SUB2, you will have no problem. Do so now with the following two commands:

MKDIR \SUB1

MKDIR \SUB1\SUB2

Notice that the parameters for the MKDIR commands use paths as absolute paths from the root. You can create these two directories with these two commands from any current directory on the disk. All of the path information necessary is in the parameters. None of the path information comes from DOS's current directory default. To see the new structure of the disk's directory system, issue the TREE command again. The output should be as follows:

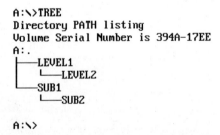

```
A:\>TREE
Directory PATH listing
Volume Serial Number is 394A-17EE
A:.
├───LEVEL1
│   └───LEVEL2
└───SUB1
    └───SUB2

A:\>
```

You can show the new branch in the directory tree containing \SUB1 and \SUB1\SUB2 by using the following command:

CHDIR \SUB1\SUB2

Your prompt should reflect the new current directory. To illustrate that you can manage other directories from the current directory, issue the following command:

DIR \LEVEL1\LEVEL2

DOS will display a listing of \LEVEL1\LEVEL2 even though the current directory for drive A is \SUB1\SUB2. You should note that the only two files in the listing are the "dot" files. In other words, the \LEVEL1\LEVEL2 directory is empty. Now you will delete \LEVEL1\LEVEL2. Issue the following command:

RMDIR \LEVEL1\LEVEL2

You can delete the directory because it is empty. Notice that the path specified in the RMDIR command is absolute. You must reference another branch in the directory tree from the root when your current directory is in another branch. For now, return to the root and look at the directory tree by issuing the following commands:

**CHDIR **

TREE

The directory tree now appears as follows:

```
A:\>TREE
Directory PATH listing
Volume Serial Number is 394A-17EE
A:.
├───LEVEL1
└───SUB1
    └───SUB2

A:\>
```

Notice that \LEVEL1\LEVEL2 is now gone. You have created and later removed part of the directory structure.

You can build further on the \SUB1 directory branch by adding an additional subdirectory to \SUB1. Issue the following command:

MKDIR \SUB1\SUB_TOO

\SUB1\SUB_TOO is at the same level as \SUB1\SUB2 and stems from the same branch. Both directories have \SUB1 as their parent directory. The output of TREE should show the new relationship as follows:

193

```
A:\>TREE
Directory PATH listing
Volume Serial Number is 394A-17EE
A:.
    ├──LEVEL1
    └──SUB1
          ├──SUB2
          └──SUB_TOO

A:\>
```

Make \SUB1\SUB_TOO your current directory with the following command:

CHDIR \SUB1\SUB_TOO

The DOS prompt should indicate the new current directory. You can make your current directory \SUB1\SUB2 using the parent "dot-dot" alias in the current directory. Issue the following command:

CHDIR ..\SUB2

The prompt should now indicate A:\SUB1\SUB2>. How did the **..** specifier in the CHDIR parameter work? Remember that in any subdirectory, DOS takes the **..** entry to represent the parent directory. In this case, the parent directory is \SUB1. When DOS saw the **..** in the path parameter, DOS assumed that \SUB1 should be substituted. The resulting parameter meant \SUB1\SUB2 to DOS. DOS was able to change to the other second level directory in the \SUB1 branch without seeing \SUB1 as a literal part of the CHDIR command's parameter.

Reviewing the Exercise

If you have completed the exercise, you have successfully created, navigated, and modified a disk's directory structure. When you work with directory management in your daily computer activities, the directory management you use will not be very different from that demonstrated in the exercise. If you observe the rules and syntax of the directory-level commands, you should be able to create a directory structure that fits your file organization categories perfectly.

A note from the author . . . If you're still a bit uncomfortable with the concept of hierarchical directories and their management, I suggest that you keep the practice disk for more exercises. You might find that practice results in proficiency in just a short amount of time. Don't be afraid to talk with other DOS users about their personal preferences for ways to arrange directories. There is no single best way.

I find that giving full, absolute path specifiers in directory commands is the surest way to work with directories. An absolute path specifier informs DOS of exactly which directory you intend the command to work with. You may want to develop the habit of using full path specifiers to avoid copying or deleting files in relatively specified directories. Don't worry about DOS getting a relative path specifier mixed-up. DOS will do what you tell it to do. Telling DOS what to do through full path specifiers helps to ensure that *you* aren't getting mixed-up.

If you use .. and relative path specifiers, always have a good sense of where you are in the directory system. There's no doubt that .. and relative paths save command keystrokes. When you use these convenient "short cuts," however, do so with care.

Putting Hierarchical Directories to Work for You

DOS supplies each disk with a root directory. Beyond the root, you can use the directory-management commands to create a directory tree in any architecture you want. DOS is flexible in allowing you to control the external look of your directory tree, while DOS manages the internal bookkeeping tasks of the DOS hierarchical directory system. Still, some planning on your part will help make your directory system design easy to use.

A note from the author . . . The following sections suggest some directory structures and tips that I use. Each DOS user is an individual and has individual tastes in creating a directory structure. You may want to consider the following suggestions for your use or as food for thought. If you already have your directories arranged, keep these suggestions in mind for the next time that you reorganize your hard disk.

Keeping a Clean Root

Because DOS defaults to the root directory of the boot disk, the root is a likely place for you to save some of your files. As long as you observe the limit to the number of root directory entries, DOS will not object. If you have a floppy-only system, you may occasionally find that the boot disk has inadequate room for all of the files you save to it. The root directory for a 360K floppy will hold 112 file entries. Both 1.2M and 1.44M floppies hold 224 entries. If you have the DOS program files on your boot floppy, you can quickly exhaust these numbers as you add small files to the boot disk. If you create a directory on your boot floppy called \WORK and log to \WORK to save files, you won't have the root directory's limit.

Subdirectories, because they are files and not fixed tables, can grow. Subdirectories do not have an entry number limit. You will most likely fill the floppy disk with file data before you fill its root directory with entries, but you will never fill a \WORK subdirectory with entries.

If you have a hard disk, consider keeping the root directory as clean as possible. Keep in the root only the few necessary files that DOS needs to get started. With an uncluttered root directory on your hard disk, you are likely to be a more efficient file manager.

Some files, however, need to be in the root of your boot disk. If you are using an AUTOEXEC.BAT file, it must reside in the root directory of the boot disk. The same rule applies to the CONFIG.SYS file, if you include one. If the disk is bootable, the hidden DOS system files will be located in the root also, but the FORMAT or SYS commands put them there. The system files will remain in the root unless you use special disk-editing software to change the hidden and system attributes so that you can erase them or move them. Be aware that if you erase or move the system files by using a third party program, DOS will not boot.

COMMAND.COM is normally in the root by virtue of the /S switch of the FORMAT command. The root of a bootable disk is a good place for COMMAND.COM. You do not have to leave COMMAND.COM in the root, however, if you make some entries in the CONFIG.SYS (Chapter 13) and AUTOEXEC.BAT (Chapter 12) files. A good directory for COMMAND.COM is \DOS. In your CONFIG.SYS file, add the following line:

SHELL=C:\DOS\COMMAND.COM C:\DOS /P

(See Chapter 13 for more information on CONFIG.SYS.)

When DOS is booted, it takes the assignment of the SHELL directive and uses the path and file name to find the command processor. Be sure not to misspell any parts of the full path name. DOS will lock up at boot time if the assignment to SHELL is a erroneous file. Of course, a working copy of DOS on a floppy will make any SHELL error (or any other hard disk boot failure) easier to recover from. Be sure that \DOS is present on the disk. Once you put this line in CONFIG.SYS, do not reboot until you have actually copied COMMAND.COM to \DOS from the root with the following command:

COPY \COMMAND.COM \DOS /V

The COPY command is covered in Chapter 9.

Notice the second occurrence of C:\DOS in the SHELL directive discussed previously. If you did not give this path in the SHELL directive, you would have to enter a line or alter an existing line in your AUTOEXEC.BAT file to change the COMSPEC environment variable. DOS uses the contents of COMSPEC to find and reload COMMAND.COM after COMMAND.COM is loaded at boot time; subsequently a transient (temporarily removable) portion of COMMAND.COM is pushed out of working memory by a large program that needs RAM space. When the program terminates, and the transient part of COMMAND.COM reloads into memory, DOS uses the COMSPEC variable to find COMMAND.COM.

At boot time, COMSPEC is set to whatever CONFIG.SYS says from the SHELL assignment. In this case, COMSPEC is C:\DOS\COMMAND.COM. If you added the COMSPEC setting to the AUTOEXEC.BAT file, be sure to find the COMSPEC line or add it if it doesn't exist yet. The line is as follows:

```
COMSPEC=C:\DOS\COMMAND.COM
```

Again, make sure that COMMAND.COM has been copied from the root to \DOS. With COMMAND.COM copied to \DOS, you can erase COMMAND.COM in the root. The erase command is as follows:

ERASE \COMMAND.COM

When you reboot, DOS finds COMMAND.COM in \DOS, and your boot disk's root directory is free of the file.

Some users keep device drivers, the programs specific to the operation of input/output devices, in the root directory. If you have these types of files in your root directory, you can move them. The next section discusses driver files.

It is not uncommon to find some batch files in a root directory. Batch files are ideal for relocation from the root because you can put them in another directory and let an alternate search path given in a PATH command lead DOS to them. The next section also gives some considerations for a home for batch files.

When you are copying a floppy disk full of files to your hard disk, it is easy to forget to use CHDIR to change the intended destination directory. If you do not use the full destination path name in the COPY command, but instead rely on the convenience of DOS defaults, you can end up with your root full of files from the floppy because of erroneous specifiers in COPY.

If your root is fairly clean (contains only a few files), you can recover from this kind of goof by copying everything in the root to an empty temporary subdirectory. When the subdirectory contains the root's normal files and the errant files, you can erase all files in the root. The hidden DOS files will remain because you cannot erase them. Now you copy the root's necessary files back to the root from the temporary directory. The root should contain only the files it contained before the goof. If you make a regular printout of the command **TREE/F**, you can double-check the root's content. When the root is back to normal, erase the temporary directory's contents. Now you're back where you started. Try your original (and erroneous) COPY command again, but this time with the correct destination parameters.

Including a Directory To Store DOS Programs

The DOS external commands and other DOS programs, such as BASICA (GW—BASIC), EDLIN, DEBUG, and setup programs, have one important element in common: these programs are all files that directly relate to the functions of DOS. Including a directory to hold these programs and their associated files is a good idea. The name for this DOS directory can be \DOS, and as the name implies, the \DOS directory is a subdirectory of the root. Some users follow the UNIX operating system's convention of keeping the utility commands in a directory called \BIN. Either name works from an organizational point of view.

When you issue a PATH command on the command line or in an AUTOEXEC.BAT file, position the \DOS entry right after the root entry. Don't forget to include the drive specifier with each alternative search path in the PATH command line. Because all of your external DOS commands are located in the second alternative search path, you should get a good response when you are working in DOS.

Many users prefer to make a subdirectory of \DOS called \DOS\DRIVERS to keep their DOS-included device drivers (those files with the SYS extensions) as well as device drivers included with applications programs or hardware. Because device drivers are loaded during the processing of CONFIG.SYS at boot time, you can place the full path name to the drivers you need in the CONFIG.SYS file and therefore eliminate the need to include a search path to the drivers with PATH. Chapter 13 covers the DEVICE directive and CONFIG.SYS. An example of a CONFIG.SYS line might be as follows:

```
DEVICE=\DOS\DRIVERS\MOUSE.SYS
```

Separating the drivers from the DOS commands can make your tree listings from the TREE command more indicative of each subdirectory's file group's function in the \DOS tree branch.

Batch files are like program files when DOS cannot locate them in the current directory. The search path set in the PATH command will locate and execute desired program and batch files located in one of the alternate search paths. Creating a \DOS\BAT directory (or similar name) for all batch files is a good idea.

Ensuring Uniform Directories for Applications Programs

Many of today's applications programs use subdirectories to store sample files, tutorials, auxiliary utilities, and your data for the applications. Most of these subdirectory-capable programs include default directory names that are used when you install the software. Most programs, however, give you the capability to choose your own names for the subdirectories instead of the default names. In most cases, you can let the package install with the default names for directories. Under one circumstance, however, you may not want to use the default names. You may want to control the names of the package's directories if you have an older version of the package and want to keep the older version. dBASE III Plus and dBASE IV, or Lotus 1-2-3 Release 2.1, 2.2, or 3, are examples of this type of situation.

If you need to keep operating an older version of a software package, for example, to maintain older data or program files, allowing the defaults to decide where the program and associated files will load is risking the loss of the old version's files. The new version may copy files with the same names as old files into the default directories because the default directories from the new version are named the same as your old directories.

Read the installation information for a package carefully before installing the software. You will not be happy if you "return" your way through the installation default directories and find that you cannot start your old version of dBASE or 1-2-3. The old version can be overwritten in installation. Pick a new set of directory names for the new package, such as \DB4 for dBASE IV or \123R3 for Lotus 1-2-3 Release 3. The contents of the previous versions' directories will then be unaltered by the installation process.

If you have an applications package that does not create directories during installation, you should think about how you want to structure your own directories for the package and its data. WordStar Release 4, for example, can be copied to a directory named \WS4. The directory or directories for your document files should be subordinate to the \WS4 directory so that all of WordStar's associated files will form a branch of the directory tree and not be spread across branches of a directory tree. You can create a \WS4\MEMOS directory for your memo documents and a \WS4\FORMS for office-form master documents.

Keeping associated files in the same branch of the directory tree also makes the job of backing up files easier. The command **BACKUP /S** backs up all files from the named directory and its subdirectories. You can make convenient partial interim backups of one branch of the directory tree if all associated files you want to back up are in that branch.

Using a Temporary Directory

On many occasions, a temporary directory comes in handy for holding files that you are readying for a final disposition. An example is the use of the temporary directory for recovering from an erroneous COPY command that deposited files in the wrong directory. You can create a directory called \TEMP to act as a temporary storage location for such files. A hard disk system with a single-floppy disk drive is not a convenient system on which to copy floppy disks. The drive gets the job done, but the COPY command, using the same drive for the source and the target, asks for multiple disk swaps. You can use the DISKCOPY command, which might require fewer swaps, but any fragmentation of the original disk is mirrored on the copy.

If you are making multiple copies of an original, a simple and speedy way to make the copy is to copy the floppy's source files to the hard disk's \TEMP directory. You can then copy the files from the \TEMP directory to the destination floppy in the sole floppy drive. The process reduces disk swapping, and the copies will be finished faster thanks to the hard disk's extra speed. When the copies are finished, you can erase the contents of \TEMP so that it will be ready for your next use.

Keeping Files in \KEEP

Sometime a file is like a favorite old shirt. You just don't know if you want to get rid of it. You leave it in a subdirectory like an old shirt in the corner of your closet. You might need it again, but then again, you might not. In either case, you may be too distracted by other issues to make a decision about its disposition when you stumble across it yet another time. Soon, you will change directories and forget about the file—that is—until your disk space gets short. Then you will be digging through the dark corners of your subdirectory closets trying to find a file or two to discard. And at "disk-space-running-out" time, you feel less equipped to make a decision about its importance than ever before. In confusion, you decide to erase the old file.

If this series of events strikes a familiar chord, you might consider creating a \KEEP directory. When you find a file that has questionable future use, but you don't want to be bothered with making a decision about its disposition at the moment, copy it to \KEEP. As always, make sure that the file will not overwrite a different file with the same name. You should always give your files descriptive names. Avoid generic names like TEMP and SAVE. You will see in the next chapter that you can always rename files as a function of COPY.

Erase the copy of the file from the subdirectory where you found it to keep that subdirectory uncluttered. When a week is up, \KEEP may have several files in it.

At this point, you may not have saved any disk space, but you have done some housecleaning in a few directories. Now comes the hard part. Before \KEEP contains more bytes of files than your floppy will hold on one disk, sit down and decide which files stay and which ones go. You will likely copy some back to their original directories. Some you will erase, and some you will copy to a "just-in-case" floppy disk for an archive copy. Before you store the floppy away, issue the following command:

DIR *d:*/**W >PRN**

d: is the name of your floppy disk. This command with the /W switch will send a wide directory report to your printer. Put the printed copy in the disk's envelope for reference. With the floppy disk holding the \KEEP "keepers," you are free to erase the contents of \KEEP. If you use this method regularly, you will develop a better sense of the files that are important; those that aren't as important, you can erase. The prices of floppy disks are low enough that you can offset the cost of a year's worth of \KEEP files on floppies the first time one of your \KEEP floppies contain that file it took you hours to create.

Summary

This chapter covered the commands which are used to manage the hierarchical directory structure. The hierarchical directory system is an important feature of DOS. Your computing experiences will be more productive when you understand and manage your directory tree effectively.

In this chapter, you learned the following key points:

❏ Subdirectories were introduced with DOS V2.0.

❏ DOS manages the directory structure internally; you manage the directory structure externally with commands.

❏ All DOS disks have a root directory.

❏ The MKDIR (MD) command creates (makes) new subdirectories.

❏ The CHDIR (CD) command changes default (current) directories.

❏ The TREE command reports your directory tree structure.

❏ The RMDIR (RD) command removes empty directories.

❏ A DOS-specific subdirectory gives better control of external DOS command path searches.

❏ Directories for applications software packages should be uniform in structure. Many applications create their own directories when the package is installed.

❏ Using a \TEMP directory can make file copying on a single floppy drive system easier.

❏ Using a \KEEP directory as part of a file's housekeeping method can keep directories less cluttered.

The directory-level commands lend themselves to practice and experimentation. You can use your existing directory layout to try variations of these commands. The concept of the path will be important to your understanding the disk-level commands presented in the next chapter. You may want to refer back to this chapter from time to time as you work with the commands that take directory parameters.

Keeping Files
in Order

9

After you have prepared your disk, installed DOS, created your key directories, and installed your applications, you are ready to start your favorite program and get down to the business of computing. In a sense, you have set up housekeeping on your PC. Working in your PC environment, however, can be like living in your home or apartment. You begin to accumulate files as by-products of computing in much the same way that you accumulate possessions as by-products of living. Most programs generate files as you work with them. You can dismiss your management responsibility for these files, as well as the program and DOS files you have on your system. If you do, however, your disks will soon be overflowing with your file "possessions."

If you don't think that you will accumulate enough files to get out of hand, take a moment to look in your garage, shed, or in that back closet. Are your possessions where you want them? Are they all useful? Can you get to them quickly when you need them? Do you remember what they are and what they are for? Are you going to go through them or rearrange them "one of these days?"

You can ask yourself these questions about your files as well. Fortunately, DOS provides useful file-management commands that make the job of keeping files in order a less tedious task than keeping your accumulated possessions in order. This chapter covers the file-level commands. DOS's file-level commands are important because you will spend most of your time during DOS sessions working with files. With a little time investment and a working knowledge of the DOS file-level commands, you will always have your computer house in order.

Key Terms Used in This Chapter

Text file   A file whose content in bytes is composed of ASCII characters which produce readable text.

Binary file   A file whose content in bytes is composed of instructions and/or data that has meaning to the PC. A binary file appears as gibberish to a human reader.

End-of-file marker   A control Z (^Z) ASCII character in a text file that denotes to DOS that the end of the usable portion of a file has been reached.

Concatenate   To join together. In DOS, to join two files into a third file.

Character string   A series or "string" of ASCII characters taken as a group.

Sorting   The alphabetical ordering of a list of items.

Changing File Names with RENAME (REN)

File renaming in DOS is a straightforward process. If you aren't satisfied with a file's name, you simply change it. The internal command RENAME or REN is your DOS tool to alter the name of an existing file. RENAME modifies a file's name, but does not change a file's content in any way.

The two command names, RENAME and REN, work in identical ways. You can use either command name to rename files.

RENAME is useful in situations other than the occasional renaming of a file when its current name isn't just right. You can rename files to temporary names or extensions in order to prevent their being overwritten in a COPY, XCOPY, or REPLACE operation. You can rename a file to a name that will match a wild-card pattern that matches other files in a directory. When a group of file names match a wild-card pattern, you can manipulate all of the files with one command. When you use wild cards with RENAME, it can be a very powerful command.

In its symbolic representation, RENAME works as in the following phrase:

RENAME from **EXISTING FILE SPECIFIER** to **NEW FILE SPECIFIER**

The syntax for the RENAME command is as follows:

RENAME *d:path***filename1.ext1 filename2.ext2**

The file to be renamed is on the disk in the default drive or *d:*, the optionally listed drive.

The file to be renamed is in the default directory or the directory listed in *path*.

The file is currently named **filename1.ext1**. Wild cards are allowed in the full file-name specifier in the file name, the extension, or both.

filename2.ext2 the new name for the file. The new file name can be literal (an actual new name) or contain wild cards. You cannot specify a drive or a path for **filename.ext2**.

Both **filename1.ext1** and **filename2.ext2** must be given.

Understanding the Operation of RENAME

RENAME changes the name in a file's directory entry. The file itself and its physical location on the disk, however, remain unchanged. RENAME takes the new file name either literally from the command line or by filling in wild cards and scanning the directory that holds the file(s) to be renamed for duplicate file names. If you use wild cards in the current file name or extension specifier, DOS will match and rename as many files as the wild cards indicate. Because a directory cannot have a duplicate file name, RENAME will not change a file to the new file name if the new file name already exists.

Understanding the General Rules of RENAME

- You can use the command names REN and RENAME interchangeably. Both command names produce identical results.

- You must supply an old file name and a new file name on the command line. Both the old file name and the new file name can contain wild cards for pattern matching.

- You cannot use RENAME to move a file from a directory or a disk to another directory or disk. To move a file, copy it to the new destination and erase the original file from the source location.

Renaming Files

The most controlled way to use the RENAME command is to issue the command with a literal old file name and new file name. You then do not have to be concerned

205

about wild cards causing unwanted renaming of pattern-matching file names. Suppose that you have a sales-report backup file, SALES.BAK, that has been prepared with your word processor. You can log to the file's disk and directory to take advantage of DOS's current defaults. Then, to give the file a more descriptive name, you can issue the following command:

RENAME SALES.BAK SALES_08.REP

You can be sure that only the desired file will be renamed because you literally specified the name of the file to be renamed. The resulting directory of the default directory will look something like this:

```
Volume in drive C is LAP TOP
Directory of C:\NAMES
.             <DIR>      8-29-89    9:29a
..            <DIR>      8-29-89    9:29a
SALES_08 REP     1664    8-01-89    2:51p
      3 File(s)    2009088 bytes free
```

After adding two more files to the default directory, you list the directory and see the following:

```
Volume in drive C is LAP TOP
Directory of  C:\NAMES
.             <DIR>      8-29-89    9:29a
..            <DIR>      8-29-89    9:29a
SALES_08 REP     1664    8-01-89    2:51p
SALES_09 REP      128    9-23-89    1:34p
EXPENSE  YTD    25372    9-23-89    8:00p
      5 File(s)    1978368 bytes free
```

Perhaps, however, you want to change the name of the EXPENSE.YTD file to a more descriptive extension with the same root name. You can specify the entire old name and an entire new name in the command line as in the previous example. An easier way, however, is to use the * wild card for the root file name and change only the extension. You can see from examining the directory listing that only one file with the root file name of EXPENSE is available for RENAME to process with a *.YTD specifier. You then issue the following command:

RENAME *.YTD *._89

The new file name for EXPENSE.YTD becomes EXPENSE._89. DOS took the *.YTD specifier to mean "Find all files with YTD extensions." DOS took the *._89 new file-name specifier to mean, "Rename the found files to _89 extensions, but keep their root file names the same."

RENAME will work in a similar way when you use the ? wild card in a file-name specifier. The ? wild card will match any character in the position that the ? occupies in the old file-name specifier. In the new file-name specifier, the ? wild card will carry that position's character out of the old file name.

One common RENAME mistake is to include a wild-card pattern that attempts to rename more than one file to the same new name. For example, if you want to indicate by the files' names that the REP extension files in this directory are no longer needed, you can use a wild card * to rename the REP files to the root file name of DONE. Because duplicate file names will appear in the directory, however, the following command will not work:

RENAME *.REP DONE.*

You immediately see the following message from DOS:

```
Duplicate file name or File not found
```

Although this message from DOS seems to indicate that the RENAME command has not been able to rename any REP files, the first REP file has been renamed. You can confirm this renaming by listing the directory with the DIR command:

```
Volume in drive C is LAP TOP
Directory of  C:\NAMES
.               <DIR>       8-29-89    9:29a
..              <DIR>       8-29-89    9:29a
DONE     REP     1664     8-01-89    2:51p
MTD_S_09 REP      128     9-23-89    1:34p
EXPENSE  _89    25372     5-10-89    8:00p
MTD_S_10_REP    1664    10-01-89    5:55p
        6 File(s)    1968128 bytes free
```

Notice that the first REP extension file in the directory has been successfully renamed to DONE.REP. RENAME issued the duplicate file message when attempting to rename the MTD_S_09.REP file. The resulting file name would have been a duplicate of the first REP file's new name; DOS will not allow two files called DONE.REP to be in the same directory.

If you are unsure as to which files a wild-card parameter will match, issue the DIR command using the exact wild-card pattern in the file specifier. DIR will then list the matching file names. Look these names over carefully to see if the RENAME command using the wild-card pattern will produce the result you expect.

Deleting Files with ERASE (DEL)

The ERASE and DEL commands remove files from the disk and return the space occupied by the deleted files back to your disk.

Both command names produce identical results; you can use ERASE and DEL interchangeably.

When you erase a file with ERASE or DEL, the file is no longer accessible by DOS, and the file's directory entry and storage space are available to DOS for additional storage of another file.

ERASE is a necessary and easy file-management command. Unless you erase unwanted or unnecessary files from a disk, the disk can eventually reach full storage capacity. If the disk is a hard disk, you need to erase files in order to use the disk for your primary data storage. ERASE is DOS's "throw-it-away" command.

Because ERASE destroys files, use the command with caution. ERASE allows wild cards in the file specifier. A momentary lapse of your attention while using ERASE can eradicate important data in the blink of an eye.

You can use either form of this command—ERASE or DEL. The syntax for the command is as follows:

ERASE *d:path***filename.ext** */P*

DEL *d:path***filename.ext** */P*

d: is the optional drive containing the disk which holds the file(s) to be erased. If you omit the drive specifier, the logged drive is used.

path is the optional directory path to the file(s) to be erased. If you omit the path specifier, the current directory is assumed.

filename.ext is the specifier for the file(s) to be erased. Wild cards are allowed in the file name and extension. A file specifier or a path specifier is required.

The */P* switch is available with V4 and later versions. Using the optional */P* switch causes ERASE to *pause* and display the name of each file to be erased before deleting the file. You answer Y to delete the file or N to leave the file intact.

Understanding the Operation of ERASE

When you issue an ERASE command, DOS locates the file's entry in the directory and marks the directory entry with a special internal indicator. DOS uses this indicator to search for available directory entries when a new file is being added to the directory. By reclaiming a deleted file's directory entry, DOS can control the expansion of a subdirectory or reclaim one of the limited root directory entries.

> **Tech note . . .** ERASE does not affect the contents of the file's allocated clusters. ERASE does not "record over" the file's data like erasing a cassette tape records over existing audio. The entire operation of ERASE involves altering DOS's bookkeeping records in the directory and the file allocation table (FAT). The directory entry for the file receives its special indicator, and the FAT cluster chain for the file is deallocated. DOS marks the file's clusters as being "free."

> **Tech note . . .** (cont.)
>
> Until another file is added to the directory or another file in any directory is expanded or added, the DOS bookkeeping records for the deleted file remain relatively intact. DOS will not, however, reverse the effect of erasing a file. To DOS, the file is gone even though the file's data is temporarily intact.
>
> Some special utilities available from third-party companies can "unerase" a file. These unerase utilities take advantage of DOS's internal file-erase methods by "fixing" the erased file's directory entry and reconstructing the erased file's cluster chain. If another file has been added, however, these unerase utilities cannot recover the erased file. If you are interested in an unerase utility, check with your dealer for a recommendation. Just remember that the unerase utilities must be used immediately if they are to work. Keeping proper backup files is the best insurance against the accidental erasure of a file.

Understanding the General Rules of ERASE

- ERASE will not erase files marked with the read-only attribute.
- ERASE will not remove a directory, erase a volume label, or erase a hidden or system file.
- If you type **DEL subdirectory_name**, DOS tries to delete all the files in **subdirectory_name**.
- When a file is erased, you cannot access the file through DOS. The file is effectively removed from the disk.
- Unless you use the /P switch (V4 only) or a parameter to include all files in a directory (such as *.*), ERASE silently erases a file(s) and issues no messages.

Erasing Unwanted Files

For an example of ERASE, suppose that you have completed and delivered a series of memos that you composed on your word processor. You want to keep the memo files on disk for your reference, but your word processor automatically creates a backup file, with a BAK extension, for each memo. Once your memos are safely delivered, you do not need the BAK files. You can erase the files with the BAK extensions one at a time, or you can issue the ERASE command as follows:

ERASE C:\WP*.BAK

In this command line, the C:\WP directory is assumed to contain the backup memo files. The *.BAK extension causes ERASE to match only the files with the BAK extension. When the command completes its work, the files with the BAK extensions are removed from the directory. Because this command line includes drive and path specifiers, you can issue the command from any logged disk and current directory and still erase the BAK files in C:\WP.

Viewing a Text File with TYPE

When you need to see the contents of a text file, you can use the TYPE command. TYPE gets its input from a file (or a device) and sends the ASCII interpretation of the file's content to the screen. You can use the MORE filter with TYPE to keep the file's text from scrolling off the screen as you view the file. You can also redirect the output of TYPE to your printer to produce a hard copy of the file.

Because TYPE enables you to see the contents of a text file, TYPE is an important file-management command. When you are cleaning up a directory or a diskette, you can use TYPE to refresh your memory about files whose names don't "ring a bell." When you are configuring your system, you can use TYPE to see the contents of your CONFIG.SYS and AUTOEXEC.BAT files. When you are installing a new applications program, you can use TYPE to see the latest instructions in the package's README.DOC or (equivalent) file. TYPE produces screen output of any character-based file.

Tech note . . . To DOS, a file is simply a stream of bytes. A byte can represent more than one kind of value in your PC. A byte can be encoded to represent a number, a computer instruction, a table, or even an ASCII character. Usually, computer professionals divide the representation categories of a byte into two general types: ASCII and binary.

An ASCII byte contains a bit code in its 8 bits that represents one of 256 possible ASCII characters. Files that are composed of bytes, all of which are ASCII representations, are called ASCII text files. The TYPE command works with ASCII text files. Not all ASCII codes, however, represent readable text characters such as letters, numbers, and punctuation symbols.

Some ASCII codes are device-control codes, which a device detects and uses to control its operation. Ctrl-S is such a control code; a device that detects Ctrl-S in a character stream stops sending its stream of characters. You use Ctrl-S to stop a display from scrolling off the screen. When the control characters are not being used for controlling a device, they can represent special characters on-screen, such as a smiling face or musical notes. Other ASCII representations make special characters on your screen, but have no device-control representations. These ASCII codes produce the lines and corners of boxes and other graphical characters.

Binary files, composed of bytes that represent instructions and data, do not have character equivalents for their contents. Only programs can read their contents meaningfully. If you were to force a binary file's content to be displayed as ASCII code, the display would be filled with random characters and graphic symbols. The display would be gibberish. When you use TYPE to display a binary file, you will see gibberish on your screen.

The syntax for the TYPE command is as follows:

TYPE *d:path***filename.ext**

d: is the optional drive that holds the disk containing the file to be typed. If you omit the drive, the default drive is assumed.

path is the optional path to the file to be typed. If you omit the path, the default directory is assumed.

filename.ext is the name of the file to be typed. You must name the file in the command line. Wild cards are not permitted.

Understanding the Operation of TYPE

TYPE is designed to display the content of a text file that contains ASCII characters. When you issue a TYPE command, DOS opens the specified file and sends the file's content to the output (normally the screen) as a stream of bytes. The bytes are displayed as ASCII characters. When DOS encounters a Ctrl-Z, the end-of-file character, the input file is closed, and the output terminates. You will learn more about the end-of-file character in this chapter's discussion of the COPY command.

When you use TYPE to view a text file, the file's content can fill the screen and begin to scroll off the screen faster than you can read it. DOS provides a solution to this problem through one of the special filter commands—MORE. MORE sends a screenful of a command's output at once and then pauses until you press a key. TYPE can be filtered by MORE in the following form:

TYPE AUTOEXEC.BAT | MORE

The | character in the command is the special DOS pipe character. A pipe character instructs DOS to send a command's output to the filter that follows the pipe character. Piping to MORE causes the output-character stream to be interrupted when the screen fills. Pressing any key starts the output again.

 If you use DOS redirection to send the output of TYPE to a printer, the printer may store characters faster than it can print the character stream. As a consequence of the printer's buffering of yet-to-be-printed characters, using Ctrl-C or Ctrl-Break will not immediately stop the printer.

Understanding the General Rules of TYPE

- Because TYPE is a character-based command, the output of TYPE stops when the first Ctrl-Z is encountered in the file being sent to a device as output. File bytes following the first Ctrl-Z will not be sent.

211

- You must give TYPE a literal file name. TYPE does not not accept wild cards in the file specifier. TYPE is therefore limited to a one-file-at-a-time use.

- TYPE interprets any file as a text file. If you use a binary file, such as a COM or EXE file as the file specifier, TYPE's output may produce graphical characters, control-character sequences, and beeps, and may hang your computer. A "hung" computer will not respond to keyboard input, and you will have to reboot.

- You can pause the output of TYPE by pressing Ctrl-S or Ctrl-Num Lock.

- You can terminate the output of TYPE by pressing Ctrl-C or Ctrl-Break.

Viewing the Contents of CONFIG.SYS with TYPE

To view the contents of a short text file, you can give a simple form of the TYPE command. In this example, suppose that you want to view the contents of your CONFIG.SYS file. Issue the following command:

TYPE \CONFIG.SYS

DOS sends the character content of CONFIG.SYS to the screen for you to view:

```
BUFFERS=15
FILES=15
DEVICE=\DOS\DRIVERS\EMM.SYS
DEVICE=\DOS\DRIVERS\ANSI.SYS
```

Using TYPE and Redirection

If you want a simple printed copy of a text file's content, you can redirect the output of the TYPE command to the printer using the special redirection character—the greater-than sign (>). Because TYPE does not format the text into pages, the printed output may not "break" at page boundaries. To print the contents of README.TXT, you can ensure that your printer is on-line and issue the following command:

TYPE README.TXT >PRN

The file is then printed by your printer. You can also redirect TYPE to another device such as COM1 or COM2. If you have a serial printer, see the MODE command in the Command Reference for more information.

Finding Strings of Text with FIND

FIND is another DOS filter command. FIND will find strings of ASCII text in files. The filter is often used in association with redirection and piping. FIND is very useful for occasions when you know some of the text that a desired file contains, but you can't recall which file contains the text. FIND, using the known text, will help you locate the file.

Issuing the FIND Filter

The syntax for the FIND Filter is as follows:

> **FIND** */C /N /V "string" d:path\filename* ...

"string" specifies the ASCII characters to be searched for. *d:path\filename* is the drive, path, and file name of the file to be searched. The ellipsis (...) indicates that more than one file can be specified.

The */C* switch changes the listing to a *count* of all lines that contain *"string"*.

The */N* switch changes the listing to include line *numbers* of the lines that contain *"string"*.

The */V* switch changes the listing to include all lines not containing *"string"*.

/C and */V* can be used together. The count displayed is the number of lines not containing *"string"*.

/V and */N* can be used together. The lines not containing *"string"* are displayed with their appropriate line numbers.

Understanding the General Rules of FIND

- Use FIND only on ASCII text files.
- The string parameter is case-sensitive. The string *LOOK* is not the same as the string *look*.
- The string is enclosed in quotes. To include a quote in a string, you type two quotes together (""). FIND will search for occurrences of ".
- The standard input device (keyboard) is used if *filename* is not specified.
- Wild cards are not allowed in *filename*.

Understanding the Operation of FIND

When used without switch options, the FIND filter reads each of the specified files and displays each line that contains a particular ASCII string. DOS takes the information that would normally go to the standard output and filters it. Lines that include the ASCII string are displayed on-screen.

If you use the /V switch, lines that include the ASCII string are not passed on to the standard output. The /C switch is used as a *counter*; the text itself is not passed to the screen. Use the /N switch to locate the line *numbers* within the text file. The line numbers assigned are the line numbers in the original text file, not just sequential numbers. For example, if the third, fifth, and sixth line in the text file contains the string, the line numbers displayed are 3, 5, and 6, not 1, 2, and 4.

Like the other filter commands, FIND is often used with redirection and piping. If you need to search a text file for lines that include certain information, it is probably more useful for you to redirect the output to a file or your printer. You can then use the list as a reference while you look at the whole of the original file using a text editor or word processor.

The FIND filter can also be used with text files as a word-search utility. Consider a situation in which you forget the name of the memo you sent to your boss. You know that it is either MEMO1, MEMO2, or MEMO3, and that you always use your boss' title *Supervisor*, in memos. You can use *Supervisor* as a search string. Type the following:

FIND "Supervisor" MEMO1 MEMO2 MEMO3

Each line in the files that contain the string *Supervisor* will be listed. The listing will be in the following form:

```
---------- MEMO1
---------- MEMO2
Supervisor of Communications
---------- MEMO3
```

The desired file is MEMO2. You can see that the line which contains the word Supervisor is listed. No lines are listed under MEMO1 or MEMO3.

Using FIND To Find Files On-Disk

The FIND command can be used to find on-disk all files that have a certain extension. To find all files that have the extension LET, type the following:

CHKDSK C: /V | FIND ".LET"

This command line forms the basis for a useful file-management tool. You can replace the search string with a string that will show you the files you want to find. The command actually pipes the output of CHKDSK to FIND. Because the /V switch is used with CHKDSK, FIND sees all of the full file names (including paths) on the disk. The search string filters all files with the extension LET and passes them to the screen.

Tapping the Power of COPY

The COPY command is the DOS workhorse. Copying files is a fundamental job for disk operating systems. DOS provides COPY with the capability to copy files as well as the capability to copy to and from logical devices. Figure 9.1 shows the COPY command used with a variety of possible inputs and two possible outputs. Three of the possible inputs consist of more than one file or logical device. DOS can join two or more inputs into one output in a process called *concatenation*. You may not ever need to use all of these COPY inputs and outputs, but they are available with the command.

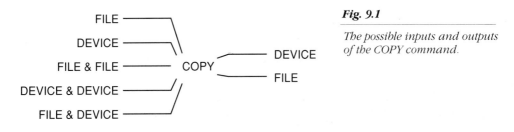

Fig. 9.1

The possible inputs and outputs of the COPY command.

A word about COPY's advanced features . . . When COPY concatenates two files, the files are joined in the output file. The files that DOS users most often concatenate are text (ASCII) files. COPY can concatenate a device's output and a file, a file and a file, or even a device's output to another device's output. The resulting output can go to a file or a device such as your printer. COPY is versatile when accepting inputs and providing outputs. You may only rarely use concatenation or device input in a COPY operation, but the capability is there.

COPY can selectively use either ASCII or binary mode for its inputs and outputs. Switches given with the command control COPY's mode selection. In ASCII mode, COPY interprets a ^Z (end-of-file marker) as the logical end of file and considers the current input file or device as finished. In ASCII mode, COPY places a ^Z as the last character in the output file or device data stream. Applications programs and DOS commands that use the ^Z end-of-file marker are accommodated by COPY. If you are worried about keeping these modes and mode switches straight, you shouldn't be. COPY uses binary mode unless you override the mode with a switch. Most users never issue a COPY command with a mode switch. Chances are good that you won't have to, either.

COPY can give the copied file a new name as part of the operation. The COPY command accepts wild cards in file specifiers to provide a versatile syntax. Through wild cards, COPY can include many source files. With drive and path parameters, COPY can reach any user file on a system from any logged drive and current directory. With a *.* source file-name specifier, COPY can copy all files from a fragmented diskette to a newly formatted diskette. By doing so, COPY eliminates any fragmentation of files on the second diskette. Even with the presence of the related commands DISKCOPY, REPLACE, and XCOPY, COPY is the most widely used file-copying command.

Don't worry about taking full advantage of COPY's range of features. In its basic form, COPY is a simple-to-issue, easy-to-understand command.

Issuing the COPY Command

In a symbolic representation, the simple COPY command looks like this:

COPY from *this source* to *this destination*

COPY always orders the parameter requirements in a direction of source to destination or target. When you include concatenation and the mode of reading and writing the files (or devices), COPY symbolically looks like this:

COPY from *source(s) in this mode* to *destination in this mode*

The symbolic mode for this example is either ASCII or binary for both the source and also the destination.

If you incorporate the symbolic view of COPY into syntax lines, you see the following syntax forms:

COPY *d1:path1***filename1.ext1**

d0:path0**filename0.ext0** */V*

For concatenation and mode control, you see the following:

COPY *d1:path1***filename1.ext1** */A/B* +

d2:path2**filename2.ext2** */A/B* +. . .

d0:path0**filename0.ext0** */A/B/V*

d1: and *d2:* are the optional source disk-drive specifiers. If you omit a source disk specifier, the logged drive is assumed.

path1\\ and *path2*\\ are optional source path specifiers. If you omit a source path specifier, the current directory is assumed.

The + character delimits source files that are to be concatenated.

filename1.ext1 and **filename2.ext2** are source file-name and extension specifiers. You must give a source path or file specifier.

The . . . signifies that other drive, path, and source file-name parameters may be included in a concatenation.

The optional /A switch invokes *ASCII* mode and affects the file specified directly preceding the switch and all files following the switch up to the file that precedes a subsequent /B switch.

The optional /B switch invokes *binary* mode and affects the file specified directly preceding the switch and all files following the switch up to the file that precedes a subsequent /A switch.

The optional /V switch causes COPY to perform a read-after-write *verification* of the output sectors of the destination file. The destination file is not compared to the source file(s) directly. Instead, DOS requests the disk's device-driver routine to make a validity check of the written data.

Understanding the Operation of COPY

COPY approaches its work serially; the command's operations occur one step at a time. The flow of COPY proceeds from source to destination. Internally, DOS assures that affected directories and FATs on the destination disk are updated correctly.

COPY does not work like DISKCOPY. DISKCOPY reads a track at a time and copies data as it is found. COPY consults the source directory and reads the source files in the order that they are found in the directory. DISKCOPY writes the destination disk with the data in an image of the source disk. COPY makes new directory entries and allocates destination files in the order that they are copied. By utilizing the FAT and directory of the destination disk, COPY can eliminate fragmentation of files when the destination disk is empty.

If the source has a reserved device name, COPY asserts the ASCII mode, reports the device's name on-screen, and awaits input from the device. If the source is not a device, COPY assumes that the source is a file. Unless a previous /A switch, an associated /A switch, or an associated + operator is present, COPY asserts the binary mode. If the current source is a file, COPY determines the full path specification for the source file, either from the command line or through defaults.

Data that is read from the input file or device is temporarily stored in a RAM buffer which fills during the input to COPY. When the buffer first fills or the end of the source file is encountered, COPY establishes the destination parameter.

If the destination is the device, COPY begins to write the contents of the buffer to the device until the buffer is empty. COPY then reads more data from the source; the cycle repeats until all data is copied from the source to the destination device.

217

If the destination is a file, COPY establishes the destination file's directory. COPY uses the given destination drive and path specifiers to locate the destination directory. Again, COPY will use default values if drive and path specifiers are omitted. The destination directory is searched from the top downward using the name of the destination file. If the destination file-name specifier contains wild cards, COPY uses the characters from the source file to match the wild-card patterns in forming the destination file name.

COPY will overwrite any existing file with the same name as the destination file unless the existing file has been made read-only through an ATTRIB command.

If you give the /V switch in the command, the copy is verified as an additional step.

Understanding the General Rules of Copy

- The source parameter must contain at least one of the following: a path specifier, a file specifier, or a device specifier

- If the source-file specifier is omitted, all files in the specified directory of the specified (or default) drive are copied. This situation is equivalent to supplying *.* as the source-file specifier.

- Additional source parameters can be specified using the + operator for concatenation.

- If the source-file parameter contains a wild card and the destination parameter is a literal file name, the destination file will be the concatenation of source files matching the pattern of the wild card.

- If COPY detects an attempt to copy a single source file to itself (same drive, directory, file name, and extension), the copy operation is aborted.

- When a device is used as a source, no drive or path specifiers should be used in the source specification.

- The optional destination parameter consists of a combination of drive, path, and file-name specifiers. An omitted drive or path specifier assumes the value of the default drive or directory. An omitted file-name specifier assumes the value of the source file-name specifier.

Respecting the COPY Command

COPY is certainly a versatile file-management workhorse. Yet even with its versatility, an errant COPY command can do nearly as much damage as an errant ERASE command, so be sure to treat COPY with respect. Many applications programs include warning messages as part of their internal file-copying commands. The DOS COPY command does not warn when it is about to overwrite existing files; it silently overwrites the files. If you confuse the source and destination when you are copying a file, you can easily copy an old file over today's work. You might not even notice the error until you need today's work. Not all mistakes with COPY, however, overwrite current data. Some mistakes just create file-management messes.

Relying on default drive and directory values when using COPY is convenient. Yet, if your current drive or directory isn't what you think it is, you can copy many files to the wrong disk or directory with one COPY command. The aftermath of cleaning the misplaced files from the erroneous directory or disk and getting the files into the correct directory or disk can be a tedious process. This can happen to you when you install new software. If you make a new directory for the package, but forget to change to the new directory with CHDIR, your next COPY command can make a mess. You will need to copy these errant files one by one to their correct directory home.

To avoid sending files to the wrong directory, check the name of the logged disk or directory. Don't forget to check the name of the current directory on other drives on your system as well. You might have forgotten that you changed floppies before a coffee break. Use the DIR command with drive and path parameters for the source and destination of your next COPY command. Viewing the directories will take a bit longer, but not as long as copying misplaced files one by one. For complete control of COPY, give the command drive, path, and file-name specifiers for both source and destination files.

Watch out for wild cards as well. You can select a source wild-card pattern that results in the inadvertent overwriting of destination files. For example, suppose that you have three reports and one graph in the files REPORT1.TXT, REPORT2.TXT, REPORT3.TXT, and REPORT3.PIX. You decide to save a standby copy of each file using a SAV extension. You issue the following command:

COPY REPORT?.* *.SAV

You intend for the ? wild card to differentiate the files by number after they are copied. The error in this reasoning is that both REPORT3.TXT and REPORT3.PIX will fit this source wild-card pattern and that both will be written to a file named REPORT3.SAV. The REPORT3.PIX copy will overwrite the existing REPORT3.SAV created as a standby copy of REPORT3.TXT. As a result, REPORT3.TXT will not have an equivalent standby copy.

Many COPY problems stem from the way a computer user develops patterns or habits when entering commands. If you are accustomed to copying a file from the default directory of your hard disk to the diskette in drive A, you are likely to develop a rhythm of entering the COPY parameters. When a different COPY situation arises, the conditioning of the previous rhythm may cause you to enter the accustomed parameters and rely on the accustomed defaults. Without thinking, you may press Enter and rapidly overwrite your good data with old data. Perhaps you pause before pressing Enter and review the command line for accuracy. If you do, you are to be congratulated. But if you get hasty from time to time, you might destroy some data with COPY.

Copying All Files in a Directory

As you add and delete files from a disk, the free space for new file information becomes physically spread around the surface of the disk. This phenomenon is called *fragmentation*. DOS allocates data storage space by finding the next available disk space. If the next available space is too small to hold an entire file, DOS uses all of that space and puts the rest of the file into the next available space. Fragmented files lower disk performance.

If you use DISKCOPY on a fragmented floppy disk, you get an exact image of the fragmented disk. To avoid copying this fragmentation, or to make an efficient copy of a fragmented floppy disk, use the COPY command. This example assumes that all of the source files are in the root directory of the source floppy. If necessary, format the destination disk and make sure that the disk contains enough room to hold all of the source files. Then copy the source files to the destination disk. To do so, place the source disk in drive A and the destination disk in drive B and type the following:

COPY A:*.* B:

This command copies all of the files on the disk in drive A to the disk in drive B, keeping the same file names. By changing to a directory on your hard disk, you can copy all of the files of the last example to that directory by using C: in place of B:. Remember, though, that you cannot use the COPY command to copy DOS's hidden system files. You need to use SYS instead.

Copying Single or Multiple Files from Disk to Disk

You can copy one file or many files to another disk for safekeeping, to move data to another computer, or for any other purpose. Simply use the COPY command with a file name or a wild card that matches the file(s) you want to move to the other disk. Put the disk with the source file(s) in drive A. Put the destination disk in drive B. Type **DIR A:** to view the files so that you can calculate the size of the file(s) you want to copy. Then type **DIR B:** to see if the destination disk contains sufficient free space. If sufficient space is on the destination disk, enter the COPY command. An example command is as follows:

COPY A:*.DOC B:/V

This command copies all files with the extension DOC to the disk in drive B, and then verifies the copy. The destination path and file name were omitted in this example, so DOS uses the current directory and accepts the original file names by default. You can omit the name of your logged drive from this example, but to be on the safe side, you should include it.

To copy one file from the source disk to a different destination disk you might enter the following:

COPY A:SPEECH.DOC B:/V

This command copies the SPEECH.DOC file from the disk in drive A to the disk in drive B. Again, the name remains the same. If you have a hard disk, you can use a command like this:

COPY A:SPEECH.DOC C:/V

This command line copies the SPEECH file from the floppy disk in drive A to the current directory of the hard disk. Similarly, you can copy from your current hard disk directory to a floppy disk:

COPY SPEECH.DOC A:

DOS finds the SPEECH file in the current directory of the logged drive C and copies it with the same name to the floppy disk in drive A.

Copying Files from Directory to Directory

One form of COPY that trips up many users is copying from one directory of a hard disk to another directory. For this example, assume that you want to copy the file C:\KEEP\SPEECH.DOC to C:\MISC\SPEECH.DOC. To take advantage of DOS defaults in the command, log to drive C: and use CHDIR to log to C:\KEEP. Now issue the following command:

COPY SPEECH.DOC \MISC

Figure 9.2 helps you visualize the directory tree of drive C before and after the command. DOS knows that SPEECH.DOC is located in the current directory of the logged drive, so you do not need to give source drive and path specifiers. \KEEP is also on the logged drive, so you do not need to give a destination drive specifier. You want the destination file to keep the name SPEECH.DOC, so you do not need to give a destination file specifier. DOS does not know the destination directory, however. Without a destination-directory specifier, DOS would use the current directory. Of course, DOS won't copy a file to itself. The destination path of \MISC is the only destination parameter that DOS needs to complete the command.

As with directory references, file references are more sure when you include the full path and file-name specifiers on the command line. Even though DOS supplies the defaults in this simplified COPY command, you can specify every part of the command and make sure that a surprise default will not deposit files in the wrong directory.

221

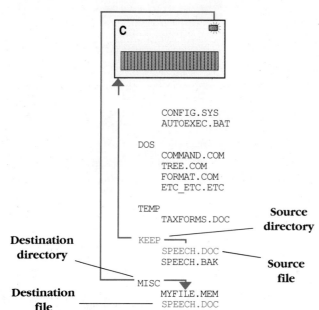

Fig. 9.2

In this example of the COPY command, a file is copied from one directory to another on the same disk.

```
C

CONFIG.SYS
AUTOEXEC.BAT

DOS
    COMMAND.COM
    TREE.COM
    FORMAT.COM
    ETC_ETC.ETC

TEMP
    TAXFORMS.DOC               Source
                              directory
KEEP
    SPEECH.DOC
    SPEECH.BAK                Source
                              file
MISC
    MYFILE.MEM
    SPEECH.DOC
```

Destination directory

Destination file

Concatenating Text Files

Although you can use COPY to concatenate any two or more files, the concatenation operation is most effective when the files are ASCII text files. Concatenating binary files results in a destination file that is not usable in most cases.

For the concatenation examples, assume that there are three text files in the current directory. All three have TXT extensions. The first file is named INTRO.TXT, the second BODY.TXT, and the third is ENDING.TXT. The contents of each file is as follows:

File	Contents
INTRO.TXT	Concatenation is
BODY.TXT	the joining of files
ENDING.TXT	into a new file.

To join the three files into a third file, you separate the source files with the + operator by using the following command:

COPY INTRO.TXT+BODY.TXT+ENDING.TXT ALL.TXT

The resulting file, ALL.TXT, contains the text from the three source files. To verify ALL.TXT, issue the following command:

TYPE ALL.TXT

TYPE sends the contents of ALL.TXT to the screen; you see the following:

```
Concatenation is the joining of files into a new file.
```

If the three source files are in order, and are the only files in the directory that contain the TXT extension, you can concatenate them in another way. To concatenate the files without using the + operator, you use a wild card in the source file name that will match only the three desired text files. You also give the destination file a literal name. The command takes the following form:

COPY *.TXT ALL.ALL

COPY works down the source directory and finds the three text files with the TXT extensions. The screen report is as follows:

```
INTRO.TXT
BODY.TXT
ENDING.TXT
        1 File(s) copied
```

If you were to name the destination file in the preceding example ALL.TXT instead of ALL.ALL, the source wild-card parameter would find ALL.TXT's directory entry at the end of the directory while the operation was in progress. Your screen would then show the following:

```
INTRO.TXT
BODY.TXT
ENDING.TXT
ALL.TXT
Content of destination lost before copy
Content of destination lost before copy
        1 File(s) copied
```

You might not concatenate files through the use of wild cards instead of the + operator on purpose. But if you get your wild cards mixed-up, you can accidentally cause a concatenation. If you are surprised during a COPY operation by a message like the preceding, suspect a wild-card mix-up.

Copying from a Device to a File

A very common and handy use of the COPY command is copying keystrokes entered from the CON (keyboard) device to a file. The resulting text file can be a batch file, a configuration file, a memo, or just about any kind of short, ASCII file.

The use of COPY with the CON device as a source parameter is so popular that many users refer to the "COPY CON command" when talking about the operation. For an example of copying the console device to a file, you can create a simple batch file that changes the current directory to \123R3 and starts Lotus 1-2-3 Release 3. The batch file is copied to the \DOS directory so that it is accessible from any directory (if you have included \DOS as a search-path alternative). The destination file's name is RUN123.BAT. After the COPY operation, LOTUS can be started from any disk or directory. The command to create the batch file is as follows:

COPY CON C:\DOS\RUN123

When you press Enter, DOS will display the cursor on the next line; the DOS prompt is not displayed. You can now start typing the file.

Enter the following line; be sure to press Enter:

C:

The cursor drops to the next line, and you enter the following line. Again, remember to press Enter.

CD\123R3

The cursor drops to the next line; enter the following:

LOTUS

The cursor drops to the next line. Press the F6 function key or the Ctrl-Z key combination to indicate the end of file. This indicates to DOS that you are finished with your input into the file. Now press Enter one last time. DOS responds with the following:

```
1 File(s) copied
```

To confirm that the new file is correct, you can use the TYPE command to review the contents of the file.

If you try this example on your system, be sure to use the appropriate directory names for DOS and Lotus 1-2-3. Also, make sure that the start command for Lotus 123 on your system is **LOTUS**.

Turning Verification On with VERIFY

The VERIFY command controls DOS's internal verify indicator. The verify indicator controls the read-after-write checking of data that is written to disk. If the verify indicator is on, data written to a disk is verified. If the verify indicator is off, the data written to disk is not verified. VERIFY is the global controller of the same verification done when COPY is issued with the /V switch. When VERIFY is on, you do not need to use /V with COPY.

VERIFY does not perform the actual verification but simply maintains the setting of the verify indicator. Data verification is the job of the device driver. The exact method that a device driver uses to verify data written to a disk varies. Thorough device drivers may read a written sector to compare with the contents of the disk buffer in memory. VERIFY ON is generally accepted as being a good validity check of data written to disk. Commands such as COPY, BACKUP, RESTORE, XCOPY, DISKCOPY, and REPLACE benefit from the VERIFY command.

Verifying data during disk writes is inherently slower than not verifying data. The verification process takes more time. In most disk-intensive activities, a program will be 20% to 40% slower during disk input/output. If you want the extra insurance of data verification, however, the slower disk operation is a small price to pay. Many users turn VERIFY on when working with critical files and then turn VERIFY off for normal DOS work.

Issuing the VERIFY Command

The VERIFY command can be issued in any of the following three forms:

VERIFY ON

VERIFY OFF

VERIFY

When you boot the computer, the default setting of VERIFY is off. Use the first form of the VERIFY syntax to turn VERIFY on.

When VERIFY is on, use the second form of VERIFY syntax to turn VERIFY off.

To see the current setting of VERIFY on-screen, use the VERIFY command with no parameter.

Understanding the General Rules of VERIFY

- If you issue VERIFY with a parameter other than ON or OFF, DOS issues the following message:

      Must specify ON or OFF

- If you issue VERIFY with no parameter, DOS will respond with VERIFY is ON or VERIFY is OFF.

- If VERIFY is on, specifying a /V switch in a COPY command will have no additional verification effect.

- You cannot use VERIFY to cause verification of a network drive.

Verifying a Critical BACKUP Operation with VERIFY

If you plan to perform a critical backup operation on your hard disk, you can add some extra insurance to the operation by turning the verify indicator on. DOS will verify each sector as it is written to the backup disk(s). To turn VERIFY on, issue the command **VERIFY ON**.

You can confirm the setting at any time from the DOS prompt by issuing the command **VERIFY**. DOS will respond as follows:

    VERIFY is ON

When you no longer want verification, you can turn the feature off with the command **VERIFY OFF**.

Unlike PROMPT and PATH, VERIFY does not export its current setting to the environment. When you issue a PROMPT or PATH command, the command's parameter is placed in the environment. DOS uses the environment string to get the setting of the prompt or the search path. VERIFY is an internal indicator or flag. DOS does not look in the environment for a VERIFY variable. DOS (or the device driver) checks the internal flag.

Selectively Updating a Disk with REPLACE

The external command REPLACE was introduced in V3.2 as a utility for updating files with different versions of the same files. REPLACE is a real boon for people who must update a disk or directory from another disk or directory. REPLACE actually copies files, but REPLACE is more selective in file copying than COPY.

You can add selectivity to the command with switches and make the updating of the target-disk files conditional on date (and time with V4) and the absence of a file. REPLACE even performs an optional search of the target disk directory's subdirectory for a replaceable file. COPY can't cross directory boundaries in a single operation; REPLACE can.

You can use REPLACE to collect the most recent versions of common files from a group of PCs to a floppy disk. You can also use REPLACE to upgrade to a new version of some software package. REPLACE is more versatile than COPY because REPLACE offers conditional copying of source files to the destination. Without switches, REPLACE will transfer files only from the source that already exists on the destination. COPY issued with the *.* wild card designation transfers all files from the source to the destination.

REPLACE is a more advanced command than COPY. You may want to experiment with replacing files on a practice floppy before trying REPLACE with your "live" files.

Issuing the REPLACE Command

The syntax for the REPLACE command is as follows:

REPLACE *d1:path1***filename.ext** **d2:***path2\\ /switches* *d1:* is the optional source drive. If you omit the source drive specifier, the current drive is assumed.

path1 is the optional path of the source files. If you omit the source path specifier, the current directory is assumed.

filename.ext is the required file name of the source file(s). Wild cards are allowed in the file name and extension.

d2: is the required target drive specifier where the files will be replaced.

path2 is the optional target path name where the files will be replaced. If the target path specifier is omitted, the current directory of the specified (or current) target disk is assumed.

/switches are optional switches shown in table 9.1.

Table 9.1
REPLACE Switches

Switch	Action
/A	Copies source files that do not exist on the target. Allows *adding* files without overwriting existing files with the same names. /A cannot be used with /S, /D, or /U.
/D	Copies source files with a more recent *date* than files on the target with the same names. /D cannot be used with /A.
/P	*Prompts* for confirmation before copying each file.
/R	Allows overwriting of *read-only* files on the target.
/S	Searches all *subdirectories* of the target directory for a file matching each source file. /S cannot be used with /A.
/U (V4)	Copies source files with a more recent date and time than files on the target with the same names. /U cannot be used with /A.
/W	*Waits* for a key to be pressed before executing REPLACE to allow disk(s) to be changed to the correct source and target.

Understanding the Operation of REPLACE

The external command REPLACE is a useful file-copying command that works at the directory level. REPLACE is a handy file-management command because it lends itself nicely to selectively updating the files from one disk from another.

When issued with no switches, REPLACE reads the source disk and directory for files matching the command line's source-file specifier. All files meeting the conditions of the source specification are transferred to the destination disk and path. Unlike COPY,

REPLACE cannot rename the files as they are copied to the destination; therefore, no file specifier is allowed (or needed) in the destination parameter.

If any optional switches are given on the command line, REPLACE performs a compatibility check of the switches to determine disallowed switch combinations. If any are found, REPLACE issues the message Parameters not compatible and then terminates (see table 9.1 for switch actions and compatibilities).

If you issue REPLACE with the /W switch specified in the command line, REPLACE will prompt you to press any key before any replacement or adding begins. This *waiting* condition allows you to change disks to those appropriate for the files you want to update.

If the /A, /D, /U, or the /P switches are specified in the command line, REPLACE will test the appropriate conditions of the source file against the destination. If the test passes, REPLACE will proceed with replacing the file. If the test fails, REPLACE will move to the next source-file candidate and test again.

If the /P switch is specified in the command line, REPLACE will *prompt* you before copying the candidate source file to the destination. You can confirm the replacement with Y or reject it with N. The file will not be replaced if you answer N; REPLACE will move on to the next candidate file.

If you use the /R switch to allow replacement of *read-only* files in addition to normal destination files, REPLACE will behave as though the destination file is not read-only and replace it. The updated file on the destination disk will not be marked as read-only.

The /S switch allows REPLACE to search all *subdirectories* of the destination directory for the file to update. You cannot use the /A (*add* a new file) switch with the /S switch. If /A were allowed with /S, REPLACE would be unable to determine which potential destination subdirectory to add the file to.

The /D switch and the /U switch add time selectivity to REPLACE. PC DOS does not include the /D switch. /D causes REPLACE to update *destination* files with source files having a more current date. /U causes REPLACE to *update* destination files with source files that have a more current time and date.

When two or more (allowed) switches are used with the command, REPLACE will consider their affects additive. The actions or selections implied by each switch will be carried out by REPLACE at the point each switch would have been carried out if it were the only switch in the command line.

Understanding the General Rules of REPLACE

- REPLACE is available with DOS V3.2 and later versions.
- REPLACE has no provision to add or update hidden or system files. To transfer system files, use the SYS command.

- You must include a source parameter with REPLACE. The source parameter can be a drive, a path, or a file name and can include all three. The file-name specifier may contain wild cards.

- If the source drive or path name is omitted, REPLACE assumes the default value for the omitted item.

- The destination parameters can include a drive and a path name but cannot include a file name. The destination drive or path or both can be omitted. REPLACE assumes default values for omitted destination parameters.

- The /A switch cannot be used with the /U, /D, or /S switches. All other switch combinations are allowed.

Updating a Directory

This example updates a directory (named \PROGRAMS) on the hard disk from a floppy disk in drive A. The floppy has been used to collect files from another computer. This REPLACE command is intended to update the files on the hard disk's \PROGRAMS directory with the more recent versions collected on the floppy.

If you look at a directory listing of \PROGRAMS, you see several files.

```
Volume in drive C is HARD DISK
Volume Serial Number is 2F7F-16CD
Directory of  C:\PROGRAMS
.               <DIR>      11-03-89   12:31p
..              <DIR>      11-03-89   12:31p
RESULT    DAT        810 08-24-88    1:32p
JUDE      DAT         56 12-12-88   10:15p
PROFILE   DAT        850 08-11-88    4:46p
RESULTS   DAT        911 08-24-88    2:46p
TESTS     DAT        488 08-26-88    3:47p
CONVERT   SYS         40 09-01-88    5:54p
GEN4SYS   BAS       6556 09-01-88    5:37p
MONITOR   BAS        993 06-22-88   12:10p
       10 File(s)    10934272 bytes free
```

A directory listing of drive A also shows several files:

```
Volume in drive A is COLLECTION
Volume Serial Number is 0000-0000
Directory of  A:\
PROCED    DOC      19712 10-29-89    7:34p
RESULT    DAT        810 08-25-88   11:06a
FRM_SR1   DAT        372 08-18-88   11:18a
JUDE      DAT         56 12-14-88   11:15p
FRM_PRL   DAT       9280 08-19-88    2:32p
PROFILE   DAT        850 08-11-88   10:46p
```

229

```
CROSS     DAT      1463 08-26-88    3:48p
RESULTS   DAT       911 08-24-88   10:55p
TESTS     DAT       488 08-28-88    2:17p
CONVERT   SYS        40 09-01-88    5:54p
GEN4SYS   BAK      6556 09-01-88    5:37p
MONITOR   BAK       993 06-22-88   12:10p
IO        BAK     22736 08-23-88   12:42p
     13 File(s)       658432 bytes free
```

Notice that some of the file names are shared between the two directories. These are the files that REPLACE will process in this example. You issue the following command:

REPLACE A:*.* C:\PROGRAMS

As REPLACE processes the files, you see the following:

```
Replacing C:\PROGRAMS\RESULT.DAT
Replacing C:\PROGRAMS\JUDE.DAT
Replacing C:\PROGRAMS\PROFILE.DAT
Replacing C:\PROGRAMS\RESULTS.DAT
Replacing C:\PROGRAMS\TESTS.DAT
Replacing C:\PROGRAMS\CONVERT.SYS
6 file(s) replaced
```

If you compare the replacement list with the files that the two directories have in common, you will see that the files are the same. The files on drive A that were not in \PROGRAMS were not copied. The files in \PROGRAMS that were not on drive A were left intact. REPLACE made the updating operation much easier than issuing a series of COPY commands.

Summary

As you can see, DOS offers useful file-management commands. You should use these commands to arrange your work and keep your computing environment clean. As you gain experience with file-management commands, you will probably want to incorporate additional switches or take more advantage of DOS defaults. In this chapter, you learned the following key points:

❏ DOS devices have names that are reserved. If you use a reserved name for a file specifier, DOS will use the specifier as a device.

❏ Some file extensions are conventionally used to indicate the type of file that the extension implies.

❏ The ^Z character marks the end of many ASCII files.

❏ The RENAME command changes the name of an existing file.

❑ The ERASE (DEL) command removes files from a directory. Erased files are no longer available to DOS.

❑ The TYPE command displays a file's content in ASCII on the screen.

❑ The COPY command concatenates and copies files and devices in binary and ASCII modes.

❑ The VERIFY command manages DOS internal verify indicator. Devices drivers check the indicator to determine whether they need to perform write verification of data.

❑ The REPLACE command selectively updates one disk's files from files on another disk.

In the next chapter, you will learn important ways to protect your data investment by making backups of your files.

Understanding Backups
and the Care of Data

10

As you use your computer, you will create a multitude of files. Many of these files will contain information you find very important. With the reliability of today's computers, it is tempting to think of your files as "being there when you need them." But as the old computer saying goes, "There are two kinds of computer users—those who have lost precious files and those who are going to." A file's data represents a time investment on your part. This chapter describes how to protect files from a variety of menaces, such as static electricity, excessive heat, and erratic electrical power.

The most important protection you can have is learning to make backup copies of your disk files. Although DISKCOPY and COPY are adequate for making "safety" copies of floppy disks, hard disk files are often too big to fit on a floppy disk or are spread across a directory structure. And yet, just one errant ERASE command given with wild cards—**ERASE *.***— can delete dozens of files from a hard disk in seconds.

What can you do for insurance against the loss of hours of work? You can always have your files duplicated on a different disk. If your primary disk fails or you issue an errant command, you have an insurance policy. For simpler file duplicating, you can use the XCOPY command. You can ensure that a copy is faithful by using the FC or COMP commands. For large backup work, you can use the DOS BACKUP and RESTORE commands.

In this chapter, you will learn the basics of these commands. Using the examples in this chapter, you will learn to back up and restore your entire hard disk. You also will learn the various switches used to adapt the XCOPY, BACKUP and RESTORE commands. The BACKUP and RESTORE commands are effective insurance against a major loss of precious files.

A note from the author . . . If you have never learned how to back up your disk files, or to produce duplicates, now is the time to learn! If you are just learning your way around DOS, this chapter is a must. Apply this chapter's information, and you may never experience the sinking feeling that comes to those who lose files. Unless you are remarkably charmed, I guarantee that the day will come when one or more of your files falls down the "bit tube."

Key Terms Used in This Chapter

Surge protector	A protective device inserted between a power outlet and a computer's power plug. Surge protectors help block power surges that can damage the computer's circuits.
Static electricity	A high voltage charge that builds on an object and that can be discharged when another object is touched. Electronic circuits can be easily damaged by static electricity discharges.
Ground	An electrical path directly to earth. A PC chassis is normally grounded. Grounds can safely dissipate static discharges.
Voltage regulator	An electrical device that keeps voltage fluctuations from reaching an electrical device. Regulators usually don't stop power surges.

Avoiding Data Loss

Today's personal computers are reliable and economical data processing machines. The PCs of today do the work of computers that a decade ago only a few fortunate users had access to. Like any machine, however, computers are subject to failures and operator errors.

Table 10.1 lists some problems and remedies for hardware and software problems that are discussed in this chapter.

Table 10.1
Hardware and Software Problems and Remedies

Problem	Remedy
Static electricity	Use anti-static liquid; an anti-static floor mat; a "touch Pad" on desk.
Overheating	Clean clogged air vents; remove objects blocking vents; use air-conditioned room during the summer.
Damaged disks	Don't leave disks to be warped by the sun; use protective covers; avoid spilling liquids on disks; store disks in a safe place; avoid magnetic fields from appliances (TVs, microwave ovens, and so on).
Software bugs	Buy tested commercial products.

Preventing Hardware Failures

Computers contain thousands of transistorized circuits. Most of these circuits have life expectancies of more than a century. A poor power source, excessive heat, and static discharges, however, can cause circuits to fail or operate erratically. Disk drives have precise moving parts with critical alignments. The potential always exists for hardware failures. If you follow the precautions presented in this section, you can reduce the likelihood of hardware failure.

Always be cautious about your computer's environment. If your power flutters and lights flicker, you might need to purchase a line *voltage regulator* from your computer dealer. Make sure that any electrical appliances you have near your computer do not pollute your power source.

Is the fan on the back of your computer choked with dust? Clean the air vents and check that your computer has room to breathe. Your computer can do unexpected things when it is too hot. Because circuits are not reliable when they overheat, you may get jumbled data. The moral is: make sure that your computer can breathe and keep its cool.

You generate *static electricity* on your body when humidity is low, you wear synthetic fabrics, or you walk on carpet. Just by touching your keyboard while carrying a static charge, you can send an electrical shudder through your computer. This can cause data jumble or circuit failure. Fortunately, you can avoid static problems by touching your grounded system cabinet before touching the keyboard. If static electricity is a serious problem for you, ask your dealer about anti-static products. These products are inexpensive and easy to use.

Preventing Software Failures

Each software program you buy is a set of instructions for the microprocessor. A small minority of software packages have flawed instructions called *bugs*. Software bugs are usually minor and rarely cause more than keyboard lock-ups or jumbled displays. The potential does exist for a software bug to cause your disk drive to operate in an erratic way, however. Fortunately, most companies test and debug their software before marketing the packages. Performing a backup of your disks is your best insurance against bugs.

About software viruses . . . Software viruses are purposefully created software bugs with the potential of great file damage. Most viruses are additional program code that is hidden in a COM file, such as COMMAND.COM. A virus most often does its damage by altering the disk's file allocation table (FAT) and marking clusters as bad or unavailable. A virus is also capable of initiating a FORMAT or destroying a disk partition table.

Viruses can "multiply" through the exchange of software between users. If you load an "infected" COM file on your PC, the virus can quickly "infect" your COMMAND.COM file. Unfortunately, you can back up an infected file, and when restored, the virus continues to do its dirty work. Your best defense against getting a virus on your system is to install only reputable software from a source who can attest to the program's operation. If you are hit by a virus, you may have to fall back to your write-protected master DOS disks and rebuild your system from the ground up.

Preventing Mistakes

As you gain skill, you will use DOS commands that can result in the unplanned loss of files. Commands such as COPY, ERASE, and FORMAT carry out their jobs as you command them. DOS has no way of knowing when a command line that you issue will have an unintended effect. For this reason, make a mental note to study what you type before you press Enter. It is easy to develop a typing rhythm that carries you straight through confirmation prompts into the clutches of disaster. Remember that you can use Ctrl-C, Ctrl-Break, and if necessary, Ctrl-Alt-Del to abandon commands. If the command that you are stopping is under way, these "panic buttons" may not contain the damage. Because you are human, you are likely to make mistakes. That's where the DOS commands that make backup data come in.

Combining Copying and Directory Management with XCOPY

The external command XCOPY is used to copy files. XCOPY also has the capability to create destination directories. Because XCOPY can create directories, the command is handy for copying a portion of your directory tree to another disk. XCOPY is certainly not limited, however, to its use in protecting data as a pseudo-backup command. XCOPY is a sophisticated copy command for which you will find many uses.

The XCOPY command, introduced with DOS V3.2, addresses the needs of three principal types of computer users: those who have more than one computer, those who have hard disks, and those who need more selectivity than the standard COPY command offers. Almost all PC users fit one or more of these categories, so XCOPY is an important command to know and use.

Issuing the XCOPY Command

XCOPY's syntax is similar to COPY's syntax, but the switches are more complex. XCOPY's syntax is as follows:

> **XCOPY** *ds:paths\filenames.exts*
>
> *dd:pathd\filenamed.extd /V /P /W /S /E /A /M /D:date*

The *source* files, designated by an *s*, are the files to be copied. If you omit the disk drive name (*ds:*), the current disk drive is used. If you omit the path name (*paths*), the current directory on the drive is used. You can use wild cards in the file name (*filenames.exts*). If you omit the file name, XCOPY assumes that you want to specify a wild card *.*, and all files in the given path will be copied. You must include at least one of the source parameters.

With XCOPY, the *destination* files are designated by the *d* in the name. File names, disk drive names, and path names are taken from DOS's current defaults. This means that if you do not specify a drive name (*dd:*), XCOPY uses the current disk drive. If you do not specify a path name (*pathd*), XCOPY uses the current disk's directory. If you omit the file name (*filenamed.extd*), the copied files retain their previous names.

A subdirectory can contain a file with the same name as the subdirectory. In some XCOPY operations, this duplicity can be a problem. A destination name might be a path name or a file name; XCOPY asks you to make the determination. XCOPY asks you whether the destination is a file name or path name.

As an example, look at the following command:

> **XCOPY C:\WORDS*.* A:\WORDS**

If you use this command to copy the files from C:\WORDS to the disk in drive A, and the disk does not have a directory called WORDS, XCOPY will display this message:

```
Does WORDS specify a filename
or directory name on the target
(F = file, D = directory)?
```

If the destination is a file name, answer F. If the destination is a directory, answer D. Unlike COPY, XCOPY creates directories on the destination disk as needed.

Understanding XCOPY's Switches

XCOPY has eight switches, which are described in this section. A complete table of XCOPY's switches can be found in the Command Reference section.

/V is the familiar *verify* switch. XCOPY verifies that it has copied the files correctly.

/W causes XCOPY to prompt and *wait* for you to insert the source disk. This switch is particularly important to users of floppy disk drives.

/P is the *pause*-and-ask switch. XCOPY displays the name of the file it will copy and asks whether the file should be copied. For the file \MYFILE.123, XCOPY will display the following prompt:

```
\MYFILE.123 (Y/N)?
```

Answer Y to copy the file or N to skip it. When you answer Y, XCOPY immediately copies the file.

The /S and /E switches affect how XCOPY handles additional subdirectories. These two switches show the true power of XCOPY. COPY limits itself to handling the files from one directory; XCOPY starts with the named or current directory and can process the files in all additional subdirectories of the directory, all lower subdirectories of these subdirectories, and so on. XCOPY traverses the subdirectory tree and can copy complete directory branches from one disk to another.

The /S switch affects the *source* and destination directories. The /S switch instructs XCOPY to copy all designated files from the current and subsequent subdirectories to a parallel set of subdirectories on the destination disk drive. As an example, look at the following command:

XCOPY C:\WORDS*.* A: /S

The command executes in the following sequence:

1. XCOPY copies all files in \WORDS to the current directory on drive A:.

2. XCOPY copies all files from WORDS\LETTERS to a subdirectory of the current directory called \LETTERS on drive A:.

3. XCOPY copies all files from the subdirectory WORDS\CONTRACTS to the subdirectory of the current directory on drive A: called \CONTRACTS.

In essence, XCOPY lifts a copy of the subdirectory tree starting at the source directory and transplants the copy to drive A:.

Note that XCOPY does not place the copied files from the subdirectories into a single directory. XCOPY places files from one subdirectory into a parallel subdirectory. If the subdirectory does not exist on the destination, XCOPY creates the subdirectory.

The /E switch affects the operation of the /S switch. If XCOPY encounters an *empty* subdirectory on the source drive, **XCOPY /S** skips the empty subdirectory. If you give the /S and /E switches, XCOPY also creates empty subdirectories on the destination drive. If you give the /E switch without giving the /S switch, the /E switch has no meaning. You must also use /S to get any action from /E.

The switches */M*, */A*, and */D:date* control which files that match the source file name will be copied. The */M* switch tells XCOPY to copy any file that has been *modified*. /M tells XCOPY to copy a file you have not previously backed up or copied with XCOPY.

In Chapter 7, you learned about the archive attribute that is stored in the directory with each file name. When you create or change a file, this attribute is turned on. XCOPY checks to see whether the archive attribute has been set. The set (on) archive attribute will be displayed as an A to the left of the file name reported by the ATTRIB command. DOS turns the archive attribute on when a file is created or modified. When you give the /M switch, XCOPY processes this file. If the attribute is not set, XCOPY skips the file.

The /A switch works like the /M switch. XCOPY will process only those files that have the *archive* flag turned on. /M clears the archive attribute after XCOPY has copied a file, however; /A does not. This difference can be important. As you will learn later in this chapter, the BACKUP command can select files based on the archive attribute. If XCOPY has cleared this flag, however, BACKUP will not process the file. If you therefore use the commands **XCOPY /M** and **BACKUP /M** (the switches have identical meaning for the two commands), the backup you make using BACKUP may not be complete. Unless you customarily use XCOPY as a backup program, avoid using the /M switch; use the /A switch instead.

The */D:date* switch selects files based on their *directory date*, which is the date of the file's creation or modification. XCOPY copies files that have been created or modified on or after the date specified.

Understanding the Operation of XCOPY

XCOPY is best described as a hybrid between COPY and BACKUP/RESTORE. XCOPY and COPY both copy files between disks. Unlike COPY, however, XCOPY does not copy files to a nondisk device, such as the printer (PRN) or the console (CON). Like BACKUP and RESTORE, XCOPY can selectively copy files and traverse the directory tree to copy files from more than one directory. XCOPY can also make a destination directory when the destination directory does not exist. This directory capability makes XCOPY useful for duplicating a directory branch to another disk.

Like COPY but unlike BACKUP, XCOPY copies files that are directly usable: you cannot use files processed by BACKUP until you have processed them with RESTORE.

Understanding the General Rules of XCOPY

- XCOPY cannot copy hidden source files.
- XCOPY will not overwrite read-only destination files.
- If a file specifier is omitted in the XCOPY syntax, XCOPY assumes the *.* full wild-card pattern as the file specifier.
- If you include the /D switch, the date specifier must be entered in the format of the system's DATE command or in the format indicated by the latest COUNTRY command.
- The /V switch performs the same read-after-write checking as the SET VERIFY ON global verify flag.
- To use XCOPY to copy empty source subdirectories, you must specify both the /S and the /E switches.

Using XCOPY Effectively

Because XCOPY can control which files should be copied by date or archive attribute, can copy complete subdirectory trees, and can confirm which files should be copied, the command has several ideal uses. One use is to copy files selectively between disks or directories. A second major use is as a "quickie" hard-disk backup command if you want to back up only a few critical files in several subdirectories. The third major use is to keep the directories of more than one computer synchronized.

With COPY, your control is limited. COPY copies all files that match the given name, which is an all-or-nothing approach. If you use the /P switch with XCOPY, however, you can select all the files that match the source file name; XCOPY will ask you if each file should be copied. You can give a single "larger" file name (a name that selects more files than necessary but covers all the files you may want to copy); then you can select individually which files you really want to copy.

XCOPY is practical to use if you want to make backup copies of less than a diskful of files from several directories. Rather than using BACKUP, you might prefer to use the command **XCOPY /A** to select files that have changed since the last backup.

This technique has one drawback; you should ensure that the files will fit on one disk. When the destination disk fills, XCOPY stops. XCOPY cannot gracefully handle full disks. You must change disks and restart the XCOPY process using the /A and /P switches to skip the files you have already copied. Also, XCOPY cannot handle an individual file that is bigger than the target disk. If you need to back up such a file, use BACKUP.

A favorite use of XCOPY is to keep synchronized the contents of the hard disks of two computers. Many people have one computer at work and another at home. If both computers have hard disks, keeping the copies of programs and data files current is a major task. Which files did you change today? Which machine has the more current version?

In such a situation, you will find especially useful the /A switch or the /D:date switch if you use the /S switch on the source and destination computers. The /S switch forces XCOPY to play a hunting game you otherwise need to perform manually. Which switch you use, /A or /D, depends on how often you copy files between the machines. If you copy files between the machines frequently, you will most likely prefer the /A switch. If you let many days pass between synchronizing your computers' contents, you may find that the /D switch works better. If you run BACKUP on the source machine between the times you use XCOPY, you must use the /D switch with XCOPY. BACKUP resets the archive attribute, and XCOPY will not catch all files that have changed.

Duplicating a Directory Branch

For this example, assume you have a subdirectory on your hard disk named \WPFILES. This subdirectory has a few word processor files in it. \WPFILES also has two subdirectories. The first, \WPFILES\DOCS, contains your current memos. The second, \WPFILES\MEMOS, contains your document files. Because these three directories are the ones you modify most, you want to keep a current set of duplicate files of those contained in the three directories. You keep the duplicates on a floppy disk because the total number of bytes of the files is less than the floppy's capacity. To copy all of the files in this directory branch to the floppy, you issue the following command:

XCOPY C:\WPFILES A:\WPFILES /S

DOS responds as follows:

```
Does WPFILES specify a filename
or directory name on the target
(F = file, D = directory)?
```

When you press F, XCOPY immediately begins to process files, and you see the following display:

```
Reading source file(s)...
C:\WPFILES\LET9_1.WP
C:\WPFILES\LET9_2.WP
C:\WPFILES\LET9_3.WP
C:\WPFILES\LET9_4.WP
C:\WPFILES\LET9_5.WP
C:\WPFILES\DOCS\SCHEDULE.DOC
C:\WPFILES\MEMOS\SALES.MEM
     7 File(s) copied
```

Because you included the /S switch, XCOPY will process the files in C:\WPFILES, C:\WPFILES\MEMOS, and C:\WPFILES\DOCS. The A:\WPFILES path specifier causes XCOPY to ask whether the name specifies a directory or a file. \WPFILES could conceivably be a user file in the root directory. The full path name of each file is echoed to the screen as it is copied to drive A. When the command completes, the \WPFILES directory branch has been copied to drive A.

In another example, if your PC experiences a hardware failure and needs to go to the shop for repairs, you can take your floppy to another PC and place the original directory branch, complete with files, on the other PC. To do so, you enter the following command:

XCOPY A: C: /S

XCOPY will reverse the above copy process by coping all of the files on drive A to their original subdirectory locations on drive C. With little DOS activity, you can access your files again. XCOPY has the advantage of copying files in a standard format. BACKUP creates a special format. With the files copied to drive A by XCOPY, you can simply choose to use that disk to access your files.

Comparing Files with COMP

The external command COMP compares two files or two sets of files to find differences in the files. Any differences are then reported on-screen. When a copied file is extremely important, you can use COMP to compare the file with the original. If any difference exists, you know on the spot that something is wrong with the copy. Normally, DOS will detect data integrity errors while reading and writing files. But if you want to be sure that two files are the same, you can ease your mind by using COMP (or FC). COMP is supplied with PC DOS V1.0 and later versions and with MS-DOS V3.3 and later versions. Check your version of DOS to determine whether you have the COMP command. MS-DOS includes a similar command, FC, which is discussed in the next section.

File comparison is a very useful file-management and integrity-checking tool. Unlike the DISKCOMP disk-level command, COMP reports differences at the file level. With COMP you can determine any of these conclusions about compared files:

- The files are identical in content and identical in size.
- The files are identical in size, but different in content.
- The files are different in size and content.

In a practical sense, COMP is useful in determining whether a file is the same as another file on a different disk or in a different directory. If the compared files have the same name, you can easily copy an older version of the named file to another disk while not realizing that the newer version in another directory is different. You might copy a file to a file name such as TEMP to have a temporary copy. After some time, you might forget which file TEMP was copied from. Using COMP with TEMP and other files will show the file that matches TEMP.

The syntax for the COMP command is as follows:

COMP *d1:path1\filename1.ext1 d2:path2\filename2.ext2*

d1: is the optional drive that contains the first file or set of files (the primary set) to be compared. If you omit the *d1:* specifier, the current drive is assumed.

path1 is the optional path to the file(s) to be compared. If you omit the *path1* specifier, the default directory is assumed.

filename1.ext1 is the optional file specifier for the file to be used as the basis of comparison. Wild cards are allowed in both the file name and extension. If you omit the file specifier but include a drive or a path, COMP assumes that the file specifier is *.*. To verify a copied file, you supply its name.

d2: is the optional drive specifier which has the second file or set of files (the secondary set) to be used in the comparison. If you omit *d2:*, but include a path or file-name specifier, the logged disk is assumed.

path2 is the optional path to the secondary set of files. If you omit the path2\ specifier, COMP assumes the default directory.

filename2.ext2 is the optional file name and extension of the secondary set of files. Wild cards are allowed in the file name and extension. If you omit the secondary set file-name specifier, COMP assumes that the secondary set files are the same name as the primary set files.

If you issue COMP with no parameters, DOS prompts you for parameters. Use COMP alone when you need to change disks after the external COMP command is loaded from disk.

Understanding the Operation of COMP

COMP reads one file and compares each byte to another file. Bytes are compared based on their relative position in the file. COMP does not care whether the bytes represent ASCII-character data or binary data. COMP does check both files for the Ctrl-Z end-of-file markers. If an end-of-file marker is not found, COMP displays the following message:

```
EOF mark not found
```

The end-of-file marker message is informational only and not an indication of a problem.

Once the COMP program is loaded into memory, you can continue to do file comparisons by answering Y to the following prompt:

```
Compare more files (Y/N)?
```

COMP will then prompt you for parameters.

You can redirect the output of COMP to the printer, but the final prompt of a comparison, Compare more files (Y/N)? as well as prompts for parameters, will be redirected to the printer. If you use redirection, you need to read the prompts from the redirection device. When you redirect the output of COMP to a file, you will have to anticipate any prompting messages because you will have no way to see prompts.

Understanding the General Rules of COMP

- If you do not specify parameters, COMP will first prompt for the primary set specifier and then for the secondary set specifier.
- As each file in the set is compared, the file-compared names are displayed.
- If the two files being compared are different sizes, COMP issues for those files the following report:

  ```
  Files are different sizes
  ```

  No further comparison of the two files is made.
- If COMP detects differences in two files of the same size, the differences are reported to the screen as byte offsets (positions in the file) and values of the differing bytes. Byte offsets and values are given in hexadecimal (base 16) notation.

- COMP reports the first 10 differences in the two files and then reports the following:

  ```
  10 Mismatches - ending compare.
  ```

- When all sets of files are compared, COMP prompts for additional comparisons.

Comparing Two Text Files with COMP

Suppose that two text files identical in size, ORIGINAL.TXT and ANOTHER.TXT, are located in the default directory of the logged drive A. By using the TYPE command, you can see the contents of the files to obtain a gauge of how they will compare. (Normally, you would compare the files first to be more efficient.) When you view the output of the two TYPE commands, you see the following for the ORIGINAL.TXT file:

```
This file contains the following numbers:
1
2
3
4
5
6
7
8
9
```

For the file ANOTHER.TXT, you see the following:

```
This file contains the following numbers:
9
8
7
6
5
4
3
2
1
```

The contents of these files are simplified lines of text for example purposes. Of course, your files would have more complex contents. To compare the two files, issue the following command:

COMP ORIGINAL.TXT ANOTHER.TXT

COMP reports as follows:

```
A:ORIGINAL.TXT and A:ANOTHER.TXT
Compare error at offset <beep> 21
File 1 = 31
File 2 = 39
Compare error at offset <beep> 24
File 1 = 32
File 2 = 38
Compare error at offset <beep> 27
File 1 = 33
File 2 = 37
Compare error at offset <beep> 28
File 1 = 34
File 2 = 36
Compare error at offset <beep> 30
File 1 = 36
File 2 = 34
Compare error at offset <beep> 33
File 1 = 37
File 2 = 33
Compare error at offset <beep> 36
File 1 = 38
File 2 = 32
Compare error at offset <beep> 39
File 1 = 39
File 2 = 31
EOF mark not found
Compare more files (Y/N)?
```

In this output, the <beep> indicator is a substitute for the PC's beep (bell) signal. COMP found 8 mismatches in the files. Because the number sequences in the files are reversed, you might expect to see 9 mismatches reported. Remember, however, that the number 5 is in the same position in both files.

Notice that COMP detected that the end-of-file marker is missing in the files. Although these files are ASCII text files, they do not contain the Ctrl-Z.

Performing a Full-File Comparison with FC

The external FC command is similar to the COMP command in that both compare files. FC, however, is a more capable command than COMP because FC can report ASCII text differences in readable text form. FC also performs binary file comparisons. FC is available with some versions of MS-DOS. FC is not available with with PC DOS.

The FC command has two general syntax forms. One form allows the /B switch for a forced *binary* comparison. The other form allows the remaining switches in an ASCII comparison. The two forms of syntax are as follows:

FC */B d1:path1***filename1.ext1** *d2:path2***filename2.ext2**

or

FC */A/C/L/LBn/N/nnnn/T/W d1:path1***filename1.ext1**
    *d2:\path2***filename2.ext2**

With the FC command, all switches *must* precede the other parameters.

d1: is the optional drive containing the first file to be compared. If the first drive specifier is omitted, the default drive is assumed.

path1 is the optional path of the directory containing the first file. If the first file's path is omitted, the default directory is assumed.

filename1.ext1 is the file name of the first file. A file name must be entered. Wild-card characters are *not* allowed.

d2: is the optional drive containing the second file to be compared.

If the second drive specifier is omitted, the default drive is assumed.

path2 is the optional path of the directory containing the second file. If the second file's path is omitted, the default directory is assumed.

filename2.ext2 is the file name of the second file. A file name must be entered. Wild-card characters are *not* allowed.

The switches are explained more fully in the next section.

Understanding the Operation of FC

FC works in two modes. FC compares two files in the ASCII mode or compares two files in the binary mode. Each mode reports its own formatted output. FC defaults to ASCII mode comparison when the files to be compared do not have EXE, COM, SYS, OBJ, LIB, or BIN extensions.

In ASCII mode, FC compares two files on a line-by-line basis. Lines from both files are held internally in a line buffer. FC uses the lines in the buffer to compare the first file to the second.

If a difference is detected by FC, the first file's name is displayed, followed by the last matching line from the first file. The first mismatching line and subsequent mismatching lines from the first file are then displayed. FC then produces output that contains the first matching line from file 1 that synchronizes the matching of file 2.

After displaying mismatch information about file 1, FC then repeats the same sequence for file 2. The file 2 name is displayed first, followed by the last matching line to file 1, followed by the mismatched lines to file 1, and ending on the first resynchronizing line of the two files.

The result of this output is a tool to identify the point of difference detection, the difference itself, and the point that the detected difference ended. You use this output as a short-cut alternative to a side-by-side comparison of the files' contents.

In the ASCII mode, FC offers several switches to modify the operation or output format of FC. Table 10.2 describes the action of each switch available in ASCII mode.

Table 10.2

FC ASCII Mode Switches

Switch	Action
/A	Instructs FC to *abbreviate* its output (V3.2 and later versions).
/C	Instructs FC to ignore the *case* of alphabetic characters.
/L	Instructs FC to do a *line-by-line* comparison on files that have EXE, COM, SYS, OBJ, LIB, or BIN extensions (V3.2 and later versions).
/LBn	Sets the number of *lines* in FC's *buffer* to *n*. The default number is 100 (V3.2 and later versions).
/N	Instructs FC to include the line *numbers* of lines reported in the output (V3.2 and later versions).
/nnnn	Establishes as *nnnn* the number of lines that must match after a difference to resynchronize FC.
/T	Instructs FC to view *tab* characters as literal characters rather than tab-expanded spaces (V3.2 and later versions).
/W	Instructs FC to ignore tabs, empty lines, and spaces.

In binary mode, FC compares two files byte for byte. At the first difference, the byte offset position in the first file is reported along with the value of the two files' bytes at the position. The offset as well as the byte values are reported in hexadecimal (base 16) form.

TIP

If you are comparing two files that are not the same, you can quickly stop the reporting of differences by using Ctrl-C or Ctrl-Break.

In binary mode, FC does not attempt to resynchronize the two files by finding an adjusted point of byte agreement. If one file has an additional byte at one offset only, not only will FC report the difference, but all subsequent bytes of the file will likely be reported.

If one file is longer than its comparison file, the binary mode will compare as many bytes as are present and then report that one file is longer. When a binary file comparison results in a long listing of differences, you may want to stop the FC operation with Ctrl-C.

Only one switch is available in the binary mode. The /B switch causes the comparison to be binary even if file extensions indicate that the files are not binary. You use the /B switch to compare two text files in binary mode. You may find situations in which you would rather have the binary-mode output format of FC than the ASCII mode format. Binary mode format reports differences as pairs of hexadecimal values. You can then see the values of characters, such as Ctrl-G (bell), that do not produce printed output.

Understanding the General Rules of FC

- When the /B (binary mode) switch is used, including the /L, /N, and /nnnn switches produces an error message from DOS. All other switches included with /B are ignored by FC.

- The internal buffer defaults to 100 lines for comparison, but can be changed with the /LBn switch.

- The default number of lines that must match in an ASCII comparison after a difference has ended is 2. The files are then considered to be resynchronized. The number of "must-match" lines can be changed using the /nnnn switch by setting nnnn to the desired value.

- Unlike the COMP command, FC requires file-name specifiers consisting of literal file names. Wild cards are not allowed.

Using FC To Compare a Copied File to its Original

Suppose you are copying the ANSI.SYS file from your hard disk to a floppy disk. The floppy will be used for an important demonstration on another PC. When the copy completes, you set the disk on the edge of your desk and go to the break room to get coffee. As you return, you notice that the disk has fallen off your desk and landed against the small transformer that runs your cassette recorder. You are worried that the magnetic field from the transformer has damaged ANSI.SYS. To verify that the copied ANSI.SYS is good, you compare it to the original by using the following command:

FC A:ANSI.SYS C:\DOS\DRIVERS\ANSI.SYS

After a few seconds, FC reports as follows:

```
fc: No differences encountered
```

Your copied ANSI.SYS seems to be good. If the file had lost its integrity, DOS might have reported a read error while accessing the file. If a change in the file was undetectable by DOS in normal reading activity, FC would begin to list the differences in hexadecimal notation. You can press Ctrl-Break to stop the listing.

Making Backup Sets with BACKUP

Compared to floppy disks, hard disks have many advantages. Hard disks are faster, have greater storage capacities and larger root directories, support multiple partitions, and never require a disk swap. A file on a hard disk can be many times the size of a file on a floppy disk. Commands like COPY and XCOPY enable you to keep a few duplicate files on a floppy for backup purposes, but DOS intends you to use another command for the big jobs. DOS provides the external BACKUP command, and its counterpart, the RESTORE command (discussed in a later section of this chapter), to enable users to maintain diskette backup sets of a hard disk's contents.

BACKUP is a modified COPY command that copies files from one disk, normally a hard disk, to another disk, normally a floppy disk. The "copies" of the files on the second disk are held in a modified format which cannot be accessed by DOS commands, other than the RESTORE command.

 BACKUP does not use the normal file format on the backup disk. Only the BACKUP and RESTORE commands can use this special file format. Backed-up files must be restored to be used.

Backup disks not only contain special copies of files; they also contain directory information about each file that enables RESTORE to copy the backup files to their original locations in the directory tree. In a way, the backup disks are a picture of the original files and directories held in suspended animation.

BACKUP can spread a single file across more than one diskette. No other DOS command can cross a disk's FAT boundary with a single file. BACKUP's capability to cross disk boundaries with a single file allows BACKUP to "copy" to additional diskettes those files that are too big to fit on a single diskette. If a BACKUP operation uses more than one diskette, each diskette is internally linked to the next diskette to form a backup set.

Backup set disks are related by the order in which they were created by BACKUP. Each disk in a set is filled to capacity until the files from the disk being backed up are complete. If a file is only partially written to a backup disk when the disk reaches full capacity, the remainder of the file is written to the next disk in the set.

Like XCOPY, BACKUP is a selective command. You can specify a directory or branch of directories, a file name, a file name patterned after a wild card, and additional selection switches. By taking advantage of BACKUP's selectivity, you can maintain more than one set of backup disks at one time, with each set having a logical purpose.

You can, for example, keep one backup set that contains every file on your hard disk. This set is insurance against data loss resulting from a hard disk failure or crash. You may have another backup set that contains only the files which have their archive attributes turned on. With an archive set for each day of the week, you can recover a week's worth of data between complete backups. When your hard disk fails, you replace it, restore using the full set, and then update with the daily set. Whatever the logical method for using BACKUP, the very presence of the BACKUP and RESTORE commands indicate that a reason exists to replicate your data.

You can lose the data on your hard disk in many ways. If you have not replicated the data, you may be forced to recreate the data wherever possible and suffer the consequences of permanent data loss where you cannot recreate data. If you have never experienced a disk-related failure, don't be overconfident. With 10 million hard-disk based DOS users working with their computers for an average of eight hours per day, over 250,000 people will experience a hard-disk related failure this year. You could be next.

Every PC user should develop a backup policy. A backup policy is simply a defined method of backing up data on a regular basis. Your policy may include making and keeping more than one backup set. Before you decide how to implement a backup policy, you should be familiar with the BACKUP command and its switches. You can pick up on the topic of the backup policy after the following section on BACKUP's syntax.

Issuing the BACKUP Command

The syntax for the BACKUP command is as follows:

BACKUP *d1:path\filename.ext* **d2:** */switches*

d1: is the optional name of the source drive that you are backing up. If you omit the drive source name, the default drive is assumed.

path is the name of the optional path holding the files you are backing up. If you omit the path name, the current directory of the specified (or default) drive is assumed.

filename.ext is the optional name of the source file(s) that you are backing up. You can use wild cards in the root file name as well as in the extension. If you omit the file-name specifier, the *.* wild-card pattern is assumed.

d2: is the required name of the destination drive where the backup disks will be written. If the destination drive name is omitted, DOS will issue an error message.

/switches are optional switches that add additional selectivity and control to the command. Table 10.3 outlines each switch and the DOS versions with which the switch can be used.

Table 10.3
BACKUP Switches

Switch	DOS Version	Action
/S	2.0 or later	Includes files from the specified directory and all subsequent *subdirectories* of the specified directory.
/M	2.0 or later	Includes files whose archive attribute is turned on.
/A	2.0 or later	*Adds* the files to be backed up to the files existing on the backup set.
/F	3.3 or later	*Formats* destination disks as part of the backup operation.
/F:size	4.0 or later	Optional *format size* is given as */F:size*.
/D	2.0 or later	Includes files created or modified on or after the *date* specified in the form */D:mm-dd-yy* or */D:mm/dd/yy*.
/T	3.3 or later	Includes files created or modified on or after the *time* specified as */T:hh:mm:ss*.
/L	3.3 or later	Writes a backup *log* entry in the file specified as */L:d:path\filename.ext* or in a file named \BACKUP.LOG in the source disk when */L* with no file specifier is used.

Understanding the General Rules of BACKUP

- Files backed up are selected by the drive, path, and file specifiers or their default values. Further selection of files is based on the optional switches.

- Unless the destination disk is a backup disk and you use the /A switch, the contents of the destination disk's root directory will be lost in the backup operation.

- If the destination disk is a hard disk, BACKUP checks for a directory named \BACKUP to store the backed up files in. The BACKUP command creates the \BACKUP directory if it does not exist already.

- If \BACKUP contains previously backed-up files, they are erased as part of the backup operation unless the /A switch is used. If the /A switch is used, and the destination disk is a hard disk, the current backup files are appended to existing backup files in \BACKUP.

- DOS V4 automatically formats the destination diskette (if it is not already formatted) as though the /F switch had been used.

- If BACKUP is formatting destination disks, the FORMAT command must be available in the current directory or accessible through a search path specified by the PATH command. The specified search path in the PATH command cannot be the destination drive.

- BACKUP will not format a hard disk even if the /F switch is given.

- The source disk cannot be write-protected because BACKUP resets each backed-up file's archive attribute.

- BACKUP does not back up the hidden DOS system files or COMMAND.COM in the root directory.

- You cannot use RESTORE V3.2 or earlier versions to restore files backed up by BACKUP V3.3 or later versions.

Determining a BACKUP Policy

The cost of performing a backup is time. The risk of not performing a backup is data loss. The gain of doing a backup is having recoverable data when original data is lost. You must weigh the cost, risk, and gains involved with backing up to determine how often is often enough to back up. The cornerstone of a good backup policy is the periodic full backup.

When you perform a full backup, all of your files are backed up. If disk disaster should strike, you can recover your data from your full backup set. You can restore the full backup set to your existing hard disk or even to a new replacement disk.

Unless you have DOS V3.3 or V4, you need to format the destination disk for the full backup set. The number of disks you need is derived from the number of bytes you will back up. When you run CHKDSK, DOS reports the number of bytes in various categories of files. A sample CHKDSK report looks like the following:

```
Volume LAP TOP      created Aug 17, 1989 6:41p
21204992 bytes total disk space
   51200 bytes in 3 hidden files
   98304 bytes in 42 directories
19404800 bytes in 1150 user files
 1650688 bytes available on disk
  655360 bytes total memory
  598784 bytes free
```

Two lines in this report apply to a disk-count calculation for BACKUP: the hidden files line and the user files line. Add the number of bytes in hidden files to the number of bytes in user files. The result is the approximate number of bytes in files that you will be backing up. In the preceding case, the number of bytes is rounded to the nearest 10,000 to 19,400,000 bytes.

Divide the rounded number by the capacity of your floppy disk drive. You can multiply your drive's capacity in K (kilobytes) by 1,000 or in M (megabytes) by 1,000,000 for a conservative estimate. In this case, you will need about 54 360K diskettes, 27 720K diskettes, 16 1.2M diskettes, or 14 1.44M diskettes. You can also use the information in table 10.4 to derive an approximation of your diskette requirements.

Table 10.4
Number of Diskettes Required for a Full Backup

Bytes to Back up	Diskette Capacity			
	360K	720K	1.2M	1.44M
10M	29	15	9	8
20M	59	29	18	15
30M	83	44	27	22
40M	116	58	35	29
70M	200	100	60	50

Because determining the exact number of disks needed to complete a backup is difficult, prepare a few more disks than you think you will need. It is easier to complete a successful backup if you err on the conservative side of a disk count.

Issuing the Full BACKUP Command

Unless you use V4 or intend to use the /F switch with V3.3, format all of your backup floppies the first time you intend to use them. Label each diskette as "Full Backup Set." When you have formatted and labeled all diskettes, you can start the full BACKUP with the following command:

BACKUP C:\ A:/S

This command tells BACKUP to start in the root directory of the hard disk and process all subdirectories on the disk. BACKUP will issue a warning message.

```
Insert backup diskette 1 in drive A:
Warning! Files in target drive
A:\ root directory will be erased.
Strike any key to continue.
```

254

Write the words "disk 1" on the first diskette's label as indicated in the screen message. Then insert the disk and press a key. DOS reports file names on-screen as they are being backed up. When the first disk is filled, BACKUP will repeat the message asking for the next disk. Again, mark the next disk's label with the sequential number that appears in the message.

The process repeats until the last file from the hard disk is processed by BACKUP. When you have completed the full backup, store the destination disks in order and in a safe place. Be sure not to mix this set with another backup set. You might accidentally try to restore a disk from the wrong set later.

Following Up with Incremental Backups

An incremental backup is a method of backing up on the full backup set only the files that are no longer current. You use a second set of disks for the incremental backup set. The number of disks in the incremental backup set depends on the number of bytes in files that have been modified since the last BACKUP. The key to making an incremental backup is the archive bit.

As you recall, BACKUP turns the archive attribute off for any file that is backed up. When you modify or create a file, DOS turns on the archive attribute for the modified or created file. BACKUP uses the /M switch to select files with their archive attribute in the on (set) state. Unless you have issued the ATTRIB command with the +A parameter or the XCOPY command with the /M switch, only changed or modified files will have their archive attributes set.

There are two basic strategies for making incremental backups. Either strategy can be combined with the full backup to comprise your backup strategy. Either incremental backup strategy uses the /M switch available with all versions of BACKUP.

The first incremental strategy or method is maintaining several small backup sets and using different sets over time. The second incremental backup method is maintaining one incremental backup set and adding files to the set over time. If your version of BACKUP supports the /A switch, the additive method is for you.

You can perform a full backup weekly or monthly or at some other interval. The incremental backup intervals should cover your risk of data loss between full backups. The time between performing incremental backups using either method depends on the amount of risk to your data you are willing to take. In a business setting, you might reduce your risk to an acceptable level by performing an incremental backup every other day. If your PC activity level is high, you might need to perform an incremental backup daily. If your PC activity is minimal, once every two weeks might be often enough to reduce your risk to a manageable level.

If you use the multiset incremental backup method, you need to ensure that you have enough formatted backup disks on hand to complete any given incremental backup. If you always keep on hand a few spare formatted backup disks, you won't be caught short when BACKUP prompts you to insert another disk.

If you use PC DOS V4, you need only keep on hand blank disks; PC DOS V4 BACKUP detects blanks and formats them on the fly. With MS-DOS V3.3 and later versions, you can always specify the /F switch and format every disk during the backup operation. Using the /F switch will slow the BACKUP operation, however, but at least you won't be caught with only blank disks and no way to complete the backup.

If you perform an incremental backup every Tuesday and Friday, and you run a full backup every two weeks, you will have four incremental backup sets accumulated before you need to repeat the backup cycle and reuse the disks. If you perform an incremental backup every Friday and a full backup on the last Friday of every month, you will need four sets of incremental backup disks, although most months would only require three. Note that the number of disks in each set will vary with the incremental time period's file-modification activity. The second backup set, for example, may be two disks one month and three disks the next month. You may need to renumber some disks from one set to another to accommodate the peaks and valleys of each set's disk requirements.

If you use the additive incremental backup method, you will have just one incremental backup set. You add files to the end disk in this set when you perform the incremental backups. An exception to adding files to the set occurs during the first incremental backup operation after a full backup. For this first incremental backup in a backup cycle, you start with the first disk in the set by omitting the /A switch from the BACKUP command line. By using this switch, you effectively reclaim the disks for reuse. The number of disks your set requires will depend on the worst case file-modification load for your full backup cycle. If you have a full backup cycle of one month, you may need five disks in your additive incremental backup cycle for 11 months out of the year, but you may need as many as ten disks during a month when you have a lot of file-creation or modification activity. Remember that you can scan the archive attributes of the files in your most heavily-used directories to get a sense of the number of bytes awaiting backup.

Issuing the Multiset Incremental Backup Command

You start one of a multiset incremental backup with the following command:

BACKUP C:\ A: /S/M

The /S switch includes all directories on the hard disk in the operation while the /M switch selects only files with their archive attribute switch set. The backup will proceed as the full backup described previously. Mark each disk in the set with the number and the date belonging to the increment for this backup. Store the completed set in a safe place and avoid mixing the disks with disks from another backup set.

If you use the additive incremental method, you will use the same command as the multiset backup method just described for the first incremental backup following a full backup. For the first incremental backup of the cycle, you will insert disk 1 of the set first.

For every other additive incremental backup besides the first one of the cycle, you issue the BACKUP command as follows:

BACKUP C:\ A: /S/M/A

BACKUP sees the /A switch and knows to add the files to the end of the backup set. BACKUP then issues the following prompt:

```
Insert last backup diskette in drive A:
Strike any key when ready . . .
```

You now insert the final disk from the last incremental backup operation. Don't start with the next reclaimed (unused in this cycle) disk. The command **BACKUP /A** needs to start off exactly where it left off in the last backup operation. When you have inserted the correct disk, press a key. The operation will proceed in the same manner as the full backup described previously.

Restoring Backed-up Files with RESTORE

The external command RESTORE is the functional counterpart of the BACKUP command. RESTORE is the only command that can read the special control information associated with files that have copied in the BACKUP format. When you need to recover backup files from a backup set, RESTORE is the command that you will use.

By issuing a literal file-name parameter with RESTORE, you can restore a single file from a backup disk. With a directory parameter and a wild-card file-name parameter, you can restore selected files to the named directory. With the /S switch, you can restore an entire hard disk with only a source drive specifier. RESTORE puts the selection of files in your control.

Like BACKUP, the RESTORE command provides additional control and selectivity through the use of numerous switches. With RESTORE's switches, you can use time, date, presence, and absence as selection criteria for files to be restored.

Issuing the RESTORE Command

The syntax of the RESTORE command is as follows:

RESTORE ds: *dd:path\filename.ext /switches*

ds: is the required source drive that holds the file(s) to be restored.

dd: is the drive that will receive the restored files.

path is the optional path to the directory that will receive the restored files. If the path specifier is omitted, the current directory of the destination disk is assumed.

257

filename.ext is the optional name of the file(s) to be restored. You can use wild cards in the file name's root and extension.

/switches are optional switches.

Table 10.5 displays the optional RESTORE switches, their actions, and the applicable versions of DOS.

Table 10.5
RESTORE Switches

Switch	DOS Version	Action
/S	2.0 or later	Restores files to the specified (or default) directory and *subdirectories.*
/P	2.0 or later	*Prompts* to confirm the restoration of a read-only file or a file modified since the last backup.
/M	3.3 or later	Restores files *modified* or deleted since the last backup.
/N	3.3 or later	Restores files that *no* longer exist on the destination disk.
/B	3.3 or later	Restores files created or modified *before* or or on the date given as */B:mm/dd/yy* or */B:mm-dd-yy.*
/A	3.3 or later	Restores files created or modified *after* or on the date given as */A:mm/dd/yy* or */A:mm-dd-yy.*
/L	3.3 or later	Restores files created or modified *later* than or at the time given as */L:hh:mm:ss.*
/E	3.3 or later	Restores files created or modified *earlier* than or at the time given as */E:hh:mm:ss.*

Understanding the Operation of RESTORE

RESTORE is the only command with the capability to read the special file format of files "copied" by the BACKUP command. RESTORE always restores files to the directory in which they were located when the files were backed up. RESTORE cannot restore files to another directory name other than the files' original directory name.

If RESTORE is restoring a file whose original directory is no longer on the destination disk, RESTORE will create the directory before restoring the file. RESTORE makes directory entries for files that are no longer on the destination disk and allocates the next available space in the FAT table for the restored file's allocation. If the destination disk is newly formatted, the restored files on the disk will not be fragmented. Files with the same full path name, but different sizes, from an additive backup set may result in a fragmented destination file after RESTORE allocates the first file of a duplicate name pair and subsequently allocates additional clusters for a larger file with the same name. As you recall, fragmentation doesn't affect the file's integrity, but may slow disk performance slightly.

Like the BACKUP command, RESTORE prompts you for the disks of the backup set. If you know the disk number which contains the file(s) that you want to restore, RESTORE will accept that disk as the first disk. You can use the /L switch with BACKUP to create a *log* file showing the names and disk numbers of files in a backup set.

Understanding the General Rules of RESTORE

- RESTORE V3.2 or earlier versions cannot restore files created by BACKUP V3.3 or later versions.
- You must give a source drive name in the command line.
- All files restored from the backup set will be placed in their original directories on the destination disk. If a source directory does not exist on the destination, the directory will be created.
- Files selected for restoration are selected from the destination drive, path, and file specifiers. Further selection is based on the included switches.
- The destination disk must already be formatted. RESTORE, unlike BACKUP, has no provision to format the destination disk.
- Files restored to a freshly formatted disk will not be fragmented.

 Most copy-protected files will not properly restore to the destination disk. Uninstall all copy-protected files using the manufacturer's procedure prior to BACKUP. Reinstall the copy-protected files after RESTORE has restored all other files.

Using RESTORE Following a Disk Failure

For the examples of the RESTORE command, assume that you are using a backup policy that includes a weekly full backup on Friday and an incremental backup each Wednesday. You will have two backup sets. The first set from Friday contains all files. The second set contains only files that were modified or created after Friday, but before Thursday.

On Thursday morning, suppose that you are saving a worksheet file when a workman begins to use a large drill next door. You notice that DOS reports the following message:

```
General Failure on drive C:
```

259

You abort the spreadsheet session and run CHKDSK to ensure that your FAT and directory system are in order. (The operation of CHKDSK is covered in Chapter 6.) DOS reports hundreds of lost clusters, and CHKDSK fills your root directory with reclaimed clusters. CHKDSK aborts after filling the root directory of your hard disk.

You have had an electrical noise-induced hard disk failure. Your hard disk most likely wrote erroneous information over valid information in the FAT. You have no choice other than to reformat your hard disk and then fall back to your backup disks. You will first need to reboot your computer with a DOS disk in drive A because your DOS utilities on your hard disk may be corrupt. After you format your hard disk, copy the external DOS commands back to the hard disk from the DOS master disk or its working copy. Use the PATH command to set a search path to the DOS directory so that DOS can locate the RESTORE command.

In the case of total disk failure, you restore your backup sets in chronological order. The first set to restore after you format your hard disk is your full backup set. Locate the disks from your full backup set and put them in their proper order. Then issue the following command:

RESTORE A: C:\ /S

DOS will prompt as follows:

```
Insert backup diskette 1 in drive A:
Strike any key when ready. . .
```

Put the first disk in drive A and press a key. DOS will respond as follows:

```
*** Files were backed up mm/dd/yy ***
```

The actual message will show mm/dd/yy as the date of the backup. DOS then prompts as follows:

```
*** Restoring files from drive A: ***
```

You will see the full path names of the files as they are being restored. When all the files from the first disk are restored to the hard disk, DOS will prompt you for the next disk in the backup set. Repeat the restoration disk prompt cycle until you have completed the restore operation.

With the full backup set restoration complete, you now must restore the incremental backup set. Because you want to restore all the files in the incremental backup set, you will use the same command as you used to restore the full backup set. The operation will proceed in the same fashion.

With both backup sets restored, you should run CHKDSK to ensure that the hard disk is in order. Keep both of your backup sets intact until you have determined that your hard disk is performing correctly. Run CHKDSK several times during the day. If all is in order, perform a full backup at the end of the day.

Using RESTORE Following an ERASE *.* Command

In another example of the use of RESTORE, assume that you have accidentally issued the **ERASE *.*** command. You thought that you were logged to your temporary directory \TEMP, but instead you were logged to your \REFLEX\DATA directory. Now all of your Reflex data files are erased. To recover your lost data, you will have to perform a selective restoration operation from your two backup sets. To restore only the files in the \REFLEX\DATA directory from the full backup set, issue the following command:

   RESTORE A: C:\REFLEX\DATA*.*

As in the complete restoration example, RESTORE will prompt you to insert the first disk. You can insert the first disk or, if you know the starting disk number that holds the Reflex files, you can insert the disk that holds the Reflex files. RESTORE will bypass any files on the source disk that are not included in the destination parameter that you gave in the command. When RESTORE does encounter a \REFLEX\DATA file, that file will be restored to the \REFLEX\DATA directory of the hard disk.

When you are sure that all files have been restored to the erased directory, you can press Ctrl-C or Ctrl-Break to abort the RESTORE operation. For safety's sake, you should insert all disks from an additive backup; a few files may have been backed up toward the end of the set.

Again, you must restore any files from the incremental set that belong in the \REFLEX\DATA directory. To restore from the incremental backup set, use the same command that you issued to restore the \REFLEX\DATA files from the full backup set.

If you maintain more than one incremental backup set, you should restore desired files from each of the incremental backup sets you have created since the last full backup and before the incident that caused the need to restore. Always restore backup sets in the order that they were created. Restore the oldest set first and the newest set last. If you restore the sets out of chronological order, you may overwrite more recent versions of files with older versions of the same files.

In situations which lend themselves to BACKUP and RESTORE, and which do not involve data loss (such as moving data from a work PC to a home PC), you can use the various RESTORE switches to ensure that you aren't moving older data to a PC that contains newer data. You can, for example, restore older files to a PC while preserving files modified or created after a specified date. Use the switches available with RESTORE to get the most from the command.

261

Summary

This chapter covered the important DOS commands and procedures that enable you to ensure the integrity of your data, and even more importantly, protect yourself from data loss. Following are the key points covered in this chapter:

❏ You can protect your computer hardware equipment by following common-sense safety precautions.

❏ You can protect yourself from "computer viruses" by purchasing only tested software.

❏ The COMP and FC commands compare a file for differences.

❏ The XCOPY command is a versatile copy command that can create subdirectories while copying.

❏ The BACKUP command is used to produce special backup disks. Backup disks are usually used for recovering lost data.

❏ The RESTORE command reads files from backup sets and restores the files to their original directories on another disk.

❏ You can protect yourself from data loss by faithfully designing and following a backup policy.

This chapter concludes Part Two of this book. In the next part, Part Three, you learn to tap the many expanded features available with DOS. You will also learn how to customize your computer system and navigate through the graphical user interface provided with DOS V4—the DOS Shell.

Part Three

Getting the Most from DOS

Using EDLIN

Using Batch Files

Configuring Your Computer and Managing Devices

Using the DOS Shell

Using
EDLIN

11

EDLIN, the mini text editor, is DOS's forgotten child. Because EDLIN is provided with every copy of DOS, the text editor has easily "outsold" Microsoft Word, WordPerfect, WordStar, or any other word processing program. Yet only a relatively small number of DOS users learn to use this simple, flexible program. As you will discover in this chapter, this neglect is undeserved.

Text editors, which actually predate word processing programs by a number of years, were originally developed for computer programmers who used them to enter and edit lists of commands for the computer. Frequently, these commands were programs eventually translated (or compiled) into the machine language understood by the computer. Programmers liked the ability to edit lines, add new lines, or move existing lines to other parts of the program.

EDLIN isn't limited to programming, however. You can use it as a handy tool to write short notes, "to-do" lists, or memos. You can use EDLIN to make changes in special configuration files used by DOS and many applications programs. The DOS CONFIG.SYS file, the Microsoft Windows WIN.INI file, and similar files for other programs are simple ASCII files you can edit with EDLIN. In Chapter 12, you will learn that EDLIN is useful for typing or editing a series of commands in special batch files.

If you understand its programming-environment heritage, you can see that EDLIN makes a lot of sense. It works with a single line at a time;

programmers write or edit commands as a series of separate lines. EDLIN provides a line number before each line; programmers use line numbers as labels to keep track of individual program lines. EDLIN enables you to move a line or a group of lines to another location in a file; programmers need these features. The EDLIN features also are handy for other text-editing chores.

Understanding EDLIN is helpful even if you use another word processing program to create ASCII files. EDLIN is fast to use. You can load EDLIN, type a few lines, and be finished in about the same time required to load a full-featured word processor. Word processors may require special syntax or formatting to produce ASCII files; EDLIN generates nothing but plain ASCII text files. Additionally, if you find yourself using someone else's computer, your favorite text editor may not be available. EDLIN nearly always is present on a PC with a hard disk.

This chapter explains how to use EDLIN to create and edit a simple memo. You'll be pleased to know you can gain EDLIN proficiency in 30 minutes or less. This chapter also contains information on additional, more advanced EDLIN commands.

A note from the author... I have used simple line editors like EDLIN for many years on mainframe computers. When full-featured word processors became available for PCs, I learned to use them as well. Although I use word processors for writing books and longer memos, I still use EDLIN much of the time. I can guarantee that if you learn EDLIN's basics, you'll use it too.

Starting EDLIN

Although EDLIN is furnished with DOS, it is a separate program. EDLIN operates like an external DOS command. The actual program is found on one of the diskettes supplied with DOS. If you use a computer that does not contain a hard disk drive, you may have to copy EDLIN from the master DOS diskettes (or a working copy) to a diskette with enough room to store a few ASCII files. The DOS disk on which EDLIN is located varies with the DOS version and disk format. With DOS V4.0 and 3 1/2-inch disks, for example, you can find EDLIN on the disk labeled *DOS Operating*. Some dealers include the EDLIN documentation in the DOS package; others feature the documentation as a separate item.

If you have a hard disk, you probably copied EDLIN to the directory (often named C:\DOS) in which you store other DOS external command programs such as XCOPY.EXE. If not, take the time now to copy EDLIN to the directory that stores your DOS files.

To run EDLIN, you simply type **EDLIN**, followed by the name of the file you want to create or edit. EDLIN itself must be located in the current directory or one of the directories listed in your DOS path (the DOS PATH command is explained in Chapter 8). If EDLIN is stored in the same directory as your other DOS files, you probably already have defined a path that allows DOS to locate it with no trouble. If the EDLIN directory is not specified in the PATH command, you can load EDLIN by changing to the directory where EDLIN resides or (if you have DOS V3.0 or later) by placing the full path name before the EDLIN commands.

Creating a Memo with EDLIN

In this section, you will learn to use EDLIN to create a simple memo. Type the following command at the DOS prompt to start EDLIN with the file MEMO.TXT:

> C>**EDLIN MEMO.TXT**

If EDLIN is located in another directory not indicated by the path, you can include the path name in the command:

> C>**C:\UTILS\EDLIN MEMO.TXT**

Either of these commands tell EDLIN to begin working with a file called MEMO.TXT in the current directory (even if EDLIN itself is located in another directory). If MEMO.TXT already exists and is smaller than about 64,000 bytes (64K), EDLIN loads it all into memory. If the file is larger than 64K, only the first 64K of the file is loaded.

 When you start editing a new file, the file name you use isn't created until the end of the editing session. Until then, EDLIN works with an intermediate file that has the root name you use, but an extension of .$$$, regardless of what you specify when you start EDLIN. The reason for this is explained later in the chapter.

For this exercise, you will create a new file called MEMO.TXT. If you want to work with a file in another directory, place the path name in front of the file name, as in the following example:

> C>**C:\DOS\EDLIN C:\MEMOS\MEMO.TXT**

This command loads EDLIN (no matter which directory is the current one) and begins work with a file called MEMO.TXT in the directory C:\MEMOS.

Once EDLIN is started, you will see the EDLIN prompt. Although the default DOS prompt is the drive name and greater-than symbol (such as A>, C>, and so on), EDLIN's prompt is a simple asterisk:

> *

When you see this prompt, EDLIN is waiting for your instructions in the form of EDLIN's commands. Each EDLIN command consists of a letter (either upper- or lowercase), which can be preceded or followed by numbers that tell EDLIN the number of lines you want to work with or the line numbers you are referring to. Some commands also enable you to specify strings of characters to search for or replace.

Inserting Text

Because the MEMO.TXT document you created in the preceding section is empty, you first need to enter some text. **I** (Insert Lines) is EDLIN's command for inserting text (even when the file is empty, text is inserted). To tell EDLIN that you want to insert text into the current file, you type the following at EDLIN's prompt:

    ***I**

EDLIN responds with the following:

    1:*

Notice that the colon is preceded by a line number, which tells you that EDLIN is currently in Insert Lines mode. If a line number, a colon, and an asterisk are the only things shown on a line, EDLIN is waiting for you to enter text.

Check the Caps Lock position on your keyboard before you start entering text. If Caps Lock is on, you may enter text with upper- and lowercase text reversed.

Now type the first line of the memo:

    1:***MEMO TO: Scott N. Hollerith, President**

Press Enter at the end of the line. EDLIN responds with the following:

    2:*

Don't confuse the asterisk shown after the line number with EDLIN's prompt. When shown with a line number, the asterisk marks the *current line*. The current line is the line currently being entered or, when you are editing lines, the line most recently edited. You will see the importance of the current line later in this chapter.

EDLIN is now ready for you to enter a second line. Type the rest of the following memo, pressing Enter at the end of each line:

    2:* **From: Otto Wirk, Research Chief**

    3:* **Subject: New Dual Processor Micro**

    4:* **Date: Sunday**

    5:*

    6:* **Our testing confirms that we should indeed**

     7 : * **include two microprocessors in the next model**

     8 : * **TLS-8E. This increases the odds that one will**

     9 : * **work. If both happen to function, they can**

    10 : * **take turns**

To leave line 5 blank, simply press Enter without typing anything. When you are finished with the memo (for the moment, anyway), stop inserting text at line 10 by pressing Enter to finish the line. Then press Ctrl-C or Ctrl-Break (hold down the Ctrl key and press C or hold down the Ctrl key and press Break). The EDLIN asterisk prompt returns.

Even though you haven't saved the memo to disk yet, suppose that you forgot to include several other staffers on the distribution list. The **I** command lets you fix this error quickly.

Type the following and press Enter:

     *5I

EDLIN responds with the following:

     5 : *

If you type a number in front of the **I** command, EDLIN enables you to enter text beginning with a new line that precedes the line you specify. In this example, EDLIN inserts a *new* line 5 in front of the *old* line 5. EDLIN renumbers the lines as necessary to accommodate the new line or lines. The line numbers aren't part of the memo you are creating; EDLIN uses line numbers only to help you keep track of the various lines currently in memory. The line numbers are not included in the file you will store to disk later.

At the **I** (Insert Lines) prompt, type this line:

     5 : * **CC: Bill Kem, Marketing; Betty Site, Testing**

Press Enter at the end of the line. A new blank line 6 appears. Because you don't want to add another line to the file, press Ctrl-C or Ctrl-Break to stop inserting lines.

Listing Text

If you want to see what the memo looks like with the addition, you can use EDLIN's **L** (List Lines) command to display the lines currently in memory. You can use the **L** command to look at a single line or a range of lines. Up to 23 lines can be shown on-screen at one time. Because the sample memo is shorter than 23 lines, you don't have to type in a range of line numbers to be displayed. Instead, specify only the first line you want displayed. Type the following:

     *1L

EDLIN responds by showing you the entire file so far:

```
 1: MEMO TO: Scott N. Hollerith, President
 2: From: Otto Wirk, Research Chief
 3: Subject: New Dual Processor Micro
 4: Date: Sunday
 5: CC: Bill Kem, Marketing; Betty Site, Testing
 6: *
 7: Our testing confirms that we should indeed
 8: include two microprocessors in the next model
 9: TLS-8E. This increases the odds that one will
10: work. If both happen to function, they can
11: take turns
```

Notice that the original blank line 5 has become line 6. In addition, only the asterisk is shown on line 6. The asterisk is not saved with the file, but it continues to mark the current line. The asterisk, like the line numbers, appears on-screen only to guide you.

For practice, list only a few lines at a time using the **L** command. Type the following:

*1,5L

EDLIN displays the first five lines of the memo—lines 1 to 5. Notice that when you type a line range, you separate the numbers with a comma instead of a hyphen, space, or other character.

You can list a single line by typing that line as the range. For example, you can type the following:

*1,1L

Editing a Line

If you listed the entire memo, you may have noticed that no period was typed at the end of the last sentence. This error can easily be fixed.

At EDLIN's * prompt, type the following:

*11

Notice that you do not type a specific command in this instance; you type just a line number at the EDLIN prompt to indicate that you want to edit line 11 of the current file. EDLIN responds by displaying the text of the specified line with the line number, colon, and asterisk prompt on the following line:

```
11:* take turns
11:*
```

No text is displayed on the second line. If you want, you can type a new line to replace the old one. Because you only want to make a small change at the end of the line, however, press F3. EDLIN displays the entire line:

```
11:* take turns
11:* take turns
```

Press the period key (.); then press Enter. EDLIN displays line 12 just as it did line 11. Press Ctrl-C or Ctrl-Break to stop editing.

The same function keys used as DOS editing keys are used with EDLIN. Recall that F3 is used to redisplay an entire command line. In the example you just worked through, F3 enables you to begin editing at the end of the specified line. If you want to replace the final word in the line, you can press Backspace four times and then type a new word. Later in this chapter, you will see how the other DOS editing keys are used with EDLIN.

For now, type **1L** at the EDLIN * prompt to list the memo. It looks much like it did before, with two changes:

```
 1: MEMO TO: Scott N. Hollerith, President
 2: From: Otto Wirk, Research Chief
 3: Subject: New Dual Processor Micro
 4: Date: Sunday
 5: CC: Bill Kem, Marketing; Betty Site, Testing
 6:
 7: Our testing confirms that we should indeed
 8: include two microprocessors in the next model
 9: TLS-8E. This increases the odds that one will
10: work. If both happen to function, they can
11:*take turns.
```

The period you typed at the end of line 11 is added, and line 11 now has an asterisk following the colon. The asterisk indicates that line 11 has been marked by EDLIN as the current line. Several EDLIN functions use the current line as a default if you don't enter a new value when you type the command. Use the **L** (List Lines) command and look for the asterisk after the line number to discover which line is the current line.

Saving Text

Before you modify the memo further, save it to disk so that you can retrieve it in this finished form later. To save the current file, you only need to end the EDLIN session with EDLIN's **E** (End Edit) command. The DOS prompt then returns. EDLIN automatically writes the file to the disk with the changes (if any) you made in the current session.

Try this technique now for practice. At the EDLIN prompt, type the following:

   *__E__

Remember to press Enter to activate the EDLIN command. The DOS prompt reappears. Notice that you don't get any "feedback," such as a message like Saving file to disk. No such message is really needed: when you exit EDLIN with the **E** command, the text is always stored. To abandon changes, use EDLIN's **Q** (Quit Edit) command to end the EDLIN session. The **Q** (Quit Edit) command is discussed in a later section of this chapter.

Printing the Memo

While you are at the DOS prompt, you can practice printing the memo. EDLIN does not have a specific print command, but to print an EDLIN file, you can use one of several DOS commands: PRINT, COPY, and TYPE.

You can use the PRINT command to copy the file to the printer. Alternatively, you can use the COPY command to copy the file to the printer. The TYPE command also can be used to redirect the file to the printer.

To print your memo, type one of the following commands at the DOS prompt:

   C>**PRINT MEMO.TXT**

   C>**TYPE MEMO.TXT>PRN**

   C>**COPY MEMO.TXT PRN**

If you have not used the PRINT command or directed output to the PRN device since the last time you rebooted, DOS may ask you to specify the print device and offer PRN as the default. If so, press Enter to confirm the default choice and start printing. If you have used DOS to print a file since you rebooted, PRINT is already resident in memory and you don't need to specify the print device.

Because you still have some work to do with MEMO.TXT, reload the file into EDLIN. To start EDLIN with an existing file, type the following:

   C>**EDLIN MEMO.TXT**

The * prompt reappears. Typing **L** after you load a file is good practice so that you can list the file and confirm that EDLIN has indeed loaded the text you intend to edit.

Deleting Lines

The last of EDLIN's basic commands is **D** (Delete Lines). As with the **L** (List Lines) command, you can work with a single line or a range of lines. The syntax is the same. Delete lines 5 and 6 of the memo by typing the following line at the EDLIN prompt:

   *__5,6D__

List the lines of the memo (type **1,11L**) to see what has happened. The memo now looks like this:

```
1: MEMO TO: Scott N. Hollerith, President
2: From: Otto Wirk, Research Chief
3: Subject: New Dual Processor Micro
4: Date: Sunday
5:*Our testing confirms that we should indeed
6: include two microprocessors in the next model
7: TLS-8E. This increases the odds that one will
8: work. If both happen to function, they can
9: take turns.
```

EDLIN again has renumbered the lines to accommodate the changes. Line 5, the line marked by the asterisk, is the current line because it is the first line that follows the lines you removed.

You can end this practice EDLIN session by typing **Q**. EDLIN asks whether you want to abort the session. Respond by pressing Y. The changes you made (deleting two lines) are not saved. The original version of MEMO.TXT remains on disk.

Learning More about EDLIN's Features

In the process of creating a memo with EDLIN, you learned some of the program's basic features. EDLIN also includes some additional editing features and commands. These are discussed in the remaining sections of this chapter.

Using EDLIN's /B Switch

EDLIN has an additional parameter, the */B* switch, that can be used when you start the program. You add the */B* switch to the initial EDLIN command at the DOS prompt, as in the following example:

C>**EDLIN MEMO.TXT /B**

The */B* switch tells EDLIN to read the entire file, based on its size as listed in the disk directory. You must type the /B as an uppercase character.

EDLIN normally reads a file only until it encounters the first end-of-file (EOF) character in the file. The EOF character is the Ctrl-Z (^Z) traditionally used to mark the end of ASCII files. Most of the time, you want EDLIN to read to the EOF character. Sometimes, however, you may want to edit a file that contains the EOF character within the file itself.

In its normal mode, EDLIN loads only the first part of such a file. By using the /B switch, you tell EDLIN to load the entire file, ignoring any Ctrl-Z characters it encounters in the file. You also can load program files (files that have the extension .COM or .EXE). Because program files are also called *binary* files, the switch is called /B. You have little reason to load such binary files; other tools like DEBUG are better suited for editing true binary files.

Understanding How EDLIN Works with Files

Remember that when you start EDLIN, it tries to find the file you specify in the current directory (or in the specified path if you precede the file name with a path name). If the file is not found, EDLIN creates the file with the extension .$$$, regardless of the extension you assigned. If you type the following, for example, EDLIN attempts to load a file called MEMO.TXT from the directory C:\MEMOS:

    C>**EDLIN C:\MEMOS\MEMO.TXT**

If EDLIN cannot find such a file, it creates a new file called MEMO.$$$.

If a new file is created, the message New file appears. When you save the file by ending the session with the **E** (End Edit) command, the file is renamed from the .$$$ extension to the .TXT extension specified when you started EDLIN.

If the C:\MEMOS\MEMO.TXT file specified when you started EDLIN is found, EDLIN copies the original file and gives it a .$$$ extension. If the file is less than 64K in size, EDLIN loads the file and displays the following message:

    End of input file

When you save the file, the original MEMO.TXT file is renamed with the extension .BAK; the temporary .$$$ file is given the original MEMO.TXT file name and becomes a permanent disk file. If you decide to quit the session without saving the file (using the **Q** command), the last version of the file on disk is retained unchanged (if you were editing an existing file). If you were working with a new file when you used the **Q** (Quit Edit) command, the temporary .$$$ file is erased.

These options and conditional statements may sound confusing, but they all boil down to one thing: EDLIN enables you to quit editing at any time without destroying the original disk version of your file.

EDLIN can work with only a limited amount of information at one time. Each line of text, for example, can have up to 253 characters, and each file can have from 1 to 65,529 line numbers, depending on file size. If the file is longer than 65,529 lines, EDLIN works with the file in sections. You can load the first section of the file into memory, work with it, and then save it to disk. EDLIN then enables you to load more of the file and work with that section. The process can be repeated until editing is complete. This section-by-section editing process is explained in the next section.

Learning Special Editing Techniques

In this chapter, you learned to edit a line by typing the line number at the EDLIN asterisk prompt. If you press Enter without typing a line number, the current line, indicated with the **L** (List Lines) command by an asterisk, is edited.

When editing a line, you can use a combination of keys to edit and change the text line. You can add information by typing up to 253 characters on the line (EDLIN wraps the line automatically at the right edge of the screen). After you have edited the line, press Enter. The cursor returns to the * prompt.

If you change your mind or make a mistake as you are editing, press Esc. This action cancels the changes to the current line. You also can cancel changes to the current line by pressing Enter when the cursor is in the first position on the current line.

You also can add special control characters such as Ctrl-Z, the end-of-file character, to your text files. To enter a control character, press Ctrl-V and then type the desired character in uppercase letters. To type a Ctrl-Z character, for example, press Ctrl-V and Z.

Another character you may want to enter is the Escape character (ASCII character #27). Batch files (discussed in Chapter 12), make use of the Escape character to send special codes to ANSI.SYS (discussed in Chapter 13). If you press the Esc key to try to enter the Escape character, a backslash (\) appears on the line, and the cursor moves to the next line, abandoning what you just typed. To enter the Escape character in a file, first press Ctrl-V and then press the left square bracket ([).

With EDLIN, you also can add graphics characters, such as those used to make a box. To add graphics characters, however, you must make sure that ANSI.SYS is installed as a device in CONFIG.SYS. You learn more about ANSI.SYS and CONFIG.SYS later in this book.

To enter a graphics character, hold the Alt key and use the numeric keypad to type the ASCII code for the character you want to insert. (A complete list of ASCII codes is found in Appendix F.) To enter a vertical bar, for example, hold the Alt key and type **179** on the numeric keypad. When you release the Alt key, a vertical bar appears on-screen.

Using the Editing Keys

You can use the function keys F1 through F6 with EDLIN to reenter and correct text lines. The function keys available for editing in EDLIN are explained in table 11.1.

Table 11.1
EDLIN Key Combinations

Key	Function
F1 or right arrow	Copies one character from the edited line to the current line.
F2 *char*	Copies all the characters from the edited line to the first occurrence of the character *char*.
F3	Copies all the remaining characters from the edited line to the current line. Pressing F3 without first typing anything on the current line copies all characters from the edited line to the current line. If you have already started to edit the current line, pressing F3 copies the remaining characters.
F4 *char*	Deletes from the keyboard buffer all characters up to *char*. Use F1 or F3 to copy the remaining characters to the current line.
F5	Copies all the characters typed on the current line into the keyboard buffer. When you press F3, the copied characters transfer to the edited line.
F6	Creates a Ctrl-Z, (^Z) end-of-file, character.
F7	Creates a null character, Ctrl-@.
Ins	Acts as a toggle switch between insert and overtype modes. After you press Ins, you can insert characters at the current cursor position. Press Ins again to turn off insert capabilities.
Del	Erases one character to the right of the current cursor position.
Esc	Causes the current line to be ignored.

Using the EDLIN Commands

Table 11.2 is a complete list of the commands available with EDLIN. Each command is listed with its function and any available parameters. The rest of this chapter describes each of these commands and their parameters in more detail.

Table 11.2
EDLIN Commands

Command	Syntax	Function
A (Append Lines)	*n***A**	Loads the next section of a file into memory if the file is too large to fit into memory
C (Copy Lines)	*sline,eline,***dline***,count***C**	Copies one or more lines within a file
D (Delete Lines)	*sline,eline,***D**	Deletes one or more lines from a file
E (End Edit)	**E**	Ends EDLIN and saves the edited file
I (Insert Lines)	*n***I**	Inserts new lines of text into the file
L (List Lines)	*sline,eline***L**	Lists the file's contents on-screen; does not change the current file
M (Move Lines)	*sline,eline,***dlineM**	Moves and relocates lines within a file
P (Page)	*sline,eline***P**	Lists the file's contents *and* changes the current line
Q (Quit Edit)	**Q**	Quits without saving changes to the file
R (Replace Text)	*sline,eline?***Rstext<F6>rtext**	Replaces text within a file
S (Search Text)	*sline,eline?***Sstext**	Searches for a specified text string
T (Transfer Lines)	*n***T***d:***filename.ext**	Transfers the contents of one file into another file
W (Write Lines)	**W**	Writes a specified number of lines to disk from memory

The following definitions are assumed in table 11.2.

<F6>   The F6 function key is pressed.

count   The number of times the procedure is to be repeated.

d: Drive name. If unspecified, the default drive is used.

dline   *Destination* line number. The text to be moved or copied is placed in front of the line number specified by *dline*.

eline	*Ending* line number. If unspecified, the operation usually affects only the *sline* (starting line).
filename.ext	A legal DOS file name.
n	An integer representing a line *number* or a total *number* of specified lines.
rtext	Series of alphanumeric characters to *replace stext*.
sline	*Starting* line number in a group of lines. If unspecified, the operation usually assumes the current or default line.
stext	Series of alphanumeric characters for which to *search*.

A—The Append Lines Command

EDLIN can hold in memory only a certain number of lines at one time. To work with larger files, you load a section of a file into memory, make your editing changes, write that section to disk, and then load the next section. The **A** (Append Lines) command is one of the tools you use to perform this process.

In actual practice, you rarely use EDLIN in this manner, because the program is somewhat clumsy for really long files. A full-featured word processor is a better choice. As a safeguard against the day when you may want or need to use EDLIN with a long file, however, you should learn to use the **A** and **W** (Write Lines) commands. They are really quite simple.

The **A** command adds the number of lines you specify from the disk and places them into memory. Lines are appended from the disk to the end of the lines currently in memory. If memory can hold no more lines, you may first need to write some of the lines already resident to disk. Otherwise, the first lines (equal to the number you have appended) will be dropped. You will learn in the next section how to write lines to disk with the **W** command.

The syntax for the **A** (Append Lines) command is as follows:

> *n***A**

n is the number of lines to place into memory.

If you see the message End of input file when you start EDLIN, you don't need the **A** command. You use **A** only when the file being edited is too large to fit in memory.

To append lines, type a number representing the total number of lines you want appended to the end of memory. Then type **A** and press Enter. The cursor returns to the * prompt.

Continue the process of writing and appending lines until you see the following message:

```
End of input file
```

After this message appears, all lines have been read into memory. If you don't use the **W** (Write Lines) command before you use **A**, you may lose previously edited corrections.

If you do not specify the number of lines to be appended, any remaining lines in the file are appended to the file in memory until available memory is 75 percent full. The number of lines will vary depending on the length of the individual lines.

W—The Write Lines Command

Use the **W** (Write Lines) command to write a specified number of lines in memory to the disk. The syntax for the **W** command is as follows:

*n***W**

n is the number of lines to write to the disk.

You don't need this command if you see the message End of input file when you start EDLIN. Use this command only when the file being edited is too large to fit into memory. Use this command before appending new lines to the file being edited. When you write, the lines are removed from memory, thus leaving room for you to append.

To use this command, type the number of lines you want to write. Type **W** and press Enter; the cursor returns to the * prompt. If you want, you can continue appending lines for editing. Continue with this process until you see the following message:

    End of input file

After this message appears, all lines have been read into memory. Using the **W** (Write Lines) command is no longer necessary because you have written the previous lines in the file to the disk, and all the remaining lines can fit into memory. Save the remaining lines in memory by ending the editing session with the **E** (End Edit) command.

If you don't specify the number of lines to be written, the remaining lines, starting from line 1, are saved to disk until available memory is 25 percent full.

C—The Copy Lines Command

You can copy one or more lines from the current file to the line number specified with the **C** (Copy Lines) command. The syntax of this command is as follows:

*sline,eline,***dline,***count***C**

sline is the starting line, and *eline* is the ending line to copy from. **dline** is the line in front of which the copied lines are to be placed, and *count* is the number of times to copy the text.

To copy lines, type the starting line number where the copying is to begin. Press the comma (,) and then type the ending line number. You have just indicated the range of lines to copy. Press the comma again and type the line in front of which the copied lines are to be inserted. If you want more than one copy of the range, press the comma and then type the number of copies you want. Finish the command by typing **C** and pressing Enter. The cursor returns to the * prompt. Use the **L** (List Lines) command to check the insertion of the copied lines. The copied lines appear in front of the specified **dline** number.

Try the following example. Start EDLIN and load MEMO.TXT (the file you created in a previous section). Then type **L** at the EDLIN prompt to see the following listing:

```
 1:*MEMO TO: Scott N. Hollerith, President
 2: From: Otto Wirk, Research Chief
 3: Subject: New Dual Processor Micro
 4: Date: Sunday
 5: CC: Bill Kem, Marketing; Betty Site, Testing
 6:
 7: Our testing confirms that we should indeed
 8: include two microprocessors in the next model
 9: TLS-8E. This increases the odds that one will
10: work. If both happen to function, they can
11: take turns.
```

Now, type the **C** (Copy Lines) command as follows:

*2,4,6C

In this syntax, 2 is the starting line, 4 is the ending line, and 6 is the destination line.

Type **L** again to see what happens:

```
 1: MEMO TO: Scott N. Hollerith, President
 2: From: Otto Wirk, Research Chief
 3: Subject: New Dual Processor Micro
 4: Date: Sunday
 5: CC: Bill Kem, Marketing; Betty Site, Testing
 6:* From: Otto Wirk, Research Chief
 7: Subject: New Dual Processor Micro
 8: Date: Sunday
 9:
10: Our testing confirms that we should indeed
```

```
11: include two microprocessors in the next model
12: TLS-8E. This increases the odds that one will
13: work. If both happen to function, they can
14: take turns.
```

EDLIN has copied lines 2 through 4 of the original memo and placed them before line 6. EDLIN then renumbered the lines from the original line 6 (which becomes line 9) on.

You can designate the number of times a range copy is repeated. For example, the command **3,3,9,7C** copies the contents of line 3 beginning at line 9, inserts the copy in front of line 9, and repeats the copy seven times. The former line 9 is renumbered as line 16.

If the starting or ending line number is omitted from the syntax of the **C** (Copy Lines) command, the current line is used as the missing parameter. If the current line is line 3, for example, and you type **3,,9C**, only line 3 is copied to line 9. If you type **,5,9C**, lines 3 through 5 are copied in front of line 9.

When you copy lines, do not overlap line numbers. Typing **2,7,5C**, for example, results in an error: lines 2 through 7 overlap line number 5.

D—The Delete Lines Command

Use the **D** (Delete Lines) command to remove one or more lines from the file being edited. You may want to use the **L** (List Lines) command to note the current line numbers before you delete. Listing lines serves as a double-check against losing important lines in your file.

The syntax of the **D** (Delete Lines) command is as follows:

> *sline,eline***D**

sline is the starting line number, and *eline* is the ending line number of the range to delete.

To delete just one line, type the line number to be deleted and then type **D**. Then press Enter. To delete line number 2, for example, type **2D** and press Enter.

To delete a range of lines, type the starting line number, a comma, and the ending line number of the range of lines to be deleted. Complete the command by typing **D** and pressing Enter. The cursor returns to the * prompt.

I—The Insert Lines Command

As you recall, the **I** command adds lines of text to a newly created file or inserts new lines of text between existing lines in an existing file or at its end. A few features of

281

this command, however, weren't explained earlier in this chapter. The syntax for the **I** (Insert Lines) command is as follows:

>   *n***I**

n is the line on which insertion is to begin.

To insert lines with EDLIN, type the line number at which you want to begin inserting lines; then type **I**. If a line number is not specified, insertion begins at the current line. If you are creating a new file, simply type **I** and press Enter; new files always begin insertion at line 1.

If you do not specify a line number, the insertion takes place before the current line. The **I** command renumbers the current line and the lines that follow to reflect the new lines added.

To insert lines at the end of the file, use the pound symbol in place of the line number (**#I**). Insertion begins after the last line number and continues until you press Ctrl-C.

L—The List Lines Command

You use the **L** (List Lines) command frequently. As you learned when you were writing MEMO.TXT, the syntax for the **L** command is as follows:

>   *sline,eline***L**

sline is the starting line, and *eline* is the ending line of the range to be listed.

You can minimize changes in line numbers if you make changes to your file by working backwards. Make the changes first to the end of the file and proceed backwards to the beginning of the file. This method leaves the early line numbers unchanged, so that you do not have to list the file after every insertion to determine the line numbers of the rest of the file.

You can use the **L** command for more than listing the entire file. To list and display a range of lines, first type the starting line number where the display is to begin. EDLIN will display 23 lines starting with the line you specify; then type **L** and press Enter. You can list a block of lines by typing the starting line number, pressing the comma key (**,**), typing the ending line number, typing **L**, and then pressing Enter.

The **L** command works like EDLIN's **P** (Page) command with one exception: **L** does not change the line EDLIN thinks of as the current line; **P** *does* change the current line number.

If you omit the starting line number, **L** starts displaying the 11 lines preceding the current line. The listing continues until the ending line number is reached. For example, if the current line were 23 and you typed **,40L** and pressed Enter, lines 12 through 30 would appear on-screen.

If you omit the ending line number, 23 lines are displayed, beginning with the starting line. If the current line were 23 and you typed **12L** and pressed Enter, lines 12 through 30 would appear on-screen.

You can reference line numbers in relation to the current line by using a plus (+) or minus (–) sign. Type **–5L** to list the five lines preceding the current line. To list the nine lines after the current line, type **+9L**.

If you cannot remember or find the current line number, use a period (**.**) to specify the current line number. To list the current line number, for example, type **.L** and press Enter. EDLIN interprets the period to mean the current line number.

Use the **L** (List Lines) command frequently with EDLIN. The **L** command can prevent you from making a mistake when using commands that affect line numbering.

P—The Page Command

Use the **P** (Page) command to list the specified block of lines on a full 23-line display. The **P** command is similar to the **L** (List Lines) command except that the current line changes each time you use **P**. Use the **P** command to move through the file being edited one page (23 lines) at a time. The syntax of the **P** command is as follows:

> *sline,eline***P**

sline is the starting line, and *eline* is the ending line of the range to be displayed.

When listing lines by page, type the line number where the block to be displayed is to begin. Then press the comma (**,**) and type the ending line number of the block. If the ending line number is omitted, the 23 lines from the starting line number are displayed. Finish the command by typing **P** and pressing Enter.

The **P** command works like the **L** command, except that **P** changes the current line. Use the Pause key or press Ctrl-S to stop the display from scrolling when you display more lines than will fit. When you use **P**, the last line displayed becomes the new current line.

If you omit the starting line, the **P** command begins the display after the current line. The listing, displaying 23 lines at a time, continues until the specified ending line is reached. If you omit the ending-line parameter, 23 lines are displayed from the starting line or the current line. If you type **12P** and press Enter, lines 12 through 35 appear on-screen. If you type only **P**, the 23 lines after the current line appear. Type **12,20P** to display lines 12 through 20. If fewer than 23 lines are in the file after the current line, typing **P** displays the lines until the lines run out.

Consider using the **P** (Page) command frequently. It can prevent you from making a mistake when you use commands that affect line numbering.

M—The Move Lines Command

The **M** (Move Lines) command moves one or more lines within a file. The **M** command is similar to the **C** (Copy Lines) command. The syntax for the **M** command is as follows:

*sline,eline,***dlineM**

sline is the starting line, and *eline* is the ending line in the range to be moved. **dline** is the destination line in front of which you want to insert the moved lines.

To move lines of text, type the starting line number of the range of lines to be moved. Press the comma (,) and then type the line number that ends the range of lines to be moved. Then press the comma and type the line number in front of which you want to move the specified range. Complete the command by typing **M** and pressing Enter.

Type **25,40,71M** to move lines 25 through 40 in front of line 71. Type **3,3,7M** to move line 3 to line number 7. Type **,+7,3M** to move the current line and the next seven lines in front of line number 3.

If you want to practice moving lines, use the MEMO.TXT file you created previously. (If the version of MEMO.TXT you modified when you copied lines is still in memory, abort the session by typing **Q**; then restart EDLIN and load MEMO.TXT.) Type **L** at the EDLIN prompt to see the following listing of MEMO.TXT:

```
 1:*MEMO TO: Scott N. Hollerith, President
 2: From: Otto Wirk, Research Chief
 3: Subject: New Dual Processor Micro
 4: Date: Sunday
 5: CC: Bill Kem, Marketing; Betty Site, Testing
 6:
 7: Our testing confirms that we should indeed
 8: include two microprocessors in the next model
 9: TLS-8E. This increases the odds that one will
10: work. If both happen to function, they can
11: take turns.
```

Type the following at the EDLIN prompt:

```
*3,3,5M
```

This command moves line 3 to a position preceding line 5. Type **L** at the EDLIN prompt to confirm this. The memo now looks like this:

```
1: MEMO TO: Scott N. Hollerith, President
2: From: Otto Wirk, Research Chief
```

```
 3: Date: Sunday
 4:* Subject: New Dual Processor Micro
 5: CC: Bill Kem, Marketing; Betty Site, Testing
 6:
 7: Our testing confirms that we should indeed
 8: include two microprocessors in the next model
 9: TLS-8E. This increases the odds that one will
10: work. If both happen to function, they can
11: take turns.
```

Q—The Quit Edit Command

Use the **Q** (Quit Edit) command to exit from EDLIN without saving the edited file. The syntax for this command is as follows:

Q

Use **Q** when you want to abort and terminate the edited file. EDLIN verifies whether you really want to abandon the edited file by displaying the following prompt:

```
Abort edit (Y/N)?
```

Press Y to abort the editing process or N to continue editing the file.

EDLIN does not create a backup when you are creating a new file. Backup files are created only when an existing file is being edited. When you use the **Q** command, a backup file is not created and the original file is not altered. If you are working on a new file and issue the **Q** command, the new file is lost.

S—The Search Text Command

Use the **S** (Search Text) command to search and locate a sequence of text characters, called a *character string*. The syntax for the **S** command is as follows:

*sline,eline?***Sstext**

sline is the starting line, and *eline* is the ending line of the range of lines to be searched. The *?* parameter produces the prompt O.K.? so that you can confirm whether you want to continue searching. If you answer Y to this prompt, the displayed line becomes the current line and the search ends. Answering N causes the search to continue. **stext** is the character string for which to search.

To search for text, type the starting line number of the text block to be searched. Press the comma (,) and type the ending line number of the text block to be searched. Press the space bar and **?** to have EDLIN prompt whether you want to stop searching. If you include this parameter, EDLIN queries you whether it should stop searching for the stext character string. To finish the command, type **S** and the text string for which you want to search. Press Enter to start the search.

If the ending line is not specified, searching continues to the end of the file. If both starting and ending parameters are unspecified, searching begins at the line following the current line and continues to the last line of the file. The last line searched that contains the **stext** character string becomes the current line. Press Esc to cancel this command.

Use the ? parameter to have EDLIN query you whether it should stop searching for the specified text string. Press Y to stop searching for text; the last line displayed becomes the current line. Pressing any other key continues the search. If you don't use the ? parameter, the text search stops on the first occurrence of the specified text string. You must issue another **S** (Search Text) command to continue the search.

If the **stext** string is not specified, EDLIN uses the value specified in the last **S** (Search Text) or **R** (Replace Text) command for the current session. When the specified text string cannot be found within the specified range of lines, the following message appears:

```
Not found
```

Remember that search strings are case-sensitive. If you specify a search string of *capital*, for example, you will not find *Capital* or *CAPITAL*.

R—The Replace Text Command

Use the **R** (Replace Text) command to replace a sequence of text characters, a *character string*, with a different character string. The syntax for the **R** command is as follows:

    *sline,eline?***Rstext<F6>rtext**

sline is the starting line of the search, and *eline* is the ending line of the search. The *?* parameter causes the prompt O.K.? to appear so that you can confirm each replacement by pressing Y or N. If you answer Y to this prompt, the replacement is made. Answering N causes the search-and-replace operation to continue, although no replacement is made at the current location. **stext** is the character string to search for, **<F6>** is the F6 key, and **rtext** is the replacement text.

To replace text, type the starting line number of the range of text to be affected by the replace operation. If you are replacing only one line, enter that line number. If you don't type a starting line number, EDLIN will start with the current default line. Press the comma (**,**) and type the ending line number of the range.

At this point, you can press **?** to have EDLIN prompt whether you want to change the displayed line. If you include this parameter, EDLIN queries you for each line that matches the search criteria. To continue with the command, type **R** and the text string for which you want to search. Then press the F6 key and type the text you want to use as the replacement. Start the command by pressing Enter.

To practice replacing text, load a fresh copy of MEMO.TXT. (If the version of MEMO.TXT you modified when you moved lines is still in memory, type **Q** to abort this EDLIN session. Restart EDLIN with the disk version of MEMO.TXT.) When MEMO.TXT is loaded, type this command at the EDLIN prompt:

> ***1,11?R TLS-8E\<F6\>TLS-8F/B1.8\<D\>**

This command tells EDLIN to search from lines 1 to 11 for the string TLS-8E. Because you have included the question mark, EDLIN asks you before replacing each occurrence of the string it finds. If you press Y when prompted, the new string, TLS-8F/B1.8, is inserted in place of the old one. List the memo to confirm that this has taken place:

```
 1: MEMO TO: Scott N. Hollerith, President
 2: From: Otto Wirk, Research Chief
 3: Subject: New Dual Processor Micro
 4: Date: Sunday
 5: CC: Bill Kem, Marketing; Betty Site, Testing
 6:
 7: Our testing confirms that we should indeed
 8: include two microprocessors in the next model
 9:*TLS-8F/B1.8. This increases the odds that one will
10: work. If both happen to function, they can
11: take turns.
```

In this example, the current line becomes the line last replaced. If the starting line number is not specified, searching begins with the line following the current line. If the ending line is not specified, searching ends with the current default line. If both starting and ending line parameters are unspecified, searching begins at the line following the current line and continues to the last line.

Use the ? parameter to have EDLIN query you whether the displayed line should be replaced. Press Y to replace the text as specified in the command line. Pressing any other key prevents changes to the displayed line, and searching continues. Use the **S** (Search Text) command to search for text without replacing it.

If you do not specify the *rtext* parameter when you type the text parameters, all occurrences of the *stext* string are deleted (replaced with nothing) from the line specified. If you type **1,4,Rmodel**, for example, any occurrence of the word *model* is deleted from the lines 1 to 4. If you don't specify either *stext* or *rtext*, EDLIN uses the values specified in the previous **R** or **S** (Search Text) commands for this session.

In some cases, memory-resident programs may reassign the value of the F6 function key. This sometimes occurs when a keyboard or control program has reassigned keys. If you have a memory-resident program that has reassigned the function keys, use Ctrl-Z as an alternative to F6 if F6 is not available to you.

T—The Transfer Lines Command

The **T** (Transfer Lines) command transfers or merges the contents of a file into the file currently being edited.

Before using the **T** command within EDLIN, check to see whether the file being merged is an ASCII file. At the DOS prompt, use the DOS TYPE command to see whether the file is readable. Make sure that the file being merged is in the same directory as the file being edited. The syntax for the **T** (Transfer Lines) command is as follows:

> *n***T***d:***filename.ext**

n is the line number in the current file where the new file is to be merged, *d:* is the drive designation for the file to be merged, and **filename.ext** is the name of the file to merge.

The **T** command merges files. To transfer lines, type the line number where the merged file contents are to be inserted. The current line is used if you don't specify a line number. Type **T** and then type the drive name for the file to be merged (for example, A:, B:, and so on). You cannot designate a directory name; this is probably the most serious drawback of the **T** command.

Type the name of the file to be merged. Press Enter. The cursor returns to the * prompt, and the contents of the merged file are inserted in front of the current default line or the specified line number.

Summary

This chapter has introduced you to the commands and functions of the DOS-provided text editor, EDLIN. Following are the important concepts discussed:

❏ EDLIN is especially useful for editing and working with short files. Running EDLIN is often quicker and easier than loading a full-scale word processor.

❏ If you routinely use large files, you may want to invest in a full-screen editor or word processing program.

❏ You load EDLIN by typing **EDLIN** and the file name to be created or edited.

❏ You can use the function keys with EDLIN to reenter and correct text lines.

❏ You can view EDLIN files by using the **L** (List Lines) or **P** (Page) command.

❏ To edit files larger than 64K, use the **W** (Write Lines) command.

❏ The **I** (Insert Lines) command enables you to insert lines in a new or existing file.

❏ EDLIN's **R** (Replace Text) and **S** (Search Text) commands enable you to quickly look for and change specific strings of text.

❏ You can move and copy lines quickly by using EDLIN's **M** (Move) and **C** (Copy) commands.

❏ To abort editing changes, exit EDLIN by using the **Q** (Quit Edit) command.

❏ To save your changes, use the **E** (End Edit) command.

With knowledge of EDLIN, you will have a convenient means to create text files, such as memos, notes, and batch files. In the next chapter, you can put EDLIN to work as you learn the basics of creating batch files.

Understanding
Batch Files

12

The idea of getting a computer to do work in convenient, manageable batches predates the personal computer by several years. The very first computers were large and expensive, and they could do only one job at a time. But even these early machines were very fast. Making them wait for keyboard input between jobs was inefficient.

Batch processing was developed to make computers more productive. Collections of tasks to be carried out consecutively were put together off-line—that is, without using the computer's resources. The chunks or batches of tasks were then fed to the computer at a rate that kept the computer busy and productive.

Today, computers are less expensive than precious human resources. Batch processing is still used to get the computer to carry out a series of tasks without wasting a lot of personnel time typing often-used or complex commands.

Batch files are available for your convenience. You can use batch files to automate a DOS process. Using a set of commands in a batch file, you actually create a new, more powerful command. After a few experiments, you probably will find this DOS facility quite handy.

In Chapter 11, you learned how to create text files with EDLIN. In this chapter, you can put that learning to use creating batch files. In the process, you will learn about batch file subcommands, the AUTOEXEC.BAT file, and some examples of batch files you can modify to suit your needs.

Key Terms Used in This Chapter

Batch file	A text file that contains DOS commands, which DOS executes as though the commands were entered at the DOS prompt. Batch files always have a BAT extension.
Subcommand	A DOS command used with batch files. These commands add more control to batch files.
Flow control	The capability to change which line in a batch file is to be processed.
Meta-string	A series of characters that takes on a different meaning to DOS than its literal meaning. DOS displays substitute text when it finds meta-strings in the PROMPT command.
Replaceable Parameters	A number preceded by a percent sign. Parameters are used in a batch file as markers for other text entered at the command line. The command-line entry for the replaceable parameter is variable.
AUTOEXEC.BAT	An optional batch file that COMMAND.COM automatically executes during the booting process. The AUTOEXEC.BAT file, usually placed in the root directory, is an ideal place to include commands that initialize the operation of a PC.

Introducing Batch Files

A *batch file* is a text file that contains a series of DOS commands. Most of the commands used in batch files are familiar to you; they are commands explained in previous chapters of this book. Other commands that control the flow of action in batch files are called the *batch subcommands*. DOS executes the commands in the batch file one line at a time, treating them as though you had issued each one individually.

Recognizing a batch file in a directory listing is easy. Batch files always have the extension BAT in their full file names. When you type a batch file's root name at the DOS prompt, COMMAND.COM looks in the current directory for that file name with the BAT extension, reads the file, and executes the DOS commands the file contains. The whole process is automatic. You enter the batch file name—DOS does the work.

You can use the PATH command early in your work session to provide DOS with alternative directories to search for the batch file you entered. As with COM and EXE files, PATH allows COMMAND.COM to find BAT files in the search path.

Batch files are useful for automatically issuing commands that are hard to remember or that are easy to mistype at the command line. A good example would be some form of the BACKUP command. BACKUP is not a difficult command, but it is a command that you will use far less frequently than you use the COPY command or the DIR command. You may find it convenient to put properly formed backup commands in batch files that you can execute with one simple batch name.

Batch files can echo or display text that you have entered into them. This text-display capability is useful for presenting instructions or reminders on the display. You can compose screens that help you execute a command or that contain syntax examples and reminders. You can even display a message of the day. A batch file is not limited to displaying text contained within it. Batch files can use the TYPE command to display text from another file.

In their advanced form, batch files can resemble computer programs. DOS has a host of special commands, called *subcommands*, that are used most often in batch files. Although you can type some of these commands at the DOS prompt, their primary application is to let you carry out other DOS functions in a more useful way. Batch subcommands introduce flow-control and decision-making capabilities into a batch file.

Understanding the Contents of Batch Files

Batch files contain ASCII text characters. You can create a text file with many word processing programs in nondocument mode. *Nondocument mode* is a setting that omits the special formatting and control characters which word processing programs use for internal purposes. Composing batch files in nondocument mode eliminates many command-syntax errors these special characters might cause.

You can also use the DOS line editor, EDLIN, to create a batch file. EDLIN is useful for creating medium-to-long batch files of 10 lines or more. The easiest way to create a very short batch file, however, is to use the COPY command by redirecting input from the CON device.

Avoid naming your batch file with the same name as a DOS command. You must avoid having two executable files on a disk with the same root name. Depending on your PATH setting and the current directory, COMMAND.COM will execute only one of the files with the duplicate name. If you give a batch file the name of an internal command, DOS will run the command instead of the batch file. If you do have a naming conflict, use the RENAME command to give the batch file a unique name.

Rules for Creating Batch Files

When you create batch files, you must follow certain rules. The following list summarizes these rules.

1. Batch files must be ASCII text files. If you use a word processor, be sure that it is in programming, or nondocument, mode.

2. The name of the batch file can be from one to eight characters long. The name must conform to the rules for naming files. It is best to use alphabetical characters in batch file names. Make the name literal.

3. The file name must end with the BAT extension.

4. The batch file name should not be the same as a program file name (a file with an EXE or COM extension).

5. The batch file name should not be the same as an internal DOS command (such as COPY or DATE).

6. The batch file can contain any valid DOS commands that you might enter at the DOS prompt. Typos will cause errors.

7. You can include in the batch file any program name that you usually type at the DOS prompt. DOS will execute the program as if you had entered its name at the prompt.

8. Use only one command or program name per line in the batch file. DOS executes batch files one line at a time.

Rules for Running Batch Files

You start batch files by typing the batch file name (excluding the extension) at the DOS prompt. The following list summarizes the rules DOS follows when it loads and executes batch files.

1. If you do not specify the disk drive name before the batch file name, DOS uses the current drive.

2. If you do not give a path, DOS searches through the current directory for the batch file.

3. If the batch file is not in the current directory, and you did not precede the batch file name with a path, DOS searches the directories specified by the last PATH command you issued.

4. If DOS encounters a syntax error in a batch file command line, DOS displays an error message, skips the errant command, and executes the remaining commands in the batch file.

5. You can stop a batch command by pressing Ctrl-C or Ctrl-Break. DOS will prompt you to confirm that you want to terminate the

batch file. If you answer No, DOS skips the current command (the one being carried out) and resumes execution with the next command in the batch file.

6. If you try to run a batch file and DOS displays an error message, you probably made a mistake when you typed the name. To check, you can view any batch file by using the following command:

   TYPE *filename*

   filename refers to the name of the batch file.

Creating a Simple Batch File

For practice, create a simple batch file. In the following example, you will use the COPY CON technique to create the file as a plain ASCII text file. Remember that you can use EDLIN or your word processor in nondocument mode to create plain ASCII text files.

A repetitive task that you perform is copying and comparing files. Tasks consisting of the same series of commands are ideal candidates for becoming batch files. Suppose that you often work with SALES.WK1 and CUSTOMER.WK1, two spreadsheet files. These files are stored in a subdirectory called \STORE on drive C. After you update each one, you then must copy the files to drive A and compare the copies to the originals. The copies on the disk in A are then ready for safekeeping or copying to (updating) another computer.

Using the console device for input, you initiate the batch file's creation by entering the following line:

   COPY CON STOREBAK.BAT

This console redirection will create a file called STOREBAK.BAT. When the cursor drops to a blank line and waits, enter the following 3 lines.

   ECHO OFF

   COPY C:\STORE A:

   COMP C:\STORE A:

Check each line before pressing Enter when you are creating a text file with COPY CON. You can use Backspace to back up on the line to correct typos. Once you press Enter, any error on the entered line is unreachable. You will have to press Ctrl-C and start the command over.

Notice the first line of the batch file. **ECHO OFF** shuts off the display of the batch file's commands to the screen. In other words, you will not see the command lines themselves on your display—only their actions. **ECHO OFF** makes the screen appear less "busy."

295

The second line of the batch file consists of a command line which copies the desired files from their source location in C:\STORE to the destination root directory of drive A.

The final line of the batch file uses COMP.COM, an external DOS command that compares the copied files to the originals. Although you can use the /V (verify) switch with COPY, using COMP is more thorough because the source and destination files are read again and compared for exactness in matching. Because COMP.COM is an external utility, the assumption is made that a PATH statement exists to the common directory that contains DOS utilities. (PATH was introduced in chapter 7 and is covered in detail later in this chapter along with AUTOEXEC.BAT.)

The final operation in the creation of SAVEBAK.BAT is the entry of the end-of-file marker. After entering the last line in the file, press F6 or Ctrl-Z (both produce the ^Z). DOS will signal as follows:

```
1 File(s) copied
```

Now that the SAVEBAK batch file is complete, you can run the batch file by typing **SAVEBAK** on the command line. Of course, it's unlikely that you have the exact directory or copying requirements that this batch file illustrates, but you can use the example as a template for your own batch file.

Understanding the AUTOEXEC.BAT File

One batch file has special significance to DOS. The full name of this batch file is AUTOEXEC.BAT. DOS automatically searches for this file in the root directory when you boot your computer. If an AUTOEXEC.BAT file is present, DOS executes the commands contained in the file.

Because the AUTOEXEC.BAT file is optional, not every PC has this file. Most users or their system managers, however, include an AUTOEXEC.BAT file of their own design on their boot disk because the file enables them to benefit from commands that automatically establish operating parameters.

AUTOEXEC.BAT is executed as a convenience to you. You can elect to omit this file, enter a few preliminary commands, and then start your PC work session. Your manual initializing will accomplish the same result as an AUTOEXEC.BAT file. But because DOS will execute the file if it is there, why not take advantage of the feature by placing those repetitive initializing commands in this special file? As a rule, AUTOEXEC.BAT files are not distributed with the DOS package because different users need varied commands. The content of each AUTOEXEC.BAT file is meant to reflect the individual start-up needs of different users.

 The installation process for DOS V4.0 creates a file called AUTOEXEC.400, which includes commands that the user might want. You can change the name of the AUTOEXEC.400 file to AUTOEXEC.BAT by using the RENAME command. DOS then executes the commands in the file upon booting. To view the contents of AUTOEXEC.400, use the TYPE command.

Nearly all users include an AUTOEXEC.BAT file in their boot disk's root directory. You do not always have to create or modify AUTOEXEC.BAT. Some software packages come with installation programs that create or modify AUTOEXEC.BAT by adding commands as one of the installation steps for the package's main program. If you have doubts about which commands you should include in your AUTOEXEC.BAT file, the following sections will give you some ideas.

The Rules for the AUTOEXEC.BAT File

The AUTOEXEC.BAT file is a privileged batch file because DOS executes its batch of commands each time you boot your computer. In every other sense, however, AUTOEXEC.BAT is like any other batch file.

You can include any commands you want in the AUTOEXEC.BAT file. When you boot your computer, DOS executes those commands. You can decide what you want the AUTOEXEC.BAT file to do, as long as you follow certain rules. The following list summarizes these rules.

1. The full file name must be AUTOEXEC.BAT, and the file must reside in the root directory of the boot disk.

2. The contents of the AUTOEXEC.BAT file must conform to the rules for creating any batch file.

3. When DOS executes AUTOEXEC.BAT after a boot, you are not prompted for the date and time automatically. You must include the DATE and TIME commands in your AUTOEXEC.BAT file if you want to retain this step in booting. Normally, you will not use DATE and TIME if you have an automatic clock.

The Contents of AUTOEXEC.BAT

Using AUTOEXEC.BAT is a great way for you to set up changeable system defaults. That is, AUTOEXEC.BAT is the place to put commands you would want to enter every time you start your system. For example, you can use AUTOEXEC.BAT to tell your computer to change to the directory that holds your most commonly used program and start the program. Used in this way, AUTOEXEC.BAT starts your program as soon as you boot your computer. The default installation of V4.0 uses this start-up technique by inserting a line in AUTOEXEC.BAT to start the DOS Shell.

The commands most frequently included in simple AUTOEXEC.BAT files are listed in Table 12.1.

297

Table 12.1
AUTOEXEC.BAT File Commands

Command	Function in the AUTOEXEC.BAT File
TIME/DATE	Uses the computer's clock to establish the correct time and date so that DOS can accurately "stamp" new and modified files. They also provide the actual time and date to programs that use the computer's internal clock.
PATH	Eliminates the need for the operator to enter the path through the keyboard after each boot.
PROMPT	Customizes the system prompt. The DOS prompt configuration can include information that makes navigating directories easier. If you include the PROMPT command in AUTOEXEC.BAT, you don't need to remember how to input the optional parameters each time you boot.
DIR	Displays a listing of the root directory as soon as the computer boots.
CD	When used with a directory path, CD takes you immediately to a directory where you normally do your work.
ECHO	Enables you to include a message as part of your start-up when used in the AUTOEXEC.BAT file. On a floppy disk system, this message can remind you to insert a program disk in drive A.

Most of these commands are self-explanatory. The more complex commands are covered in the following sections.

The PATH Command

You know how to issue the PATH command to tell DOS where to search for COM, EXE, and BAT files. In this section, you will learn how to put into the AUTOEXEC.BAT file the PATH command that contains the search paths. With this information, DOS will know the search path as soon as you boot the computer. The benefit to you is that you won't have to remember to issue a PATH command or include an external command's path in a command line.

For example, suppose that you create a directory on your hard disk called \DOS. To tell DOS to search the \DOS directory, you enter the following command:

PATH C:\DOS

If you want DOS to search in the root directory first, the \DOS directory next, and another directory—such as \TEMP—last, you enter the following:

PATH C:\;C:\DOS;C:\TEMP

Notice that semicolons (;) separate the three directory names. The semicolons tell DOS to search the alternative directories in the search path in order as you issued them. In other words, if the external command or program is not in the current directory, DOS looks at the first alternate directory in the path setting. If the command or program is not located in the first alternative directory, DOS moves to the next alternative and searches that directory. DOS will continue searching each alternative path in turn until the file is found, or until the alternatives are exhausted.

The path you include in the AUTOEXEC.BAT file becomes DOS's default search path. Of course, you can change this default path. Simply issue the PATH command with a new path or set of paths at the DOS prompt.

The PROMPT Command

You are familiar with what your DOS prompt looks like: A> or B> if you use floppy diskettes, or C> if you have a hard disk. In fact, the default DOS prompt is the letter of your current drive and the > symbol. DOS enables you to change the look of the prompt. You can, for example, change the prompt so that it provides more information or makes DOS appear more friendly. By using the PROMPT command, you can change the DOS prompt to a wide variety of looks that can include useful system information. The symbolic syntax for the PROMPT command is as follows:

PROMPT *text*

text is any combination of words or special characters. The words can be literal, such as *HELLO*, or random, such as *12 XXX*. The characters that DOS treats as special characters are called *meta-strings*. DOS sees meta-strings as instructing, "Don't show what I say. Show what I mean."

Understanding Meta-strings

A meta-string consists of two characters, the first of which is always the dollar sign (**$**). When DOS sees a dollar sign in a PROMPT-assignment command, DOS expects the character that follows to have a special meaning. The dollar sign and the character that follows comprise the meta-string. DOS interprets meta-strings to mean something other than the literal meaning of the characters. When DOS displays its prompt, the meta-string supplies the replacement text.

Including the meta-string **$t** in the PROMPT command tells DOS, "My meaning is the current time in HH:MM:SS." Placed in the DOS prompt, **$t** prints the current system time.

299

Meta-strings are used in the PROMPT command to substitute for characters that DOS would otherwise interpret literally. For example, DOS recognizes the symbols >, <, and the vertical bar (|) as reserved command-line characters. Any time you enter one of these characters directly, COMMAND.COM assumes that you are trying to establish redirection. You may, however, want to include one or more of the redirection symbols in a prompt. Unless DOS is tipped off that you aren't trying to redirect a command, DOS will fail to use the redirection symbols correctly. The meta-string substitutes can solve your problem. All of the redirection symbols have meta-string equivalents so that you can use them in PROMPT text. You must substitute the appropriate meta-string in order to cause these special characters to appear in the prompt. Otherwise, DOS tries to act on the characters in its usual interpretive way.

Redirection symbols aren't the only characters that benefit from having meta-string assignments. Some meta-strings represent information that DOS knows. Using these information-based meta-strings makes your prompt an information point in its own right.

Table 12.2 summarizes meta-string characters and their meanings to the PROMPT command.

Table 12.2
Meta-Strings for Use with the PROMPT Command

Meta-string	Displayed information or result
$_	Carriage return/line feed (moves the cursor to the beginning of the next line)
$b	The vertical bar character (	)
$d	The current date
$e	The Esc character
$g	The greater-than sign (>)
$h	The Backspace character (moves the cursor one space to the left)
$l	The less-than sign (<)
$n	The current disk drive name
$p	The current drive and path
$q	The equal sign (=)
$t	The system time
$v	The DOS version

Customizing Your Prompt

You can use the meta-string characters with the PROMPT command to produce your own DOS prompt. PROMPT allows words or phrases in addition to meta-strings. You can experiment with different combinations of meta-strings and phrases.

When you find a combination that you like, type the PROMPT command followed by the meta-string and phrase. Then, each time you boot your computer, your custom prompt will appear. Issuing the PROMPT command alone with no parameters restores the prompt to its default, which is the drive name and the greater-than sign (C>).

If you want your prompt to tell you the current DOS path, type the following command:

PROMPT THE CURRENT PATH IS $P

If your current location is drive C in the \DOS directory, this PROMPT command would produce the following prompt:

```
THE CURRENT PATH IS C:\DOS
```

By adding the > sign (using the meta-string **$G**), the command would be as follows:

PROMPT THE CURRENT PATH IS PG

Your DOS prompt would then appear as the following:

```
THE CURRENT PATH IS C:\DOS>
```

Examining a Sample AUTOEXEC.BAT File

The contents of each user's AUTOEXEC.BAT file may vary, but most AUTOEXEC.BAT files will contain a few of the same commands. You can create examples using COPY CON, EDLIN, or a text editor of your choice. The following sample of an AUTOEXEC.BAT file executes useful start-up commands.

DATE
TIME
PATH=C:\DOS;C:\KEEP;C:\;
PROMPT PG
CD\BATCH
DIR
ECHO Good Day, Mate!

301

The following explains each line of the file.

DATE

Uses the computer's clock to establish the correct date so that DOS can accurately "date stamp" new and modified files.

TIME

Uses the computer's clock to establish the correct time so that DOS can accurately "time stamp" new and modified files.

PATH=C:\DOS;C:\KEEP;C:\;

Instructs DOS to search the named subdirectories to find files that have EXE, COM, or BAT extensions.

PROMPT PG

Customizes the system prompt to show the current drive and path and the greater-than (>) character. By including the PROMPT command in the AUTOEXEC.BAT file, you eliminate the need to remember how to input the parameters for PROMPT each time you boot.

CD\BATCH

Makes \BATCH the current directory. This, presumably, is the directory that contains your batch files to start programs on your hard disk.

DIR

Displays a listing of the current directory as soon as the computer boots.

ECHO Good Day, Mate!

Displays the on-screen message "Good Day, Mate!" as part of your start-up procedure.

Examining an Existing AUTOEXEC.BAT File

Most computers already have an AUTOEXEC.BAT file in the root directory of the hard disk or on the bootable floppy disk. Remember that packaged software sometimes creates or adds to the AUTOEXEC.BAT file when you install the software on your hard disk or floppy disk.

You can easily see if AUTOEXEC.BAT exists in your root directory or on your logged floppy disk. If your hard disk is the logged drive, change to the root directory by typing **CD **. You can look at the directory listing of all the files with BAT extensions by typing the following:

DIR *.BAT

You can view the contents of AUTOEXEC.BAT on-screen by typing the following:

TYPE AUTOEXEC.BAT

To get a printed copy of the AUTOEXEC.BAT file, you can redirect output to the printer by using the following command:

TYPE AUTOEXEC.BAT >PRN

If you choose not to print out a copy of your AUTOEXEC.BAT file, make sure that you write down the contents before you make any changes. Be sure that you copy the syntax correctly. This copy will serve as your worksheet.

You can use your copy of AUTOEXEC.BAT to see whether a PROMPT or PATH command is contained in the batch file. If you want to add or alter PROMPT or PATH commands, jot the additions or changes on your worksheet. Use your paper copy of the AUTOEXEC.BAT file to check for proper syntax in the lines you change or add before you commit the changes to disk.

Making a Backup Copy of the Existing File

Always make a backup copy of your existing AUTOEXEC.BAT file before you make any changes in the file. Save the current version by copying it with a different extension. Type the following command and press Enter:

COPY AUTOEXEC.BAT AUTOEXEC.OLD

The contents of AUTOEXEC.BAT will be copied to the file AUTOEXEC.OLD. You now can modify your AUTOEXEC.BAT file by using EDLIN or your word processor, or you can use COPY CON to create a new AUTOEXEC.BAT file. If you find that the new AUTOEXEC.BAT file does not work or does not do what you want, you can always erase the new file. Then, using the COPY command, you can copy the AUTOEXEC.OLD file to AUTOEXEC.BAT and be back where you started.

Creating an AUTOEXEC.BAT File

You create the AUTOEXEC.BAT file in the same way that you create any other batch file. Making sure that the root directory is the current directory, type the following command:

COPY CON AUTOEXEC.BAT

Enter the commands that you have decided should make up the file. Type one command per line and correct any mistakes before you press Enter. When you finish, press F6 or Ctrl-Z, and then press Enter to write the new file to disk. Now when you boot your computer, DOS executes your new AUTOEXEC.BAT file.

If your AUTOEXEC.BAT file is going to be more than a few lines long, or if it already exists and you are modifying it, use EDLIN or another text processor. EDLIN will give you far more control than a straightforward COPY CON operation.

The advantages of multiple AUTOEXECs ... Technically speaking, there is only one AUTOEXEC.BAT file. But you can have the benefit of several "versions" by giving different extensions to files with the name AUTOEXEC. You can then activate an alternative version by using an operation involving the RENAME and COPY commands.

You can use in the extensions any character that DOS normally allows in file names. The extensions BAK, OLD, NEW, TMP, and .001 are just a few examples. By giving AUTOEXEC.BAT a unique new name, such as AUTOEXEC.TMP, you can activate any other AUTOEXEC file by renaming it AUTOEXEC.BAT.

This method is handy if you want to include commands for some activity such as automatically starting a monthly spreadsheet. When the monthly work is done, and you no longer need to concentrate on the spreadsheet as soon as you boot, you can activate your normal AUTOEXEC.BAT file by changing its temporary name back to AUTOEXEC.BAT.

Understanding Batch File Parameters

You can create quite sophisticated batch files using only DOS commands and the simplest batch subcommands. The batch files created so far in this chapter carry out exactly the same functions every time you use them. You may want a batch file to perform an operation on different files each time you use it, however, even though the commands in the batch file are fixed. You can use the same batch file to do different things by taking advantage of batch file parameters.

A review of parameters in general helps you understand batch file parameters. In DOS, many commands accept additional information when you issue the command. COPY is an example of such a command. The name of the file you want to copy, the destination to which you want to copy the file, and any additional switches you enter are all parameters. *Parameters* can be defined as the additional information you type after you type the command name at the DOS prompt. Commands (or command programs) can use whatever information is in the parameters.

Consider the following command:

COPY FORMAT.COM B: /V

Every word or set of characters separated by a space, comma, semicolon, or other valid delimiter is a parameter. FORMAT.COM, B:, and /V are parameters. Each parameter controls some aspect of the COPY command. In this example, the parameters tell COPY to copy the file FORMAT.COM from the default disk to the disk in drive B and to verify that DOS has correctly made the copy.

Batch files also use parameters, but in a different manner from commands. When you type the name of the batch file at the DOS prompt, you can include up to nine parameters. DOS assigns a variable name to each of these parameters. You can use the variable name in your batch file in the form of a variable marker numbered from 0 to 9. You precede the marker number with a percent sign (%) to inform DOS that you are specifying a replaceable parameter.

Understanding Variable Markers

This section examines how variable markers can be used in a batch file. If you want to practice including parameters in a batch file, use a text editor or the COPY CON technique to create a file called TEST.BAT. Type the following line into the file:

ECHO Hello, %1

Now type **TEST**, press the space bar, type your first name, and press Enter. The results should display on-screen like this:

```
C>TEST JOHN
C>ECHO Hello, JOHN
Hello, JOHN
C>
```

To see how DOS replaces the parameters, create another batch file called TEST1.BAT. Type the following line into this file:

ECHO %0 %1 %2 %3 %4 %5 %6 %7 %8 %9

After you create this file, type **TEST1**, a space, then type your first name, your last name, your street address, your city, your state, ZIP code, and age, each separated by a space. The following is the screen display:

```
C>TEST1 JOHN SMITH 1234 PIONEER STREET ANYTOWN IN 46032 42
C>ECHO TEST1 JOHN SMITH 1234 PIONEER STREET ANYTOWN IN 46032 42
TEST1 JOHN SMITH 1234 PIONEER STREET ANYTOWN IN 46032 42
C>
```

The batch file command instructs DOS to display on-screen the parameters 0 through 9. These parameters worked out to be the following:

Parameter	Word
%0	TEST1
%1	JOHN
%2	SMITH
%3	1234
%4	PIONEER
%5	STREET
%6	ANYTOWN
%7	IN
%8	46032
%9	42

Now, try to "shortchange" DOS by not specifying a sufficient number of parameters to fill each expected variable marker. Run TEST1 again, but this time give only your first name. You should see something like the following:

```
C>TEST1 JOHN

C>ECHO TEST1 JOHN

TEST1 JOHN

C>
```

DOS displayed the batch file name and your first name. No other information was echoed to the screen. Although not enough parameters were specified, DOS replaced the unfilled markers with nothing. In this case, the empty markers did no harm.

Some commands that you use in a batch file, however, may require that a replaceable parameter not be empty. For example, if you include DEL in a batch file with a replaceable parameter, and the parameter is empty, you will see the following error message:

```
Invalid number of parameters
```

You can use the IF subcommand (discussed later in the chapter) to avoid errors like this one.

Constructing a Batch File Using Parameters

In this section, you will learn how to construct a batch file that takes advantage of parameters. Suppose that you use several computers daily, but one of the hard disk systems is your primary "workhorse" where you store the files you want to keep from all of the computers you use.

Suppose that you use diskettes to move information between computers. You usually delete the file from the diskette after the file has been copied back to a hard disk. Deleting the file "cleans" the file out of the process so the file won't be accidentally copied to the hard disk again later. You use the following steps to transfer data from a floppy disk to a hard disk:

1. Copy file from the diskette to the hard disk.
2. Erase the file from the diskette.

To simplify this process, you can create a batch file called C&E.BAT (copy and erase). Type the following commands in the file:

COPY A:%1 C:%2 /V

ERASE A:%1

To use the C&E.BAT file, type the following at the DOS prompt:

C&E *oldfilename newfilename*

The first parameter, *oldfilename*, represents the name of the file you want to copy from the floppy disk to the hard disk; *newfilename* is the new name for the copied file (if you want to change the file name as it is being copied).

Suppose that you put a diskette containing the file NOTES.TXT into drive A and want to copy the file to the hard disk. Type the following at the DOS prompt:

C&E NOTES.TXT

Here's what the screen looks like:

```
C>COPY A:NOTES.TXT C: /V
1 file(s) copied
C>ERASE A:NOTES.TXT
C>
```

Notice that even though you didn't type the parameter *newfilename*, DOS carried out the batch file, keeping the same file name during the copy. DOS copied NOTES.TXT from drive A to drive C and then deleted the file on the diskette in drive A. The %2 parameter was "dropped," and the file did not get a new name when it was copied.

One of the benefits of constructing a batch file that copies a file using parameters is that you can use a path name as the second parameter. By specifying a path name, you can copy the file from the floppy disk to a different directory on the hard disk. To copy NOTES.TXT to the directory called WORDS, for example, type the following:

C&E NOTES.TXT \WORDS

The screen display is as follows:

```
C>COPY A:NOTES.TXT C:\WORDS /V
1 file(s) copied
C>ERASE A:NOTES.TXT
C>
```

Because \WORDS is a directory name, DOS knows to copy the file NOTES.TXT into the directory \WORDS. DOS does not give the new file the name WORDS. DOS isn't doing anything unusual here. DOS is simply following the rules of syntax for the COPY command. The batch file takes advantage of these syntax rules.

A note from the author . . . To understand batch files, patience and persistence are important. I've seen many PC users avoid using batch files only to try one or two examples and then pick up the concept rapidly. These same users now produce batch files that anyone would be proud of. Give yourself a chance to learn batch files by practicing with the examples in this chapter. You can use the examples as templates for your own situation. Once you get into the rhythm of composing batch files, you will have harnessed one of DOS's greatest features.

Your use of batch files is not limited by your own imagination. If you pick up almost any copy of a personal computer magazine, you'll find a few useful batch files introduced in a feature or an article. You can use these featured batch files directly or as the basis for your own special situation.

Even if you don't regularly create your own batch files, you will find use for some knowledge of batch file principles. Many programs are started by batch files rather than the name of the actual program file. The DOS Shell is a perfect example. With your knowledge of batch files, you can type the contents of any batch file to see what the batch operation is up to.

Many applications programs install the main files through the commands included in an installation batch file. You will understand how an installation will proceed if you can read the contents of the installing batch file. Knowing what the batch file will do can help you avoid installation conflicts. For instance, I install 5 1/4-inch disk-based software from drive B because my drive A is a 3 1/2-inch drive. Many installation batch files, however, look for the files to be installed on drive A. To avoid this conflict, I modify a version of the installation batch file by changing all references to drive A: to drive B:. By running my modified installation batch file, the new software installs without a hitch.

I recommend working with batch files as a meaningful introduction to programming. The batch subcommands give batch files the kind of internal flow and decision-making that programming languages offer. Of course, you shouldn't expect batch files to equal the versatility of an actual program. But batch files certainly can assume a programming flavor. Use batch files, and you will have a method to greatly increase DOS's utility.

Using the Batch File Subcommands

Included in DOS are special commands called *batch subcommands*. Table 12.3 is a complete list of batch subcommands for DOS V3 through V4.

Any of the subcommands listed in table 12.3 can be used in a batch file. Most of them can be used at the DOS system level as well. For example, you can type **ECHO** at the DOS prompt, with or without an argument. DOS either displays the string you type after ECHO or, if you provide no argument, tells you whether ECHO is ON or OFF. You can type **PAUSE** at the DOS prompt; DOS will pause. Neither of these commands is of much use at the DOS prompt. The FOR..IN..DO command structure, however, can be quite useful at the operating-system level to carry out repetitive commands.

The following sections explain each of the batch subcommands and their uses.

Table 12.3
Batch File Subcommands for DOS V3 and V4

Subcommand	Action
@	Suppresses the display of a line on-screen (DOS V3.3 and later).
CALL	Runs another batch file and returns to the original batch file (DOS V3.3 and later).
CLS	Clears the screen and returns the cursor to the upper left corner of the screen.
COMMAND	Invokes a second copy of the command processor, COMMAND.COM, to call another batch file.
ECHO	Turns on or off the display of batch commands as they execute. Also can display a message on-screen.
FOR..IN..DO	Allows the use of the same batch command for several files. The execution "loops."
GOTO	Jumps to the line following the specified label in a batch file.
IF	Allows conditional execution of a command.
PAUSE	Halts processing until a key is pressed. Displays the message `Press a key to continue. . .`
REM	Displays a message on-screen or allows for batch comments that describe the intent of an operation.
SHIFT	Shifts the command-line parameters one parameter to the left.

Introducing REM and ECHO

As you learned earlier in this chapter, the ECHO command does two things. ECHO ON and ECHO OFF turn on and off the display of lines from batch files as the commands are executed. ECHO is also used to display messages.

When ECHO is used to display messages, the command parallels the REM (remark) command, which also displays messages on-screen. ECHO can display a message with a maximum length of 122 characters; REM can display 123 characters (the 127-character DOS command-line limit, minus the length of the command, minus a space).

The ECHO setting affects REM. If ECHO OFF is set, no REM message appears on-screen. If ECHO ON is set, REM messages are displayed. A message following the ECHO command, on the other hand, always appears on-screen, regardless of whether ECHO OFF has been issued. If you always want a message in your batch file to appear, use ECHO rather than REM.

You can put both ECHO and REM to good use in a batch file. When you review a batch file some time after you create it, you may have forgotten why you used certain commands, or why you constructed the batch file in a particular way. Leave reminders in your batch file with REM statements. Comments in REM statements don't appear on-screen when you issue the ECHO OFF command, and the comments make the batch file self-documenting, which you and other users will appreciate later. If you want the batch file to display particular messages, use ECHO. Messages set with ECHO appear on-screen whether or not you set ECHO OFF.

Controlling the Display with CLS

The DOS CLS command can be used at any time at the DOS prompt to clear the screen. In batch files, CLS is used commonly after the ECHO OFF command. The reason CLS follows the ECHO OFF command is that the ECHO OFF command itself appears on-screen. To keep the screen clear, issue the CLS command as shown:

ECHO OFF

CLS

With DOS V3.3 or later versions, you can use the @ feature to prevent the ECHO OFF command from appearing on-screen. Replace the preceding two command lines with the following single line:

@ECHO OFF

Because **@** is the first character on the line, ECHO OFF does not appear on-screen, and the ECHO OFF command stays in effect until the end of the batch file. Using the @ feature does not clear the screen, however. If you want to clear the screen when you start a batch file, use the CLS command in the batch file.

Branching with GOTO

With the DOS GOTO command, you can jump to another part of your batch file. The DOS GOTO command uses a label to specify the destination. A *label* is a batch file line that starts with a colon and is followed by a one-character to eight-character name. The label name can be longer than eight characters, but only the first eight characters are significant as a label.

When DOS encounters a GOTO command in the batch file, DOS starts at the beginning of the batch file and searches for a label matching the one specified by GOTO. DOS then jumps to the line in the batch file following the line with the label.

As an example, the batch file TEST2.BAT is listed here. This file is similar to the TEST.BAT batch file you created previously, with the addition of the GOTO and PAUSE subcommands.

```
:START
ECHO Hello, %1
PAUSE
GOTO START
```

If you invoke the batch file by typing **TEST2 DAVID**, the screen shows the following:

```
C>TEST2 DAVID
C>ECHO Hello, DAVID
Hello, DAVID
C>PAUSE
Strike a key when ready... <space>
C>GOTO START
C>ECHO Hello, DAVID
Hello, DAVID
C>PAUSE
Strike a key when ready... ^C
Terminate batch job (Y/N)? Y
C>
```

The batch file began by echoing the message that included the name DAVID. The file then paused so that you could press a key before it continued. After you pressed a key (in this example, the space bar), DOS executed the GOTO START command. DOS then jumped to the line following :START and continued. When DOS paused a second time in this example, Ctrl-C was pressed to stop the batch file. DOS asked whether you wanted to stop the batch file. In this example, the response was Y for yes, so DOS stopped processing the batch file and returned to the system prompt.

311

This type of batch file causes DOS to loop continuously until you type the Ctrl-C or Ctrl-Break sequence.

Using the IF Command

The IF subcommand is a "test-and-do" command. When the condition is true, IF executes the command on the same line. When the condition is false, IF ignores the line. The DOS IF subcommand works like the IF statement in the BASIC programming language. The subcommand can be used to test one of three conditions:

- The ERRORLEVEL of a program
- Whether a string is equal to another string
- Whether a file exists

Using IF To Test ERRORLEVEL

The first condition IF can be used to test is ERRORLEVEL. A better name for this condition would have been "exit level." ERRORLEVEL is a code some programs leave for DOS when they finish executing. In DOS V3.3 and later versions, only the BACKUP, GRAFTABL, KEYB, REPLACE, RESTORE, and XCOPY commands leave an exit code. Many other programs use exit codes, however.

An exit code of zero (0) usually means that everything is okay. Any number greater than 0 usually indicates that something went wrong when the program terminated. For example, no files were found, the program encountered an error, or the operator aborted the program. Including an IF command in a batch file enables you to test ERRORLEVEL to see whether a program worked properly.

If the exit you test for is equal to or greater than the number you specify in the batch file, the ERRORLEVEL condition is true. You can think of this condition as a BASIC-like statement:

    IF ERRORLEVEL > number THEN do this

The IF ERRORLEVEL command is most useful with any of the noncopyrighted public-domain utilities for user keyboard input. These utilities have names such as INPUT.COM, ASK.COM, and the like. When your batch file uses these utilities, it can pause and wait for keyboard input. The utility puts a value in ERRORLEVEL related to the scan code of the key pressed. You can then make your batch file branch or perform some other task based on the key pressed. A batch file does not accept keyboard input except when the input is provided on a batch-file command line.

Using IF To Compare Strings

The second condition the IF command can be used to test is whether string 1 equals string 2. The IF *string1 == string2* condition is normally used with parameters and variable markers. An example is a batch file you can create called ISIBM.BAT. This batch file contains the following single line:

IF %1 == IBM ECHO I'm an IBM computer

If you type **ISIBM IBM** at the DOS prompt, you see the following:

```
I'm an IBM computer
```

If you type something other than **IBM** as the first parameter, nothing appears on-screen.

If you don't provide enough parameters with the IF command, DOS replaces the parameter marker with nothing. Because DOS does not like to compare null parameters, it displays the message Syntax error and aborts the batch file.

To avoid the syntax-error problem, first test whether a parameter is empty before trying another test. You can see the general technique in this revised version of ISIBM.BAT:

IF "%1" == "" GOTO NOTHING

IF %1 == IBM GOTO IBM

ECHO What computer are you?

GOTO END

:IBM

ECHO I'm an IBM computer

GOTO END

:NOTHING

ECHO Pardon me, I could not hear you.

:END

:END is often used as a convenient GOTO label when none of the IF conditions are met. In this batch file, when the IF statements do not branch to NOTHING or IBM, the message What computer are you? appears, and the batch file branches to END. Because nothing follows the END label, the batch file quits.

The first line puts quotation marks around %1 and tests to see whether %1 is empty (is the same as a double set of quotation marks, or a null). If %1 is null (meaning ISIBM was called with no parameters), the line effectively reads as follows:

IF "" == "" GOTO NOTHING

This line traps the error condition of too few batch-file parameters. If you need to check for a nonexistent parameter, use this format.

The quotation marks around the variable marker were used in this example because quotation marks are easy to understand, especially for BASIC programmers. In truth, a comparison with any letter, number, or symbol can do the job. One common procedure is to use a single period instead of the quotation marks, as shown in the following example:

IF %1. == . GOTO NOTHING

If no parameter is entered for %1, DOS interprets the line as follows:

IF . == . GOTO NOTHING

Use the syntax that is easiest for you to remember and understand.

If %1 equals nothing, DOS branches to the line following the label NOTHING, and the message Pardon me, I could not hear you. appears on-screen.

If %1 equals something other than nothing, DOS does not branch to NOTHING; instead, it executes the second line in the batch file. The second line of the revised ISIBM.BAT file tests to see whether **IBM** was entered. Notice that GOTO statements are used to jump around the parts of the batch file that should not be executed. If %1 equals IBM, the message I'm an IBM computer appears. If the parameter is not nothing, and is not IBM, the message What computer are you? appears.

When using the IF subcommand, remember that DOS compares strings literally. Uppercase characters compare differently than lowercase characters. If you invoke ISIBM.BAT by typing **ISIBM ibm**, DOS compares the lowercase *ibm* to the uppercase *IBM* and decides that the two strings are not the same. The IF test fails, and I'm an IBM computer does not appear on the display.

Using IF To Look for Files

The third condition you can use the IF subcommand to test is IF EXIST *filename*. This IF condition tests whether the file *filename* is on-disk. If you want to test for a file on a drive other than the current drive, put the disk drive name in front of *filename* (for example, **IF EXIST B:CHKDSK.COM**).

You can use IF EXIST when starting your word processor. Perhaps you use a file called TEMP.TXT to store temporary files, or to write blocks to read into other documents. You can use IF EXIST to test for the existence of the file, and erase the file if it does exist.

Your batch file, called WORD.BAT, would look like the the following:

ECHO OFF

CLS

CD \DOCUMENT

IF EXIST TEMP.TXT ERASE TEMP.TXT

\WORDS\WP

**CD **

In this batch file, ECHO is shut off and the screen is cleared. The current directory is changed to \DOCUMENT, the directory where you store your word processing documents.

Next, IF EXIST tests for the existence of TEMP.TXT. If the file does exist, it is erased. Next, your word processor WP is started from the \WORDS subdirectory.

Notice the last line of the batch file: **CD **. When your word processor starts, the batch file halts. When you quit your word processor, control is given back to the batch file which has one line to process. **CD ** changes the directory back to the root directory, and then the batch file ends.

Using NOT with IF

You also can test for the opposite of these three IF conditions. That is, you can test whether a condition is false by adding the word NOT after IF. For example, you can use the following statement to check whether a file does not exist on the disk:

IF NOT EXIST *filename*

If the result of the statement is true (the file does not exist), the command following the IF statement is executed.

You can also test for NOT ERRORLEVEL or NOT string1 == string2. In any event, the command at the end of the IF test activates only if the condition if false, that is, if the condition does NOT occur.

Using FOR..IN..DO

FOR..IN..DO is an unusual and extremely powerful batch subcommand. The subcommand's syntax is as follows:

FOR %%*variable* **IN (***set***) DO** *command*

variable is a one-letter name that takes on the value of each item in *set*. The double percent sign (%%) in front of the variable is important. If you use a single percent sign, DOS confuses the symbol with the parameter marker and does not work properly.

set is the list of the items, commands, or disk files you want *variable* to take the value of. You can use wild-card file names with this parameter. You also can use drive names and paths with any file names you specify. If you have more than one file name or other item in the set, use a space or comma between the names. *command* is any valid DOS command that you want to perform for each item in *set*.

Using a FOR..IN..DO Batch File

An interesting example of the use of FOR..IN..DO is a simple batch file that compares file names on a diskette with file names on another diskette or a hard disk subdirectory. To see how this batch file works, copy some files to a diskette, either from another diskette or from a hard disk subdirectory. Create the batch file CHECKIT.BAT and type the following in the file:

```
@ECHO OFF
IF "%1"=="" GOTO END
FOR %%a IN (B: C: D: E: b: c: d: e:) DO IF "%%a"=="%1" GOTO COMPARE
GOTO END
:COMPARE
%1
CD \%2
FOR %%a IN (*.*) DO IF EXIST A:%%a ECHO %%a is on this disk also.
:END
```

Put the diskette you want to compare in drive A and then type the following:

CHECKIT *drive<space>directory*

Notice that the directory you want to compare is optional, but if you specify it, you must separate it from the drive name with a space. This convention is followed because two batch file parameters (%1 and %2) are used to store the letter of the drive and the directory name. If you don't specify a directory name, the root directory of the drive you specify is used. If you type **CHECKIT B: \games**, for example, the file searches drive A for the B:\games directory.

When the CHECKIT batch file is called, DOS first checks whether %1 is empty (if no parameters were provided when the command was issued). If %1 is empty, DOS branches to the end of the file. Otherwise, DOS goes to the third line and checks whether a valid drive letter was entered; valid drive letters are B:, C:, D:, E:, b:, c:, d:, or e:. (If your system has more or fewer drives, change this list to reflect your configuration). If an invalid drive letter is found, DOS branches to the end of the batch file. You must invoke this batch file with the drive name and the colon, separated by no space, or the comparison will fail.

If the specified drive is valid, CHECKIT accesses the COMPARE section of the file. The first thing COMPARE does is to change the currently logged drive to the drive specified by %1. COMPARE then changes to the subdirectory specified by %2. If %2 is empty, the root directory of the disk is used. If %2 is a valid subdirectory name for that disk, the default directory is changed to %2. The **CD** command is valid even when %2 is null; no Syntax error appears in this instance. A Syntax error appears only when a null parameter makes the statement invalid.

The eighth line looks at all the files in the current directory to see whether a file with the same name as the one you specified when you invoked CHECKIT exists on drive A. If a match is found, the message filename is on this disk also appears on-screen.

Using FOR..IN..DO at the DOS Prompt

You may find that you want to issue commands like the ones in CHECKIT on an ad hoc basis at the DOS prompt. Instead of using the batch file for the preceding example, you can manually change subdirectories and then type the FOR..IN..DO line (the line that does all the work in the batch file) at the DOS prompt. If you do use FOR..IN..DO outside a batch file, DOS requires that you enter only one of the percent signs.

Another use for FOR..IN..DO can come if you have copied files from a diskette to the wrong subdirectory on a hard disk. You can delete the files from the hard disk using FOR..IN..DO.

Using FOR..IN..DO with Other Commands

FOR..IN..DO works equally well with commands and file names. Instead of naming a set of files, you can name a series of commands you want DOS to carry out. Consider the following example:

FOR %%a IN (COPY ERASE) DO %%a C:*.*

In a batch file, this line first copies all the files on drive C to the current directory and then erases the files from drive C. You can put a replaceable parameter in the line instead of explicitly naming the drive and file specifications:

FOR %%a IN (COPY ERASE) DO %%a %1

To use this batch file, you must first change to the destination directory (for example, D:\BAK). When you invoke this version of the batch file, you type the files you want copied and removed. If you name the batch file MOVER.BAT, you can type the following to invoke the file:

MOVER C:\WP

MOVER.BAT copies all the files in the subdirectory C:\WP to D:\BAK and then erases the files in C:\WP. This file works much like the C&E.BAT file created earlier in this chapter.

Moving Parameters with SHIFT

The SHIFT subcommand moves the parameters in the command one parameter to the left. SHIFT tricks DOS into accepting more than 10 parameters. The diagram of SHIFT is as follows:

%0 ← %1 ← %2 ← %3 ← %4 ← %5 . . .

↓

bit bucket

In this diagram, parameter 0 is dropped. The old parameter 1 becomes parameter 0. The old parameter 2 becomes parameter 1; parameter 3 becomes 2; parameter 4 becomes 3; and so on.

The following batch file, SHIFTIT.BAT, is a simple example of the use of the SHIFT command:

:START
ECHO %0 %1 %2 %3 %4 %5 %6 %7 %8 %9
SHIFT
PAUSE
GOTO START

Suppose that you type the following:

SHIFTIT A B C D E F G H I J K L M N O P Q R S T U V W X Y Z

The screen shows the following:

```
SHIFTIT A B C D E F G H I
Press a key to continue. . .
```

Notice that the batch-file name is displayed because %0 holds the name of the batch file before the first shift. Press a key to continue; ECHO now shows the following:

```
A B C D E F G H I J
Press a key to continue. . .
```

In this case, the file name has been dropped into the bit bucket. %0 now equals A. All the parameters have shifted one to the left. Press a key to continue; SHIFT continues moving down the list of parameters you typed initially. Press Ctrl-C when you want to stop.

SHIFT has many uses. You can use it to build a new version of the C&E.BAT file created in Chapter 11. The following modified version of the copy-and-erase batch file, called MOVE.BAT, shows a use for SHIFT:

```
:LOOP
COPY %1 C: /V
ERASE %1
SHIFT
IF NOT %1. == . GOTO LOOP
```

This batch file copies and erases the specified file or files. This batch file assumes nothing about the files to be copied; you can specify a disk drive, a path, and a file name. The batch file copies the files to the current directory on drive C, and then erases the files from the original disk or directory.

The last two lines shift the parameters to the left, test whether any parameters remain, and then repeat the operation if necessary.

Running Batch Files from Other Batch Files

On some occasions, you may want to run a batch file from another batch file. This section discusses three ways to run batch files from other batch files. One method is a one-way transfer of control. The other two ways show you how to run a second batch file and return control to the first batch file. These techniques are useful if you want to build menus with batch files or use one batch file to set up and start another batch file.

Calling a Batch File at the End of Another

The first method of calling a second batch file is simple. Include the root name of the second batch file as the final line of the first batch file. The first batch file runs the second batch file as if you had typed the second batch file's root name at the DOS prompt. To run BATCH2.BAT, for example, the final line of BATCH1.BAT is as follows:

```
BATCH2
```

DOS loads and executes the lines from BATCH2.BAT. Control passes in one direction—from the first batch file to the second. When BATCH2.BAT finishes executing, DOS displays the system prompt. You can consider this technique an interbatch-file GOTO. Control goes to the second file but doesn't come back to the first file.

Calling a Batch File with CALL

In all versions of DOS, you can call a second batch file from the first, execute the second batch file, return to the first batch file, and continue processing the first batch file. With DOS V3.0 through V3.2, you use COMMAND, the DOS command processor. With DOS V3.3 and V4, you can use either the COMMAND or the CALL subcommand.

The syntax of the CALL subcommand is as follows:

> **CALL** *d:path\filename parameters*

d:path is the optional disk drive and path name of the second batch file you want to execute. *filename* is the root name of the second batch file. You can place the CALL subcommand anywhere in the first batch file. DOS executes the batch file named by the CALL subcommand, returns to the first batch file, and executes the remainder of the first batch file. When you type the CALL subcommand, you can specify any *parameters* you want to pass to the batch file you're calling.

Understanding CALL Batch Files

The following three batch files demonstrate how CALL works. If you use DOS V3.3 or later, type these files into your computer. You can use uppercase or lowercase letters; uppercase letters are used here to highlight information. (If you use a version of DOS earlier than V3.3, do not type these files yet; some of the features used in these files do not work with versions before V3.3, as noted in the following discussion.)

BATCH1.BAT

```
@ECHO OFF
REM This file does the setup work for demonstrating
REM the CALL subcommand or COMMAND /C.
ECHO This is the STARTUP batch file
ECHO The command parameters are %%0-%0 %%1-%1
CALL batch2 second
ECHO CHKDSK from %0
CHKDSK
ECHO Done!
```

BATCH2.BAT

> **ECHO This is the SECOND batch file**
> **ECHO The command parameters are %%0-%0 %%1-%1**
> **CALL batch3 third**
> **ECHO CHKDSK from %0**
> **CHKDSK**

BATCH3.BAT

> **ECHO This is the THIRD batch file**
> **ECHO The command parameters are %%0-%0 %%1-%1**
> **ECHO CHKDSK from %0**
> **CHKDSK**

The first line of BATCH1.BAT sets ECHO OFF. With DOS V3 and V4, when you set ECHO OFF, it stays off. With DOS V2, ECHO turns back on each time a new batch file starts. The next two lines in BATCH1 are REM comments. Because ECHO is OFF, the REM statements do not display when the batch file runs.

The next two ECHO lines are similar for all three batch files. The first of the two lines identifies the batch file being used. The second of the two lines shows the zero parameter (the name by which the batch file was invoked) and the first parameter (the first argument) for the batch file. Notice that to display the strings *%0* and *%1*, you must use two percent signs (%%0 and %%1). If you use a single percent sign, DOS interprets the string as a replaceable parameter and does not display the actual symbol *%*.

The CALL statement in the first and second batch files invokes another batch file. In the first batch file, BATCH2.BAT is invoked. In the second batch file, BATCH3.BAT is invoked. In each case, a single argument is passed to the batch file being called: the word *second* to BATCH2.BAT and the word *third* to BATCH3.BAT.

Each batch file then displays its name (by using the %0 variable) as the file invoking the CHKDSK command, and then invokes CHKDSK. When DOS encounters the end of the batch file, DOS returns to the invoking batch file.

Analyzing the Results of CALL Batch Files

After you type the batch files explained in the preceding section, make sure that your printer is ready. Press Ctrl-PrtSc to turn on the printer and then type **BATCH1 FIRST**. When the printer is finished, toggle off the printer's capability to print echoed lines by pressing Ctrl-PrtSc again. If you do not have a printer to record the information displayed on-screen, press Ctrl-S to pause the screen as needed. When you have viewed the screen, press Ctrl-S again to "unpause" the screen display.

Check the printout or the screen display for the number of bytes of available RAM each time CHKDSK runs. Following is an abbreviated screen output from a PS/2 computer when **BATCH1 FIRST** is typed:

```
This is the STARTUP batch file
The command line parameters are %0-BATCH1 %1-FIRST
This is the SECOND batch file
The command line parameters are %0-batch2 %1-second
This is the THIRD batch file
The command line parameters are %0-batch3 %1-third
CHKDSK from batch3
Volume MODEL 60    created Apr 24, 1989 5:10p

   . . .
   654336 bytes total memory
   453744 bytes free
CHKDSK from batch2
Volume MODEL 60    created Apr 24, 1989 5:10p

   . . .
   654336 bytes total memory
   453840 bytes free
CHKDSK from batch1
Volume MODEL 60    created Apr 24, 1989 5:10p

   . . .
   654336 bytes total memory
   453936 bytes free
DONE!
C>
```

Each time you use the CALL command, DOS temporarily uses 96 bytes of RAM until the called batch file finishes running. Because DOS uses free memory, you can run out of memory if you use many batch file CALL commands (although this is not likely). Not many people create long, "nested" calls. The accumulated memory-usage problem occurs only when batch files continue to call other batch files. A single batch file can use the CALL command as many times as desired and use only the same 96 bytes of RAM for each call.

You can use batch files like the ones described in this section with versions of DOS earlier than V3.3 by making two changes. First, delete the @ character in the first line of BATCH1.BAT. The @ feature is not available with versions of DOS earlier than V3.3. Second, change the reference to CALL in BATCH1.BAT and BATCH2.BAT to COMMAND /C. You then can run the batch files.

Calling a Batch File with COMMAND /C

If you use a version of DOS earlier than V3.3, you can use the command interpreter to call other batch files. If you use V3.3 or later versions, you can use either CALL or COMMAND to call other batch files. The syntax of the COMMAND subcommand is as follows:

COMMAND /C *d:path\filename string*

One difference between the syntax of CALL and COMMAND is that you *must* use COMMAND's /C switch. The /C switch accepts a single string (*d:path\filename string*) that can include spaces and any other information. COMMAND.COM is a program that loads and executes *string*. When COMMAND.COM executes *string*, two copies of COMMAND.COM are in memory: the original and the one executing *string*. When *string* is finished executing, the second copy of COMMAND.COM leaves memory, and the original copy regains control.

If you use COMMAND /C in the example batch files, the results are almost identical to the results when CALL is used. Each copy of COMMAND.COM, however, uses more memory than the CALL subcommand. The amount of memory used by COMMAND.COM varies among versions of DOS, but is less than 4K.

Another difference between CALL and COMMAND /C is worth noting. Because COMMAND loads a new version of COMMAND.COM, any changes you make to the environment are lost when you return to the batch file that invoked COMMAND. If you invoke another batch file with CALL and then change the environment, the changes are made to the copy of the environment currently used by that batch file. This distinction can be important if you write batch files that make changes to the environment as a way of "flagging" processes you carry out. With COMMAND /C, the current batch file does not know what happened; any batch files you run later also do not inherit the changed environment. If you use CALL, the environment changes are "permanent" and are available to the current batch file later on, as well as to other programs run by the same command processor.

To better understand this process, look at the following example. Because these batch files use the CALL command, they work with DOS V3.3 or later versions.

TEST1.BAT

```
ECHO OFF
SET VAR1=VAR1
COMMAND /C TEST2
CALL TEST3
```

TEST2.BAT

```
SET VAR2=VAR2
```

TEST3.BAT

SET VAR3=VAR3

Run the files by typing **TEST1** and pressing Enter. When the files are finished running, type **SET** (the DOS command that displays the environment) to see something like the following:

```
PATH=C:\BATCH;C:\MS-DOS;C:$\UTILS;C:\
COMSPEC=C:\MS-DOS\COMMAND.COM
VAR1=VAR1
VAR3=VAR3
```

Look at the last two lines. If the SET command lists the variables currently in memory, what happened to VAR2? It was set when TEST1.BAT used COMMAND /C to invoke TEST2.BAT. Because DOS loaded a new copy of COMMAND.COM to run TEST2.BAT, however, the variable VAR2 was lost when DOS returned to the original copy of COMMAND.COM to continue processing TEST1.BAT. Because CALL was used to invoke TEST3.BAT, however, VAR3 is not lost when DOS returns to TEST1.BAT.

Summary

Batch files can make your computer do the hard work for you. They can replace repetitive typing with commands executed automatically. As you work with batch files, remember the following key points:

❏ You must give batch files the extension .BAT.

❏ You invoke batch files by typing the root name of the batch file and pressing Enter. You can specify an optional disk drive name and path name in front of the batch file name.

❏ You can use in a batch file any command you can type at the DOS prompt.

❏ AUTOEXEC.BAT is a special batch file that DOS calls when booting.

❏ Each word (or set of characters) in a command separated by a delimiter is a parameter. When you use a batch file, DOS substitutes the appropriate parameters for the variable markers (%0 to %9) in the file.

❏ You can use the ECHO subcommand to turn on or off the display of DOS commands being executed by the batch file.

❑ The PAUSE subcommand causes the batch file to suspend execution and then displays a message on screen.

❑ Use the REM subcommand to leave comments and reminders in your batch file; the comments do not display on-screen.

❑ Use the CLS subcommand to clear the screen completely.

❑ The GOTO subcommand can be used to create a loop in the batch file.

❑ IF tests for a condition or for the opposite condition.

❑ FOR..IN..DO can repeat a batch-file command for one or more files or commands.

❑ SHIFT shifts command parameters to the left.

❑ The @ character suppresses the display of a single line from a batch file.

❑ COMMAND /C and CALL can be used to invoke a second batch file and return control of the computer to the first batch file.

In the next chapter, you will learn about configuring your computer system. In this way, you can tailor your use of DOS to your needs.

Configuring Your Computer and Managing Devices

13

DOS provides you with the means to do more than just manage disks and files. With DOS, you can also manage your PC's adjustable features. A great deal of flexibility is built into DOS. The default configuration of DOS may be fine for millions of users, but if you need to make some changes to better suit your needs, or to fine-tune your computer system, DOS provides you with that capability. DOS also provides commands that control how devices do their jobs. This chapter looks at configuration and device control.

DOS's flexibility translates into many more choices for you to make. To make intelligent choices, you must understand exactly how DOS is configured. Luckily, DOS makes fine-tuning your computer relatively simple. You do not need to learn arcane techniques or undergo painful *sysgen* (system generation) procedures as do mainframe managers. Customizing DOS is as easy as collecting a few commands in a plain ASCII file and rebooting.

Key Terms Used in This Chapter

CONFIG.SYS	A special text file that DOS reads during booting to find and execute configuration directives.
Directive	A special assignment command that DOS uses to configure a PC's resources at boot time.

Expanded memory   Special RAM that DOS accesses as a device. Expanded memory conforms to the LIM 3.2 or 4.0 standard.

Extended memory   Memory at addresses above 1M on 80286-, 80386-, and 80486-based PCs. Extended memory is not available for program use without special provisions in programs.

Device driver   A special program file, usually with a SYS extension, that DOS can load through a configuration directive. Device drivers control specific items of hardware.

Disk cache   A specialized intelligent buffer that DOS can use to increase the efficiency of disks.

RAM disk   A disk-like implementation of RAM through a device driver. DOS can access a RAM disk as it would a standard disk.

Understanding CONFIG.SYS

Perhaps you either do not have a CONFIG.SYS file or have never examined the CONFIG.SYS file placed on your hard disk by the person who installed your computer. Maybe you know only that CONFIG.SYS contains the following lines that someone said you needed:

```
BUFFERS = 15
FILES   = 10
```

If you are to use CONFIG.SYS to your advantage, you should understand more about it. This section provides an explanation.

After DOS starts, but before the AUTOEXEC.BAT file is invoked, DOS looks in the root directory of the boot disk for a file called CONFIG.SYS. If DOS finds CONFIG.SYS, DOS attempts to carry out the commands in the file before proceeding with the AUTOEXEC.BAT file. You cannot abort this configuration file by pressing Ctrl-C or Ctrl-Break as you can with AUTOEXEC.BAT.

Like AUTOEXEC.BAT, CONFIG.SYS is a plain ASCII text file that lists on separate lines special commands, called *directives*. You use a fairly limited set of directives as legal commands in CONFIG.SYS. As you will see, however, you can accomplish quite a lot with those commands.

If you have a CONFIG.SYS file, you can view its contents by using the following command at the DOS prompt:

TYPE CONFIG.SYS

If you do not have a CONFIG.SYS file, you can create it with the command **COPY CON CONFIG.SYS**. You also can create or edit an existing file using the

DOS EDLIN text editor or a word processor that can output plain ASCII text. (EDLIN is explained in Chapter 11).

The CONFIG.SYS file contains the directives that alter some of DOS's functions and features. Table 13.1 lists the directives you can use in your CONFIG.SYS file and describes the functions they control.

Table 13.1
CONFIG.SYS Directives

Directive	Action
BREAK	Determines when DOS recognizes the Ctrl-Break sequence
BUFFERS	Sets the number of file buffers DOS uses
COUNTRY	Sets country-dependent information
DEVICE	Allows different devices to be used with DOS
FCBS	Controls file-handling for DOS V1
FILES	Sets the number of files to be used at one time
INSTALL	Installs specific memory-resident programs (DOS V4)
LASTDRIVE	Specifies the highest disk drive on the computer
REM	Flags a line as a remarks line (DOS V4)
SHELL	Informs DOS what command processor should be used and where the processor is located
STACKS	Sets the number of stacks that DOS uses
SWITCHES	Disables extended keyboard functions (DOS V4)

This chapter discusses the most important of the CONFIG.SYS directives listed in table 13.1. The directives you probably use most are FILES, BUFFERS, and DEVICE; you may want to pay special attention to the discussions of these directives. Directives not discussed in this chapter are explained in the Command Reference.

Some applications software packages make recommendations for you to add directives to CONFIG.SYS. Some peripheral hardware devices that you add to your PC may also make recommendations. Be sure to consult the manuals that come with these products to determine whether you need to alter CONFIG.SYS to satisfy the requirements of new software and devices.

Telling DOS When To Break

In this book, you learned that Ctrl-Break and Ctrl-C are helpful—but not foolproof—panic buttons used to stop commands. The response from a Ctrl-Break or Ctrl-C are not instantaneous. Only an "oh-no" second may have passed from the time you pressed the panic button until DOS responded, but you still had time to wonder what took so long for DOS to pay attention. The reason is that DOS is busy doing other things most of the time and only looks for Ctrl-Break at intervals. The BREAK directive (identical to the DOS BREAK command) tells DOS when to check for this key sequence. BREAK does not enable or disable this feature.

If you set BREAK ON in CONFIG.SYS, DOS checks to see whether you have pressed Ctrl-Break whenever a program requests some activity from DOS (performs a DOS function call). If you set BREAK OFF, DOS checks for a Ctrl-Break only when DOS is working with the video display, keyboard, printer, or asynchronous serial adapters (the ports at the back of the computer).

If you use programs that do a lot of disk accessing but little keyboard or screen work, you may want to set BREAK ON. This setting enables you to break out of the program if something goes awry or if you simply want to stop DOS to do something else.

The syntax structures for the BREAK directive are as follows:

BREAK=ON

BREAK=OFF

Because the default setting for this directive is BREAK=OFF, you do not have to specify the directive at all if you do not want to set BREAK on.

Using BUFFERS To Increase Disk Performance

The BUFFERS directive tells DOS how many disk buffers to use. BUFFERS uses an area of RAM set aside by DOS to temporarily store data. The stored data in BUFFERS is disk data which is read into the RAM when DOS accesses a disk. Before the introduction of disk-caching programs (which also keep disk information in memory), the BUFFERS directive had the potential for the greatest impact on disk performance. With disk information in buffers (memory), DOS can sometimes work with data in the buffer instead of accessing the disk. This directive was changed significantly for DOS V4. The earlier version of BUFFERS is discussed first, followed by a discussion of DOS V4 enhancements.

A *buffer* is a reserved area of RAM set up by DOS to store information read from disk. If you have configured your system with enough buffers, DOS frequently finds the information it needs in buffered memory. Instead of idling for a few hundred million cycles during a disk access, your microprocessor may be able to go back to work in as little as a thousand cycles if the information is in a buffer. If your program makes only an occasional disk access, you might not notice the difference that the BUFFERS directive makes. If you are using a disk-intensive program, however, the difference can be dramatic.

Why memory buffers are efficient . . . You do not have to be a computer expert to know that RAM is a lot faster than disk memory. RAM access speed is rated in nanoseconds (one billionth of a second); hard disks boast of access to data in as little as 18 to 28 milliseconds (thousandths of a second.) To translate that into human terms, the difference is like someone saying, "I'll get that for you in a second," or "I'll find that for you in eleven-and-a-half days." Clearly, whenever you can fetch data from RAM instead of from the disk, you are way ahead. You will see how this concept is taken to its near-ultimate in the discussion of IBMCACHE.SYS and SMARTDRV.SYS later in this chapter.

A single buffer is about 512 bytes long (plus 16 bytes for overhead). The BUFFERS directive controls how many disk buffers your computer uses. The syntax for the BUFFERS directive is as follows:

BUFFERS = *nn*

nn is the number of disk buffers you want. With versions of DOS before V4, you can have any number of buffers from 1 to 99. If you do not give the BUFFERS directive, DOS uses a default value of from 2 to 15. The default number of buffers depends on the type of disk you have, the amount of memory in your computer, and the version of DOS you use. Table 13.2 lists the different buffer configurations.

Table 13.2
Default Number of Disk Buffers

DOS Version	Number of BUFFERS	Hardware
DOS pre-V3.3	2	floppy disk drives
	3	hard disk
DOS V3.3/V4	2	360K floppy disk drive
	3	any other hard or floppy disk drive
	5	more than 1284K of RAM
	10	more than 256K of RAM
	15	more than 512K of RAM

You can use fewer BUFFERS than the default numbers shown in table 13.2. Unless you use a disk-caching program, however, you may find you want more, rather than fewer, buffers.

Understanding How DOS Uses Disk Buffers

When DOS is asked to get information from a disk, DOS reads information in increments of whole sectors (512 bytes). Excess data not required from that sector is left in the buffer. If this data is needed later, DOS does not need to perform another disk access to retrieve the data. Similarly, DOS tries to reduce disk activity when it writes information to the disk. If less than a full sector is to be written to the disk, DOS accumulates the information in a disk buffer. When the buffer is full, DOS writes the information to the disk. This action is called *flushing the buffer*. To make sure that all pertinent information is placed into a file, DOS also flushes the buffers when a program "closes" a disk file.

When a disk buffer becomes full or empty, DOS marks the buffer to indicate that the buffer has been used recently. When DOS needs to reuse the buffers for new information, it takes the buffer that has not been used for the longest time.

The net effect of DOS's use of buffers is to reduce the number of disk accesses DOS performs by reading and writing only full sectors. By reusing the least-recently used buffers, DOS retains information more likely to be needed next. Your programs and DOS run faster.

If your program does much *random* disk work (reading and writing information in different parts of a file), you may want to specify a higher number of buffers. The more buffers you have, the better the chance that the information DOS wants is already in memory (the disk buffer).

Some programs do not benefit much from using disk buffers. If your program mainly does *sequential* reads and writes (reading or writing information from the start of the file straight through to the end), using disk buffers does not give you a considerable advantage.

Fine-Tuning with Buffers

The number of disk buffers you should have depends on the programs you run on your computer and how much memory you have. If your day-to-day use of the computer does not involve accounting or database work (which uses files with small groups of data), the correct number of buffers is from 10 to 20. If you do accounting or database work, you should have between 20 and 40 buffers (or more, if you use expanded memory with DOS V4). If you use many subdirectories, using more disk buffers can increase your computer's performance.

Because each disk buffer takes 528 bytes of memory, every two disk buffers you use costs just over 1K of RAM. If you use many memory-hungry programs and terminate-and-stay-resident (TSR) utilities, you may need to use a minimal number of buffers simply to preserve precious RAM.

Even if memory is no problem, DOS has a "magic" range for disk buffers. DOS V3 and V4 slow down if you specify between 40 and 60 disk buffers. This happens because DOS spends more time searching the buffers for information than reading or writing the disk. Depending on the programs you run, you may find that specifying more than 30 buffers causes the system to become sluggish.

Start with 10 disk buffers if you use a floppy disk system; start with 20 buffers for a hard disk system. Fine-tune the number by increasing or decreasing the number by 1 to 5 buffers every few hours or once a day. Then reboot DOS and examine its performance. Your performance test need only be a subjective "feel" of a favorite, disk-intensive program's performance. Keep doing this until you think you have the best performance. You do not need to be exact, but just get the general "feel" of the computer's performance with different numbers of buffers.

These rules of thumb go out the window if you use sophisticated programs with memory-management routines of their own. If you have a disk cache (explained in a later section), for example, most of the work done by buffers is handled automatically—and more intelligently. Memory managers for 386 computers, such as Quarterdeck's QEMM-386, set up their own disk buffers. If you fall into either of these categories, set the CONFIG.SYS BUFFERS directive to a relatively low number, such as 2. This action enables DOS to read a whole sector or two into memory, but doesn't waste memory on buffers that really aren't needed.

Understanding DOS V4 BUFFERS Options

DOS V4 added important options to the BUFFERS directive. The numbers of buffers you can set with DOS V4 was increased to 10,000—if you have expanded memory. In addition, you can now use something called a "look-ahead" buffer to increase disk efficiency.

DOS V4 introduced support for expanded memory, and BUFFERS is one of the features that can use it. If you add the /X switch to the BUFFERS directive in your CONFIG.SYS file, DOS uses expanded memory to store buffered information. Calculate the number of buffers you can fit in the memory you have (each buffer is 528 bytes).

You must have an Expanded Memory Adapter or a 386-expanded memory manager to use the /X switch with the BUFFERS directive.

Look-ahead buffers are special buffers that DOS uses to store sectors that are ahead of the sector requested by a DOS read operation. A look-ahead buffer requires 512 bytes of memory. You can specify from 0 to 8 look-ahead buffers. If you specify 5 look-ahead buffers, for example, every time DOS reads a sector from your disk, it also reads the following five sectors. Reading the additional sectors is simple for DOS because the read/write head is already positioned and operating to read the first sector.

If your application or DOS needs one of the sectors already read, DOS finds the sectors in the look-ahead buffer and does not have to make another disk access. As you can see, the look-ahead buffer can be a powerful performance enhancer.

The syntax for the expanded-memory and look-ahead-buffer features is as follows:

BUFFERS = *buffers, look-ahead_buffers /X*

Including the directive **BUFFERS = 1000,8 /X**, for example, tells DOS to set aside 1,000 buffers and 8 look-ahead buffers, using expanded memory. If enough expanded memory is not available, the directive is ignored, and DOS reverts to the default buffer value. To be sure that you have enough memory for the buffers you want to specify, use the DOS V4 MEM command. The default is 1 look-ahead buffer; if you want to use look-ahead buffers, a good value to start with is 8.

Installing Device Drivers with DEVICE

Device drivers are special software additions to DOS's basic input/output system. DOS is supplied with a wealth of device drivers you can use to make better use of your current—and future—computer hardware equipment. Some add-on hardware comes with device-driver files that enable the hardware to function on your system. To make DOS aware of the device drivers you want to use, include the DEVICE directive in the CONFIG.SYS file. The syntax for the DEVICE directive is as follows:

DEVICE = *d:path\filename.ext /switches*

 You do not have to include spaces on either side of the equal sign in this syntax. Spaces around the equal sign are optional.

d: is the disk drive where the device-driver file resides, *path* is the directory path to the device-driver file, and *filename.ext* is the name of the device-driver file. */switches* are any switches needed by the device-driver software.

You can load as many device drivers as you need, but you must use a separate DEVICE line for each driver you install. As each device driver is loaded, DOS extends its control to that device. Remember that the device driver must be accessible when DOS starts. For convenience, floppy disk users should place device-driver files in the root directory. Hard disk users can make a special subdirectory called DRIVERS or SYS and put the driver files in this directory, out of the way of daily files. If you put the driver files in a separate subdirectory, add the directory path name to the device-driver file name, as in the following examples:

DEVICE = C:\DOS\DRIVERS\ANSI.SYS

DEVICE = C:\SYS\ANSI.SYS

The preceding sections in this chapter introduced techniques of using memory efficiently with the BUFFERS directive. The following sections show you how to gain extra horsepower from your system with some device drivers. Some of these drivers are supplied with DOS; others are supplied with the mouse, printer, or other software.

Understanding Disk Caches

Strictly speaking, the IBMCACHE.SYS device-driver file is not part of DOS (IBMCACHE.SYS is included on the Reference Disk for the IBM PS/2 Models 50, 60, and 80). Some versions of DOS come with the SMARTDRV.SYS file; other versions of DOS do not have it. If your version of DOS does not include the file, you will need to purchase Microsoft Windows to get SMARTDRV.SYS. No discussion of device drivers is complete without an understanding of disk-cache systems. The concepts discussed in this section apply to both of these programs as well as other caching programs.

You can think of IBMCACHE.SYS and SMARTDRV.SYS as large, smart buffers. Like a buffer, a disk cache operates from a section of RAM that you request from DOS. Both a disk cache and a disk buffer accumulate information going to the disk or coming from the disk. When information is read from the disk, the information is placed in a buffer or cache; the information requested by the program is sent to the program. Like a buffer, a disk cache can read more information than was requested by the program. When information is written to the disk, the information can be stored in the buffer or cache until the buffer or cache is full; the information is then written to the disk.

Most caches have a "write-through" feature: the cache writes information to disk frequently to avoid data loss if the system is turned off or loses power. Smart caches eliminate redundant writes by putting information on disk only when the data is different from what is there already.

If you use a cache or buffers, your program performance improves because slow disk accesses are replaced by higher-speed memory-to-memory transfers.

Although a DOS disk buffer is a form of a disk cache, a good caching program outperforms a buffer. Disk caches are better performers because they have more "intelligence" than buffers. You may find that the performance of a disk cache is hampered if you make the cache too large or too small. Test the different applications you use and vary the size of the cache to find the optimum performance.

A disk cache remembers which sections of the disk have been used most frequently. When the cache must be recycled, the program keeps the more-frequently used areas and discards those less-frequently used. Buffers, as you recall, are recycled based on how old the buffer is, regardless of how frequently the buffer is used. Disk-cache recycling is more efficient.

In an absolutely random disk access, where program and data files are scattered uniformly across the disk, the cache method of recycling the least-frequently used area is more efficient than the buffer method of recycling the oldest area. A cache tends to keep in memory the areas of the disk that are most heavily used.

Like the DOS V4 BUFFERS directive, many disk caches have look-ahead capabilities, a technique in which the cache reads more sectors than the program requests.

In many cases, using a disk cache to help with disk activity is preferable to using a RAM disk program like RAMDRIVE.SYS (discussed later in this chapter). A RAM disk helps only with files copied to the RAM disk (loading a program with overlays into a RAM disk may be better than using a cache to speed up a slow disk). The cache's activity is effortless and transparent to the user; a RAM disk requires separate directives to access the needed files.

> **Tech note ...** Some programs are too large to fit completely in your PC's memory. These programs load a core part of themselves into memory and access additional parts from *overlay* files as needed. When a new section of the program is needed, the appropriate overlay for that section is read in from disk into the area occupied by the current overlay. The term "overlay" comes from this process of overlaying sections of program space in memory with new sections. RAM disks enable rapid switching of active overlays because the overlay disk files are actually in memory, not on a disk. You must copy any needed overlay files to the RAM disk before starting the application. Of course, you must configure the application to look for its overlays on the RAM disk.

A disk cache is also preferable to a RAM disk because the cache offers more protection against losing information. There is a greater probability of losing information when files are written to a RAM disk than when files are written to the cache. The cache, like a DOS buffer, holds the information for only a few seconds before writing it to the disk. During this brief period, the information is at risk. If power is lost to the RAM disk, however, all files on the disk are destroyed. You must issue commands to copy the information in the RAM disk to the safety of a hard disk; the RAM disk does not do this automatically.

In two situations, however, a RAM disk is preferable to a disk cache. First, when you need to copy files between diskettes on a computer with a single floppy disk drive, copying to and from the RAM disk is convenient. You first copy the files to the RAM disk, change diskettes, and then copy the files from the RAM disk to the second diskette. A disk cache cannot help you copy files between diskettes.

Second, you may prefer to use a RAM disk if you frequently use nonchanging files that can be placed completely on the RAM disk. A good example is Turbo Lightning; you can place its dictionary and thesaurus files on a RAM disk. Because you access these files frequently—but rarely the same spots in the files—having the files on a RAM disk provides better performance than having the files in a disk cache.

Installing IBMCACHE.SYS

IBMCACHE.SYS is a file that accompanies any IBM PS/2 that uses extended memory (this excludes the Models 25 and 30). IBMCACHE is a disk-caching program specifically made for PS/2 computers. IBMCACHE.SYS is found on the Reference Disk that comes with the computer.

To install IBMCACHE.SYS the first time, you must run the program IBMCACHE from the Reference Disk. Because the IBMCACHE.COM program and the IBMCACHE.SYS disk cache itself are hidden files on the diskette, you cannot copy the files to your computer using the DOS COPY command. You have to install the disk cache.

First, start up DOS on your PS/2 system. After DOS is running, insert the Reference Disk in drive A and type the following:

A:IBMCACHE

Your screen should look something like that in figure 13.1. The highlighted bar should be over the first option, Install disk cache onto drive C:. When you press Enter to select the option, a window pops up giving the information shown in figure 13.2. Press Y to install the cache. The pop-up window goes away, the floppy disk and hard disk lights go on, and a message that the cache is installed appears in another window (see fig. 13.3). Press Enter to continue.

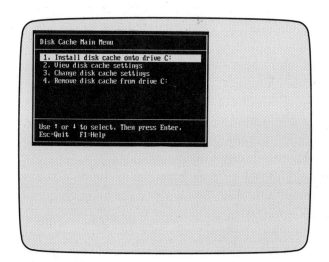

Fig. 13.1

Initial installation screen for IBMCACHE.

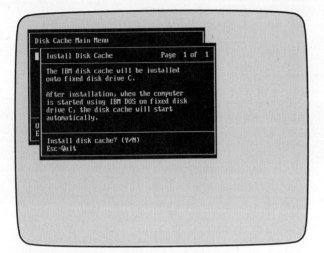

Fig. 13.2

IBMCACHE installation information.

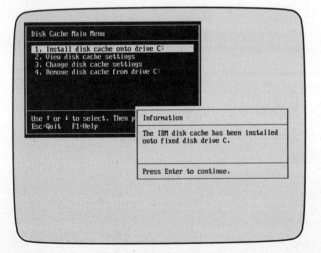

Fig. 13.3

Successful installation of IBMCACHE.

If you have extended memory, move the highlighted bar on the Disk Cache Main menu to option 3, Change disk cache settings, by tapping the down-arrow key twice. Press Enter. The Change Disk Cache Settings screen appears as shown in figure 13.4. The following sections explain how to use this screen.

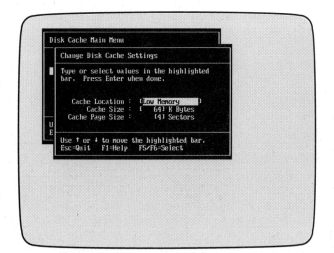

```
Disk Cache Main Menu

  Change Disk Cache Settings

  Type or select values in the highlighted
  bar.  Press Enter when done.


      Cache Location :  [Low Memory    ]
         Cache Size :  [   64] K Bytes
    Cache Page Size :     [4] Sectors


  Use ↑ or ↓ to move the highlighted bar.
  Esc=Quit   F1=Help   F5/F6=Select
```

Fig. 13.4

*The Change Disk Cache
Settings screen.*

Changing the Cache Size

The initial size of the cache is 64K. A computer with 1M of memory has 384K of extended memory. You may want to expand the size of the cache to incorporate all the extended memory, or you may want to save some of the memory for a RAM disk.

The latest computer systems, particularly 386-based systems, may use some extended memory to "shadow" ROM code in faster RAM. If you have a VGA board or other peripherals, some ROM may be mapped into extended memory, which decreases the amount of extended memory that can be used as a cache.

If you want to change the size of the cache, press the down-arrow key on the Change Disk Cache Settings screen to move to the Cache Size option. Press F5 to reduce the cache size; press F6 to increase the size. Try pressing the F5 and F6 keys to see some of the possible sizes for the cache. Alternatively, you can type the desired cache size.

If you do not use a RAM disk in extended memory, use all the extended memory for the cache by specifying a cache size of 384K. If you use a RAM disk in extended memory, use the leftover memory for the cache. Subtract the size, in K, of the RAM disk from 384K; then use the resulting figure as the size of the cache.

You may notice that the size choices offered when you press F5 or F6 do not match your calculations. If you do not see a number that matches your calculations, simply type the number you want.

Changing the Cache Page Size

The final option on the Change Disk Cache Settings screen is `Cache Page Size`. This option specifies the number of sectors to be read whenever DOS reads any information from the disk. Regardless of how many sectors a program requests that DOS read, DOS always reads the number of sectors you specify here (in this respect, the page size is similar to a look-ahead buffer). DOS always reads the minimum amount of sectors required; if you specify a page size larger than what is required, more sectors are read. This strategy is excellent for programs that start at the beginning of a file and read to the end, but may not be good for programs that read files randomly.

The starting value for `Cache Page Size` is 4 sectors. The values 2, 4, and 8 are valid for this option. Do not change this value initially. No single optimum value can be given for this option; you and your programs must determine the best value. Run your system for several hours or days. If you find the performance of some of your programs declining slightly, rerun IBMCACHE and change this value to 2. You reduce the number of sectors to be read because your programs are reading files randomly rather than sequentially; DOS is wasting time reading sectors that are not used by the program.

Once you have finished changing disk-cache options, press Enter. You see a message stating that the changes you made have been saved (see fig. 13.5). Press Enter again to return to the DOS prompt.

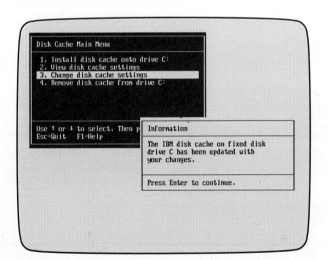

Fig. 13.5

The successful change of IBMCACHE options.

To start the cache program, restart DOS by pressing Ctrl-Alt-Del; you soon should see the following message:

```
Disk Cache Version 1.0
Copyright 1987 by IBM Corp.
Allocating Cache Buffers
Cache Initialization Complete
```

The cache has been successfully installed. Whenever you boot DOS, the cache is reinstalled.

Changing the IBMCACHE Settings in CONFIG.SYS

If you want to change options after the cache has been installed, you can either rerun IBMCACHE or edit the IBMCACHE line in your CONFIG.SYS file (when you installed the cache, the CONFIG.SYS file was altered to include this line). The syntax for the IBMCACHE.SYS program is as follows:

DEVICE = *d:path***IBMCACHE.SYS** *cachesize /E or /NE /Psectors*

d:path is the optional disk drive and path name for the IBMCACHE.SYS program, and *cachesize* is the size of the cache in kilobytes.

The /E and /NE switches designate where the cache is to be placed. /E designates extended memory, and /NE designates the 640K of low memory. You can use either switch, but not both.

/Psectors designates the number of disk sectors that DOS should read at once. *sectors* can be set to 2, 4, or 8. Notice that, unlike many DOS switches, no colon is used to separate the P from the number of sectors.

Installing SMARTDRV.SYS

MS-DOS V4 includes a a disk-cache program called SMARTDRV.SYS. (SMARTDRV.SYS also comes with Microsoft Windows.) You can use SMARTDRV.SYS instead of IBMCACHE.SYS, if you want. This section explains how to install and use SMARTDRV.SYS.

No installation program is necessary for SMARTDRV.SYS. To install this program, all you have to do is put a correctly worded directive in CONFIG.SYS. The syntax for installing SMARTDRV.SYS is as follows:

DEVICE = *d:path***SMARTDRV.SYS** *size /A*

d:path is the optional disk drive and path name for the SMARTDRV.SYS program, and *size* is an optional parameter that specifies how much memory you want SMARTDRV to use. The default size is 256K.

The /A switch tells SMARTDRV to use expanded memory, if it is *available,* or to use extended memory as expanded memory. If this switch is not used, SMARTDRV uses extended memory.

After you insert the SMARTDRV.SYS directive in CONFIG.SYS and boot the computer, you see something like the following message:

```
Microsoft SMARTDrive RAM Cache version x.xx
Cache Size: 256K in 80286 Extended Memory
```

The version number and size of the cache vary depending on how SMARTDRV was set up.

Using RAMDRIVE To Make a RAM Disk

RAM disks are given a drive allocation letter such as D or E. You can use RAM disks just like an ordinary drive, but you lose the contents of the drive when you turn off the computer.

Another device driver you can install is RAMDRIVE.SYS (also called VDISK.SYS in PC DOS). This program enables you to install an imaginary disk in memory. Like buffers and disk caches, a RAM disk is much faster than ordinary disk access.

To install RAMDRIVE and create an imaginary (or virtual) disk, just insert a line in CONFIG.SYS. The syntax to invoke RAMDRIVE from CONFIG.SYS is as follows:

DEVICE = *d:path***RAMDRIVE.SYS** *bbbb sss ddd /E:max or /X*

If you use PC DOS, your syntax will use VDISK in place of RAMDRIVE.

d: is the disk drive, and *path* is the directory path for RAMDRIVE.SYS. The options for RAMDRIVE are listed in table 13.3 and described in the following sections.

Table 13.3
RAMDRIVE Options

Option	Description
bbbb	The size (in K) of the RAM disk
sss	The size (in bytes) of the RAM-disk sectors
ddd	The number of directory entries (files) for the RAM disk
/E:max	The switch for extended memory use
/X	The DOS V4 switch for expanded memory use (some versions of DOS use /A instead of /X)

Understanding RAMDRIVE Options

This section describes the parameters you can use with the RAMDRIVE.SYS program. The arrangement of the options is shown in the syntax line in the preceding section.

The RAMDRIVE *bbbb* option can range from 1K to the maximum amount of memory available minus the 64K that DOS requires for other programs. For most PCs and compatibles, the maximum amount of memory is 640K. ATs and compatibles can have up to 16M of RAM, so you can set up more than one RAMDRIVE with these computers. You can, for example, conceivably set up one 3M and three 4M virtual disks (*virtual disk* is another name for RAM drive).

The default value of *bbbb* is 64K. With DOS V3.2, V3.3, and V4, RAMDRIVE automatically reduces the RAM disk's size if you forget to leave 64K of memory free for your programs. With DOS V3.0 and V3.1, if you specify a value for *bbbb* larger than the amount of your computer's RAM, RAMDRIVE uses the default value of 64K. If you have less than 64K of memory available, RAMDRIVE displays an error message and cannot be installed.

The *sss* option refers to the size of the sectors for RAMDRIVE. You can specify one of three sector sizes: 128, 256, or 512 bytes. The default sector size is 128 bytes. (DOS enables you to specify the sector size for a RAM disk; DOS disks usually use a sector size of 512 bytes.) Set *sss* to 512 if you store larger files on the RAM disk or if you want to maximize disk speed when you use the RAM disk. If you store many small files, set *sss* to 256 or 128 so that less space is wasted. If you set a smaller sector size, the disk must be read more often, but the space in the RAM disk is used more efficiently.

The *ddd* option refers to the number of directory entries for the RAM disk. Each file you store on the RAM disk uses one directory entry. Because the volume label that RAMDRIVE creates takes one of the directory entries, *ddd* actually specifies the number of files, minus 1, that your RAM disk can hold. You can specify a value for *ddd* from 2 to 512 files; the default is 64. Set the number of directories based on the size of the RAM disk and the size of the files you are storing.

/E is the switch RAMDRIVE uses to access extended memory—that is—memory above the one million-byte point. With the /E switch, RAMDRIVE uses 768 bytes of regular memory, but places the RAM disk itself in extended memory. If you use the /E switch, the maximum size of the RAM disk is 4M. You can use multiple RAM disks, limited only by the amount of available extended memory and DOS's regular memory. Because each RAMDRIVE uses 768 bytes of regular memory, specifying many RAM disks may reduce regular memory below 64K. If this happens, the last RAM disk you try to install does not install.

DOS V3.0 uses the */E* switch alone; later versions add the *max* parameter to the switch. *max* is the maximum number of sectors that can be transferred at one time from the RAM disk. Certain programs, primarily communications programs, may lose characters if the CPU's attention is directed to the RAM disk for too long. If you have such a problem, set *max* to 7 or less. Otherwise, omit the parameter or specify **/E:8**.

If you have enough extended memory, you can set up several RAM disks. Just specify additional **DEVICE = RAMDRIVE.SYS** statements in CONFIG.SYS. Each statement invokes a fresh copy of RAMDRIVE and installs additional RAM disks.

To use a RAM disk that has the features of a 360K, double-sided diskette, for example, use this command line:

DEVICE = RAMDRIVE.SYS 360 512 112

If you want a RAM disk that uses all the extended memory on a computer with 1M of RAM, use this command line:

DEVICE = RAMDRIVE.SYS 384 512 112 /E:8

This statement creates a RAM disk of 384K (384K is the difference between 1M of RAM and 640K of conventional memory), with 512-byte sectors and 112 directory entries. The **/E:8** switch tells DOS to install the RAM disk in extended memory and transfer 8 sectors to and from the RAM disk at a time. If you omit the /E switch, DOS installs the RAM disk in the 640K of DOS memory.

If you use DOS V4, you can use the /A parameter, which enables you to use expanded memory (instead of extended memory) for the RAM disk. To use this switch, you must load the expanded-memory driver (such as XMA2EMS.SYS) before loading RAMDRIVE.SYS. You cannot use both the /A and /E switches for the same RAM disk. You can create different RAM disks, however, some using extended memory and others using expanded memory, if you have enough memory available. Simply insert multiple DEVICE statements in CONFIG.SYS.

Learning More about RAM Disks

The amount of RAM in your computer, the programs you use, and the convenience of a RAM disk play a part in determining the size of RAM disk you use—or whether you even should use a RAM disk. This section helps you determine whether you should bother using a RAM disk, and if so, what size may help you the most.

Both CHKDSK and MEM (DOS V4) report your available system memory. You can use either command to help determine your system's available memory.

A RAM Disk in 640K of Memory

Although all computers can accommodate a RAM disk, your computer may not be able to accommodate a RAM disk while using other programs. When DOS V4.01 is loaded on a computer with 640K of memory, for example, 581K is left for programs to use (640K is actually 655,360 bytes). DOS V4.01, using the CONFIG.SYS FILES and BUFFERS directives and the ANSI.SYS device driver, uses about 74K of RAM.

If you use Lotus 1-2-3 Release 2.2 on a computer with this setup, you must have 223K of RAM for the program, plus enough memory left over for worksheets. Loading 1-2-3 leaves 358K for worksheet creation. If you create a RAM disk in the remaining 358K of conventional memory, you decrease the memory you can use for a worksheet.

As another example, dBASE IV uses 412K of RAM, leaving 169K of memory. Although dBASE IV does not use RAM for workspace in the same way as 1-2-3, you may limit some features of dBASE IV, such as running DOS commands from dBASE, if you create a RAM disk.

The bottom line is this: if you have only conventional memory, you may find that a RAM disk does not optimize your use of memory. Exceptions exist, of course. If the program you use does not take up a lot of memory, you may be able to use a RAM disk. You may want to limit the size of the RAM disk to no more than 100K, however.

If you set up a 100K RAM disk, you cannot store a large quantity of information on the RAM disk. You probably would use the RAM disk only for temporary storage of rather small files. You may want to use the following directive in your CONFIG.SYS file:

DEVICE = C:\RAMDRIVE.SYS 100 128 64

This statement creates a 100K RAM disk, with 128-byte sectors and 64 directory entries. Because the RAM disk uses some of the allocated space for the directory and file-allocation table (FAT), only 98.9K is actually usable.

The small sector size of 128 bytes is assigned in this example to maximize the performance of the RAM disk. If you set up the disk with 128-byte sectors, and the disk contains 10 files of 600 bytes each, 92.5K is available for further storage. If you set up the RAM disk with 512-byte sectors and have the same files, only 89K would be available.

Because one file does not share a sector with another file, a single 600-byte file uses five 128-byte sectors, wasting 40 bytes. The same 600-byte file uses only two 512-byte sectors; however, 497 bytes are wasted. From this example, you can see that using a small sector size has advantages.

If you plan to store only one or two larger files on the 100K RAM disk, however, you may be better off setting a larger sector size. You realize a time savings when fewer, larger sectors are read or written rather than more, smaller sectors.

The size of the directory also influences the usable size of the RAM disk: the larger the directory, the more room is needed to track files. A 100K RAM disk set up to store 64 files has 98.9K available for storage. The same 100K RAM disk with a directory size of 192 files has only 94.9K for storage. You get a 4-percent larger disk by using the smaller directory size. Practically speaking, you rarely store more than 64 files on a 100K RAM disk, anyway.

A RAM Disk in Expanded or Extended Memory

If your computer has either extended or expanded memory, you may find that a RAM disk is worthwhile. With expanded or extended memory, the actual memory used by the RAM disk is located outside the conventional memory used by programs. You can create a RAM disk without giving up program memory. If you decide to use a RAM disk on a computer with expanded or extended memory, the issue is how large the RAM disk should be and what settings you should use.

If you have expanded memory and use a program like Lotus 1-2-3 Release 2.01 or 2.2, you have more of a decision of how much expanded memory to dedicate to a RAM disk, because 1-2-3 can store data in expanded memory. Creating a RAM disk in expanded memory decreases the amount of expanded memory that 1-2-3 can use. If you have 2M of expanded memory, for example, you may find that you can set aside as much as 512K for a RAM disk without affecting programs that use expanded memory.

If your computer has extended memory, you must decide how much extended memory to use as a RAM disk, if any. Programs such as Lotus 1-2-3 Release 3 use a DOS extender to make extended memory available to the program for data storage. Creating a RAM disk in extended memory, then, decreases the amount of memory available to programs that use DOS extenders.

Regardless of whether you have extended or expanded memory, you also must decide what you can use that memory for in addition to programs. You may want to use some of that memory for SMARTDRV.SYS or IBMCACHE.SYS, for example. If the programs you use are disk-oriented rather than RAM oriented (dBASE is disk-oriented; 1-2-3 is RAM-oriented), you can use expanded or extended memory for a large disk cache. The use of a large disk cache may make a RAM disk obsolete, however, because the disk cache speeds access to your data files.

If you create a RAM disk in expanded or extended memory, you will probably create a disk larger than one created in conventional memory. When you create a larger RAM disk, you can vary the settings for sector size and directory size. The values you give for these settings, however, still depend on the quantity and size of the files to be stored on the RAM disk.

If you create a 512K RAM disk, for example, you may find that a sector size of 512 bytes is adequate, even if you store small files on the RAM disk. You may also find that a directory size of 64 is adequate because you seldom store more than 64 files on a RAM disk. If, however, you plan to use the RAM disk to help you copy files from one diskette to another, change the directory value to 112. This is the total number of files that can be stored in the root directory of a 360K diskette.

To create a 512K RAM disk with 512-byte sectors and 112 directory entries in expanded memory, include the following directive in CONFIG.SYS:

DEVICE = C:\RAMDRIVE.SYS 512 512 112 /A

To create the same RAM disk in extended memory, include this directive:

DEVICE = C:\RAMDRIVE.SYS 512 512 112 /E

These directives create a RAM disk adequate for temporary storage. Remember the word *temporary*; when the power goes out, you lose what is on the RAM disk. Back up important files on the RAM disk to the hard disk or diskettes.

 Because RAM disks are memory-based devices, they lose their contents when you reboot or turn your PC's power off. You must copy the contents of a RAM disk to a conventional disk file before rebooting or powering down to prevent such a loss. If you (or your applications program) are creating or modifying RAM disk files, it is a good idea to copy regularly the files to an actual disk in case an unexpected power failure occurs.

Naming Disk Drives

The logical disk-drive names (the drive letters) that DOS assigns to disks created by DRIVER.SYS (see the Command Reference) and RAMDRIVE.SYS depend on the placement of the directives in the CONFIG.SYS file. You may try to use the wrong disk drive name if you do not know how DOS assigns drive names.

Normally, CONFIG.SYS directives are not order-dependent. That is, you can give the directives in any order, and the computer does not change how the directive operates.

RAMDRIVE.SYS and DRIVER.SYS do not have the same independence, however. You can load RAMDRIVE.SYS and DRIVER.SYS in any order—the device drivers work, but the disk-drive names change. Whenever DOS encounters a block-device driver (that is, any device that transfers data in blocks, rather than in bytes), DOS assigns the next highest drive letter to the device. The order is first come, first assigned.

If you load a copy of RAMDRIVE.SYS on a system with a single logical hard disk, for example, DOS assigns the name D to the RAM disk. If you load a second copy of RAMDRIVE.SYS, DOS assigns the name E to the second RAM disk. Even if the system has only one floppy disk drive, the first RAM disk is assigned the name D; the letter B is reserved for a second floppy disk drive.

If you load a copy of DRIVER.SYS for the external floppy disk drive instead of RAMDRIVE on the same computer, DOS assigns the external disk drive the name D. If you load another copy of DRIVER.SYS for the same external drive, DOS assigns the logical name D to this disk drive.

Remember that additional hard disks or additional logical disks add to the starting letter of drives created by CONFIG.SYS. Suppose that the hard drive on a 44M system has the drive names C and D. Additional partitions of the hard disk are assigned the next available drive letters before drives created by CONFIG.SYS directives are named. (Hard disks are partitioned with the FDISK command, explained in Chapter 6, and are

347

assigned driver letters whether or not you use DRIVER.SYS.) For this reason, the second partition of the hard disk is named D. RAMDRIVE, if used, is assigned the drive name E. DRIVER.SYS, if used instead of RAMDRIVE, is assigned the drive name E.

The potential for further confusion comes when several block-device (disk-like) drivers are loaded. The order of loading, determined by the order of the directives in the CONFIG.SYS file, determines the names assigned by DOS.

If you load RAMDRIVE.SYS first and DRIVER.SYS second, the RAM disk may be named D and the DRIVER.SYS disk is one letter higher . If you switch the lines so that DRIVER.SYS is loaded first, the disk drive names are switched as well. The DRIVER.SYS disk is named D and the RAM disk is named E.

Using Expanded Memory with DOS V4

Two device drivers, XMA2EMS.SYS and XMAEM.SYS, are provided with DOS V4 to enable you to use expanded memory with your system. Although these drivers are intended for IBM memory adapters, you can successfully use the drivers with other brands, including the Orchid RamQuest 50/60 memory add-on.

Some implementations of DOS V4 call the XMAEM.SYS file EMM386.SYS.

Using the XMA2EMS.SYS Driver

You can use XMA2EMS.SYS if you have either an expanded memory adapter or an 80386-based computer with the XMAEM.SYS driver installed. The syntax used to install this driver is as follows:

DEVICE = XMA2EMS.SYS *FRAME* = *xxxx P254* = *yyyy P255* = *zzzz /X:aa*

xxxx can be any page from address C000 to E000, where the address reflects a 64K page. *P254* and *P255* represent 16K pages of memory used by FASTOPEN and BUFFERS, respectively, to perform their functions in expanded memory. (FASTOPEN and BUFFERS are covered in other sections of this chapter). *yyyy* and *zzzz* are memory addresses of the pages you want to use for these functions.

The */X:aa* switch is used to keep the driver from using less than the maximum total available memory. If you supply a value for *aa* in multiples of 16K pages, XMA2EMS.SYS uses only that amount for expanded memory specification (EMS). If you specify **/X:8**, for example, 128K of EMS memory is defined for use from the total memory on your expanded or extended memory board.

Consult the manuals furnished with your applications programs and peripherals to determine how to allocate expanded memory in your system.

Users of early versions of DOS V4.0 reported serious problems with IBM's EMS support. The V4.0 EMS support implemented expanded memory in a different way than most other available EMS drivers. In particular, you could run into trouble if you told DOS to use expanded memory when you installed FASTOPEN and BUFFERS from CONFIG.SYS. DOS V4.01 corrected this bug.

Using the XMAEM.SYS Driver

The XMAEM driver is designed to be used with 80386-based systems. It enables you to use extended memory that can be addressed as though it were EMS memory. You can use this driver to define the number of 16K pages of extended memory to be devoted to expanded memory.

Some implementations of DOS V4 call the XMAEM.SYS file EMM386.SYS.

If you want to address extended memory as EMS memory, use the following syntax:

DEVICE = XMAEM.SYS *aa*

aa is the number of pages to allocate (divide the amount of memory by 16 to calculate this figure). The XMAEM.SYS driver must be loaded before XMA2EMS.SYS in your CONFIG.SYS file. Refer to the software and hardware manuals for your system to install this driver properly.

Accessing Files through FCBS

Some DOS users find the FCBS directive indispensable. It enables you to use useful, but antiquated, programs written for DOS V1 with later versions of DOS.

FCB is an acronym for *file control block*. FCBs serve as one way a program can access a file. This method of file access was used by DOS V1 to communicate with programs. Later versions of DOS borrow a UNIX-like method for controlling files, called *handles* (discussed in "Using the FILES Directive" later in this chapter). Although FCBs can be used with any version of DOS, handles can be used only with DOS V2, V3, or V4.

To use the FCBS directive in the CONFIG.SYS file, use this syntax:

FCBS = *maxopen, neverclose*

maxopen is the maximum number of unique FCBs that programs can open at one time, and *neverclose* is the number of FCBs that DOS cannot reuse automatically. You must specify *maxopen*, which can be a number from 1 to 255. The default value is 4. The optional *neverclose* parameter must be a number less than or equal to *maxopen*. If you do not specify *neverclose*, the default value is 0. Set these values by trial and error. If you set certain values and then run the program, and the program cannot open all the required files (a message to this effect appears), set the FCBS parameters to higher values.

Although the IBM documentation states that FCBs are closed only when you use the SHARE command for a local area network (LAN), this is not true with DOS V3.0 and V3.1. If you use an older program that does not support path names, the program uses FCBs, and you should set the FCBS directive.

You pay a small price in RAM to use the FCBS directive. For each number above 4 that *maxopen* exceeds, DOS uses about 40 bytes. Considering that most people have 256K or more of RAM in their computers, the use of this extra RAM should not be a problem.

Using the FILES Directive

As the FCBS directive decreases in importance with the later versions of DOS, the FILES directive increases. FILES is the DOS V2, V3, and V4 directive used to enable UNIX-like or XENIX-like file handling. UNIX and XENIX—and later versions of DOS—use a file *handle* (a number corresponding to the file name) instead of file-control blocks to access files. You never have to deal with file handles directly. Your program gives the operating system the name of the file or device you want to use. The operating system gives back to your program a handle—a two-byte number. From that point on, your programs use the handle, rather than the FCB, to manipulate the file or device.

To include the FILES directive in CONFIG.SYS, use the following syntax:

FILES = *nn*

nn is the number of files you want opened at any time. The maximum is 255, and the minimum is 8. If you give a FILES directive with a number less than 8, or if you omit this directive, DOS makes the number 8. Each additional file over 8 increases the size of DOS by 39 bytes.

The name FILES is somewhat deceiving because handles are used by both files and devices. For example, standard devices such as the display, keyboard, or printer automatically receive 1 file handle each. If you do not specify the FILES directive, DOS starts with 8 file handles and immediately takes 5 handles for the standard devices, leaving only 3 handles for your programs. Including this directive in your CONFIG.SYS file is a good idea:

FILES = 10

This directive establishes 10 file handles, which should be enough for most programs. If a program displays an error message about file handles, edit CONFIG.SYS and increase the number of handles to 15 or 20 (if you are using dBASE III Plus, use 20 files). These higher numbers are sufficient for most existing programs.

Some applications programs automatically increase the FILES directive in CONFIG.SYS to the number required for the application's correct operation.

Using LASTDRIVE To Change the Number of Disk Drives

The LASTDRIVE directive informs DOS of the maximum number of disk drives on your system. Generally, LASTDRIVE is a directive used with networked computers or with the pretender commands (such as SUBST).

If you do not use the LASTDRIVE directive, DOS assumes that the last disk drive on your system is E. If you give DOS a letter corresponding to fewer drives than are physically attached to your computer, DOS ignores the directive. The LASTDRIVE directive enables you to tell DOS how many disk drives, real or apparent, are on your system. Suppose that you have a system with two floppy disk drives and a hard disk partitioned into three drives (C, D, and E). If you issue the directive **LASTDRIVE = D**, DOS ignores the directive because it knows the last drive is E.

If you want to use the LASTDRIVE directive in CONFIG.SYS, use the following syntax:

LASTDRIVE = x

x is the alphabetical character for the last disk drive on your system. The letters A through Z, in uppercase or lowercase, are acceptable.

You have a good reason to use the LASTDRIVE directive if you want to use multiple RAM disks. Suppose that you have a system with two floppy disk drives (drives A and B) and a hard drive (drive C). You create two RAM drives (drives D and E). To create a third RAM drive, you must issue the directive **LASTDRIVE = F** so that you can control the third RAM drive as drive F.

Another reason you may want to use LASTDRIVE is to establish logical disk drives. A *logical* disk drive can be a nickname for a subdirectory (see the SUBST command later in this chapter and in the Command Reference section). A logical disk drive may also be another partition of the hard disk. A logical disk drive is just a name. DOS "thinks" that the logical disk drive is real.

351

Using the SHELL Directive

The SHELL directive was originally implemented to enable programmers to replace the DOS command processor (COMMAND.COM) with other command processors. The directive now has two additional functions: You can place the command processor in any directory—not just in the boot disk's root directory—and you can expand the size of the environment. The *environment* is an area of RAM, set aside, in which named variables are assigned values. Commands such as PATH and PROMPT store their current settings in environment variables. You can see the contents of the environment by issuing the SET command.

SHELL is a tricky directive that should be used cautiously. Giving the wrong SHELL directive can "lock up" your system. Until you understand the directive, do not use it in your CONFIG.SYS file.

When you do need to use the directive to move COMMAND.COM from the root directory or to increase the size of the environment, have handy another DOS diskette that can start up your computer. If you make a mistake, reboot with this diskette and then correct the mistake in the SHELL directive.

You may want to keep COMMAND.COM in a directory other than the root directory to make it harder for computer "viruses" to locate the file. Another reason is to protect the file when you copy a diskette containing another copy of COMMAND.COM. If you accidentally copy the diskette to the root directory, you won't overwrite your version of COMMAND.COM.

The SHELL directive is slightly different for DOS V3.0 and later versions. The syntax for the SHELL directive in DOS V3.0 is as follows:

> **SHELL** = *d:path***filename**.*ext d:\\path* **/P**

The syntax for SHELL for DOS V3.1 through V4.0 is as follows:

> **SHELL** = *d:path***filename**.*ext d:\\path* **/P** */E:size*

d:path is the name of the disk drive and the subdirectory path to the command processor you want to use. *d:path* is optional but should be given. **filename**.*ext* is the name of the command processor. The root name is required, and the extension is needed only if the file does not use the extension COM.

The second *d:\\path* parameter is the disk drive and path name to the command processor. DOS uses this information to set the COMSPEC environment variable. This drive and path name should duplicate the first disk drive and path name. Although this drive and path are optional, they should be given.

SHELL has two switches under versions prior to V4.0: **/P** and */E:size*. DOS V4 adds a new switch to COMMAND.COM; */MSG* can be used with the SHELL.

The */MSG* switch tells DOS to load DOS *messages* into RAM when it loads COMMAND.COM. This enhancement can speed up operation somewhat and increases the amount of memory DOS uses only by about 1K.

The **/P** switch instructs DOS to load and keep resident a copy of the command processor. The **/P** switch is also called the **permanent** switch. Without the **/P** switch, DOS loads COMMAND.COM, executes the AUTOEXEC.BAT file, and immediately exits. If you omit the **/P** switch, you then must reboot the system using a different disk.

/E:size is an optional switch that sets the amount of random-access memory used for the *environment.* If you see the message Out of environment space, use the SHELL directive with the /E switch to specify a larger space for environment variables.

If you use /E, the size of DOS increases by the amount of space you add to the normal starting value for the environment. The SHELL directive does not use any additional memory except when it increases the size of the environment.

DOS V3.2, V3.3, and V4.0 start with an environment size of 160 bytes. You can specify a size from 160 to 32,767. If you give a size number greater than 32,767, DOS uses 32,767. If you give a number smaller than 160 or give a nonsense size (such as a letter), DOS uses 160 bytes for the environment.

If the size you specify is not evenly divisible by 16, DOS adjusts it to the next higher multiple of 16. For example, if you specify 322, DOS automatically adjusts the size to 336.

DOS V3.1 uses a different system for size: the number of 16-byte paragraphs for the environment. DOS V3.1 starts with an environment size of 128 bytes. You can change the size with the SHELL directive from 11 (11 × 16, or 176 bytes) to 62 (62 × 16, or 992 bytes). If you use a number less than 11 or greater than 62, DOS V3.1 displays an error message and ignores the /E switch.

Understanding DOS V4 CONFIG.SYS Commands

In addition to the new device drivers, DOS V4 provides three additional CONFIG.SYS directives: REM, SWITCHES, and INSTALL.

Using the REM Directive

REM enables you to insert remarks in your CONFIG.SYS file. You can leave notes to yourself (or others) explaining what particular lines do. This kind of documentation in a CONFIG.SYS file is especially helpful if you use non-DOS device drivers for your hardware. You also can remove temporarily a CONFIG.SYS statement by prefacing it with a REM directive. When you test a new configuration, you can enable only those features you want by removing the word *REM*.

To use the REM directive, use the following syntax:

   REM *remarks*

Using the SWITCHES Directive

SWITCHES turns off Extended Keyboard functions. This directive works like the ANSI.SYS /K switch. The syntax for this directive is as follows:

   SWITCHES = /K

Some software cannot work with the Extended Keyboard. If you use this directive to disable the Extended Keyboard for that software, the software should function properly.

Using the INSTALL Directive

INSTALL enables you to load from the CONFIG.SYS file certain utility programs that remain in memory. In versions of DOS before V4, you had to load these programs from the DOS prompt or through a batch file such as AUTOEXEC.BAT. DOS V4 supports loading any of the following programs using INSTALL:

   FASTOPEN.EXE

   KEYB.COM

   NLSFUNC.EXE

   SHARE.EXE

The Command Reference can provide more information about these programs. Loading these programs from CONFIG.SYS instead of from AUTOEXEC.BAT can result in a memory savings of several kilobytes per program.

The syntax for using INSTALL in CONFIG.SYS is as follows:

   INSTALL = *d:path\program*

d:path is the disk and path information, and *program* is the name of the utility you want to load. You may be able to use INSTALL with some non-DOS utilities such as SideKick and Keyworks. The program you install with this directive must have the extension COM or EXE; you cannot install a file such as a batch file.

Gaining More Speed with FASTOPEN

Although FASTOPEN is not a CONFIG.SYS directive, it is appropriate to discuss it after the INSTALL directive. FASTOPEN, introduced with DOS V3.3, can be used only with hard drives. Where buffers store information moved from disk to user memory, FASTOPEN allocates memory to store directory information. FASTOPEN partially solves a performance problem not resolved by the CONFIG.SYS BUFFERS directive. BUFFERS helps when your computer reads or writes information to several files, and helps most when disk activity is isolated to a file's few key portions.

If you use many of the same files during the day, however, particularly small files that DOS can read or write in one cluster, BUFFERS is not a major benefit. The time DOS spends traversing the subdirectory system and opening the files may take more time than actually reading or writing the files.

FASTOPEN caches directory information, holding in memory the locations of frequently used files and directories. Directories are a type of file, not accessible by users, that DOS reads and writes in a manner similar to other files. A part of the directory entry for a file or subdirectory holds the starting point for the file in the file allocation table (FAT). Because DOS typically holds the FAT in the disk buffers, FASTOPEN was developed to hold directory entries in memory.

FASTOPEN is not a complex command, but you must do a little work before you can use it effectively. FASTOPEN's syntax is as follows:

>   **INSTALL =** *d:path***FASTOPEN**.*EXE* d: *= nnn*
>
>   or
>
>   *d:path***FASTOPEN**.*EXE* **d:** *= nnn*

You use INSTALL and the .EXE extension only if you use this line in CONFIG.SYS. If you issue this command at the DOS prompt, omit these items and type the rest of the command.

d:path is the disk drive and path to the FASTOPEN.EXE file. The **d:** following the file name is the name of the hard drive you want FASTOPEN to act on; you must specify this part of the command. *nnn* is the number of directory entries that FASTOPEN should cache. Each file or subdirectory requires one directory entry, and you can enter a value from 10 to 999. If you do not specify a value for *nnn*, DOS defaults to 34.

If you use DOS V4, you can use several additional parameters with this command, as shown in the following syntax line:

>   **INSTALL =** *d:path***FASTOPEN**.*EXE* **d:** *= (nnn, mmm) /X*
>
>   or
>
>   *d:path***FASTOPEN**.*EXE* **d:** *= (nnn,mmm) /X*

The new *mmm* parameter refers to the number of fragmented entries (the DOS manual calls them "continuous space buffers") for the drive. Using this parameter improves performance when files on your hard disk become fragmented. The values you can use for *mmm* can range from 1 to 999. DOS has no default value for fragmented entries. If a value is not given, the feature is not active.

The /X switch is similar to the /X switches of other commands. This switch enables FASTOPEN information to reside in expanded memory.

You can use FASTOPEN on as many disks as you want. Note, however, that the total number of directory entries or fragmented entries FASTOPEN can handle is 999. If you issue the command for several disk drives, the sum of *nnn* values or the sum of *mmm* values cannot exceed 999. This limit is FASTOPEN's physical limit.

The practical limit of *nnn* is between 100 and 200 per disk. If you specify a value much higher, DOS wades through the internal directory entries slower than it reads information from the disk. Additionally, each directory entry stored in memory takes 35 bytes. Considering the speed-and-memory trade-off, the 100-to-200 limit yields adequate performance.

Using too small a number for *nnn* can be a disadvantage as well. When directory entries are recycled, the least-recently used entry is discarded if a new entry is needed. If the *nnn* value is too small, DOS discards entries it may still need. The object is to have enough entries in memory so that FASTOPEN operates efficiently, but not so many that FASTOPEN wastes time wading through directory entries.

At the very least, *nnn* must exceed the number of subdirectories you travel to get to the "deepest" subdirectory. The minimum value for *nnn* is 10; this value often exceeds the number of levels in your directory organization. Suppose that you have a directory structure such as \DOS\BASIC\TEST. The deepest "level" is 3 down from the root, much less than DOS's default of 10. A not terribly scientific guideline is to start with 100 and fine-tune up or down by 5 until you "feel" the right performance.

The value you specify for *mmm* depends on how fragmented your files are. Use the command **CHKDSK *.*** in subdirectories where you store data files to get a report of fragmentation. The more fragmentation, the larger the value you should assign to *mmm*. A general rule is to use for *mmm* a value that is twice the number of *nnn*s as your *mmm* entry.

You should observe two restrictions about using FASTOPEN. First, the disk drive you name cannot be one on which you use JOIN, SUBST, or ASSIGN, because these commands do not create "real" drives. Second, if you load a disk-drive device driver through AUTOEXEC.BAT rather than through CONFIG.SYS (some manufacturers provide a driver that must be started from a batch file or from the DOS prompt rather than from CONFIG.SYS), you must use FASTOPEN *after* you have defined all disk drives. FASTOPEN can become confused if you add additional disk drives after you have invoked FASTOPEN.

Making a CONFIG.SYS File

Following is a sample CONFIG.SYS file for an IBM AT or PS/2 Model 60:

```
DEVICE = C:\SYS\SJDRIVER.SYS /M
DEVICE = C:\SYS\HPSCANER.SYS
DEVICE = C:\SYS\XMA2EMS.SYS FRAME = C000 P254 = D000 P255 = D400 /X:32
DEVICE = C:\SYS\IBMCACHE.SYS 1900 /E /P8
LASTDRIVE = G
BUFFERS = 10,5 /X
COUNTRY = 001,,C:\SYS\COUNTRY.SYS
DEVICE = C:\SYS\DISPLAY.SYS CON = (,437,1)
SHELL = C:\DOS\COMMAND.COM C:DOS /P /MSG
DEVICE = C:\SYS\ANSI.SYS /L
REM DEVICE = C:\SYS\VDISK.SYS 360 /X:8
INSTALL C:\DOS\FASTOPEN.EXE C: = (100,50) /X
FILES = 30
```

Examining this specialized file can provide you with some useful tips for building a customized CONFIG.SYS file of your own.

This sample file assumes that you have a subdirectory called \SYS on your hard disk and that device drivers are in this subdirectory. You may actually use a different subdirectory.

The first two lines load special third-party device drivers needed to operate an HP ScanJet scanner. Consult the syntax recommendations of your software or hardware vendors to see exactly how to phrase your own DEVICE directives when installing such drivers.

The LASTDRIVE and BUFFERS directives were explained earlier in this chapter. Only 10 buffers are used because the IBMCACHE program reduces the need for a larger number of buffers.

Several other directives are included in the CONFIG.SYS file for various reasons. For example, the COUNTRY directive and DEVICE = DISPLAY.SYS statement enable the use of code pages. The SHELL directive tells DOS where the command processor is located, passes the directory of the command processor to COMSPEC, and makes memory-resident the messages COMMAND.COM uses. ANSI.SYS is loaded as a device driver so that ANSI-compatible programs can use ANSI.SYS to control the screen. FILES is set to 30 to allow up to 30 files to be open at once.

Notice the line where VDISK.SYS is loaded. In the listing shown, the line is commented out using the REM directive. When you use a directive only on occasion, you may find it convenient to leave the directive in the CONFIG.SYS file, preceding it with the REM directive so that DOS "ignores" the rest of the line. When you need a RAM disk, simply edit the CONFIG.SYS file and remove REM from the line. When you

357

do not want to use the directive, edit the CONFIG.SYS file and add REM to the beginning of the directive. The alternative is typing the complete directive whenever you need it and erasing it completely when you do not need it.

Redirecting File I/O with the DOS Pretender Commands

Because DOS manages disks in a logical rather than a strictly physical way, DOS can "pretend" that a disk's identity is different than the disk's name really is. DOS provides three commands that pretend that a disk's identity has changed. ASSIGN redirects disk operations from one disk to another. JOIN attaches an entire disk as a subdirectory to the directory structure of another disk. SUBST makes a directory of a disk appear to commands as a separate disk. When you issue commands that contain drive parameters, these pretender commands can alter the identity of the underlying drives. The next sections examine these commands.

Using the ASSIGN Command

The external command ASSIGN is used to redirect all DOS input and output (I/O) requests from one drive to another. Each drive is a DOS device; by using the ASSIGN command, DOS can interrogate a different disk than the one actually specified on a command line.

The syntax for the ASSIGN command is as follows:

    ASSIGN d1=d2 ...

d1 is the drive letter for the original disk drive; **d2** is the drive letter for the reassignment.

The ellipsis (**...**) indicates that more than one drive can be reassigned on a single command line.

Understanding the Operation of ASSIGN

When you issue the ASSIGN command, DOS redirects all I/O requests for **d1** to **d2**. If you assign drive A to drive C, all commands referring to drive A will actually be sent to drive C.

The ASSIGN command should be used sparingly. If it is not required for a particular purpose, do not use it. Certain programs may require disk information that is not available from the reassigned drive.

Understanding the General Rules of ASSIGN

- You can use an optional colon after the drive letter with DOS V4 only.
- Remove any ASSIGN settings before running FDISK, PRINT, FORMAT, BACKUP, or RESTORE.
- Do not use ASSIGN if either JOIN or SUBST are being used.
- Do not use ASSIGN prior to using the APPEND command.
- Beware of using CHDIR, MKDIR, RMDIR, LABEL, APPEND, and PATH with any drives reassigned.
- DISKCOPY and DISKCOMP do not recognize any drive reassignments.
- **d1** and **d2** must both physically exist in the computer.

Using ASSIGN To Reassign Drives

Some early versions of programs may not be able to use drives other than drive A or B. In many cases, if you reassign drives A and B to drive C, you can run an otherwise uncooperative program on a hard disk.

In some cases, by reassigning a drive, you can avoid having to use a floppy disk to run a program. Certain programs assume that their program floppy disk is located in drive A. Reassignment of drive A to the hard disk results in the program being directed by DOS to the hard disk instead of to the floppy drive.

To use the ASSIGN command to assign drive A to drive C, you type the following:

ASSIGN A=C

If you now issue a directory command to drive A or drive C, you will get a directory listing for drive C.

Typing just **ASSIGN** at the prompt removes all the reassignments previously made.

Joining Two Disk Drives with JOIN

The ASSIGN command makes an entire disk drive appear to have a different drive letter than its real value. The JOIN command is used to add a disk drive to the directory structure of another disk.

The external command JOIN enables you to have a floppy disk that appears to be part of a hard disk. The directory structure on the floppy disk is added to the directory structure of the hard disk. You can also use JOIN if you have two hard disks—drive C and drive D. You use the command to attach drive D to a subdirectory on drive C.

359

To connect disk drives, use the following form:

JOIN d1: *d2:***directoryname**

To disconnect disk drives, use this form of the command:

JOIN d1: /D

To show currently connected drives, use the following form:

JOIN

d1: is the disk drive to be connected. DOS calls this drive the *guest disk drive.*

d2: is the disk drive to which **d1:** is to be connected. DOS calls *d2:* the *host disk drive.*

directoryname is a subdirectory in the root directory of *d2:*, the host drive. DOS calls **directoryname** the *host subdirectory.* **directoryname** holds the connection to **d1:**, the guest drive.

The */D* switch *disconnects* the specified guest disk drive from its host.

Understanding the Operation of JOIN

Hierarchical directories and associated commands are discussed in Chapters 7 and 8. The JOIN command reassigns a drive to a subdirectory position on a different disk. Any directory hierarchy on the reassigned disk becomes a part of the other disk's hierarchical structure.

Using the terminology of a directory tree, the JOIN command can be thought of as grafting a second tree onto the first. The second tree is positioned at least one level down the structure. The grafting point must be assigned a name so that DOS can refer to it. In this way, the root directory of the reassigned disk is given a new name. All directories below the root directory on this reassigned drive have this new name as part of their path.

DOS internally converts all I/O requests to this new subdirectory—and all layers below the subdirectory—into a drive assignment with the appropriate path.

Understanding the General Rules of JOIN

- **directoryname** must either be empty or not exist.
- You cannot join a directory to the current directory.
- You cannot join to the root directory of a drive.
- When a drive is joined to another, you will not be able to access **d1:**.
- The entire drive is joined with the JOIN command.

- You cannot specify a networked drive either as **d1:** or *d2:*.
- Do not use the JOIN command with ASSIGN or SUBST.
- Remove any JOIN settings before running DISKCOPY, DISKCOMP, FDISK, PRINT, FORMAT, BACKUP, or RESTORE.
- Beware of using CHDIR, MKDIR, RMDIR, LABEL, APPEND, and PATH with any drives reassigned.

Using JOIN To Connect Drives

To JOIN drive B to drive C as a subdirectory called \DRIVEB, type the following:

JOIN B: C:\DRIVEB

Typing just **JOIN** at the prompt displays any drive reassignments. In this example, the following message appears:

```
B: => C:\DRIVEB
```

To remove a joined drive, type the following:

JOIN B: /D

The JOIN command can be used to overcome the limitations of DOS. The command is not, however, an ideal solution in all cases. Certain commands must not be used when JOIN is in effect. Joining two logical partitions on a single drive overcomes the 32MB partition barrier. Choosing to use the JOIN command is a compromise between full DOS functionality and the benefit of a larger partition.

Substituting a Drive Name for a Path with SUBST

The external command SUBST is an opposite of the JOIN command. Instead of grafting a second disk onto the tree structure of another disk, the SUBST command splits a disk's directory structure into two. In effect, the SUBST command creates an alias disk drive name for a subdirectory.

The syntax for the SUBST command has several different forms.

To establish an alias, use the following form:

SUBST d1: *d2:***pathname**

To delete an alias, use this form:

SUBST d1: /D

To see the current aliases, use this form:

SUBST

d1: is a valid disk drive name that becomes the alias or nickname. **d1:** may be a nonexistent disk drive.

*d2:***pathname** is the valid disk drive name and directory path that will be nicknamed **d1:**.

Understanding the Operation of SUBST

The SUBST command replaces a path name for a subdirectory with a drive letter. Once a SUBST command is in effect, DOS translates all I/O requests to a particular drive letter back to the correct path name.

As the default, DOS assigns the LASTDRIVE= parameter a value of E. Higher drive designators, however, can be made by inserting a **LASTDRIVE=** parameter into the CONFIG.SYS file. DOS then establishes each of the drive letters up to an including the specified LASTDRIVE as DOS devices. When you use the SUBST command, DOS understands that you are referring to a device.

The alias drive "created" by the SUBST command inherits the directory tree structure of the subdirectory reassigned to a drive letter.

Understanding the General Rules of SUBST

- **d1:** and *d2:* must be different.
- You cannot specify a networked drive either as **d1:** or *d2:*.
- **d1:** cannot be the current drive.
- **d1:** must have a designator less than the value in the LASTDRIVE statement of CONFIG.SYS.
- Do not use SUBST with ASSIGN or JOIN.
- Remove any SUBST settings before running DISKCOPY, DISKCOMP, FDISK, PRINT, FORMAT, LABEL, BACKUP, or RESTORE.
- Beware of using CHDIR, MKDIR, RMDIR, APPEND, and PATH with any drives reassigned.

Using SUBST To Reference a Path

SUBST is commonly used in two different situations. If a program is being used that does not support path names, the SUBST command is used to assign a drive letter to a directory. The program then refers to the drive letter, and DOS translates the request into a path. If, for example, the data for a program is stored in C:\WORDPROC, you can type the following:

SUBST E: C:\WORDPROC

You tell the program that the data is stored in drive E.

When the substitution has been made, you can issue the following command:

SUBST

The following message will appear:

```
E: => C:\WORDPROC
```

To disconnect the substitution of drive E for the C:\WORDPROC directory, you type the following:

SUBST E: /D

The other use for SUBST is to reduce typing long path names. Typing long path names can be a tedious process when a PC is used by more than one person. Each user may have a separate section of the hard disk for storing data files, but common areas of the disk are used to store the programs. If the paths \USER1\WORDDATA and \USER1\SPREDATA exist on drive C, the typing needed to reach files in the directories can be reduced by entering the following command:

SUBST E: C:\USER1

Issuing a directory command on drive E produces the following listing:

```
Volume in drive E is HARD DISK C
Directory of  E:\
 .              <DIR>      06-02-88    2:07p
 ..             <DIR>      06-02-88    2:07p
WORDDATA        <DIR>      05-01-89   11:59a
SPREDATA        <DIR>      06-02-88    2:08p
        4 File(s)      77824 bytes free
```

The volume label given is the label from drive C, but the directory itself is the contents of C:\USER1.

As with JOIN and ASSIGN, the choice to use this command is a compromise. In some situations is it beneficial, you must be aware of the commands not to be used when SUBST is in effect.

Changing the Command Prompt with PROMPT

Unless it has been altered, the command prompt shows the current drive and a greater-than sign (C>). The PROMPT command enables you to change from this standard display to a more informative and friendly prompt.

The most basic form of the PROMPT command was introduced in Chapter 7. Typing **PROMPT pg** at the command prompt changes that prompt to give you the full path on the disk. This new prompt enables you to see the current directory at all times. If you have a hard disk, this display is the minimum prompt setting recommended. Navigating subdirectories is very difficult if you do not know your current position.

The PROMPT command offers many other features as well. In its most extensive form, the command requires the ANSI.SYS device driver. However, even without using the ANSI.SYS device driver, many different command prompts can be chosen.

Issuing the PROMPT Command

The syntax for the PROMPT command is

    PROMPT *string*

string consists of text and/or a series of character pairs. Each character pair, called a *meta-string*, consists of a dollar sign followed by one of the following characters:

    t d p v n g l b q h e _

The string can contain any text or any number of meta-strings in any order. Table 13.4 lists the different meta-strings.

Table 13.4
Meta-Strings for Use with the PROMPT Command

Meta-string	Displayed information or result
$_	Carriage return/line feed (moves the cursor to the beginning of the next line)
$b	Vertical bar character (	)
$d	Date
$e	Esc character
$g	Greater than sign (>)
$h	Backspace (moves the cursor one space to the left)
$l	Less than sign (<)
$n	Current drive
$p	Current path
$q	Equal sign (=)
$t	Time
$v	DOS version

Understanding the Operation of PROMPT

The **PROMPT pg** command introduced in Chapter 7 shows the current path followed by the greater-than sign. Consider, for example, the following command:

PROMPT Date: $d Time: t_pg

This command displays the following prompt:

```
Date: Mon 09-18-1989 Time: 2:35:07.23p
C:\WP\MEMOS>
```

Two of the meta-strings require further explanation. The Esc character (**$e**) is used in association with the ANSI.SYS driver. In the same way that the dollar sign is used to indicate to DOS that the next character is a meta-string, the Esc character is used to signal ANSI.SYS that the next few characters are an ANSI.SYS command. Appendix H provides the special meanings of the Esc character sequences.

You must include the directive **DEVICE=ANSI.SYS** in your CONFIG.SYS file to use the Esc sequences. ANSI.SYS contains screen device driver codes capable of providing enhanced control over the appearance of the screen.

You can use the Backspace character (**$h**) to remove characters from the prompt. For example, in the preceding PROMPT example, the seconds and hundredths of a second in the displayed prompt are more of a distraction than helpful. You might, therefore, alter the command using the meta-string for the Backspace character as follows:

PROMPT Date: $d Time: thhhhhhh$_pg

The result is the following improved prompt:

```
Date: Mon 09-18-1989 Time: 2:35
C:\WP\MEMOS>
```

If you do not like the current prompt, type **PROMPT** alone at the command prompt, and DOS will reset the prompt to the current drive and a greater-than sign (such as C>). Keep in mind that if you are using subdirectories, the best practice is to use **PROMPT pg** as the minimum prompt.

Using Other Device Control Commands

DOS provides other commands to control devices and report system information. All of these other commands are available in the Command Reference section. Following are brief descriptions of some of the commands you may want to use.

The SET command displays the current environment settings and enables you to make new variable assignments.

The PRINT command enables you to print text files on your printer while you continue to do other PC work. This "background" printing is a great time saver for many DOS users.

The MODE command is a multifaceted device-control command. MODE can establish the height and width of your screen's lines and characters and control the speed of your serial ports. MODE can redirect the output from a parallel printer port to a serial port. In a more esoteric form, MODE can be used in association with code page support for international character sets on the PC. You will want to browse the MODE section of the Command Reference.

In addition to these listed commands, Appendix A, the "DOS Survival Guide," is a guide to DOS commands, explaining briefly what each DOS command does. You will want to study Appendix A and refer to the Command Reference for details on commands that you might find useful in your DOS work.

Summary

In this chapter, you learned the following important points:

❏ DOS can alter system settings through instructions in the CONFIG.SYS file.

❏ The CONFIG.SYS file must be in the root directory of the boot disk. When you alter CONFIG.SYS, the changes do not occur until DOS is rebooted.

❏ You can tell DOS when to look for the Ctrl-Break key sequence.

❏ Disk buffers make DOS work faster by placing requested information in RAM.

❏ Disk caches, such as the DOS IBMCACHE program, can speed up certain disk operations.

❏ RAMDRIVE, the DOS RAM-disk software, can speed disk operations if your computer has sufficient random-access memory.

❏ DOS V4 enables the use of expanded memory.

❏ DOS V1 used a different method of accessing files; this method can be reproduced with later versions of DOS by using the FCBS directive.

❏ The FILES directive sets the number of files DOS can open at any one time.

❏ The LASTDRIVE directive specifies the letter of the last disk drive installed in your system.

❏ You can replace the command processor DOS uses by invoking the SHELL directive.

❏ You can alter the look of the DOS prompt using the PROMPT command with text and meta-strings.

❏ You can cause DOS to pretend that a drive's identity is different than it really is with JOIN, SUBST, and ASSIGN.

Using the
DOS Shell

14

The DOS Shell program available with DOS V4 is a graphical user interface that replaces the DOS command line with easy-to-use and easy-to-understand menus. The DOS Shell was introduced in Chapter 3; this chapter expands the coverage of the Shell.

The DOS Shell has several commendable features: you do not need much memory or a graphics monitor, you can use the Shell with a mouse, and the Shell comes free with DOS V4.

Learning to use the DOS Shell can also serve as an introduction to more complex systems like Microsoft Windows and OS/2's Presentation Manager. You can use the Shell to learn to install programs, manage the file system, and use pull-down menus; you use many of these concepts with Windows or another shell.

Even if you don't intend to use the Shell yourself, you probably will encounter it at one time or another, so you should learn to use it. This chapter explains what you need to know if you encounter the Shell when you sit down at a colleague's computer.

Key Terms Used in This Chapter

Shell   A program that acts as a user interface to the features and capabilities of an operating system.

Mouse pointer The arrow-shaped screen icon that indicates the position of the mouse's attention.

Selection cursor An area of highlighted text that shows where selected action will occur.

Scroll bar   An icon-based area of the screen that serves to move the items through the window.

Pull-down menu Additional selection items that drop down when an item from a horizontal list of items is selected.

Text mode   Screen mode available to all PC users. In text mode, all screen presentation is composed of ASCII characters.

Graphics mode Screen mode available to users of PCs equipped with graphics adapters. In graphics mode, screen presentation utilizes bit-mapped graphics.

Getting To Know the Shell Menu Tree

The DOS Shell has a series of menus arranged in branching, tree fashion. The topmost menu provides a list of functions from which you can choose. These choices may include DOS commands, utility programs, or submenus that provide further selection lists.

The Shell main menu is called the Start Programs/Main Group menu. The main menu is the jumping-off point to each of the other DOS Shell functions and submenus. From this menu, you can load programs or access additional menus (see fig. 14.1).

If you have any familiarity with menu trees, you will notice that the DOS Shell menu tree is odd: it is "split" into two sections that are not directly connected. This is done so that you can do several things with DOS Shell menus.

You can, for example, access various programs and utilities provided by the Shell. These functions include DOS commands, your own applications programs, and special DOS Shell utilities such as the File System or the Change Colors functions. The functions are accessed through the Main Group menu and the submenus beneath it.

You can also modify the Shell itself. You can add programs, move programs to other parts of the menu, or modify how the programs are started by the DOS Shell. You also can add new groups of programs (submenus) to the tree, or change the order in which groups of programs appear in the menus.

Fig. 14.1

Menu structure of the DOS Shell.

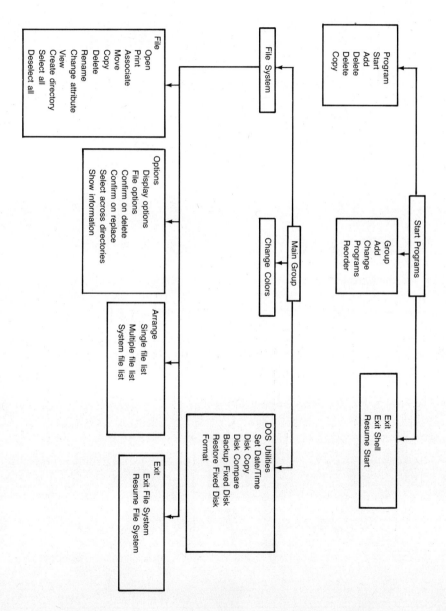

Finally, you can disable the Shell—or leave it entirely. That is, you can exit from the DOS Shell and return to the DOS prompt. The Shell is unloaded from memory and is no longer available to you until you type **DOSSHELL** again.

You can also temporarily exit from the Shell by using the Command Prompt option from the Main Group menu or by pressing Shift-F9. If you exit from the Shell this way, the Shell remains in memory and can be recalled when you type **EXIT** at the DOS prompt.

To differentiate between the two main types of functions, DOS V4 sets up two different menus—Main Group and Start Programs. You can switch back and forth between these menus at any time by pressing F10. The Start Programs action bar contains the `Program`, `Group`, and `Exit` options which enable you to start or modify programs or groups of programs. The Main Group menu enables you to access any of the programs listed; you can also select one of the four options on this menu to display the associated submenu. Each of these menus is described later in this chapter.

Understanding the Shell Display Modes

The Shell can be displayed in one of four modes, depending on the type of monitor you have. Figure 14.2 shows the main menu in 25-line color graphics mode. This mode is used by most DOS V4 users who have Enhanced Graphics Adapter (EGA) or Video Graphics Adapter (VGA) color monitors. If you have a VGA or EGA monochrome monitor, your screen also looks like the one in figure 14.2. The mouse cursor (if you have a mouse) is displayed as an angled arrow.

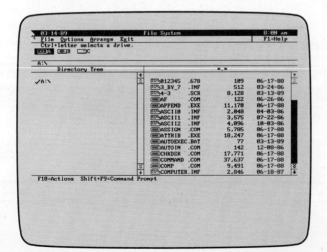

Fig. 14.2

The DOS Shell menu in 25-line color graphics mode.

The DOS Shell also operates in text mode (see fig. 14.3). If you have a monochrome or Color Graphics Adapter (CGA) monitor, this is the mode for you. You can set up your system to display in text mode even if you have a VGA or EGA monitor, but you gain no advantages. The mouse cursor is displayed as a graphics box in text mode.

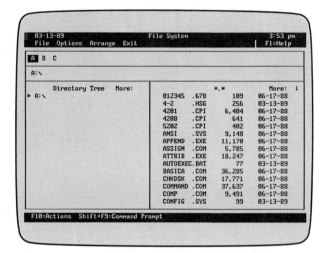

Fig. 14.3

The DOS Shell menu in text mode.

Third and fourth modes are available for use with VGA monitors: 30-line color and black-and-white graphics modes (see fig. 14.4). These modes have the advantage of displaying five extra lines on-screen. The text is slightly smaller and may be more difficult to read on some monitors. With a good-quality monitor, however, this mode is worth using. The chief advantage comes when you display directories, because an additional five file names can be shown on a single screen without scrolling.

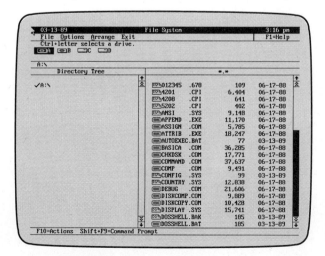

Fig. 14.4

The DOS Shell menu in 30-line black-and-white graphics mode.

Scrolling Text

Before you read about the Start Programs and Main Group menus, you should know how to move the selection cursor around the screen. You can use the mouse or the arrow keys to move the selection cursor around the Shell menus.

Many of the boxes and screens displayed by the DOS Shell include text. This text may be too long to show in the space allotted. If you don't have a mouse, you can see more text by using the PgUp, PgDn, and the left- and right-arrow keys to scroll the "window" to a new position.

If you have a mouse, you can use it to move the selection cursor beyond the boundaries of the window. You may not want to take your hand from the mouse to use the keyboard controls to scroll. If you use a mouse in text mode, you can point to the arrows(s) next to the word `More:` (see fig. 14.5). Graphics-mode mouse users, on the other hand, can use the special scroll bars to scroll text (see fig. 14.6).

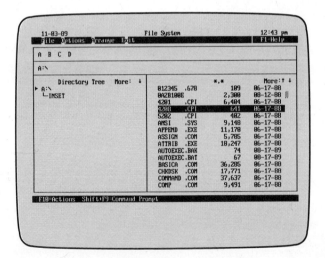

Fig. 14.5

Scroll arrows are used to scroll information in text mode.

The scroll bar has the following components:

- A single-line arrow box at the top and bottom of the bar. Clicking the cursor inside these boxes scrolls text up or down one line at a time.

- A page scroll box, indicated by double arrows, located below the top single-line box and above the bottom single-line box. Clicking these boxes moves text up or down one page at a time.

- A slider box located between the scroll boxes. You can position the cursor on this box, press and hold the mouse button, and drag the slider box up or down. The text window moves with the slider.

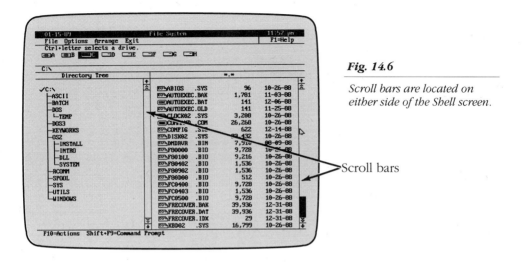

Fig. 14.6

Scroll bars are located on either side of the Shell screen.

Scroll bars

You use the scroll bar extensively with the DOS Shell File System. In the next section, you can practice using the scroll bar as you explore the help screens. If you do not have a mouse, remember that you can use the arrow keys and the PgUp and PgDn keys to scroll.

Using the Help System

The Shell's help system is *contextual*. That is, DOS looks at the menu item currently highlighted and provides information about that selection. You can go from that help screen to other help screens to get help on additional topics. Figure 14.7 shows a typical help screen.

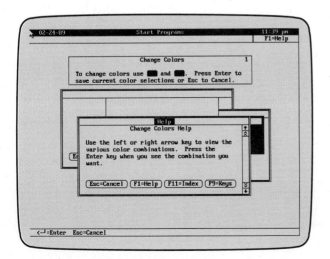

Fig. 14.7.

The Change Colors help screen.

Notice that four boxes appear at the bottom of the help screen, labeled Esc=Cancel, F1=Help, F11=Index, and F9=Keys. If you press F1 (or click the F1=Help box), you receive help on how to use the help system. If you press F11 or click the F11=Index box, you see an index of topics on which you can receive help. If you press F9 or click the F9=Keys box, you see a list of special key assignments. Press Esc or click the Esc=Cancel box to return to the main menu.

Figure 14.8 shows the Index menu for the help system. You can use this screen to obtain an introduction to the help system or to get help on topics like the File System or Start Programs menu. Select the desired index item, read the help text, and when you finish with that selection, press F11 to return to the Index menu. If you press Esc, you return to the help screen from which you called the index.

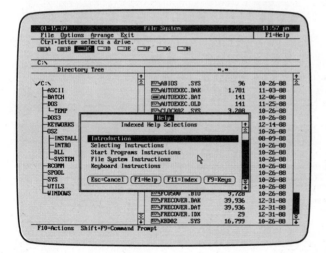

Fig. 14.8

The Help system's Index menu.

The availability of help information varies depending on the menus you have on-screen. Note that when you add your own programs to the Shell, you can, if you want, type help instructions of your own. Then, anyone accessing that program can press F1 to see your special tips in the form of a help screen.

Using the Start Programs Menu

The Start Programs menu is the action bar at the top of the Shell screen. The menu can include a display of the date and time. If you press F1, the menu also displays a help prompt. The action bar shows three pull-down menu headings: Program, Group, and Exit. One of these is *highlighted*; that is, it is displayed in a different color or in reversed tones. If none of the three items is highlighted, the Start Programs menu is not active. To activate the Start Programs menu, press F10. If a menu other than Start Programs is on-screen, select the Exit option from the action bar at the top of the screen to exit the current menu before pressing F10.

Pull-down menus appear when you select a heading; they are lists of choices displayed beneath the headings. You can make selections from menus by moving the cursor keys to the desired choice and pressing Enter, clicking the mouse button, or typing the underlined menu-option character.

To select options with a mouse, move the cursor directly to one of the menu headings. The mouse cursor is a block in text mode and an arrow in graphics mode. Click the mouse button once to select the option you want.

Whether or not you have a mouse attached to your system, you can select a menu by typing the underlined letter associated with that menu heading, for example, Program, Group, or Exit.

When you have made a selection from the Start Programs menu or the action bar, the highlight drops down to the first item on the pull-down menu. You can move the highlighted line with the up-arrow and down-arrow keys or with the mouse. If you move the highlighting with the cursor keys, the highlight cycles back to the beginning when you reach the bottom of the list or to the bottom when you reach the top of the list.

To select one of the pull-down submenu items, highlight it and then press Enter or click the left mouse button. Alternatively, type the underlined letter of the option you want to select. To exit a pull-down menu, press Esc.

When you use the Shell, you may notice that some menu options are followed by three ellipsis dots (...). The dots are DOS's way of telling you that this option is not an action in itself but a gateway to another menu. That submenu provides a list of functions from which you can choose. Menu options that are themselves headings for submenus are always indicated by three trailing dots.

Follow these steps for a quick introduction to using the menus:

Step 1. If the action bar is not activated (none of the three selections is highlighted), activate it by pressing F10.

Step 2. Use the left-arrow and right-arrow keys to move the highlight to the Program selection on the action bar. Press the down-arrow key and then Enter, or press P to select Program and activate the Program menu.

Step 3. When the pull-down Program menu appears, move the cursor to the Add... selection using the down-arrow key; press Enter. Alternatively, press A.

The Add Programs screen appears. Because you are just exploring menus and do not want to add a program at this time, press Esc to remove this menu from the screen and return to the Main Group menu.

Step 4. Pull down the Group menu. You can do this in one of two ways:

- Press F10 to activate the action bar. Then move to the Group selection by using the right-arrow key and pressing Enter or simply by pressing G.

- If the Program menu is pulled down, move directly from the Program pull-down menu to the Group pull-down menu by pressing the right-arrow key. You don't have to go "through" the Group heading to reach the Group menu.

Step 5. When the Group menu appears, move the cursor to the Add... selection and press Enter, or simply press A.

The Add Group screen appears. Because you don't want to add any groups now, press Esc. The Main Group menu appears again.

Step 6. Move the cursor to the Exit heading on the action bar. You can do this by choosing either of the options in Step 4.

The Exit menu appears with two choices: Exit Shell or Resume Start Programs. Move the selection cursor to Resume Start Programs and press Enter.

Using Function Keys

The following sections describe the function keys you use with the DOS Shell program.

The F1 Key

If you need help, press the F1 function key. A series of text screens with useful information appears (refer to "Using the Help System" earlier in this chapter). You can page through the help screens by using the PgUp and PgDn keys. The following keys can be used with the help screens:

Key	Function
Esc	Returns to the menu
F1	Provides instructions on how to use the help system
F9	Displays a list of the special-key definitions
F11 or Alt-F1	Displays an index of available help screens

The Shift-F9 Key

Any time you use the DOS Shell, you can perform a DOS function and then return to the DOS Shell. When you press Shift-F9, you see a DOS command prompt and a reminder that you can return to the Shell by typing **EXIT**.

When you access the DOS prompt in this way, the DOS Shell remains loaded and available for use. You can carry out DOS functions, or even load and run other programs if you have sufficient memory available.

Return to the Shell by typing **EXIT** at the DOS prompt and pressing Enter.

Tech note . . . The Shift-F9 key starts a secondary command processor. The same action occurs when you issue the DOS **COMMAND** command. When you start a secondary command processor, typing the **EXIT** command is the signal to DOS that you want to return to the primary command processor. When you are in the DOS Shell, COMMAND.COM has loaded and executed SHELLC.COM; typing **EXIT** after accessing the DOS prompt returns control to SHELLC.COM.

The F10 Key

The F10 key moves the cursor to the Start Programs action bar if the cursor is located in the Main Group menu, or to the Main Group menu if the cursor is located in the action bar.

Using the Program Submenu

To use the Program pull-down menu, select Program from the action bar. If the cursor is located in the Main Group menu, press F10 to activate the Start Programs action bar, and then select the Program option with the mouse or keyboard. The Program pull-down submenu looks like the one in figure 14.9.

If you use the Shell in graphics mode, some of the choices on the menu may be dimmed or blurred to indicate that they are not presently available. If you use the Shell in text mode, the underlined letter is replaced by an asterisk to indicate that the choice is not available or appropriate at the moment.

The Main Group listing shows all the programs and groups of programs that you can select from the Shell. Because this list is not a directory listing, you must add and delete the entries that appear on the list. You use the Program submenu to make these changes to the Main Group listing.

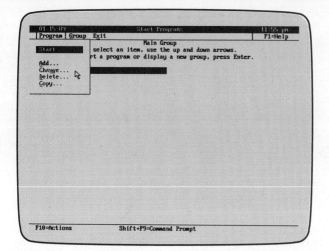

Fig. 14.9

The Program submenu.

You use the Start option from the Program submenu to start the program highlighted on the Main Group screen. You use the Add... option to put additional programs in the Main Group list. You use the Change... option to modify the guidelines or parameters used to load a specific program from the Shell. You can use this option to change certain information (such as the path DOS uses to find the program) about a program already available from the Shell. You use the Delete... option to remove programs from the menu entirely. You use the Copy... option to duplicate a given program in another menu. (You then can delete that program from the old menu if you want to move the program rather than simply duplicate it.) The following sections explore each of the choices on the Program submenu.

Starting a Program

The Start option on the Program submenu is used to start the program or utility highlighted on the lower part of the Main Group screen. If the item is an applications program, DOS attempts to load the program using the specifications you supplied when the program was added to the Main Group. (Adding programs is explained in the next section.)

Other methods of starting programs are described in "Starting Programs" and "Associating a File" later in this chapter.

Adding a Program

Adding a program to the DOS Shell is simple. You can add single programs or you can group related programs (using the Group option on the action bar). You can have up to 16 entries on the Main Group screen, where each entry is either a single program or the name of a group of programs. If the entry is a group name, it is followed by three dots (such as DOS Utilities...) to indicate that a menu of choices is presented when that entry is selected. When you select the Add... menu option from the Program submenu, the screen shown in figure 14.10 appears.

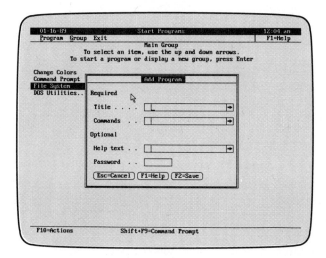

Fig. 14.10

The Add Program panel.

Of the four parameters you can type on the Add Program panel, two are required and the other two are optional. The first required parameter is the title, or label, to appear on the Main Group screen. The title can have up to 40 characters and can contain spaces, upper- or lowercase letters, or graphics characters.

The second required parameter is the set of commands needed to load the program. You can provide the commands in one of two ways: You can type all the commands needed to load the program, using up to 500 characters, on the Commands line. Alternatively, you can type all the commands in a batch file and call the batch file from the Commands line by typing **CALL** and the name of the batch file. Following is a sample batch file you can use to start the KEYWORKS program (located in the \KEYWORKS directory):

```
@ECHO OFF
C:
CD \KEYWORKS
KEYWORKS
CD \
```

The Add Program panel enables you to provide two optional parameters. First, you can create your own help text, which will be displayed when you highlight the title on the Main Group screen and press F1. You can type up to 478 characters of help text. The Shell neatly displays this information in pages that you can scroll through. You may want to enter help text to explain what the program is or how it is to be used.

381

The second optional parameter you can provide is a password of up to eight characters. A password limits access to the program. If you provide a password, you must type it before the Shell will load, change, copy, or delete that program.

If you decide to use a password, be sure to write it down in a safe place or find some other way to remember it. If you forget what the password is, you will not be able to perform any of the functions in the Add Program panel.

The DOS Shell enables you to customize the Add Program entries even more extensively. Because you can create interactive menu selections (to ask for information "on the fly"), the Shell can be even more versatile than most batch files. The following sections explain how you can customize the entries you make with the Add Program panel.

Creating Customized Menu Options

Because you can tailor the parameters for each entry you add, you can create menu options for quite specialized operations.

The following steps explain how to create a Main Group menu selection that backs up all changed files in the C:\BATCH subdirectory on your hard disk to a floppy disk. If you don't have a C:\BATCH subdirectory, substitute the name of a directory you do have.

Step 1. Insert a blank, formatted disk in drive A.

Step 2. From the action bar, pull down the Program menu and select
`Add Program`.

Step 3. Type the following title on the Add Program panel:

Back Up Batch Subdirectory

Step 4. Press Tab to move to the `Commands` line and type the following lines:

ECHO INSERT BACKUP DISK IN DRIVE A:<F4>
PAUSE<F4>
XCOPY C:\BATCH A:\ /M

Do not type the characters <F4>; instead, press F4 at the end of the first and second lines. You will see two vertical lines apeear when you press F4.

Step 5. Press Tab again to move to the `Help text` line and type the following:

Copies any batch files that have changed since they were last copied. Files are copied to the floppy disk in drive A.

Step 6. Press Tab one more time to move to the Password line and type
this password:

XCOPY

Step 7. Click the F2=Save box or press F2 to save this new program.

The Back Up Batch Subdirectory selection appears in the Main Group menu.

Test this new menu item by selecting it a few times. To use this program, you must
type the password **XCOPY**. In "Changing a Program" later in this chapter, the
Change... option is used to remove the password.

Using Prompt Panels

You can create another menu entry that performs almost the same function as the
Back Up Batch Subdirectory option created in the preceding steps; the new
menu entry enables you to specify the source and destination drives and directories.

Using prompt panels, you can ask for information in a sophisticated manner. Prompt
panels are created by typing a pair of brackets ([]) on the Commands line of the Add
Program panel. In the entry you just created, for example, you can prompt the user
for the source and destination subdirectories by replacing **C:\BATCH** and **A:** with
brackets, as in the following:

XCOPY [] [] /M

The Shell displays a Program Parameters panel for each set of brackets you type,
and the user types the parameters in the panel. Unfortunately, new users may not
know which parameters are required; you will need to provide specific instructions
to avoid confusion. To solve this problem, the Shell enables you to specify prompts to
replace the default Program parameters panel with something more meaningful.
You can customize the prompt panel by including three different options within
the brackets:

Option	Meaning
/T"title"	Specifies the title for the prompt panel
/I"instructions"	Specifies any further instructions
/P"prompt"	Labels the line where the parameters are typed

The strings you type within quotation marks for the /T and /I options can be up to
40 characters long; the string you type for /P can be up to 20 characters long. What
you type is made clear in the following example where you create a new Main Group
option called Back Up A Directory:

Step 1. Insert a blank, formatted disk in drive A.

Step 2. From the action bar, pull down the Program menu and select
Add Program.

Step 3. Type the following title:

> **Back Up a Directory**

Step 4. Press Tab to move to the Commands line and type the following as one line, without pressing F4:

> **XCOPY [/T"Source Directory" /I"Full drive/path of source directory" /P"Drive/path..."] [/T"Destination Directory" / I"Drive/path of destination directory" /P"Drive/path..."] /M**

Step 5. Press Tab again to move to the Help text line and type the following:

> **Copies to the destination directory any files in the source directory that have changed since they were last copied.**

Step 6. Press Tab one more time to move to the Password line and type the following:

> **XCOPY**

Step 7. Click the F2=Save box or press F2 to save this new entry.

The Back Up Directory selection appears in the Main Group menu.

When you select this menu item, you are prompted with screens like those shown in figures 14.11, 14.12, and 14.13.

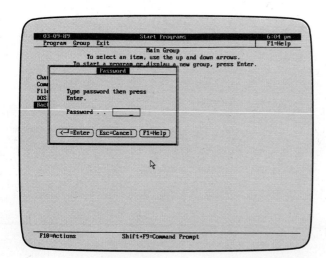

Fig. 14.11

The Password prompt panel.

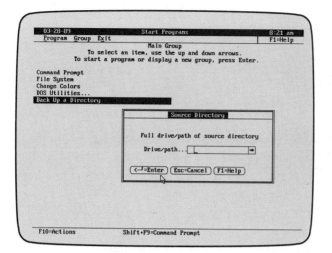

Fig. 14.12

The customized Source Directory prompt panel.

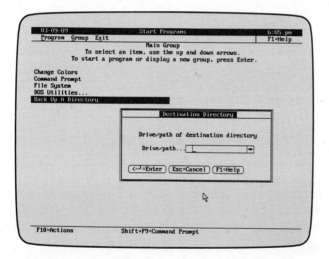

Fig. 14.13

The customized Destination Directory prompt panel.

In addition to the prompt panel, you can use a number of other commands to customize the Add Program parameters. These powerful facilities are described in the next section.

Using Additional Add Program Parameters

You can use additional parameters on the Add Program panel's Commands line to customize the program you add. This section describes these additional parameters.

The */F"drive:\path\filename"* parameter checks to see that the file specified by *drive:\path\filename* actually exists before you continue with the procedure.

Suppose that you want to run a program from a floppy disk. Before continuing, you can check to see that the correct floppy disk is loaded.

The *%n* parameter is similar to the variable markers used in batch files. Replace the *n* with a whole number from 1 to 10 and place the parameter anywhere in the Commands line. When you enter a value for each parameter in the prompt panels, the new value is substituted for %n. Suppose that you type the following on the Commands line:

COPY [/T"Enter filename" /P"Filename..." %1] B: | |ERASE %1

When this program is called, a prompt panel appears, asking you to enter a file name. The file name you type is stored in %1 and used as a parameter to copy the file to drive B. The same file is then erased by the second command, **ERASE %1**. (Remember that you create the set of double vertical bars (| |) in the preceding syntax line by pressing F4.)

The */D"text"* parameter defines an initial or *default* value for the entry field within the brackets. If you press Enter instead of typing something in the prompt panel, the default text is used. Suppose that you type the following on the Commands line:

XCOPY [/T"Source directory" /P"Directory..." /D"C:\BATCH"] A:

If you do not enter a value when the prompt panel appears, the program uses C:\BATCH as the default source directory.

You can use */D"%n"* to specify as the default a variable marker defined earlier in the command string. Suppose that the Commands line is as follows:

COPY [/T"Enter filename" /P"Filename..." %1] B: | |ERASE
**   [/T"Erasing File" /P"File..." /D"%1"]**

This line prompts you to enter a file name for %1, copies that file to drive B, and prompts you for the name of another file to erase. If you do not provide a new file name, the program erases the first file.

Sometimes, if you choose to type something other than the default value, you don't want to force yourself to erase the default supplied. The Shell provides a parameter to help you out: */R*. If you include this parameter, the default value shown is erased as soon as you start to type something else.

The */L"n"* parameter defines the *length* of the entry field. The letter *n* can be a number from 0 to 128. If you don't use /L"n", the entry field is 128 characters long. If you specify /L"0", you cannot type any characters in response to the prompt, but you must press Enter to proceed.

The */M"e"* parameter causes the Shell to check whether the file name entered actually exists. If it doesn't, you are asked to substitute a different name. Consider the following example:

COPY [/T"Enter filename" /P"Filename..." /M"e" %1] B:

The /M switch used with the XCOPY command in the preceding section is different than this /M"e" parameter. The XCOPY switch discussed in the previous section appears outside the brackets and does not specify "e".

These instructions take effect only if the file name specified by %1 actually exists. Otherwise, the prompt panel is repeated until you enter a valid file name.

The */C"%n"* parameter passes a variable defined in one program to another program in the group. The variable must already be defined; that is, the first program must be used after the computer is turned on and before the program containing /C"%n" is used. Imagine that you have the following two Main Group entries:

```
Copy a Program to Drive A:
Erase a Program Copied to Drive A:
```

The first entry's Commands line looks like this:

COPY [/T"Enter filename" /P"Filename..." %1] A:

The second entry's Commands line looks like this:

ERASE [/C"%1"]

If you run the first program, you don't have to enter the name of the file to be erased; the name of the file you copied is supplied as the default. The %1 parameter retains the value of the %1 defined by the most recently used program. If you had another menu option that used %1, and that option was selected more recently, its value for %1 would be used in the ERASE option. If you use /C"%n", you may want to pair the options that use it.

The /# parameter must be used outside the prompt-panel brackets. /# substitutes the drive letter (followed by a colon) from which the Shell was started. The /@ parameter also must be used outside the brackets; it substitutes the path from which the Shell was started. No backslash is included in the substituted path name. You can use both the /# and /@ parameters to default to the drive and directories used to run the Shell.

Changing a Program

Now that you understand how to use the Add... option to add a program to the Main Group list, changing an existing program should be easy.

For this exercise, use the Back Up Batch Subdirectory program you created earlier. You cannot change any of the default menu entries, such as Command Prompt, File System, DOS Utilities..., or Change Colors; you can change only those entries you have added yourself.

Follow these steps to change an existing program:

Step 1. Highlight the program to be changed.

Step 2. Pull down the Program menu and select Cha<u>n</u>ge...

The Change Program panel appears. This panel looks like the Add Program panel shown in figure 14.10, except for the title. Existing information about the selected entry appears on the various lines of this panel.

Step 3. Change any aspect of the entry you want.

In this example, press Tab to move the cursor to the Password line and delete the password.

Step 4. Click the F2=Save box or press F2 to save the changed entry.

Now you can use the Back Up Batch Subdirectory entry without entering a password.

Deleting a Program

You may want to delete from the Main Group list a program that you no longer use. The program itself is not removed, only the menu entry.

To delete a program, follow these steps:

Step 1. Highlight the entry you want to delete.

Step 2. Pull down the Program panel and select <u>D</u>elete....

The Delete Program panel appears. This panel asks you to confirm or abort the process. Delete Program is the default option.

Step 3. Press Enter to delete the selected entry.

Back Up Batch Subdirectory has been removed from the Main Group list.

Copying a Program

You can copy a Main Group entry; the DOS Shell has no prohibition against having two programs in the same group with the same name, but such an arrangement has little point. You can also copy a program to a subgroup. In this exercise, you copy the Back Up a Directory entry you created in a previous section to another DOS Utilities... group:

Step 1. Highlight the entry you want to copy in the Main Group list.

For this example, highlight Back Up a Directory.

Step 2. Pull down the Program panel from the action bar and choose `Copy....`

Step 3. Highlight the group where you want to copy the entry.

In this example, move the cursor to DOS Utilities... and press Enter; alternatively, double click with the mouse. The DOS Utilities... menu appears.

Step 4. Click `F2=Copy` or press F2 to copy the program to the new group.

`Back Up a Directory` now appears both in the Main Group and the DOS Utilities... menus.

Using the Group Submenu

The Group submenu is easy to use once you know how to add, change, delete, and copy programs from the Main Group list. As you will see, groups in the Main Group can have subgroups of their own. You may find yourself building menus several levels deep so that you can group a large number of programs together conveniently. The Group submenu is shown in figure 14.14.

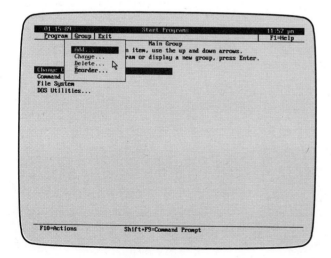

Fig. 14.14

The Group submenu.

Notice that the Group submenu has four choices. Three of them will be familiar: `Add...`, `Change...`, and `Delete....` You learned to use these options on the Program submenu. The fourth, `Reorder...`, enables you to change the arrangement of programs in the group listing. Each option is described in the following sections.

Adding a Group

You can add a group to a menu if fewer than 16 entries appear on the Group menu with which you are working. To add a group, follow these instructions:

Step 1. Pull down the Group menu from the action bar.

Step 2. Choose the Add... option.

The Add Group menu appears. This menu contains the following four entries: Title, Filename, Help text, and Password.

Step 3. Enter a title.

The title is the name that appears in the group menu; the title can be up to 37 characters long. The Shell adds the trailing dots automatically.

Step 4. Type a file name.

The file name is the name under which this new menu is to be stored. The file name can have 8 characters; the Shell automatically adds the .MEU extension.

Step 5. Add optional help text and a password, if you want.

Step 6. Click the F2=Save box or press F2 to save the new group entry.

The new title appears in the group menu. Now use the Add Program panel to add program files to this group.

Changing a Group

You can change the parameters used to define a group just as you can change a program. You cannot change the default DOS subgroups, such as File System, DOS Utilities..., or Change Colors; however, you can add, change, or delete programs within these groups. Just select the group you want to modify by highlighting it in the current group and pressing Enter. Alternatively, double click the group with the mouse. You then can access the Program or Group menus within the subgroup.

To change the parameters of a group you have added yourself, follow these directions:

Step 1. Highlight the name of the group.

Step 2. Pull down the Group menu from the action bar.

Step 3. Select Change....

The Change Group menu appears. This menu looks like the Add Group menu, except that the current information about the selected group appears in the fields.

Step 4. Use the Tab key to move to the field you want to change and make your changes.

Step 5. Click the F2=Save box, or press F2 to save the changes.

Deleting a Group

You can remove a group you have added yourself with the Delete... option in the Group menu. Follow these directions:

Step 1. Highlight the name of the group to be deleted.

Step 2. Pull down the Group menu.

Step 3. Select the Delete... option.

Step 4. Confirm that you want to delete the group by pressing Enter.

The group is removed from the menu.

Changing the Order of a Group's Listings

Placing the menu items you use most near the top of the group listing is convenient; you can then find these items more quickly. You can place menu items in any order you want. To move an entry from one place to another in the menu list, follow these steps:

Step 1. Highlight the menu item to be moved.

Step 2. Pull down the Group menu.

Step 3. Choose Reorder....

A prompt appears on-screen under the group title, telling you to move the highlight to the new position and press Enter.

Step 4. Use the cursor keys or the mouse to move the highlight to the position you want the selected menu item to appear in the group. Press Enter.

The menu item has been moved.

You can repeat these steps as often as necessary to produce the order you want for a given group.

Creating a New Main Group Menu

Perhaps you want to create an entirely new Main Group menu. You may want to move the Command Prompt option to a special subgroup that has password protection. If you make this change, users who know the password can use the command prompt; others cannot.

You may find that certain Main Group entries, such as Change Colors, are rarely used. The DOS Shell does not enable you to delete entries from the Main Group, however. What do you do? The following exercise shows you a way around that roadblock.

In this exercise, you will create a new subgroup that includes all the programs you want in your Main Group except for the DOS defaults. You then cause the Shell to use the new subgroup as the Main Group instead. You haven't deleted anything from the Main Group; you have just scrapped it and substituted a new one with the files you want. The old Main Group can become a subgroup under the new Main Group. As confusing as this may sound, the procedure is relatively simple, as you will see in the exercise that follows:

Step 1. With the Main Group menu on-screen, pull down the Group menu from the action bar.

Step 2. Choose Add....

Step 3. Type a name for the new group that is to become the new Main Group.

For this example, type **NEW** as the name. The Shell later substitutes the name Main Group for you, so the name you choose at this point is almost irrelevant.

Step 4. Press Tab to move to the Filename line. Type **NEW** as the name under which to save this menu.

DOS automatically adds the extension .MEU.

Step 5. Type any help text you want.

Do not type a password; putting a password on the menu that will be your Main Group is not a good idea.

Step 6. Click the F2=Save box or press F2 to save this entry.

Your new group appears in the present Main Group listing.

Next, you copy the programs you want to appear in the new Main Group (called NEW) from the existing Main Group.

Step 7. Highlight a program you want to copy.

The program can be in the current Main Group, or it can be in one of the other subgroups you have created. The program cannot be one of the default DOS programs, such as Change Colors.

Step 8. With the group where the program to be copied is located on-screen, pull down the Program panel from the action bar.

Step 9. Choose the Copy... option.

A prompt reminds you to press F2 when the group to which you want to copy the program is on-screen.

Step 10. Move to the NEW group.

If you are copying a program from a subgroup, press Esc to exit from the subgroup and return to the current Main Group. Then select the NEW group with the cursor or mouse. If you are copying a program from the Main Group, simply choose NEW.

Step 11. Press F2 when the NEW group is on-screen.

The selected program is copied to the NEW group.

Step 12. Repeat Steps 7 through 11 until all the programs you want copied to the NEW group have been duplicated.

Now you must substitute the NEW group for the current Main Group. The Main Group is stored in a file called SHELL.MEU. Your DOSSHELL.BAT file contains the following line:

```
/MEU:SHELL.MEU
```

This statement tells the Shell to load the SHELL.MEU file as the Main Group when the Shell starts up. To use the NEW.MEU file instead, edit DOSSHELL.BAT and substitute **NEW.MEU** for **SHELL.MEU** in this statement. You can use EDLIN or any other ASCII text editor to edit batch files. To do this, follow these steps:

Step 1. Exit from the Shell (use the Exit option on the Main Group).

Step 2. Load DOSSHELL.BAT into your text editor. Find the line containing /MEU:SHELL.MEU. Replace SHELL.MEU with NEW.MEU and save the file.

Step 3. Reload the DOS Shell using DOSSHELL.BAT.

The NEW group is now the Main Group menu and is labeled as such. However, you don't have access to any of the default DOS functions formerly available from the Main Group. To resolve this problem, add the old Main Group as a subgroup to the new Main Group with these directions:

Step 1. From the new Main Group, pull down the Group menu.

Step 2. Select Add....

Step 3. Type a name for the old Main Group. For example, type
Shell Utilities.

Step 4. On the `Filename` line, type **SHELL.MEU**.

Step 5. Type any help text you want.

Step 6. If you want to protect this group with a password, type one
on the `Password` line.

Step 7. Click the `F2=Save` box or press F2 to save the new group parameters.

The `Shell Utilities` group appears in the new Main Group.
`Shell Utilities` now contains the DOS Shell functions such as
DOS Utilities ... and Change Colors.

Using the Exit Submenu

The third pull-down menu in the Start Programs action bar is the Exit menu. Two options are provided on this menu: you can either exit the DOS Shell entirely, or you can return to the Start Programs action bar.

If you elect to leave the DOS Shell, you cannot return to it unless you reload it by typing **DOSSHELL** at the DOS prompt. If you want to leave the Shell temporarily, use the Shift-F9 key described earlier in this chapter.

Using the Main Group Menu

The following sections explain the various options on the Main Group menu.

Starting Programs

You don't have to start a program from the Program submenu. In fact, you may seldom start a program from the action bar; you can use a much faster method.

You can start programs directly when the Main Group menu is active. Simply highlight the selection you want and then press Enter or click the mouse button. The program starts exactly as if you had chosen it using the `Start...` option from the Program submenu.

Using the Command Prompt

The Command Prompt option in the Main Group menu enables you to access the DOS V4 prompt temporarily. After you finish executing DOS commands, return to the Shell by typing **EXIT** at the DOS prompt and pressing Enter.

Using the File System Menu

The DOS Shell File System is available from the Main Group menu and enables you to perform many functions with your files. Because accessing a directory of those files is the most rudimentary of those functions, the directory feature is a good introduction to the File System.

To access the directory, select `File System` from the Main Group menu. DOS reads the current disk and displays the screen shown in figure 14.15.

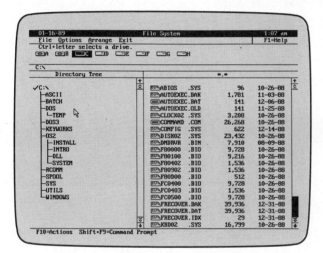

Fig. 14.15

The File System menu.

The menu displayed has four options: `File`, `Options`, `Arrange`, and `Exit` (each of these options is described in the following sections). The display shows letters or icons (depending on whether your Shell is in graphics or text mode) representing the disk drives available in your system. The current disk drive is highlighted.

The split-screen display shows you two key pieces of information. On the left is a directory tree that shows how the files are arranged on your disk.

The right side of the display lists the files on the current disk drive. This list looks much like that shown by the DIR command from the DOS prompt. If you use graphics mode, each file has an icon or character next to it that indicates the type of file it is. The icons look like miniature documents. This side of the display gives the same information available from the DOS prompt: the file name, extension, size, date, and so forth.

In many cases, not all the files on a disk can be displayed on-screen at once. The DOS Shell provides several ways to scroll back and forth through a listing of file names. If you have a graphics-based system and a mouse, you can use the scroll bar. If you do not have a mouse or if you are using a text-based Shell, use the cursor keys. Before using either method, you must make sure that the file-display panel is active by highlighting an option on the panel.

To view a directory of a different disk, select from the third line of the display the letter or icon representing the desired disk drive. If the drive area is active, you can select a drive by holding down the Ctrl key and pressing the letter corresponding to that drive (Ctrl-A, Ctrl-B, and so forth) or by clicking the drive icon with the mouse. Press the Tab key to make the drive area active.

So far, the directory listing available from the Shell is much like that shown by the DOS DIR command. However, you can also sort directories, display specified files, and perform other tasks from the Shell, as described in the following sections.

Using the File System File Option

As shown in figure 14.16, the File System File submenu lists 12 options, divided into 3 groups. These options are described in the following sections.

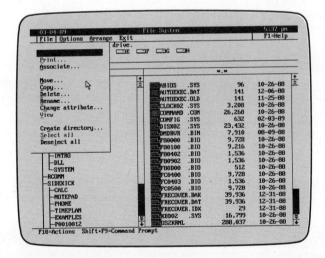

Fig. 14.16

The File submenu.

Opening a File

You can start an applications program by double clicking the mouse pointer on an appropriate file entry in the File System directory listing. If you don't have a mouse, use the arrow keys to highlight the desired entry and press Enter. DOS runs the file if it is a valid EXE, COM, or BAT file. If you have used the Associate... option (described later in this chapter) to link a file extension to an application, you can start a program by clicking a data file.

You also can start a program by choosing the Open... option from the File menu when a file is highlighted in the directory listing. Alternatively, you can type a file name when the Open File panel appears (see fig. 14.17). In the Open File panel, you can type an associated file name and the options to be passed to the application when the file is opened.

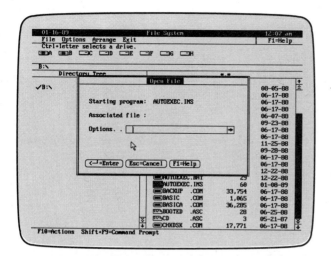

Fig. 14.17

The Open File Panel

Printing a File

The DOS Shell File System includes a Print... option, similar to the one available at the DOS prompt except that the switches used at the prompt are not readily available in the Shell.

You can create a separate program that includes the PRINT command along with parameters that enable you to enter switches. The Shell's Print... option, however, is generally used only to get a quick printout of an ASCII file, so creating such a program is probably not worth your while.

In ASCII mode, the File System's Print... option works quite well. You must load PRINT.COM from the DOS prompt for the option to work, however. Once you have loaded PRINT.COM, follow these steps to print a file:

Step 1. Mark in the File System's directory listing the file or files you want to print.

Step 2. Pull down the File menu.

Step 3. Choose Print....

Each file you mark is submitted to DOS for printing. A panel confirming that the file has been submitted for printing appears, displaying the name of each file in turn.

Associating a File

The Associate... option enables you to specify to the Shell which applications programs are associated with various file extensions. After you have associated particular applications programs with particular file extensions, you can automatically start one of those applications by simply selecting a data file used by the application.

This procedure of selecting an associated data file is a third way to start a program. You have already learned how to start a program from the Main Group or subgroup listings, and you also know how to use the Program panel in the action bar to start a program.

To associate an applications program with specific file extensions, follow these steps:

Step 1. Choose the applications program or programs you want to associate with specific extensions.

The programs can be COM or EXE files, or BAT batch files that load COM or EXE files.

Step 2. Highlight the file or files by pressing the space bar or by moving the mouse pointer to the file's name and clicking.

You may have to change the current disk drive or directory to locate the application. Ideally, the applications programs you select use a single default file extension, such as PCX for Publisher's Paintbrush or PC Paintbrush, DOC for DisplayWrite 4, WP for WordPerfect, WKQ for Quattro, BAS for BASIC programs, and so on. You can associate a total of 20 extensions with your applications programs where no two applications are associated with the same extension. (See Chapter 5 for a list of commonly used file extensions.)

Step 3. Pull down the File menu in the action bar and choose the Associate... option.

If you have marked several files, the first file name appears. If the file does not have a valid extension (COM, EXE, or BAT), you are told that the extension is invalid and are asked to choose between skipping the file or entering a different extension.

Step 4. If the file is a valid application or batch file, use the Extensions line to type the extension or extensions you want to associate with that application.

Type only the one to three characters of the extension, not the period. If you type more than one extension, separate the entries with a space.

Step 5. When you have typed the extensions for a given application, press Enter.

The Prompt for Options panel appears. In this panel, you specify whether you want the Shell to pause and ask for options when it loads the application or load the application directly. Some programs enable you to specify something at the DOS prompt, such as the file to be edited. You can choose Prompt for options if you want to provide this capability. If your application doesn't enable you to do this, or if you simply don't want this option, select Do not prompt for options.

Step 6. After choosing either Prompt for options or Do not prompt for options, press Enter.

The Associate... information is stored in a file called SHELL.ASC. Any time you try to open a file with an ASC extension, the Shell instead opens the application you have associated with that extension. The Shell does not actually open the data file you have selected. You can type the file name when prompted if you have told the Shell to prompt for options when a data file with that extension is selected. The DOS Shell cannot pass the file name directly to the application.

Moving a File

You can select the Move... option from the File menu if you need to move a file or files quickly from one subdirectory to another or if you need to send a file to a disk for archiving.

The Move... option works just like the Copy... option (described in the next section), except that after you have moved the file to the new directory or disk, the file is erased from the old location. The names of the files you have marked in the file listing appear on the From: line; you specify the destination on the To: line.

If you have activated the Confirm on Delete choice in the File System Options menu, the Shell asks you for confirmation before removing the old file.

Copying a File

You already should be familiar with the DOS COPY command (described in Chapter 9). Use these instructions if your system has two floppy disk drives. You should have the DOS Shell loaded and the Start Programs menu on your screen.

Step 1. Place into drive A a blank, formatted disk.

Step 2. Place into drive B a disk containing files you want to copy.

Step 3. Select File System from the Main Group menu.

The File System menu appears. Make sure that drive B is selected. If it isn't, select it with the mouse, or press the Tab key to highlight the drive spefiecier, and then press Ctrl-B.

Step 4. Select the File menu from the action bar.

Press F10, if necessary, to activate the action bar. You can pull down the File menu with the mouse, or you can press F to select the menu. Note that the Copy... option is blurred, shaded, or marked with an asterisk, depending on your display mode.

Step 5. Choose the Select all option from the File menu.

The Copy... option becomes available.

Step 6. Choose the Copy... option.

You see a panel like the one shown in figure 14.18.

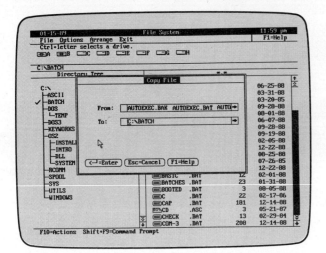

Fig. 14.18

The Copy File panel.

The Copy File panel has two lines on which you can enter information. The From: line enables you to enter the name of the file or files to be copied. Because you have chosen the Select all option, each of the file names on the disk appear one after another on the line. Not all the names appear at once because the line has room for just a few. You can use the scroll bar to scroll through the listing, if you want.

Use the mouse or press Tab to move to the To: line and type the name of the destination drive or directory. If drive A does not appear on the line, press Del to delete what appears there, type **A:**, and then press Enter.

The light on drive B goes on first, and then the light on drive A goes on. The lights alternate for a minute or so as each file is copied from drive B to drive A. The name of the file being copied appears on the Copy File screen, along with the information that file 1 of x, 2 of x, or 3 of x, and so on, is being copied (where x is the number of files you selected). You always know how many files remain to be copied. Finally, a screen message tells you that DOS has successfully copied all the files.

Deleting a File

Before selecting the Delete... option, make sure that no files are selected that you do not want to delete. Highlight only the files you do want to remove, and then select the Delete... option from the File menu.

A panel pops up listing the selected files. Press Enter to start deleting the files. A confirmation panel appears for each file; you can choose to skip the current file and continue; or you can delete the file. You confirm the deletion of each file for all the files you selected. You can disable the confirmation step by using the File System Options menu described later in this chapter.

Renaming a File

To rename a file, choose Rename... from the File menu. A panel pops up with fields in which you type the old file name and the new file name.

Changing a File's Attributes

File attributes are discussed in Chapter 7. You can change file attributes with the DOS Shell as well as with the DOS ATTRIB command. You can use the Shell's Change attribute... option in batch mode to change several files one after another. You can also use the utility in global mode to change many files all at once in exactly the same way. You also can use the utility to change a single file. To change a file's attributes, follow these steps:

Step 1. From the file listing, select the file or files you want, marking them with the space bar or mouse.

Step 2. Pull down the File menu and choose Change attribute....

The Change Attribute menu appears. You can choose to change all selected files one at a time or simultaneously.

Step 3. Choose either 1. One at a time or 2. All selected files at once. Press Enter.

If you choose to change all selected files one at a time, each of the file names appears in turn on the File: line of the next panel. You select the desired attributes for each file. If you elect to change all selected files at one time, no file names appear, and you select attributes to be applied to all the files. Either way, the hidden, read-only, and archive attribute selections appear.

Step 4. Choose the attributes you want to change.

You can move the highlight by using the mouse or cursor keys. Press the space bar to toggle the attribute on or off. (If the attribute is on, pressing the space bar turns it off, and vice versa.)

Step 5. When you have set the attributes as you want them for a given file, press Enter.

The attributes are changed on the disk. If you have selected more than one file, the next file name appears in the panel, and you can repeat Steps 4 and 5 until the last file is changed.

Viewing a File

The View option enables you to look at the contents of ASCII files. You can page through the files by pressing the PgUp and PgDn keys.

To view a file, select it from the file list (either by using the mouse or by pressing the space bar when the file name is highlighted). Then pull down the File menu from the action bar and select View. The File View panel appears, as shown in figure 14.19. When you have finished viewing the file, press Esc to return to the File System.

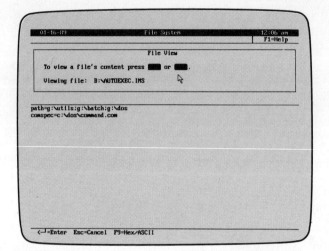

Fig. 14.19

The File View panel.

Creating a Directory

To make a new directory from the Shell File System, select Create directory... from the File menu. A panel appears, and you can type the name of the directory to be created.

Selecting All Files

To highlight all the files in the current directory (you may want to do this to copy or delete them all at one time), choose the Select all option from the File menu. All the files in the directory are highlighted.

Deselecting All Files

To reverse the preceding procedure and deselect all the files in the directory, use the Deselect all option from the File menu. All the highlighted files in the directory are deselected.

Using the File System Options Option

The File System Options menu has three entries: Display options..., File options..., and Show information..... Each of these entries is described in the following sections.

Selecting Display Options

The Display options... selection in the Options menu enables you to specify the order in which files are shown in the File System. The panel that appears when you select Display options... lists the following items:

    Name Extension Date Size Disk order

Select one of these items to sort your directory files by file root, file extension, creation or modification date, file size, or the order in which the files appear on the disk. Use the cursor keys or mouse to select the option you want.

Selecting File Options

The File options... selection enables you to specify how the Shell is to perform certain functions. You can select any or all of these options:

Option	Description
Confirm on delete	Requires the Shell to ask you before erasing a file. If you do not select this option, the Shell erases files without presenting a confirmation panel.
Confirm on replace	Causes the Shell to prompt you for confirmation before copying a file over another file with the same name.
Select across directories	Enables the Shell to choose files even if the files are in different directories.

Showing File Information

Figure 14.20 shows a typical Show Information panel, which displays four categories of information under the headings File, Selected, Directory, and Disk. The panel shows information about the file currently highlighted in the file listing.

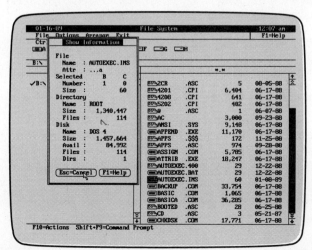

Fig. 14.20

The Show Information panel.

The `File` section of the Show Information panel displays the file's name (including the extension) and attributes. Each attribute set is indicated on the `Attr` line by a character: *r* for read-only, *h* for hidden, *s* for system, and *a* for archive bit. Any of these characters, none of them, or all four may appear on the line, depending on the file.

To the right of the `Selected` heading in the panel appear the names of the drives currently stored in the Shell's buffer. If more than one drive is "memorized," this entry and the `Number` and `Size` entries have two columns, one for each of the drives. The `Number` entry indicates how many files have been marked in the directory listing for that drive. The `Size` entry shows the total number of bytes taken up by the selected files in that drive.

The `Directory` section of the panel displays the name of the currently selected directory, the total size of all the files in that directory, and the total number of files in that directory.

The `Disk` section covers information about the disk drive itself. The `Name` entry is the label applied during formatting or with the LABEL command. The `Size` entry represents the total disk space, and the `Avail` entry signifies the free space available for new files. The `Files` entry shows the number of files stored on the disk. The last entry, `Dirs`, shows the number of subdirectories on the disk.

Although certain utility programs provide the same information as the Show Information panel, this panel gives DOS users easy access to all this data, in one place.

Using the File System Arrange Option

The File System Arrange menu is a powerful tool that enables you to choose files from a single file listing (the default option), from multiple windows that show file listings for two disks or directories, or from the current directory.

The Multiple File List Option

You use the Multiple file list option from the Arrange menu to show two file lists on-screen. To learn to use the multiple windows, follow these steps:

Step 1. Make sure that the File System menu is on-screen, pull down the Arrange menu, and choose `Multiple file list`.

The screen shows two panels, one above the other (see fig. 14.21). Each panel consists of a directory-tree section and a file-listing section. The current drive and directory listing appears in the top panel; the other buffered drive or directory appears in the bottom panel. Each panel displays fewer lines than its corresponding single-file listing would display.

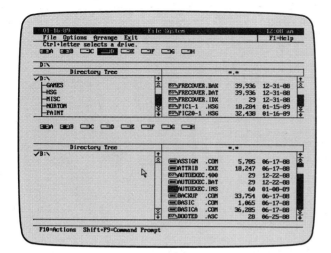

Fig. 14.21

The Multiple file list.

Step 2. Use the mouse or Tab key to move from one panel to the other.

You can scroll through each of the listings and manipulate the directory tree of each individually.

Step 3. If you want to select another drive for an active panel, move the mouse pointer to the drive symbol you want and click. Alternatively, hold the Ctrl key and press the letter associated with the desired drive.

Each panel has its own drive-selector line, so you can change the drive for each panel.

Step 4. To return to the single-file list, pull down the Arrange menu and choose Single file list.

The System File List Option

You can select the System file list option from the Arrange menu to show only the DOS system files for the currently selected disk.

Using the File System Exit Option

To exit the File System, access the File System Exit menu and select Exit File System. The Main Group/Start Programs menu appears. If you select Resume File System, the File System menu reappears.

Using Change Colors

If you have a color monitor, you can select one of four combinations of colors in which to display the Shell. To choose one of these combinations, access the Change Colors utility from the Main Group. A screen showing the color combinations appears.

Use the right and left arrows to move through the four choices. When you see a combination you like, press Enter. The Shell saves that choice and uses it for the rest of the current session as well as all subsequent sessions.

Using the DOS Utilities Menu

The DOS Utilities... menu enables you to access several standard DOS commands. When each is selected, a panel appears in which you can type the standard parameters DOS requires for each of the commands. In all respects, these commands behave exactly the same as if you had typed them at the DOS prompt. These commands are available on the DOS Utilities... menu for your convenience. Refer to the following chapters for descriptions of these commands:

DOS Utilities Option	DOS Command	Chapter Reference
Set Date/Time	TIME and DATE	3
Disk Copy	DISKCOPY	5
Disk Compare	DISKCOMP	5
Backup Fixed Disk	BACKUP	10
Restore Fixed Disk	RESTORE	10
Format	FORMAT	6

Installing DOS V4 and the Shell with SELECT

You can use the SELECT utility that comes with DOS to do more than install the Shell; you can use it to install DOS also. SELECT can create diskettes you can use to boot from your floppy disk drive (much like the DOS V3 SELECT utility); SELECT also can copy DOS to your hard disk. The SELECT utility is not completely new; the utility was introduced in DOS V3 to prepare a diskette for use with various country codes and keyboard combinations. If you had no need to change country codes, however, you probably never had occasion to use SELECT. In versions of DOS before V4, SELECT worked only with diskettes.

SELECT is menu-oriented and contains complete help instructions. Complete instructions on installing DOS V4 are found in Appendix C, "Installing DOS."

The SELECT utility creates for you a batch file, DOSSHELL.BAT, that actually starts the DOS Shell. The DOSSHELL.BAT file is the key to the configuration that the DOS Shell will use. You can modify the key set-up parameters in the DOSSHELL.BAT file by editing the file. The next section looks at a sample DOSSHELL.BAT file.

Understanding a Sample DOSSHELL.BAT File

The SELECT utility creates for you a batch file similar to the DOSSHELL.BAT file described in this section. Your file may differ slightly depending on the options you selected and the changes you made to this file.

    (1) @ECHO OFF

    (2) C:

    (3) CD \DOS

    (4) SHELLB DOSSHELL

    (5) IF ERRORLEVEL 255 GOTO END

    (6) :COMMON

    (7) @SHELLC/MOS:PCIBMDRV.MOS/TRAN/COLOR/DOS/MENU/MUL/SND/MEU
        :SHELL.MEU/CLR:SHELL.CLR/PROMPT/MAINT/EXIT/SWAP/DATE

    (8) :END

    (9) CD \

 Each line in this sample batch file is numbered for easy reference. The line numbers are not part of the batch file, however, and should not be included if you copy this file or create one of your own from scratch.

Following are explanations of each line of the sample DOSSHELL.BAT file.

Line 1: Turns off the echoing of commands so that they are not displayed on-screen as DOS carries them out.

Line 2: Changes the current drive to drive C in case you happen to be using some other drive at the time you call DOSSHELL.BAT.

Line 3: Changes the current directory to \DOS, in which the programs you need to run the Shell are stored.

Line 4: Summons a program called SHELLB.COM, which loads some key functions into memory. These functions take up less than 4K of DOS memory. SHELLB.COM also performs two other tasks that enable the remaining Shell programs to load:

- First, SHELLB.COM checks for any errors that might prevent the Shell from running properly. If any errors are found, a value of *255* is loaded into the special DOS memory register that stores the current ERRORLEVEL setting.

- Second, SHELLB.COM notes the name of the batch file you want to use to call up the DOS Shell. The default name is DOSSHELL. In network environments, customized batch files can be used for each note using the Shell on the same server.

Line 5: Checks to see whether SHELLB.COM found any errors by checking whether ERRORLEVEL equals 255. If an error was found, control passes to line 8 (:END), and the batch file terminates. If this happens, you may have to run the SELECT program again, making sure you correctly define your system.

Line 6: Marks the beginning of the portion of the batch file that calls the SHELLC.COM program. When you run a program from the DOS Shell or leave the Shell to access the DOS prompt, DOS returns to this line in the batch file to reload the Shell. You must be careful to specify to SHELLB.COM the name of the file you want to use; you also must use only the :COMMON label to mark this point in the batch file. If you don't specify the name of the file, DOS does not know where to look. If you use some label other than :COMMON, DOS cannot find the correct starting place.

Line 7: Does most of the work in setting up the DOS Shell. A detailed examination of this line appears in the following section.

Line 8: Marks the end of the section of the batch file that calls SHELLC.COM.

Line 9: Changes the current subdirectory to the root directory.

Customizing the Shell

This section first examines the options listed in line 7 of the sample DOSSHELL.BAT file and then discusses those options not included in the sample batch file. Line 7 of the sample file calls the SHELLC.COM program and specifies a list of options that customize the Shell. When including options in your DOSSHELL.BAT file, remember that no spaces can precede the slashes for the options in the SHELLC line.

A few of the options for customizing the Shell can regulate a user's interaction with the Shell. In particular, notice the function of the /PROMPT, /EXIT, and /MAINT options that can keep a user from leaving or modifying the Shell.

The /MOS: Option

The /MOS: option enables you to specify the mouse driver to be used with the DOS Shell. Include this option only if you use a mouse with the Shell. The IBM mouse, for example, uses the PCIBMDRV.MOS driver. The Shell also provides the PCMSDRV.MOS driver for the Microsoft serial mouse and the PCMSPDRV.MOS driver for the Microsoft parallel mouse. One of these three drivers should work with your mouse; each requires only 1K of memory. You must specify one of these three drivers if you have a mouse; other drivers do not work with the Shell. You should find these drivers in the same directory as the Shell programs. DOS deactivates these drivers when the Shell is not active so that these drivers do not conflict with any other mouse drivers you may use.

The /TRAN Option

The /TRAN option activates the transient mode of the Shell. In *resident* mode, the DOS Shell and the buffers it uses are loaded into memory and stay there. The buffers use all available memory (unless you limit the buffer size with the /B: option, described later in this chapter). If the Shell operates in resident mode, the Shell works faster because DOS doesn't have to access the hard disk. Because the entire Shell is available in memory for instant access in resident mode, however, you have less free memory for other uses. For more information on buffers, refer to Chapter 13.

In *transient* mode, the Shell uses only 3.5K of memory and stores the other information it needs on the hard disk. Because you run other programs from the Shell (you do not exit the Shell before starting another program), limiting the amount of RAM the Shell uses is a good idea if you want memory available for such RAM-hungry programs as Ventura Publisher.

The /COLOR Option

If you do use a color monitor, the /COLOR option activates the Change Colors utility in the Main Group menu. If you omit this option from DOSSHELL.BAT, you cannot change the colors of the Shell. The Change Colors selection still appears in the Main Group menu.

The /DOS Option

The /DOS option makes the File System selection available on the Main Group menu. If you omit the /DOS option from DOSSHELL.BAT, you cannot perform any File System functions such as copying files and viewing directories. You can always modify DOSSHELL.BAT to include the /DOS option later.

409

The /MENU Option

The /MENU option activates the Start Programs main menu. If you don't specify this option, you can access only the File System menu. (If you don't specify the /DOS option or the /MENU option, you cannot do anything.)

The /MUL Option

When the /MUL option is specified, the Shell keeps track of the information obtained from the last two drives accessed. Having the Shell keep track of this information can speed up File System operations such as displaying the directory tree and listing files, because the Shell doesn't have to access the disk to recall the information.

The /SND Option

The /SND option activates the sounds you hear when working with the Shell (it does not control the sounds made by programs you start from the Shell). Unless you work in a "quiet zone," you may want the added feedback that your computer's various beeps can provide.

The /MEU: Option

The /MEU: option enables you to define the name of the menu file used for the Main Group menu. The default file is SHELL.MEU. If you want to use the SHELL.MEU file, you don't have to include the /MEU: option at all.

If you want to create a new Main Group menu, specify a file other than SHELL.MEU. Suppose that you deleted the Change Colors utility and also want to remove it from the Main Group menu. To do this, create a new subgroup menu that has the headings you want and provide the menu with a file name (refer to "Adding a Group" later in this chapter). Edit the DOSSHELL.BAT file so that the /MEU: option includes the new menu file name.

The /CLR: Option

The /CLR: option enables you to specify the name of the file containing the DOS Shell color scheme you have selected. The default file is SHELL.CLR. If you want to use the default file, you don't have to include the /CLR: option at all. If you want, you can write different versions of DOSSHELL.BAT, each specifying a different color-scheme file. You create color schemes using the Change Colors option on the Main Group menu (refer to "Using Change Colors" later in this chapter).

The /PROMPT Option

The /PROMPT option enables you to switch from the Shell to the DOS command prompt so that you can carry out functions or run other programs. The /PROMPT option enables the Shift-F9 key and the Command Prompt option on the Main Group menu. To return to the Shell after you have accessed the DOS prompt, type **EXIT** at the DOS prompt.

If you omit the /PROMPT option, you are "stuck" inside the Shell with no means of quick access to DOS (other than exiting from the Shell entirely).

The /MAINT Option

The /MAINT option provides access to the various action-bar commands that appear in the submenus (such as Add... and Change...). If you omit /MAINT, you can use only the commands found in the group listings themselves. Each of the Main Group programs and utilities are accessible if you omit /MAINT, but you cannot add or change programs and groups. In the File System, you can view directories and the directory tree if you omit /MAINT, but you cannot copy or delete files, create directories, and so on. In short, including /MAINT enables you to change the Shell; omitting /MAINT prevents you from accessing commands that change the Shell.

The /EXIT Option

The /EXIT option activates the action-bar selection that enables you to unload the Shell and return complete control to DOS. If you do not specify /EXIT, you are "trapped" in the Shell. If you also do not specify the /PROMPT option, you cannot access the DOS prompt unless you reboot the system.

The /SWAP Option

The Shell can maintain a file that stores the buffered information about files and directories used by the File System. If you specify the /SWAP option, DOS stores this information on disk in a temporary file. This file helps speed up the reloading of the Shell when you exit from a program. Like the /MUL option, /SWAP can speed up the operation of the Shell; you can specify both of these options if you want.

The /DATE Option

When you specify the /DATE option, the date and time are displayed in the DOS Shell title bar and are updated every minute. You may not want to use the /DATE option if you have installed the Shell on a computer with a nonfunctional clock.

The Shell options described in the following sections do not appear in the sample batch file, but you may want to include them in your own DOSSHELL.BAT file.

The /ASC: Option

The DOS Shell A̲ssociate... function enables you to correlate various file extensions with particular applications programs. You can use A̲ssociate... to pair the DOC extension with your word processing program, for example, or the WKQ extension with your Quattro spreadsheet program. When you select a file with an "associated" extension, the Shell automatically loads the correlated application for you.

DOS stores the links between file extensions and application programs in a file called SHELL.ASC. If your computer has several users, you may want to store each user's associations in a different file. (You create the association file by selecting File System from the Main Group menu, selecting the File option, choosing A̲ssociate..., and filling out the displayed screen.) Use the /ASC: option to specify the name of another association file.

The /ASC: option allows more flexibility in loading programs. You don't have to know which file contains the program you want to start; you can just select the file you want to access and let DOS find and start the associated program file.

The /B: Option

The /B: option enables you to limit the amount of memory that the Shell uses in resident mode for its *buffers*. Specify the size in whole kilobytes. If you want to limit to 8K the amount of RAM the Shell uses for buffers, for example, specify **/B:8**. If you don't use the /B: option, DOS uses all available memory for buffers. Omitting the /B: option usually does not cause problems.

The /CO1, /CO2, and /CO3 Options

Use the /CO1, CO2, or /CO3 option to specify the video-graphics mode the Shell is to use. The mode you choose must be compatible with your display adapter and monitor. You can use some of these options with more than one type of monitor. Try several to see which are compatible with your system and use the one you prefer. The options and their associated modes are listed in the following chart:

Option	Mode
/CO1	EGA 640 × 350 16-color mode; produces an 80-column, 25-line display (in technical terms, video mode 10H)
/CO2	VGA 640 × 480 black-and-white mode; produces an 80-column, 30-row display (in technical terms, video mode 11H)
/CO3	VGA 640 × 480 16-color mode; produces an 80-column, 30-row display (in technical terms, video mode 12H)

The /TEXT Option

The */TEXT* option instructs the Shell to use *text* mode for CGA monitors or Monochrome Display Adapter (MDA) monitors. These video modes are 3 and 7, respectively.

The /COM2 Option

Ordinarily, the Shell uses the COM1 serial port for the mouse. If you include the */COM2* option, the Shell uses COM2 for the mouse.

The /LF Option

The */LF* option changes the mouse driver's configuration so that you use the right button instead of the left button with the Shell. This option is useful for left-handed people. Because this option controls only the action of the mouse within the Shell, and not in programs started from the Shell, switching mouse buttons may be confusing.

Summary

As you can see, the DOS Shell adds a new dimension to using DOS. Even if you are comfortable with DOS at the DOS prompt, you will want to explore the DOS Shell and try some of the configuration exercises in this chapter. Important points covered in this chapter include the following:

❏ You can choose to "balance" your system between maximum DOS function and maximum memory space.

❏ You can change the DOS Shell by altering the DOSSHELL.BAT file.

❏ Many of the features of the Shell can be disabled or activated, as you prefer.

❏ Customized shells can be prepared for different users.

❏ The Shell's menus are arranged in tree fashion.

❏ You can add or change the program names that appear on the Shell menu.

❏ You can help users by adding customized prompt and help panels to the menu choices.

❏ The DOS Shell File System system enables you to copy or delete multiple files using the menus.

❏ The File System enables you to change the attributes of files.

❏ You can choose the order in which the File System displays files.

❏ Files can be erased automatically after they are copied to another disk or directory.

❏ You can associate an application with the file extensions its data files use. As a result, the application is loaded automatically when you attempt to open the data file.

❏ You can specify whether the File System asks for confirmation before deleting or overwriting files.

❏ The Shell provides an extensive Show Information listing.

❏ You can view the directories of more than one disk or subdirectory at one time by using the Multiple file list option.

❏ You can change the screen colors in which the Shell appears.

❏ Several DOS commands, such as DISKCOPY, TIME, and Date, are available on the DOS Utilities... menu.

❏ The DOS Shell is installed with the SELECT program.

The next part of the book, Part Four, contains the comprehensive Command Reference. The Command Reference lists, in alphabetical order, the commands available with DOS. The commands are shown with syntax, applicable rules, and examples. You can use the information in the Command Reference both as a reference when you have problems and as a source of practical advice and tips.

Part Four

Command Reference

Command
Reference

ASSIGN
ATTRIB
BACKUP
BATCH
BREAK
CHCP
CHDIR
CHKDSK
CLS
COMMAND

This DOS Command Reference indexes and describes the DOS commands. The commands are presented with the command name appearing first, followed by the versions of DOS to which the command applies.

Next, the terms *internal* and *external* indicate whether the command is built into DOS or is disk-resident. A brief description of the command's purpose immediately follows the title line. Each command entry illustrates the syntax in one or more syntax lines showing how to invoke the command. Occasionally, a command may have a long and a short form, equally valid as command terms in a syntactical structure. In these instances, both forms are illustrated. When switches can be used in the command line, these are listed and defined.

Notes give further information about the command, amplifying the purpose, giving insight into its efficient use, or otherwise acquainting you with the scope of the command. As appropriate, cautionary notes are included to help you avoid particular pitfalls associated with a command. A reference may be given directing you to a chapter within the body of the book that treats the command at greater length. Finally, at least one example of how to use the command is given. You will see more than one example when a command has varied uses.

Command Reference Conventions

Great effort has been taken to make the DOS Command Reference as easy as possible to use. Yet to understand fully the syntax lines discussed you must be familiar with a few conventions. These conventions signal key properties of the terms shown in the command line, indicating what is mandatory or merely optional, and what components of the syntax line are variable. Conventional substitute forms also stand in place of the variable terms you will use.

Expressing File Names

To represent a file name, you will see the following:

   d:path**filename.ext**

The *d:* represents a drive designation and can be any valid drive letter that is available on your computer.

path\ represents a single subdirectory or a path of subdirectories on a valid drive. This shows the path to the file.

filename.ext represents the full file name and its extension. When specifying a file name, you must give the extension if one exists. When a file has no extension, you will omit this portion of the file name specification. The **.ext** is always shown in the syntax line as a reminder to supply this if, in fact, the name bears an extension.

When the syntax specifies an external command, you will see a command line that resembles the following:

   dc:pathc**command_name**

The *dc:* represents the *drive* that contains the command. Again, this can be any valid drive letter that is on your computer.

pathc\ represents the subdirectory or *path* of subdirectories that leads to the command.

command_name is any valid DOS command. **FORMAT**, for example, may replace **command_name** in an actual line. When entering the command name, you do not need to specify the extension.

418

If FORMAT.COM resides in drive C in the subdirectory path \DOS\DISK, the syntax line

> *dc:pathc***FORMAT**

means that you can type

> **C:\\DOS\\DISK\\FORMAT**

to start formatting a disk.

Using Upper- and Lowercase Letters

In any syntax line, not all elements of the syntax can be represented in a literal manner. For example, *filename.ext* can represent any file name with any extension. It also may represent any file name with no extension at all. However, command names and switches can be represented in a literal way. To activate FORMAT.COM, you must type FORMAT.

Any literal text that you can type in a syntax line will be shown in uppercase letters. Any text that you can replace with other text (variable text) will be shown in lowercase letters.

As an example, the syntax line

> **FORMAT d:**

means that you must type **FORMAT** to format a disk. However, **d** can be replaced by any valid disk drive letter. If **d:** is to be drive A, then you would type

> **FORMAT A:**

Mandatory vs. Optional

Not all parts of a syntax line are essential when typing the command. You must be able to distinguish mandatory parts of the syntax line from those that are optional. Any portion of a syntax line that you see in **bold** letters is mandatory; whatever you see in *italic* is optional.

It is not always mandatory to type the drive and the path that contains a command. For example, if FORMAT.COM is in the \DOS directory on drive C:, and your current directory is C:\DOS, you do not have to type the drive and path to start FORMAT.COM. In this instance, the syntax form can omit this information:

   *C:\DOS***FORMAT**

If you have FORMAT.COM residing on a drive and directory other than shown in this example, the syntax would be represented as

   *dc:pathc***FORMAT**

where *dc:pathc* is variable text and optional, and **FORMAT** is literal text to type and is mandatory.

Pulling It All Together

Look at this sample syntax line:

   *dc:pathc***FORMAT d:** *⁄S⁄1⁄8⁄V⁄B⁄4⁄N:ss⁄T:tt ⁄V:label ⁄F:size*

The drive and path pointing to the command are both optional and variable, indicated by the italic, lowercase type. All of the switches are optional. The switches are in uppercase, signifying literal text. A few options for the *⁄N, ⁄T, ⁄V,* and *⁄F* switches are variable.

The only mandatory items in the syntax line are the command **FORMAT** and the drive to format, **d:**.

APPEND

V3.3, V4—External

Instructs DOS to search the directories on the disks you specify for nonprogram/
nonbatch files.

Syntax

> *dc:pathc***APPEND** */X /E d1:path1;d1:path2;d2:path1;...*

DOS V4 additional switches indicate the following:

> *dc:pathc***APPEND** */X:on /X:off /PATH:on /PATH:off*

dc:pathc are the disk drive and directory that hold the command.

d1:path1, d1:path2, d2:path1 are valid disk drive names and paths to the
directories you want DOS to search for nonprogram/nonbatch files. The three
periods (...) represent additional disk drive and path names.

Switches

/X	Redirects programs that use the DOS function calls SEARCH FIRST, FIND FIRST, and EXEC.
/X:ON	Same as /X (DOS V4 only).
/X:OFF	Turns this feature off (DOS V4 only).
/E	Places the disk drive paths in the environment.
/PATH:ON	Turns on the search for files that have a drive or path specified (DOS V4 only).
/PATH:OFF	Turns off search for files that have drive or path specified (DOS V4 only).

Notes

The first time you execute APPEND, the program loads from the disk and installs
itself in DOS. APPEND then becomes an internal command and is not reloaded
from the disk until you restart DOS. You can give the /X and /E switches only
when you first invoke APPEND. You cannot give any path names with these two
switches.

If an invalid path is encountered, such as a misspelled path or one that no
longer exists, DOS skips the path and does not display a message.

Do not use APPEND with RESTORE. The RESTORE command searches for files
in the directories on which you have used APPEND. If you use the /N or /M

switch with RESTORE, the correct files may not be processed. Before you use RESTORE, be sure that you have deactivated APPEND.

Examples

APPEND is the complement of PATH. Whereas PATH searches for program and batch files, APPEND searches for all other files.

Before using APPEND to set search paths, use the following form:

APPEND /E /X

After you run APPEND with the switches, you can tell APPEND which directories to search. For example, to search the directories C:\DOS and C:\DOS\UTILS, use the following form:

APPEND C:\DOS;C:\DOS\UTILS

To disable the APPEND command, type this form:

APPEND;

ASSIGN   V2, V3, V4—External

Instructs DOS to use a disk drive other than one specified by a program or command.

Syntax

To reroute drive activity, use the following form:

*dc:pathc***ASSIGN d1=d2 ...**

dc:pathc are the disk drive and directory that hold the command.

d1 is the letter of the disk drive that the program or DOS normally uses.

d2 is the letter of the disk drive that you want the program or DOS to use instead of the usual drive.

The three periods (**...**) represent additional disk drive assignments.

Switch

(None)

Notes

ASSIGN reroutes a program, causing it to use a disk drive that is different from the one the program intends. A program "thinks" that it is using a certain disk drive, when in fact the program is using another. You should use ASSIGN primarily for programs that were written to work only with drives A and B, but which you want to load and run from your hard disk.

Do not use a colon after the disk drive letter for **d1** or **d2**. You can use a space on either side of the equal sign.

You can give more than one assignment on the same line. Use a space between each set of assignments, as in the following example:

ASSIGN B=C A=C

Examples

To assign all activity for drive A to drive C, use the following form:

ASSIGN A = C or ASSIGN A=C

To clear any previous drive reassignments, type only the following command:

ASSIGN

ATTRIB   V3, V4—External

Displays, sets, or clears the read-only or archive attributes of a file.

Syntax

*dc:pathc***ATTRIB** *+R −R +A −A d:path***filename.ext** */S*

dc:pathc are the disk drive and directory that hold the command.

+R sets a file's read-only attribute on.

+A sets a file's archive attribute on.

−R sets a file's read-only attribute off.

−A sets a file's archive attribute off.

d:path are the disk drive and directory holding the files for which the attribute will be displayed or changed.

filename.ext is the name of the file(s) for which the read-only attribute will be displayed or changed. Wild cards are permitted.

Switch

/S Sets or clears the attributes of the specified files in the specified directory and all subdirectories to that directory.

Notes

With the DOS V3 addition of ATTRIB, users have more control over the DOS read-only and archive file attributes. ATTRIB sets or clears these attributes. When the file is marked as read-only, it cannot be altered or deleted. When the archive attribute is on, the file can be processed by using the commands **BACKUP /M**, **XCOPY /M**, or **XCOPY /A**.

For more information, see Chapter 7.

Examples

Use the following to set the read-only and archive attributes for the file MEMO.TXT on:

ATTRIB +R +A MEMO.TXT

To turn off the read-only attribute of MEMO.TXT, type:

ATTRIB –R MEMO.TXT

To see the read-only and archive attributes for MEMO.TXT, type:

ATTRIB MEMO.TXT

BACKUP   V2, V3, V4—External

Backs up one or more files from a hard disk or floppy disk onto another disk.

Syntax

*dc:pathc***BACKUP** *d1:path\\filename.ext* **d2:** */S /M /A /D:date /T:time /F /L:dl:pathl\\filenamel.extl*

dc:pathc are the disk drive and directory that hold the command.

d1:path are the hard disk or floppy disk drive and the directory to be backed up.

filename.ext specifies the file you want to back up. Wild cards are allowed.

d2: is the hard or floppy disk drive that receives the backup files.

Switches

/S	Backs up all *subdirectories*, starting with the specified or current directory on the source disk and working downward.
/M	Backs up all files *modified* since their last backup.
/A	*Adds* the file(s) to be backed up to files already on the specified floppy disk drive.
/D:date	Backs up any file that was created or changed or after the specified *date*.
/T:time	Backs up any file that was created or changed on or after the specified *time* on the specified date (given with the /D switch).
/F	*Formats* the destination floppy disk if the floppy disk is not formatted. DOS V4 formats the target floppy disks automatically without the use of this switch.
/F:size	With DOS V4, *formats* the destination floppy disk according to the *size* specified. If you have a 1.2M disk drive, but only 360K floppy disks, you can specify /F:360 to format the 360K disk in the 1.2M drive.
/L:dl:pathl\filenamel.ext	Creates a *log* file.

Notes

If you have a hard disk, you should become familiar with BACKUP and its companion program RESTORE. BACKUP makes a copy of files from a source disk to a destination disk. With BACKUP, you are prompted to insert disks by number in sequential order until all specified files are backed up. You should number each disk with the number that BACKUP assigns.

You must give both a source and a destination for BACKUP. Neither disk can be a networked disk and neither can be used in an ASSIGN, SUBST, or JOIN command.

If you back up onto diskettes with BACKUP from a version of DOS prior to V3.3, you must have enough formatted diskettes before invoking the BACKUP command. BACKUP does not work on unformatted or non-DOS diskettes. If you have too few formatted diskettes, you will need to stop and restart BACKUP. With V3.3 or V4 of DOS, you may use the /F switch to format unformatted disks.

For more information, see Chapter 10.

Examples

To back up the entire hard disk C to floppy disks in drive A, type

BACKUP C:\ A: /S

To back up all files on or after a specified date, type

BACKUP C:\ A: /S /D:08/21/89

To back up all files modified since the last backup and add those files to the last backup disks, use the following form:

BACKUP C:\ A: /S /M /A

Batch Command   V1, V2, V3, V4—Internal

Executes one or more commands contained in a disk file.

Syntax

*dc:pathc***filename** *parameters*

dc:pathc are the disk drive and directory that hold the command.

filename is the root name of the batch file.

parameters are the parameters to be used by the batch file.

Notes

A batch file is an ASCII text file that contains DOS commands as well as the special batch subcommands. A batch file is useful for performing repetitive tasks, such as issuing commands to start programs.

For more information, see Chapter 12.

Batch Subcommand
CALL   V3.3, V4

Runs a second batch file, then returns control to the first batch file.

Syntax

CALL *dc:pathc***filename** *options*

dc:pathc are the disk drive and directory that hold the command.

filename is the root name of the called batch file.

options are the parameters to be used by the batch file.

Notes

Use the CALL command to run a second batch file from another batch file. When the second file is finished, DOS resumes processing the remaining commands located in the first file.

For more information, see Chapter 12.

Batch Subcommand
ECHO   V2, V3, V4

Controls the display of batch commands and other messages as DOS executes batch subcommands.

Syntax

To display a message, use the following form:

ECHO *message*

To turn off the display of commands and batch command messages, use the following form:

ECHO OFF

To turn on the display of commands and messages, use the following form:

ECHO ON

To check the status of ECHO, use the following form:

ECHO

message is the text of the message to be displayed on-screen.

Notes

For unconditional on-screen display of a message, use the command **ECHO message**. This means that the message you designate will be displayed whether ECHO is on or off.

When ECHO is on, a batch file displays commands as DOS executes each line. The batch file also displays any messages from the batch subcommands.

When ECHO is off, a batch file does not display its commands as DOS executes them. The batch file also does not display messages produced by other batch

427

subcommands. Exceptions to this rule are the `Strike a key when ready` message generated by the PAUSE subcommand and any ECHO message command.

For more information, see Chapter 12.

Batch Subcommand FOR..IN..DO

Allows iterative processing of a DOS command.

Syntax

FOR %%variable IN (set) DO command

variable is a single letter.

set is one or more words or file specifications. The file specification is in the form *d:path***filename.ext**. Wild cards are allowed.

command is the DOS command to be performed for each word or file in the set.

Notes

You can use more than one word or a full file specification in the set. You must separate words or file specifications by spaces or by commas.

%%variable becomes each literal word or full file specification in the set. If you use wild-card characters, FOR..IN..DO executes once for each file that matches the wild-card file specification.

For more information, see Chapter 12.

Batch Subcommand GOTO

Transfers control to the line following a label in the batch file.

Syntax

GOTO label

label is the name used for a marker in a batch file. Although more than eight characters can be used, only the first eight characters of **label** are significant.

Notes

When the command **GOTO label** is executed, DOS jumps to the line following **label** and continues execution of the batch file. **label** is used as a marker in a batch file and must be preceded by a colon. You do not use a colon in the GOTO statement, however.

For more information, see Chapter 12.

Batch Subcommand
IF

V2, V3, V4

Allows conditional execution of a DOS command.

Syntax

IF *NOT* **condition command**

NOT tests for the opposite of **condition** and executes the command when the condition is false.

condition is the basis of the test and can be any of the following:

ERRORLEVEL number	DOS tests the exit code (0 to 255) of the program. If the exit code is greater than or equal to the number, the condition is true.
string1 == string2	DOS compares these two alphanumeric strings to find whether they are identical.
EXIST *d:path***filename.ext**	DOS tests whether *d:path***filename.ext** are in the specified drive or path (if given) or on the current disk drive and directory.

command is any valid DOS batch file command.

Notes

For the IF subcommand, if **condition** is true, **command** is executed. If **condition** is false, **command** is skipped and the next line of the batch file is immediately executed. For the IF NOT subcommand, if **condition** is false, the command is executed. If **condition** is true, **command** is skipped, and the next line of the batch file is immediately executed.

For **string1 == string2**, DOS makes a literal, character-by-character comparison of the two strings. The comparison is based on the ASCII character set, and upper- and lowercase letters are distinguished.

When you are using **string1 == string2** with the parameter markers (%0-%9), neither string may be null (empty, or nonexistent). If either string is null, DOS displays a syntax error message and aborts the batch file.

For more information, see Chapter 12.

Batch Subcommand
PAUSE
V1, V2, V3, V4

Suspends batch file processing until a key is pressed and optionally displays a message.

Syntax

PAUSE *message*

message is a string of up to 121 characters.

Notes

Regardless of the ECHO setting, DOS displays the message:

```
Strike a key when ready
```

DOS suspends processing of the batch file until you press any key. Afterward, DOS continues processing the batch file lines. To end processing of a batch file, press Ctrl-Break or Ctrl-C.

For more information, see Chapter 12.

Batch Subcommand
REM
V1, V2, V3, V4

Displays a message within the batch file.

Syntax

REM *message*

message is a string of up to 123 characters.

Notes

The optional message can contain up to 123 characters and must immediately follow the word REM. When DOS encounters a REM subcommand in a batch file, DOS displays the message if ECHO is on. If ECHO is off, DOS does not display the message.

For more information, see Chapter 12.

Batch Subcommand
SHIFT   V2, V3, V4

Shifts command line parameters one position to the left when a batch file is invoked.

Syntax

SHIFT

Notes

When you use SHIFT, DOS moves the command line parameters one position to the left. DOS discards the former first parameter (%0).

For more information, see Chapter 12.

BREAK   V2, V3, V4—Internal

Determines when DOS looks for a Ctrl-Break sequence to stop a program.

Syntax

To turn on BREAK, use the following form:

BREAK ON

To turn off BREAK, use the following form:

BREAK OFF

To determine whether BREAK is on or off, use the following form:

BREAK

Switch

(None)

Notes

The setting of BREAK depends on the type of work you will be doing on the computer. When BREAK is on, DOS checks for a Ctrl-Break sequence whenever

431

a program uses a DOS device. The Ctrl-Break key then causes the program to halt.

With BREAK set to off, the default setting, DOS checks for a Ctrl-Break key sequence only when the program writes to the screen or the printer, reads the keyboard, or reads/writes from the serial adapter. With BREAK set to off, a user is less likely to halt a program with Ctrl-Break.

For more information, see Chapter 13.

CHCP   V3.3, V4—Internal

Changes or displays the code page (font) used by DOS.

Syntax

CHCP *codepage*

codepage is a valid three-digit code page number.

Switch

(None)

Notes

CHCP is a system-wide code-page (font) changer. CHCP simultaneously resets all affected devices to the changed font. MODE works similarly, but changes only one device at a time.

You must use NLSFUNC prior to issuing this command.

Examples

To display the current code page, type the command:

CHCP

To change the current code page to 850 (Multilingual), type the command, followed by the code number:

CHCP 850

CHDIR or CD   V2, V3, V4—Internal

Changes or shows the path of the current directory.

Syntax

CHDIR *d:path*

or, using the short form:

CD *d:path*

d:path are valid disk drive and directory names.

Switch

(None)

Notes

You have two methods for maneuvering through the hierarchical directories with CD: (1) starting at the root, or top, directory of the disk and moving down, or (2) starting with the current directory and moving in either direction.

To start at the root directory of a disk, you must begin the path with the path character (\), as in \ or **B:**. When DOS sees \ as the first character in the path, the system starts with the root directory. Otherwise, DOS starts with the current directory.

For more information, see Chapter 8.

Examples

To display the current directory, type the command:

CD

To move to the single directory \DOS, use:

CD \DOS

To move to the second-level directory \DATA\MEMOS, use this form:

CD \DATA\MEMOS

CHKDSK   V1, V2, V3, V4—External

Checks the directory and the file allocation table (FAT) of the disk and reports disk and memory status. CHKDSK can also repair errors in the directories or in the FAT.

Syntax

*dc:pathc***CHKDSK** *d:path\filename.ext /F/V*

dc:pathc are the disk drive and directory that hold the command.

d: is the disk drive to be analyzed.

path\filename.ext are the directory path and the file name(s) to be analyzed.

Switches

/F   Fixes the file allocation table and other problems if errors are found.

/V   Shows CHKDSK's progress and displays more detailed information about the errors the program finds. (This switch is known as the verbose switch.)

Notes

CHKDSK shows you the following items of information:

1. Volume name and creation date (only disks with volume labels)

2. Total disk space

3. Number of files and bytes used for hidden or system files

4. Number of files and bytes used for directories

5. Number of files and bytes used for user (normal) files

6. Bytes used by bad sectors (flawed disk space)

7. Bytes available (free space) on disk

8. Bytes of total memory (RAM)

9. Bytes of free memory

In DOS V4, CHKDSK also reports the following:

1. Total bytes in each allocation unit

2. Total allocation units on the disk

3. The available allocation units on the disk

An allocation unit equates to a cluster.

CHKDSK checks a disk's directories and the FAT. The command also checks the amount of memory in the system and determines how much of that memory is free. If CHKDSK finds errors, it reports them on-screen before it makes a status report.

You must direct CHKDSK to make repairs to the disk by giving the /F switch. CHKDSK asks you to confirm that you want the repairs made before the program proceeds.

Do not combine different versions of CHKDSK and DOS. Do not, for example, use CHKDSK from any increment of DOS V2 with DOS V3 or later versions, or you may lose files.

CHKDSK will not process a directory on which you used the JOIN, ASSIGN, or SUBST commands.

For more information, see Chapter 6.

Examples

To analyze the current disk drive, type the following command:

CHKDSK

To analyze a disk in another drive and display all the files on the disk, type the following form:

CHKDSK B: /V

CLS   V2, V3, V4—Internal

Erases the display screen.

Syntax

CLS

Switch

(None)

Notes

This command clears all information on the screen and places the cursor at the home position in the upper left corner. This command affects only the active video display, not memory.

For more information, see Chapter 4.

COMMAND   V2,V3,V4—External

Invokes a second copy of COMMAND.COM, the command processor.

Syntax

*dc:pathc***COMMAND** */E:size /P /C string*

dc:pathc are the disk drive and the directory that hold the command.

string is the set of characters you pass to the new copy of the command interpreter.

Switches

/E:size	Sets the *size* of the *environment*. Size is a decimal number from 160 to 32,768 bytes, rounded up to the nearest multiple of 16.
/P	Keeps this copy permanently in memory (until the next system reset).
/C	Passes the string of commands (the string) to the new copy of COMMAND.COM and returns to primary processor.

Notes

COMMAND is an advanced DOS command not recommended for newcomers to DOS. Consult the DOS *Technical Reference* manual for more information about this command.

COMMAND is most often used with the SHELL directive. This combination allows you to relocate COMMAND.COM from the root directory of a disk to a subdirectory.

Example

You can use COMMAND with DOS versions from V2.0 through V3.2 to emulate the CALL command found in V3.3 through V4.01. To use COMMAND in a batch file to call a batch file named MOVE.BAT, use the following form:

COMMAND /C MOVE

COMP   V1, V2, V3, V4—External

Compares two sets of disk files. This command is not available with some DOS versions. If COMP is not available on your version of DOS, see the FC command.

Syntax

*dc:pathc***COMP** *d1:path1\filename1.ext1*
d2:path2\filename2.ext2

dc:pathc are the disk drive and the directory that hold the command.

d1:path1 are the drive and the directory containing the first set of files to be compared.

filename1.ext1 is the file name for the first set of files. Wild cards are allowed.

d2:path2 are the drive and the directory containing the second set of files to be compared.

filename2.ext2 is the file name for the second set of files. Wild cards are allowed.

Special Terms:

d1:path1\\filename1.ext1 is the *primary* file set.

d2:path2\\filename2.ext2 is the *secondary* file set.

Switch

(None)

Notes

COMP is the utility for comparing files. Use the command to verify that files on which you used the COPY command are correct. Also, use COMP to check a known good program copy against a questionable copy. If a program once functioned properly but now acts strangely, check a good backup copy of the file against the copy you are using. If COMP finds differences, copy the good program to the disk you are using.

Files with matching names but different lengths are not checked. A message is printed indicating that these files are different.

After 10 mismatches (unequal comparisons) between the contents of two compared files, COMP automatically ends the comparison and aborts.

For more information, see Chapter 10.

Examples

To compare the file IBM.LET that resides in the current directory of drive C and in drive A, type the following form:

COMP A:IBM.LET C:IBM.LET

To compare all the files in C:\WORDS\LETTERS with the files on drive A, type the following form:

COMP C:\WORDS\LETTERS*.* A:*.*

or this form:

COMP C:\WORDS\LETTERS A:

Configuration Subcommand
BREAK
V3, V4—Internal

Determines when DOS looks for a Ctrl-Break or Ctrl-C to stop a program.

Syntax
BREAK = ON

or

BREAK = OFF

Switch
(None)

Notes
The setting for BREAK in the CONFIG.SYS file works in the same manner as setting BREAK from the DOS prompt.

For more information, see Chapter 13.

Example
To set DOS to check for the Ctrl-Break key sequence, type the following in your CONFIG.SYS file:

BREAK = ON

Configuration Subcommand
BUFFERS
V2, V3, V4—Internal

Sets the number of disk buffers set aside by DOS in memory.

Syntax
BUFFERS = nn

If you are using DOS V4.0 or V4.01, use this form:

BUFFERS = nn,*mm /X*

nn is the number of buffers to set, in the range of 1 to 99. If you have DOS V4, you may set a maximum of 10,000 buffers, using the /X switch.

mm is the number of sectors, from 1 to 8, that can be read or written at a time. The default is 1 buffer.

Switch

/X   Uses expanded memory for buffer storage.

Notes

Buffers provide the memory for DOS to store data that is in transit between a disk drive and user RAM. The use of buffers is desirable. When reading from a disk, DOS checks first to see if the information is in a buffer. The information, if found in the buffer, is transferred to user memory—the disk is not accessed and computer time is saved. For programs, such as database programs that read and write to the disk often, the more buffers you have, the more time you will save, because the data is more quickly accessible. A program that does not access the disk often, such as a spreadsheet program, does not gain any speed from a larger buffers setting.

For more information, see Chapter 13.

Example

To set your CONFIG.SYS file so that DOS uses 20 disk buffers, enter the command in the following form:

BUFFERS = 20

Configuration Subcommand COUNTRY   V3, V4—Internal

Instructs DOS to modify the input and display of date, time, and field divider information.

Syntax

COUNTRY = nnn

If you are using DOS V3.3 or later, use the following form:

COUNTRY = nnn*,mmm,d:path\filenamef.extf*

nnn is the country code.

mmm is the code page.

d:path are the drive and directory that contain *filenamef.extf*

439

filenamef.extf is the file that contains the country information; that is, COUNTRY.SYS.

Switch

(None)

Notes

If *filenamef.extf* is not in the root directory of your hard disk, you must specify the drive and path containing *filenamef.extf*.

You cannot mix code pages with country codes. If you use the country code 001 for the United States, you cannot use also the code page code for another country, for example, 863 for French Canada.

Example

To set a country code in your CONFIG.SYS file for the United Kingdom, enter the following form:

COUNTRY = 044

Configuration Subcommand
DEVICE   V2, V3, V4—Internal

Instructs DOS to load, link, and use a special device driver.

Syntax

DEVICE = *d:path***filename.ext** *options*

d:path are the disk drive and the directory that hold the device driver.

filename.ext is the root file name and optional extension of the device driver.

options are any parameters or switches that may be used with a device driver.

Switch

(None)

Notes

The device command is used to attach devices to DOS. The *device driver*, as it is called, can be a program that controls a physical device attached to the computer, such as a mouse. Or the device driver can be a program that creates a logical, or non-real, device.

For more information, see Chapter 13.

Example

To install ANSI.SYS in your CONFIG.SYS file, use this form:

DEVICE = C:\DOS\ANSI.SYS

This example assumes that ANSI.SYS is located in the drive C: \DOS subdirectory.

Configuration Subcommand
DRIVPARM   V4—Internal

Defines or changes the parameters of a block device, such as a disk drive (with MS-DOS only).

Syntax

DRIVPARM = /D:num */C /F:type /H:hds /I /N /S:sec /T:trk*

Switches

/D:num   Specifies the drive number, **num**, ranging from 0 to 255, where drive A=0, drive B=1, drive C=2, etc.

/C   Specifies that the drive supports *change-line*, meaning that the drive has sensor support to determine when the drive door is open. When the drive door is open, the drive is sensed as empty.

/F:type   Determines the type of drive. *type* is one of the following:

type	Drive specification
0	160K/320K/180K/360K
1	1.2M
2	720K
3	Single-density 8" disk
4	Double-density 8" disk
5	Hard disk
6	Tape drive
7	1.44M

Type 2 is the default if you do not specify /F.

441

/H:hds	Specifies the total number of drive heads, where *hds* is a number from 1 to 99. The default for *hds* is 2.
/I	Used if you have a 3 1/2-inch drive connected internally to your floppy drive controller, but your ROM BIOS does not support a 3 1/2-inch drive.
/N	Specifies that your drive or other block device is not removable—a hard disk, for example.
/S:sec	Used to specify the total number of sectors per side on the drive. *sec* can be a number from 1 to 999.
/T:trk	Used to specify the number of tracks per side of a disk or the total number of tracks per tape. *trk* can be a number from 1 to 99.

Notes

You have great flexibility in adding block devices to your computer. Make sure that you specify the correct type of device, number of heads, and number of sectors. Incorrect values will cause the device to work incorrectly or not at all.

Example

To specify an internal 3 1/2-inch, 1.44M drive that will be drive B and will support change-line, use the following form:

DRIVPARM /D:1 /C /F:7 /I

Configuration Subcommand
FCBS   V2, V3, V4—Internal

Specifies the number of DOS file control blocks that can be open simultaneously and how many always remain open.

Syntax

FCBS = maxopen, *neverclose*

maxopen is the number of FCBs that can be open at any given time. The default is 4.

neverclose is the number of FCBs that are always open. The default value is 0.

Switch

(None)

Notes

FCBS is rarely used. DOS began using file handles rather than File Control Blocks, beginning with V2.0. The number of programs available that use FCBs is diminishing. All major commercial programs as of this printing use file handles. However, if you find a DOS V1 program using FCBs that you find helpful, you will need to use the FCBS setting.

For more information, see Chapter 13.

Example

To specify in your CONFIG.SYS file to allow 10 open files, 5 of which always remain open, use the following form:

FCBS 10,5

Configuration Subcommand
FILES   V2, V3, V4—Internal

Specifies the number of file handles open at any given time.

Syntax

FILES = nnn

nnn is the number, from 8 to 255, of file handles that may be open at any given time. The default value is 8.

Switch

(None)

Notes

Starting with DOS V2.0, you use the FILES directive in the CONFIG.SYS file to specify the maximum number of files that DOS can have open at one time. For some programs, such as spreadsheet programs, a setting of FILES = 15 may be adequate. With database programs, however, you should set FILES for 20 or greater. Database programs often open several files at a time.

DOS began using file handles rather than File Control Blocks, beginning with V2.0. The number of programs available that use FCBs is diminishing. All major commercial programs as of this printing use file handles. Still, you may find a DOS V1 program using FCBs that you find helpful, for which you will use the FCBS setting.

For more information, see Chapter 13.

Example

To allow as many as 20 files open at one time, type the following form in your CONFIG.SYS file:

FILES = 20

Configuration Subcommand
INSTALL   V4—Internal

Starts program from CONFIG.SYS. Valid programs to start with INSTALL are FASTOPEN, KEYB, NLSFUNC, and SHARE.

Syntax

INSTALL = *dc:pathc***filename.ext** *options*

dc:pathc are the disk drive and the directory that hold the command.

filename.ext is the name of the file, which may be FASTOPEN.EXE, KEYB.COM, NLSFUNC.EXE, or SHARE.EXE.

options are any parameters the command spedified by **filename.ext** requires to function.

Switch

(None)

Notes

INSTALL gives DOS the capability to load some programs from CONFIG.SYS. When a program is loaded from CONFIG.SYS rather than at the DOS prompt, less memory is used.

For more information, see Chapter 13.

Example

To start SHARE.EXE in your CONFIG.SYS file using INSTALL, type the form:

INSTALL = C:\\DOS\\SHARE.EXE

This directive assumes that SHARE.EXE is in the directory \\DOS on drive C.

Configuration Subcommand
LASTDRIVE

V3, V4—Internal

Sets the last valid drive letter acceptable to DOS.

Syntax

LASTDRIVE = x

x is the alphabetical character for the highest system drive. The highest default drive letter is E.

Switch

(None)

Notes

If you use the SUBST command to assign drive letters to subdirectories, use the LASTDRIVE statement to increase the usable drive letters. Also, users of a local area network can use the LASTDRIVE statement to identify the highest letter that can be assigned as a drive letter to a subdirectory.

For more information, see Chapter 13.

Example

If you want to use a drive letter of J, type in your CONFIG.SYS file the following form:

LASTDRIVE = J

Configuration Subcommand
REM

V4—Internal

Places remarks or hide statements in the CONFIG.SYS file.

Syntax

REM *remark*

Switch

(None)

Notes

You may find REM useful in the CONFIG.SYS file to document commands in the file. For example, if you place the DRIVPARM command in your CONFIG.SYS file, you may place a REM statement on the line before the DRIVPARM command to explain the type of drive you are installing.

For more information, see Chapter 13.

Example

To place a remark in your CONFIG.SYS file to explain another entry, you can type something like the following:

REM internal 3 1/2-inch, 1.44M, B:, change-line
DRIVPARM /D:1 /C /F:7 /I

Notice that the REM statement explains the DRIVPARM line.

Configuration Subcommand
SHELL   V3, V4—Internal

Changes the default DOS command processor.

Syntax

SHELL = *d:path***filename.ext** *parameters*

d:path are the drive and the directory where DOS can find the command processor to be used.

filename.ext is the root file name and optional extension of the command processor.

parameters are the optional parameters that the command processor uses.

Switch

(None)

Notes

Most users will not replace COMMAND.COM with another command processor. However, many users wish to reposition COMMAND.COM to a subdirectory. The SHELL command can help accomplish this task.

You may find REM useful in the CONFIG.SYS file to document commands in the file. For example, if you place the DRIVPARM command in your CONFIG.SYS file, you may place a REM statement before the DRIVPARM command to explain the type of drive you are installing.

For more information, see Chapter 13; also see COMMAND in this Command Reference.

Example

To place COMMAND.COM in the \DOS directory on drive C:, use the following form:

SHELL = C:\DOS\COMMAND.COM /P

Configuration Subcommand
STACKS   V3.3, V4, V4.01—Internal

Allots memory storage when a hardware interrupt occurs.

Syntax

STACKS = n,m

n is the number of stacks to allot. The default for computers using the 8088/8086 microprocessor is 0, whereas the default for those computers using the 80286, 80386sx and 80386 is 9.

m is the size in bytes of each stack. The default for computers using the 8088/8086 microprocessor is 0, whereas the default for those computers using the 80286, 80386sx and 80386 is 128.

Switch

(None)

Notes

You will find that the default stacks are adequate for normal usage. However, if you begin receiving the error message `Fatal: Internal Stack Failure, System Halted`, you should increase the stacks. If the error persists after increasing the number of stacks, increase the size of each stack.

Example

To allocate 12 stacks rather than the default 9, type the following form:

STACKS = 12,128

COPY

V1, V2, V3, V4—Internal

Copies files between disk drives and/or devices, either keeping the file name or changing it.

Syntax

To copy a file, use the following form:

COPY /A/B *d1:path1***filename1.ext1**/A/B
d2:path2\\filename2.ext2/A/B/V

To join several files into one, use the following form:

COPY /A/B *d1:path1***filename1.ext1**/A/B
+ d2:path2\\filename2.ext2/A/B +...

d1:path1 and *d2:path2* are valid disk drive names and directories.

filename1.ext1 and *filename2.ext2* are valid file names. Wild cards are allowed.

The three periods (**...**) represent additional files in the form *dx:pathx/ filenamex.extx*.

Special Terms:

The file being copied *from* is the *source file*. The names containing 1 and 2 are the source files.

The file being copied *to* is the *destination file*. This file is represented by a 0.

Switches

/V   *Verifies* that the copy has been recorded correctly.

The following switches have different effects on the source and the destination.

For the source file:

/A   Treats the file as an ASCII (text) file. The command copies all the information in the file up to, but not including, the first end-of-file marker (Ctrl-Z). Anything after the end-of-file marker is ignored.

/B   Copies the entire file (based on its size as listed in the directory) as if it were a program file *(binary1)*. Any end-of-file markers (Ctrl-Z) are treated as normal characters, and the EOF characters are copied.

For the destination file:

/A   Adds an end-of-file marker (Ctrl-Z) to the end of the ASCII text file after it is copied.

/B   Does not add the end-of-file marker to this binary file.

Notes

The meanings of the /A and /B switches depend on their positions in the line. The /A and /B switches affect the file that immediately precedes the switch and all that follow the switch until another /A or /B is encountered. When one of these switches is used before any file name, the switch affects all following files until contradicted by another /A or /B switch.

For more information, see Chapter 9.

Examples

To copy the file MEMO.TXT from the current directory on the default drive A to the directory C:\WORDS, type the following form:

COPY MEMO.TXT C:\WORDS

To copy the file MEMO.TXT from the current directory on drive C to the current directory on drive A, type the following form:

COPY MEMO.TXT A:

To copy the file MEMO.TXT from \WORDS on the current drive to drive A and change the name to MEMO.LTR, type the following form:

COPY \WORDS\MEMO.TXT A:MEMO.LTR

CTTY

V2, V3, V4—Internal

Changes the standard input and output device to an auxiliary console, or back from an auxiliary console to the keyboard and video display.

Syntax

CTTY device

device is the device you choose as the new standard input and output device. This name must be a valid DOS device name.

Switch

(None)

Notes

The CTTY command was designed so that a terminal or teleprinter, rather than the normal keyboard and video display, can be used for console input and output. This added versatility has little effect on most personal computer users.

Example

To change the standard input and standard output from the default console to the first communications port, type the form:

CTTY COM1

DATE   V1, V2, V3, V4—Internal

Displays and/or changes the system date.

Syntax

DATE *datestring*

datestring is in one of the following forms:

mm-dd-yy or *mm-dd-yyyy* for North America

dd-mm-yy or *dd-mm-yyyy* for Europe

yy-mm-dd or *yyyy-mm-dd* for East Asia

mm is a one- or two-digit number for the month (1 to 12).

dd is a one- or two-digit number for the day (1 to 31).

yy is a one- or two-digit number for the year (80 to 99). The 19 is assumed.

yyyy is a four-digit number for the year (1980 to 2099).

The delimiters between the day, month, and year can be hyphens, periods, or slashes. The result displayed will vary, depending on the country code set in the CONFIG.SYS file.

Switch

(None)

Notes

When you boot DOS, it issues the DATE and TIME commands to set your system clock. If an AUTOEXEC.BAT file is on the boot disk, DOS does not display a prompt for the date or time. You can include the DATE or TIME commands in the AUTOEXEC.BAT file if you want these functions to be set when DOS is booted. If your computer has a battery backed-up clock, as the AT-class computers do, you do not need to enter the date or time until the battery wears out.

DOS uses the date and time. When you create or update a file, DOS updates the directory with the date you entered. This date shows which copy is the latest revision of the file. The DOS BACKUP command uses the date in selecting files to back up.

For more information, see Chapter 3.

Example

To change the date, at the DOS prompt, type the following form:

DATE 12-15-89

If you type only **DATE**, you will see the set date and be prompted to enter a new date.

DEL

V1, V2, V3, V4—Internal

Deletes files from the disk.

DEL is an alternative form of the ERASE command and performs the same functions. See ERASE for a complete description.

DIR

V1, V2, V3, V4—Internal

Lists any or all files and subdirectories in a disk directory.

Syntax

DIR *d:path\filename.ext /P/W*

d: is the drive holding the disk you want to examine.

path is the path to the directory you want to examine.

filename.ext is a valid file name. Wild cards are permitted.

Switches

/P   Pauses when the screen is full and waits for you to press any key.

/W   Gives a wide (80-column) display of the file names. Information about file size, date, and time is not displayed.

Notes

The DIR command displays the following information:

Disk volume name, if any

Name of the directory (its complete path)

Name of each disk file or subdirectory

Number of files

Amount, in bytes, of free space on the disk

The DIR command, unless otherwise directed, shows also the following:

Number of bytes occupied by each file

Date/time of the file's creation/last update

The DIR command finds the disk files or subdirectories on the disk. This command shows only the files and subdirectories in the specified or the default directory.

For more information, see Chapter 4.

Examples

To examine the directory of the current disk and current directory, type the command:

DIR

To examine the \DOS directory on the current drive, and pause after each screen view of files, type the following form:

DIR \DOS /P

DISKCOMP   V1, V2, V3, V4—External

Compares two diskettes on a track-for-track, sector-for-sector basis

Syntax

*dc:pathc***DISKCOMP** *d1: d2: /1 /8*

dc:pathc are the disk drive and the directory that hold the command.

d1: and *d2:* are the disk drives that hold the diskettes to be compared. These drives may be the same or different.

Switches

/1   Compares only the first side of the diskette, even if the diskette or disk drive is double-sided.

/8   Compares only 8 sectors per track, even if the first diskette has a different number of sectors per track.

Notes

DISKCOMP compares, track-for-track, the contents of two compatible diskettes. Although you can use this command with any two compatible, or nearly compatible, diskettes, its most effective use is in comparing originals with diskettes that have been duplicated with DISKCOPY.

If you are using a diskette system and do not give a drive name, the first floppy disk drive (usually drive A) is used. If you specify only one drive, it is used for the source and destination disk. If, however, you are on a hard disk and do not specify a drive name, you will receive an error message:

```
Invalid drive specification
Specified drive does not exist,
or is non-removable
```

Only compatible diskettes should be compared. The two diskettes must be of the same capacity.

Do not use DISKCOMP with a disk drive on which you have used the ASSIGN, JOIN, or SUBST commands.

For more information, see Chapter 5.

Examples

If you want to compare the disk in drive A to the disk in drive B, type the form:

DISKCOMP A: B:

If you have only one floppy disk drive, but must compare two diskettes, you can type the form:

DISKCOMP A: A:

or the form

DISKCOMP A:

DISKCOPY

Copies the entire contents of one diskette to another on a track-for-track basis, making an exact duplicate. DISKCOPY works only with diskettes.

Syntax

> *dc:pathc***DISKCOPY** *d1: d2: /1*

dc:pathc are the disk drive and the directory that hold command.

d1: is the floppy disk drive that holds the source diskette.

d2: is the floppy disk drive that holds the destination diskette.

Switch

> */1* Copies only the first side of the diskette.

Special Terms:

The diskette you are copying from is the *source* or first diskette.

The diskette you are copying to is the *destination* or second diskette.

Notes

DISKCOPY makes identical copies of diskettes. The command automatically evaluates the size of the source diskette and makes an exact copy of it on another disk drive. If the destination diskette is not formatted or is formatted differently, DISKCOPY reformats the diskette to the same size as the source diskette. For example, if the source diskette is double-sided with nine sectors per track, and the destination diskette is single-sided with eight sectors per track, DISKCOPY reformats the destination diskette and makes it double-sided with nine sectors per track. Then the information is copied to the destination diskette.

If you give only one valid floppy disk drive name, this drive is used as both the source and destination for the copy, provided your system has only a single floppy disk drive. If your system has two floppy disk drives, giving only one valid disk drive name results in the message:

```
Invalid drive specification error.
```

You can use DISKCOPY to copy only disks with the same capacity. You cannot, for example, disk copy a 360K disk to a 1.2M disk.

For more information, see Chapter 5.

Examples

If you want a duplicate of the disk in drive A in drive B, type the form:

DISKCOPY A: B:

If you have only one floppy disk drive, but must duplicate two diskettes, you can type the form:

DISKCOPY A: A:

or the form:

DISKCOPY A:

ERASE   V1, V2, V3, V4—Internal

Removes one or more files from the directory.

Syntax

You can use the command form:

ERASE *d:path***filename.ext**

or the form:

DEL *d:path***filename.ext**

With DOS V4, you can add the /P switch in the form:

ERASE *d:path***filename.ext** */P*

or with its alternative command:

DEL *d:path***filename.ext** */P*

d:path are the disk drive and the directory holding the file(s) to be erased.

filename.ext is the name of the file to be erased. Wild cards are allowed.

Switch

/P   With DOS V4, this switch prompts you before erasing the file with the message `filename.ext, Delete (Y/N)?`

Notes

ERASE, or its short form DEL (delete), removes files. The directory entry for each erased file is altered so that DOS knows the file is not in use. The space occupied by each file erased from the disk is freed.

If you specify *.*, or no file name, when you give a disk drive name and/or path name, DOS displays the following prompt:

```
Are you sure (Y/N)?
```

If you answer Y, all files in the specified directory are erased; If you answer N, no files are erased.

You cannot ERASE either the current (.) or the parent (..) directory from a subdirectory. To remove a directory, you must use RMDIR.

For more information, see Chapter 9.

Examples

To erase the file MEMO.TXT, type the following form:

ERASE MEMO.TXT

or the alternative command form:

DEL MEMO.TXT

To erase all the files in the directory C:\MEMOS, type the form:

ERASE C:\MEMOS

or the form:

DEL C:\MEMOS

To erase all the files in C:\MEMOS using DOS V4 and be prompted before each file is erased, type the form:

ERASE C:\MEMOS /P

or this form:

DEL C:\MEMOS /P

EXE2BIN   V1.1, V2, V3—External

Changes suitably formatted .EXE files into .BIN or .COM files.

Syntax

*dc:pathc***EXE2BIN** *d1:path1***filename1.ext1**
d2:path2\filename2.ext2

dc:pathc are the disk drive and the directory that hold the command.

d1:path1 are the disk drive and the directory holding the file to be converted.

filename1.ext1 is the root name and extension of the file to be converted.

d2:path2 are the disk drive and the directory for the output file.

filename2.ext2 is the root name and extension of the output file.

Special Terms:

The file to be converted is the *source* file.

The output file is the *destination* file.

Switch

(None)

Notes

EXE2BIN is a programming utility that converts .EXE (executable) program files to .COM or .BIN (binary image) files. The resulting program takes less disk space and loads faster. This conversion, however, may be a disadvantage in future versions of DOS. Unless you use a compiler-based language, you may never use this command.

For further information about EXE2BIN, see the DOS *Technical Reference* manual.

EXIT   V2, V3, V4—Internal

Leaves a secondary command processor and returns to the primary one.

Syntax

EXIT

Switch

(None)

Notes

This command has no effect if a secondary command processor is not loaded or was loaded with the /P switch.

FASTOPEN

V3.3, V4—External

Keeps directory information in memory so that DOS can quickly find frequently needed files.

Syntax

> *dc:pathc***FASTOPEN d:**=*nnn*...

For DOS V4, additional syntax is as follows:

> *dc:pathc***FASTOPEN d:**=*(nnn,mmm)*... /X

dc:pathc are the disk drive and the directory that hold the command.

d: is the name of the disk drive containing directory information to be held in memory.

nnn is the number of directory entries to be held in memory (10 to 999).

mmm is the number of fragmented entries for the drive (1 to 999).

... designates additional disk drives in the forms **d:**=*nnn* or **d:**=*(nnn,mmm)*.

Switch

> /X Tells DOS to use expanded memory to store the information buffered by FASTOPEN.

Notes

FASTOPEN was added to DOS V3.3 and retained in DOS V4. This command caches directory information on files and can be used on any disk drive. The value of using the command on a RAM disk is questionable, however.

FASTOPEN works by keeping directory information in memory. Because disk buffers already hold the file allocation table information, FASTOPEN allows DOS to search memory for a file or a subdirectory entry, to locate quickly the corresponding FAT entry, and to open the file. If you have many files and use FASTOPEN effectively, you can increase DOS's performance significantly.

If you give *nnn*, the value must be between 10 and 999, inclusively. FASTOPEN's minimum value is 10 or the maximum level of your deepest directory plus 1, whichever value is greater.

The sum of *nnn* for all successful FASTOPEN commands cannot exceed 999.

For more information, see Chapter 13.

Examples

To keep in memory the location of up to 90 files residing on drive C, use the following form:

FASTOPEN C:=90

With DOS V4, to track as many as 90 files in memory from drive C that may be fragmented, you can use the following form:

FASTOPEN C:=(90,10)

FC

Compares two sets of disk files.

Syntax

*dc:pathc***FC** */A /B /C /L /LB x /N /T /W /n*
*d1:path1***filename1.ext1** *d2:path2***filename2.ext2**

dc:pathc are the disk drive and the directory that hold the command.

d1:path1 are the drive and the directory containing the first set of files to be compared.

filename1.ext1 is the file name for the first set of files. Wild cards are allowed.

d2:path2 are the drive and the directory containing the second set of files to be compared.

filename2.ext2 is the file name for the second set of files. Wild cards are allowed.

Special Terms:

d1:path1\\filename1.ext1 is the *primary* file set.

d2:path2\\filename2.ext2 is the *secondary* file set.

Switches

/A	Abbreviates ASCII comparison displays.
/B	Forces a binary file comparison.
/C	Causes DOS to disregard case of letters.
/L	Compares files in ASCII mode.

/LBx	Sets internal buffer to x lines.
/N	Displays line numbers for ASCII comparisons.
/T	Suppresses expansion of tabs to spaces.
/W	Compresses tabs and spaces.
/n	Sets the number of lines (1-9) to match (the default is 2).

Notes

FC is a file comparison program similar to COMP, but more powerful (see COMP in this Command Reference). With FC, you can compare either source or binary files.

Source files are batch files, or files that contain text, such as program listings. Binary files are program files, usually bearing the extension .COM or .EXE.

For more information, see Chapter 10.

Examples

To compare MEMO.LET to MEMO.BAK, type the form:

FC MEMO.LET MEMO.BAK

To find the proper syntax for File Compare, type the command:

FC

FIND   V2, V3, V4—External

Displays from the designated files all the lines matching or not matching (depending on the switches used) the specified string. This command can also display the line numbers.

Syntax

*dc:pathc***FIND** */V/C/N* **"string"** *d:path\\filename.ext...*

dc:pathc are the disk drive and the directory that hold the command.

string is the set of characters you want to find. As shown in the syntax line, you must enclose **string** in quotation marks.

d:path are the disk drive and the directory that hold the file.

filename.ext is the file you want to search.

... designates additional files to be searched.

Switches

/V   Displays all lines that do *not* contain **string**.

/C   Counts the number of times that **string** occurs and displays that number on the screen.

/N   Displays the number of the line that contains **string**, with the number placed in front of the line.

Notes

FIND is one of several filters provided with DOS V3 and V4. The command can find either lines that contain **string** or those that do not. FIND also can number and count lines rather than display them.

This filter is useful when it is combined with DOS I/O redirection. You can redirect the output of FIND to a file by using the > redirection symbol. Because FIND accepts a sequence of files to search, you do not have to redirect the input to FIND.

If you use switches with FIND, you must place them between the word **FIND** and the **string**. Most DOS commands require you to place switches at the end of the command line.

You must enclose **string** in quotes. To include the quote character in part of the string, use two quote characters together.

For more information, see Chapter 9.

Examples

To display each occurrence of the string *print* in the file HELP.TXT, type the form:

FIND "print" HELP.TXT

To find all files in a directory that were created or modified on July 9, 1989, type the following form:

DIR | FIND "7-09-89"

FORMAT   V1, V2, V3, V4—External

Initializes a disk to accept DOS information and files; also checks the disk for defective tracks and optionally places DOS on the floppy or hard disk.

Syntax

*dc:pathc***FORMAT d:** */S/1/8/V/B/4/N:ss/T:tt*

With DOS V4, you also may add the */V:label* and */F:size* switches:

*dc:pathc***FORMAT d:** */S/1/8/V/B/4/N:ss/T:tt /V:label /F:size*

dc:pathc are the disk drive and the directory that hold the command.

d: is a valid disk drive name.

Switches

/S	Places a copy of the operating system on the disk so that it can be booted.
/1	Formats only the first side of the floppy disk.
/8	Formats an eight-sector floppy disk (V1).
/V	Writes a volume label on the disk.
/B	Formats an eight-sector floppy disk, leaving the proper places in the directory for any operating system version, but does not place the operating system on the disk.
/4	Formats a floppy disk in a 1.2M disk drive for double-density (320K/360K) use.
/N:ss	Formats the disk with *ss* number of sectors, with *ss* ranging from 1 to 99.
/T:ttt	Formats the disk with *ttt* number of tracks per side, with *ttt* ranging from 1 to 999.
/F:size	Formats the disk to less than maximum capacity, with *size* designating one of the following values:

Drive	Allowable Values for *size*
160K, 180K	160, 160K, 160KB, 180, 180K, 180KB
320K, 360K	All of above, plus 320, 320K, 320KB, 360, 360K, 360KB
1.2M	All of above, plus 1200, 1200K, 1200KB, 1.2, 1.2M, 1.2MB
720K	720, 720K, 720KB
1.44M	All of above, plus 1440, 1440K, 1440KB, 1.44, 1.44M, 1.44MB

/V:label	Transfers volume label to formatted disk. Replaces label with 11-character name for new disk.

Notes

You must format each diskette or hard disk before using it. FORMAT actually performs several tasks. The program sets up each track and sector on the disk so that it accepts information. Special information is recorded, such as track headers (one for each track), sector headers (one for each sector), and CRC (cyclic redundancy check) bits to ensure that the recorded information is accurate.

FORMAT destroys information previously recorded on the diskette or hard disk, so do not FORMAT a diskette or hard disk that contains useful information.

For more information, see Chapter 6.

Examples

To format the disk in drive A, type the following form:

FORMAT A:

To format the disk in drive A and transfer DOS to the disk, type the following form:

FORMAT A: /S

To format a 720K diskette in a 1.44M drive A, type the following form:

FORMAT A: /N:9 /T:80

With DOS V4, type the form:

FORMAT A: /F:720

GRAFTABL

V3, V4—External

Loads into memory the tables of additional character sets to be displayed on the Color/Graphics Adapter (CGA)

Syntax

*dc:pathc***GRAFTABL** *codepage /STATUS ?*

dc:pathc are the disk drive and the directory that hold the command.

codepage is the three-digit number of the code page for the display.

Switches

/STATUS   Shows the current active code page.

?   Displays instructions for GRAFTABL.

Notes

The IBM Color/Graphics Adapter in graphics mode smears characters in the 128-to-255 range of ASCII characters. National-language characters and many graphics characters are in this range. GRAFTABL produces a legible display of these ASCII characters.

GRAFTABL does not affect characters in the A/N (alphanumeric), or text, mode. GRAFTABL should be used only on systems that have the Color/Graphics Adapter.

Examples

To load a table of graphics characters in memory, type the form:

GRAFTABL

To display the current code page table in memory, type the form:

GRAFTABL /STATUS

or the shorter form:

GRAFTABL /STA

GRAPHICS   V2, V3, V4—External

Prints the graphics-screen contents on a suitable printer.

Syntax

*dc:pathc***GRAPHICS** *printer /R /B /LCD*

With DOS V4, you can add the name of a file containing printer information:

*dc:pathc***GRAPHICS** *printer d:path\\filename.ext/R /B /LCD /PRINTBOX:x*

dc:pathc are the disk drive and the directory that hold the command.

printer is the type of IBM Personal Computer printer you are using. The printer can be one of the following:

COLOR1	Color printer with a black ribbon
COLOR4	Color printer with an RGB (red, green, blue, and black) ribbon, which produces four colors
COLOR8	Color printer with a CMY (cyan, magenta, yellow, and black) ribbon, which produces eight colors
COMPACT	Compact printer (not an option with V4.0 and V4.01)

GRAPHICS	Graphics printer and IBM ProPrinter
THERMAL	Convertible Printer

With DOS V4, you also may specify the following printer:

GRAPHICSWIDE	Graphics Printer and IBM ProPrinter with 11-inch wide carriage

filename.ext is the name of the file containing printer information (DOS V4 only). If no file name is specified, DOS uses the name GRAPHICS.PRO.

Switches

/R	Reverses colors so that the image on the paper matches the screen—a white image on black background.
/B	Prints the background color of the screen. You can use this switch only when the printer type is COLOR4 or COLOR8.
/LCD	Prints the image as displayed on the PC Convertible's LCD display.
/PRINTBOX:x	Prints the image and uses the print box size *id* represented by *x*. This value must match the first entry of a Printbox statement in the printer profile (DOS V4 only), such as *lcd* or *std*.

Notes

The GRAPHICS command enhances your print screen capability. Normally, when you press Shift-PrtSc or Print Screen, a copy of the screen is sent to your printer. If, however, the screen is displaying graphics, you cannot send a copy of the screen to the printer. With GRAPHICS loaded in memory, you are able to send graphics screens to the printer by pressing the key to print the screen.

Example

To load GRAPHICS in memory so that you can print a graphics screen on an IBM Graphics printer or compatible, type the command:

GRAPHICS

JOIN
V3.1, V3.2, V3.3, V4—External

Produces a single directory structure by connecting one disk drive to a subdirectory of another disk drive.

Syntax

To connect disk drives, use the following form:

> *dc:pathc***JOIN d1:** *d2:***dirname**

To disconnect disk drives, use this form of the command:

> *dc:pathc***JOIN d1: /D**

To show currently connected drives, use the following form:

> *dc:pathc***JOIN**

dc:pathc are the disk drive and the directory that hold the command.

d1: is the disk drive to be connected. DOS calls this drive the *guest disk drive.*

d2: is the disk drive to which **d1:** is to be connected. DOS calls *d2:* the *host disk drive.*

\\dirname is a subdirectory in the root directory of *d2:*, the host drive. DOS calls **\\dirname** the *host subdirectory.* **\\dirname** holds the connection to **d1:**, the guest drive.

Switch

/D   Disconnects the specified guest disk drive from its host.

Notes

The JOIN command, introduced with DOS V3.1, combines two disks into a single disk. The guest disk logically (apparently) becomes a subdirectory to the host disk.

JOIN does not affect the guest disk drive, only the way you access the files on that disk drive. You cannot exceed the maximum number of files in the guest disk's root directory. In the host subdirectory, size of a single file cannot exceed the guest disk's size. Similarly, a single file cannot span more than one disk.

Use the JOIN command with caution. When a JOIN is active, certain DOS commands work differently and some should not be used at all. While joined, the guest disk drive appears to be a host subdirectory. You cannot issue a DIR or CHKDSK command using the letter of the guest disk drive. You must first break the connection, then use DIR or CHKDSK on the former guest.

You must specify the host subdirectory name. This subdirectory must be a level-one subdirectory; that is, it must belong to the root directory of the host disk drive and not to another subdirectory. If the host subdirectory does not exist, JOIN creates one. If the subdirectory exists, it must be empty (it must have only the entries **.** and **..**), or DOS displays an error message and aborts the connection. When you break the connection, the newly created subdirectory remains. You can use this subdirectory later for another JOIN command or delete the subdirectory by issuing the RMDIR command.

For more information, see Chapter 13.

Examples

To join the diskette in drive A to C:\MNT, type the following form:

JOIN A: C:\MNT

To display the current join status, type the following command:

JOIN

JOIN displays the current assignments. If the preceding example is in effect, DOS displays this message:

```
A: => C:\MNT
```

To disconnect drive A from the JOIN to C:\MNT, type the following form:

JOIN A: /D

KEYB   V2, V3, V4—External

Changes the keyboard layout and characters to one of five languages other than American English.

Syntax

To change the current keyboard layout, use the following form:

*dc:pathc***KEYB** *keycode, codepage, d:path\\KEYBOARD.SYS*

To specify a particular keyboard identification code, use this form:

*dc:pathc***KEYB** *keycode, codepage, d:path\\KEYBOARD.SYS /ID:code*

To display the current values for KEYB, use the following form:

*dc:pathc***KEYB**

dc:pathc are the disk drive and the directory that hold the command.

keycode is the two-character keyboard code for your location.

codepage is the three-digit code page that will be used (437, 850, 860, 863, or 865).

d:path\\KEYBOARD.SYS are the drive and the path to the KEYBOARD.SYS file.

Switch

/ID:code   is the code for the enhanced keyboard that you want.

Notes

Previously, KEYB was a set of five programs, featuring one for each of the five national languages that DOS supported. DOS V3.3 codified the five programs into one program.

When KEYB is active, it reassigns some alphanumeric characters to different keys and introduces new characters. The new layout and characters vary among the supported languages.

If you do not specify a *codepage*, DOS uses the default code page for your country. The default code page is established by the COUNTRY directive in CONFIG.SYS or, if the COUNTRY directive is not used, by the DOS default code page. KEYB attempts to activate the default code page.

Example

To display the current keyboard code and code page, type the command:

KEYB

LABEL   V3, V4—External

Creates, changes, or deletes a volume label for a disk.

Syntax

*dc:pathc***LABEL** *d:volume_label*

dc:pathc are the disk drive and the directory that hold the command.

d: is the disk drive whose label will be changed.

volume_label is the disk's new volume label.

Switch

(None)

Notes

You can easily identify your disks by giving each one a *volume_label*, which is simply an electronic label for a disk. Volume labels appear when you use the DIR, TREE, or CHKDSK commands.

Do not use LABEL on a disk in any drive that is affected by the SUBST or ASSIGN commands, because DOS labels the "real" disk in the disk drive instead.

For more information, see Chapter 6.

Examples

To change the current label to MY_DISK, type the form:

LABEL MY_DISK

To display the current label of the disk in drive B and have the option to change the label, type the command:

LABEL B:

MEM   **V4—External**

Displays the amount of used and unused memory, allocated and open memory areas, and all programs currently in the system.

Syntax

*dc:pathc***MEM** */PROGRAM /DEBUG*

dc:pathc are the disk drive and the directory that hold the command.

Switches

/PROGRAM	Displays programs that are in memory, including the address, name, size, and type of each file for every program. Also shows current free memory.
/DEBUG	Displays programs that are in memory, including the address, name, size, and type of each file for every program. Also displays system device drivers and installed device drivers, as well as all unused memory.

Notes

You can use MEM to display information on how memory is being used. MEM displays statistics for conventional memory and also for extended and expanded memory if the latter two are available. You cannot specify /PROGRAM and /DEBUG at the same time.

For more information, see Chapter 13.

Example

To display the current memory usage, type the command:

MEM

MKDIR or MD

V2, V3, V4—Internal

Creates a subdirectory.

Syntax

MKDIR *d:path***dirname**

or the short form:

MD *d:path***dirname**

d: is the disk drive for the subdirectory.

path\\ indicates the path to the directory that will hold the subdirectory.

dirname is the subdirectory you are creating.

Switch

(None)

Notes

MKDIR, or the short form MD, makes subdirectories. You can create as many subdirectories as you want, but remember that DOS accepts no more than 63 characters, including backslashes, for the path name. Do not create too many levels of subdirectories with long names, or the path to the directory may exceed 63 characters.

You cannot create a directory name that is identical to a file name in the current directory. For example, if you have a file named MYFILE in the current directory, you cannot create the subdirectory MYFILE in this directory. If the file is named MYFILE.TXT, however, the names will not conflict when you create the MYFILE subdirectory.

For more information, see Chapter 8.

Examples

To create the subdirectory \\WORDS on the current drive, type the form:

MKDIR \\WORDS

or the short form:

MD \WORDS

MODE

V1, V2, V3, V4—External

This command has numerous forms that will be treated in this reference as separate commands. Generally, MODE sets the printer characteristics, keyboard rate, the video display, and the Asynchronous Communications Adapter. This command controls redirection of printing between parallel and serial printers. MODE also controls code page switching for the console and printer. Other functions differ according to DOS implementation.

MODE
PRINTER

V1, V2, V3, V4—External

Sets the IBM printer characteristics.

Syntax

*dc:pathc***MODE LPTx:***cpl,lpi,P*

With DOS V4 or V4.01, you can use the following form:

*dc:pathc***MODE LPTx** *COLS=cpl LINES=lpi RETRY=ret*

dc:pathc are the disk drive and the directory that hold the command.

x: is the printer number (1, 2, or 3). The colon is optional.

cpl is the number of characters per line (80, 132).

lpi is the number of lines per inch (six or eight).

P specifies continuous retries on time-out errors.

ret tells DOS what to do when a time-out error occurs. You can choose from the following options:

ret	*Action*
E	Return the error when port is busy (default).
B	Return busy when port is busy.
R	Return ready when port is busy (infinite retry).
NONE	Take no action.

471

Switch

(None)

Notes

You must specify a printer number, but all other parameters are optional, including the colon after the printer number.

If you do not want to change a parameter, enter a comma for that parameter.

The characters-per-line and lines-per-inch portions of the command affect only IBM and Epson printers and others that use Epson-compatible control codes.

Examples

To set the printer on LPT1 to 132 characters per line, 8 lines per inch, and keep checking for the printer's busy condition, type the following form:

MODE LPT1:132,8,P

With DOS V4, you can use the following form:

MODE LPT1 COLS=132 LINES=8 RETRY=B

MODE
DISPLAY TYPE   V3, V4—External

Switches the active display adapter between the monochrome display and a graphics adapter/array (Color/Graphics Adapter, Enhanced Color/Graphics Adapter, or Video Graphics Array) on a two-display system, and sets the graphics adapter/array characteristics.

Syntax

*dc:pathc***MODE dt**,*y*

or the form:

*dc:pathc***MODE** *dt*, **s**, *T*

With DOS V4.0 or V4.01, you can use the following form:

*dc:pathc***MODE CON**: **COLS**=*x* **LINES**=*y*

dc:pathc are the disk drive and the directory that hold the command.

dt is the display type, which may be one of the following:

40   Sets the display to 40 characters per line for the graphics display.

80   Sets the display to 80 characters per line for the graphics display.

BW40   Makes the graphics display the active display and sets the mode to 40 characters per line, black and white (color disabled).

BW80   Makes the graphics display the active display and sets the mode to 80 characters per line, black and white (color disabled).

CO40   Makes the graphics display the active display and sets the mode to 40 characters per line (color enabled).

CO80   Makes the graphics display the active display and sets the mode to 80 characters per line (color enabled).

MONO   Makes the monochrome display the active display.

s shifts the graphics display right (**R**) or left (**L**) one character.

T requests alignment of the graphics display screen with a one-line test pattern.

x specifies the number of columns to display; 40 or 80 columns are possible.

y specifies the number of lines on the display, applicable only to EGA and VGA displays. EGA values are 25 and 43; VGA adds the value 50.

Switch

(None)

Notes

For the first form of the command, you must enter the display type (**dt**); all other parameters are optional. For the second form of the command, you must enter the shift parameter **s** (which is an R or an L for right or left); the display type (dt) and test pattern (T) are optional.

The **s** (R or L) parameter works only with the Color/Graphics Adapter; the display does not shift if you use this command with any other adapter. The T parameter, conversely, causes the test pattern to be displayed with any graphics adapter (Convertible, EGA, or VGA). If you use the parameter with the Monochrome Adapter, DOS responds with an error message.

Color is not displayed automatically when you use the CO40 or CO80 parameter for the display type. Programs that use color, however, can be displayed in color.

Examples

To set your 80-column color monitor into Black and White mode, type the form:

MODE BW80

If you have a VGA display and want to display color, with 80 columns and 50 lines of text, type the form:

MODE CO80,50

Or, if you have DOS V4, type the form:

MODE CON COLS=80 LINES=50

MODE
COMMUNICATIONS   V1.1, V2, V3, V3.3, V4—External

Controls the protocol characteristics of the Asynchronous Communications Adapter.

Syntax

*dc:pathc***MODE COMy***: **baud**, parity, databits, stopbits, P*

With DOS V4 or V4.01, you can use the following form:

*dc:pathc***MODE COMy***: **BAUD=baud** PARITY=parity DATA=databits STOP=stopbits RETRY=ret*

dc:pathc are the disk drive and the directory that hold the command.

y*:* is the adapter number (1, 2, 3, or 4); the colon after the number is optional.

baud is the baud rate (110, 150, 300, 600, 1200, 2400, 4800, 9600, or 19200).

parity is the parity checking (None, Odd, or Even; in DOS versions before V4.0, use N, O, E, or M for Mark and S for Space).

databits is the number of data bits (7 or 8; 5 or 6 in V4).

stopbits is the number of stop bits (1 or 2; 1.5 in V4).

P represents continuous retries on time-out errors.

ret tells DOS what to do when a time-out error occurs. You can choose from the following options:

ret	*Action*
E	Return the error when port is busy (default).
B	Return busy when port is busy.
R	Return ready when port is busy (infinite retry).
NONE	Take no action.

Switch

(None)

Notes

You must enter the adapter's number, followed by a space and a baud rate. If you type the optional colon, it must immediately follow the adapter number. All other parameters are optional.

If you do not want to change a parameter, enter a comma for that value.

The 19200 baud rate is valid only for PS/2 computers. If you try to use the 19200 baud rate on a PC or compatible, DOS displays an `Invalid parameter` message and takes no further action.

If the adapter is set for continuous retries (P or RETRY=B) and the device is not ready, the computer appears to be locked up. You can abort this loop by pressing Ctrl-Break.

Examples

To set up your communications port for 9600 baud, even parity, 8 databits, 1 stop bit and continuous retry, use the following form:

MODE COM1:9600,E,8,1,P

or the optional form:

MODE COM1:96,E,8,1,P

With DOS V4, you can use the form:

MODE COM1 BAUD=9600 PARITY=EVEN DATA=8 STOP=1 RETRY=B

MODE
SERIAL PRINTER
V2, V3, V4—External

Forces DOS to print to a serial printer rather than a parallel printer.

Syntax

*dc:pathc***MODE LPTx***: = ***COMy***:*

dc:pathc are the disk drive and the directory that hold the command.

x*:* is the parallel printer number (1, 2, or 3). The colon is optional.

y*:* is the Asynchronous Communications Adapter number (1, 2, 3 or 4).

Switch

(None)

Notes

This form of MODE is useful for systems that have only a serial printer. When used, the serial printer receives all the output usually sent to the system printer (assuming that the serial printer is connected to the first Asynchronous Communications Adapter). This output includes the print-screen (Shift-PrtSc) function.

Before you issue the MODE LPT=COMy command, use the MODE COMn: command to set up the serial adapter used for the serial printer.

Example

To redirect output meant for LPT1: to COM1:, first initialize COM1: with the previous MODE command. Then type the form:

MODE LPT1 = COM1

MODE
CODEPAGE PREPARE
V3.3, V4, V4.01—External

Determines the code pages to be used with a device.

Syntax

*dc:pathc***MODE device CODEPAGE PREPARE =
((codepage***, codepage,* **. . .)** *dp:pathp***pagefile.ext)**

or the form:

> *dc:pathc***MODE device CP PREP = ((codepage**, *codepage*, . . .**)**
> *dc:pathp***pagefile.ext***)*

dc:pathc are the disk drive and the directory that hold the command.

device is the device for which code page(s) will be chosen. You can select one of the following devices:

CON*:*   The console

PRN*:*   The first parallel printer

LPTx*:*   The first, second, or third parallel printer (**x** is 1, 2, or 3)

codepage is the number of the code page(s) to be used with the device. The following are valid numbers:

437	United States
850	Multilingual
860	Portugal
863	French Canadian
865	Denmark/Norway

The ellipsis (. . .) represents additional code pages.

dp:pathp are the disk drive and directory holding the code page information.

pagefile.ext is the file holding the code page (font) information. Currently, the DOS-provided code page files are as follows:

4201.CPI	IBM ProPrinter
4208.CPI	IBM Proprinter X24 and XL24
5202.CPI	IBM Quietwriter III Printer
EGA.CPI	EGA/VGA type displays
LCD.CPI	IBM Convertible LCD display

Switch

(None)

Notes

MODE CODEPAGE PREPARE is used to prepare code pages (fonts) for the console (keyboard and display) and the printers. You should issue this subcommand before the MODE CODEPAGE SELECT subcommand, except for the IBM Quietwriter III printer, which holds font information in cartridges. If the needed code page is in a cartridge and the code page has been specified to the PRINTER.SYS driver, no PREPARE command is needed.

Examples

To prepare the code pages 850, 863, and 865 for use with an EGA or VGA display, type the form:

MODE CON CODEPAGE PREPARE = ((850, 863, 865) C:\EGA.CPI)

For code pages 850 and 863 for an IBM ProPrinter Model 4201 attached to LPT1, type the form:

MODE LPT1 CP PREP = ((850, 863) C:\4201.CPI)

MODE
CODEPAGE SELECT   V3.3, V4, V4.01—External

Activates the code page used with a device.

Syntax

*dc:pathc***MODE device CODEPAGE SELECT = codepage**

or

*dc:pathc***MODE device CP SEL = codepage**

dc:pathc are the disk drive and the directory that hold the command.

device is the device for which code page(s) will be chosen. You can select one of the following devices:

CON:	The console
PRN:	The first parallel printer
LPTx:	The first, second, or third parallel printer (**x** is 1, 2, or 3)

codepage is the number of the code page(s) to be used with the device. The valid numbers are as follows:

437	United States
850	Multilingual
860	Portugal
863	French Canadian
865	Denmark/Norway

Switch

(None)

478

Notes

MODE CODEPAGE SELECT activates a currently prepared code page or reactivates a hardware code page. You can use MODE CODEPAGE SELECT only on these two types of code pages.

Examples

To activate the prepared 863 font for use with an EGA or VGA display, type the form:

MODE CON CODEPAGE SELECT = 863

To activate the prepared 850 font for use with the printer attached to LPT1, type the form:

MODE LPT1 CP SEL = 850

MODE
CODEPAGE REFRESH V3.3, V4, V4.01—External

Reloads and reactivates the code page used with a device.

Syntax

*dc:pathc***MODE device CODEPAGE REFRESH**

or the short form:

*dc:pathc***MODE device CP REF**

dc:pathc are the disk drive and the directory that hold the command.

device is the device for which code page(s) will be chosen. You can select one of the following devices:

CON*:* The console

PRN*:* The first parallel printer

LPTx*:* The first, second, or third parallel printer (**x** is 1, 2, or 3)

Switch

(None)

Notes

MODE CODEPAGE REFRESH downloads, if necessary, and reactivates the currently selected code page on a device. Use this command after you turn on your printer or after a program corrupts the video display and leaves the console code page unusable. You do not give a code page to MODE CODEPAGE REFRESH, because the command uses the last selected code page for the device.

Examples

To reactivate the code page for the video display, type the form:

MODE CON: CODEPAGE REFRESH

or the short form:

MODE CON: CP REF

MODE
CODEPAGE STATUS   V3.3, V4, V4.01—External

Displays a device's code page status.

Syntax

*dc:pathc***MODE device CODEPAGE** */STATUS*

or the short form:

*dc:pathc***MODE device CP** */STA*

dc:pathc are the disk drive and the directory that hold the command.

device is the device for which code pages are chosen. You can select one of the following devices:

CON*:*   The console

PRN*:*   The first parallel printer

LPTx*:*   The first, second, or third parallel printer (**x** is 1, 2, or 3)

Switch

/STATUS   Displays the status of the device's code pages. If you prefer, you can use **/STA** rather than the complete **/STATUS.**

Notes

MODE CODEPAGE /STATUS shows the device's current code-page status.

MODE /STATUS displays the following information about the device:

a. The selected (active) code page, if one has been selected.

b. The hardware code page(s).

c. Any prepared code pages.

d. Any available positions for additional prepared code pages.

Here is a sample output for the command:

```
Active codepage for device CON is 437
hardware codepages:
    Codepage 437
prepared codepages:
    Codepage 850
    Codepage not prepared
MODE Status Codepage function completed
```

Examples

To display the status of the console's code page, type the form:

MODE CON CODEPAGE /STATUS

or the short form:

MODE CON CP

MODE
CONSOLE RATE/DELAY   V4—External

Adjusts the rate at which the keyboard repeats a character.

Syntax

*dc:pathc***MODE CON RATE=x DELAY=y**

dc:pathc are the disk drive and the directory that hold the command.

x is a value that specifies the character-repeat rate. You can select a value between 1 and 32.

y is a value that specifies the delay between the initial pressing of the key and the start of automatic character repetition. This value can be 1, 2, 3, or 4, representing delays of 1/4 second, 1/2 second, 3/4 second, and one full second, respectively.

Switch

(None)

Notes

On some keyboards, you may want characters to repeat faster when you hold down a key. On others, however, the keys may repeat too fast or may start repeating too quickly. Use this command to vary the speed and delay of key repeat.

Example

To set the keyboard rate to 10 and the delay to 2, enter the following form:

MODE CON RATE=10 DELAY=2

MODE
STATUS   V4—External

Displays the status of a specified device or of all devices that can be set by MODE.

Syntax

*dc:pathc***MODE** *device* /**STA***TUS*

dc:pathc are the disk drive and the directory that hold the command.

device is the optional device to be checked by MODE.

Switch

/**STA***TUS*   The mandatory switch to check the status of a device or devices. If you prefer, you can enter just /**STA** rather than the complete /**STATUS**.

Notes

This command enables you to see the status of any device that you normally set with MODE. Typing **MODE LPT1 /STA**, for example, displays the status of the first parallel port.

Examples

To display the current status of the console, type the following form:

MODE CON /STATUS

MORE

V2, V3, V4—External

Displays one screen of information from the standard input device and pauses while displaying the message —More—. When you press any key, MORE displays the next screen of information.

Syntax

*dc:pathc***MORE**

dc:pathc are the disk drive and the directory that hold the command.

Switch

(None)

Notes

MORE is a DOS filter that enables you to display information without manually pausing the screen.

MORE is similar to the TYPE command, but automatically pauses after each screen of information.

One screen of information is based on 40 or 80 characters per line and 23 lines per screen. MORE, however, does not always display 23 lines from the file. Rather, the command acts intelligently with long lines, wrapping those that exceed the display width (40 or 80 characters). If one of the file's lines takes 3 lines to display, MORE displays a maximum of 21 lines from the file, pauses, and shows the next screen of lines.

For more information, see Chapter 9.

Examples

To use redirection to display TEST.TXT one screen view at a time, type the following form:

MORE <TEST.TXT

To display a sorted directory one screen at a time, type the following form:

DIR | SORT | MORE

NLSFUNC

V3.3, V4—External

Supports extended country information and allows use of CHCP.

Syntax

> *dc:pathc***NLSFUNC** *d:path\\filename.ext*

dc:pathc are the disk drive and the directory that hold the command.

d:path are the disk drive and the directory holding the country information file.

filename.ext is the country information file. With DOS V3.3, this information is contained in the file COUNTRY.SYS.

Switch

(None)

Notes

NLSFUNC loads support for extended country information and enables you to use the CHCP (Change Code Page) command. When you load NLSFUNC, DOS increases in size by 2,672 bytes.

You must load NLSFUNC only if your programs use the extended country information that is available from DOS, or if you want to use the CHCP command to change code pages. Your program's documentation should tell you if NLSFUNC is required.

Examples

To load NLSFUNC, assuming that the file COUNTRY.SYS is in the root directory of your disk, type the following command:

NLSFUNC

To load NLSFUNC when COUNTRY.SYS is in the directory C:\DOS, type the following form:

NLSFUNC C:\DOS\COUNTRY.SYS

PATH   V2, V3, V4—Internal

Tells DOS to search specific directories on specified drives if a program or batch file is not found in the current directory.

Syntax

> **PATH** *d1:path1;d2:path2;d3:path3;...*

d1:, *d2:*, and *d3:* are valid disk drive names.

path1, *path2*, and *path3* are valid path names to the commands you want to run while in any directory.

The ellipsis (...) represents additional disk drives and path names.

Switch

(None)

Notes

PATH is a useful command in hierarchical directories. Directories containing utility programs, system programs, or batch files can be established and used from anywhere on the disk. PATH enables the directories that you specify to be searched for your programs; you do not need to type the path each time.

Always specify an absolute path that starts with a disk's root directory (\ ) rather than a relative path starting with the current directory. By specifying an absolute path, you need not be concerned with the current directory.

If you specify more than one set of paths, the following rules apply:

   a. The path sets must be separated by semicolons.
   b. The search for the programs or batch files is made in the order in which you give the path sets. First, the current directory is searched. Then *d1:path1* is searched, then *d2:path2*, *d3:path3*, and so on, until the command or batch file is found.

If you give invalid information when assigning a path, such as an invalid disk drive, a bad delimiter, or a deleted path, DOS does not display an error message. When the path is being searched for a program or batch file, DOS skips a bad or invalid path. If, however, you give an invalid disk drive name, DOS displays an `Invalid drive in search path` message when it searches the path for a program or batch file.

PATH affects the execution of only program (.COM or .EXE) files or batch (.BAT) files. This command does not work with data files, text files, or program overlays.

For more information, see Chapter 7.

Examples

To set a search path for C:\DOS, C:\UTILS, and the root directory, type the following form:

PATH C:\DOS;C:\UTILS;C:

To display the current path setting, type the following command:

PATH

PRINT

V2, V3, V4—External

Prints a list of files while the computer performs other tasks.

Syntax

> dc:pathc**PRINT** /D:device /B:bufsiz /M:maxtick /Q:maxfiles
> /S:timeslice /U:busytick d1:path1\\filename1.ext1 /P/T/C
> d2:path2\\filename2.ext2/P/T/C . . .

dc:pathc\\ are the disk drive and the directory that hold the command.

d1: and d2: are valid disk drive names.

path1\\ and path2\\ are valid path names to the files for printing.

filename1.ext1 and filename2.ext2 are the files you want to print. Wild cards are allowed.

The ellipsis (. . .) represents additional file names in the form dx:pathx\\filenamex.extx.

Switches

You can specify any one of the following switches, but only the first time you start PRINT:

/D:device	Specifies the device to be used for printing. *device* is any valid DOS device name. (You must list this switch first whenever you use it.)
/B:bufsiz	Specifies the size of the memory buffer to be used while the files are printing. *bufsiz* can be any number from 1 to 16,384.
/M:maxtick	Specifies in clock ticks the maximum amount of time that PRINT has for sending characters to the printer every time PRINT gets a turn. (A tick is the smallest measure of time used on PCs. A tick happens every 1/18.2 [0.0549] seconds.) *maxtick* can be any number from 1 to 255. Default is 2.
/Q:maxfiles	Specifies the number of files that can be in the queue (line) for printing. *maxfiles* can be any number from 4 to 32. Default is 10.
/S:timeslice	Specifies the number of slices in each second. *timeslice* can be a number from 1 to 255. Default is 10.
/U:busytick	Specifies in clock ticks the maximum amount of time for the program to wait for a busy or unavailable printer. *busytick* can be any number from 1 to 255.

You can specify any one of the following switches whenever you use PRINT:

/P   Queues up the files (*places* in the line) for printing.

/T   *Terminates* the background printing of any or all files, including any file currently being printed.

/C   *Cancels* the background printing of the file(s).

Notes

PRINT controls the background printing feature of DOS V3 and V4. The command has been significantly improved since DOS V2.

During the *background printing* process, DOS orders a specified printer to print a disk-based file while the computer itself performs a separate task, such as running a program. Because the computer must devote most of its time and attention to the non-printing task, that task is in the *foreground*. PRINT gets less attention from the computer, and therefore is called a *background* task. When the cursor sits at the system prompt (A>), PRINT receives most of the computer's time.

You can specify any of the switches from the first set (/D, /B, /M, /Q, /S, and /U) only when PRINT is first used. If you give the /D switch, you must make it the first switch on the line. You can give the remaining five switches in any sequence before you specify a file name.

For more information, see Chapter 13.

Examples

To enable background printing to the LPT1 device, type the following form:

PRINT /D:LPT1

Once PRINT is enabled, to start the files MEMO.TXT, LETTER.TXT, and REPORT.PRN printing, type the following form:

PRINT MEMO.TXT /P LETTER.TXT REPORT.PRN

If the three files begin printing, to cancel LETTER.TXT, type the following form:

PRINT LETTER.TXT /C

To cancel all jobs that are queued for printing type this form:

PRINT /T

PROMPT

V2, V3, V4—Internal

Customizes the DOS system prompt (A>, the A prompt).

Syntax

PROMPT *promptstring*

promptstring is the text to be used for the new system prompt.

Special Terms:

A *meta-string* produces a prompt that you designate. The meta-string is comprised of a $ character, followed by a single character. To use certain characters (for example, the < or the > I/O redirection symbols), you must enter the appropriate meta-string to place the desired characters in your *promptstring*. Otherwise, DOS immediately attempts to interpret the character.

All meta-strings begin with the dollar sign ($) and have two characters, including the symbol $. The following list contains meta-string characters and their meanings:

Character	Meaning
$	$, the dollar sign
_ (underscore)	Line feed, (moves to the first position of the next line)
b	|, the vertical *b*ar
e	The *E*scape character, CHR$(27)
d	The *d*ate, like the DATE command
h	The backspace character, CHR$(8), which erases the previous character
g	>, the *g*reater-than character
l	<, the *l*ess-than character
n	The curre*n*t disk drive
p	The current disk drive and *p*ath, including the current directory
q	=, the e*q*ual sign
t	The *t*ime, like the TIME command
v	The DOS *v*ersion number
Any other	Nothing or null; the character is ignored

Switch

(None)

Notes

The PROMPT command gives users control over the DOS system prompt. With hierarchical directories, you will find it helpful to display the current path on your disk drive. For that reason, you may want to set the system prompt to the following:

PROMPT $p

Any text entered for *promptstring* becomes the new system prompt. You can enter special characters by using the meta-strings. If you do not enter the *promptstring*, the standard system prompt reappears (A>).

For more information, see Chapter 13.

Examples

To set the current prompt to display the date, then the path in brackets on the next line, type the form:

PROMPT D_[$P]

To return the prompt to the default (C> for example), type the command:

PROMPT

RECOVER   V2, V3, V4—External

Recovers a file with bad sectors or a file from a disk with a damaged directory.

Syntax

To recover a file, use the following form:

*dc:pathc***RECOVER** *d:path***filename.ext**

To recover a disk with a damaged directory, use this form:

*dc:pathc***RECOVER d:**

dc:pathc are the disk drive and the directory that hold the command.

d:path are the disk drive and the directory holding the damaged file.

filename.ext is the file to be recovered.

Switch

(None)

Notes

RECOVER attempts to recover either a file with a bad sector or a disk with a directory containing a bad sector. DOS tells you if a file has bad sectors by displaying a disk-error message when you try to use the file. To recover a file with one or more bad sectors, type **RECOVER d:filename.ext**.

If the damaged file is a program file, the program probably cannot be used. If the file is a data or text file, some information can be recovered. Because RECOVER reads the entire file, make sure that you use a text editor or word processor to eliminate any garbage.

Example

To recover the file MEMO.TXT that contains a few bad sectors, type the form:

RECOVER MEMO.TXT

RENAME or REN   V1, V2, V3, V4—Internal

Changes the name of the disk file(s).

Syntax

RENAME *d:path***filename1.ext1 filename2.ext2**

or the short form:

REN *d:path***filename1.ext1 filename2.ext2**

d:path\ are the disk drive and the directory holding the file(s) to be renamed.

filename1.ext1 is the file's current name. Wild cards are allowed.

filename2.ext2 is the file's new name. Wild cards are allowed.

Switch

(None)

Notes

RENAME, or the short form REN, changes the name of a file on the disk. Because you are renaming an established disk file, the file's drive or path designation is given with the old name so that DOS will know which file to rename.

Wild-card characters are acceptable in either the old or the new name. Be careful, however, when you use these characters, because they can be troublesome. You may not be able to rename all files, as DOS may try to use duplicate names.

For more information, see Chapter 9.

Examples

To rename the file MEMO.TXT to SMITH.MMO, type the form:

REN MEMO.TXT SMITH.MMO

To rename all the files in C:\LETTERS to change their extension from TXT to LTR, type the form:

REN C:\LETTERS*.LTR *.TXT

REPLACE   V3.2, V3.3, V4—External

Replaces files on one disk with files of the same name from another disk; adds files to a disk by copying them from another disk.

Syntax

*dc:pathc***REPLACE** *ds:paths***filenames**.*exts* **dd:***pathd* /A/P/R/S/W

With DOS V4, you can add a /U switch:

*dc:pathc***REPLACE** *ds:paths***filenames**.*exts* **dd:***pathd* /A/P/R/S/W/U

dc:pathc are the disk drive and the directory that hold the command.

ds:paths are the disk drive and directory holding the replacement file(s).

filenames.exts are the replacement files. Wild cards are allowed.

dd:*pathd* are the disk drive and the directory whose file(s) will be replaced.

In the fragment *ds:paths***filenames**.*exts*, *s* represents the *source*. The source is the file that will be added to a directory or that will replace an existing file in the directory.

In the fragment *dd:pathd*, *d* represents the *destination*. The destination can be either the file to be replaced or the disk and directory where a new file will be added. DOS refers to the destination as the *target*.

Switches

/A   *Adds* files from the source disk that do not exist on the destination disk.

/P   Displays a *prompt* asking if the file should be replaced or added to the destination.

/R   Replaces files on the destination disk even though the files' *read-only* attribute is on.

/S   Replaces all files with matching names in the current directory and its subordinate *subdirectories*. The /S switch does not work with the /A switch.

/W   Causes REPLACE to prompt and *wait* for the source floppy disk to be inserted.

/U   Replaces only those files of a date and time earlier than the source files (DOS V4).

Notes

The REPLACE command, added with DOS V3.2, is a modified COPY program that can selectively update or add files to one or more directories.

You can use this command to replace one or a few files that are duplicated in several subdirectories. You also can use the command to update a major applications program or even DOS itself. REPLACE is especially useful because it can search subdirectories for files to replace.

REPLACE replaces or adds files based on the matching of file names. The command disregards drive names, directory names, and file contents, searching only for the appropriate file names and extensions. REPLACE can quickly find older files and replace them with their updated versions.

For more information, see Chapter 9.

Examples

To search the current directory of drive A for files with a .COM extension, then copy over files with matching names in C:\DOS, type the following form:

REPLACE A:*.COM C:\DOS

Any .COM file on A is not copied if its name does not match a file in the directory C:\DOS.

To use the command above to replace only matching files in C:\DOS and any directories below C:\DOS, type the form:

REPLACE A:*.COM C:\DOS /S

RESTORE

V2, V3, V4—External

Restores one or more backup files from one disk onto another. This command complements BACKUP.

Syntax

> *dc:pathc***RESTORE d1:** *d2:path\\filename.ext /S /P /M /N*
> */B:date /A:date /L:time /E:time*

dc:pathc are the disk drive and the directory that hold the command.

d1: is the disk drive holding the backup files.

d2: is the disk drive that will receive the restored files.

path is the path to the directory that will receive the restored files.

filename.ext is the file that you want to restore. Wild cards are allowed.

Switches

/S Restores files in the current directory and all its subordinate *subdirectories*. When this switch is given, RESTORE re-creates any necessary subdirectories that have been removed, and then restores the files in the re-created subdirectories.

/P Causes RESTORE to *prompt* for your approval before restoring a file that was changed since the last backup or before restoring a file that is marked as read-only.

/M Restores all files that have been *modified* or deleted since the backup set was made.

/N Restores all files that *no longer* exist on the destination.

/B:date Restores all files that were created or modified on or *before* the *date* you specify.

/A:date Restores all files that were created or modified on or *after* the *date* you specify.

/L:time Restores all files that were created or modified at or *later* than the *time* you specify.

/E:time Restores all files that were created or modified at or *earlier* than the *time* you specify.

Notes

BACKUP and RESTORE V3.3, V4, and V4.01 are modified from earlier versions. BACKUP V3.3 and later versions place all backed-up files in one larger file and maintain a separate information file on the same disk. In V3.3 and later, RESTORE handles the new and old backup file formats, which means that these later versions will restore backups created by any version of BACKUP.

You can use the RESTORE command only on files that you have saved with the BACKUP command.

RESTORE prompts you to insert the backup diskettes in order. If you insert a diskette out of order, RESTORE prompts you to insert the correct diskette.

Be cautious when you restore files that were backed up while an ASSIGN, SUBST, or JOIN command was in effect. When you use RESTORE, clear any existing APPEND, ASSIGN, SUBST, or JOIN commands. Do not use RESTORE /M or RESTORE /N while APPEND /X is in effect. RESTORE attempts to search the directories for modified or missing files. APPEND tricks RESTORE into finding files in the paths specified to the APPEND command. RESTORE then might act on the wrong files and fail to restore files as you want. Give the **APPEND;** command to disable APPEND.

For more information, see Chapter 10.

Examples

To restore an entire backup set of disks from drive A to drive C, type the form:

RESTORE A: C:\ /S

To restore the file MEMO.TXT from the backup disks in drive A to C:\LETTERS, type the form:

RESTORE A: C:\LETTERS\MEMO.TXT

To restore all files from the disks in drive B to C:\REPORTS, type this form:

RESTORE B: C:\REPORTS

RMDIR or RD   V2, V3, V4—Internal

Removes a subdirectory.

Syntax

RMDIR *d:***path**

or the short form:

RD *d:***path**

d: is the drive holding the subdirectory.

path is the path to the subdirectory. The last path name is the subdirectory you want to delete.

Switch

(None)

Notes

RMDIR, or the short form RD, removes subdirectories from the disk. RMDIR is the opposite of MKDIR (make directory).

When you remove a subdirectory, it must be empty except for the current directory file (.) and any parent directory files (..). You cannot remove the current directory. To do this, you must first move to another directory, then use RMDIR to remove the previous current directory. If you attempt to remove a subdirectory that is not empty or is the current directory, DOS displays an error message and does not delete the directory.

For more information, see Chapter 8.

Examples

To remove the directory C:\LETTERS when drive C is the current drive, type the form:

RD \LETTERS

or when drive A is the current drive, type the form:

RD C:\LETTERS

To remove the directory REPORTS from the path C:\DATA\REPORTS, type the form:

RD C:\DATA\REPORTS

The directory REPORTS is removed; DATA is not removed. Note: all directories must be empty of files before they can be removed.

SELECT   V3, V4—External

Creates a disk with the DOS files and configures the CONFIG.SYS and AUTOEXEC.BAT files for your country. For DOS V4, SELECT was expanded to a full-featured, menu-oriented DOS installation utility.

Syntax

For DOS V3, use the following form:

> *dc:pathc***SELECT** *ds: dd:pathd* **countrycode keycode**

dc:pathc are the disk drive and the directory that hold the command.

ds: is the source disk drive.

dd:pathd is the destination disk drive and directory.

countrycode is a valid country code from the COUNTRY.SYS device driver.

keycode is a valid key code that can be set with KEYB.

Switch

(None)

Notes

The SELECT program helps you set up DOS on a new disk. SELECT V3.3, which is different from earlier versions, works with any hard or floppy disk. SELECT V3.2 and earlier versions work only with floppy disks.

For V4 and V4.01, SELECT has been modified even further. With these versions, SELECT is the program that starts when you boot your computer from the DOS Install disk. SELECT V4 enables you to configure and format your hard disk, install the DOS Shell, and then set up the CONFIG.SYS and AUTOEXEC.BAT files.

Example

To prepare a disk in drive A from your hard disk drive C for use with a French country code, type the form:

> **SELECT C: A: 437 FR**

SET   V2, V3, V4—Internal

Sets or shows the system environment.

Syntax

To display the environment, type the command:

> **SET**

To add to or alter the environment, use this form:

SET name=*string*

name is the string you want to add to the environment.

string is the information you want to store in the environment.

The *environment* is the portion of RAM reserved for alphanumeric information that can be examined and used by DOS commands or user programs. For example, the environment usually contains COMSPEC, which is the location of COMMAND.COM; PATH, the additional paths for finding programs and batch files; and PROMPT, the string defining the DOS system prompt.

Switch

(None)

Notes

SET puts information in memory for later use by invoked batch files or programs. The command is most commonly used to store the directory path to data files or program overlays. An invoked program examines the RAM where the SET information is stored, then issues the proper commands to find the needed data or program overlays.

For more information, see Chapter 13.

Examples

To set an environment variable WPPATH to be equal to C:\WORDS\LETTERS, type the form:

SET WPPATH=C:\WORDS\LETTERS

To delete the environment variable WPPATH from the environment, type the form:

SET WPPATH=

SHARE   V3, V4—External

Enables DOS support for file and record locking.

Syntax

*dc:pathc***SHARE** */F:name_space /L:numlocks*

dc:pathc are the disk drive and the directory that holds the command.

Switches

/F:*name_space*   Sets the amount of memory space (*name_space* bytes large) used for file sharing.

/L:*numlocks*   Sets the maximum number (*numlocks*) of file/record locks to use.

Notes

SHARE is the DOS V3 and V4 program for file and record locking.

You use SHARE when two or more programs or processes share a single computer's files. After SHARE is loaded, DOS checks each file for locks whenever the file is opened, read, or written. If a file has been opened for exclusive use, an error message results from any subsequent attempt to open the file. If one program locks a portion of a file, an error message results if another program attempts to read or write the locked portion.

You must use SHARE if you use DOS V4 and V4.01 and have a hard disk formatted larger than 32M. For convenience, you can use INSTALL in the CONFIG.SYS file to activate SHARE.

Example

To install SHARE with the default file space (/F) of 2048 bytes and number of locks (/L) of 20, type the command:

SHARE

SORT   V2, V3, V4—External

Reads lines from the standard input device, performs an ASCII sort of the lines, then writes the lines to the standard output device. The sorting may be in ascending or descending order and may start at any column in the line.

Syntax

*dc:pathc***SORT** /R /+c

dc:pathc are the disk drive and the directory that hold the command.

Switches

/R   Sorts in reverse order. Thus, the letter Z comes first, and the letter A comes last.

/+c   Starts sorting with column number *c*.

Notes

SORT is a general-purpose sorting program that has been changed significantly since DOS V2. With V3 and V4, SORT is a powerful filter, but it does have some limitations. One limitation, for example, is that it cannot sort a file larger than 63K.

SORT uses the ASCII sequence with some exceptions. SORT treats numbers as characters.

With DOS V3 and V4, SORT handles alphabetic characters intelligently, giving upper- and lowercase characters the same treatment. SORT V2 treats these characters differently. In the ASCII characters the uppercase A precedes the uppercase Z, but the lowercase a comes after the uppercase Z.

With V3 and V4, SORT also is intelligent in sorting certain ASCII characters in the range of 128 to 225, which includes foreign language characters and symbols. SORT V3 and V4 can handle most files containing non-English text.

For more information, see Chapter 9.

Examples

To sort the lines in the file WORDS.TXT and display the result on the screen, type the form:

SORT < WORDS.TXT

To sort the lines in the file WORDS.TXT and place the result of the sort in the file WORDS.SRT, type the form:

SORT < WORDS.TXT > WORDS.SRT

To produce a sorted directory listing, type the form:

DIR | SORT

To produce a directory listing sorted by extension, type this form:

DIR | SORT /+10

SUBST   V3.1, V4—External

Creates a disk drive alias for a subdirectory; used principally with programs that do not use path names.

Syntax

To establish an alias, use the following form:

*dc:pathc***SUBST d1:** *d2:***pathname**

To delete an alias, use this form:

*dc:pathc***SUBST d1: /D**

To see the current aliases, use this form:

*dc:pathc***SUBST**

dc:pathc are the disk drive and the directory that hold the command.

d1: is a valid disk drive name that becomes the alias or nickname. **d1:** may be a nonexistent disk drive.

*d2:***pathname** are the valid disk drive name and the directory path that will be nicknamed **d1:**.

Switch

/D   Deletes the alias.

Notes

SUBST enables you to use a disk drive name rather than a disk drive name and directory path name. SUBST also enables you to use files in subdirectories with programs that do not allow path names, such as programs written for DOS V1.

If you need several SUBST commands, use the LASTDRIVE command in your CONFIG.SYS file. Without this command, the normal LASTDRIVE is E.

While SUBST is in effect, certain DOS commands should be used with caution, others should be avoided, and some should not be used at all. When used on the alias disk, for example, MKDIR and RMDIR actually make or remove subdirectories from subdirectory *dirname*. Other commands that you should avoid or use with care are: CHKDSK, ASSIGN, JOIN, LABEL, BACKUP, DISKCOPY, DISKCOMP, FDISK, FORMAT, and RESTORE.

For more information, see Chapter 13.

Examples

To assign the directory path C:\WORDS\LETTERS the drive designation E, type the form:

SUBST E: C:\WORDS\LETTERS

To display all current substitutions, type the command:

SUBST

For the above substitution, you would see the message:

```
E: => C:\WORDS\LETTERS
```

To deactivate the above substitution, type the form:

SUBST E: /D

SYS V1, V2, V3, V4—External

Places a copy of DOS on the specified disk.

Syntax

*dc:pathc***SYS d:**

dc:pathc are the disk drive and the directory that hold the command.

d: is the disk drive that will receive the copy of DOS.

Switch

(None)

Notes

The SYS command places a copy of IO.SYS and MSDOS.SYS (or IBMBIO.COM and IBMDOS.COM on IBM's version) on the target disk. You also must copy COMMAND.COM onto the target disk to enable the disk to load and execute the disk operating system.

SYS V1 and SYS with DOS V2, V3, and V4 have few differences. SYS V2 and V3 check the destination disk to see if enough space is available for DOS. Then SYS displays an error message if space is not available. SYS V1 places DOS on the floppy disk even if the proper space is unavailable. If you run SYS V1 on a floppy disk with existing files, some of the disk's files' information can be lost.

For more information, see Chapter 6.

Example

To place the two hidden DOS files on the empty disk in drive A, type the command form:

SYS A:

TIME

V1.1, V2, V3, V4—Internal

Sets and shows the system time.

Syntax

TIME *hh:mm:ss.xx*

hh is the one- or two-digit number for hours (0 to 23).

mm is the one- or two-digit number for minutes (0 to 59).

ss is the one- or two-digit number for seconds (0 to 59).

xx is the one- or two-digit number for hundredths of a second (0 to 99).

NOTE: Depending on the country code's setting in your CONFIG.SYS file, a comma may be the separator between seconds and hundredths of seconds.

Switch

(None)

Notes

TIME is used to set the computer's internal 24-hour clock. The time and date are recorded in the directory whenever you create or change a file. This information can help you find the most recent version of a file when you check your directory.

If you do not enter the time when starting up most PCs, the time defaults to 00:00:00.00. If you want your system to use the correct time, you must set it.

Many computers retain the time of day through a battery-backed circuit. The real-time clock is read and displayed when you start the computer. Such clocks usually are accurate to within one minute a month, which is about the same accuracy as a digital watch. After you boot your computer, DOS uses the software time clock, which suffers the same inaccuracies as the PC clock.

If you enter a valid time, DOS accepts the new time and displays no other message. If you type the TIME command but do not enter the time, DOS responds:

```
Current time is hh:mm:ss.xx
Enter new time
```

If DOS displays the correct time, simply press Enter, and the time is not reset. If you want to change the time setting, enter a valid time in the DOS format. DOS accepts the new time without displaying another message.

For more information, see Chapter 3.

Examples

If you wish to set the current time to 3:15 pm, type the form:

TIME 15:15

To display the current time and optionally reset the time, type the command:

TIME

TREE V2, V3, V4—External

Displays all the subdirectories on a disk and optionally displays all files in each directory.

Syntax

*dc:pathc***TREE** *d: /F*

With DOS V4, you may add the /A switch:

*dc:pathc***TREE** *d:path\\ /F /A*

dc:pathc are the disk drive and the directory that hold the command.

d:path are the disk drive and directory holding the disk you want to examine.

Switches

/F   Displays all files in the directories.

/A   Uses graphics characters available to all code pages.

Notes

The TREE command displays all directories on a disk so that the user does not have to enter every directory, run a DIR command, and search for every <DIR> file (subdirectory). The /F option also displays the name of every file in every directory.

TREE shows one directory or file name on a line and can quickly scroll off the screen. If you want a copy of the entire tree, you can redirect the output to the printer.

For more information, see Chapter 8.

Examples

To display a listing of all directories and subdirectories of the current disk drive, type the command:

TREE

If you have DOS V4 and want to use graphics characters available to all code pages, type the form:

TREE /A

TYPE   V1, V2, V3, V4—Internal

Displays a file's contents on-screen.

Syntax

TYPE *d:path***filename.ext**

d:path are the disk drive and the directory holding the file that will be displayed.

filename.ext is the file that will be displayed on-screen. Wild cards are not permitted.

Switch

(None)

Notes

The TYPE command displays a file's characters on the video screen. You can use TYPE to see a file's contents.

Strange characters appear on the screen when you use TYPE on some data files and most program files, because TYPE tries to display the machine-language instructions as ASCII characters.

The output of TYPE, like most other DOS commands, can be redirected to the printer by adding **>PRN** to the command line or by pressing Ctrl-PrtSc. (Don't forget to press Ctrl-PrtSc again to turn off the printing.)

You cannot predict what will happen if you print when you TYPE a program file or a data file that contains control characters. Because of the unpredictable nature of using TYPE to redirect the contents of a program file to the printer, avoid using TYPE with program files.

For more information, see Chapter 9.

Example

To display the contents of the file MEMO.TXT that resides in the \WORDS directory, type the following form:

TYPE \WORDS\MEMO.TXT

VER   V2, V3, V4—Internal

Shows the DOS version number on the video display.

Syntax

VER

Switch

(None)

Notes

The VER command displays a one-digit DOS version number, followed by a two-digit revision number, reminding you which DOS version (V2.0 through V4.01) the computer is using.

For more information, see Chapter 6.

VERIFY   V2, V3, V4—Internal

Sets the computer to check the accuracy of data written to a disk to ensure that information is recorded properly.

Syntax

To show the verify status, type the command:

VERIFY

To set the verify status, use this form:

VERIFY ON

or the reverse form:

VERIFY OFF

Switch

(None)

Notes

VERIFY controls new data, checking on the disk to ensure correct recording of the data. If VERIFY is off, DOS does not check the data; if VERIFY is on, DOS checks the data. VERIFY does not affect any other DOS operation.

Two factors affect the trade-off between VERIFY ON and VERIFY OFF. If VERIFY is on, data integrity is assured. If VERIFY is off, you can write to the disk faster. It usually is safe to leave VERIFY off. If you are working with very important data or are using BACKUP, you are wise to turn VERIFY on.

For more information, see Chapter 9.

VOL
V2, V3, V4—Internal

Displays the disk's volume label, if a label exists.

Syntax

> **VOL** *d:*

d: is the disk drive whose label you want to display.

Switch

(None)

Notes

This command is similar to LABEL. The main difference is that, whereas LABEL changes a disk label, VOL only displays the disk label.

For more information, see Chapter 6.

Example

If you want to display the label of the disk in drive A, type:

> **VOL A:**

XCOPY
V3.2 and later—External

Selectively copies files from one or more subdirectories.

Syntax

> *dc:pathc***XCOPY** *ds:paths***filenames.exts**
> *dd:pathd\filenamed.extd /A/D/E/M/P/S/V/W*

dc:pathc are the disk drive and the directory that hold the command.

ds:paths are the source disk drive and the directory holding the file(s) that will be copied.

filenames.exts is the file that will be copied. Wild cards are allowed.

dd:pathd are the destination disk drive and the directory to receive the copied file(s). DOS refers to the destination drive as the *target*.

filenamed.extd is the new name of the file that is copied. Wild cards are allowed.

Switches

/A   Copies files whose *archive* flag is on, but does not turn off the archive flag (similar to the /M switch).

/E   Creates parallel subdirectories on the destination disk even if the created subdirectory is *empty*.

/D:date   Copies files that were changed or created on or after the date you specify. The date's form depends on the setting of the COUNTRY directive in CONFIG.SYS.

/M   Copies files whose archive flag is on (*modified* files) and turns off the archive flag (similar to the /A switch).

/P   Causes XCOPY to prompt you for approval before copying a file.

/S   Copies files from this directory and all subsequent subdirectories.

/V   Verifies that the copy has been recorded correctly.

/W   Causes XCOPY to prompt and wait for the correct source floppy disk to be inserted.

Notes

XCOPY is the extended COPY command. Although XCOPY runs more slowly than COPY, XCOPY offers more features and greater versatility. For example, XCOPY gives you greater control in selecting the files that will be copied. You can select the file's archive attribute and directory data and confirm the files individually before they are copied. The XCOPY command also enables you to copy through more than one directory. The command is most useful as an alternative to the DOS BACKUP command or when you want to maintain files between two computers that are "in sync" (two systems with hard disks or a "base" station and a laptop).

When the destination floppy disk is full, XCOPY pronounces the destination full and stops. Change floppy disks and reissue the command. The files that were copied have their archive attribute off, and XCOPY skips these files. XCOPY copies the files that have not yet been copied.

For more information, see Chapter 10.

Examples

To copy all files from the root directory of drive C to drive A, type the form:

XCOPY C:\ A:

To copy all files from the directory C:\WORDS and all directories beneath C:\WORDS to the disk in drive A, type the form:

XCOPY C:\WORDS A: /S

Any directories beneath C:\WORDS will be created on drive A, and the associated files will be copied to their respective directories on drive A.

To copy all files from the directory C:\WORDS with the extension TXT to the disk in drive A, type the following form:

XCOPY C:\WORDS*.TXT A:

Part Five

Appendixes

DOS Survival Guide

Use this guide to determine the command you need in order to accomplish a specific task. Then refer to the Command Reference for details about the use and syntax of the command. Note that an asterisk may follow some of the commands, which designates a directive to be set in the CONFIG.SYS file.

To	Use
Analyze a disk	CHKDSK
Automatically find files	APPEND, PATH
Automatically run a file at start-up	AUTOEXEC.BAT
Back up files	BACKUP, COPY, XCOPY
Back up disks	BACKUP, DISKCOPY
Change a code page	CHCP, KEYB, MODE
Change the active display	MODE
Change the baud rate	MODE
Change the console	CTTY
Change the current directory	CHDIR (CD)
Change the current disk drive	d:

To	Use
Change disk buffers	BUFFERS*
Change the disk label	LABEL
Change the environment	SET
Change file attributes	ATTRIB
Change a file name	RENAME (REN)
Change/set location of the command interpreter	SHELL*
Change program input	<
Change program output	>, >>
Clear the video display	CLS
Combine disks	JOIN
Combine files	COPY
Compare disks	DISKCOMP
Compare files	COMP
Concatenate files	COPY
Connect disk drives	JOIN
Control Ctrl-Break	BREAK, BREAK*
Control verification of files	VERIFY
Copy backup files	RESTORE
Copy disks	DISKCOPY, COPY, XCOPY
Copy files	COPY, REPLACE, XCOPY
Create a subdirectory	MKDIR (MD)
Display available RAM	CHKDSK, MEM
Display the current code page	CHCP, MODE
Display the date	DATE
Display environment	SET
Display a list of files	DIR, CHKDSK /V, TREE /F
Display national-language characters	CHCP, GRAFTABL, KEYB, MODE
Display the time	TIME
Display the version of DOS	VER

To	Use
Display the volume label	VOL, LABEL, DIR, CHKDSK
Erase a character	Left arrow, or Backspace
Erase a directory	RMDIR (RD)
Erase a disk label	LABEL
Erase files	DEL, ERASE
Execute several DOS commands with one command	Batch file
Find disk free space	CHKDSK, DIR
Find a file	CHKDSK /V, TREE /F
Find a word or phrase in a file	FIND
Freeze the video display	Ctrl-Num Lock, Pause
Ignore a line	Esc
Load file-sharing software	SHARE
Pause the display	Ctrl-Num Lock, Pause, Ctrl-S
Pipe output between programs	|
Place DOS on a disk	SYS, FORMAT /S
Prepare a disk	FORMAT, FDISK
Print the display	Shift-PrintSc, GRAPHICS
Print graphics	GRAPHICS
Print on the display and the printer	Ctrl-PrintSc
Print a file	PRINT, >, >>
Print from the background	PRINT
Reassign disk drives	ASSIGN, JOIN, SUBST
Reassign printers	MODE
Restore backup files	RESTORE
Repair a file	RECOVER
Remove a directory	RMDIR (RD)
Remove files	DEL, ERASE
Repair a disk	RECOVER, CHKDSK
Run a program	program_name

To	Use
Set alternative directories for data files	APPEND
Set alternative directories for programs	PATH
Set the country code	COUNTRY*
Set/change a code page	MODE, KEYB
Set/change checks on file writing	VERIFY
Set/change communications ports	MODE
Set/change displays	MODE
Set/change an environmental variable	SET
Set/change internal stacks	STACKS*
Set/change printers	MODE
Set/change the system date	DATE
Set/change the system prompt	PROMPT
Set/change the system time	TIME
Sort a file	SORT
Speed DOS	BUFFERS*, FASTOPEN
Stop a running program	Ctrl-Break, Ctrl-C
Stop a running program and reset the computer	Ctrl-Alt-Del
Unfreeze the video display	Any key
Update files	REPLACE
Use a different disk drive	d:, ASSIGN, SUBST
Use a new device	DEVICE*
Use a subdirectory in place of a disk	SUBST

DOS
Messages

DOS messages fall into two groups: *general* and *device error* messages. The larger group of general messages is listed here first, followed by the device error messages. Both lists are organized alphabetically.

General DOS Messages

The following messages may appear when you are starting DOS or using your computer. Messages that occur only when you are starting DOS are marked (start-up). Most start-up errors mean that DOS did not start and that you must reboot the system.

Most of the other error messages mean that DOS terminated the program and returned to a system prompt, such as A> or C>.

```
Access denied
```

ERROR: You or a program attempted to change or erase a file that is marked as read-only or is in use. If the file is marked as read-only, you may change the read-only attribute with the ATTRIB command.

```
Attempted write-protect violation
```

WARNING: The floppy disk you are trying to format is write-protected. If the disk is the one you want to format, remove the write-protect tab (for minifloppies) or move the write-protect tab down (for microfloppies). If the floppy disk in the drive is the wrong floppy disk, put the correct disk in the drive and try the command again.

```
Bad command or filename
```

ERROR: The name you entered is not valid for invoking a command, a program, or a batch file. The most frequent causes are the following: (1) you misspelled a name; (2) you omitted a needed disk drive or path name; or (3) you gave the parameters without the command name, such as typing **myfile** instead of **ws myfile**, where the **ws** specifying WordStar is omitted.

Check the spelling on the command line. Make sure that the command, program, or batch file is in the location specified (disk drive and directory path). Then try the command again.

```
Bad or Missing Command Interpreter
```

Error (start-up): DOS cannot find COMMAND.COM, the command interpreter. DOS does not start.

If you are starting DOS, this message means that COMMAND.COM is not on the start-up disk or that a version of COMMAND.COM from a previous version of DOS is on the disk. If you have used the SHELL directive in CONFIG.SYS, the message means that the SHELL directive is improperly phrased or that COMMAND.COM is not where you specified. Place another disk that contains the operating system (IBMBIO.COM, IBMDOS.COM, and COMMAND.COM) in the floppy disk drive, and then reset the system. After DOS has started, copy COMMAND.COM to the original start-up disk so that you can boot DOS.

If this message appears while you are running DOS, there are several possible explanations: COMMAND.COM has been erased from the disk and directory you used when starting DOS, a version of COMMAND.COM from a previous version of DOS has overwritten the good version, or the COMSPEC entry in the environment has been changed. You must restart DOS by resetting the system.

If resetting the system does not solve your problem, use a copy of your DOS master disk to restart the computer. Copy COMMAND.COM from this disk to the offending disk.

```
Bad or missing filename
```

WARNING (start-up): The device driver filename was not found; an error occurred when the device driver was loaded; a break address for the device driver was beyond the RAM available to the computer; or DOS detected an error while the driver was being loaded into memory. DOS will continue its boot, but will not use the device driver file name.

If DOS loads, check your CONFIG.SYS file for the line DEVICE=filename. Make sure that the line is spelled correctly and that the device driver is where you specified.

If this line is correct, reboot the system. If the message reappears, copy the file from its original disk to the boot disk and try starting DOS again. If the error persists, the device driver is bad, and you should contact the dealer or publisher who sold you the driver.

```
Batch file missing
```

ERROR: DOS could not find the batch file it was processing. The batch file may have been erased or renamed. With DOS V3.0 only, the disk containing the batch file may have been changed. DOS aborts the processing of the batch file.

If you are using DOS V3.0 and you changed the disk containing the batch file, restart the batch file and do not change the disk. You may need to edit the batch file so that you will not need to change disks.

If the batch file includes a RENAME command, causing the originating batch file name to change, edit the batch file so as to prevent renaming when processed again.

If the file was erased, re-create the batch file from its backup file, if possible. Edit the file to ensure that the batch file does not erase itself.

```
Compare error at offset xxxxxxxx
```

INFORMATION: The files you are comparing are not the same. The difference occurs at xxxxxxxx bytes from the beginning of the file. The number given is in hexadecimal format, base 16. The values for the differing bytes in the files are displayed also in hexadecimal format.

```
Cannot load COMMAND, system halted
```

ERROR: DOS attempted to reload COMMAND.COM, but the area where DOS keeps track of available and used memory was destroyed, or the command processor was not found in the directory specified by the COMSPEC=entry. The system halts.

This message indicates either that COMMAND.COM was erased from the disk and directory you used when starting DOS, or that the COMSPEC= entry in the environment has been changed. Restart DOS from your usual start-up disk. If DOS does not start, the copy of COMMAND.COM has been erased. Restart DOS from the DOS start-up or master disk and copy COMMAND.COM onto your usual start-up disk.

Another possible cause of this message is that an errant program corrupted the memory allocation table, where DOS tracks available memory. Try running the same program that was in the computer when the system halted. If the problem occurs again, the program is defective. Contact the dealer or publisher who sold you the program.

```
Cannot start COMMAND, exiting
```

ERROR: You or one of your programs directed DOS to load an additional copy of COMMAND.COM, but DOS could not load it. Either your CONFIG.SYS FILES directive

517

is set too low or you do not have enough free memory for another copy of COMMAND.COM.

If your system has 256K or more and FILES is less than 10, edit the CONFIG.SYS file on your start-up disk and use FILES=15 or FILES=20. Then restart DOS.

If the problem occurs again, either you do not have enough memory in your computer or you have too many resident or background programs competing for memory space. Restart DOS and do not load any resident or background programs you do not need. If necessary, eliminate unneeded device drivers or RAM-disk software. Another alternative is to increase the amount of RAM in your system.

Configuration too large

ERROR (start-up): DOS could not load itself because either you specified in your CONFIG.SYS file too many FILES or BUFFERS, or you specified too large an environment area (/E switch) to the SHELL command. This problem should occur only on systems with less than 256K.

Restart DOS with a different disk; then edit the CONFIG.SYS file on your boot disk, lowering the number of FILES, BUFFERS, or both. You can also edit the CONFIG.SYS file to reduce the size of the environment, either in addition to lowering the number of FILES and BUFFERS or as an alternative solution. Restart DOS with the edited disk.

Another alternative is to increase the RAM in your system.

Current drive is no longer valid

WARNING: You have set the system prompt to PROMPT $p. At the DOS system level, DOS attempted to read the current directory for the disk drive and found the drive no longer valid.

If the current disk drive is set for a floppy disk, this warning appears when you do not have a disk in the disk drive. DOS reports a Drive not ready error. Give the F command to fail or the I command to ignore the error. Then insert a floppy disk into the disk drive or type another drive designation.

The invalid-drive error also can happen if you have a current networked or SUBST disk drive that has been deleted or disconnected. Simply change the current drive to a valid disk drive.

Disk boot failure

ERROR (start-up): An error occurred when DOS tried to load itself into memory. The disk contained IBMBIO.COM and IBMDOS.COM, but one of the two files could not be loaded. DOS did not start.

Try starting DOS from the disk again. If the error recurs, try starting DOS from a disk you know is good, such as a copy of your DOS start-up or master disk. If this action fails, you have a disk-drive problem. Contact your dealer.

Disk unsuitable for system disk

WARNING: FORMAT detected on the floppy disk one or more bad sectors in the area where DOS normally resides. Because DOS must reside on a specified spot on the disk, and this portion is unusable, you cannot use the floppy disk to boot DOS.

Try reformatting this floppy disk. Some floppy disks format successfully the second time. If FORMAT gives this message again, you cannot use the floppy disk as a boot floppy disk.

Divide overflow

ERROR: A program attempted to divide by zero. DOS aborts the program. Either the program was incorrectly entered or it has a logical flaw. With well-written programs, this error should never occur. If you wrote the program, correct the error and try the program again. If you purchased the program, report the problem to the dealer or publisher.

This message can also appear when you are attempting to format a RAM disk with DOS V3.0 and V3.1. Make sure that you are formatting the correct disk, and try again.

Drive or diskette types not compatible

ERROR: When using DISKCOMP or DISKCOPY, you specified two drives of different capacities. You cannot, for example, DISKCOMP or DISKCOPY from a 1.2M drive to a 360K drive. Retype the command using like drives.

Duplicate filename or File not found

ERROR: While using RENAME (or its short form REN), either you attempted to change a file name to a name that already existed, or the file to be renamed does not exist in the directory. Check the directory for the conflicting names. Make sure that the file name exists and that you have spelled it correctly. Then try again.

Enter current Volume Label for drive d:

WARNING: you are attempting to format a hard disk that has a volume label. Enter the exact volume label to proceed with the format; if you do not want to enter a volume label, press Enter.

EOF mark not found

INFORMATION or WARNING: You may receive this message when using COMP to compare files. This message is informational if the files you are comparing are program files, but the message is a warning if the files you are comparing are text files. The message indicates that COMP could not find the customary end-of-file marker (EOF marker), which is Ctrl-Z or 1A hex. COMP came to the end of the file before it found the EOF marker.

Error in COUNTRY command

WARNING (start-up): The COUNTRY directive in CONFIG.SYS is either improperly phrased or has an incorrect country code or code page number. DOS continues its start-up but uses the default information for the COUNTRY directive.

After DOS has started, check the COUNTRY line in your CONFIG.SYS file. Refer to Chapter 18 and make sure that the directive is correctly phrased (using commas between country code, code page, and COUNTRY.SYS file) and that any given information is correct.

If you detect an error in the line, edit the line, save the file, and restart DOS.

If you do not find an error, restart DOS. If the same message appears, edit your CONFIG.SYS file. Re-enter the COUNTRY directive and delete the old COUNTRY line. The old line may contain some nonsense characters that DOS can see but are not apparent to your text-editing program.

Error in EXE file

ERROR: DOS detected an error while attempting to load a program stored in an EXE file. The problem is in the relocation information DOS needs to load the program. This problem can occur if the EXE file has been altered in any way.

Restart DOS and try the program again, this time using a backup copy of the program. If the message appears, the program is flawed. If you are using a purchased program, contact the dealer or publisher. If you wrote the program, use LINK to produce another copy of the program.

Error loading operating system

ERROR (start-up): A disk error occurred while DOS was loading itself from the hard disk. DOS does not start.

Restart the computer. If the error keeps occurring after several tries, restart DOS from the floppy disk drive. If the hard disk does not respond (that is, you cannot run DIR or CHKDSK without getting an error), you have a problem with the hard disk. Contact your dealer. If the hard disk does respond, use the SYS command to put another copy of DOS onto your hard disk. You also may need to copy COMMAND.COM to the hard disk.

Increase to 15 or 20 the number of FILES in the CONFIG.SYS file of your start-up disk. Restart DOS. If the error recurs, you may have a problem with the disk. Use a backup copy of the program and try again. If the backup copy works, copy it over the offending copy.

If an error occurs in the copying process, you have a flawed floppy disk or hard disk. If the problem is a floppy disk, copy the files from the flawed disk to another disk and reformat or retire the original disk. If the problem is the hard disk, immediately back up your files and run RECOVER on the offending file. If the problem persists, your hard disk may be damaged.

```
File allocation table bad, drive d
Abort, Retry, Fail?
```

WARNING: DOS encountered a problem in the file allocation table of the disk in drive d. Enter R for Retry several times. If this does not solve the problem, use A for Abort.

If you are using a floppy disk, attempt to copy all the files to another disk and then reformat or retire the original disk. If you are using a hard disk, back up files on the disk and reformat it. The disk will be unusable until it has been reformatted.

```
File cannot be copied onto itself
```

ERROR: You attempted to copy a file to the same disk and directory containing the same file name. This usually happens when you misspell or omit parts of the source or destination drive, path, or file name. This also may happen when you are using wild-card characters for file names. Check your spelling and the source and destination names, and then try the command again.

```
File creation error
```

ERROR: A program or DOS attempted to add a new file to the directory or to replace an existing file, but failed.

If the file already exists, use the ATTRIB command to check whether the file is marked as read-only. If the read-only flag is set and you want to change or erase the file, use ATTRIB to remove the read-only flag; then try again.

If the problem is not the read-only flag, run CHKDSK without the /F switch to determine whether the directory is full, the disk is full, or some other problem exists with the disk.

```
File not found
```

ERROR: DOS could not find the file that you specified. Either the file is not on the current disk or in the current directory or you specified incorrectly the disk drive name, path name, or file name. Check these possibilities and try the command again.

```
filename device driver cannot be initialized
```

WARNING (start-up): In CONFIG.SYS, either the parameters in the device driver `filename` are incorrect, or the DEVICE line is in error. Check for incorrect parameters, and check for phrasing errors in the DEVICE line. Edit the DEVICE line in the CONFIG.SYS file, save the file, and restart DOS.

```
Incorrect DOS Version
```

ERROR: The copy of the file holding the command you just entered is from a different version of DOS.

Get a copy of the command from the correct version of DOS (usually from your copy of the DOS start-up or master disk), and try the command again. If the disk you are using has been updated to hold new versions of the DOS programs, copy the new versions over the old ones.

```
Insert disk with batch file
and strike any key when ready
```

INFORMATION: DOS is attempting to execute the next command from a batch file, but the disk holding the batch file is not in the disk drive. This message occurs for DOS V3.1 and later versions. DOS V3.0 gives a fatal error when the disk is changed.

Put the disk holding the batch file into the disk drive and press a key to continue.

```
Insert disk with \COMMAND.COM in drive d
and strike any key when ready
```

INFORMATION and WARNING: DOS needed to reload COMMAND.COM but could not find it on the start-up disk.

If you are using floppy disks, the disk in drive d (usually A) probably has been changed. Place a disk holding a good copy of COMMAND.COM in drive d and press a key.

```
Insert diskette for drive d and strike
any key when ready
```

INFORMATION: On a system with one floppy disk drive or a system using DRIVER.SYS that makes more than one logical disk drive out of one physical disk drive, you or one of your programs specified the tandem disk drive d (such as A or B). This drive is different from the current disk drive.

If the correct disk is in the disk drive, press a key. Otherwise, put the correct disk into the floppy disk drive and then press a key.

```
Insufficient disk space
```

WARNING or ERROR: The disk does not have enough free space to hold the file being written. All DOS programs terminate when this problem occurs, but some non-DOS programs continue.

If you think that the disk has enough room to hold the file, run CHKDSK to see whether the disk has a problem. Sometimes when you terminate programs early by pressing Ctrl-Break, DOS is not allowed to do the necessary clean-up work. When this happens, disk space is temporarily trapped. CHKDSK can "free" these areas.

If you simply have run out of disk space, free some disk space or use a different disk. Try the command again.

If you loaded a resident program like PRINT, GRAPHICS, SideKick, or ProKey, restart DOS and try the command before loading any resident program. If this method fails, remove any unneeded device driver or RAM-disk software from the CONFIG.SYS file and restart DOS. If this action fails, your computer does not have enough memory for this command. You must increase your RAM to run the command.

```
Intermediate file error during pipe
```

ERROR: DOS is unable to create or write to one or both of the intermediate files it uses when piping information between programs. The disk is full; the root directory of the current disk is full; or DOS cannot find the files. The most frequent cause is running out of disk space.

Run the DIR command on the root directory of the current disk drive. Make sure that you have enough free space and enough room in the root directory for two additional files. If you do not have enough room, create room on the disk by deleting or copying and deleting files. You may also copy the necessary files to a different disk with sufficient room.

One possible cause of this error is that a program is deleting files, including the temporary files DOS uses. If this is the case, you should correct the program, contact the dealer or program publisher, or avoid using the program with piping.

```
Internal stack over flow
System halted
```

ERROR: Your programs and DOS have exhausted the *stack*, the memory space that is reserved for temporary use. This problem is usually caused by a rapid succession of hardware devices demanding attention (interrupts). DOS stops, and the system must be turned off and on again to restart DOS.

The circumstances that cause this message are generally infrequent and erratic, and they may not recur. If you want to prevent this error from occurring at all, add the STACKS directive to your CONFIG.SYS file. If the directive is already in your CONFIG.SYS file, increase the number of stacks specified.

```
Invalid COMMAND.COM in drive d
```

WARNING: DOS tried to reload COMMAND.COM from the disk in drive d and found that the file was from a different version of DOS. You will see a message instructing you to insert a disk with the correct version and press a key. Follow the directions for that message.

If you frequently use the disk that was originally in the disk drive, copy the correct version of COMMAND.COM to that disk.

```
Invalid COMMAND.COM, system halted
```

ERROR: DOS could not find COMMAND.COM on the hard disk. DOS halts and must be restarted.

COMMAND.COM may have been erased, or the COMSPEC variable in the environment may have been changed. Restart the computer from the hard disk. If you see a message indicating that COMMAND.COM is missing, the file was erased. Restart DOS from a disk and recopy COMMAND.COM to the root directory of the hard disk or to wherever your SHELL directive indicates if you have used this command in your CONFIG.SYS file.

If you restart DOS and this message appears later, a program or batch file is erasing COMMAND.COM or is altering the COMSPEC variable. If a batch file is erasing COMMAND.COM, edit the batch file. If a program is erasing COMMAND.COM, contact the dealer or publisher who sold you the program. If COMSPEC is being altered, either edit the offending batch file or program, or place COMMAND.COM in the subdirectory your program or batch file expects.

```
Invalid COUNTRY code or code page
```

WARNING (start-up): Either the COUNTRY code number or the code page number given to the COUNTRY directive in the CONFIG.SYS file is incorrect or incompatible. DOS ignores the COUNTRY directive and continues to start.

Check the COUNTRY directive in your CONFIG.SYS file. Refer to Chapter 18 and make sure that the correct and compatible country code and code page numbers are specified. If you detect an error, edit and save the file and restart DOS.

```
Invalid date
```

ERROR: You gave an impossible date or used the wrong kind of character to separate the month, day, and year. This message is also displayed if you enter the date by using the keypad when the keypad is not in numeric mode.

```
Invalid directory
```

ERROR: One of the following errors occurred: (1) you specified a directory name that does not exist, (2) you misspelled the directory name, (3) the directory path is on a different disk, (4) you forgot to give the path character (\) at the beginning of the name, or (5) you did not separate the directory names with the path character. Check your directory names, make sure that the directories exist, and try the command again.

Invalid disk change

WARNING: The disk in the 720K, 1.2M, or 1.44M disk drive was changed while a program had open files to be written to the disk. You will see the message Abort, Retry, Fail.

Place the correct disk in the disk drive and type R for Retry.

Invalid drive in search path

WARNING: Either a specification you gave to the PATH command has an invalid disk drive name or a named disk drive is nonexistent or hidden temporarily by a SUBST or JOIN command.

Use PATH to check the paths you instructed DOS to search. If you gave a nonexistent disk drive name, use the PATH command again and enter the correct search paths. If the problem is temporary because of a SUBST or JOIN command, you can again use PATH to enter the paths, but leave out or correct the wrong entry. Or you can just ignore the warning message.

Invalid drive or file name

ERROR: Either you gave the name of a nonexistent disk drive or you mistyped the disk drive, file name, or both.

Remember that certain DOS commands (such as SUBST and JOIN) temporarily hide disk drive names while the command is in effect. Check the disk drive name you gave, and try the command again.

Invalid drive specification

ERROR: This message is given when one of the following errors occurs: (1) you have entered the name of an invalid or nonexistent disk drive as a parameter to a command; (2) you have specified the same disk drive for the source and destination, which is not permitted for the command; or (3) by not giving a parameter, you have defaulted to the same disk drive for the source and the destination. Remember that certain DOS commands (such as SUBST and JOIN) temporarily hide disk drive names while the command is in effect. Check the disk drive names. If the command is objecting to a missing parameter and defaulting to the wrong disk drive, explicitly name the correct disk drive.

Invalid drive specification
Specified drive does not exist,
or is non-removable

ERROR: One of the following errors occurred: (1) you gave the name of a nonexistent disk drive, (2) you named the hard disk drive when using commands for floppy disks only, (3) you did not give a disk drive name and defaulted to the hard disk when using commands for floppy disks only, or (4) you named or defaulted to a RAM-disk drive when using commands for a "real" floppy disk only.

525

Remember that certain DOS commands (such as SUBST and JOIN) temporarily hide disk drive names while the command is in effect. Check the disk drive name you gave, and try the command again.

```
Invalid environment size specified
```

WARNING: You have given the SHELL directive in CONFIG.SYS.

The environment-size switch (/E:size) contains either nonnumeric characters or a number that is less than 160 or greater than 32,768.

If you are using the SHELL /E:size switch of DOS V3.1, size is the number of 16-byte paragraphs, not the number of bytes.

Check the form of your CONFIG.SYS SHELL directive; the form needs to be exact. There should be a colon between /E and size; there should be no comma or space between or within the /E: and the size characters; and the number in size should be greater than or equal to 160 but less than or equal to 32,768.

```
Invalid number of parameters
```

ERROR: You have given either too few or too many parameters to a command. One of the following errors occurred: (1) you omitted required information, (2) you forgot a colon immediately after the disk drive name, (3) you put a space in the wrong place or omitted a needed space, or (4) you forgot to place a slash (/) in front of a switch.

```
Invalid parameter
```

or

```
Incorrect parameter
```

ERROR: At least one parameter you entered for the command is not valid. One of the following errors occurred: (1) you omitted required information, (2) you forgot a colon immediately after the disk drive name, (3) you put a space in the wrong place or omitted a needed space, (4) you forgot to place a slash (/) in front of a switch, or (5) you used a switch that the command does not recognize. For more information, check the explanation of this message in the Command Reference under the command you were using when the message occurred.

```
Invalid partition table
```

ERROR (start-up): While you were attempting to start DOS from the hard disk, DOS detected a problem in the hard disk's partition information.

Restart DOS from a floppy disk. Back up all files from the hard disk, if possible. Run FDISK to correct the problem. If you change the partition information, you must reformat the hard disk and restore all its files.

```
Invalid path
```

ERROR: One of the following errors has occurred: (1) the path name contains illegal characters, (2) the name has more than 63 characters, or (3) one of the directory names within the path is misspelled or does not exist.

Check the spelling of the path name. If needed, do a DIR of the disk and make sure that the directory you have specified does exist and that you have the correct path name. Be sure that the path name contains no more than 63 characters. If necessary, change the current directory to a directory "closer" to the file and shorten the path name.

```
Invalid path or file name
```

ERROR: You gave a directory name or file name that does not exist, used the wrong directory name (a directory not on the path), or mistyped a name. COPY aborts when it encounters an invalid path or file name. If you used a wild card for a file name, COPY transfers all valid files before it issues the error message.

Check to see which files already are transferred. Determine whether the directory and file names are spelled correctly and whether the path is correct. Then try again.

```
Invalid STACK parameter
```

WARNING (start-up): One of the following errors has occurred to the STACKS directive in your CONFIG.SYS file: (1) a comma is missing between the number of stacks and the size of the stack, (2) the number of stack frames is not in the range of 8 to 64, (3) the stack size is not in the range of 32 to 512, (4) you have omitted either the number of stack frames or the stack size, or (5) either the stack frame or the stack size (but not both) is 0. DOS continues to start but ignores the STACKS directive.

Check the STACKS directive in your CONFIG.SYS file. Edit and save the file, and then restart DOS.

```
Invalid switch character
```

WARNING: You have used VDISK.SYS in your CONFIG.SYS file. VDISK encountered a switch (/), but the character immediately following it was not an E for extended memory. DOS loaded VDISK and attempted to install it in low (nonextended) memory. Either you misspelled the /E switch, or you left a space between the / and the E. Edit and save your CONFIG.SYS file, and then restart DOS.

```
Invalid time
```

ERROR: You gave an impossible time or used the wrong kind of character to separate the hour, minute, and second. This message is also displayed if you enter the time by using the keypad when the keypad is not in numeric mode.

```
Memory allocation error
Cannot load COMMAND, system halted
```

ERROR: A program destroyed the area where DOS keeps track of in-use and available memory. You must restart DOS.

If this error occurs again with the same program, the program has a flaw. Use a backup copy of the program. If the problem persists, contact the dealer or program publisher.

```
Missing operating system
```

ERROR (start-up): The DOS hard disk partition entry is marked as "bootable" (able to start DOS), but the DOS partition does not have a copy of DOS on it. DOS does not start.

Start DOS from a floppy disk. Use the SYS C: command to place DOS on the hard disk, and then copy COMMAND.COM to the disk. If this command fails to solve the problem, you must back up the existing files, if any, from the hard disk; then issue FORMAT /S to put a copy of the operating system on the hard disk. If necessary, restore the files that you backed up.

```
No free file handles
Cannot start COMMAND, exiting
```

ERROR: DOS could not load an additional copy of COMMAND.COM because no file handles were available.

Edit the CONFIG.SYS file on your start-up disk to increase the number of file handles (using the FILES directive) by five. Restart DOS and try the command again.

```
No room for system on destination disk
```

ERROR: The floppy disk or hard disk was not formatted with the necessary reserved space for DOS. You cannot put the system on this floppy disk.

```
Non-System disk or disk error
Replace and strike any key when ready
```

ERROR (start-up): Either your disk does not contain IBMBIO.COM and IBMDOS.COM, or a read error occurred when you started the system. DOS does not start.

If you are using a floppy disk system, put a bootable disk in drive A and press a key.

The most frequent cause of this message on hard disk systems is that you left a nonboot disk in drive A with the door closed. Open the door to disk drive A and press a key. DOS will boot from the hard disk.

```
Not enough memory
```

ERROR: The computer does not have enough free RAM to execute the program or command.

If you loaded a resident program like PRINT, GRAPHICS, SideKick, or ProKey, restart DOS and try the command again before loading any resident program. If this method fails to solve the problem, remove any unneeded device driver or RAM-disk software from the CONFIG.SYS file and restart DOS again. If this option fails also, your computer does not have enough memory for this command. You must increase your RAM to run the command.

```
Out of environment space
```

WARNING: DOS is unable to add any more strings to the environment from the SET command. The environment cannot be expanded. This error occurs when you load a resident program, such as MODE, PRINT, GRAPHICS, SideKick, or ProKey.

If you are running DOS V3.1 or a later version, refer to the SHELL directive in Chapter 17 (on customizing DOS) for information about expanding the default space for the environment. DOS V3.0 has no method to expand the environment.

```
Path not found
```

ERROR: A file or directory path that you named does not exist. You may have misspelled the file name or directory name, or you may have omitted a path character (\) between directory names or between the final directory name and the file name. Another possibility is that the file or directory does not exist in the place you specified. Check these possibilities and try again.

```
Path too long
```

ERROR: You have given a path name that exceeds the 63-character limit. Either the name is too long or you omitted a space between file names. Check the command line. If the phrasing is correct, you must change to a directory that is closer to the file you want and try the command again.

```
Program too big to fit in memory
```

ERROR: The computer does not have enough memory to load the program or the command you invoked.

If you have any resident programs loaded (such as PRINT, GRAPHICS, or SideKick), restart DOS and try the command again without loading the resident programs. If this message appears again, reduce the number of buffers (BUFFERS) in the CONFIG.SYS file, eliminate unneeded device drivers or RAM-disk software, and restart DOS again. If these actions do not solve the problem, your computer does not have enough RAM for the program or command. You must increase the amount of RAM in your computer to run this command.

```
Sector size too large in file filename
```

WARNING: The device driver `filename` is inconsistent. The device driver defined a particular sector size for DOS but attempted to use a different size. Either the copy of the device driver is bad, or the device driver is incorrect. Make a backup copy of the device driver on the boot disk and then reboot DOS. If the message appears again, the device driver is incorrect. If you wrote the driver, correct the error. If you purchased the program, contact the dealer or software publisher.

Syntax error

ERROR: You phrased a command improperly by (1) omitting needed information, (2) giving extraneous information, (3) putting an extra space in a file name or path name, or (4) using an incorrect switch. Check the command line for these possibilities and try the command again.

Too many block devices

WARNING (start-up): There are too many DEVICE directives in your CONFIG.SYS file. DOS continues to start but does not install any additional device drivers.

DOS can handle only 26 block devices. The block devices created by the DEVICE directives plus the number of block devices automatically created by DOS exceed this number. Remove any unnecessary DEVICE directives in your CONFIG.SYS file and restart DOS.

Top level process aborted, cannot continue

ERROR (start-up): COMMAND.COM or another DOS command detected a disk error, and you chose the A (Abort) option.

DOS cannot finish starting itself, and the system halts.

Try to start DOS again. If the error recurs, use a floppy disk (if starting from the hard disk) or a different floppy disk (if starting from floppy disks) to start DOS. After DOS has started, use the SYS command to put another copy of the operating system on the disk, and copy COMMAND.COM to the disk. If DOS reports an error during the copying, the disk is bad. Either reformat or retire the floppy disk, or back up and reformat the hard disk.

Unable to create directory

ERROR: Either you or a program has attempted to create a directory, and one of the following has occurred: (1) a directory by the same name already exists; (2) a file by the same name already exists; (3) you are adding a directory to the root directory, and the root directory is full; or (4) the directory name has illegal characters or is a device name.

Do a DIR of the disk. Make sure that no file or directory already exists with the same name. If adding the directory to the root directory, remove or move (copy, then erase) any unneeded files or directories. Check the spelling of the directory name and make sure that the command is properly phrased.

```
Unrecognized command in CONFIG.SYS
```

WARNING (start-up): DOS detected an improperly phrased directive in CONFIG.SYS. The directive is ignored, and DOS continues to start; but DOS does not indicate the incorrect line. Examine the CONFIG.SYS file, looking for improperly phrased or incorrect directives. Edit the line, save the file, and restart DOS.

DOS Device Error Messages

When DOS detects an error while reading or writing to disk drives or other devices, one of the following messages appears:

```
type error reading device
```

or

```
type error writing device
```

The `type` is the type of error, and `device` is the device at fault. If the device is a floppy disk drive, do not remove the disk from the drive. Refer to the possible causes and corrective actions described in this section, which lists the types of error messages that may appear.

```
Bad call format
```

A device driver was given a requested header with an incorrect length. The problem is the applications software making the call.

```
Bad command
```

The device driver issued an invalid or unsupported command to device. The problem may be with the device driver software or with other software trying to use the device driver. If you wrote the program, it needs to be corrected. For a purchased program, contact the dealer or publisher who sold you the program.

```
Bad format call
```

The device driver at fault passed an incorrect header length to DOS. If you wrote this device driver, you must rewrite it to correct the problem. For a purchased program, contact the dealer or publisher who sold you the driver.

```
Bad unit
```

An invalid subunit number was passed to the device driver. The problem may be with the device driver software or with other software trying to use the device driver. Contact the dealer who sold you the device driver.

    Data

DOS could not correctly read or write the data. Usually the disk has developed a defective spot.

    Drive not ready

An error occurred while DOS tried to read or write to the disk drive. For floppy disk drives, the drive door may be open, the disk may not have been inserted, or the disk may not be formatted. For hard disk drives, the drive may not be properly prepared—you may have a hardware problem.

    FCB unavailable

With the file-sharing program (SHARE.EXE) loaded, a program that uses the DOS V1 method of file handling attempted to open concurrently more file control blocks than were specified with the FCBS directive.

Use the Abort option (see the end of this section). Increase the value of the FCBS CONFIG.SYS directive (usually by four), and reboot the system. If the message appears again, increase the number again and reboot.

    General failure

This is a catchall error message not covered elsewhere. The error usually occurs for one of the following reasons: (1) you are using an unformatted disk; (2) the disk drive door is open; (3) the floppy disk is not seated properly; or (4) you are using the wrong type of disk in a disk drive, such as formatting a 360K disk in a 1.2M disk drive.

    Lock violation

With the file-sharing program (SHARE.EXE) or the network software loaded, one of your programs attempted to access a file that is locked. Your best choice is Retry. Then try Abort. If you choose A, however, any data in memory will be lost.

    No paper

The printer is either out of paper or not turned on.

    Non-DOS disk

The FAT has invalid information. This disk is unusable. You can Abort and run CHKDSK to learn whether any corrective action is possible. If CHKDSK fails, your other alternative is to reformat the disk. Reformatting, however, will destroy any remaining information on the disk.

If you use more than one operating system, the disk has probably been formatted under the operating system you are using and should not be reformatted.

```
Not ready
```

The device is not ready and cannot receive or transmit data. Check the connections, make sure that the power is on, and check to see whether the device is ready. For floppy disk drives, check to make sure that the disk is formatted and is properly seated in the disk drive.

```
Read fault
```

DOS was unable to read the data, usually from a disk. Check the disk drive doors and be sure that the disk is inserted properly.

```
Sector not found
```

The disk drive was unable to find the sector on the disk. This error is usually the result of a defective spot on the disk or of defective drive electronics. Some copy-protection schemes also use the defective spot to prevent unauthorized duplication of the disk.

```
Seek
```

The disk drive could not find the proper track on the disk. This error is usually the result of a defective spot on the disk, an unformatted disk, or drive-electronics problems.

```
Write fault
```

DOS could not write the data to this device. Perhaps you inserted the disk improperly or you left the disk drive door open. Another possibility is an electronics failure in the floppy or hard disk drive. The most frequent cause is a bad spot on the disk.

```
Write protect
```

The disk is write-protected.

Note: One of the previously listed messages (usually Data, Read fault, or Write fault) appears when you are using a double-sided disk in a single-sided disk drive or a 9-sector disk (V2 and later) with DOS V1. DOS will display one of these error messages, followed by the line

```
Abort,Retry,Fail?
```

for DOS V3.3, V4.0 and V4.01 or

```
Abort,Retry,Ignore?
```

for versions of DOS before V3.3.

533

If you press A for Abort, DOS ends the program that requested the read or write condition. Typing R for Retry causes DOS to try the operation again. If you press F for Fail or I for Ignore, DOS skips the operation and the program continues. Some data may be lost, however, when you use Fail or Ignore.

The order of preference, unless stated differently under the message, is R, A, F or I. You should retry the operation at least twice. If the condition persists, you must decide whether to abort the program or ignore the error. If you ignore the error, data may be lost. If you abort, data still being processed by the program and not yet written to the disk will be lost.

Installing
DOS

C

To install MS-DOS V3.3 and earlier versions, and PC DOS V4.0, read carefully the instructions in this appendix.

Use the disks that come in the DOS package to make a working copy of DOS. You will use the working copy with your computer, and you should store the original DOS disks in a safe place.

Before you insert any of the disks that came in your DOS package into a drive, ensure that the disk is write protected. 5 1/4-inch floppy disks must have their write-protect notches covered by an adhesive, opaque tab. (In some cases, the write-protect notch on 5 1/4-inch disks is not cut and, therefore, the disk is permanently write-protected.) 3 1/2-inch floppies have a write-protect window with a sliding shutter that must be open for the disk to be write-protected.

There are several versions of DOS, and various vendors of computers use specific instructions that pertain only to their versions of DOS. Check your DOS manual for instructions that may apply to your version of DOS. The general instructions in this appendix allow you to make a working copy of DOS on a floppy disk for use with this book. Remember to use the disks that came in your package only to create working copies of your original disks.

Installing MS-DOS Versions 3.3 and Earlier

Versions of DOS up to V3.3 usually contain a DOS system disk and a supplemental files or diagnostics disk. You will need the DOS system disk for this operation. To make a bootable working disk, you will perform the following steps:

1. Boot your computer using the DOS system disk.
2. Copy the DOS system disk to a new floppy disk.
3. Label the new floppy disk.

Booting with the DOS System Disk

Locate your DOS system disk and insert it into drive A. Turn the computer on. If it is already on, press and hold down the Ctrl and Alt keys and press the Del key. Your computer will boot from the DOS disk. Booting will take from a few seconds to a couple of minutes. When your computer beeps and displays screen information, read the display. If the message NON SYSTEM DISK or an equivalent message appears, you have chosen the wrong disk from your DOS package. Repeat this procedure with the correct disk. If you are prompted for the date and time, enter the current date and time. When the computer displays the DOS prompt (almost always A>), your system is successfully booted.

Copying the DOS System Disk

The disk-copying operation makes a working copy of your system disk. If your package has a system disk 1 and a system disk 2, you will need to repeat this operation to copy both disks. You can optionally repeat this operation to make a working copy of the DOS supplemental or diagnostics disk or other disks from your package. In all cases, **ensure that the DOS package disks are write-protected.**

Type **DISKCOPY** and be sure to press Enter. DOS will prompt you to insert a disk or disks. Follow the sequence DOS leads you through. When DOS refers to the *source* disk, you will insert the DOS system disk from your DOS package into the drive specified. When DOS refers to the *target* disk, insert the blank disk into the drive DOS specifies. Depending on your system's memory and the number of drives you have, the DOS messages to insert disks will vary. Because the DOS system disk is write-protected, you will be safe from accidental insertion of the wrong disk. When the DISKCOPY operation for the disk is complete, DOS will ask if you want to make another copy. Answer Y for yes if you want to copy the other disks in the DOS package. Answer N for no if you have just one system disk to copy. When you have finished copying the disk(s) and answer N to the prompt, DOS redisplays the A> prompt.

Labeling the Copies

Remove all disks from the drives. Place a label on the DOS working disk. Be careful not to touch the disk's internal surface. To write on a disk's label, use a felt-tipped pen, not a ball point pen or a pencil. If you must use a ball point pen, write on the label *before* putting it on the disk. Put the disk back into its jacket if it is a 5 1/4-inch disk. Put the original DOS disks back in their holders for safe storage away from heat, moisture, and electrical fields.

Label the copy of the system disk "DOS Working Master." If you made additional disks from your package, label them now using the "Working" description along with the name on the original disk. Because you will use the working DOS disk to learn DOS commands, there is a chance that you could erase the disk. For additional safety, you should write-protect the working copy now.

To test the working DOS disk, insert it into drive A and press Ctrl, Alt, and Del together to warm boot your system. The computer will display the DOS prompt again, and you can proceed with the exercises in this book.

Installing PC DOS V4.0

PC DOS V4.0 for IBM systems comes with an installation program called SELECT. The SELECT program can configure the DOS Shell to suit your computer's configuration. SELECT enables you to install PC DOS V4.0 on floppy disks or on a hard disk. The following procedure shows you how to create working copies of DOS V4.0 on floppy disks. You can then use the working copies with examples in this book.

Note that PC DOS V4.0 is an operating system for IBM computers and may not work satisfactorily on other computers.

Memory Requirements for DOS V4.0 Installation

To install PC DOS V4.0, your computer must have at least 256K of random-access memory (RAM). If your system has less, ask your dealer about options to upgrade your memory. DOS V4.0's DOS Shell can be fully installed if you have at least 360K of RAM.

Floppy Disk Installation

If you are installing DOS V4.0 on 5 1/4-inch disks, you will need the five 5 1/4-inch 360K disks that came with your DOS V4.0 package and four blank 5 1/4-inch 360K disks to create the working copies.

If you are installing DOS on a 3 1/2-inch 1.44M disk, you will need the two 3 1/2-inch 720K disks that came with your package and one blank 3 1/2-inch 1.44M disk to create the working copy.

If you are making the installation on a 3 1/2-inch 720K disk, you will need the two 3 1/2-inch 720K disks that came with your package and two blank 3 1/2-inch 720K disks to create the working copies.

The disks that came with the package must be write-protected. For 3 1/2-inch disks, open the write-protect shutter. For 5 1/4-inch disks, cover the write-protect notch with an adhesive write-protection tab. The original 5 1/4-inch DOS disks are normally write-protected permanently.

Special Key Assignments for Installation

SELECT uses some of your keyboard keys for special purposes during installation. Press F1 and then F9 to see a reminder of these special key assignments. The following table summarizes the special keys in SELECT.

Table A-1
Special Key Assignments for Installation

Key	Function
Tab	Moves the cursor to the next choice.
Arrow keys	Move the cursor in the direction of the arrow key.
Enter	Takes you to the next step. (Be sure to first read information presented by SELECT.)
Esc	Takes you back to the preceding SELECT screen. Information typed on the current screen is not saved.
PgUp/PgDn	Move through HELP information when it is displayed.
F1	Brings help information to the screen. During certain operations, help is not available.
F3	Discontinues the installation process.
F9	Shows special key assignments when you view the HELP screen.

Running SELECT

If you are installing DOS V4.0 onto 360K floppies, label the four blank disks "Startup," "Shell," "Working 1", and "Working 2." If you are installing onto 720K floppies, label the two blank disks "Startup" and "Shell." If you are installing onto a 1.44M floppy, label the new disk "Startup." These new disks should *not* be write-protected at this time. Make sure, however, that the original disks are write-protected.

Insert the DOS V4.0 INSTALL disk in drive A. Now press and hold down the Ctrl and Alt keys and then press Del. If your system's power is off, turn the power on instead. This step will reboot your computer and start the SELECT program.

SELECT will present an opening identification screen and ask you to press Enter to continue. If, for some reason, you don't want to continue at this point, press Esc. SELECT will ask you to pick a drive where DOS is to be installed. Depending on your hardware, this drive could be A, B, or the hard disk C. For this installation, select A or B. Use the up- or down-arrow keys to highlight your selection. Then press Enter.

During SELECT's operation, you will be asked to switch disks several times. Confirm the disk's identity by checking its label before you proceed. SELECT is designed to pick options on the installation screens that correspond to your computer's configuration. You will be safe letting SELECT make its choices. Any choices will be highlighted, and you can select them by pressing Enter.

When the installation process is complete, you can remove the DOS original V4.0 disks and store them in a safe place. The Startup disk that SELECT created will be your working DOS disk. If you have a 360K floppy system, some of the DOS external commands may be found on the Working 1 and Working 2 disks.

SELECT creates two files, AUTOEXEC.400 and CONFIG.400. These files can be renamed AUTOEXEC.BAT and CONFIG.SYS at a later time. The two files tailor the way your computer starts and configures. You learn more about these files in Chapter 12.

To see what files reside on the working disks, use the **DIR /W** command (Chapter 4). Any working disk that shows the file COMMAND.COM can be used to start DOS from drive A. Normally, the Startup disk will serve as your working DOS disk. The Shell disk will start the DOS Shell. You can exit the Shell and go to the DOS prompt to do the exercises in this book.

Hard Disk Installation

CAUTION: If you do not know how to prepare your hard disk, you can inadvertently select an installation option that can cause permanent loss of data from your hard disk. This section on hard disk installation is intended for experienced users. Please use caution.

You can optionally run the installation operation to install V4.0 onto your hard disk, but you should follow certain precautions before hard disk installation. If your computer is on a local area network (LAN), consult the network administrator before attempting to install V4.0 on your system. If you share backed-up files with other computer users under the guidance of a lead user, ask the lead user to become familiar with the implications of BACKUP and RESTORE before proceeding with hard disk installation of V4.0.

If you bought your computer and DOS V4.0 from a dealer, ask the dealer to assist you with hard disk installation of DOS. If you have another operating system already installed on your hard disk, such as OS/2, XENIX, or UNIX, you will need to read and understand the IBM DOS V4.0 *Getting Started* manual's discussion. For hard disk installation of PC DOS 4.0, you will need one new or blank floppy disk, which SELECT will use to record your configuration options during the installation.

If you are familiar with the DOS FDISK command and understand the implications of preparing a hard disk, you can follow the procedures for installing DOS 4.0 on a hard disk. If you do not know about FDISK, do not select hard disk installation from SELECT's options. SELECT does not require you to run FDISK, but SELECT does prompt you for selections which are based on the functions of FDISK.

SELECT optionally installs DOS 4.0 to your hard disk if a hard disk is detected. SELECT allows you to automatically partition your hard disk if it does not have a primary DOS partition. SELECT then formats the hard disk after it has performed the partitioning step. Hard disks that are already partitioned prior to running SELECT are not partitioned again by SELECT if you allow SELECT to make its own choices at the prompts. If you have a new hard disk which has no partition on it, SELECT will volunteer this step as part of the installation process.

If your hard disk has already been partitioned and formatted, SELECT will copy the hidden system files to your hard disk from the DOS V4.0 disk. You can optionally specify a directory to hold the DOS V4.0 commands and utilities. By default, SELECT copies the commands and utilities as well as the Shell files to the \DOS directory. Any command or utility files with duplicate names in the directory you choose will be replaced during V4.0 installation.

SELECT detects hard disks that need only upgrading of the DOS version to 4.0. Except for changing the DOS files, SELECT leaves the existing file system intact if no partitioning or formatting of the hard disk is required.

Because DOS V4.0 supports partitions larger than 32M, users who have hard disks with capacities greater than 32M may elect to remove existing partitions and install one large partition to take advantage of V4.0's larger partition-size capability. Remember that removing a partition will destroy the files in that partition.

The booklet, *Getting Started,* which comes with the PC DOS V4.0 package, devotes several sections to hard disk installation. You should consider that booklet the source for additional information about installing PC DOS V4.0.

Preparing Your
Hard Disk

D

IMPORTANT: *Some dealers install the DOS operating system and applications programs on your hard disk before you receive your computer. If only DOS has been installed, you may skip the steps in these first two sections, which describe two of the processes for setting up the hard disk. If, however, you choose to complete the steps in these sections, you must complete both sections before proceeding to the final section.*

If your dealer has installed some applications programs, such as an accounting package, a word processor, or a data management program, you should not complete the steps outlined in the first and second sections of this appendix.

Before you can use your hard disk, you must perform three distinct processes: (1) assign the disk one or more partitions by using FDISK, (2) format the hard disk by using FORMAT, and (3) set up the hard disk for daily operations using several DOS commands. Before beginning these processes, you must have DOS up and running on your computer.

If you have an IBM Personal Computer AT, you must run the SETUP program before starting the steps outlined in the sections of this appendix. The information on SETUP is located in the Installation and Setup manual for your Personal Computer AT. In the setup procedure, you will be asked for the disk drive type. Currently, all IBM 20-megabyte disk drives are type 2, and all IBM 30-megabyte disk drives are type 20. If you are unsure of your disk drive type, remove the cover of your AT and read the large number on the front of the disk drive.

If you have an IBM PS/2 Micro Channel computer (Model 50, 50Z, 60, 70, or 80), you should boot the system from the Reference Disk. Follow the instructions, and the system will automatically configure itself for the hard disk and adapter cards you have installed.

FDISK is slightly different for DOS V3 and DOS V4. Each is addressed in separate sections in this appendix.

Using FDISK with DOS V3.2 and Earlier Versions

FDISK works a little differently with DOS V3.2 and earlier versions than it does with DOS V3.3. The differences are noted as they occur in the following instructions.

The hard disk of your computer can be used by more than one disk operating system. To accommodate the people who use more than one operating system, IBM provides the FDISK program, which divides the hard disk into partitions. Each partition is used with a different operating system.

Most people use only DOS. The instructions given in this first section are for setting up your hard disk for a single DOS partition.

Step 1. Insert your DOS start-up disk (one of the disks that came with your DOS program) into the first disk drive.

This drive will be the left or top disk drive. Close the disk drive door. Start your computer by either turning on the power if the computer is off or pressing Ctrl-Alt-Del if the computer is on. (Hold down the Ctrl and Alt keys and then press the Del key.)

Step 2. If you are not using a Personal Computer AT, type the correct date and press Enter. Separate the month, day, and year with hyphens.

If you are using an AT, check the date. If the date is incorrect, enter the correct date and then press Enter. Remember that the date was incorrect.

Step 3. If you are not using an AT, enter the correct time.

Because DOS uses a universal, 24-hour clock, add 12 to afternoon and evening hours. Separate the hours, minutes, and seconds with colons. You don't need to enter the hundredths of seconds.

If you are using an AT, check the time. If the time is incorrect, enter the correct time and press Enter. If the time is off by more than a minute or two, remember this fact.

You should now see the DOS prompt:

        A>

Step 4. Type **FDISK** and press Enter.

The screen should look something like the following:

```
IBM Personal Computer
Fixed Disk Setup Program Version 3.20
(C)Copyright IBM Corp. 1983, 1985
FDISK Options
Current Fixed Disk Drive: 1
Choose one of the following:
     1. Create DOS Partition
     2. Change Active Partition
     3. Delete DOS Partition
     4. Display Partition Data
     5. Select Next Fixed Disk Drive
Enter choice: [1]
```

Step 5. Choose option 1 by pressing Enter.

For DOS V3.2 and earlier, if the following message appears, a DOS partition has already been created on your hard disk:

```
DOS partition already exists
```

You should skip this section and the next one on formatting your disk. Press the Esc key to return to DOS.

If this message does not appear, and you have DOS V3.2 or an earlier version, your screen should look something like this:

```
Create DOS Partition
Current Fixed Disk Drive: 1
Do you wish to use the entire fixed
disk for DOS (Y/N)............? [Y]
```

Step 6. Press Enter to inform FDISK that DOS should use the entire hard disk.

The red light for the hard disk should go on briefly, and the following message should appear:

```
System will now restart
Insert DOS disk in drive A:
Press any key when ready...
```

543

Step 7. Press any key.

Because the DOS disk is already in drive A, DOS will restart. Answer the date and time questions again (Steps 2 and 3) and then proceed to the next section on formatting the hard disk.

Using FDISK with DOS V3.3 and V4

Step 1. After you have booted DOS, load the disk with FDISK in drive A.

For DOS V3.3 this will be the Operating disk; for DOS V4, the Install disk. At the A> prompt, type the following:

FDISK

You'll see a screen like this one:

```
                IBM DOS Version 4.00
              Fixed Disk Setup Program
          (C) Copyright IBM Corp. 1983, 1988
                    FDISK Options
     Current fixed disk drive:1
     Choose one of the following:
          1. Create DOS Partition or Logical DOS Drive
          2. Set active partition
          3. Delete DOS Partition or Logical DOS Drive
          4. Display partition information
          5. Select next fixed disk drive
     Enter choice:[ ]
     Press Esc to exit FDISK
```

For DOS V3.3, option 2 in this display reads Change Active Partition, and option 4 reads Display Partition Date. DOS V3.3 allows you to have more than one bootable partition, so it is possible to use FDISK to change the active (bootable) partition from one to another. DOS V4. allows you only to activate the primary DOS partition.

With either version of DOS, option 5 is displayed only if your system has more than one hard disk.

Step 2. Choose option 1.

A menu appears, which looks like this one:

```
        Create DOS Partition or Logical DOS Drive
Current fixed disk drive:1
    1. Create Primary DOS Partition
    2. Create Extended DOS Partition
    3. Create Logical DOS Drive(s) in the
       Extended DOS Partition
Enter choice:[ ]
```

The heading will be slightly different with DOS V3.3, but the menu choices are the same. The primary DOS partition is the bootable partition (under DOS V4.0), and cannot be divided into more than one logical drive. If you want to have more than one logical drive, you must divide your disk into both primary and extended DOS partitions. Menu option 3 will let you create those logical drives.

DOS V4.0 also will enable you to create a primary DOS partition that is larger than 32 megabytes. The extended DOS partition can also be larger than 32 megabytes, and the logical drives there *also* may be larger than 32 megabytes. Note that you cannot create a partition of exactly 32 megabytes; if you choose 32, FDISK will substitute 31.

Step 3. Choose option 1 to create the primary DOS partition.

The screen you will see will look like the one that follows.

```
            Create Primary DOS Partition
Current fixed disk drive: 1
Do you wish to use the maximum available size for a Primary
DOS Partition and make the partition active (Y/N).....? [Y]
Press Esc to return to FDISK options.
```

Step 4. Decide how much of your hard disk you want to allocate to the primary partition.

If you want to use the entire hard disk for a single partition, even if you are using DOS V4 and the partition is more than 32 megabytes, press Y. If you press N, DOS will report on available space and ask you to enter the amount to be set aside for this partition. With DOS V3.3, enter the number of megabytes to be allocated. With DOS V4.0, you may enter either the number of megabytes or the percentage. For example, with a 44-megabyte disk, you could type either 22 or 50% to allocate half for the primary partition. When you have selected the amount of space to allocate, press Enter. You'll be returned to the main menu.

Step 5. Choose option 2 from the main menu to make the primary partition active, so that you'll be able to use it to boot your computer.

If you want to create additional DOS partitions, because you have another physical hard disk or have not set aside the entire disk as the primary partition, follow the next

545

steps. Otherwise, press the Esc key and you are finished with FDISK. Go to the section "Using FORMAT To Prepare Your Hard Disk" to format your hard disk.

If additional partitions can be created on your disk, FDISK will automatically take you to the next menu, which looks like this:

```
Create Extended DOS Partition
Current fixed disk drive:1
Partition Status  Type   Size in Mbytes  Percentage of Disk Used
C:1       A      PRI DOS   22                  50%
Total disk space is 22 Mbytes (1 Mbyte  =   1048576 bytes)
Maximum space available for partition is 22 Mbytes (50%)
Enter partition size in Mbytes or percent of disk space (%) to
create an Extended DOS Partition..................[22]
Press Esc to return to FDISK options.
```

C:1 in the first column indicates the drive letter and the number assigned to the DOS partition. The A indicates that the partition is active; PRI DOS shows that it is the primary DOS partition. The Size and Percentage columns show the amount of space already used for the primary partition and any other DOS partitions you may already have created.

Step 6. Enter the amount of space to be allocated to the next partition.

Just as you did when you created your primary partition, you may enter the size of the extended partition(s) in megabytes or (with DOS V4.0) in percentages.

Step 7. Now create logical disk drives in the partition if you want to divide it into separate drives.

Each time you create an extended partition, FDISK will show you the following screen:

```
  Create Logical DOS Drive(s) in the Extended DOS Partition
No logical drives defined
Total Extended DOS Partition size is 22 Mbytes
(1 MByte = 104857 bytes)
Maximum space available for logical drive is 22 Mbytes
(50%)
Enter logical drive size in Mbytes or percent of disk space
(%)...[ ]
Press Esc to return to FDISK options.
```

DOS V3.3 does not show all the information provided in this DOS V4 screen, such as the size of a megabyte, or the percentage of the disk used. However, the concept is the same. Enter the space in megabytes only, rather than percentages, if you have DOS V3.3.

Step 8. Repeat Steps 5–7 to create additional partitions.

When you have created all the partitions and logical drives you want, press Esc to return to the FDISK menu. You may exit to DOS from there.

Using FORMAT To Prepare Your Hard Disk

The FORMAT command performs several functions. It lays out individual sections of the disk that DOS uses to store your programs and data. FORMAT creates the housekeeping areas so that DOS can keep track of your programs and files. The command also places the key parts of DOS on your hard disk.

To do its job, FORMAT permanently removes any files stored on the hard disk. *If you have on your hard disk any files you want to keep, do not perform the steps in this section.*

Step 1. With the DOS start-up disk in the floppy disk drive and the door closed, start the FORMAT program by typing the following:

FORMAT C: /S /V

Then press Enter. The light on the floppy disk drive should go on for a few seconds. You should see this message:

```
WARNING, ALL DATA ON NON-REMOVABLE DISK
DRIVE C: WILL BE LOST! Proceed with Format (Y/N)?
```

Step 2. Because you do want to format the hard disk, press Y and then press Enter.

You should see the following message:

```
Formatting...
```

The red light for the hard disk will stay on for two to four minutes, depending on the type of hard disk you have.

After FORMAT has completed its first stage, the message Format complete will appear. Within a few seconds, FORMAT will provide the message System transferred. This informs you that DOS has been placed on the hard disk.

Then you should see the following message:

```
Volume label (11 characters, ENTER for none)?
```

Step 3. Type a volume name that contains up to 11 characters.

This name will appear whenever you display a list of files on the hard disk and at several other times also. After you have typed the name, press Enter.

Step 4. Test the setup of your computer.

Open the floppy disk drive door and press the Ctrl-Alt-Del keys (hold down the first two keys while pressing the Del key). This sequence should restart DOS from the hard disk.

The floppy disk drive light should come on, followed by the hard disk drive light. Then the computer should beep. The computer will attempt to load DOS from the floppy disk drive. Several seconds later, the computer will try to load DOS from the hard disk. Within 20 seconds, DOS should ask you for the date.

Answer the date and time messages if they appear, as you did in steps 1 and 2 in the first section. You have now successfully prepared the hard disk to start DOS. Go to the next section on setting up files on your hard disk for daily use.

If you don't see a message about the date, either you did not press the Ctrl, Alt, and Del keys correctly, or you were not successful in preparing your hard disk. Try pressing Ctrl-Alt-Del again. If you do not see the date and time messages within 30 seconds, close the disk drive door, restart DOS from the floppy disk (press Ctrl-Alt-Del again), return to Step 1, and repeat the instructions in this section again.

Setting Up the Hard Disk for Daily Use

Because only basic setup commands are used for this setup procedure, the procedure will work for DOS V2, V3, and V4. However, some of the special capabilities of DOS V3 and V4 are not used. (If you have DOS V4, you may prefer to set up your hard disk using SELECT.)

Your hard disk is now ready to store and retrieve information under DOS. In this section, you will copy the DOS programs to the hard disk and also create some files for customizing DOS. If your computer uses minifloppy disk drives, you will have extra steps in this section because DOS comes on more than one minifloppy disk.

First, you'll restart DOS to ensure that your computer is working properly. In this section, remember to end each line you are asked to type by pressing Enter.

Step 1. Check that the DOS start-up disk is in the floppy disk drive and that the disk drive door is closed.

Step 2. Make the hard disk the current disk drive.

You do so by typing **C:**. Don't forget to press the Enter key afterward. The DOS prompt should look like this:

```
C>
```

Step 3. Create a subdirectory called BIN by typing

       MKDIR \BIN

Later you will place the DOS programs in this subdirectory.

Step 4. Create a subdirectory in BIN called SYS by typing

MKDIR \BIN\SYS

Here you will place the DOS device-driver software (files ending in SYS).

Step 5. Create another subdirectory in BIN called SAMPLES by typing

MKDIR \BIN\SAMPLES

This subdirectory is where you will place the BASIC programs on the DOS Supplemental Programs or Operating disk.

Step 6. Make BIN the current directory by typing

CHDIR \BIN

Step 7. Copy all files from the DOS start-up disk to the current directory (BIN) on the hard disk by typing

COPY A:*.* C: / V

You will see the name of each file as it is copied. Then you'll see a message like the following:

```
36 files copied
```

Remember that the number of files on the disk (and the number of files copied) will vary, depending on your version of DOS.

Step 8. Copy all files ending with SYS to the SYS directory by typing

COPY *.SYS SYS /V

You will see a message indicating that two files have been copied.

Step 9. Remove the two SYS files from the BIN subdirectory by typing

ERASE *.SYS

Because you have safely copied (in step 8) the files to the SYS subdirectory, you can remove them from BIN.

Step 10. Take the DOS start-up disk out of drive A. Put the disk back into its protective envelope. Put the DOS Operating disk into drive A and close the drive door.

Step 11. Copy to the current directory (BIN) the program files with .COM extensions on the Operating disk by typing

COPY A:*.COM C: /V

Step 12. Copy to the current directory (BIN) the program files with .EXE extensions on the Operating disk by typing

COPY A:*.EXE C: /V

Step 13. Copy the BASIC sample programs to the SAMPLES subdirectory of the hard disk by typing

COPY A:*.BAS \SAMPLES /V

You should see a message indicating that 13 files have been copied.

You have now copied most of the files from the DOS disk to the hard disk. The files you did not copy are not important.

Step 14. Remove the Operating disk and store it and the start-up disk in a safe place. (Remember that if you have DOS V4, your disks have other names, such as Install and Operating 1, Operating 2, and Operating 3.)

Step 15. Make the root (topmost) directory of the hard disk the current directory by typing

**CD **

Step 16. Begin to create a CONFIG.SYS file by typing the following command:

COPY CON CONFIG.SYS

The DOS prompt (C>) will disappear.

Step 17. Now type the following lines. Be sure to check your typing before you press Enter at the end of each line. If you make a mistake and you have already pressed Enter, perform Step 20 and then return to Step 16.

BUFFERS = 20
DEVICE c:\bin\sys\ansi.sys
FILES = 20
FCBS = 12,12 LASTDRIVE = F

Step 18. If you live in the United States or the English-speaking provinces of Canada, type the following line:

COUNTRY = 001

Step 19. If you want to use a RAM disk on a PC XT or an AT with 640K of memory or less, type the following line:

DEVICE = c:\bin\sys\vdisk.sys 180 512 64

550

If you want to use a RAM disk on a Personal Computer AT with more than 640K of memory, type the following line instead:

DEVICE = c:\bin\sys\vdisk.sys 180 512 64 /e:8

If you do not want to use a RAM disk, skip this step and continue with Step 20.

Step 20.   The cursor should be at the beginning of a blank line. If not, press Enter. Then press the F6 key.

A ^Z should appear. Press Enter again. The hard disk light should come on briefly, and you should see the message 1 file(s) copied. The DOS prompt will reappear.

You have just created a CONFIG.SYS file for your computer.

Step 21.   To begin creating an AUTOEXEC.BAT file, type the following line:

COPY CON AUTOEXEC.BAT

The DOS prompt should disappear again.

Step 22.   Now type the following lines:

ECHO OFF
PATH=C:\BIN;C:

As before, check your typing before you press Enter at the end of each line (for this step and the next two steps). If you notice a mistake after you have pressed Enter, perform Step 26 and then return to Step 21.

Step 23.   If you are in the United States or the English-speaking provinces of Canada, go to Step 24.

Step 24.   If you have an IBM Color/Graphics Adapter (CGA) on your computer, type the following line as well:

GRAFTABL

Step 25.   If you have a Personal Computer AT, continue with step 26. Otherwise, type the following lines:

DATE
TIME

Step 26.   The cursor should be at the beginning of a blank line. If not, press Enter. Then press the F6 key.

A ^Z should appear. Press Enter again. The hard disk light should come on briefly, and you should see the message 1 file(s) copied. The DOS prompt (C>) will reappear.

You have just created an AUTOEXEC.BAT file for your computer.

Step 27. Test the setup you have just created. Make sure that the floppy disk drive door is open. Press the Ctrl-Alt-Del sequence to restart DOS. In one minute, you should see the following lines if you used the VDISK line in your CONFIG.SYS file:

```
VDISK  Version 2.0 virtual disk D:
VDISK Buffer size:          180 KB
VDISK Sector size:          512
VDISK Directory entries:     64
VDISK Transfer size:          8
```

If you are not using a Personal Computer AT or PS/2, DOS will ask for the date and time. Provide this information. The DOS prompt, C>, should appear. If you are using a Personal Computer AT, the DOS prompt should appear; you should not see a request for the date or time.

If you see a message about a file not found, a syntax error, or some other problem, repeat steps 16–27. If the same message appears again, repeat the entire procedure, beginning at the point where you create the \BIN directory.

The final test is to run the CHKDSK program. Type **CHKDSK**. If you see a message that says something about a bad command or a file not found, return to Step 21 and try creating your AUTOEXEC.BAT file again. If, after restarting DOS and typing CHKDSK, you get the same message, the DOS files did not get copied correctly. Try repeating Steps 6, 7, and 9.

You're finished! DOS is set up on your computer and is ready to go. When you start your computer, make sure that the door to the floppy disk drive is open. When you turn on the power or press Ctrl-Alt-Del, DOS will automatically start from the hard disk.

A Note to Personal Computer AT Owners

If you discovered that the date or time for your computer was incorrect, the correct date or time you gave to DOS is kept until the computer is turned off or until DOS is restarted. When you use DOS's DATE and TIME commands to set the computer's date and time, DOS versions prior to V3.3 do not set the battery-backed clock/calendar of the AT.

To change the internal date and time of the Personal Computer AT, you must run the SETUP program again. Directions for using SETUP are in the Installation and Setup manual that comes with your computer.

Changes between Versions of DOS

Several major changes occurred between DOS V2 and V3. Additional revisions occurred between DOS V3–3.3 and between V3.3 and V4.0. All these changes are described briefly in this appendix.

Changes between DOS V2.x and DOS V3.0

DOS V3.0 offers several new commands, changed commands, and changed features.

New CONFIG.SYS Features

The following CONFIG.SYS directives are available in V3.0:

COUNTRY	Allows DOS to change its date, time, and other characteristics for international use
FCBS	Controls DOS's reactions to a program's use of DOS V1 file handling
LASTDRIVE	Sets the last real or nonreal disk drive that DOS will use
VDISK.SYS	Provides additional RAM (virtual) disk space

The undocumented SWITCHAR directive was dropped.

New Commands

The following commands were added to DOS V3.0:

ATTRIB — Enables the user to set the read-only attribute of a file

GRAFTABL — Allows legible display of some graphics characters if you use the Color/Graphics Adapter in medium-resolution graphics mode

KEYBxx — Changes the keyboard layout for different languages

LABEL — Enables a user to add, change, or delete a disk's volume label

SELECT — Enables a user to customize the start-up disk for use with languages other than English

SHARE — Provides file sharing (file and record locking)

Changed Commands

The following commands were changed between DOS V2 and V3:

BACKUP and RESTORE — Includes the backing up of floppy disks and enables backups to be placed on another hard disk

DATE and TIME — Supports international date and time formats

FORMAT — Includes the /4 switch to format 360K floppy disks on 1.2M disk drives; also warns when a hard disk is to be formatted

GRAPHICS — Includes support for the IBM Personal Computer Compact and Color Printers

Changed Features

With DOS V3.0, a drive name and a path name can now be specified before an external command or program name. You can run programs that do not reside in the current directory or in a directory specified in the PATH command.

Changes between DOS V3.0 and V3.1

The following changes were made between DOS V3.0 and V3.1.

New Commands

The following commands are available under DOS V3.1:

JOIN	Enables the user to connect the directory structures of two different disk drives, thus creating "one" disk drive
SUBST	Enables a subdirectory to be used as though it were a disk drive

DOS V3.1 supports the IBM PC Network commands.

Changed Commands

The following commands were changed in V3.1:

LABEL	Prompts the user before deleting a volume label
SHELL	Includes the */E:size* switch; *size* in 16-byte paragraphs
TREE	Displays files in the root directory when the */F* switch is used

Changes between DOS V3.1 and V3.2

The following changes were made between DOS V3.1 and V3.2.

New CONFIG.SYS Features

STACKS	Sets the number and size of the DOS internal stacks

The DRIVER.SYS device driver was added to support various-sized floppy disks, particularly 720K microfloppy drives on Personal Computers.

New Feature

Support for the IBM Token Ring was added.

New Commands

REPLACE	Selectively updates files in one or many directories; adds missing files to a directory
XCOPY	Copies files from one or more directories to another; selectively copies files

Changed Commands/Directives

ATTRIB	**+A/–A** switch added; controls the archive attribute of files
COMMAND	*/E* switch added; supports the environment size
DISKCOPY/DISKCOMP	Supports 720K floppy disks
FORMAT	Supports formatting of 720K floppy disks; requests verification before formatting a nonremovable disk that has a volume label; disk drive name required
SELECT	Formats the hard disk and copies DOS files
SHELL	*/E:size* switch specifies the environment size in bytes, not 16-byte paragraphs

Changes between DOS V3.2 and V3.3

The following changes were made between DOS V3.2 and V3.3.

New CONFIG.SYS Options

The following device drivers for use with the DEVICE directive were added:

DISPLAY.SYS	Supports code pages (multiple fonts) on EGA, VGA, and PC Convertible displays
PRINTER.SYS	Supports code pages (multiple fonts) on the IBM ProPrinter and Quietwriter III printers

New Features

Support was added for 1.44M microfloppy disks, for COM4: and 19,200 baud rates, and for switchable code pages (international character fonts).

New Commands

The following commands were added to DOS V3.3:

APPEND	A PATH-like command for data files
CHCP	Provides code page changing
FASTOPEN	Provides a directory-caching program for hard disks
NLSFUNC	Provides support for additional character sets (code pages) and for country-dependent information

Changed Commands/Directives

The following commands and CONFIG.SYS directives were changed for DOS V3.3:

ATTRIB	Has the /S switch to change the attributes of files in subdirectories
BACKUP	Has the /F switch to format floppy disks, the /T switch to back up files based on their time, and the /L switch to produce a log file; also places all backed-up files into a single file
batch files	Adds support for using the environment variable (*%variable%*), @ for suppressing display of a line, and the CALL subcommand for running a second batch file and returning control to the first batch file
BUFFERS	Default buffers based on random-access memory in the computer
COUNTRY	Adds support for code pages and a separate country information file (COUNTRY.SYS)
DATE and TIME	Sets the computer's clock/calendar
DISKCOPY/DISKCOMP	Supports 1.44M floppy disks
FDISK	Supports multiple logical disks on a large hard disk
FORMAT	Adds the /N switch for number of sectors and the /T switch for number of tracks
GRAFTABL	Supports code pages; also supports additional devices and higher baud rates

KEYB	Replaces the KEYBxx programs and supports additional layouts
MODE	Supports code pages; also supports additional devices and higher baud rate
RESTORE	Adds the /N switch to restore erased or modified files, the /B switch to restore files modified before a given date, and the /L and /E switches to restore files modified after or before a given time
SHELL	Default environment size changed from 128 to 160 bytes

Changes between DOS V3.3 and V4

The following changes were made between DOS V3.3 and DOS V4.

New CONFIG.SYS Features

INSTALL	Allows loading of terminate-and-stay-resident programs that were previously loaded from the DOS command prompt or in the AUTOEXEC.BAT file; includes FASTOPEN.EXE, KEYB.COM, NLSFUNC.EXE, and SHARE.EXE
REM	Allows the insertion of remarks in a CONFIG.SYS file, which DOS will ignore when the computer is booted
SWITCHES	Disables Enhanced Keyboard functions so that software that cannot use those functions will remain compatible
XMA2EMS.SYS	A new device driver for expanded memory
XMAEM.SYS	Allows emulation of an expanded memory adapter on 80386 machines

New Features

A new user interface, the DOS Shell, allows the running of programs and the management of files using a graphics- or text-oriented menu system. Many error messages were changed, and error checking was refined.

New Commands

MEM	Provides a report on available conventional, extended, and expanded memory, and lists how much of each is unused
TRUENAME	Lists the actual name of a drive or directory affected by a JOIN or SUBST command

Changed Commands/Directives

The following commands and CONFIG.SYS directives were changed between DOS V3.3 and V4:

ANSI.SYS	Gained three new parameters: /X, which redefines keys added to Enhanced Keyboards; /L, which tells DOS to override any applications program that resets the number of screen rows to 25; and /K, which turns off extended keyboard functions to comply with noncompatible software
APPEND	Can ignore file operations that already include a drive or path in the original specification
BACKUP	Automatically formats target floppy disks if necessary
BUFFERS	Allows the /X switch, which tells DOS to use expanded memory; specify up to 10,000 buffers and ,1 to 8 look-ahead buffers
CHKDSK	Shows the disk's serial number and tells the size and number of allocation units
COUNTRY	Provides support for Japanese, Korean, and Chinese characters—on special Asian hardware only
DEL/ERASE	Includes /P, which allows you to verify each file name before it is deleted
DIR	Shows the disk's serial number
DISPLAY.SYS	Checks hardware and automatically chooses the most appropriate type of active display if you don't specify an adapter type
FASTOPEN	May be loaded from CONFIG.SYS, and has the /X parameter, which tells DOS to use expanded memory
FDISK	Supports larger disk partitions and has easier-to-use menus and displays

559

FORMAT	Has a */V:label* parameter, which lets you specify the label on the command line as you start to format a disk, and a new */F:size* parameter, which allows you to indicate the size of a floppy disk when you want to format the disk for less than its maximum capacity
GRAFTABL	Supports code page 850
GRAPHICS	Supports EGA and VGA adapters and can support more printers
KEYB	Has a */ID.nnn* parameter, which can be used to choose a specific keyboard for countries like France, Italy, and Great Britain that have more than one Enhanced Keyboard
MODE	Lets you specify the keyboard rate and number of lines displayed on the screen; has parameters for the COM ports
PRINTER.SYS	Has enhanced support for the IBM ProPrinter
REPLACE	Has the */U* parameter, which tells DOS to update files that have a date and time more recent than that of a file with the same name on the target disk
SELECT	Enhanced to install DOS
SYS	Changed to allow specification of an optional source drive
TIME	Allows either a 12-hour or 24-hour clock, depending on the country code in use
TREE	Includes graphics and indentations to show various subdirectory levels
VDISK.SYS	Has the */X* parameter, which tells DOS to use expanded memory, and the */E* parameter, which tells DOS to use extended memory

DOS Control and
Editing Keys

Control Keys

Enter, Return, or ⏎	Tells DOS to act on the line you just typed
←	Backs up and deletes one character from the line
Ctrl-C Ctrl-Break	Stops a command
Ctrl-Num Lock Ctrl-S	Freezes the video display; pressing any other key restarts the display
PrtSc Print Screen	Prints the contents of the video display (print-screen feature)
Ctrl-PrtSc Ctrl-Print Screen Ctrl-P	Echoes lines sent to the screen to the printer also; giving this sequence a second time turns off this function (printer echo feature)
Ctrl-Alt-Del	Restarts DOS (system reset)

Editing Keys

When you type a line and press Enter, DOS copies the line into an input buffer. By using certain keys, you can use the same line over and over again. The following keys enable you to edit the input buffer line. When you press Enter, the new line is placed into the primary input buffer as DOS executes the line.

|←	Moves to the next tab stop
→|	
Esc	Cancels the current line and does not change buffer
Ins	Enables you to insert characters in the line
Del	Deletes a character from the line
F1 or →	Copies one character from the previous command line
F2	Copies all characters from the previous command line up to, but not including, the next character you type
F3	Copies all remaining characters from the previous command line
F4	Deletes all characters from the previous command line up to, but not including, the next character you type (opposite of F2)
F5	Moves the current line you are typing into the buffer but does not allow DOS to execute the line
F6	Produces an end-of-file marker when you copy from the console to a disk file

Special Key Definitions within the DOS Shell

DOS V4 assigns special functions to some of the keys used with the Start Programs menu.

Enter or ↵	Places the information you select or type into memory
Esc	Cancels the current function
F1	Displays a series of text screens with help information
PgUp PgDn	Scrolls through "pages" of information
F2	Saves the information typed in an entry field and completes the copy operation in Start Programs

F3	Returns you to the DOS command prompt from Start Programs and the File System; cancels copying operations in Start Programs
F4	Creates the		marker that separates the commands used to start a program
F9	Displays key assignments within HELP; returns an entry field to its original value; switches the View function between ASCII and hexadecimal format
Shift-F9	Takes you to the DOS command prompt; typing **EXIT** returns you to the DOS Shell
F10	Moves the cursor to the action bar if the cursor is located in the Main Group or to the Main Group if the cursor is located in the action bar
Space bar	Selects or deselects a file name
Tab	Moves the selection cursor to different areas of the File System screen

Key Assignments within the DOS Shell's HELP Feature

DOS V4 provides a context-sensitive help feature for all selectable items and entry fields. Within HELP, special function key assignments assist you in using HELP.

Esc	Returns you to the menu
F1	Provides instructions on how to use HELP
F9	Lists the special key definitions in HELP
F11 or Alt-F1	Displays an index of available HELP screens

563

ASCII and Extended ASCII Codes

G

This appendix presents the ASCII, Extended ASCII, and Extended-Function ASCII codes. In the tables, a ∧ represents the Control (Ctrl) key. For example, ∧C represents Ctrl-C.

ASCII Codes

The codes for the American Standard Code for Information Interchange (ASCII) are presented in the following table.

Decimal	Hex	Octal	Binary	Graphic Character	ASCII Meaning
0	0	0	00000000		^@ NUL (null)
1	1	1	00000001	☺	^A SOH (start-of-header)
2	2	2	00000010	●	^B STX (start-of-transmission)
3	3	3	00000011	♥	^C ETX (end-of-transmission)
4	4	4	00000100	♦	^D EOT (end-of-text)
5	5	5	00000101	♣	^E ENQ (enquiry)
6	6	6	00000110	♠	^F ACK (acknowledge)
7	7	7	00000111	·	^G BEL (bell)

Decimal	Hex	Octal	Binary	Graphic Character	ASCII Meaning
8	8	10	00001000	∙	^H BS (backspace)
9	9	11	00001001	○	^I HT (horizontal tab)
10	A	12	00001010	○	^J LF (line feed - also ^Enter)
11	B	13	00001011	σ	^K VT (vertical tab)
12	C	14	00001100	♀	^L FF (form feed)
13	D	15	00001101	♪	^M CR (carriage return)
14	E	16	00001110	♫	^N SO
15	F	17	00001111	✿	^O SI
16	10	20	00010000	►	^P DLE
17	11	21	00010001	◄	^Q DC1
18	12	22	00010010	↕	^R DC2
19	13	23	00010011	‼	^S DC3
20	14	24	00010100	¶	^T DC4
21	15	25	00010101	§	^U NAK
22	16	26	00010110	▬	^V SYN
23	17	27	00010111	↨	^W ETB
24	18	30	00011000	↑	^X CAN (cancel)
25	19	31	00011001	↓	^Y EM
26	1A	32	00011010	→	^Z SUB (also end-of-file)
27	1B	33	00011011	←	^[ESC (Escape)
28	1C	34	00011100	∟	^\ FS (field separator)
29	1D	35	00011101	↔	^] GS
30	1E	36	00011110	▲	^^ RS (record separator)
31	1F	37	00011111	▼	^_ US
32	20	40	00100000		Space
33	21	41	00100001	!	!
34	22	42	00100010	"	"
35	23	43	00100011	#	#
36	24	44	00100100	$	$
37	25	45	00100101	%	%
38	26	46	00100110	&	&
39	27	47	00100111	'	'
40	28	50	00101000	(	(
41	29	51	00101001	)	)
42	2A	52	00101010	*	*
43	2B	53	00101011	+	+
44	2C	54	00101100	,	,
45	2D	55	00101101	-	-
46	2E	56	00101110	.	.
47	2F	57	00101111	/	/
48	30	60	00110000	0	0
49	31	61	00110001	1	1
50	32	62	00110010	2	2
51	33	63	00110011	3	3
52	34	64	00110100	4	4
53	35	65	00110101	5	5
54	36	66	00110110	6	6
55	37	67	00110111	7	7
56	38	70	00111000	8	8
57	39	71	00111001	9	9

Decimal	Hex	Octal	Binary	Graphic Character	ASCII Meaning
58	3A	72	00111010	:	:
59	3B	73	00111011	;	;
60	3C	74	00111100	<	<
61	3D	75	00111101	=	=
62	3E	76	00111110	>	>
63	3F	77	00111111	?	?
64	40	100	01000000	@	@
65	41	101	01000001	A	A
66	42	102	01000010	B	B
67	43	103	01000011	C	C
68	44	104	01000100	D	D
69	45	105	01000101	E	E
70	46	106	01000110	F	F
71	47	107	01000111	G	G
72	48	110	01001000	H	H
73	49	111	01001001	I	I
74	4A	112	01001010	J	J
75	4B	113	01001011	K	K
76	4C	114	01001100	L	L
77	4D	115	01001101	M	M
78	4E	116	01001110	N	N
79	4F	117	01001111	O	O
80	50	120	01010000	P	P
81	51	121	01010001	Q	Q
82	52	122	01010010	R	R
83	53	123	01010011	S	S
84	54	124	01010100	T	T
85	55	125	01010101	U	U
86	56	126	01010110	V	V
87	57	127	01010111	W	W
88	58	130	01011000	X	X
89	59	131	01011001	Y	Y
90	5A	132	01011010	Z	Z
91	5B	133	01011011	[	[
92	5C	134	01011100	\	\
93	5D	135	01011101	]	]
94	5E	136	01011110	^	^
95	5F	137	01011111	_	_
96	60	140	01100000	'	'
97	61	141	01100001	a	a
98	62	142	01100010	b	b
99	63	143	01100011	c	c
100	64	144	01100100	d	d
101	65	145	01100101	e	e
102	66	146	01100110	f	f
103	67	147	01100111	g	g
104	68	150	01101000	h	h
105	69	151	01101001	i	i
106	6A	152	01101010	j	j
107	6B	153	01101011	k	k

Decimal	Hex	Octal	Binary	Graphic Character	ASCII Meaning
108	6C	154	01101100	l	l
109	6D	155	01101101	m	m
110	6E	156	01101110	n	n
111	6F	157	01101111	o	o
112	70	160	01110000	p	p
113	71	161	01110001	q	q
114	72	162	01110010	r	r
115	73	163	01110011	s	s
116	74	164	01110100	t	t
117	75	165	01110101	u	u
118	76	166	01110110	v	v
119	77	167	01110111	w	w
120	78	170	01111000	x	x
121	79	171	01111001	y	y
122	7A	172	01111010	z	z
123	7B	173	01111011	{	{
124	7C	174	01111100	|	|
125	7D	175	01111101	}	}
126	7E	176	01111110	~	~
127	7F	177	01111111	Δ	Del
128	80	200	10000000	Ç	
129	81	201	10000001	ü	
130	82	202	10000010	é	
131	83	203	10000011	â	
132	84	204	10000100	ä	
133	85	205	10000101	à	
134	86	206	10000110	à	
135	87	207	10000111	ç	
136	88	210	10001000	ê	
137	89	211	10001001	ë	
138	8A	212	10001010	è	
139	8B	213	10001011	ï	
140	8C	214	10001100	î	
141	8D	215	10001101	ì	
142	8E	216	10001110	Ä	
143	8F	217	10001111	À	
144	90	220	10010000	É	
145	91	221	10010001	æ	
146	92	222	10010010	Æ	
147	93	223	10010011	ô	
148	94	224	10010100	ö	
149	95	225	10010101	ò	
150	96	226	10010110	û	
151	97	227	10010111	ù	
152	98	230	10011000	ÿ	
153	99	231	10011001	Ö	
154	9A	232	10011010	Ü	
155	9B	233	10011011	¢	
156	9C	234	10011100	£	

Decimal	Hex	Octal	Binary	Graphic Character
157	9D	235	10011101	¥
158	9E	236	10011110	Pt
159	9F	237	10011111	ƒ
160	A0	240	10100000	á
161	A1	241	10100001	í
162	A2	242	10100010	ó
163	A3	243	10100011	ú
164	A4	244	10100100	ñ
165	A5	245	10100101	Ñ
166	A6	246	10100110	ª
167	A7	247	10100111	º
168	A8	250	10101000	¿
169	A9	251	10101001	⌐
170	AA	252	10101010	¬
171	AB	253	10101011	½
172	AC	254	10101100	¼
173	AD	255	10101101	¡
174	AE	256	10101110	«
175	AF	257	10101111	»
176	B0	260	10110000	░
177	B1	261	10110001	▒
178	B2	262	10110010	▓
179	B3	263	10110011	│
180	B4	264	10110100	┤
181	B5	265	10110101	╡
182	B6	266	10110110	╢
183	B7	267	10110111	╖
184	B8	270	10111000	╕
185	B9	271	10111001	╣
186	BA	272	10111010	║
187	BB	273	10111011	╗
188	BC	274	10111100	╝
189	BD	275	10111101	╜
190	BE	276	10111110	╛
191	BF	277	10111111	┐
192	C0	300	11000000	└
193	C1	301	11000001	┴
194	C2	302	11000010	┬
195	C3	303	11000011	├
196	C4	304	11000100	─
197	C5	305	11000101	┼
198	C6	306	11000110	╞
199	C7	307	11000111	╟
200	C8	310	11001000	╚
201	C9	311	11001001	╔
202	CA	312	11001010	╩
203	CB	313	11001011	╦
204	CC	314	11001100	╠
205	CD	315	11001101	═
206	CE	316	11001110	╬

Decimal	Hex	Octal	Binary	Graphic Character
207	CF	317	11001111	⊥
208	D0	320	11010000	⊥
209	D1	321	11010001	⊤
210	D2	322	11010010	π
211	D3	323	11010011	⊔
212	D4	324	11010100	⊢
213	D5	325	11010101	F
214	D6	326	11010110	π
215	D7	327	11010111	╫
216	D8	330	11011000	╪
217	D9	331	11011001	⌐
218	DA	332	11011010	⌐
219	DB	333	11011011	█
220	DC	334	11011100	▄
221	DD	335	11011101	▌
222	DE	336	11011110	▐
223	DF	337	11011111	▀
224	E0	340	11100000	∝
225	E1	341	11100001	β
226	E2	342	11100010	Γ
227	E3	343	11100011	π
228	E4	344	11100100	Σ
229	E5	345	11100101	σ
230	E6	346	11100110	μ
231	E7	347	11100111	τ
232	E8	350	11101000	Φ
233	E9	351	11101001	Θ
234	EA	352	11101010	Ω
235	EB	353	11101011	δ
236	EC	354	11101100	∞
237	ED	355	11101101	φ
238	EE	356	11101110	∈
239	EF	357	11101111	∩
240	F0	360	11110000	≡
241	F1	361	11110001	±
242	F2	362	11110010	≥
243	F3	363	11110011	≤
244	F4	364	11110100	⌠
245	F5	365	11110101	⌡
246	F6	366	11110110	÷
247	F7	367	11110111	≈
248	F8	370	11111000	°
249	F9	371	11111001	·
250	FA	372	11111010	·
251	FB	373	11111011	√
252	FC	374	11111100	n
253	FD	375	11111101	²
254	FE	376	11111110	∎
255	FF	377	11111111	

Extended ASCII Keyboard Codes

Certain keys cannot be represented by the standard ASCII codes. To represent the codes, a two-character sequence is used. The first character is always an ASCII NUL (0). The second character and its translation are listed in the following table. Some codes expand to multi-keystroke characters.

If an asterisk (*) appears in the column *Enhanced Only*, the sequence is available only on the Enhanced Keyboards (101- and 102-key keyboards).

Enhanced Only	Decimal Meaning	Hex	Octal	Binary	Extended ASCII
*	1	01	001	00000001	Alt-Esc
	3	03	003	00000011	Null (null character)
*	14	0E	016	00001110	Alt-Backspace
	15	0F	017	00001111	Shift-Tab (back-tab)
	16	10	020	00010000	Alt-Q
	17	11	021	00010001	Alt-W
	18	12	022	00010010	Alt-E
	19	13	023	00010011	Alt-R
	20	14	024	00010100	Alt-T
	21	15	025	00010101	Alt-Y
	22	16	026	00010110	Alt-U
	23	17	027	00010111	Alt-I
	24	18	030	00011000	Alt-O
	25	19	031	00011001	Alt-P
*	26	1A	032	00011010	Alt-[
*	27	1B	033	00011011	Alt-]
*	28	1C	034	00011100	Alt-Enter
	30	1E	036	00011110	Alt-A
	31	1F	037	00011111	Alt-S
	32	20	040	00100000	Alt-D
	33	21	041	00100001	Alt-F
	34	22	042	00100010	Alt-G
	35	23	043	00100011	Alt-H
	36	24	044	00100100	Alt-J
	37	25	045	00100101	Alt-K
	38	26	046	00100110	Alt-L
*	39	27	047	00100111	Alt-;
*	40	28	050	00101000	Alt-'
*	41	29	051	00101001	Alt-'
*	43	2B	053	00101011	Alt-\
	44	2C	054	00101100	Alt-Z
	45	2D	055	00101101	Alt-X
	46	2E	056	00101110	Alt-C
	47	2F	057	00101111	Alt-V
	48	30	060	00110000	Alt-B
	49	31	061	00110001	Alt-N
	50	32	062	00110010	Alt-M
*	51	33	063	00110011	Alt-,

Enhanced Only	Decimal Meaning	Hex	Octal	Binary	Extended ASCII
*	52	34	064	00110100	Alt-.
*	53	35	065	00110101	Alt-/
*	55	37	067	00110111	Alt-* (keypad)
	57	39	071	00111001	Alt-space bar
	59	3B	073	00111011	F1
	60	3C	074	00111100	F2
	61	3D	075	00111101	F3
	62	3E	076	00111110	F4
	63	3F	077	00111111	F5
	64	40	100	01000000	F6
	65	41	101	01000001	F7
	66	42	102	01000010	F8
	67	43	103	01000011	F9
	68	44	104	01000100	F10
	71	47	107	01000111	Home
	72	48	110	01001000	↑
	73	49	111	01001001	PgUp
	74	4A	112	01001010	Alt-— (keypad)
	75	4B	113	01001011	←
	76	4C	114	01001100	Shift-5 (keypad)
	77	4D	115	01001101	→
	78	4E	116	01001110	Alt-+ (keypad)
	79	4F	117	01001111	End
*	80	50	120	01010000	↓
*	81	51	121	01010001	PgDn
*	82	52	122	01010010	Ins (Insert)
	83	53	123	01010011	Del (Delete)
	84	54	124	01010100	Shift-F1
	85	55	125	01010101	Shift-F2
	86	56	126	01010110	Shift-F3
	87	57	127	01010111	Shift-F4
	88	58	130	01011000	Shift-F5
	89	59	131	01011001	Shift-F6
	90	5A	132	01011010	Shift-F7
	91	5B	133	01011011	Shift-F8
	92	5C	134	01011100	Shift-F9
	93	5D	135	01011101	Shift-F10
	94	5E	136	01011110	Ctrl-F1
	95	5F	137	01011111	Ctrl-F2
	96	60	140	01100000	Ctrl-F3
	97	61	141	01100001	Ctrl-F4
	98	62	142	01100010	Ctrl-F5
	99	63	143	01100011	Ctrl-F6
	100	64	144	01100100	Ctrl-F7
	101	65	145	01100101	Ctrl-F8
	102	66	146	01100110	Ctrl-F9
	103	67	147	01100111	Ctrl-F10
	104	68	150	01101000	Alt-F1
	105	69	151	01101001	Alt-F2
	106	6A	152	01101010	Alt-F3

Enhanced Only	Decimal Meaning	Hex	Octal	Binary	Extended ASCII
	107	6B	153	01101011	Alt-F4
	108	6C	154	01101100	Alt-F5
	109	6D	155	01101101	Alt-F6
	110	6E	156	01101110	Alt-F7
	111	6F	157	01101111	Alt-F8
	112	70	160	01110000	Alt-F9
	113	71	161	01110001	Alt-F10
	114	72	162	01110010	Ctrl-PrtSc
	115	73	163	01110011	Ctrl-←
	116	74	164	01110100	Ctrl-→
	117	75	165	01110101	Ctrl-End
	118	76	166	01110110	Ctrl-PgDn
	119	77	167	01110111	Ctrl-Home
	120	78	170	01111000	Alt-1 (keyboard)
	121	79	171	01111001	Alt-2 (keyboard)
	122	7A	172	01111010	Alt-3 (keyboard)
	123	7B	173	01111011	Alt-4 (keyboard)
	124	7C	174	01111100	Alt-5 (keyboard)
	125	7D	175	01111101	Alt-6 (keyboard)
	126	7E	176	01111110	Alt-7 (keyboard)
	127	7F	177	01111111	Alt-8 (keyboard)
	128	80	200	10000000	Alt-9 (keyboard)
	129	81	201	10000001	Alt-0 (keyboard)
	130	82	202	10000010	Alt-— (keyboard)
	131	83	203	10000011	Alt-= (keyboard)
	132	84	204	10000100	Ctrl-PgUp
*	133	85	205	10000101	F11
*	134	86	206	10000110	F12
*	135	87	207	10000111	Shift-F11
*	136	88	210	10001000	Shift-F12
*	137	89	211	10001001	Ctrl-F11
*	138	8A	212	10001010	Ctrl-F12
*	139	8B	213	10001011	Alt-F11
*	140	8C	214	10001100	Alt-F12
	141	8D	215	10001101	Ctrl-↑/8 (keypad)
	142	8E	216	10001110	Ctrl-— (keypad)
	143	8F	217	10001111	Ctrl-5 (keypad)
	144	90	220	10010000	Ctrl-+ (keypad)
	145	91	221	10010001	Ctrl-↓/2 (keypad)
	146	92	222	10010010	Ctrl-Ins/0 (keypad)
	147	93	223	10010011	Ctrl-Del/. (keypad)
	148	94	224	10010100	Ctrl-Tab
*	149	95	225	10010101	Ctrl-/ (keypad)
*	150	96	226	10010110	Ctrl-* (keypad)
*	151	97	227	10010111	Alt-Home
*	152	98	230	10011000	Alt-↑
*	153	99	231	10011001	Alt-Page Up
*	155	9B	233	10011011	Alt-←
*	157	9D	235	10011101	Alt-→
*	159	9F	237	10011111	Alt-End

Enhanced Only	Decimal Meaning	Hex	Octal	Binary	Extended ASCII
*	160	A0	240	10100000	Alt-↓
*	161	A1	241	10100001	Alt-Page Down
*	162	A2	242	10100010	Alt-Insert
*	163	A3	243	10100011	Alt-Delete
*	164	A4	244	10100100	Alt-/ (keypad)
*	165	A5	245	10100101	Alt-Tab
*	166	A6	256	10100110	Alt-Enter (keypad)

Extended Function ASCII Codes

The following extended codes are available only with the Enhanced Keyboards (101/102-key keyboards); the codes are available for key reassignment only under DOS V4.0. The keys include the six-key editing pad and the four-key cursor-control pad. To reassign these keys, you must give the **DEVICE = ANSI.SYS /X** directive or the enable extended function codes escape sequence (**Esc[1q**). All extended codes are prefixed by 224 decimal (E0 hex).

Decimal	Hex	Octal	Binary	Extended ASCII Meaning
71	47	107	01000111	Home
72	48	110	01001000	↑
73	49	111	01001001	Page Up
75	4B	113	01001011	←
77	4D	115	01001101	→
79	4F	117	01001111	End
80	50	120	01010000	↓
81	51	121	01010001	Page Down
82	52	122	01010010	Insert
83	53	123	01010011	Delete
115	73	163	01110011	Ctrl-←
116	74	164	01110100	Ctrl-→
117	75	165	01110101	Ctrl-End
118	76	166	01110110	Ctrl-Page Down
119	77	167	01110111	Ctrl-Home
132	84	204	10000100	Ctrl-Page Up
141	8D	215	10001101	Ctrl-↑
145	91	221	10010001	Ctrl-↓
146	92	222	10010010	Ctrl-Insert
147	93	223	10010011	Ctrl-Delete

ANSI Terminal Codes

All ANSI terminal codes are preceded by an Escape (ESC) character and a left bracket ([). The Escape character is 27 decimal or 1b hexadecimal.

Cursor-Control Sequences

For the cursor-control sequences, if a value is omitted, the default value of 1 is used.

Cursor Position

Horizontal and Vertical Position

ESC[#;#H ESC[#;#f	The first # is the row (vertical coordinate); the second # is the column (horizontal coordinate). The starting value for either coordinate is 1 (also the default value).

Cursor Up

ESC[#A   # is the number of rows to move up.

Cursor Down

ESC[#B   # is the number of rows to move down.

Cursor Forward

ESC[#C   # is the number of columns to move forward (right).

Cursor Backward

ESC[#D   # is the number of columns to move backward (left).

Device Status Report

ESC[6n   Inputs through the keyboard a cursor report on the current cursor position.

Cursor Position Report

ESC[#;#R   Reports the current cursor position. The string is returned by the ANSI console and is eight characters long. The first # is the two-digit row number; the second # is the two-digit column number.

Save Cursor Position

ESC[s   Saves the current cursor position in the driver. The position can be restored by using ESC[u.

Restore Cursor Position

ESC[u   Sets the cursor to the horizontal and vertical position that was saved.

Erasing

Erase Display

ESC[2J   Erases the display and also moves the cursor to the Home
                  position (the upper left corner of the screen).

Erase to End of Line

ESC[K   Erases from the current cursor position to the end of the
                  current line.

Modes of Operation

For all ANSI-operation-mode control codes, if a parameter is omitted, the default
value of 0 is used.

Set Graphics Rendition

ESC[#;...;#m   Sets the character attributes by the following parameters. The
                  attributes remain in effect until the next graphics rendition
                  command.

Parameter	Meaning
0	All attributes off (normally white on black)
1	Bold on (high intensity)
4	Underscore on (IBM Monochrome Display only)
5	Blink on
7	Reverse (inverse) video on
8	Cancel on (invisible characters black on black)
30	Black foreground
31	Red foreground
32	Green foreground
33	Yellow foreground
34	Blue foreground
35	Magenta foreground
36	Cyan foreground

Parameter	Meaning
37	White foreground
40	Black background
41	Red background
42	Green background
43	Yellow background
44	Blue background
45	Magenta background
46	Cyan background
47	White background

Set Screen Mode

Esc[=#h   Sets the screen width or type based on #

    (for parameter 7 only)

Esc[=7h   Turns on the wrap at end-of-line; long lines automatically
Esc[?7   wrap onto subsequent lines.

Reset Screen Mode

Esc[=#1   Resets the screen width or type based on # (in the
following list).

    (for parameter 7 only)

Esc[?71   Turns off wrap at end-of-line; long lines are truncated at
Esc[=71   the end-of-line.

Parameter	Meaning
*0	40 × 25 monochrome
*1	40 × 25 color
*2	80 × 25 monochrome
*3	80 × 25 color
*4	320 × 200 color
*5	320 × 200 monochrome
*6	640 × 200 monochrome
*7	Wrap at end-of-line (set mode); or do not wrap and discard characters past end of line (reset mode).

Parameter	Meaning
*14	640 × 200 color
*15	640 × 350 monochrome
*16	640 × 350 color
*17	640 × 480 monochrome
*18	640 × 480 color
*19	320 × 200 color

*Available with DOS V4.0 and later versions.

Keyboard Key Reassignment

Reassign Keyboard Keys

Esc[sequencep   Sets the sequence typed by the named key.

sequence can be in the form of #;#; ...# (where # represents the one-, two-, or three-digit code for an ASCII character), or "string" (a string of characters within double quotation marks), or any combination of the two provided that # and "string" are separated by a semicolon.

Esc[#;#;...;p

or

Esc["string"p

or

Esc[#;"string";#;#;"string";#p

The first ASCII code (the first #) defines which key or keystrokes (such as a Ctrl-character combination) are being reassigned. However, if the first code in the sequence is 0 (ASCII Nul), the first and second codes designate an Extended ASCII key sequence. See Appendix G for the set of ASCII codes and the set of Extended ASCII codes.

The remaining numbers (#) or characters within the "string" are the replacement characters typed when that key or keystroke combination is pressed. Any nonnumeric characters used in the replacement must be placed within double quotation marks.

Enable/Disable Extended Keys on Enhanced Keyboards

Esc[1q	Enables assignment of the extended keys on the Enhanced Keyboard. The sequence is the same as using the /X switch for the ANSI.SYS directive.
Esc[0q	Disables assignment of the extended keys on the Enhanced Keyboard.

ANSI.SYS Keyboard Scan Codes

Function Keys

Function keys	Alone	With Shift	With Ctrl	With Alt
F1	59	84	94	104
F2	60	85	95	105
F3	61	86	96	106
F4	62	87	97	107
F5	63	88	98	108
F6	64	89	99	109
F7	65	90	100	110
F8	66	91	101	111
F9	67	92	102	112
F10	68	93	103	113

Alphanumeric Keys with Alt Key Pressed

A	30	J	36	S	31	1	120
B	48	K	37	T	20	2	121
C	46	L	38	U	22	3	122
D	32	M	50	V	47	4	123
E	18	N	49	W	17	5	124
F	33	O	24	X	45	6	125
G	34	P	25	Y	21	7	126
H	35	Q	16	Z	44	8	127
I	23	R	19			9	128
						0	129

Note: The numerals are those on the top row of the typewriter area, not the numeric keypad or the function keys.

Cursor Pad Keys

Key	*Alone*	*With Ctrl*
Up arrow	72	
Down arrow	80	
Left arrow	75	115
Right arrow	77	116
Home	71	119
End	79	117
Page Up	73	132
Page Down	81	118
Insert	82	
Delete	83	

Other special code combinations include the following:

Key Combination	*Code*
Alt-hyphen (–)	130
Alt-equal sign (=)	131
Ctrl-asterisk (* on numeric keypad)	114
Shift-Tab	15
Ctrl-Alt-Num Lock	55
Ctrl-Alt-Scroll Lock	56

Code Page Tables

Code Page 437 (United States)

Hex Digits 1st→ 2nd↓	0-	1-	2-	3-	4-	5-	6-	7-	8-	9-	A-	B-	C-	D-	E-	F-
-0		►		0	@	P	`	p	Ç	É	á	░	└	┴	α	≡
-1	☺	◄	!	1	A	Q	a	q	ü	æ	í	▒	┴	╤	β	±
-2	☻	↕	"	2	B	R	b	r	é	Æ	ó	▓	┬	╥	Γ	≥
-3	♥	‼	#	3	C	S	c	s	â	ô	ú	│	├	╙	π	≤
-4	♦	¶	$	4	D	T	d	t	ä	ö	ñ	┤	─	╘	Σ	⌠
-5	♣	§	%	5	E	U	e	u	à	ò	Ñ	╡	┼	╒	σ	⌡
-6	♠	▬	&	6	F	V	f	v	å	û	ª	╢	╞	╓	µ	÷
-7	•	↨	'	7	G	W	g	w	ç	ù	º	╖	╟	╫	τ	≈
-8	◘	↑	(	8	H	X	h	x	ê	ÿ	¿	╕	╚	╪	Φ	°
-9	○	↓	)	9	I	Y	i	y	ë	Ö	⌐	╣	╔	┘	Θ	∙
-A	◙	→	*	:	J	Z	j	z	è	Ü	¬	║	╩	┌	Ω	·
-B	♂	←	+	;	K	[	k	{	ï	¢	½	╗	╦	█	δ	√
-C	♀	∟	,	<	L	\	l	|	î	£	¼	╝	╠	▄	∞	ⁿ
-D	♪	↔	-	=	M	]	m	}	ì	¥	¡	╜	═	▌	φ	²
-E	♫	▲	.	>	N	^	n	~	Ä	Pt	«	╛	╬	▐	ε	■
-F	☼	▼	/	?	O	_	o	⌂	Å	ƒ	»	┐	╧	▀	∩	

Code Page 860 (Portugal)

Hex Digits 1st → 2nd ↓	0-	1-	2-	3-	4-	5-	6-	7-	8-	9-	A-	B-	C-	D-	E-	F-
-0		►		0	@	P	`	p	Ç	É	á	▦	└	╨	α	≡
-1	☺	◄	!	1	A	Q	a	q	ü	À	í	▒	┴	╤	β	±
-2	●	↕	"	2	B	R	b	r	é	È	ó	▓	┬	╥	Γ	≥
-3	♥	‼	#	3	C	S	c	s	â	ô	ú	│	├	╙	π	≤
-4	♦	¶	$	4	D	T	d	t	ã	õ	ñ	┤	─	╘	Σ	⌠
-5	♣	§	%	5	E	U	e	u	à	ò	Ñ	╡	┼	╒	σ	⌡
-6	♠	▬	&	6	F	V	f	v	Á	Ú	ª	╢	╞	╓	μ	÷
-7	•	↨	'	7	G	W	g	w	ç	ù	º	╖	╟	╫	τ	≈
-8	◘	↑	(	8	H	X	h	x	ê	Ì	¿	╕	╚	╪	Φ	°
-9	○	↓	)	9	I	Y	i	y	Ê	Õ	Ò	╣	╔	┘	Θ	•
-A	◙	→	*	:	J	Z	j	z	è	Ü	¬	║	╩	┌	Ω	·
-B	♂	←	+	;	K	[	k	{	Í	¢	½	╗	╦	█	δ	√
-C	♀	∟	,	<	L	\	l	|	Ô	£	¼	╝	╠	▄	∞	ⁿ
-D	♪	↔	-	=	M	]	m	}	ì	Ù	¡	╜	═	▌	∅	²
-E	♫	▲	.	>	N	^	n	~	Ã	Pt	«	╛	╬	▐	ε	■
-F	☼	▼	/	?	O	_	o	△	Â	Ó	»	┐	╧	▀	∩	

Code Page 850 (Multilingual)

Hex Digits 1st→ 2nd↓	0-	1-	2-	3-	4-	5-	6-	7-	8-	9-	A-	B-	C-	D-	E-	F-
-0		►		0	@	P	`	p	Ç	É	á	▓	└	ð	Ó	-
-1	☺	◄	!	1	A	Q	a	q	ü	æ	í	▓	┴	Ð	β	±
-2	●	↕	"	2	B	R	b	r	é	Æ	ó	▓	┬	Ê	Ô	=
-3	♥	‼	#	3	C	S	c	s	â	ô	ú	│	├	Ë	Ò	¾
-4	♦	¶	$	4	D	T	d	t	ä	ö	ñ	┤	─	È	õ	¶
-5	♣	§	%	5	E	U	e	u	à	ò	Ñ	Á	┼	ı	Õ	§
-6	♠	▬	&	6	F	V	f	v	å	û	ª	Â	ã	Í	µ	÷
-7	•	↨	'	7	G	W	g	w	ç	ù	º	À	Ã	Î	þ	¸
-8	◘	↑	(	8	H	X	h	x	ê	ÿ	¿	©	╚	Ï	Þ	°
-9	○	↓	)	9	I	Y	i	y	ë	Ö	®	╣	╔	┘	Ú	¨
-A	◙	→	*	:	J	Z	j	z	è	Ü	¬	║	╩	┌	Û	·
-B	♂	←	+	;	K	[	k	{	ï	ø	½	╗	╦	■	Ù	¹
-C	♀	∟	,	<	L	\	l	|	î	£	¼	╝	╠	▬	ý	³
-D	♪	↔	-	=	M	]	m	}	ì	Ø	¡	¢	=	¦	Ý	²
-E	♫	▲	.	>	N	^	n	~	Ä	×	«	¥	╬	Ì	¯	■
-F	☼	▼	/	?	O	_	o	△	Å	ƒ	»	┐	¤	▬	´	

Code Page 863 (Canada-French)

Hex Digits 1st → 2nd ↓	0-	1-	2-	3-	4-	5-	6-	7-	8-	9-	A-	B-	C-	D-	E-	F-
-0		►		0	@	P	`	p	Ç	É	¦	▒	└	╨	α	≡
-1	☺	◄	!	1	A	Q	a	q	ü	È	'	▒	┴	╤	β	±
-2	●	↕	"	2	B	R	b	r	é	Ê	ó	▓	┬	╥	Γ	≥
-3	♥	‼	#	3	C	S	c	s	â	ô	ú	│	├	╙	π	≤
-4	♦	¶	$	4	D	T	d	t	Â	Ë	¨	┤	─	╘	Σ	⌠
-5	♣	§	%	5	E	U	e	u	à	Ï	¸	╡	┼	╒	σ	⌡
-6	♠	▬	&	6	F	V	f	v	¶	û	³	╢	╞	╓	µ	÷
-7	•	↨	'	7	G	W	g	w	ç	ú	·	╖	╟	╫	τ	≈
-8	◘	↑	(	8	H	X	h	x	ê	¤	Î	╕	╚	╪	Φ	°
-9	○	↓	)	9	I	Y	i	y	ë	Ô	┌	╣	╔	┘	Θ	•
-A	◙	→	*	:	J	Z	j	z	è	Ü	┐	║	╩	┌	Ω	·
-B	♂	←	+	;	K	[	k	{	ï	¢	½	╗	╦	█	δ	√
-C	♀	∟	,	<	L	\	l	|	î	£	¼	╝	╠	▄	∞	ⁿ
-D	♪	↔	-	=	M	]	m	}	=	Ù	¾	╜	═	▌	ø	²
-E	♫	▲	.	>	N	^	n	~	À	Û	«	╛	╬	▐	ε	■
-F	☼	▼	/	?	O	_	o	△	§	ƒ	»	┐	╧	▬	∩	

Code Page 865 (Norway)

Hex Digits 1st→ 2nd↓	0-	1-	2-	3-	4-	5-	6-	7-	8-	9-	A-	B-	C-	D-	E-	F-
-0		►		0	@	P	`	p	Ç	É	á	░	└	╨	α	≡
-1	☺	◄	!	1	A	Q	a	q	ü	æ	í	▒	┴	╤	β	±
-2	●	↕	"	2	B	R	b	r	é	Æ	ó	▓	┬	╥	Γ	≥
-3	♥	‼	#	3	C	S	c	s	â	ô	ú	│	├	╙	π	≤
-4	♦	¶	$	4	D	T	d	t	ä	ö	ñ	┤	─	╘	Σ	⌠
-5	♣	§	%	5	E	U	e	u	à	ò	Ñ	╡	┼	╒	σ	⌡
-6	♠	▬	&	6	F	V	f	v	å	û	ª	╢	╞	╓	µ	÷
-7	•	↨	'	7	G	W	g	w	ç	ú	º	╖	╟	╫	τ	≈
-8	◘	↑	(	8	H	X	h	x	ê	ÿ	¿	╕	╚	╪	Φ	°
-9	○	↓	)	9	I	Y	i	y	ë	Ö	⌐	╣	╔	┘	Θ	∙
-A	◙	→	*	:	J	Z	j	z	è	Ü	¬	║	╩	┌	Ω	·
-B	♂	←	+	;	K	[	k	{	ï	ø	½	╗	╦	█	δ	√
-C	♀	∟	,	<	L	\	l	|	î	£	¼	╝	╠	▄	∞	ⁿ
-D	♪	↔	-	=	M	]	m	}	ì	Ø	¡	╜	═	▌	ø	²
-E	♫	▲	.	>	N	^	n	~	Ä	Pt	«	╛	╬	▐	ε	■
-F	☼	▼	/	?	O	_	o	⌂	Å	ƒ	¤	┐	╧	▬	∩	

The tables in this Appendix are reproduced courtesy of IBM.

Index

593

611

More Computer Knowledge from Que

MS-DOS User's Guide, Special Edition
Developed by Que Corporation

A special edition of Que's best-selling book on MS-DOS, updated to provide the most comprehensive DOS coverage available. Includes expanded EDLIN coverage, plus **Quick Start** tutorials and a complete **Command Reference** for DOS Versions 3 and 4. A **must** for MS-DOS users at all levels!

Order #1048
$29.95 USA
0-88022-505-X, 900 pp.

Upgrading and Repairing PCs
by Scott Mueller

The ultimate resource for personal computer upgrade, repair, maintenance, and troubleshooting! This comprehensive text covers all types of IBM computers and compatibles—from the original PC to the new PS/2 models. Defines your system components and provides solutions to common PC problems.

$27.95 USA
Order #882
0-88022-395-2
750 pp.

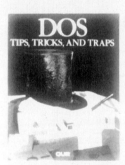

DOS Tips, Tricks, and Traps
by Chris DeVoney

This series of tips and techniques includes information on batch files, printer operation and use of floppy and hard disks for MS-DOS or PC DOS users.

Order #847
$22.95 USA
0-88022-376-6, 450 pp.

Managing Your Hard Disk, 2nd Edition
by Don Berliner

Learn the most efficient techniques for organizing the programs and data on your hard disk! This hard-working text includes management tips, essential DOS commands, an explanation of new application and utility software, and an introduction to PS/2 hardware.

$22.95 USA
Order #837
0-88022-348-0
600 pp.